PRAISE
FATAL V...

"Mr. McGinniss has delivered ... *Vision* smells of integrity, and that's one of the many things about it that make it irresistible to read, even if its vision of the human soul is somewhat bleak and frightening."
—Christopher Lehmann-Haupt, *The New York Times*

"This is a wisely observant, well-written, understated book full of truths about people. . . . McGinniss has exercised his customary skill here, far transcending the gore and creepy-crawliness. The mysteries in his story are both eerie and profound."
—Robert Stone, *Harper's Magazine*

"A HAUNTING, ENGROSSING BOOK . . . the terrifying resonance when the most chilling facts curl out of those things we think we know and trust the most. Mac-Donald was one of those things." —*Chicago Sun-Times*

"A POWERFUL JOB OF REVEALING AN ABERRANT MIND IN ALL ITS INTRICACY." —*People*

"FASCINATING, FIRST-RATE . . . COMPULSIVELY READABLE." —*Newsday*

"A HAUNTING HORROR STORY TOLD IN COMPELLING DETAIL." —*Newsweek*

"EXTRAORDINARY, COMPELLING . . . a book of depth and maturity." —*The Philadelphia Inquirer*

continued . . .

FATAL VISION

Including the 1985 Afterword and the 1989 Epilogue

Joe McGinniss

A SIGNET BOOK

SIGNET
Published by New American Library, a division of
Penguin Group (USA) Inc., 375 Hudson Street,
New York, New York 10014, USA
Penguin Group (Canada), 90 Eglinton Avenue East, Suite 700, Toronto,
Ontario M4P 2Y3, Canada (a division of Pearson Penguin Canada Inc.)
Penguin Books Ltd., 80 Strand, London WC2R 0RL, England
Penguin Ireland, 25 St. Stephen's Green, Dublin 2,
Ireland (a division of Penguin Books Ltd.)
Penguin Group (Australia), 250 Camberwell Road, Camberwell, Victoria 3124,
Australia (a division of Pearson Australia Group Pty. Ltd.)
Penguin Books India Pvt. Ltd., 11 Community Centre, Panchsheel Park,
New Delhi - 110 017, India
Penguin Group (NZ), 67 Apollo Drive, Rosedale, Auckland 0632,
New Zealand (a division of Pearson New Zealand Ltd.)
Penguin Books (South Africa) (Pty.) Ltd., 24 Sturdee Avenue,
Rosebank, Johannesburg 2196, South Africa

Penguin Books Ltd., Registered Offices:
80 Strand, London WC2R 0RL, England

Published by Signet, an imprint of New American Library, a division of Penguin Group (USA) Inc. Previously published in a G. P. Putnam's Sons edition.

First Signet Printing (Premium Edition), August 2012
10 9 8 7 6 5 4 3 2 1

The author gratefully acknowledges permission from Front Line Management
Company, Inc., to reprint lyrics from "Heartache Tonight" by Don Henley,
Glenn Fry, Bob Seger, and J. D. Souther, copyright © Cass County Music &
Red Cloud Music & Gear Publishing & Ice Age Music ASCAP, 1979; permis-
sion from Music Music Music Inc. to reprint lyrics from "The Ballad of the
Green Berets," words and music by Barry Sadler and Robin Moore, copyright
© Music Music Music Inc., 1963, 1964 & 1966; and permission from Dwarf
Music, Inc., to reprint lyrics from "I Shall Be Released," words and music by
Bob Dylan, copyright © Dwarf Music, 1967, 1970.

 REGISTERED TRADEMARK—MARCA REGISTRADA

Printed in the United States of America

AUTHOR'S NOTE

In the interest of protecting the privacy of individuals whose real identities are not central to the true story told here, certain names and other descriptive details have been altered in several instances.

ACKNOWLEDGMENTS

Through fifteen years and five books the one constant in my professional life has been my agent, Sterling Lord. For his grace, strength, ingenuity, and generosity during the particularly trying period which encompassed the composition of this work I would like to thank him.

For her immense confidence, her extraordinary and infectious enthusiasm, and her considerable editorial skills, I would like to thank Phyllis Grann of G. P. Putnam's Sons, without whom—it is entirely possible—this book would never have come to fruition.

In addition, for the most capable and conscientious job of copyediting ever done on a manuscript of mine—as well as for patience and forbearance far beyond the call of duty—I would like to express gratitude to David Frost.

The author would also like to express thanks to the Edward J. Doherty Foundation for its generous financial assistance, and to those officials of the U.S. government who, in compliance with the Freedom of Information Act, made available various materials which proved to be of considerable use.

FOR NANCY

THE BALLAD OF THE GREEN BERETS

Fighting soldiers from the sky,
Fearless men who jump and die.
Men who mean just what they say,
The brave men of The Green Beret.
Silver wings upon their chests,
These are men, America's best,
One hundred men we'll test today,
But only three win The Green Beret.

Trained to live off nature's land,
Trained to combat, hand to hand.
Men who fight by night and day,
Courage take from The Green Beret.
Silver wings upon their chests,
These are men, America's best,
One hundred men we'll test today,
But only three win The Green Beret.

Back at home a young wife waits,
Her Green Beret has met his fate.
He has died for those oppressed,
Leaving her this last request.
Put silver wings on my son's chest,
Make him one of America's best,
He'll be a man they'll test one day,
Have him win The Green Beret.

Is this a dagger which I see before me,
The handle toward my hand? Come,
      let me clutch thee:
I have thee not, and yet I see thee still.
Art thou not, fatal vision, sensible
To feeling as to sight? or art thou but
A dagger of the mind, a false creation,
Proceeding from the heat-oppressed
      brain?

MACBETH, II, 1, 33

INTRODUCTION

He's full of fun, plus noise and vim.
There's really no one quite like him.

> —inscription beneath
> Jeffrey Robert MacDonald's
> high school yearbook
> photograph

I first met Dr. Jeffrey MacDonald in Huntington Beach, California, on a hot and cloudless Saturday morning in June of 1979.

He was living in a $350,000 condominium just off the Pacific Coast Highway, fifty miles south of Los Angeles, and ten miles from St. Mary's Hospital in Long Beach, where he served as director of emergency medicine. There were parking spaces for cars in front and boats in back and Dr. MacDonald had one of each: in his driveway a rare Citroën-Maserati with JRM-MD license plates, and, docked just behind the sliding glass doors of his living room, a thirty-four-foot yacht, the *Recovery Room*.

He was thirty-five years old, five feet, eleven inches tall, well muscled and deeply tanned. He wore a tight-fitting short-sleeved shirt. He had a strong handshake and a quick smile. There were gold rings on his fingers, a gold watch on his wrist, and a gold chain around his neck. His blond hair was just beginning to turn gray.

At Patchogue High School on Long Island he had

been president of the student council, quarterback of the football team, and king of the senior prom. His graduating class had voted him not only Most Popular but also Most Likely to Succeed. He had attended Princeton University and the Northwestern University Medical School. His internship year had been spent at the Columbia Presbyterian Medical Center in New York City. Upon its completion he had enlisted in the Army and had volunteered to serve as a Green Beret.

It had been almost ten years since his wife and two daughters had been murdered in the family apartment at Fort Bragg, North Carolina, and he had first been accused of killing them. In less than a month he would be returning to North Carolina to stand trial.

He took me to eat at a little restaurant just down the highway from where he lived. The Citroën-Maserati handled the trip comfortably without being extended much past second gear.

We sat at a large table outside, surrounded by fresh flowers and hanging plants. The waitresses made a fuss over Dr. MacDonald—he was, apparently, a regular—and he, in turn, administered hugs and dispensed free medical advice.

He ordered for both of us: a lavish, Los Angeles–style brunch. Fresh juice, fresh melon, *huevos rancheros,* fried potatoes, coffee, white wine. He said the trial would be held in federal court in Raleigh, North Carolina.

From the start, he had claimed that the murders had been committed by a band of Manson-like intruders who had burst into the apartment in the middle of the night, in February 1970, stabbing him and knocking him unconscious and then slaughtering his pregnant wife and two young daughters.

The Army had cleared him of all charges nine months after the crimes, following the longest pre-court-martial hearing in military history, but his dead wife's stepfather—at first his most impassioned defender—had turned bitterly against him, MacDonald said, and had hounded him throughout the years that followed.

After a 1975 indictment, the charges had again been dismissed—this time by a federal appeals court, on grounds that he had already been denied his constitutional right to a speedy trial—but the U.S. Supreme Court had recently vacated that ruling, clearing the way for the impending trial, which would be, MacDonald said, "an obscene charade."

"It's inconceivable to me," he said over a second pot of coffee, "that more than nine years after the night my family was killed and I came so close to being killed myself, I can still pick up a newspaper and see myself called a murder suspect in the headlines.

"My only consolation is that in a few weeks it will finally be over. For nine years I've been haunted—both by the loss of my family, and by this ridiculous accusation that for some reason I killed them myself. The normal assumption might be that this is the sort of thing that gets easier with time. Well, I'll tell you something. It doesn't.

"It's always there. You speak at a medical conference and it's there. You ask a girl out and it's there. You wonder, 'How much does she know? How much should I tell her on the first date?'

"And for the past three months—knowing it would definitely come to trial—I've been under more stress than at any time since 1970. I'm not sleeping, I'm not eating well"—he pointed to his half-empty plate—"I'm showing irritability at work. It's going to be a terrible ordeal to go back there, to relive the whole thing, but at this point, in a way, I'm almost looking forward to the trial. Maybe this will finally clear the air."

After the meal, Jeffrey MacDonald took me back to his condominium. There was a Jacuzzi just off his master bedroom, wall-to-wall carpeting, a lot of glass. Glass-topped tables, sliding glass doors, and large mirrors lining the walls. I had never before been in a home in which such a large percentage of wall space had been given over to mirrors.

Hot sunlight shimmered on the water beyond the dock but air conditioning kept the interior of the condominium cool. He poured me a glass of fruit juice and asked if I would like to go with him to North Carolina, in order to write a book about the case.

For years, he said, he had resisted such an idea, refusing all who had approached him with book or movie proposals. Publicity of any sort in regard to the deaths of his wife and daughters caused him pain. He had struggled hard to put the past behind him and leave it there. But now that this would no longer be possible—now that his nightmare finally was building toward its climax—he'd changed his mind. He was frustrated. He was angry. He felt abused by the judicial process. Perhaps, after all, it was time for the full story to be told.

A few days later I received an invitation to a party. It had been sent by the Long Beach Police Officers Association.

Dear Friend,

> *As you may already know, the time is drawing near for the trial of Jeffrey R. MacDonald vs. the U.S.*

A group of "Jeff's Friends" has organized in an effort to lend both financial and emotional support during this crucial time. We have planned a dinner, a dance, and raffle as a means of showing our support. The date to remember is June 18, a Monday. There will be a sumptuous gourmet dinner at Bogart's in Marina Pacifica beginning at 7 P.M, and to round out the evening there will be a dance in Bogart's Disco beginning at 8 P.M.

Tickets for the dinner are $100 per person, which includes admission to the disco. For those who are able to give more, there will be a Golden Circle Table, seating with Jeff, for $500 per person, which also includes admission to the disco.

During the dance there will be a lively auction of unusual one-of-a-kind items and services (bring your checkbook). We will also draw and announce the winner of the Hawaii Vacation for 2.

The evening promises to be filled with good friends, good fun, good feelings. So please circle June 18th on your calendar and help us send Jeff back to North Carolina on an emotional high.

It was a perfectly lovely evening in every way. The food was superb, fine wines were available, and at the Golden Circle Table there was no shortage of champagne. For three dollars, one could even purchase a bright yellow bumper sticker which said FREE THE FORT BRAGG ONE.

Everyone to whom I spoke—doctors, policemen, former girlfriends, even an old Princeton roommate—exuded admiration and affection for Dr. MacDonald. Superlatives were the order of the night. He was the best and the brightest, the strongest and gentlest, the most loving and most worthy of love. Everyone thought the world of Jeff. He seemed almost too good to be true.

I watched as the subject of this intense adulation moved slowly from table to table, chatting easily, smiling often, his new girlfriend, Candy Kramer, glowing softly at his side. She was twenty-two, blond and cheerful, and just launched on her career as an airline stewardess.

Dressed in an impeccably tailored cream-colored suit and charming everyone in his path, MacDonald had about himself something of the aura of Robert Redford in *The Candidate*—with, perhaps, faint, distant echoes of Gatsby.

In addition to directing the fourteen-doctor group that handled all emergency services for St. Mary's, he was an instructor at the UCLA medical school, author of a forthcoming textbook on emergency medical techniques, founder and director of the first Long Beach Paramedical Squadron, medical director of the Long Beach Grand Prix auto race, past president of the Southern California chapter of the Heart Association, the first person ever granted honorary lifetime membership in the Long Beach Police Officers Association, and a nationally known lecturer on the subject of recognition and treatment of child abuse.

Whichever he was, victim or killer—and there did not seem to be a middle ground—Jeffrey MacDonald had clearly succeeded in putting a great deal of time and space between himself and the events of February 17, 1970.

In the lotus land of Southern California he had insulated himself behind layer upon layer of wealth, prestige, creature comfort, and professional accomplishment.

Yet now, across all that time and space, the past had reached out to claim him. From almost a decade ago, from 3,000 miles away, voices were calling him back.

Back to the darkest hours of a cold and rainy February night and to the cramped little apartment at 544 Castle Drive in which his wife and daughters had lived the final, terrible moments of their lives.

Jeffrey MacDonald had no choice. He had to go. Even before they raffled off the trip to Hawaii, I had decided to go with him: back to North Carolina to live with him during the trial. And then, perhaps, further back, into the past, along whatever tangled paths I might discover, to wherever it was they might lead.

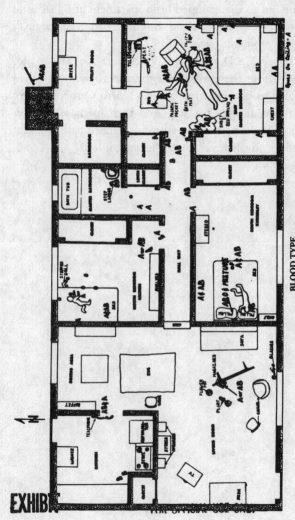

BLOOD TYPE

Colette MacDonald   A   Kimberly MacDonald   AB

Jeffrey MacDonald   B   Kristen MacDonald   O

PART ONE

THE SHADOW
OF DEATH

Let that day be darkness;
let not God regard it from above,
neither let the light shine upon it.
Let darkness and the shadow of death stain it;
let a cloud dwell upon it;
let the blackness of the day terrify it.
As for that night, let darkness seize upon it;
let it not be joined unto the days of the year,
let it not come into the number of the months.

—Job, 3:4–6

1

On May 31, 1963, from her mother and stepfather's apartment overlooking Washington Square in New York City, Colette Stevenson, who was twenty years old and had just completed her sophomore year at Skidmore College in Saratoga Springs, New York, wrote a letter to her boyfriend, Jeffrey MacDonald, who was about to finish his second year at Princeton.

My darling,

Just a short note to tell you what I could say briefly (i.e., I need you) and something which will take a lifetime to say—I love you.

Whenever I get depressed here, or impatient to do something, I take out some of your letters. Then I realize that any boredom now of mine, any spur of the moment ideas about jumping on a bus to see you, are important now because I'm not with you—but with all this summer and all our lives, I can at least leave you alone long enough to get some good marks on your exams.

It's just that knowing you are so close—only an hour and a half away—it's much worse than being at Skidmore. You are so close but I don't want to come down. I do want to come down but I can't let my selfishness get the best of me this time. I rationalize and say it won't be long, but darling that doesn't help because I miss you until I am in your arms again.

This might sound a little blunt coming from your shy, demure girlfriend, but at this exact moment I wish I had my tongue in your mouth. I wish I could be with you, loving you with every part of myself. I miss you, sweetheart, so much.

I've been thinking a lot about this summer and about riding in a car with you again and being with you again and loving you (still) (yet) (forever) and I'm getting excited . . .

Oh, by the way, at the risk of sounding very ultra-redundant again—I adore you.

Yours forever,
Colette

p.s. Hope your tests are going O.K. I'm thinking of you all day, every day.
p.p.s. You've just got to read Lord of the Flies. *It was really great.*

She got pregnant that summer and they were married in September in a small Catholic church in Greenwich Village. She dropped out of Skidmore and they rented a house in Princeton, where Kimberly, their first daughter, was born in April of 1964.

He left Princeton at the end of his junior year to enroll in medical school. Their second daughter, Kristen, was born during his third year at Northwestern.

He completed his internship in June of 1969 and was inducted into the Army on July 1. In September, following a physician's basic training course at Fort Sam Houston, Texas, and paratroop training at Fort Benning, Georgia, he was assigned to duty as a medical officer at Green Beret headquarters, Fort Bragg.

Colette and the children joined him there. They moved into a little garden apartment at the end of a row of garden apartments in a married officers' housing area known as Corregidor Courts. The address was 544 Castle Drive.

At Christmas, in a card sent to friends from Northwestern, Colette said:

> *We are having a great, all expense paid vacation in the Army. It looks as if Jeff will be here in North Carolina for the entire two years, which is an immense load off my mind at least. Life has never been so normal nor so happy. Jeff is home every day at 5 and most days even comes home for lunch—By the way, been having such a good time lately that we are expecting a son in July.*

It rained in Fayetteville, North Carolina, on the night of Monday, February 16, 1970, and into the early hours of Tuesday morning.

It had been raining off and on for a week. A cold, demoralizing February rain which had turned the sandy soil muddy but which had brought no new life to the brown winter grass.

At Fort Bragg, situated less than ten miles from downtown Fayetteville, the night had begun uneventfully. The military police patrol assigned to the Corregidor Courts housing area had responded to only one call since coming on duty at 11:30 P.M. and that had been from a captain having trouble with his oil burner. At least half a dozen times the two-man patrol had driven past 544 Castle Drive and had neither seen nor heard anything out of the ordinary. On a Monday night in February, the combination of cold and rain apparently was enough to have kept the streets almost deserted.

Then, at 3:40 A.M., a Fayetteville telephone operator received a call from a man who asked in a very faint voice that the military police and an ambulance be sent to 544 Castle Drive.

"Is that on post or off post?" the operator asked.

She did not receive an answer to her question. Instead, there was only silence on the line. She put the call through to MP headquarters at Fort Bragg.

At 3:42 A.M. a desk sergeant heard the caller say:

"Five forty-four Castle Drive . . . Help . . . Five forty-four Castle Drive . . . Stabbing . . ."

Then, apparently, the caller dropped the phone. The sergeant heard a clunking noise, as if the receiver had hit a wall or floor.

For thirty seconds, maybe sixty, there was silence. Then the caller was back, speaking this time in a voice that the sergeant described as "almost too weak to be a whisper."

"Five forty-four Castle Drive . . . Stabbing . . . *Hurry!* . . ."

Again, there was only silence on the line.

Within ten minutes there were a dozen military policemen at the scene, milling about on the front steps or standing on the walk that led up to the house. The red lights and blue lights of their jeeps and patrol cars flashed in the raw and misty darkness.

The front door was locked. The blinds were drawn. Inside, the house seemed dark and silent. A lieutenant knocked. There was no response. He knocked harder.

One MP suggested that they break down the door. The lieutenant said no. This was, after all, an officer's residence. He tried once more, banging as hard as he could. Then he started back toward his car, thinking he would call the provost marshal to ask about obtaining a search warrant.

On his way, he said, "Somebody check the back door."

A sergeant trotted around the side of the house. Two other MPs started to follow. They were only halfway around, however—and the lieutenant was only halfway to his car—when they met the sergeant coming back. He was no longer trotting, but running now as fast as he could.

"Tell them to get Womack ASAP!"

Womack is the name of the Fort Bragg hospital. ASAP is a military acronym that means "as soon as possible." In this context, it meant: *"Emergency!"*

The back door was open, though a screen door outside it was closed. The rear entrance led through a small utility room into the master bedroom.

Colette MacDonald, who was twenty-six years old at the time of her death, lay on her back, legs apart, on the floor next to the bed. One eye was open, one breast exposed, and one arm was extended over her head.

She was covered with blood. A torn and bloodstained blue pajama top had been draped across part of her chest. Her own pajamas, which had been pink, were dark with blood. Her face and head were battered and covered with blood and more blood had soaked—perhaps still was soaking—into the rug on which she lay.

Her husband, Captain Jeffrey R. MacDonald, M.D., also twenty-six, lay next to her, motionless. He wore only blue pajama bottoms. He was face down with his head on her chest and one arm wrapped around her neck.

"Just like with a girlfriend," an MP sergeant described it later. "As if he was crying on her shoulder."

A small paring knife lay on the rug near a dresser. A bedspread and sheet—saturated with blood—lay rumpled together near the doorway that led to the hall. On the headboard of the double bed, in letters eight inches high, the word PIG had been written in blood.

Jeffrey MacDonald began to moan. An MP ran to his side.

"Check my kids," MacDonald whispered. "I heard my kids crying . . ."

An MP ran down the hall. He took two steps inside a darkened bedroom on his left. He shined his flashlight on the bed.

Kimberly MacDonald, five years old, lay on her left side. The covers were pulled up to her shoulders and tucked beneath her. Blood covered her mattress and pillow. There was a large wound, through which bone protruded, on her cheek. There also were a number of gaping stab wounds in her neck.

The MP backed quickly out of the room and stepped to a doorway on the opposite side of the hall. Shining his light on the bed in that room he saw the body of an even smaller child.

Kristen MacDonald, two years old, also lay on her left side. Her left arm was outstretched. A nearly empty baby bottle lay next to her mouth. A large stuffed dog stood near the bed, its wide-eyed face pointed toward her.

Her blond hair, her head, and her face were un-
marked, but she had been stabbed many times in the
chest and back. Her pajamas, sheets, and mattress were
soaked with blood, and more blood had run down the
side of her bed to form a large pool on the floor.

Leading away from this pool, toward the doorway,
was a footprint in blood that appeared to have been
made by the bare foot of an adult human being.

In the master bedroom, Jeffrey MacDonald was trying
to speak.

"Four of them . . . She kept saying, 'Acid is groovy . . .
Kill the pigs' . . ."

He seemed to be laboring for breath.

"Why did they do this to me? . . . I can't breathe . . .
I need a chest tube . . ."

He was shivering, his teeth were chattering, his muscles seemed to tighten as he shook. Suddenly, his eyes
closed and he went limp. A military policeman began to
administer mouth-to-mouth resuscitation. MacDonald
revived. He began struggling, trying to push the MP
away.

"I've got to check my kids!"

"Don't worry, sir. Someone is down there taking care
of them."

"Fuck me! I gotta see my kids! Take care of my kids!
Leave me alone!"

He pushed harder and raised himself to a sitting position. Then he looked down at the body of Colette.

"Jesus Christ!" he cried. *"Look at my wife!"* Then he
mumbled, "I'm gonna kill those goddamned acid heads.
I don't know why in the hell I fuck with them. I'm not
gonna help them anymore."

There had been four of them, MacDonald told the

MPs. Two white men, one black, and a woman with long blond hair who had been wearing a floppy hat and high boots and who had been holding a candle. He also told the military police that he was a doctor and he had been stabbed and he thought he was going into shock. If that happened, he said, they should elevate his legs and keep him warm and make sure he did not swallow his tongue.

An ambulance arrived. Two medics wheeled a stretcher through the living room and down the hallway to the bedroom. MacDonald was placed on the stretcher.

As he was being wheeled back down the hall, past the bedroom of his older daughter, Kimberly, he suddenly reached out, grabbed the edge of the doorway, and, struggling hard against the two medics and a military policeman, managed to pull himself halfway off the stretcher.

"Goddamn MPs!" he shouted. "Let me see my kids!"

With some difficulty, the MP and the medics restrained him. They then proceeded through the hallway, down the two steps that led to the living room, and out the front door of 544 Castle Drive.

Once outside, Jeffrey MacDonald lay quietly. His eyes were closed and a sheet was pulled up to his chin. He was wheeled quickly down the front walk, through the chilly, misty darkness, past a small group of neighbors that had gathered, and toward the flashing lights of the waiting ambulance.

The Voice of Jeffrey MacDonald

I can still remember when I first met Colette. We were in eighth grade, in the junior high school on South Ocean Avenue in Patchogue, and she was walking down the hallway with her best friend, June Desser.

June was thin, taller than Colette, very attractive, but I thought Colette was more attractive: much softer appearing. She had sort of a vulnerable look.

I was standing in the doorway of my homeroom up on the fifth floor, the highest floor, of the Patchogue Junior High School, and they walked past and Colette turned around and looked at me and I looked back and they just kept going. But I had the distinct impression—that I can still see today—that she was interested and wanted to say hello, but she was a little hesitant or tentative about doing so.

I remember then for about a week I kept trying to find out who was the good-looking blonde who was always with the other blonde. Some people told me they were sisters and some people told me they weren't. But they had their reputation of being kind of aloof. And

Colette, of course, was from a reasonably wealthy family by Patchogue standards, and they were considered kind of upper-class, and I really couldn't seem to find out that much about her.

Anyway, I met her again like two weeks later, in passing, and eventually I found out what her full name was and where her homeroom was, and we met on and off in the hallways, and, I believe, in one class. I finally had her in a—in either a history or an English class. And we started talking and eventually I found out where she lived and I drove my bicycle over to her house one day and we met that way.

Those were seemingly—in retrospect now—painful times. Driving past her house on a bicycle until she noticed you, and then she'd call you over and you'd stand outside and talk in kind of a confused fashion—not trying to be forward or aggressive but trying to talk to her and get to meet her and know her better. And this would go on for hours.

The person she lived next to was Timmy Cohane. He was a kid who'd had polio and had a weakened leg, with a brace, and he was one of Colette's best friends. I ended up becoming a good friend of his, too, and we used to go out and play basketball together at his house, but a lot of the reason I was over there was so I could end up seeing Colette.

She would come over and sit on the fence and we eventually struck up this relationship and I ended up asking her out to the movies. It was either in the last part of eighth grade or the first part of ninth grade that we went to the Rialto Theater and sat in the balcony and held hands and watched *A Summer Place,* with Troy Donahue, and I think the blonde was Connie Stevens.

We sat through it twice because we were so stunned

by its beauty, and it was always sort of our movie. Colette and I always felt that we were those two people, falling in love. It was a beautiful thing to us in ninth grade.

And that song—"Theme from *A Summer Place*"—was always a very good song for us. We fell in love to that song and whenever we heard it, it was, you know, a tremendous reminiscence. It was a tiny bit melancholy, as all love songs are to young people when they're falling in love, but it was a good melancholy, and we always—either of us—would turn up the radio when that song came on.

Now, of course, if I—still to this day when I hear that song, I get this big flood of sadness and nostalgia—and Colette and warm eyes and her blond hair and her warmth and me holding her in the theater as a ninth-grader.

2

In the ambulance, on the way to the hospital, Jeffrey MacDonald told the attendant that he needed fluids, that he was going into shock, that he was about to pass out. He spoke again of the attack: the female intruder had said, "Groovy, hit him again." He also spoke briefly of his wife. She had called out, "Help me, Jeff. Help me, Jeff," he said, but he had been attacked before he was able to get to her. Then he exclaimed: "My God, she was pregnant!"

In the emergency room, an orderly placed a Vaseline gauze bandage over a small wound in the right side of MacDonald's chest through which blood was bubbling. That was the only injury which seemed to require immediate attention.

"He wanted to know where his family was," the orderly would later tell investigators. "Why weren't they here? He mentioned something about two Negro males, one white male, and one female—she was wearing a white hat and white boots. She was carrying a candle and she was saying, 'Acid is groovy' and 'Kill the pigs.'" According to the orderly, MacDonald said the intruders had been wearing "hippie-style" clothing.

"He said he woke up in the hallway and could see his wife and she had a knife sticking out of her chest and he crawled over to her and he said he pulled the knife out and saw that she wasn't breathing. He said the children were saying, 'Daddy, Daddy.' Then he said, 'Why would they do this to my wife? She never hurt anyone.'"

The doctor on duty in the emergency room made a quick examination and noted three injuries in addition to the chest wound: a bruise on the left side of the forehead, the skin of which was not broken; and superficial stab wounds of the abdomen and upper left arm. None of MacDonald's wounds required stitching.

His blood pressure was 120 over 70, his pulse 78, respiration rate 26, and temperature 99—all considered normal vital signs. The emergency physician gave him no treatment at all. In listening to MacDonald's chest, however, the doctor noted decreased breath sounds on the right side, indicating the possibility of a partially collapsed lung, a diagnosis which was confirmed by chest X-ray.

Of far more concern than his physical condition was MacDonald's emotional status. He was both tearful and angry during his first moments at the hospital and seemed agitated to the point of hysteria.

Screaming and cursing, he berated a nurse who approached to ask his Social Security number, and there was concern that he might jump up from the litter upon which he'd been placed—just as, pushing and swearing, he had tried to struggle free of the military police and medics who had wheeled him out of 544 Castle Drive.

"Am I gonna be all right, Doc? Am I gonna be all right?" MacDonald asked the emergency physician.

"Yes," said the doctor, "I think you are."

"What about my wife and kids?"

The doctor—who already had been informed that this patient's family had just been murdered—did not want to upset him any further.

"They'll be okay," the doctor said.

"What do you mean, they'll be okay?" MacDonald said. "They're dead, aren't they?"

The second doctor to examine MacDonald was the surgical resident on duty, Benjamin Klein. He observed the same injuries that the first doctor had, and in addition noted, on the left side of the chest, "four puncture type wounds along a linear track, spaced rather evenly, about two to three millimeters apart."

The military policeman who had given MacDonald mouth-to-mouth resuscitation had observed the same marks. To him, they had appeared to be scratches, "like where someone had dug their nails into him."

Repeatedly, MacDonald asked why his wife and children had not yet been brought to the hospital.

"Why aren't they here yet? How come they're so slow? The ambulance ought to be here by now." On several occasions, he said of Colette, "She never hurt anyone," and added that, "the kids were great." "He said he was awakened from sleep," Dr. Klein said. "I believe he was in the living room, sleeping on the sofa. He said he was awakened by somebody beating on him, and his wife was screaming, and there was a blond female holding a candle, saying something like, 'Kill the pigs,' and there were three men, one of them a Negro.

"There was a man with a bat and a man with a knife—some sort of sharp instrument—and the man with the bat hit him and somebody was jabbing at him with the sharp instrument and he was dancing around trying to avoid them, and he said he could still hear his wife screaming.

"He mentioned something about his own wounds, that he'd seen a little bubble from his right chest, and—I did not get the exact timing interval but he said he examined his children. He said they didn't have any pulses and that he went on to his wife. She had a lot of blood on her. He said she looked very bad. That was his statement: 'She looked very bad.'

"He also said, 'Be sure to tell the MPs and the CID [the Army's Criminal Investigation Division] that I pulled the knife that was in her chest out. Tell the MPs and the CID I pulled the knife from my wife's chest and threw it on the floor.'"

The third doctor to see MacDonald was Merrill Bronstein, the staff surgeon on call, who had been awakened at home by a 4:45 A.M. call from the resident. Bronstein knew MacDonald from moonlighting work each had done in the emergency room of a civilian hospital in Fayetteville and Bronstein had been extremely impressed by MacDonald, both as a person and as a physician.

The relationship had not yet blossomed into close personal friendship, but once MacDonald had shown Bronstein a picture of one of his daughters on a pony he had bought them for Christmas, and more recently—in fact, within ten days of February 17—he had asked Bronstein, whose own wife was pregnant, to recommend an obstetrician for Colette.

Stunned by the news of the murders, Bronstein arrived at the hospital shortly after 5 A.M. to assume responsibility for the care of Jeffrey MacDonald.

"When I first came in," Bronstein said, "he was in a

glass cubicle in the intensive care unit. He was tearful and very upset. Continually asking where his family was. At one moment talking about one thing and at the next moment talking about something else, but always very agitated. How could they do this to him? How could this have happened? What was this country coming to?

"I was concerned about his emotional status. That was the thing that affected me the most, the thing that impressed me the most, the thing that I had the greatest difficulty, as a physician, in dealing with.

"He was very upset and I was very concerned for him and because he was kind of hysterical, I thought—I wanted him to be sedated. I wanted to give him a narcotic to relax him and I wanted to give him a barbiturate to help him sleep.

"So I went over him thoroughly. I went over his scalp and hair, and I especially went over his reflexes. I did a neurological examination because, generally, when a person has had a head injury—which I felt he had, because he had a bruise and he said there had been times when he had lost consciousness—you withhold those drugs.

"So I did go over him very thoroughly, and then I gave him those drugs. I gave him a fair amount of them. I may have done it mainly for my own comfort. I mean, you know, it's no joke: I hate to see a grown man cry."

Two hundred milligrams of the sedative Nembutal—a not insignificant amount—was administered intravenously at 5:30 A.M., at which time, according to the hospital nursing notes, Jeffrey MacDonald was "hysterical and crying." Fifteen minutes later, 100 milligrams of the tranquilizer Vistaril were added. By 6 A.M., according to his chart, MacDonald was "resting quietly."

"But I never really accomplished what I intended,"

Bronstein said. "I mean, I never really knocked him out or made him incoherent in any way."

As he had to the surgical resident, MacDonald described to Merrill Bronstein what had transpired at 544 Castle Drive. There was one detail which Bronstein recalled with particular clarity.

"He told me at one point he had looked down at a man's hand and saw—he thought it was an icepick. He told me to remind him to tell the FBI it was an icepick. He said this several times: he remembered looking down and seeing a blade that looked like an icepick, and he said to remind him to tell them about it."

MacDonald also asked Bronstein to call his mother and his in-laws on Long Island and—without informing them of what had happened—to tell them to come to Fort Bragg right away.

"He made me promise to stay with him, to be with him when he told them what had happened. On the other hand, he wanted to know what had happened. He was—one minute he would say that he wanted me to be with him when he told them what had happened, and yet he would ask *me* what had happened.

"He would continually ask where was his wife, where were the kids, were they dead? Why weren't they here? Why wasn't I with them? He wanted me to be with him, yet he wanted me to go out and see what was going on. In other words, there was a question in my mind if he knew that his wife and children were dead."

It was shortly after 5:30 A.M. when the phone rang at the home of Colette MacDonald's mother and stepfather, Mildred and Freddy Kassab. Mildred Kassab answered it. The caller identified himself as a doctor from Womack Hospital and asked to speak to her husband.

"He's in the shower," Mildred Kassab said, "but you can tell me whatever it is. I'm not a hysterical person."

"In that case," Merrill Bronstein said, "you'd better locate Captain MacDonald's mother and get down here as fast as you can."

The first agent of the Army's Criminal Investigation Division to reach 544 Castle Drive on the morning of February 17 was William Ivory, who arrived just as Jeffrey MacDonald was being wheeled out the front door.

Ivory was the CID agent on duty that night. He was thirty years old and had grown up in Somerville, Massachusetts, on the outskirts of Boston. Before becoming an Army detective, Ivory had worked for a while as a truck driver, and then as a security guard at a Sylvania electronics plant. He was married and had two children of his own.

Ivory had been dozing on a cot at CID headquarters when, shortly before 4 A.M., he had heard voices coming over the military police radio at what seemed a higher than normal pitch. There was a sense of urgency in the voices which brought Ivory fully awake.

When he heard the word *stabbing* he went to the radio in his office and inquired of the MPs at the scene whether there had been any fatalities. Told that there had been, he gathered some evidence-processing equipment, alerted the CID photographer, and drove to 544 Castle Drive.

The streets were deserted. A light rain was falling. The ground was already wet from the heavy rain that had fallen earlier in the night. The temperature was not much above 40 degrees.

Ivory reached the apartment at 4:10 A.M. There was, he noted, "quite a stir in the neighborhood. People were coming to their doors, coming to the house, to see what had happened."

There were more than a dozen military policemen still clustered inside the apartment. Ivory stepped into the living room and was told what had happened by the lieutenant in charge.

Looking down the hallway, Ivory could see the body of Colette MacDonald lying on the master bedroom floor. He walked to it. He got down on one knee. He studied the wounds to see if there was any active bleeding. There was not. He looked at the chest for signs of respiration. There were none. Whatever she had been for twenty-six years, she was now simply a battered, bloody corpse.

Ivory noted the torn and bloody blue pajama top that had been laid across her chest and the white Hilton Hotel bathmat on her abdomen.

He saw the word PIG written in blood on the headboard.

He saw the paring knife—a small, wooden-handled knife with a bent blade and the brand name "Geneva Forge" stamped in the handle—lying not far from the body.

By the feet of Colette MacDonald, he saw the pocket from the blue pajama top. This was only lightly flecked with blood.

He saw a large stain—it looked like urine—on the exposed bottom sheet of the double bed. And he saw, rumpled together in a corner, the blood-soaked bedspread and top sheet from the bed.

"Now I'll show you the children," the lieutenant said.

Kimberly MacDonald's bedroom was dark. The lieutenant shined his flashlight on the bed. Ivory, using the tip of his pen so as not to blur any possible fingerprints, flipped on the light switch.

He could see a bookcase filled with books and games. A child's record player sharing a tabletop with a collection of dolls. A Pink Panther piggy bank on a windowsill. And the body of five-year-old Kimberly MacDonald in her bed, her skull fractured, a piece of cheekbone protruding from her face, and the numerous gaping stab wounds in her neck.

The process was repeated in the bedroom of Kristen MacDonald, where, amid the gore, Ivory noted the bare, bloody footprint leading away from the girl's bed.

Ivory went next door to use a neighbor's telephone. He called half a dozen CID agents and told each of them to call more. He also called the chief of the Fort Bragg CID, Franz Joseph Grebner. Then he asked the neighbors—a warrant officer, his wife, and three teenaged children—if they had heard any noise. "Any sounds of a break-in, a fight, any disturbance at all?"

They said they had not.

Ivory asked the warrant officer to accompany him next door to identify the bodies. "It's a pretty rough scene," he said, "but I'd appreciate it."

In bathrobe and slippers, Jeffrey MacDonald's next-door neighbor accompanied Ivory to 544 Castle Drive. The first time the neighbor had met MacDonald had been in September, when MacDonald had asked to borrow his lawn mower. The last time he'd been inside the apartment had been on Christmas afternoon when MacDonald had invited him and his wife over for a drink. His sixteen-year-old daughter had been employed frequently by the MacDonalds as a babysitter.

He followed Ivory from room to room.

"Yes," he said, "that's Krissy."

"Yes," he said, "that's Kim."

"Yes," he said, "that's Mrs. MacDonald."

At that point the CID photographer arrived. He did not stay long, however. He became nauseated at the sight of the bodies and Ivory had to escort him from the scene. Ivory returned to the neighbor's house to again use the phone and request that the director of the CID photo lab come himself.

In response to Ivory's calls, more agents began to arrive. Fort Bragg's chief law enforcement officer, the provost marshal, came to the scene with an assistant. Despite the raw chill in the air, the crowd of neighbors and bystanders grew larger. By the time Franz Joseph Grebner reached 544 Castle Drive, shortly after 5 A.M., there were so many people already there that he could not find a place to park his car.

Once inside the apartment, Grebner received a briefing from Ivory. They knew only what they had seen and what MacDonald had told the military police: that he'd been attacked by a group of hippies as he lay sleeping on his living room couch.

Franz Joseph Grebner looked slowly around the living room. He had spent nineteen years in CID and had seen a lot of crime scenes and this one did not look to him the way it should. When one considered that it was an area in which a life-and-death struggle had taken place between a Green Beret officer and four intruders who had obviously been in some sort of murderous frenzy and at least some of whom had been armed, there seemed remarkably few signs of disorder.

A coffee table was tipped on its side next to the couch, its lower edge resting on a stack of magazines. An empty flowerpot stood upright on the floor, its plant spilled out alongside it. A pair of eyeglasses with a speck of blood on an outer lens lay in a corner of the room.

That was it. That was the sum total of the disarray.

And in a dining area immediately adjacent to the living room nothing at all had been disturbed. Plates remained balanced on edge in an unstable china cabinet and Valentine cards still stood upright on a table.

Grebner had been in poker games which had left premises in worse condition. He called the CID laboratory at Fort Gordon, Georgia, and asked them to send a team of technicians to the scene.

At 6 A.M., just as the first chilly gray light began to spread across the drizzly sky, three weapons were found. A bloodstained club, measuring 31 by 1¼ by 1¼ inches, lay just outside the back door. Two blue threads were stuck to it with blood. Twenty feet away, lying side by side beneath a bush, were an icepick and a second paring knife. This knife bore the trade name "Old Hickory," and its blade was not bent but straight. The blades of both the knife and icepick—like the blade of the knife found on the bedroom floor—appeared to have been wiped clean of blood.

At 8 A.M. medics arrived to remove the bodies of Jeffrey MacDonald's wife and daughters. Kristen's body was lifted from its bed and placed on a stretcher in the hallway. The body of her sister was carried from the room across the hall and laid upon the same stretcher. A Catholic chaplain made the sign of the cross and spoke a few words of prayer. Then the medics lifted the stretcher and carried it out of the house. They returned, with a separate stretcher, for Colette.

*   *   *

Using tongs, Ivory removed the bath mat from her abdomen and placed it in a plastic bag. Then, again using tongs, he lifted the torn and bloody blue pajama top from her chest. As he did, he could see that not only had the garment been ripped down the front, along a seam, but that across the back there were dozens of neat, round holes—there would turn out to be forty-eight altogether—that looked as if they had been made with an icepick.

Three hours earlier, Ivory had seen Jeffrey MacDonald wheeled, apparently unconscious, to an ambulance. Dozens of icepick holes in the back of his pajama top, Ivory assumed, meant dozens of icepick holes in his back.

Ivory immediately dispatched an agent to Womack Hospital with instructions to interview MacDonald as soon as possible in an attempt to get a better description of the intruders and a more detailed account of the attack. Indeed, Ivory feared that it might already be too late. He did not think it likely that a man with that many wounds was going to survive for very long.

Then, with the pajama top sealed inside a plastic bag, Ivory watched as medics lifted the body of Colette MacDonald from the floor. She had been dead long enough by this time for the process of rigor mortis to have begun. Her neck and the upper portion of her body had grown rigid.

As the medics lifted her, by the shoulders and legs, her head did not slump backward, and Ivory, who was standing close by, saw, directly beneath her head, a dark clot of blood about the size of his fist and, sticking up from the clot, pigtail fashion, something which appeared to be a thread. A blue thread.

He got down on his hands and knees and removed the thread from the blood clot with tweezers and placed it in a plastic vial. Then, looking within the body outline that he had drawn with yellow Magic Marker on the rug, he noticed more threads—perhaps as many as two dozen altogether. These threads were not microscopic. They ranged in length from 1 to 2½ inches and all appeared identical to those used in the manufacture of the torn blue pajama top that had been found on Colette Mac-Donald's chest.

This immediately struck William Ivory as peculiar. He could not understand how—if, as seemed obvious, the torn blue pajama top had been placed on top of Colette Mac-Donald's body after it had come to rest on the floor—so many threads from it could have wound up underneath.

During the next hour, Ivory continued to gather evidence. He soon discovered additional blue threads. There would turn out to be eighty-one altogether, scattered across the entire room. Two were even found beneath the headboard of the bed, where the word PIG had been written in blood.

Ivory also found two pieces of latex rubber on the rug. One was the size of a dime, the other the size of a quarter. They looked like they might have come from a rubber glove.

A few minutes later, as he unfolded the pile of bloody bedding that lay in the corner of the master bedroom, he found a finger section of a disposable rubber surgeon's glove. The section seemed to have been torn at its base, as might happen if one were removing such a glove in a hurry. Also, it was stained, as if someone wearing such a glove had dipped a finger in blood, as one might if one were preparing to write in blood on the headboard of a bed.

The Voice of Jeffrey MacDonald

In the summer, during high school, Colette would go over to Fire Island. She stayed with her friend Bonnie Brown. Bonnie's father owned a big construction company and owned part of Davis Park or Leisure Beach over on Fire Island. Very wealthy guy. Big political influence-type guy. And one summer—either after our freshman year or sophomore year in high school—she started dating this kid who was a sophomore or a junior at Purdue.

I had been unable to get ahold of her and eventually went over one day on the ferry, and I remember very clearly being up on the second deck, and Colette was sitting down on the dock, on a seat that was right under the harbormaster's booth, with Bonnie Brown.

I got off the ferry and saw them and Bonnie looked embarrassed and Colette looked mortified. But I walked up to her and she greeted me and then there was sort of this pregnant pause and she said she had to tell me something and I said what was that, and she told me that she was seeing someone else and that we were really not going together anymore.

And I remember my world fell apart. A tremendously empty feeling, just like sort of destroyed. Tried to be brave about it in front of Colette but was really, really devastated.

I walked around aimlessly and got back on the ferry a short while thereafter and took the ferry back to Patchogue and that was the end of it until we really started dating again when I was a freshman at Princeton and she was a freshman at Skidmore.

I believe her relationship with Dean Chamberlain had been severed by that time. Dean was a tall, kind of gawky, not bad-looking, left-handed kid who was the son of an art teacher at Patchogue Junior-Senior High School. They dated fairly heavily the senior year.

To be honest, Dean was a jerk as far as I was concerned. I always thought he was a nitwit. He was bigger than most kids at the time. I think he was only about six-two or six-three, but he grew up to that height very early so when we were in like ninth grade he was tall, he was a big kid, but he wasn't a tough kid or anything—he was just a jerk.

I could never understand Colette's fascination with him because he was a nonsupportive sort of drain on her. And they'd play all these dumb little games like, "If you leave me, I won't be able to live," and all this stuff. You know, really juvenile stuff. I didn't think much of him at all. I didn't like him, never liked him.

It's funny, several things happened when I first went to Princeton. I went through this incredible transformation. I really don't know how it came about, but I suddenly decided that I wanted to become a doctor. I sort of came to a conclusion—kind of abruptly, as I remember it—that medicine was the thing for me. I transmitted this rather casually in a phone call to my parents who were, I think, stunned by the suddenness and the seeming casualness of the decision, and yet I seemed so positive.

Suddenly, in this first week of being at Princeton and this new, glorious experience in an Ivy League school, and meeting all these exciting people, it just came to me that I wanted to be a physician. That it was a field where I could sort of be on my own, make whatever I wanted to out of myself. That I could have a variety of possible specialties and sub-specialties that all sounded exciting—especially surgery at that time. Which is funny, because most of the kids I grew up with became cops or gas station owners or fishermen or carpenters or things like that.

I think that, in retrospect, my family doctor had something to do with it. I always remember him as being sort of Ivy League–ish; he always wore, um, soft desert boots, and, like, brown pants and a tweed jacket, although he was young and, you know, kind of attractive. And I always thought of him as being a neat sort of professional guy. I mowed his lawn, as a matter of fact, for a whole summer, and we had talked a little bit about it and he always encouraged me to go into medicine.

Our family doctor before that, Dr. Swenson, was kind of a big, rough-looking guy who seemed a little rough to me. He had a pock-marked face and—the only exam I ever remember was him examining my mother and I was there in the room, which I remember very clearly because he took her blouse off and I had never seen my mother without any clothes on, and he did a breast examination, and I was thinking to myself, "I hope he doesn't hurt my mother while he does that," and I remember seeing her without any clothes on.

* * *

Anyway, it was only a week or two after that that I started thinking of Colette. It was weird, my birthday was coming up on October 12 and I wrote her a letter, like on October 7 or October 5 or something like that. It was very strange because I was thinking of my birthday coming up and I wrote to Colette out of the clear blue.

I wrote her a long, kind of emotional letter saying that I was now at school and she was at school and we'd had such fantastic times in the past, and times were changing and life was moving on, and—oh, geez, it's embarrassing, I remember it now—it was a sophomoric letter telling her how incredible our experience had been together and how much she had meant to me, and again I repeated that wouldn't it be fantastic if we could get together again, and I even closed it with, like, a four-line poem. Aaagh! I feel like—it's weird to think about that.

I got a letter back from her. Umm, it was funny, it was kind of tantalizing, it wasn't, like, by return mail. It wasn't prior to my birthday. It was, like, three or four or five days later, so it was, like, close to a two-week wait. I got a card for my birthday in which she apologized for being late but said she was so busy, and a letter. And the letter was very revealing in that she also opened up to me like I had opened up to her. She felt, I think, a little lonely at college, like everyone, I think, does the first couple of months. You're—you know—away from the parents, away from the home womb, and out in the big world, et cetera.

But it was a great letter. And I remember—oh, it was—it's so clear now! I remember sitting in my room in Witherspoon Hall, a fifth-floor walkup in Princeton, and getting this letter from Colette in that beautiful handwriting of hers, and my heart jumped.

She didn't say, like, "I love you." She said things like we'd had such a great relationship and it was difficult to be away from home and it was such a shock and a surprise and it made her feel so good to get this long letter from me, and she was surprised that I had opened up to her as much as I did.

I remember specifically, she kept coming back to our relationship and she sort of left the door open for it, like, "It would be nice to hear from you again. Maybe you could even come up to see me sometime." Words to that effect.

And I remember I sort of leaped at it in my mind. It sounded like so much more than the words actually said, and I remember being on top of the world and going to class for the next several days thinking how fantastic it was that we were gonna possibly begin seeing each other.

And it was not too long after that that I first went up to Skidmore. I don't remember exactly which weekend but it was in the fall and it was an off weekend for football—in other words, the Princeton Tigers were not playing at home, they were away—and I took a bus up and I remember that slight, sweaty-palmed, heart-pounding feeling, like: what was going to happen? How was it going to go?

3

By 7:30 A.M., the extent to which Jeffrey MacDonald's right lung was impaired by the puncture had increased from 20 to 40 percent and the chief of surgery at Womack Hospital decided to insert a chest tube as a precautionary measure. MacDonald was given 50 milligrams of Demerol intravenously at 7:30 and again an hour later to alleviate the discomfort caused by this procedure, but he remained conscious throughout and in fact, at about 8 A.M., even asked if a friend could come to visit.

The friend was an unmarried Green Beret lieutenant named Ron Harrison, who had been a frequent visitor to the MacDonald residence throughout the fall and winter.

Unlike MacDonald, Harrison did have combat experience in Vietnam and would soon have more, and spoke often of having participated in covert Special Forces operations.

From the start of their relationship, MacDonald—the doctor fresh from civilian life—had seemed extremely proud that a "real" Green Beret like Ron Harrison was

willing to consider him an equal, and Harrison had become MacDonald's best friend at Fort Bragg.

Harrison had, in fact, been the last person to see the
MacDonald family alive. It had been on Saturday, Valentine's Day. During the afternoon, Jeff had taken Colette
and the girls down to Hamlet, a small town sixty miles
from Fort Bragg, to show them the hospital at which he
had just begun moonlighting. That evening, after supper—as he did about two or three times a week—
Harrison had visited 544 Castle Drive. Colette had
served Jell-O and cookies, and the three adults had sat in
the living room chatting, while Kimberly and Kristen
had watched television.

Harrison had left at about 10 P.M. At four the next
morning, MacDonald had awakened and had driven
back to Hamlet Hospital, where, from 6 A.M. Sunday to
6 A.M. Monday, he had worked in the emergency room.
It had been a quiet day by emergency room standards—
an average of only one patient per hour—and on Sunday
night he had even managed a few hours' sleep on a cot.

Awakened at 6 A.M. Monday, he had driven back to
Fort Bragg, showered, eaten breakfast, changed into his
military uniform, and gone to work. MacDonald was
preventive medical officer for a Special Forces unit at
Fort Bragg. His work was mostly clerical: he was responsible for the sanitation of mess hall and latrines, and for
filling out the monthly venereal disease report.

Monday had been an ordinary, quiet day. In late afternoon, he had gone to the gym to play basketball for an
hour and then had come home and had taken his daughters to feed the pony he had bought them for Christmas.

He had showered again after that and had changed
into an old pair of blue pajamas. Supper had been rushed
because Colette was hurrying to get to an evening class

at the North Carolina University extension at Fort Bragg.

He had put Kristen to bed at about 7 P.M. and then had fallen asleep on the living room floor. At 8 P.M. Kimberly had awakened him so that he could watch *Laugh-In* with her. It was her favorite television show, and she especially enjoyed watching it with her father.

At 9 P.M., Kimberly had gone to bed. Colette had come home about forty minutes later, having stopped after class to drop off a female friend and to pick up a half gallon of milk for the next morning.

Six hours later, the Fayetteville operator had received the first call for help.

At 8 A.M., Ron Harrison, who had heard on his car radio as he was driving to work that there had been some sort of tragedy in the Corregidor Courts housing area, and who had discovered, upon reaching his office, that the tragedy had been the murder of Jeffrey MacDonald's wife and children, was told that MacDonald wanted him to come to the hospital.

Harrison arrived soon after the chest tube had been inserted. MacDonald appeared to him—as he had appeared to everyone else who had seen him that morning—to be extremely distraught and agitated. He was twitching from side to side in his bed with such force that Harrison was afraid he might dislodge the tube.

Harrison approached the bed and said, "Calm yourself, Jeff. Calm yourself."

MacDonald looked up and began to cry. He said, "They clubbed me, Ron. They clubbed me and I couldn't get to her."

Harrison was standing at the bedside. MacDonald reached out and grabbed Harrison's arm as he spoke. So hard did he squeeze it that that night, when Harrison removed his uniform shirt, he noticed bruises on his forearm, caused by the pressure of MacDonald's fingers.

During the morning and afternoon, MacDonald was interviewed by agents of both the CID and FBI. The CID agent remarked later that MacDonald had displayed surprisingly little emotion when describing the attack upon him and its aftermath—except when he talked about discovering the body of Kristen. "He would talk about the wife and he would talk about the older girl," the agent said. "He just didn't want to talk about Kristen."

MacDonald told both agents that after his wife's return from class, they had watched television together, sitting on the couch and sipping a liqueur. They had seen a Bob Hope special and Glen Campbell and the eleven o'clock news. Shortly after the start of Johnny Carson, Colette, who was four and a half months pregnant, had gone to bed. MacDonald had stayed up to watch the rest of Johnny Carson. At 1 A.M., still not tired, he had read the last fifty pages of a paperback novel he'd started earlier. At some point, he had heard his younger daughter, Kristen, start to cry, and he had brought her a bottle of chocolate milk. Finishing the novel at 2 A.M., he had washed the dinner dishes. Then he prepared to go to bed, but had found his younger daughter in bed with his wife and had found also that she had wet the bed. He had carried her back to her own room and had placed her in bed. Then, not wanting to awaken his wife in order to change the wet sheet, he had taken a blanket from Kristen's room and had returned to the living room and had immediately fallen asleep on the couch.

He did not know how long he had slept, but the next sound he'd heard had been the sound of his wife shouting, *"Jeff, Jeff, help!"* And, *"Jeff, Jeff, why are they doing this to me?!"* At the same time, he had heard his older daughter, Kimberly, screaming, *"Daddy, Daddy, Daddy, Daddy, Daddy!"*

As he opened his eyes, he saw four people standing over him: a black man wearing an Army fatigue jacket with sergeant's stripes on the sleeve, two white men, one of whom had a mustache and wore a red-hooded sweatshirt, and the blond woman in the floppy hat, holding a candle in front of her face. She wore high boots and a short skirt. He could not recall the exact color of the boots but said they were so wet they appeared to be black. "They were all wet," he said. "The water was just dripping off them, like they had just walked in out of the rain."

"Acid is groovy . . ." the woman was chanting. "Kill the pigs . . . Acid and rain . . ."

As he had tried to sit up, the black man had hit him on the side of the head with a baseball bat. As he grabbed for it, he found it to be slippery, as if it were covered with blood.

Struggling with the intruders, MacDonald had suddenly felt a sharp pain on the right side of his chest. At first, he had thought, "This guy throws a hell of a punch," but then he looked down and saw the glint of a blade—an icepick blade.

He said he wrestled his way off the end of the couch and toward the two steps that led up from the living room to the hallway. At that point, he fell forward and passed out. When he regained consciousness—he did not know how much time had passed—the house was silent and dark and he was shivering so hard his teeth were chattering. His pajama top, bloody and torn, was twisted around his wrists.

He had gone from room to room and had discovered

the bodies of his wife and daughters. He had felt for pulses and heartbeats, and tried in each case to administer mouth-to-mouth resuscitation, but had heard only gurgling sounds, indicating that blood and air were escaping through the lungs.

He had pulled a small knife from his wife's chest. He had covered her with his torn pajama top. He had gone to the back door to look for signs of the intruders. He had gone to the hall bathroom to check the extent of his own injuries. He had used first the bedroom telephone and then the kitchen phone to call for help. The operator, he said, would not accept his complaint until he had given her his Social Security number.

One of the white males, he said—the shorter one—had been wearing lightweight gloves. They could have been surgical gloves. He kept several pairs of surgical gloves around the house. Colette had used them while washing dishes.

Two floors below, in the basement morgue, autopsies were performed.

Colette had been stabbed nine times in the neck and seven times in the chest with a knife. One of the wounds had put a hole through her major pulmonary artery—the vessel that carries blood from the heart to the lungs. This had caused massive bleeding into her chest cavity and into the sac surrounding her heart. That had been what had killed her: the bleeding, both internal and external.

She had also been stabbed twenty-one times in the chest with an icepick. The thrusts had been so powerful that the blade of the icepick had been driven into her chest up to the hilt.

She had been hit at least six times in the head with a club: once on each temple, causing lacerations in which the skin was torn right down to the skull; once in the middle of the forehead, fracturing her skull; once on top of her head; once across the jaw, near the chin; and once above the right ear, that blow, too, delivered with enough force to break the skin.

In addition, both of Colette MacDonald's arms had been broken. The pathologist described these as "defensive type injuries." He said they had apparently been sustained as she had held her arms up in front of her face, in an attempt to ward off the blows. Both bones in the right forearm were broken and one of the bones in the left forearm was broken twice.

During the autopsy, a male fetus of four to five months' gestation was removed from her womb, a blond hair, about six inches long, was found stuck with blood to the palm of one hand, and a piece of what appeared to be human skin was removed from beneath a fingernail.

Kimberly had died from being hit with a club, at least twice, on the right side of her head.

The blows had shattered her skull and caused extensive bruising of her brain. The largest fracture line extended almost the entire length of the right side of her skull, and there were many other, smaller fractures. The blows had been of such severity as to have caused coma, and quite likely death, soon after they were delivered.

It was apparently after she was already unconscious and near death that she was stabbed with a knife on the right side of her neck. The pathologist could determine this from the relatively small amount of bleeding at the wound sites, indicating little or no blood pressure at the time these injuries were sustained.

The neck wounds cut through her windpipe and some came out the other side. Because of overlapping, it was not possible to obtain an exact count, but there appeared to be eight to ten separate incisions.

Kimberly also had been hit once with a club on the left side of her face. That blow had been delivered with such force that it produced multiple fractures of the cheekbone and nose, and left the piece of cheekbone protruding through the skin.

Thirty-three separate incisions were found in Kristen's body.

She had been stabbed twelve times in the back with a knife, four times in the chest, and once in the neck. Two of the knife wounds were deep enough to have penetrated the heart.

In addition, she was found to have approximately fifteen shallow puncture wounds in her chest, such as could have been caused by an icepick, if the person wielding it had been stabbing with minimal force.

Kristen also had a number of cuts on her hands—in one instance, down to the bone of a finger—indicating that she, like her mother, had been holding her hands up in front of her, trying to protect herself.

A blue thread was found beneath one of her fingernails.

An investigator was sent to Jeffrey MacDonald's office, to examine the contents of his desk drawers. He found an envelope that had been mailed from Honolulu on February 14—Valentine's Day—with no return address.

Inside the envelope was a Valentine's card. Printed on it were dozens of reproductions of a woman's lips: bright red, slightly parted, poised for a kiss. The printed message said, "Thinking of You." The card was signed, "Love, Jo."

Also in the envelope was a copy of a column Joan Didion had recently written for *Life* magazine. Titled "A Problem in Making Connections," the column described how Didion and her husband had gone to Hawaii for a vacation in lieu of seeking a divorce.

Jeffrey MacDonald's mother and Colette's mother and stepfather reached the hospital in early afternoon, still not knowing why they had been summoned.

As soon as he saw them, MacDonald cried out: "They're all dead! Colette and Kimmy and Kristy are dead! They killed them all!"

Colette's mother stepped to the side of his bed.

He looked up at her and started to sob.

"I couldn't protect her," he said. "She was so good and you gave her to me and I couldn't take care of her."

The Voice of Jeffrey MacDonald

That was the weekend, by the way, that first weekend up at Skidmore, that Colette and I first made love. We had not made love in high school. Colette was a very private person and maintained a tremendous code that she was true to, and, you know, it took a long time to get past that first kiss at the back door.

To this day, I think that she probably had not made love with anyone, but she may have. She may have slept with Dean Chamberlain. I suspect she probably did sleep with the sophomore from Purdue that summer on the beach, but that's not for sure. I suspect more likely that she did sleep with Dean Chamberlain in their later romance in high school. But again that's not for sure. She was a delicate, feminine person and you didn't want to upset her or go too far. It was this delightful combination of wanting to spend more time with her and be more physical, and wanting also to live up to her standards and not do that right now because maybe she didn't think it was right then, or her inhibitions were too high at that moment.

I had made love with a few girls that I had been dating in high school, but far and away the only girl that I really made love to at any length was Penny Wells. Junior year ended up being the heavy year together. It may have been senior year, actually. It was part of the senior year. At that point, Penny had a new car, I did not have a car, and she eventually ended up picking me up sometimes and driving me around in her new Chevy—her father was a Chevrolet dealer.

We had a good time together, especially physically. In our senior year we were sleeping together, and, um, we had an incredibly physical thing. Very torrid, as a matter of fact, regards our physical attraction for each other. It was instantaneous and long-lasting and repetitive. Anywhere—in the car, the drive-in movie, at parties, at her house, at my house, on dates, the whole bit. And it was just sort of endless, we just couldn't stop.

Penny was a—is a very beautiful girl. She was sort of a plastic princess. I don't mean to say that derogatorily— she's an extraordinarily good-looking woman. I don't know if she's still good-looking now, but she certainly was then. She was a little bit of an airhead, maybe, but she was very dependent on me and I liked that.

I always liked Penny. I'm not sure I was ever in love with her as I see love now, but I suppose I was in high school love with her, whatever that means. I thought of her a lot. There was a tremendous amount of tumultuous physical energy between us and we had an amazing amount of sexual experience together, which was not my first time, but it was certainly my first real affair with anyone: the first time that there was any sustained amount of sexual energy passing between myself and any—and a woman. And it was without question the first time for Penny.

In the fall, Penny came down to Princeton for two weekends, but it became clear that something was missing in the relationship. Penny seemed out of place at Princeton. I know that—I don't mean that to sound snobby, it's just that things didn't fit.

She seemed ill at ease, she was a little uncomfortable with my friends, she didn't understand that on other weekends we were hitchhiking into New York and going down into Greenwich Village and seeing the beatniks and Joan Baez and Bob Dylan and people like that. She seemed to come from working-class Patchogue and not to be changing at all.

And the fact that she was studying to be a dental technician—it just seemed like such a different world. The difference in our approach to life, I think, intellectually was sharpened all of a sudden. It crystallized. We really didn't have that much to say.

We did make love. We made love endlessly. I remember one weekend when she arrived we had a particularly tumultuous episode on the, ah, on the, ah, on my bed in my little room up on the fifth floor of Witherspoon Hall. And as a matter of fact, Penny came down for weekends, I believe, all the way into the spring of that year.

But her letters were this incredible disappointment in which nothing really was said except we talked about the weather and how her training was going and how my school was going, but there was none of the discussion of events or thought processes, or meaningful discussions of any kind, whereas I got these brilliant letters from Colette in which there was so much said and unsaid and so much between the lines. And her Skidmore life sounded so exciting. With Penny, though we made love extremely vigorously and openly and passionately many, many times, sometimes in succession—we had the strength and vigor of incredibly sexed seventeen-year-olds—there just wasn't any of the mental meeting of the minds that Colette and I always had.

In any event, regards Colette, our first episode was very, very tentative. There was no forceful taking. She never flung herself upon me. It was hesitant on both our parts, Colette especially so, but myself also, which is not my usual nature, and, for instance, not the way Penny and I had made love.

The first episode with Colette was in the motel room I was staying at in Saratoga Springs. And, strange as it sounds, the ah—she did it kind of as a joke, I think—she always laughed about it afterwards—the motel she got me a room in was the Grand Union, believe it or not. We first made love in that motel.

She was very frightened. I was caring for her and babying her and gently taking her through it. She was totally unfamiliar with, for instance, the actual act itself, and positioning. I remember it seemed like an eternity of patience on my part—I'm not patting myself on the back at all—it just seemed like it took hours and hours to gradually get her to relax. Her legs were shaking and she was extremely frightened.

As a matter of fact, she cried quietly—just like in the movies, I'm embarrassed to say—afterwards. And I remember consoling her and holding her very tightly for a long time and asking her why she was crying, and she said, emphatically, that she didn't have any pain, it wasn't that at all. It was sort of, she said, a cry of happiness—that she seemed so fulfilled.

The weekend, then, was an extremely romantic one. We walked together, we had dinner together in restaurants. I remember coming over to pick her up and waiting in the waiting room at her residence at Skidmore and feeling sort of flushed and in love, and her roommate and her friends would, one by one, come down to the sitting room and sort of giggle and look at me, and some of them came in and said hello. And I remember the discreet and some not so discreet smiles as they went back and discussed me.

But I felt proud to be with Colette and it was a new and very exciting time for us, and I remember we did go back to the motel probably three times to make love. It was not easy at all. Like I say, it was so apprehensive and so slow, um, and we did it so gingerly and I didn't want to hurt her and she seemed to be easily hurt. She seemed to be extremely tender and more feminine than at any time I had ever known her. It just increased all my feelings for her probably tenfold.

4

OFFICER'S WIFE, CHILDREN FOUND SLAIN AT FORT BRAGG, said the headline across the top of the front page of the Fayetteville newspaper, in the largest type used since the assassination of John F. Kennedy. VICTIMS OF HIPPIE CULT?

The story said that the wife and two daughters of Jeffrey MacDonald apparently had been murdered by members of a "ritualistic hippie cult" who burst through the rear door of the residence, "shouting, 'LSD is great! LSD is great!' while the family slept."

The provost marshal was quoted as saying, "During the struggle, the captain managed to make his way to the bedroom but was stabbed several times and finally knocked unconscious by a blow or blows on the head."

Fort Bragg is the largest military base in the United States. In addition, it is an open post, meaning that access is unrestricted. No guards monitor visitors and no fences separate the more than 50,000 residents from the surrounding civilian population.

Not including tank trails, there are more than thirty

points of entrance to and exit from Fort Bragg, at least half of them on well-traveled roads. A four-lane state highway traverses the base, passing within 100 yards of Castle Drive. Thus, it had been no simple matter to launch a predawn search for four suspected killers described only as two white males, one black male, and one white female with long blond hair, high boots, and a floppy hat, and an Army spokesman said that despite military police roadblocks which had been thrown up around the base within minutes of the discovery of the bodies, the killers had managed to slip away. A massive search had been launched, however, and it was expected that the assailants would be quickly apprehended. In the meantime, Captain MacDonald was reported in "satisfactory" condition at Womack Hospital.

An accompanying story described the rapidly worsening drug problem in the Fayetteville area, the result of American soldiers smuggling back large quantities of narcotics from Vietnam. The county sheriff was quoted as saying that more heroin arrests had been made in the six months leading up to the murders than in the preceding fifteen years. He estimated that up to two thousand "hippies" had recently taken up residence in and around Fayetteville, living in "ramshackle houses."

"They mob up together," the sheriff said. "They live like animals, with quilts on the floor. They don't have any bed. They paint all kinds of pictures and decorations."

That such individuals were capable also of grotesque acts of violence had been graphically demonstrated less than six months before by members of the Charles Manson cult.

While the Manson killings had horrified, however, and no doubt, in some instances, titillated, they had not *threatened* in any significant way. That satanic cult members could murder a Hollywood starlet in her Beverly Hills home was certain to produce lurid headlines and extensive reportage, but it was an occurrence which seemed light years removed from the world in which most Americans lived.

This new outburst of homicidal violence was, in some ways, more alarming. Sharon Tate had been a prominent movie actress whose fame, conspicuous beauty, and opulent lifestyle might much more understandably—insofar as such madness can ever be understood—have attracted the twisted, pathological attention of the devil-worshiping misfits who made up the Manson cult.

Colette MacDonald, on the other hand, had been the childhood sweetheart of the all-American boy. Her mate had been not an *outré* film director, but a Princeton man, a doctor, a dedicated young Army officer. One of the very best and brightest: a Green Beret. If she and her children—asleep in their own beds on the largest military base in the United States—could not be protected from drug-crazed demons in the night, then there was no longer safety anywhere. Not only was America losing the war in Vietnam, it was faring no better at home.

At first, then, in addition to being so ghastly and horrid in themselves, the MacDonald murders were widely perceived as yet another clear sign among many—indeed, a particularly lurid sign—that the disintegration of the American social fabric, which had accelerated so rapidly and flamboyantly through the mid and late 1960s, would continue—in an even more destructive form—into the decade that had just begun.

After two days had passed with no arrests, the local papers reported that "waves of terror" had engulfed Fort Bragg, especially in the vicinity of Corregidor Courts.

Husbands refused to report for night duty. Doors were double- and triple-locked. Military police, attempting to query neighborhood residents, found women afraid to open their doors, even in daylight, even to uniformed personnel. More than ninety new gun permits were issued on the base within forty-eight hours of the murders, and pawnshops throughout Fayetteville reported an unprecedented demand for firearms.

The obvious similarities to the Manson killings— intruders in the night chanting "Acid is groovy," the word PIG written in blood, the fact that Colette MacDonald, like Sharon Tate, had been pregnant—brought dozens of out-of-town newspaper reporters to Fayetteville. With little hard news to report (on February 18, the Army's only announcement was that a "specially trained team of criminologists" had arrived from the Fort Gordon laboratory), such papers as the New York *Daily News* resorted to running stories on the city's ambience.

"Young girls from all over the country follow the Green Beret glamour and the highly polished jump boots into this town," one feature began. They lived in "rickety old wooden houses on the outskirts," the rent for which was paid "by young men from Fort Bragg who want to get away from military life.

"Speed, hash, whammies, pot, pills—they're all here. Carried into the communes by vets of Vietnam who have seen plenty of action and already at 18 or 19 are looking for a way out of it all."

The desire for information about the background of Jeffrey MacDonald—the Green Beret doctor from the Ivy League who had somehow survived the bizarre, maniacal assault—became almost insatiable.

An interview with his immediate superior yielded the

information that MacDonald was "an unusually good soldier, willing to work eighteen to twenty hours a day."

MacDonald's younger sister, arriving from her home in Schenectady, New York, described him as an "athletic intellectual" who had "breezed through Princeton in three years" and who loved to read—"especially adventures, philosophy, and poetry." She said he had become a doctor because of his compassion for humanity. "He just didn't like to see things die."

On February 19, under considerable media pressure and with no suspects yet apprehended, the Army made Lt. Ron Harrison available for a press conference, at which it was expected that—as the Green Beret who had known the family best—he would provide a more intimate glimpse of the family's life at Fort Bragg.

Harrison began by saying that Jeffrey MacDonald was "an outstanding person in any walk of life. A very intelligent, very perceptive person, very kind, and, I'm certain, a great father."

He liked to help people, Harrison said. "He was always available for counseling." He was also a man interested in many things. Harrison mentioned several: "Special Forces, parachuting, baseball, football, boxing, the kids' horse, what Kimmy did yesterday afternoon, Colette's class at school."

Colette had been, quite simply, "Number one," Harrison said. "A very innocent person, very, very sweet." She and her husband, Harrison added, had been extremely happy about her new pregnancy.

Then he described for the press his final visit to 544 Castle Drive on the night of Valentine's Day. Nothing out of the ordinary had occurred, just a couple of Green Berets sitting around eating Jell-O and cookies—but there had been one incident which, in retrospect, struck him as "odd" and "ironic."

Speaking very softly and slowly, Harrison explained that Jeffrey MacDonald had just received the new issue of *Esquire* magazine in the mail. It was the March 1970 issue. There was a picture of Lee Marvin on the cover, and next to it the caption: "Evil Lurks in California—Lee Marvin Is Afraid."

Almost the entire issue was devoted to articles about witchcraft cults and drug orgies and violence in California. Among the stories to which MacDonald had specifically called Harrison's attention—saying, "Hey, Ron, you've got to take a look at this, it's really wild"—had been one which described how an "acid queen" with long blond hair, attended by a "retinue of four," had consummated a candlelit LSD orgy by copulating with a black swan.

Another story dealt with the murder of Sharon Tate by members of the Charles Manson cult.

Mention was made of the fact that Tate had been pregnant when she was killed, and that the word PIG had been written in her blood on the headboard of her bed.

A funeral service was held on Saturday, February 21. "Hunched over in pain from the stab wound in his chest," according to newspaper accounts, Jeffrey Mac-Donald walked "dry-eyed, with head bowed," into the John F. Kennedy Memorial Chapel in the Special Forces area of Fort Bragg. A squadron of Green Berets in dress uniform carried the three silver caskets—one full-sized, two smaller—into the church.

MacDonald sat in the front row, next to Colette's mother and stepfather. His own mother sat directly behind him. The chaplain read from the Book of Job. "Job, too," the chaplain said, "lost a couple of his children."

MacDonald seemed able to control his emotions until the final moments of the service. Then, the newspapers reported, "sobs shook his shoulders," and he emerged from the chapel "with tears running down his handsome face," and returned directly to his hospital bed.

Very early on the morning of Sunday, February 22—the morning after the funeral—Freddy Kassab borrowed Jeffrey MacDonald's white 1965 Chevrolet Impala convertible and drove to 544 Castle Drive.

He parked across the street from the apartment. It was empty and sealed and, as a crime scene under continuing investigation, guarded by military police. For more than two hours, Kassab sat alone, staring at it.

He was a portly, balding man, fifty years old. He had been born in Montreal to wealthy Syrian parents and had been educated in European private schools. As a child he had learned to speak French fluently and had worn his first tuxedo at the age of six.

At the age of eighteen, he had enlisted in the Canadian Army and had been assigned to intelligence work. He had served as a liaison with the French resistance, making half a dozen parachute drops behind enemy lines. He had been wounded four times during the war and while he was on a mission in Italy his young Scottish wife and infant daughter had been killed by a German bomb dropped on London.

Kassab had returned to North America after the war and his life had become somewhat more prosaic. He moved to an apartment in New York City, remarried, and found work at a Sears, Roebuck store in Brooklyn, where he sold washing machines.

In 1957, while on Long Island, overseeing a housing development in which his mother held a financial interest, he met an interior decorator named Mildred Stevenson. She was the mother of two children and her husband had committed suicide a year before. Kassab's second marriage, which had produced no children, was in the process of divorce. Within a year he married Mildred Stevenson, becoming stepfather to her seventeen-year-old son, Bobby, and to her thirteen-year-old daughter, Colette.

The Kassabs enjoyed an extensive European honeymoon, sailing first class on the *Liberté*. Their drink of choice was Dom Perignon. Later, while touring the Monte Carlo casinos to which Freddy, as a child, had accompanied his wealthy father, they spent time in the company of King Farouk.

In the decade that followed however, the Kassabs had fared less well than expected financially. Mildred's decorating career did not prove profitable and a dress shop which they opened in her hometown of Patchogue proved too posh for community standards and had to be sold at a loss.

They sold their home in Patchogue and moved to the apartment on Washington Square. Within a few years, however, that, too, was surrendered and they returned to Long Island where Freddy found work as a salesman for a firm which distributed liquid egg yolk in large quantity to manufacturers of macaroni, baked goods, and mayonnaise.

Throughout this period of financial disequilibrium, there were two constants in the life of Freddy Kassab. One was his wife, Mildred, for whom his love was deep and strong, and the other was his stepdaughter, Colette. Stepdaughter, he felt, was an awkward, formal term, and one which did not even begin to reflect the depth of feeling that had grown between Freddy and Colette. He thought of her and spoke of her as if she had always been his daughter—as if she were a reincarnation of the infant daughter in London he'd scarcely seen—and his feeling was reciprocated in full. He was, to Colette, not a stepfather, but a father, replacing the father who had killed himself.

Freddy Kassab had quickly become acquainted with Jeffrey MacDonald. Colette, it seemed, was virtually obsessed with this bright, energetic, and extraordinarily charming classmate. She doodled his name—JEFF—in double block letters everywhere: in her schoolbooks, in her mother's cookbooks, and on the desk blotter in the Kassab living room.

While they were dating, in junior high school, Freddy Kassab would often drive them to the movies. Even after they stopped seeing one another—following Colette's summer flirtation with the student from Purdue—Jeff continued to show up at the Kassab house. Unbidden, he would mow the lawn in summer, and shovel the driveway in winter. More than once, he would leave a surprise gift for Colette on the back steps of the house, ringing the doorbell and then disappearing before anyone could come to answer it.

With Colette at Skidmore and Jeff at Princeton—and with Jeff having announced his intention to pursue a career in medicine—both Freddy and Mildred were delighted at the resumption of the relationship. Jeff was so obviously a special young man: so full of drive, of ambition, of intelligence. To both Freddy and Mildred it was gratifying to think that Colette would someday be this doctor's wife.

Neither, however, was prepared for the call they received on the afternoon of August 30, 1963—a call from Mildred's sister in Patchogue, with whom Colette had been living for the summer (the summer which had begun with her letter to Jeff from Washington Square).

"Don't be upset," Colette's Aunt Helen said "but Jeff and Colette have just been to see me, and she's pregnant. They're on their way in to tell you right now."

The Kassabs stood at their living room window, looking out at the street below. They saw Jeff and Colette arrive and park the car. They watched as three times Jeff and Colette, hand in hand, circled the building on foot, trying to build up the courage to ascend.

Mildred, in particular, was horrified at the news. Not that Colette had been intimate with Jeff: as mother and daughter, they'd had frank talks about that subject long before, and it was Mildred's view (which Freddy, with his old-world values, did not fully share) that Colette, at age twenty—three years older than Mildred had been at the time of her own first marriage—was competent to make her own decisions in that regard.

What appalled Mildred were the stupidity, the carelessness, and now the consequences involved in getting pregnant while only halfway through college. Particularly when the father was facing four years of medical school after that.

Mildred suggested an abortion, but neither Jeff nor Colette would hear of it. Their minds were already made up: they would be married. When the Kassabs persisted in expressing an opposing point of view, Jeff went to the telephone and called his mother. She drove in immediately from Long Island to lend her voice to Jeff and Colette's side of the argument.

Neither Freddy nor Mildred had ever before met Dorothy MacDonald, but both were impressed by her forceful personality—a characteristic also so apparent in her son. She rode over all objections the Kassabs raised.

Others might have their futures ruined by such a happenstance, but not Jeff. Nothing would stop him. His drive was too strong. Once he set a goal he would achieve it. He would continue at Princeton and then go on to medical school and become a doctor as planned. Colette could now be with him every step of the way, sharing the joy he would feel in his accomplishments, as well as sharing with him the joys of parenthood.

A wedding date was set for two weeks hence. One hundred people were invited. The wedding was held in a Catholic church because Jeffrey MacDonald was a Catholic, and the reception was at the Fifth Avenue Hotel. It all cost a lot more than Freddy Kassab could afford, but he acted as maître d' for the entire affair and everyone agreed that they had never seen him more charming or radiant.

The years that followed had gone much as Jeffrey MacDonald's mother had predicted, with the exception that the joys of parenthood were soon amplified by the presence of a second child.

Freddy Kassab had stayed in close touch with Colette throughout her marriage. In addition to the frequent family visits, he had made it a practice to call her at least twice a week on the WATS line from his office, often taping the conversations and replaying them for Mildred at night.

In September 1969, when Jeff was transferred from Fort Benning to Fort Bragg, Freddy had driven Colette and the children to their new home. He and Mildred had returned for a Christmas visit, and it was the memory of that time which was affecting him most strongly now, as he sat in tearful silence in the white convertible on Castle Drive.

He remembered, in particular, Christmas morning.

He had risen early, as was his custom, and at about 6 A.M., as he had been making coffee in the kitchen, Jeff had come out of the bedroom and had said, "I've got a surprise for the kids and I want you to come down and take a look."

The two of them had dressed quickly and quietly and had driven a few miles to the stable which housed the pony Jeff had bought. Returning to the apartment, Jeff had told Colette that he'd ordered a gift for the children but that the department store had fouled it up. If they would all get in the car, however, he could at least take them down and show it to them in the window.

They had started down Bragg Boulevard toward Fayetteville, but had quickly turned off on a side road. Colette had asked why. Jeff had been vague, saying, "Well, I've got to stop here and pick something up."

Then they reached the corral and got out of the car and Jeff said, "I want you to see something over here," and he and Freddy led them over and showed them the pony.

For years, Jeff and Colette had told friends that their dream was to someday have a farm in Connecticut, with five children, horses, and lots of dogs. Jeff would practice at a university hospital—probably Yale—and Colette would have her teaching certificate. This Christmas pony was the first tangible step—other than the two children, with the third due in July—toward that goal.

Colette had been so happy, Freddy Kassab recalled, that it had taken her almost half an hour to stop crying.

Residents of Castle Drive were now beginning to emerge from their apartments, some in bathrobes, just bending over to pick up the Sunday paper from the stoop. It would soon be time for Freddy Kassab to return to his grieving wife. But he lingered just a few minutes longer in front of 544 Castle Drive. This was the last place he had seen Colette and Kimberly and Kristen alive and it seemed as close as he would ever be to them again.

The bodies were flown north at 1 P.M. Sunday, in the cargo hold of the Piedmont Airlines plane on which Freddy and Mildred Kassab and Jeffrey MacDonald's mother rode.

Five days earlier they had flown down together, their nervous, apprehensive curiosity gradually giving way to a stifling, overwhelming sense of dread.

Now, as they flew back in silence, there remained nothing to dread. The worst had happened—the worst that could ever happen to anyone—and its effects would govern the remainder of their lives.

Mildred Kassab stared out the window of the plane. The one thought that tormented her above all others was a recollection of her final conversation with Colette.

She had called from Long Island late Sunday afternoon—less than thirty-six hours before Colette's death. Jeff had been working his twenty-four-hour shift at Hamlet Hospital, and Colette, five months pregnant, had been stuck without a car, in February, in the small, cramped apartment on the Southern military base, with her two children bored and restless and confined to the apartment by the rain.

Colette had asked if she could bring Kimberly and Kristen north for a visit. Mildred had looked out at the backyard, where snow was falling. In the fall, the Kassabs had begun construction of a swimming pool. When completed, they felt, it would be something that the children could enjoy for years to come. Now, however, in mid-February, it was just a deep hole in the ground, surrounded by tall piles of slippery, snow-covered dirt.

Mildred had thought that it might pose a hazard for Kimberly and Kristen. So instead of saying, "Catch the first flight tomorrow," she had responded with words that would haunt her the rest of her life.

"Wait until spring," she had said.

Now, on the plane, she was suddenly struck by the unwelcome thought that Colette had not had to wait until spring after all. And that she and the children were coming north not for a visit, but to stay.

The Voice of Jeffrey MacDonald

Through that year, my freshman year at Princeton, Colette clearly became the love of my life. There was no question about it. That was the year our love flowered.

I remember your heart would just leap into your throat at a phone call or when you'd see her return address on a letter and you would joyously finish school on a Friday at noon and start hitchhiking or taking the bus up to Skidmore.

It was an enormously exciting time but it was also a delicate time because Colette was not at all like my prior girlfriends. She was very delightful and warm but yet she had this little bit of aloofness about her which some people took to mean snottiness, but it was never that, it wasn't that at all. If anything, it was timidity on her part. As I got to know her well and we fell in love and whatnot, I realized that it wasn't from a real aloofness, but more from a hesitancy and a slight fear of the world in general.

Basically, she was a very shy person without too much self-confidence. She did not at all have the sort of widespread contact that I enjoyed or my brother or my sister enjoyed, and she kind of leaned on my self-confidence and we had—that was part of our relationship: she liked my leadership and I liked her vulnerability and femininity.

She was always questioning and bright and intuitive and alert, but she had this—sort of an underlying anxiety at all times—very soft and feminine and attractive in a way—and it was nice, sort of, to be her—her boyfriend and her protector.

We were writing each other constantly. I remember I wrote her a long, um, poem, several pages in length, and she thought it was extremely romantic. I think, probably, in retrospect, it was one of the worst things ever written. It was terrible. It was very sophomoric. But I remember that she kept it and—it was, you know, a sophomoric thing to do, but we were young and in love.

I was pretty active in my pursuit. You know, it was okay for me to go to New York and possibly pick up a girl, or even have Penny Wells down on a weekend, but it wasn't special anymore. There was nothing neat about that. The specialness was Colette.

She said she had occasional other dates and I think that's true. As a matter of fact, I remember one specific weekend during the winter. I called her and she apologized—you know, I was going to go up to see her on short notice—and she apologized profusely because she had a blind date arranged by her roommate.

The blind date came over from Dartmouth for the weekend, and I remember spending the whole time kind of jealous and angry and hurt, and waiting all through the week for a letter, which I got about Friday of the following week, in which she said the weekend was a bust.

Whether that was a transparent lie or not, it certainly

lifted my spirits. I remember, like, refalling in love when I got the letter saying that her weekend with the blind date was a disaster, the guy from Dartmouth was a quote, animal, unquote, which was what we all kidded everyone from Dartmouth about being.

I remember Thanksgiving of that freshman year. Colette was not going to come down, which seemed very strange, and she told me that it was because of funds. She didn't have the funds to come down. And I remember thinking how weird that was, with Freddy and Mildred living in such, you know, supposed splendor in Greenwich Village.

And I know this sounds ridiculous and self-serving, but it's not. I sent her something like thirty dollars or forty dollars for her bus ticket down to New York. Now I know it sounds ridiculous, but I remember writing to her and sending her either, like, two twenty-dollar bills or a forty-dollar check, and told her don't be absurd, you know, come down for Thanksgiving, it would be very lonely for you to be up there at Skidmore.

And I remember her calling me and thanking me, and then she invited me in. Now, I wasn't there the whole weekend, I don't remember exactly how long, but I stayed overnight at the apartment in Greenwich Village, on Washington Square, and the things that I remember most were two things.

One was the walk through the Village, because it was one of those beautiful fall days and we were holding hands and we were very much in love, and we stopped at an outdoor café, and we went through the park at the end of Fifth Avenue and watched the organ grinders and the, the, you know, ah, the people at the time when there were a lot of guitar players, um, and we thought, you know, that Greenwich Village was super, um, that it was neat and artsy-craftsy, et cetera, cetera, and we had a very, like, lovely day.

I also remember that night, the nice dinner we had at Freddy and Mildred's apartment. Mildred was a good cook and the dinners were always a little more formal than I was used to at my house. My house was very casual.

At Mildred's, you know, everyone sat in certain places and you stood behind a chair until the table was all ready to go and then we all sat down and certain, ah, ceremony was always performed with the wine, and, ah, it was much more formal.

We kind of enjoyed it. Colette and I were learning from it and it seemed very chic, although we used to occasionally make light of it and think that Freddy and Mildred were blowhards about it, that they were a little pretentious.

But the other thing I remember about that night is when Mildred and Freddy went to bed, Colette and I sat up. I was sleeping on the couch in the living room. It was a long, I believe, green couch which they'd had for a long time. It was a very expensive couch. Colette had set up the bed—you know, set up the sheet and the pillowcases and the pillow and blanket and stuff, and we were sitting out there talking and we began kissing and ah, making out, as it were, um, and Colette, ah, got a little flustered and said that she really shouldn't be doing this at home.

She didn't want Freddy walking out or Mildred walking out and, you know, I said fine and she went to bed, and I remember it was very strange because this was a little atypical of Colette: she came out about twenty minutes later and lay down on the couch with me, very quietly and a little apprehensively, and we began kissing and—and caressing each other.

We ended up making love, and I remember it was one of those exquisite times where we were trying to be so incredibly quiet, and it was one of those times that Colette, ah—it was sort of the excitement of doing something, I guess, ah, that we shouldn't have been doing, and in a place where we shouldn't have been doing it, and the threat of Mildred and Freddy walking out at any moment, but it was more exciting than even usual, and she was sort of, like, giving herself to me by coming out of her room and getting into bed with me, and it was the first time that this had ever really happened because we had just recently begun making love, and we—it was a—incredible, very exciting session. We talked about this for years afterwards, in fact, as one of our most memorable lovemaking sessions.

We never openly discussed whether she or I had slept with anyone else. She always avoided the subject of Penny Wells. She was not really jealous of Penny. She always felt, like, unthreatened by her, but she didn't see any need to discuss it. I think she wondered what the attraction was between Penny and I, but we never talked about it. I never told her that we'd had a tremendous physical thing going and, you know, we never discussed it. We sort of avoided those topics.

We did talk about her feelings for Dean. Never about potential lovemaking with Dean. I'm not sure if she made love with Dean Chamberlain or not. My strong impression is that she didn't. She always implied that in conversation. We never talked—I never said to her, "Were you a virgin?" I never said to her: "Did you ever make love to Dean Chamberlain?" It always seemed like sort of a too-jealous thing to ask, and too immature, and

I—we always tried to respect each other more than that. She never, for instance, said to me: "Did you make love with Penny Wells?" I think we tried to be honest with each other and so we skirted that type of question.

We did make love in some wild places, though. I remember one Saturday morning I was up seeing her—as a matter of fact, I believe it was Happy Pappy weekend at Skidmore, and Freddy Kassab did not go up, I went up. I believe this episode was Happy Pappy weekend. I may be incorrect. Happy Pappy weekend possibly was during the winter.

But in any case, on Saturday morning—it may have been a later weekend in the spring, because it was warm—she took me out to the Saratoga racetrack. They were either not running or the horses were running later in the day, but there were workouts going on at the track. In other words, there were grooms working horses and I remember there were, oh, you know, probably fifty or a hundred people wandering around the stands, and there were people cleaning up. There were people mowing the lawn and doing the hedges and stuff like that, so the horses must have been in session.

And Colette and I were walking in the infield, carrying a blanket, and, I believe, lunch, and we ended up making love under the blanket in broad daylight, very slowly and gently. We thought, of course, being very secretive and no one could possibly see us, but I'm sure anyone who passed within two hundred yards of us could see that we were making love.

And I remember that summer one night we went down to a park in Patchogue—we were watching a big softball game. I was playing on some softball leagues, and Colette used to love to come and watch me play. But this was not one of my games. This was like an A-League game—these guys eventually went to the Jones Beach world tournament.

But we went down to watch and got bored around the third or fourth inning and we walked out into the outfield, behind the fence, and we eventually ended up making love under our blanket while the game was going on—just out of the arc lights, just at the fringe of the lights. And I remember thinking what an adventure it was, and Colette felt the same way—that here we were making love only 400 feet from this whole crowd of people watching this big softball game.

5

The laboratory team from Fort Gordon spent four days inside 544 Castle Drive.

In addition to the eighty-one blue threads in the master bedroom, they found nineteen in the bedroom of Kimberly MacDonald, the majority of them under the covers that had been tucked up around the dead girl. Two threads were found in Kristen's bedroom, but in the living room, where Jeffrey MacDonald had said his pajama top had been torn during his struggle with the intruders, no fibers from it were found. A CID agent with a magnifying glass spent hours on his hands and knees, searching through the nap of the living room carpet, but all he found was some confetti from a child's game and a few strands of tinsel which had fallen, weeks earlier, from the family Christmas tree.

Investigators found not only fibers, but splinters. These splinters, which were bloodstained and which appeared to have broken off the club that had been found outside the back door, were located in all three bedrooms of the apartment, including Kristen's, although Kristen had not been attacked with the club. No splinters, however, were found in the living room, where Jeffrey MacDonald said the intruders had struck him.

There was, of course, a great deal of blood in all three bedrooms.

In the master bedroom, in addition to that which had soaked the carpet, sheet, and bedspread, several drops of blood—forming a circle about six inches in diameter—were found just inside the room, near the doorway that led to the hall.

There were also spatters of blood on the walls and one more blood-streaked indentation on the ceiling—a mark which suggested to investigators that a club from which blood had already been dripping had been raised high above the head of whoever had wielded it, in preparation for the striking of a particularly forceful blow.

A similar indentation was found on the ceiling of Kimberly's bedroom and spatters of blood were found high on the wall above her bed. Additional, larger drops of blood formed a trail in the hallway between her room and the master bedroom.

Across the hall, in Kristen's bedroom, there were blood spatters on the wall above the bed, blood in large quantity on the top sheet, blood stains on the side of the bed, and a large, heavy stain on the floor next to the bed. This, of course, was in addition to the bloody footprint which led away from her bed toward the doorway.

Blood also was found elsewhere in the apartment. There were traces on the door to a hall closet that contained a large stock of medicinal supplies, such as prescription drugs, syringes, hypodermic needles, and disposable scalpel blades.

Several drops, as Ivory had noted, had dripped onto the right side of the sink in the hall bathroom, and, as Ivory had also noted, five drops, each about the size of a dime, had dripped onto the kitchen floor, beneath the sink, directly in front of a cabinet. When Ivory got down on his hands and knees and opened the cabinet door, he found, in the extreme left rear corner, tucked away behind a can of Ajax, a sack of potatoes, some scrubbing brushes, and a pile of old rags, an opened box which contained several packages of Perry Pure Latex Disposable Surgeon's Gloves.

There were certain places, however, where blood was not found.

No blood was found, for instance (nor were any fingerprints), on either of the two telephones that Jeffrey MacDonald had said he'd used to call for help after checking the blood-drenched members of his family for signs of life and attempting to resuscitate them.

No blood was found on the floor of the hallway where MacDonald had said he'd lain face down and unconscious after having already been stabbed in the chest.

And, with two small exceptions, no blood was found anywhere in the living room where MacDonald had said he'd been attacked. The two exceptions were the speck on the outer lens of the eyeglasses which were identified as belonging to MacDonald, and a bloody smear, having roughly the configuration of a fingertip, across the top of the March 1970 issue of *Esquire* magazine—the issue with Lee Marvin on the cover.

Examination of the word PIG on the headboard led technicians to conclude that it had been written by a right-handed person in full control of his motor faculties who had used the first two fingers of his right hand, those fingers encased in a thin covering such as a rubber surgical glove, and who had found it necessary to return to the source of the blood at least once in order to obtain sufficient quantity to enable him to complete the writing of the word. Jeffrey MacDonald was right-handed.

Examination of the blood on the kitchen floor—focusing on the extent to which it had splattered—led the CID to the conclusion that it had dripped from a height of between twenty and thirty inches—as it would have if someone bleeding from a small wound in the chest had crouched or knelt in front of the cabinet in order to remove something from inside it.

William Ivory paid a return visit to Jeffrey MacDonald's next-door neighbors. He asked again if they were certain they had heard nothing from 544 Castle Drive during the early morning hours of February 17. The warrant officer's wife said no, she was not certain at all. She was, in fact, now certain that she *had* heard sounds coming from the apartment, but in the first shock of learning what had happened she had been afraid to mention it.

The way the apartments were laid out along Castle Drive, the neighbors actually lived above the MacDonalds, although the entrances to the apartments were adjacent to one another. The master bedroom of the upstairs apartment was, thus, directly above the MacDonald master bedroom. The warrant officer's wife now said she could remember having been awakened by the sound of Colette MacDonald's loud and angry voice. She could not recall what words had been spoken, but she emphasized the anger in her voice.

Her sixteen-year-old daughter also spoke again to Ivory. Her bedroom was directly above the MacDonald living room. Often, in the past, she had been able to hear conversations from the apartment below, or the sound of a phonograph or television.

Sometime after she had gone to bed on the night of Monday, February 16, she said, she had been awakened by a sound from below. It had not been either the phonograph or television. Nor had it been the sound of a struggle between Jeffrey MacDonald and four intruders who were clubbing and stabbing him. She had heard nothing of the sort.

What she had heard, she said, had been the sound of a male voice—it had sounded to her like the voice of Jeffrey MacDonald—either sobbing loudly or laughing hysterically.

When asked at a press conference whether MacDonald was considered a suspect in the murders of his family, the Fort Bragg provost marshal said, "There are a lot of suspects. Captain MacDonald is certainly a witness."

The Voice of Jeffrey MacDonald

Interestingly enough, Colette and I do think that we know exactly when she got pregnant with Kimberly. It was sometime in late July or early August after sophomore year. I don't remember the exact date but I remember the moment very clearly.

We were at her Aunt Helen's, where Colette was staying for that summer. We had been spending every available moment—I mean *every* waking moment—together. I would stay over there until 11 or 12 or 1 every night and then go home. We were by now sleeping together fairly openly but we were not, of course, taking precautions except haphazardly—occasionally using condoms and occasionally using withdrawal, and trying the rhythm method, but our lovemaking had increased greatly through the trips up to Skidmore and her trips down to Princeton and our vacations together and now the summertime, and our love was in full bloom, there was no question about it.

We were already talking at this time of when would we be getting married. Never from the viewpoint of—I never said to her, "Colette, will you marry me?" It was from the viewpoint of, when do you think it would be possible for the two of us to really be together, and it was always done in a sort of roundabout, mildly mysterious fashion. We never openly said to each other, "We're going to be married for the rest of our lives," but we talked in this kind of code about right after college we would— it would be permanent, and, um, you know, won't—isn't life fantastic now that we're together and seeing each other almost every day.

But we were absolutely positive that Kimberly was conceived when we were making love one night about 11:30. Helen had gone to bed and we were sitting in the car at Helen's house and I was kissing Colette goodnight at the back door and we kept kissing each other and kissing each other and finally we moved over to the hammock, believe it or not, that was in the backyard, and we were in the hammock, fooling around—I mean, you know, kissing each other, basically—and then we started petting and gradually more and more clothes came off and by now it was probably 12 or 12:30 at night and we were in the hammock and Colette was very gently saying no, you can't, you know, we're not taking any precautions, and I was saying we have to, we have to, I promise I'll pull out—as usual—and we were extremely passionate, you know, passionately making love and it—we sort of exploded and we lay there in each other's arms and we did something which for us was not that common. Umm, normally we made love once and occasionally, like especially on the honeymoon I remember we made love many times in one day, but we did not have this, this, this, ah, like need between us to make love two or three times a day. We usually made love once, or something like that.

But I remember this specific night we lay there and twenty minutes later we were making love again, and we stayed there until about 1:30 or 2 in the morning, in the hammock, in each other's arms, and I remember neither of us felt any, like, ah, guilt or, um, negative feelings about this.

We were totally in love at this point. We really were throwing ourselves at each other and there was a feeling that both Colette and I had that it was just such an explosion that it had to have been that night that she got pregnant. Colette always said that she could tell.

Anyway, it wasn't two weeks later that Colette came to me, kind of embarrassed and apologetic, and said she was two or three or four or five days late on her period and that she was going to have to go see the doctor. I told her at first that that was nonsense and, with more hope than fact, I told her she was just missing her period because she was scared. And she—you know, we were scared, there's no question about it. We didn't know what it meant for her schooling, for my schooling, our life, and yet there was this element of, ah, sudden excitement between us.

I'm not saying we were proud of what we did. We went to my mother and father first and told them with much fear and trepidation and were vastly relieved when they seemed to handle it so gracefully, ah, and gently. Ah, there wasn't even like a burst of anger.

There was, ah, some sadness and resignation but actually I remember being astutely surprised—*acutely* surprised—at my father and mother handling it so gently, talking to us that we had to make a decision, um, marriage number one, adoption number two, and abortion number three.

We immediately in our own minds threw out adoption. We wrestled for a day or two with the thought of abortion, but, ah, we clearly were opposed to that. Colette and I were very much in love. Neither of us at the time, ah, really believed in abortion. Colette was much more anti-it than I was. I wasn't pro or anti, I just had never thought about it, but when it was us facing it, it was an uncomfortable and an ugly thought. Neither of us liked it, neither of us really wanted it. We struggled with it for several days, and we mutually came to that conclusion—that we would not have an abortion, that we couldn't get an abortion, that we just couldn't face each other, and that we didn't want that and we loved each other and why shouldn't we just go ahead and get married?

Freddy, on the other hand, and Mildred, were very clear that the decision should be, ah, number one: abortion. Their explanation, which was very open, was that the pregnancy and marriage at this time would hurt my career. They were worried about my medical career and they stated it. But once we decided to get married, then Mildred made no bones about the fact that she wouldn't mind having a physician as a son-in-law.

Our wedding day was a little bit overcast. We were afraid that it wasn't gonna be a nice day but it ended up being nice. It was a little windy, but it was September in New York and it was beautiful. It was a little cool, too, as I remember. I don't think it ever really got hot that day, but I remember being in a nice breeze and it was a beautiful day and the wedding went off very, very smoothly, very beautifully. Everything was just super. It was a really nice wedding.

We stayed that night at the Hotel Pierre up on Central Park South, had a nice room, and despite the fact that we had just left the reception we decided to really show off and order from room service, so we ordered, I believe, like, at ten o'clock at night, steak sandwiches and champagne and it was something like $60 or some incredible cost like that and she and I both almost fell over.

It was a very exciting time. We had a very lovely night. It was a funny night because we were tentative, despite the fact that we'd been sleeping together for at least a year and she was already pregnant. It seems a little silly but in fact we really were—it really was like a honeymoon night. We were very tentative and I'd say gentle with each other. It was sort of the beginning of our real life together.

The honeymoon was kind of a funny time. It was, um—I don't have one word to describe the honeymoon by any means. There was a certain amount of hesitancy. There was a little chagrin because Colette was pregnant. We had this sort of feeling of adventure that we were embarking on this great life adventure together, and that somehow we always knew we would do that ever since we met in the eighth grade, and now we were fulfilling that.

And yet you have to remember it was 19, um, 63, and it wasn't common for college kids, especially at Princeton, to have to get married all of a sudden and have a child. As a matter of fact, we had to ask permission to be married at Princeton at that time. So it was, you know—there was a whole host of confusing emotions.

We drove up to Cape Cod and—the week is a little blurry, to be honest. I have some great remembrances of us walking together through, I guess it's Provincetown at the end of Cape Cod, and eating the salt water taffy and going in all the shops. It was a quiet time, of course. It was after Labor Day. And it was so beautiful. We had one or two rainy days—no, two or three rainy days out of the week and only two or three sunny days, but we enjoyed both. We were kind of oblivious to the weather. And we had a super time. We were arm in arm, and we would eat a late breakfast and a great big dinner and walk around and shop.

I had been passed a lot of envelopes all through the reception. People kept, you know, coming up, wishing us congratulations and giving me envelopes like they do at Polish or Italian weddings.

And when we got to this motel in Provincetown, we sat on the bed and we took out the suitcase—we had thrown all these envelopes and cards and everything, without really looking at them the first night, into the suitcase—and the next night we're up in Cape Cod and we undid all these envelopes and we had almost $3,000 sitting in front of us, which at that time—in 1963—was an extraordinary sum of cash.

I still remember this very clearly. We were sitting at the edge of the bed—I was, as a matter of fact, on the left side, sitting on the bed looking down toward the foot, and Colette was on the right side and her back was a little to me as she was opening some of the letters, and my back was a little to her.

We both turned and looked at each other after the first couple of letters and she was squealing sort of with delight as she opened each letter, and I ended up letting her open the majority of them because it was so much fun to watch her, and they kept making this mound of money and cash and checks and, like I say, it ended up to right around $3,000, and we were just stunned.

We just—it was sort of hilarious—we didn't sort of

know what to do with that much money. So we put it all in a big wad and put some rubber bands around it and put it back in the suitcase. But I remember we had a super week.

One dinner we had was the best of the whole honeymoon. It was, I think, like about the second or third night. We found this Portuguese restaurant which we went back to later in the week, which is always a mistake. You can't really re-create.

We had a—the second dinner was nice also but the first dinner was like magic. It was the first time we had— we ordered a strange wine, I believe it was a Portuguese wine, and we had a Portuguese dish, and I don't remember what it was, but I remember everything was spicy, and we tried everything, with entrées and soup and the salad and then the main course, which was seafood. We both picked seafood but they were done Portuguese-style and they were very zesty, spicy hot.

We had the absolute, most delightful evening. It's one of the best evenings I think we ever had. We laughed and giggled the whole time and had the bottle of champagne at least, and then we went back to the motel and had a super night.

I think we realized then, it was about the third day of the honeymoon—although we really had no bad feelings, bad premonitions, we had hesitancy—and at that point, about the second or third day of the honeymoon, we felt that, sort of, we could conquer the world. That the union was so fine and so much fun and held so much promise and fulfillment for both of us.

6

The bodies of Colette MacDonald and her two daughters were buried in a Long Island cemetery on Monday, February 23. Immediately afterward, Freddy and Mildred Kassab retreated to the seclusion of their home. They pulled down the blinds to shut out the light and had their phone number changed to prevent any incoming calls. In their grief they wanted total isolation.

Jeffrey MacDonald's mother did not have the time to plunge deeply into mourning. She left the gravesite and drove immediately to New Hope, Pennsylvania, to meet with a psychiatrist concerning difficulties being experienced by her older son, Jay.

The previous November, in apparent reaction to a drug overdose, Jay, who was a year and a half older than Jeffrey, and who, like Jeffrey, had been named Most Popular male during his senior year of high school, had suffered a schizophrenic break with reality. This had resulted in his arrest and confinement to a state mental hospital after he had assaulted his mother on a street corner.

A police report prepared at the time said that Jay "struck his mother several times about the body," and that it had been necessary for officers to "physically subdue" him. The incident had occurred on November 7, at the corner of Windsor Avenue and Montauk Highway in the town of Brightwaters, New York. Jay had been brought to a local precinct house and examined by a police psychiatrist who recommended transfer to Central Islip State Hospital.

Jeff had been called home on emergency leave from Puerto Rico, where he had been on a training exercise with his Green Beret unit. Jay had been released from the hospital within a week and had returned to his part-time job as a bartender at a Greenwich Village tavern called the Shortstop.

On the morning of February 17, having been informed by Freddy Kassab that she was to accompany them on the urgent and ominous trip to Fort Bragg, Dorothy MacDonald had tried, unsuccessfully, to reach Jay by telephone.

The next day, while at Fort Bragg, she learned that Jay—having heard the news of the murders on the radio—had suffered a relapse and had once again required hospitalization.

A close family friend named Bob Stern, who was in the computer business and who had access to a private plane, had obtained Jay's release from the hospital in order that the two of them might fly to Fort Bragg to attend the funeral on February 21. Afterward, Stern had flown back to New York with Jay and had helped him transfer his belongings from the Greenwich Village apartment he was sharing with a merchant seaman to the Stern home in New Hope, Pennsylvania, about thirty miles north of Philadelphia. Arrangements had been made for Jay to recuperate at the Stern residence while undergoing psychotherapy as an outpatient.

Dorothy MacDonald was a sturdy, energetic woman of fifty who was employed as a school nurse. Since her husband's unexpected death of lung disease at the age of forty-eight, four years earlier, she had noted a steady deterioration in her older son's emotional well-being. Since his November breakdown, she had devoted an enormous amount of time and energy to efforts to aid his recovery. Now she was faced with him in a state of relapse and with her younger son, Jeffrey, recovering from injuries sustained during the assault which had resulted in the murder of his wife and children.

After visiting Jay and the Stern family, and meeting with a psychiatrist in nearby Doylestown, Jeffrey Mac-Donald's mother drove back to Fort Bragg on Tuesday, February 28, to return to his hospital bedside.

Jeffrey MacDonald remained in Womack Hospital for nine days. He looked pale and said he felt exhausted. He complained of frequent, severe headaches and of an inability to sleep. An armed guard was stationed outside his door to protect him from any attempts at further violence by the four intruders who he said had massacred his family. The chest tube used to reexpand his lung did not function properly, and it became necessary to insert a second tube. He was seen twice by a Green Beret psychiatrist, a major with a shaved head and a handlebar mustache. "Normal grief process continues," the major noted at the conclusion of his second visit.

On Thursday, February 26, his lung having healed without further complication, MacDonald was discharged from Womack Hospital and was assigned to a room in Bachelor Officers' Quarters. The armed guard that had been stationed outside his hospital room was withdrawn.

Upon hearing of this development, MacDonald's mother confronted his commanding officer. She demanded to know why the guard had been removed, particularly since, in an unsupervised BOQ room, her son would be in more danger of an attack by murderous intruders than he had been while hospitalized. She was told that law enforcement officials at Fort Bragg did not feel that her son was in danger.

"That makes it sound," Dorothy MacDonald said, "like you suspect Jeff may be involved."

The commanding officer assured her, without attempting to explain the contradiction, that her son was not considered a suspect. He said, in fact, that having just gone through such an ordeal, Captain MacDonald was now free to take some time off, and added that Mrs. MacDonald could retain her visitor's suite, in order to remain close to her son, as long as she wished.

That evening, Jeffrey MacDonald said he found his new room unbearably depressing. He said he could not yet cope with solitude. He spent the night on his mother's couch.

MacDonald, however, was indeed a suspect at that time. Even before his release from the hospital, military authorities—while continuing to refuse public comment (newspapers reported that a "shroud of secrecy" had enveloped the investigation)—had concluded that the young captain was the *primary* suspect in the murders.

In a report never publicly released, the Fort Bragg provost marshal expressed the opinion that "the accuracy, similarity, and location of the wounds strongly indicates actions of one individual with expertise on vulnerability—killing as rapidly and mercifully as possible without creating any noise."

He added the observation that all the knife wounds were "deep, and in a relatively small area of the bodies," and that there had been "no disfiguring and no sexual molestation," indices which, to him, pointed away from drug-crazed hippies, and toward the one man—husband, father, and physician with an interest in surgery—known to have been in the apartment at the time that the murders occurred.

The provost marshal's opinion was shared by Franz Joseph Grebner and the two CID investigators—William Ivory and Robert Shaw—who were working most exhaustively at the crime scene. The three of them, within days, had come to believe it highly likely that Jeffrey MacDonald had—for reasons unknown—killed his wife and children and had then—in an attempt to escape detection—staged a scene designed to make the murders look like the work of drug-crazed intruders, even going so far as to puncture his own lung in the process.

As early as Monday, February 23, the provost marshal had informed the FBI that they could cease their nationwide search for the four killer hippies. He said a preliminary consideration of the physical evidence did not indicate that any civilians had been involved in the commission of the crimes.

Nonetheless, pending laboratory analysis, the "evidence" against MacDonald was nonexistent. Thus, at the beginning of March, when Dorothy MacDonald asked if she could take her son to the seashore for a few days of rest and recuperation, no one at Fort Bragg felt there was any basis for not granting her request.

So, during the first week of March, Jeffrey MacDonald and his mother drove to Myrtle Beach, South Carolina, for what she hoped would be a restorative time near the salt water to which he had always been attracted as a child.

Later, MacDonald would recall that trip:

"We drove down in my white Chevy, the white '65 Chevy convertible with the black top. It was a really nice car, it wasn't souped up or anything, it was a handsome convertible for the time. I'm sure I did the driving, because that would be my normal personality, and I can see us driving along this two-lane highway. It seemed to run indefinitely. It was almost an extraordinarily long four-hour drive.

"We talked aimlessly about things, not seriously ever about Colette, Kim, Krissy, or that night. We talked about other things, about Jay. I believe I knew at this time that Jay was having problems. I don't think I was aware of the depth of his problems. I knew there was something going on up north."

In early March, however, the air was chilly, the sky dark, and many of the better motels and restaurants not yet open.

"We stayed at a motel which I would rate as one star out of four stars—possibly a half star instead of one. The rooms were drafty and it was a cold weekend on the beach. It was gray, overcast, windy—like forty-five to fifty degrees, which was perfect for my mood. It was just how I felt. It was as though the cumulonimbus that were scudding across the skies were a reflection of me, rather than a clear sky that would draw me out of this depression we were in.

"We found the food to be sort of unpleasant. I don't remember anything that we ate, but I remember that we were displeased with (A) the accommodations and (B) the food. We had a couple of crummy meals. The town was almost shut down because it was the off season.

"We did walk on the beach, though. I remember my mother was frustrated and anxious because things were not turning out like she hoped. She had hoped it would be warm and sunny. I think she sensed what I've always known about myself, and what later years proved to be correct: that I *do* recover with the sun. I need the sun. Basking in the sun rejuvenates me physically and emotionally. A long, sunny weekend is the best possible cure for me. But that was not to be.

"My mother was trying to give me space, and yet she wanted the weekend at least to have something nice to try to lighten the load, so therefore she was frustrated and anxious, and I was the one who had to turn and say to her, 'Relax, that's okay. We'll just—we'll walk on the beach anyway.' So we did.

"But actually, walking on the beach was not a good thing for me at that time. It was a melancholy thing. I'm not a beach walker. I'm a much more active person than that. So I was walking along the surf remembering both my father and my family and trying to forget the recent tragedy, and I had to keep turning from my mother so as to not let her see me cry, which is my way, right or wrong."

As MacDonald's mother recalled it: "The time that was spent at the shore was very quiet. We would have a quiet breakfast, go to bed early, rest, and so forth. He complained of a headache and I'd give him an aspirin, you know, just to reduce it. We picked up shells, and he just walked. He walked for hours along the beach. I did not question him. I never probed. I could not ask questions. I felt that other people had. I was the mother of a young man whose wife and children had been murdered and my concern was to give solace and to try and help him bear this agonizing burden. When he wept, I was trying to tell him that it was really rough and I understood and that we would just have to go on from that point. And sometimes he would weep, and he would say, 'I loved them so much, Mom. You know I loved them so much.'"

Back at Fort Bragg, on March 6, Jeffrey MacDonald wrote a letter to the Kassabs.

> *Dear Fred and Mildred—*
>
> *Apparently it was not just a bad dream—the magnitude of our loss is something I'm still trying to comprehend.*
>
> *I know this won't help you in your grief but I want you to know that I loved Colette more than anything in the world. I know she was happy as long as we were together, and I will never be the same person without her.*
>
> *Although my family is gone, it helps me just a little to remember that Colette and Kim and Kristy and I had as much happiness in our short years together as most families have in a lifetime. Colette truly loved you both and would want you to remember the happier times.*
>
> *Love,*
Jeff

The Voice of Jeffrey MacDonald

The year at Princeton was incredibly great. I was in absolute love with Colette and I thought having Kimberly was neat and we had tons of people over to the house. We had just moved into a house on Bank Street, right off Nassau Street, across from the university, and we had some great times: the big dinner that Colette and I learned to cook for all our friends, mainly spaghetti, but we had some others and our house became as I knew my house in Patchogue, where my parents were the entertainers of everyone. Colette and I had sort of taken over this role at Princeton. We were the hit of the campus, so to speak.

Of course, that was the year that Bill Bradley became a big star and the next year he went on to superstardom, but we were good friends with Cosmo Iacavazzi, who was the all-American football player at Princeton at the time, and I remember he used to come over to eat and we had a blast together.

I was so proud of Princeton, and being a member of Tiger Inn, the eating club. It wasn't Ivy or Cottage, which were the rich boys' clubs, but it was, you know, one of the top five for sure, and it was *the* jock club—Cosmo Iacavazzi was a member—and Colette w²s proud of me being in there.

We had some difficult times. I remember there was a football weekend and we had invited my parents and we had tickets for the game and everything, but my father was always an enigma—you never really could figure out what was gonna happen next. He was very ambivalent about a lot of things. He was proud of me being at Princeton but he was also upset a little bit that it was maybe too snooty a place—in other words, it was too pseudo-intellectual, and it was perhaps a little bit left-leaning, and more importantly it wasn't the working people, it was the phonies of the world that were going there.

My father was essentially an unschooled person. He was extremely bright, a voracious reader, an intellectual at heart but one who tried to hide his intellectual—both capabilities and desires—under a barrel. He would have liked the world to have believed that he was rough and tough and non-intellectual, in fact a laborer, and he would occasionally make what sounded like racist comments, either about racism or other religious groups like Presbyterians or Methodists or whatever.

He was raised by his great-grandmother in Gardner, Massachusetts. His own mother had gotten married at fifteen, just like *her* mother had done, and just like *her* mother had had to leave *her* behind to go off and find a way to earn a living, she had had to do the same thing when her husband left her. She moved to New York when my father was very young, leaving him with this great-grandmother who spoke French and who was, apparently, a very tough woman and very dominating.

He became an electrical designer. He had gone to

technical school, and essentially he was a draftsman. He worked at the Brookhaven National Laboratory, and even though he never finalized his engineering degree, he never really forgave the intellectually elite community for not recognizing him as an engineer. He always resented that he was being paid less to do full engineer's work, just because he was a designer and did not have a degree.

There's no question that he was the leader and ruler of our family. His presence—it's almost beyond comprehension how important he was to the family. His presence was huge, wherever he was and in whatever setting he was in. He was a very magnetic person, not a shy person, a lot of charm and grace, always a gentleman and chivalrous—he treated women in a chivalrous fashion which now, of course, would be considered chauvinistic—but his hold on the family, even to this day, is staggering.

My Dad *was* the family, and that's the truth. He was a phenomenal person with an incredible presence. I think no matter how strong my Mom got—and this is a little unfair but it's simply a fact from my viewpoint—no matter how strong my Mom is and was, my Dad was still the main mug. He was a dominating force in all of our lives. There's no question that he was the most important force in my brother's and sister's psyches—my brother, incidentally, was clearly favored by my father, simply because he was firstborn—and, I suspect, also in mine.

He was not a peaceful man by any means. He terrified us when he was angry, and a mere look, or the *thought* of him being angry would completely silence us and stop any problem. Also, he constantly railed against the domination by women that he saw in the world, and his background, of course, is very consistent with that. Never to his dying day did he forgive the women of this world for attempting to rule and take over, and many was the time—especially when he'd had a little too much to drink—I heard him say that a domineering woman was the most dangerous creature on God's earth.

In keeping with that, he was not a warm, loving father. He was a little distant, especially physically. My father was super-masculine and he never really touched us or hugged us or kissed us, because that was unmanly. He could never express his love for us. We all knew it was there, but we never heard it spoken and never felt a physical embrace.

What he demanded most were two things: absolute obedience, and achievement. In my family, any indication that you couldn't keep up or couldn't be superior in every field—or try harder and overcome whatever adversity it was—was a sign of weakness.

And what I remember *most* clearly about him, I suppose, were the trips we would take on Sundays to visit my grandmother—his mother—in Malverne, where she had finally wound up living. It was a harrowing experience to go forty-five miles along the old 1950s back roads between Patchogue and Malverne with an impatient, angry father driving the car, bitching constantly about the inadequacies of every other driver on the road.

He was always very tense and angry on these trips, and he was extremely vituperative toward other drivers. His frequent expression was he wished he had a Sherman tank, or he wished he was driving a big cement truck and he could just squash the other cars.

But anyway, at Princeton, we had this big weekend all set up, and one of the highlights of these weekends was bringing your parents to the club for dinner. And I remember that my father was already sick and was having difficulty walking long distances, and the day was a trial for him because we had done so much and walked so much and we had to walk from the club at lunchtime to go down to Palmer Stadium, which was a pretty good walk for him, being short of breath, and then walk back and have dinner.

And I'll never forget how incensed he got that we had black waiters in little white, short jackets serving us in the club. He became furious, and as a matter of fact we got into an argument at the club over that, the particulars of which elude me, but I was embarrassed about his anger.

The black help and the short white jackets were uncomfortable to him at best, and snobby and pseudo-intellectual and effete at worst, and we had a little, sort of, scene that day together, and I'm kind of sorry, of course, that it occurred. We didn't have that much time together from then on, and I remember with some sadness that this occurred.

From time to time I brought Colette to the club, the Tiger Inn, and, um, she was funny, she was a little ambivalent. She didn't like the idea of clubs at Princeton because they seemed a little, um, white-glovish, too much like something Mildred would like, but she also kind of enjoyed the status, and also the fact that the Tiger Inn was considered a really good club—one of the top five for sure, and it was *the* jock club—and she was proud of me being in there. We went over and had lunch and dinner many times, especially on football weekends, and she was kind of proud of that. And, um, there were no other relationships going on at all during this year. There was—I wasn't seeing anyone or doing anything. I was coming home. You know, we had a good year.

*   *   *

Kimmy's birth was, of course, traumatic, no question about it. Colette, you know, does not—did not—like pain. We had joked for a long time about natural childbirth and she had even made a little pretense at beginning classes for natural childbirth but she was advised not to by her physician and advised not to by me. I knew Colette very well and I felt that as soon as the first pain came the plans for natural childbirth would go out the window. And indeed they did.

Colette is a feminine, gentle person. She was not a sturdy frontier woman. She, you know—she was very motherly. Especially later on, with two kids, she was an incredibly good mother. But at this point, you know, she was reasonably frail.

Like, for instance, she's left-handed, you know, and so she was—she had this funny-looking shot on the basketball court, and she could dribble only intermittently well, sometimes with both hands. But very feminine and pretty and it's distressing to see her with the hair, you know, a little scraggly, and sweating and grunting and complaining about the pain.

So I'd hold her hand and talk her through it, and we were doing the breathing—the breathing things. And she was very reassured that I was there, there's no question about that. I'm not just saying that. I really have a—always have felt very strongly that she did trust me implicitly, and the fact that I was there holding her hand was very important to her.

I did leave at one point for about an hour. It was something to do with canceling classes or something like that. I may have had to run over to a chemistry lab to hand in a paper or tell my lab partner that I wasn't going to be there, or something like that, and came right back.

But the doctor arrived shortly thereafter, checked her, and what happened was he examined her a couple of times, and he clearly had a frown on his face after the second or third examination. Then they took X rays and another OB man was there also, and it turned out the baby was too large for Colette's pelvis type, so basically the doctor and I told her together.

We came in together and said, "It's not progressing well, and we think that we're probably gonna have to do a Cesarean section." The doctor and I then had a discussion about whether I would be in the Cesarean section room. I didn't particularly want to, not because I was squeamish, I just—I didn't see any reason to be there. And I always felt that it would sort of impede the doctor. I still believe that to this day, by the way, about other couples when they ask me. But he was not at all in favor of me being in there, so as we mutually discussed it, it became clear that it was clearly better that I wasn't in there.

So I sat outside the operating room in a little, you know, sort of waiting area, and read a *Reader's Digest* and a *Look* magazine, then reread the *Look* magazine and paced a little and had a cup of coffee and, I guess, the usual parent routine, new to me but not new to anyone else.

Finally, you know, he came out from the operating room—it seemed like an eternity, by the way—and said that everyone was fine and that we had a—ah, a girl, and that the baby was happy and healthy and Colette seemed to be doing fine but she was exhausted from the long, sort of nonproductive labor.

I saw the baby, oh, it wasn't immediately. It was more like half an hour, an hour later, and the baby, quite honestly, to me she did not look that pretty. Everyone kept saying what a pretty baby Kimmy was. She was cute, but she wasn't, you know, an elegant-looking baby.

Anyway, she was healthy and appeared happy. And Colette was certainly healthy and seemed to do fine. But she was sort of knocked out from the surgery, and she was very wan in the recovery room but happy that everything came out okay.

Mildred had come to help out at the house, and she and I were hitting it off better at this time than ever before or since. We had a good time. We went to dinner together, I showed her around Princeton a little bit, she met our friends. She was staying at the house, in one of the bedrooms. Didn't, of course, like the house. Felt it was, you know, not clean enough. Felt that it was not nearly up to the standards that her daughter should be kept in. But I handled myself well, you know, through all of this, and she liked that. I was clearly in charge of the family, and it was working out well for Colette.

Anyway, our friends had a nice, joyous reaction. We did the pass-out-the-cigar routine, and all my friends stopped by. Cosmo Iacavazzi, who was the all-American football player, stopped by. He was a good friend at the time. We were in Tiger Inn together.

And his wife, whose name I forget, who was a great cook. She cooked her spaghetti sauce, by the way, with the pork chops and chicken in the sauce and then they scooped out the pork chop and chicken and didn't serve that, and just used sausage and meatballs left in the sauce for the meat. But the flavoring was with the pork chops and chicken, and it was a great spaghetti sauce. It was a true, great real Italian homemade spaghetti sauce, and it would take her a whole day and she made it once a week. And she wasn't even really Italian. Cosmo Iacavazzi's mother had to teach her how to cook that. She always recalled that as one of her traumatic events of getting married to Cosmo.

Anyway, they came over and we had planned this big thing for when Colette came home from the hospital. But she—she was very worn out. She had lost some blood at surgery and it took a little while to get her back on her feet, so she wanted it a little more quiet. Two or three weeks later, though, we had all our friends over and *I* cooked spaghetti one night. It was a positive time in our lives, and I remember sort of how proud it was to be, you know, a father.

7

Freddy and Mildred Kassab visited the cemetery every day in March, bringing fresh flowers each time. Other than that, they went nowhere and spoke to no one. No one called; no one visited; letters of sympathy piled up unanswered.

Though neither she nor her husband felt the desire to eat, Mildred suddenly found herself with an inexplicable but irresistible compulsion to bake. She baked pies, cakes, cookies, and bread, at all hours of the day and night. The aroma of her baking filled the air. Soon, the refrigerator was full, then the freezer. Still, she baked, stacking loaves of bread on kitchen counters.

Mildred seldom spoke to her husband; he very seldom spoke to her. There was, they both felt, nothing to say: nothing would ever be worth saying again. Words could neither soothe nor heal, nor undo death, so the Kassabs existed, side by side, in a silent darkness beyond words.

A shipment of clothing arrived from 544 Castle Drive: the contents of Colette's and the children's drawers and closets. Items that had been deemed of no evidentiary importance.

Mildred sat alone in her bedroom, sorting the clothes, suffering new stabs of agony every time she came across a little dress or coat she recognized. Worst of all was handling Colette's nursing bras and maternity girdles. The new baby would have been born in July.

On routine errands, Mildred would see a pregnant woman and start to cry. She would see a bearded, long-haired hippie and feel an almost uncontrollable surge of hate. She could not understand why the killers had not yet been apprehended. Mildred was not a strong woman, physically—only five feet one inch tall and very thin—but her grief and rage were immense. At Womack Hospital, that first afternoon, she had said to Jeffrey MacDonald: "If I ever found her [the blonde in the floppy hat] I would tear out her eyes and her tongue and turn her loose." Her desire for vengeance was undiminished. It was the only feeling left to her, other than pain.

Eventually, she had to stop her baking. The kitchen could no longer contain what she produced. Yet not a single piece of cake nor slice of bread was ever eaten. She and her husband were utterly without appetite.

At the cemetery, she would whisper to Colette, "Help us . . . help us . . ." Then she and Freddy would return home.

At seventeen, Mildred Kassab had married a man ten years older than she was. His name was Cowles Stevenson and he had owned a luncheonette in downtown Patchogue: an undistinguished, working-class town on the south shore of Long Island, physically quite near but socially worlds removed from such fashionable resort communities as the Hamptons and Amagansett.

Mildred had wanted a baby right away: a girl whom she could dress up in fine and fancy clothes. When she became pregnant she and her husband transformed one room of their small rented house into a nursery. They pasted silver stars on a pale blue ceiling and nursery rhyme characters on peach pastel walls. They painted yellow and white ducks on the floor. In a closet, they hung a little fur coat and a row of tiny, frilly dresses. Mildred decided that if the baby were female she would name it Colette, after its father.

The baby was female, but stillborn. That had been the first Colette.

A second pregnancy resulted in another female infant—the second Colette—also stillborn.

A year later, the third Colette was born. The baby died within weeks, however, following surgery to relieve an intestinal obstruction.

Mildred did have a healthy male child, and then, four years later, on May 10, 1943, she gave birth to the fourth Colette—the one who would live—the one who would marry Jeffrey MacDonald.

One Friday evening in the spring of 1955 Mildred was returning home from having picked up her son at a friend's house. As she opened the door to her garage, the car headlights illuminated the interior and she could see her husband's bathrobe hanging from the rafters. In the same instant, she realized he was in it.

Cowles Stevenson had left no note. He had not seemed depressed. There had been no sudden trauma in their life. Mildred told friends she had no idea what had driven her husband to suicide.

Colette, who was twelve at the time, had been spending the night at a friend's house. Her Aunt Helen had broken the news to her because Mildred could not bring herself to do so. Her father's death was the one thing, in later years, that Colette would never talk about: not to her mother, not to her friends, not to her eventual husband, Jeffrey MacDonald. When she met Freddy Kassab a year later, she told her mother right away that she hoped the two of them would marry, "so that everything can be the way it used to be again." After the marriage, Colette began immediately to refer to Freddy as her father; never did she call him her stepfather, nor would she permit her friends to do so.

Mildred had arrived at the Princeton Medical Center in April of 1964, the day after Kimberly was born. Colette had been holding the baby at her breast when her mother had walked into the room. Looking up from her bed, Colette had reached out and had handed the infant to Mildred.

"Here, Mom," Colette had said, her eyes moist. "Here is one of your lost little girls."

Now they were lost forever, all of them, and— immersed in her pain and surrounded by late-winter gloom—Mildred Kassab felt that she did not want to lay eyes upon or speak to another human being ever again.

The Kassabs' solitude was interrupted only once: On March 19, when CID agent William Ivory arrived at their home to ask questions about Colette's relationship with Jeffrey MacDonald.

Ivory had been on Long Island for a week, interviewing residents of Patchogue who had known MacDonald since childhood. He had compiled a summary of their comments in a notebook.

—"The best student I ever had," said a former English teacher.

—"Possibly the finest kid ever to come through the Patchogue High School," said another. "I am still waiting to see his equal."

—"He is absolutely not capable of doing this."

—"He is incapable of any such action."

—"Jeff and Colette got along beautifully. I was especially impressed by how proud they seemed to be of their kids, with the way Jeffrey exhibited his affection for the babies."

—"The kid I knew could not possibly have been involved in this."

—"The Jeffrey MacDonald I knew would not have done this."

—"Not Jeff. Absolutely, not Jeff."

An agent who accompanied Ivory to Patchogue remarked that MacDonald seemed to be "Li'l Abner with straight-A marks," and even the Fort Bragg provost marshal was prompted to comment that from all outward appearances, "It was as if the all-American girl had married the all-American boy."

Freddy and Mildred Kassab, in their grief and isolation, sang his praises with special fervor.

Colette's mother told Ivory that she had encouraged her daughter's relationship with MacDonald from its inception. She said that there had been no one in Patchogue—no one she had ever met anywhere—who had seemed to her a finer prospective husband for her daughter.

The marriage, though it had come about sooner than it otherwise would have, because of Colette's pregnancy, had been ideal from its first day to its last. The Kassabs told Ivory that they had maintained extremely close contact with Colette and that at no time had she ever seemed less than totally satisfied with her domestic situation.

During their Christmas visit to Fort Bragg, the Kassabs had found the atmosphere to be joyous. And, as late as Sunday afternoon, February 15—only thirty-six hours before her death—Colette had sounded the way she always did: calm, untroubled, content; at peace with herself and her life, and looking forward with great anticipation to the birth of her third child in July. Perhaps, she had told her mother, this would be the son that Jeff had always wanted.

The Voice of Jeffrey MacDonald

I think, you know, if there was a low point to the marriage, it was the summer after our year in Princeton. That was a bad summer. We were living at my Mom and Dad's house—I believe we took over my Mom and Dad's bedroom and they moved upstairs—and my sister Judy was there, and my brother Jay was in and out, and it was tight.

Also, I was gone too much of the time. I worked out at Montauk, managing the building of three hundred houses and I had never been in construction in my life. I was totally faking it. I was superintendent on the job at age eighteen or nineteen, managing hundreds and hundreds of workmen—in way over my head, but making like four hundred dollars a week, which was tremendous money at that time.

But I was out there most of Monday through Friday and then when I came home I spent the weekend over on Fire Island driving a beach taxi. I made about three hundred and fifty or four hundred dollars on the weekends, so I was making over seven hundred for sure and some weeks up to a thousand dollars.

Well, not a thousand. About eight-fifty was the highest week—that was the July 4th weekend as a matter of fact—but it was a hard, long summer, and things were a little tense between Colette and I because I was away so much and when I was home I was too tired to pay good attention.

I would be aggravated. I would, you know, ascribe it to the tiredness of the week—we needed to build up money for the coming school year, that was our rationale—but having the young baby at home, having Colette with my parents, um, maybe it did seem a little easier to find those weekends of work over at Fire Island.

But I didn't spend much time with Colette. I didn't spend much time with Kimberly. And Colette was a little uptight, I'm sure, about having to live with Mom and Dad. And I think the relationship may have been at a low ebb.

But the nadir—the absolute bottom in our relationship—was the trip to Chicago in September for the start of my four years in medical school. We were driving a 1959 blue Chevy station wagon and we packed it up and got the maps out and found out where Chicago was—we had never been to Chicago—and plotted our course. The Chevy was overloaded and we were towing a trailer and I was full of optimism about a new challenge ahead, but Colette, I think, in all honesty, was a little frightened.

You know, we had Kim so we weren't just two people bumming around and the trip was long and tiring, the car loaded down, hot, the end of summer, me tired, and ah, the relationship with Colette and Kim was, you know, a little brittle.

And if you've ever driven to Chicago it's an awesome experience, because you drive across the Midwest for hours and hours and hours of wheat fields and cornfields, and then finally off in the distance you see this mushroom of ugly, gray-brown smoke and that is the beginning of the industrial complex in Indiana: East Gary, Indiana; East Chicago, Indiana; Gary, Indiana; and the south end of Lake Michigan. And from that point, around the corner of the lake, back up behind the lake to Chicago was, about, oh, thirty-five or forty miles and twenty miles of it leading into Chicago were the slums of Chicago, the South Side.

I can still remember driving through the South Side of Chicago—and I had never in my wildest dreams ever imagined that there would be a city that we would be going to with literally twenty miles of slums, including miles of these high-rise tenement apartments with the laundry hanging out the windows and no windows in a lot of the apartments.

And of course the signs were confusing and we had gotten on the wrong freeway and we got off several times—this is with a heavy trailer and the car overloaded and Kim having a tough trip—and it was raining—and I looked over at Colette and she was crying. That moment was probably the low point, um, in our relationship.

My initial impulse was to be angry: why was she crying? We were starting this great new adventure. But then—I think uncharacteristically for me at the time—I thought better of it and realized that it was the better part of valor to realize that things were a little tense.

And I remember looking over at her, with Kimberly crying, too, and both of us hot and tired from the trip and also hot and tired from the summer, from maybe three months of not having a good relationship—and I remember pulling off and asking for final directions at one of those crummy gas stations on the turnpike or freeway or whatever it's called going into Chicago from Gary, Indiana, and I remember resolving to myself that we would make, you know, a better go of it, and turning to Colette.

And I remember I held her in the front seat of the car, which was not like me. It was not like me to hug her and console her. It was much more like me to be a little more distant and formal, but I held her and talked to her. And she calmed down immediately. In fact, she brightened considerably. Much more so than a few soothing words would make it seem. It was, I think, the fact that I pulled off to the side of the road and held her, talked to her, and said that things would be okay. That we'd make it financially and emotionally and medical school was going to be a snap.

It was really strange, but it was like one of those instances in time: something really flowed between us and we sort of strengthened our resolve. In fifteen or twenty minutes we seemed to really—a lot of the summer fell away, and Colette ended up laughing and saying, "Yes, this is what we want: medical school and your medical degree, and then we go on from there."

Freshman year in medical school was a tough year, there's really no other way to describe it. Scholastically it was very hard. I was working around the clock almost nonstop. I was a medical student, so this was not an uncommon syndrome, and I was Jeff the medical student, so I worked harder than most. It was definitely a year of trials.

In any event, our apartment was tiny—a very small, city-style, one-bedroom apartment, and we set up the playpen for Kim in the living room, and it was the centerpiece, sort of. We had the bedroom to ourselves, but we had a very tiny kitchen. In fact, Colette couldn't buy too many groceries at once because the kitchen was so small, and she was kind of tied up with Kim, you know, pretty well tied down to home, so there was always that normal amount of, I think, frustration and small aggravations. My greatest remembrance of the apartment, to be honest, was the uh, the tiny kitchen and Colette working feverishly in there to prepare meals for us.

One thing was, we had the beginnings of the fraternity thing in medical school, which was not a big deal, but—and I was never rah-rah fraternity—but we were rushed for these fraternities and I eventually joined Nu Sigma Nu.

Sophomore year was, I think, our most difficult. We lost the apartment we'd had right across from the medical school, and I had to look for one and found one in our price range in a bad area, a poor white area, several miles north.

Chicago has several pockets of poor whites—and I mean from Appalachia, where they walk around barefoot through the streets of Chicago—and a lot of bars and honky-tonks, and it's a very low-rent district.

The apartment was decent inside, and seemed very secure, but to be honest, Colette, I'm sure, was very uncomfortable. Home alone with Kim in a bad neighborhood when I was down at school so much, and, you know, I also had some part-time jobs.

Then that was the year when we went home for Christmas and found my father was getting sicker. It was not emphysema and it did not seem to be cancer of the lung, and no one could figure out why he was getting so radically ill. It turned out he had Hammond-Rich Syndrome, or pulmonary fibrosis of unknown etiology, which is mildly familial and always gives us cause for thought.

In any case, Dad was home sick, and I remember that that Christmas vacation was a time when we sat and talked a lot. I did some work in the bedroom to make it more comfortable for him, put up some bookshelves and a shelf for a radio, and better lighting, and made his bedroom a little more comfortable and felt that we sort of made our peace with each other.

I am forever thankful for that Christmas vacation because I think my Dad and I got to know each other better then than we ever had our whole life. I think we really sealed our love and friendship, as late as it was, on that vacation. He had an incredible grasp of people, intuitively, and I think he knew me and knew me well and loved me, but, still, I didn't have enough communication with him, and to this day believe—I wish I had told him one more time, a little more clearly, how much I loved him, maybe allowing him then to tell me that he also loved me. Who knows? In any event, he died shortly thereafter—March 5, 1966.

Junior year was the start of the better years for us. We moved to a real nice house in the suburbs, a two-family house in a middle-class area and we lived on the second floor, and we had trees in the front yard and backyard. We were living in a much better lifestyle, and it was a much nicer area of town. Also I became the sports chairman for Nu Sigma Nu, this fraternity that I had joined. We had teams in football, softball, and basketball and I was very active in that.

The people that lived below us was a Thai couple— you know, a Thai from Thailand. He was a surgical resident, a super guy, very good surgeon. As a matter of fact, I did my first appendectomy because of him.

I had scrubbed with him on several cases. Of course, the medical student is low on the totem pole, but he liked my answers to some questions and also liked my aggressiveness, and I remember specifically one evening about 8 o'clock I was walking through the hall, this was at Wesley Memorial Hospital, and we were supposed to be through with our work around 5:30 or 6 during a surgical clerkship, and this was not my night on call, and this resident from Thailand saw me and said he thought I was off for the evening, and I said, well, I was just finishing an interesting workup, and getting ready for rounds the next morning, and he said, "Well, have you ever done an appendectomy?"

It turned out he had a patient in the emergency room, so I said, "Sure, I've done appendectomies," and he kind of looked at me and smiled a little bit and said, "Okay, let's go then. I want you to be my first assistant, and maybe you'll do it."

Well, you know, this is a big thing for a junior in medical school: This is a big thing for an *intern*. So I jumped for it, I said, "Sure, no problem," and we went upstairs, changed into scrub suits, and scrubbed in, and then we went into the operating suite and it was, like a teenage boy, as I remember, I would say, like fourteen or something, um, fourteen or about sixteen, I think he was.

And we did an appendectomy—actually, I did it. I was on the right side and I had the scalpel and it took [laugh] it seemed like it took forever. The nurse was going crazy because the scrub nurses like to think they run the rooms, and when this resident said, "Dr. MacDonald is going to be doing this appendectomy," the nurses sort of smiled at each other and groaned and said, "Oh, no, here we go: a first."

I assured them that it wasn't the first, but an hour and a half later, in what should have been twenty or thirty minutes, they knew it had been a first and so did the surgical resident and so did I. But the patient did fine. He in fact did have a hot appendix, and we took it out, and he did very well with no complications.

In any case, as I was going into surgery I remember calling Colette and telling her that I was going in to do an appendectomy and would be late for dinner, and she said, "What dinner? You were supposed to be here at six." And it was now 8:30 or 9 and I was telling her I wouldn't be home until midnight, and the following night, of course, was the night I was on call, so to make a long story short, I got home real late and Colette was sitting up waiting and we had a little glass of liqueur together, and she, I remember, was very pleased by how excited I was after my first experience as an operating surgeon. And we talked about it for 45 minutes or so and went to bed.

"Now this was the year that we [laugh] found out that Colette was pregnant with Kristy. This was exciting to both of us. I remember, we thought about it for about five minutes after we found out and then we were overjoyed. We never had any hesitation at all about the happiness about having Kristy.

Kimmy, of course, had been conceived out of wedlock, so to speak. And that was, you know, threatening to us both. It did—it was a big thing, it was a big step, and it meant we were getting married and living together and having a child, and so—and there was the haste of getting ready for a wedding and everything, you know, while going back to Princeton—so that was a more difficult conceptual thing to get through, no pun intended.

Kristy was a much more joyous occasion. In fact, that Colette was pregnant, neither of us felt that this was any major catastrophe at all. We kind of looked forward to it. And the closer we got to the delivery, you know, Colette slowed down. I tried to pitch in a little more with Kim and the home, and we got ready. Kristy was born in May, and although this was a happy event, it was the time of the near-tragedy with Colette.

Colette had had a very difficult time with Kimmy, had gone into a long, difficult labor and eventually Cesarean section, and with Kristy what happened was she was going into normal labor and then, very precipitiously, the fetal heart tones dropped and the doctor had to operate in a hurry-up fashion.

I was in the room while she was in labor but I left for the surgery. I—I felt very uncomfortable. My normal aggressiveness was all gone in the face of Colette's surgery and she seemed to be well and Kristy was fine so I went home.

When I went back early the next morning to see Colette she looked terrible. She looked white as a sheet and she was soaked with perspiration and I walked over to her and I said, "Honey, are you okay?" She said she felt fluttery in her chest and she felt like she was going to die.

I reached down to feel her pulse and I remember very specifically thinking that I can't feel her pulse but that's okay, I'm gonna not let her know that I can't really feel her pulse very well. Then I looked for her intravenous and her intravenous was *out*. There wasn't any intravenous going and she was clearly in early shock.

So I went out and yelled for the nurse and when the nurse came I said, "Where the hell is her IV?" and the nurse said, "The doctor is on his way," and I said, "I don't care about the doctor. I want to know where her IV is and what's her blood pressure," and I grabbed her chart from the rack and her blood pressure had been going down for several hours and her pulse had been going up and I said, "What the hell is going on here? You don't even have a handle on your patient! That's my wife in there!"

And she said, "Now, relax. You're not allowed to go back in," and I said, "Not allowed to go back in?!" I said, "I'm the one who's treating her now." So I went back inside and the nurse came in with an IV cart and she started to stick Colette but she couldn't get one going so I grabbed it from her and told her to find me another nurse who knew what the hell she was doing.

And she left the room—very upset, by the way—and I started the IV and shortly thereafter a very excited nurse and the doctor arrived and I took him out in the hallway—or, *he* took *me* out in the hallway—and I told him that she was in shock, that she had a belly pain, that she had a very fast pulse and a low blood pressure and she looked terrible.

And he said, "Well, she's probably having some bleeding in her tummy from the surgery," and that, in fact, is what it was. They ended up doing a second operation right away and she got several blood transfusions and they opened her up and found an arterial bleeder—a little artery that had had a ligature around it but the ligature had slipped off and she was pumping blood into her tummy and had bled several quarts. She only has eleven pints, you know. Five and a half quarts in a 170-pound male, so she probably only has nine and a half to begin with and she had bled a good half of that into her stomach. So she was in real trouble when I found her. It was very close. She, I think for a while there, was in a very risky situation.

Anyway, that episode sort of, um, intensified our feelings for each other. I almost lost her, and it, um, it meant something. It just, ah—Colette became a more intense, a more real need for me then because I had almost lost her. And when she came home from the hospital she in turn felt a new dependence on me.

She was always dependent on me, she was never really an independent person, but when she came home from the hospital—she was tireder now, much tireder than she would have been, and her recovery took a little longer—there was a new ability to lean on me, and to hug me once in a while when she wanted to, not when I wanted to. I had to keep up my school duties, of course, but we were able to have more interplay than before.

Our senior year, we had the nice house, we had Kim and Kris and both of them were doing fine, Colette had recovered nicely by now, and I made Alpha Omega Alpha, which was the honorary society in medical school for the top 10 percent of the students, and that was a real honor. I felt very good about that.

It was also the time that we were applying for internships and, I believe it was in the early fall, several of us went together to make a circuit of areas that we wanted to visit for potential internships.

I was being wooed by Northwestern Hospital to be an intern there because my record was so good in medical school, but Colette and I felt that we wanted to get out of Chicago, so I took off on an internship tour with two of my classmates and good friends.

We went out to the West Coast and we did the Los Angeles, San Diego, San Francisco tour, and I was kind of impressed, but not as impressed as I thought I would be, but the tour was kind of fun, it was kind of a bachelor night out.

One of the guys was married, and one was not, and I was married to Colette, but to be honest, we had a blast on this trip. We went out every night and had plenty of beer and drinks, and I remember being a little stunned by the openness of the girlie shows in Los Angeles and San Francisco. We went to a place called the Body Shop in Los Angeles, and I remember thinking, gee, I hadn't seen anything quite like this, where the audience participation took place.

And we went to Carol Doda's Condor Club up in San Francisco, and there was some famous competitor of hers then, had a club two doors away and we went to that one and we did this whole tour and had an absolute blast.

I ended up liking San Francisco General best, as far as the hospitals went. It was the most dynamic, most exciting, most trauma-filled, clearly a knife-and-gun-club atmosphere, the surgeons were clearly in charge, but its ranking wasn't quite yet up to that of some of the others.

So I ended up, to make a long story short, ranking Columbia Presbyterian first on my application, simply because I felt it was the best hospital that I had seen or heard of except for Mass General, and I had decided that I didn't want to go to Boston. I don't know what I decided that on, I just decided that I really didn't want to go the Boston route, and Columbia Presbyterian always seemed to be number two in the country, behind Mass General, so I applied, had a good interview, liked it—it was a little awesome, the structure is so gigantic and overwhelming that I, um, it was, it's a magnificent place, but I didn't have any warm, dynamic feelings for it like I did for San Francisco General, but when we got ranked that spring I got Columbia Presbyterian, my first choice. I'm not sure Colette was really that happy about it, but it was such a hard-to-get internship, it was so impressive that that overwhelmed us, and I remember my friends, even Bob McGann who got into Mass General, number one in our class, was impressed.

We worked hard, even in senior year. Colette was taking in papers for typing, and doing lots of babysitting for pay, in addition to taking care of Kimmy and Kristy, and I was having all my odd jobs—working at the Chicago *Tribune* employees' clinic as well as doing autopsies over at the VA Hospital, and Colette was now taking English classes at Northwestern.

But we still seemed to find time for each other and for the kids and still to go out socially. We liked Rush Street and the nightclubs, and we went to Mr. Kelly's several times, and we even tried some of the jazz clubs in the South Side. And we ate at a lot of ethnic places—there was a little Greek place over near Cook County Hospital, and we tried Mexican food for the first time and we found the Italian places that we liked, and we went to movies and we stayed out late, and we went to the Playboy Club—I had a key to the Playboy Club—and we also had a lot of people over for dinner. Our house was kind of more of a social center than some of our other friends' houses.

The kids were doing fine this senior year, and the sports teams that we were involved in [laugh] did very well, too. We had a blast, I remember, in the winter tournament in basketball.

8

Even after her return from Myrtle Beach, Jeffrey Mac-
Donald's mother did not go home. She took an indefi-
nite leave of absence from her school nursing job and
remained with her son at Fort Bragg. They ate breakfast
together every morning and dinner together every night.
Accompanied frequently by Ron Harrison, they would
go on shopping trips in Fayetteville and to the movies in
the evening.

Often, MacDonald and his mother would also go to
Franz Joseph Grebner's office to inquire about what
progress was being made in the investigation. On these
occasions, the young Green Beret captain would wait in
an outer office while his mother went in to speak to
Grebner. The dominant role she was assuming began to
strike the CID chief as peculiar. "She leads him around,"
Grebner would remark to associates, "like a little kid
who's just wet his pants."

Grebner, however, did not have a great deal of time to
devote to speculation about the nature of the relationship between Jeffrey MacDonald and his mother. Even

before the MacDonald murders he had been a man under considerable stress. Though the CID detachment at Fort Bragg was supposed to consist of forty-four accredited investigators, it was, through attrition and general understaffing, down to seventeen men during the early months of 1970. This despite the fact that at any given time there were approximately 250 unsolved felonies under investigation at the base.

There were an average of four murders per month in the Fort Bragg–Fayetteville area for the investigation of which the CID eventually assumed responsibility. And, in addition to numerous other deaths due to suicide, training accident, motor vehicle accident, and narcotics overdose, there were rapes, robberies, and—as the Cumberland County sheriff had noted—a narcotics problem which had reached epidemic levels.

Since February 17, Grebner had felt greatly burdened by the fact that the MacDonald investigation had not gone as smoothly as it should have. Though he personally, like Ivory and Shaw, the agents actively involved in the case, and like the Fort Bragg provost marshal, had little doubt that Jeffrey MacDonald was, indeed, the murderer of his family and that the story of the drug-crazed hippies was fabrication, the number of investigatory loose ends was threatening to unravel the whole case.

For example, contrary to what the provost marshal had told the press, roadblocks had never been established. As an open post from which there were more than a dozen exits on well-traveled routes, Fort Bragg could not have been sealed in time to prevent the killers—had there been killers—from escaping. All that had been done in the first moments after the discovery of the bodies was to call the morning shift of military police in early and to have them check cars at random, looking for one containing two white men, one black man, and a girl with a floppy hat and long blond hair. By 6 A.M., even this ineffectual attempt at search had been discontinued because of the heavy buildup of traffic on post.

Still, the first impression Grebner had formed upon arriving at 544 Castle Drive remained with him: there were no hippies; there was only Jeffrey MacDonald, the Green Beret doctor who for reasons as yet unknown had exploded into a murderous rage and had then just as quickly regained enough presence of mind to stage the scene, develop his story, and stick to it.

The case against MacDonald would have to be based entirely upon circumstantial evidence. Under the most favorable of conditions (i.e., a well-preserved crime scene and an impeccably conducted investigation), such cases were difficult to win, and, as Grebner was learning to his increasing dismay, the MacDonald case did not even come close to meeting those criteria.

MacDonald's pajama bottoms, for example—potentially crucial evidence—had been discarded by a hospital orderly in the emergency room and had been burned with the rest of the hospital trash.

In addition, the MPs assigned to guard the exterior of 544 Castle Drive on the morning of February 17 had allowed the Fort Bragg trash collectors to empty the MacDonald garbage cans before any CID agent had thought to examine the rubbish for possible evidence—such as a bloodstained pair of disposable rubber surgeon's gloves.

Such gloves, of course, could as easily have been flushed down the toilet. But before this thought had occurred to agents at the scene (four days after the murders), the laboratory technicians from Fort Gordon had been making such regular use of the toilet facilities as to assure that evidence disposed of by such means would have been long since carried into the main sewer lines and lost forever.

Blunders by lab technicians had not stopped there. When one, using a saw, had attempted to remove the bloody footprint from the floor of Kristen's room, the boards on which the print had been made had separated and the print itself had been destroyed.

Even back at the laboratory, inexcusable mistakes continued to be made. The piece of skin found beneath Colette's fingernail, for instance, had inexplicably been lost. And lost, too, was the vial which contained the blue fiber that had been scraped from beneath the fingernail of Kristen.

Nonetheless, by mid-March, the laboratory at Fort Gordon was forwarding to the Fort Bragg CID findings which, in Grebner's view, strengthened considerably the case against Jeffrey MacDonald.

It was proved by microscopic analysis, for instance, that the loose fibers found in the three bedrooms of 544 Castle Drive were, in fact, identical in composition to those used in the manufacture of Jeffrey MacDonald's torn blue pajama top. It was also determined that the rubber glove fragments found in the master bedroom were identical in chemical composition to the surgical rubber gloves that had been kept beneath the MacDonald kitchen sink.

In addition, based upon comparison with the "known hair samples" taken from the MacDonald apartment, the laboratory reported that the blond hair found in the palm of Colette MacDonald's hand was her own and not that of a blond-haired intruder.

CID investigators were also informed that no fingerprints—neither Jeffrey MacDonald's nor anyone else's—were present on the handle of the Geneva Forge paring knife which he said he had pulled from his wife's chest. Nor were there prints on any of the other weapons. The club, however, was found to contain paint stains which were identical in chemical composition to paint on homemade bookshelves in the bedroom of Kimberly MacDonald.

By far, the most important laboratory finding had to do with blood analysis. While examination of a sample of Jeffrey MacDonald's blood and urine "did not indicate the presence of dangerous drugs" and demonstrated that he "was not under the influence of alcohol," it was determined, against all statistical probability, that each of the four members of MacDonald's family had possessed a different blood type.

Colette MacDonald's blood was Type A.

Jeffrey MacDonald's blood was Type B.

Kimberly MacDonald's blood was Type AB.

Kristen MacDonald's blood was Type O.

Thus, by mid-March it was possible for investigators to determine where within the apartment the blood of each family member could be found. The thrust of this evidence—the story told by the blood—seemed, to William Ivory, to Franz Joseph Grebner, and to Robert Shaw, to contradict more strongly than anything before it the story that Jeffrey MacDonald had told.

The laboratory eventually identified the location and type of every stain and drop of blood inside the MacDonald apartment and on the weapons found outside. From this huge mass of fact, a few details stood out in bold relief:

—The drops of blood which formed the six-inch cir[cle] near the entrance to the master bedroom were in the [Type] AB blood of Kimberly MacDonald. Her blood w[as] found on the rumpled sheet and on the torn blue pajama top in the master bedroom, and it was her blood which formed the trail of drops between the master bedroom and her own room, in which her body had been found.

—The Type A blood of Colette MacDonald was found in the bedroom of Kristen. There were spatters of it on the wall above the bed and a heavy stain on the top sheet of Kristen's bed. In addition, the footprint leading away from the bed—a print made by the bare foot of Jeffrey MacDonald—had been made not with Kristen's Type O blood but with the Type A blood of her mother. Colette's blood was also found, in large quantity, on the bedspread and sheet that had been rolled up together and deposited on the master bedroom floor.

—The Type B blood of Jeffrey MacDonald was found in significant quantity in only two locations within the apartment: on the kitchen floor in front of the cabinet that contained the box of rubber gloves, and on the right side of the hall bathroom sink, in a pattern suggesting it might have dripped from the right side of the chest of a person who had stood in front of the sink while making a neat, clean incision between two ribs—an incision, perhaps, only one centimeter long, and just deep enough to puncture a lung without doing any other damage.

With the hysteria that had swept over Fort Bragg in the first days after the murders having abated (in the absence of any further homicidal outbursts), Grebner was inclined to proceed cautiously. He wanted as much evidence as possible available to him before he summoned MacDonald for a formal interrogation.

To himself he could justify this approach by saying that since flight would be an admission of guilt, it was unlikely that MacDonald would flee, and since the murders had been—he was certain—the result of an explosion of rage which had built up within the confines of a troubled domestic situation, MacDonald did not pose a threat to anyone else at Fort Bragg.

The young doctor had returned to duty and was now in residence in the BOQ room assigned to him, and, for the moment—despite ever increasing impatience on the part of superiors who wanted a quick announcement that an arrest had been made—Franz Joseph Grebner was content to let the matter lie, hoping that the worst of the mistakes had already been made and that the strands of circumstantial evidence, in time, would weave themselves into a noose.

Besides, the longer he waited, the more Grebner learned. He had learned, for example, that the Valentine found in MacDonald's desk had been sent by Josephine Kingston, the wife of Col. Robert Kingston, MacDonald's first commanding officer, who had been transferred to Vietnam in the fall.

On Saturday, April 4, Jeffrey MacDonald located an unfurnished apartment not far from Fort Bragg and convenient to the civilian hospital in Fayetteville where he was working emergency-room shifts during his off-duty hours. He decided that he would prefer to live off post.

On Sunday, April 5, his mother finally went back to Long Island.

On the morning of Monday, April 6, he was summoned to the headquarters of the Fort Bragg Criminal Investigation Division. Upon his arrival he was directed to the office of Franz Joseph Grebner.

Six weeks had elapsed since the murders and the Fort Bragg provost marshal, as well as his superiors, both at

Fort Bragg and at the Pentagon, were by now extremely impatient. Since the provost marshal's own mind—like Grebner's—had been made up long ago, he had grown weary of saying "No comment" when asked about the investigation's progress, and wearier still of reading newspaper stories about how the Army's apparent inability to crack the case was just one more example of the incompetence that was leading to the loss of the war in Vietnam, and to the public's complete loss of faith in the military.

Daily, the provost marshal would receive pressure from above, and, daily, he would make Franz Joseph Grebner aware of it. By April 6, the CID chief—despite his unease in regard to the incomplete nature of the investigation—felt he had no choice but to act. Perhaps, he thought, once MacDonald was made aware of the evidence the CID had assembled, he could be persuaded to confess.

In preparation for the interview, Grebner, who before joining the Army had been a school superintendent in South Dakota, summoned William Ivory and the other agent—Robert Shaw—who had done the majority of the investigative work on the case. The two detectives took seats on either side of Grebner's desk. A gray, armless chair was positioned alongside the desk, facing Grebner and the windows behind him. Grebner took a tape recorder out of the desk. Having long ago misplaced the microphone stand, he propped the microphone on top of some books on his desk and asked that MacDonald be sent in.

MacDonald, in uniform—planning, in fact, to go to his office—stood directly in front of Grebner's desk. He smiled, then looked quickly at the unfamiliar—and unsmiling—faces of Ivory and Shaw. He still had no idea that the Army investigators considered him their prime suspect.

Motioning to the armless chair alongside his desk, Grebner told MacDonald to take a seat. He then turned on the tape recorder.

"Before we begin," he said, as the smile faded from Jeffrey MacDonald's face, "I would like to advise you of your rights."

The Voice of Jeffrey MacDonald

Internship year, though, the year at Columbia Presbyterian, was a very tough year, a down year, a brutal year. There were months when I worked the entire month, every other night on. That meant thirty-six hours straight at the hospital and only twelve off, and you never really got the full twelve, it was always eleven or ten or nine and a half, and I had to go home, clean up, eat, see the kids, play with them, see Colette, catch up on the news, fall asleep, then get up at four or five in the morning and go back on rounds at 6 A.M.

Basically, it was a horrendous year. Really bad from the point of view of my workload, lack of family interaction, and total physical exhaustion.

Now, that was not my doing. And I refuse to take any, um, negative credit for working too hard. That's just the way it was being an intern at one of the best hospitals in the world. But our apartment in Bergenfield, New Jersey, was hot and cramped and not nearly as pretty as what we had just come from in Chicago, plus the neighborhood was not nearly as nice.

Of course, intellectually, Columbia Presbyterian was very exciting. As a medical learning experience it was phenomenal, and I became one of the hot interns, there was no question about it.

On chest surgery I scrubbed at some of the open hearts which were—you know, this was still big news in 1969. These were very tense operations and different surgeons handled the tenseness in different ways.

One of my most vivid recollections was I was assisting the most brutal of these surgeons—this guy was a pusher and shover and swearer and a knife-thrower, and he had an awesome reputation for pushing interns out of the way and being nasty to them.

And I was assisting and I did something he didn't like and he pushed me. I didn't say anything, just did my job, and he asked me some questions and I answered them and then something happened that he didn't like—he wanted me to move or something—and he, really hard, gave me an elbow in the middle of the chest and I just sort of gave him a very light elbow back and I said, "I don't have to take that from you. You know, you don't need me here at the table. I seem to be in your way, but if I'm not in your way and you want me here, then you'll have to treat me as a physician."

And there was silence in the room and I probably broke out in a sweat, but I was just so furious that I just sort of stood there thinking I was correct and maintained my position and the surgeon didn't say anything.

For the next two weeks he treated me as an absolute gentleman and finally sat me down and asked me if I wanted to be on the thoracic surgery service, which I thought was phenomenal. I thought he would throw me out of my internship but I had stood up to him because it just seemed so outrageous that he was physically abusing physicians who were assisting him. I just reacted and sort of pushed him back with my right elbow and he had hit me with his left elbow, and I said, "If you want me in here you'll have to treat me like a gentleman." And then he offered me a position on the service. I thought that was phenomenal.

But the year, on the whole, wasn't filled with a whole lot of fun. We did have brief spurts, you know, nights out together. I remember one specifically, I think it may have been for my birthday, my brother Jay was taking us out, and he met us somewhere in Brooklyn.

He was in his Cadillac and we had the Chevy and we made three or four stops at his Italian hangouts, and then we followed him for what seemed like miles and miles and miles and miles through side streets, and the neighborhood kept getting worse and worse.

It started out industrial, then it was residential, then it got shabby residential, then it got tenement, then it got abandoned slums, and pretty soon we went, it must have been, half a mile through a slum in which there was nothing but abandoned tenements and these shells of cars that were up on cinder blocks or just down on the axles, no tires on them—they're colloquially referred to as "Brooklyn Foxholes"—when the shooting starts, everyone dives for an abandoned car.

But we eventually came to this little side street and it was jam packed with cars that people were getting in and out of, and then there was a parking lot across the street and you'd pull up to this place and a guy was standing at the front door with a white shirt with no tie, open at the collar, and the sleeves were rolled up to his big biceps, and he took the car, talking in an Italian accent, and you went inside.

Jay had already told me that it was a real place—that, you know, people did carry guns into the restaurant and the lot of the guys were heavy-duty Mafia types, and we went in and that's in fact what it was: Monte's Venetian Room.

We were treated to this grand and glorious nine- or ten-course Italian meal with three or four courses of pasta, and it took all night, from seven-thirty till about midnight.

And I can still remember, Colette and I were just stuffed, we couldn't move, we felt like gluttons, and then we had the ice cream and coffee—Coffee Paradise— where they put in some anisette and a twist of lemon peel while they strike a match at the same time and it all flames up and they drop the burned lemon peel in the cup.

Jay and several of the Italian guys were ordering bowls of these noodles mixed with peas—shells mixed with peas—for dessert, and Jay proceeded to eat at least a quart of these noodles after, you know, after this incredible nine- or ten-course meal in which we had chicken and steak and fish and several orders of different type of pasta, and salads, and we had started off with a great big bowl of meatballs in the middle of the table, and everyone had a fork and you'd just spear a meatball and keep eating until this several gallons of meatballs were gone and all of these guys had their shirt sleeves rolled up and their pearl stickpins—they undo their tie and then cross their tie in front of themselves and put their stickpin through it so they can leave the collar open—and the women all have beehive hairdos and minks, mink stoles around these sequined dresses. All this in Monte's Venetian Room, this little restaurant in the middle of Brooklyn, in the sleaziest area I've ever seen.

*   *   *

Occasionally we'd go down to Greenwich Village and just bum around for the evening and sit at the different cafés and hear some of the folk singers, which was nice for us, especially because we had done it when we were at Princeton that last year, and it was already sort of reminiscing to get back to Greenwich Village, and we were decrying how it had changed.

Then antiwar people had taken it over and there were draft card burnings and red berets everywhere, when we were just out to have a good time for the evening. We weren't raging conservatives by any means, but we were middle of the road and we felt all the disruption was destructive of our country's ability to end the war with some honor in Southeast Asia.

Actually, I was reasonably right-wing, I sort of believed what the president said and thought that the citizens of the country had a duty to do what was ordered by the president. I guess I'd been raised that way. My father always felt that it was not only your duty but your right to join the service and go fight for your country, and it never seemed like a bad thing to me. If there was an undeclared war, it was only because of some left-wing liberals in Congress that didn't have the sense to see what my father had seen and what the other fathers saw and what all of us could see: that Vietnam needed defending and we were the ones who should be helping to defend it.

This was, of course, at the height of the war, and the doctors were being drafted either right after their internship or during or after their residency. Most people were trying to stay out, but Colette and I were not having a good year. I wasn't home much and when I was I was tired and cranky and Colette was tired and cranky and we

didn't have sex as much and there was a lot of pressure—
on both of us, on the marriage, on the children—and
sometime during the middle of that year I gradually
came to the realization that I didn't mind the idea of going into the service.

There was no question about the fact that Colette was
unhappy about my decision but there was never any argument. It was kind of strange, I actually looked forward
to the challenge of something new. I kind of looked at it
as an adventure, whereas Colette saw it as, ah, somewhat
of an abandonment of the family, and, um, a year without me and a chance for me getting killed and the whole
bit.

At the time, this didn't bother me at all. What did
sound good was a year or two away from the high pressure environment that I'd been in for the last five years,
four of medical school and this horrendous year of the
internship.

I was exhausted from the year, there's just no question, and Colette was exhausted physically and mentally
from coping with the two kids and too small an apartment. There was a little tension in the air. Not tension,
but uneasiness, about me going into the Army, there's
no question about that. Colette was definitely uneasy.
She was uncomfortable. She would rather I didn't go in
the Army.

I had, I think, about fifteen days between the end of
internship and when I had to report to Fort Sam Houston, and Colette and I took a vacation, you know, to get
away from the year that we had just had and try to sort of
remeet, you know, retouch base with each other as we
were heading towards the, um, the Army.

It was not in the Bahamas, which was where we had
gone a couple of years before. It was somewhere in the

Caribbean more distant than the Bahamas. I want to say Aruba but I can't be sure of that.

We'd had a wonderful, a very warm time in the Bahamas. There, we dug for clams and we snorkel-dived and we made love on the beach, and I clearly remember going to the casino, Colette and I being a little young, and neophytes at the time, and a little uncomfortable in the glittery atmosphere of this small casino in Nassau.

But this second trip was a different style. We were sort of, you know, I was exhausted from the year, there's just no question, and Colette was exhausted physically and mentally from coping with the two kids and too small an apartment, so we spent time just recuperating. It was a, you know, a quieter type of trip.

We just sort of had nice breakfasts and late lunches, and we had long slow dinners with, with wine. We walked around a little bit, we toured the island, and it wasn't very—a very pretty island. I—I think it was Aruba. Anyway, it wasn't very pretty. We had a nice time but there was a little tension in the air. Not tension, but uneasiness, about me going into the Army, there's no question about that.

Colette was definitely uneasy. She was uncomfortable. She would rather I didn't go in the Army. But she also respected me, you know, for sort of joining up at that point, making a firm decision, being the, you know, the leader of the family and deciding it was a better time to take the break now that we had had this very tough year, and that—might as well go in and get it over with. But it was also unsettling. I mean, you know, her husband and the father, um, of her children would be leaving for, you know, indeterminate period of time, so, you know, it was uneasy.

9

It was 9:30 A.M. Trucks were grinding by outside an open window. A radio on the desk next to Grebner's was tuned to a pop music station. Grebner informed MacDonald that he had the right to remain silent and the right to request an attorney, and that, even if he chose to answer questions, he would retain the right to stop at any time. Grebner added, however, that what MacDonald did say could be used against him in any future judicial proceeding.

The microphone lay eighteen inches from Jeffrey MacDonald's right elbow, which rested on the edge of Grebner's desk. Ivory and Shaw sat silently. The majority of their waking hours since February 17 had been spent inside 544 Castle Drive. Both men had gazed deeply into the wounds that had been inflicted on Jeffrey Mac-Donald's wife and children. For the rest of their lives, both would carry with them visions of what they had seen. Both men, like Grebner, were by now convinced that Jeffrey MacDonald was the murderer. This was their first close look at him.

MacDonald glanced up at the ceiling, he glanced

down at the floor. He cleared his throat, he looked past Grebner's shoulder, out the window. He said he understood what Grebner had just told him and that he was willing to answer any questions the agents might have.

"All right," Grebner said. "Just go ahead and tell us your story."

MacDonald cleared his throat again and began. He spoke quickly, with little inflection, as he described for the first time, formally, on record, the details of his struggle with the intruders. MacDonald did not yet know how much—or what—the CID knew. He was not yet aware of the story the physical evidence had told. And so, on this first Monday morning of April 1970, he could not realize that the account he was about to render would stick to him like tar for years afterward, in all its messy, inconvenient detail, despite his many attempts to cleanse himself of it as his understanding of the physical evidence, and its implications, increased.

"Let's see, Monday night my wife went to bed and I was reading and I went to bed about—somewheres around two o'clock, I really don't know, I was reading on the couch and my little girl Kristy had gone into bed with my wife.

"And I went in to go to bed and the bed was wet. She had wet the bed on my side so I brought her in her own room and I don't remember if I changed her or not—gave her a bottle and went out to the couch, 'cause my bed was wet, and I went to sleep on the couch.

"And then the next thing I know I heard some screaming—at least my wife but I thought I heard Kimmy, my older daughter, screaming also, and I sat up. The kitchen light was on and I saw some people at the foot of the bed [*sic*].

"So I don't know if I really said anything or I was getting ready to say something, this happened real fast. You know, when you talk about it, it sounds like it took forever but it didn't take forever.

"And so I sat up and at first I thought it was—I just could see three people and I don't know if I—if I heard the girl first, or—I think I saw her first. I think two of the men separated sort of at the end of my couch and I keep—all I saw was some people, really.

"And this guy started walking down between the coffee table and the couch and he raised something over his head and just sort of then—sort of all together—I just got a glance of this girl with kind of a light on her face. I don't know if it was a flashlight or a candle but it looked to me like she was holding something. And I just remember that my instinctive thought was that, 'She's holding a candle. What the hell is she holding a candle for?' But she said—before I was hit the first time—'Kill the pigs. Acid's groovy.' Now that's all—that's all I think I heard before I was hit the first time and the guy hit me in the head. So I was knocked back on the couch and then I started struggling to get up and I could hear it all then. Now I could—maybe it's really, you know—I don't know if I was repeating to myself what she just said or if I kept hearing it, but I kept—I heard, you know, 'Acid is groovy. Kill the pigs.'"

MacDonald's voice was sharp, his sentences running together. His words had the sound of dice rattling in a cup.

"And I started to struggle up and I noticed three men now and I think the girl was kind of behind them, either on the stairs or at the foot of the couch behind them. And the guy on my left was a colored man and he hit me again, but at the same time, you know, I was kind of struggling. And these two men, I thought, were punching me. Then I—I remember thinking to myself that—see, I work out with the boxing gloves sometimes. I was then. And I kept—'Geez, that guy throws a hell of a punch,' because he punched me in the chest and I got this terrific pain in my chest.

"And so I was struggling and I got hit on the shoulder or the side of the head again and so I turned and I—I grabbed this guy's whatever it was. I thought it was a baseball bat at the time. And I had—I was holding it. I was kind of working up it to hold on to it.

"Meanwhile, both these guys were kind of hitting me and all this time I was hearing screams. That's what I can't figure out. So, let's see, I was holding—so, I saw the—all I got a glimpse of was some stripes. I told you, I think, they were E-6 stripes, there was one bottom rocker, and it was an Army jacket, and that man was a colored man and the two men—other men—were white, and I didn't really notice too much about them.

"And so I kind of struggled and I was kind of off balance 'cause I was still halfway on the couch and half off, and I was holding on to this. And I kept getting this pain either in—you know, like sort of in my stomach and he kept hitting me in the chest.

"And so I let go of the club and I was grappling with him and I was holding his hand in my hand and I saw, you know, a blade. I didn't know what it was, I just saw something that looked like a blade at the time.

"And so then I concentrated on him. We were kind of struggling in the hallway right there at the end of the couch and then really the next distinctive thing, I thought that—I thought that I noticed—I saw some legs, you know, that—not covered. Like I saw the top of some boots. And I thought I saw knees as I was falling. I saw—saw some knees on the top of boots and I told, I think, the investigators, I thought they were brown.

"The next thing I remember, though, was lying on the hallway—at the end of the hallway floor, and I was freezing cold and it was very quiet and my teeth were chattering and I went down and—to the bedroom."

MacDonald's voice suddenly weakened and his cadence slowed.

"And, ah, I had a—I was dizzy, you know, I wasn't really, ah, real alert, ah, and I, ah—my wife was lying on the—the floor next to the bed, and there—there was a—a knife in her—upper chest."

He was sobbing his words now, rather than speaking them, and trying repeatedly to clear his throat.

"So I took that out and tried to give her artificial respiration but the air was coming out of her chest, so . . . umm . . . I went and checked . . . the kids . . . and, ah . . ."

There was a long pause as MacDonald wept. Grebner and Ivory and Shaw waited in silence. The loudest sound in the room was that of an up-tempo Al Hirt trumpet on the radio.

". . . And they were, ah . . . had a lot of, ah . . . blood around. So I went back into the bedroom and I—by this time I was finding it real hard to breathe and—" He sighed deeply. "I was dizzy. So I, ah, picked up the phone and I, ah, told this asshole operator that it was, ah—my name was Captain MacDonald and I was at 544 Castle Drive and I needed the, ah, MPs and a doctor and an ambulance and she said, ah, 'Is this on post or off post?'—something like that. And I started yelling at her. I said, ah—finally I told her it was on post and she said, 'Well, you'll have to call the MPs.'

"So I dropped the phone and I went back and I

checked my wife again, and now I was—I don't know. I assume I was hoping I hadn't seen what I had seen or I—I was starting to think more like a doctor.

"So I went back and checked for pulses. You know, carotid pulses and stuff. And I—there was no pulse on my wife and I was—I felt I was getting sick to my stomach and I was short of breath and I was dizzy and my teeth were chattering 'cause I was cold. And so I didn't know if I was going—I assumed I was going into shock because I was so cold. That's one of the symptoms of shock—you start getting shaking chills.

"So I got down on all fours and I was breathing for a while and then I realized that I had talked to the operator and nothing really had happened with her. But, ah, in any case, when I went back to check my wife I then went to check the kids and a couple of times I had to—thinking that I was going into shock and not being able to breathe.

"Now, I—you know, when I look back, of course, it's merely a symptom, that shortness of breath. It isn't—you weren't really that bad. But that's what happens when you get a pneumothorax, you—you think you can't breathe.

"And, ah, I had to get down on my hands and knees and breathe for a while and I went in and checked the kids and checked their pulses and stuff. And, ah—ah, I don't know if it was the first time I checked them or the second time, to tell you the truth, but I had all—you know, blood on my hands and I had little cuts in here and in here [pointing to his midsection], and my head hurt, so when I reached up to feel my head, you know, my hand was bloody, and so I—I think it was the second circuit 'cause by that time I was—I was thinking better, I thought. And I went into that, ah—I went into the bathroom right there and looked in the mirror and didn't—nothing looked wrong. I mean there wasn't really even a cut or anything.

"So, I ah, then I went out in the hall and I couldn't breathe, so I was on my hands and knees in the hall and I—it kept hitting me that really nothing had been solved when I called the operator.

"And so I went in and—this was in the—you know, in the middle of the hallway there, and I went the other way, I went into the kitchen, picked up that phone and the operator was on the line. My other phone had never been hung up.

"And she was still on the line and she said, 'Is this Captain MacDonald?' I said, 'Yes, it is.' And she said, 'Just a minute.' And there was some dial tones and stuff and then this sergeant came on and he said, 'Can I help you?' So I told him that I needed a doctor and an ambulance and that some people had been stabbed and that I thought I was going to die.

"And he said, 'They'll be right there,' so I left the phone and I remember, ah, going back to look again, and the next thing I knew, ah, an MP was giving me mouth-to-mouth resuscitation next to, ah—next to my wife.

"Now I remember I saw—I don't know if it was the first or second trip into the bedroom to see my wife, but, ah, I saw that the back door was open, but that's ah, that's immaterial, I guess."

MacDonald stopped. Grebner and Ivory and Shaw remained silent. On the radio, Nat "King" Cole was singing "Ramblin' Rose."

"When you woke up," Grebner said after more than thirty seconds of silence, "there were three men there?"

"The first time? You mean when I was on the couch?"

"Yes."

"Right. Well, I—yeah. Now, I—sir, you know, let me say one thing now." There seemed a new edge of anxiety in MacDonald's voice. "You know, when you say something it sounds cut and dried, but this thing happened— I'm sure it didn't take more than eight or ten seconds, when I think back about it.

"You know, I mean I've been in fights before and, Christ, you think it's an eternity, and, ah, when it's over it's less than a minute. But I'm sure this was a matter of seconds, and, ah, I'd just woken up and it was dark, and—I think it was three men, right, because I remember specifically struggling with three people in front of me and seeing a fourth—seeing the girl. And, really, all I saw of her was some long, stringy blond hair and—and a big hat."

"You say this man with the sergeant stripes on came toward you. Where did he strike you first? In the head?"

"Right, right. I mean I was just sitting—I was just sitting in bed [*sic*]. I was just getting ready to say something like, 'What the hell are you—what's going on here?' when I could hear screaming, and really, it isn't a matter of like running at me or anything, 'cause it was only a step. The point is, he was closer than the others and I remember thinking that he was raising something and they—I really didn't even defend myself. I mean it was really too—too fast. I just sort of sat up and as I looked and saw these people he was doing this at, really—at the same time. And he hit me.

"And, ah—I mean they weren't shouting or anything. There wasn't any, ah—I mean she wasn't jumping up and down and screaming, ah, you know, 'Kill him!' The point was, it all seemed—you know, when you see it like in *Easy Rider*. I made the mistake of going to see that film. They have all these stop-action things. Well, that's what it seemed like. All I really see is these real fast glimpses of what happened."

"Captain MacDonald," Shaw said, speaking in a voice so flat and dry that he might have been an airline pilot addressing a cabin filled with passengers, "you told one of the other investigators earlier that you were wearing a pajama top that was pulled over your head or something like that."

"Right, well, all I know is that, ah—well, when I was struggling now—after I had been hit the first time and I was struggling with these guys and my—somehow my pajama top—I don't know if it was ripped forward or pulled over my head. I don't think it was pulled over my head. I don't remember actually, like, backing my head through it.

"But all of a sudden it was all around my hands and it was in my way and I remember that I was holding this thing in my hands—the guy's hand—that—that I couldn't maneuver very well. My hands were kind of wrapped up in the—in the thing.

"And as they were punching me I was kind of using that a little bit, you know, holding it, 'cause this guy, I thought, was really punching me in the chest, you know, and in the stomach, 'cause I—I was getting hit across here [pointing again to the midsection of his body].

"So, in effect, I was blunting everything by, you know, holding this up. And I couldn't get my hands free—out of this thing. And I remember I ended up, when I was laying on the floor—I forgot to say that—when I woke up on—it was still all around my hands and everything, and I took it off as I was going in the bedroom. And after I took this knife out of my wife's chest, I—you know, ah, keeping her warm. You know, to treat shock, elevate the legs and keep them warm."

"Was Colette alive then?" Shaw asked.

"I—I don't think so, sir, because, ah, medically, I don't think she could have been, because when I gave her mouth-to-mouth I remember distinctly the bubbles were coming out of her chest. She was just lying there, very still, and made no response at all. I didn't take her pulse initially. All I did was see her and"—he cleared his throat—"take the knife out of her chest, and—and breathe into her mouth, really. So I don't know, but I assume not. She just—you know, I've seen a lot of dead people."

"Did you try to move her anyplace?"

"Geez, I don't know, sir. I don't think so. I mean maybe—there's a green chair there. Maybe she was leaning against it. I don't remember specifically, no, but, you know, if she was lying a little crooked, in my compulsive manner I might have straightened her out a little bit, or something. But I honestly don't remember that. I can't—I can't say yes to that. I don't remember moving her. I don't think I moved her body at all."

Then Ivory asked, "What part of the hallway were you laying in?"

"Originally?"

"Yeah."

"Ah, down near the end. Down near the couch end."

"Where did the struggle actually take place?" Grebner asked.

"Right—right at the end—right at the, ah, foot of the couch."

"Right at the foot of the couch?"

"This wasn't a big deal, you know. I wasn't James Bond, like—like all my readings. It didn't work out the way it's supposed to work out, ah—come charging through. It was just kind of a scene around me that I was grabbing things and holding on, basically. And I remember that at one time when I let go of the—this club that, ah—you know, I tried to hit a couple people and I think I hit the guy with the club once, but, ah, nothing very spectacular, let me tell you."

As the morning wore on, the three CID men, with Shaw doing most of the questioning, led MacDonald through his story again; step by step.

At Womack Hospital, MacDonald said (though this was not supported by his medical records), it had been discovered that he had "a whole bunch of little puncture marks across my abdomen. I guess we ended up with fourteen of them, or something like that."

"These injuries," Shaw said, in his dry, sterile voice, "were these from these assailants? These people that were in your house?"

"Well, I assume so," MacDonald said.

Then, with no change of tone, Shaw let the cat spring from the bag, claws exposed: "You didn't do it yourself, did you?"

"No."

Almost without pause, though with an even higher pitch of nervousness in his voice, MacDonald continued with a long, rambling explanation of how he'd had to persuade the doctors at the hospital that his lung really was punctured and that the insertion of a chest tube would be required. For almost five minutes he talked nonstop, as if by piling enough other words on top of it, he could smother Shaw's almost gentle but exceedingly ominous query.

By the time MacDonald had finished, Shaw had decided to simply let his skepticism lie in the room for a while, smoldering, as he explored other avenues.

"What were you doing before Colette went to bed?" he asked. "What transpired in the house that evening? She went to school?"

"Right. The kids and I were lying on the living room floor watching TV and when they went to bed I just read for a while. Nothing—I think I was reading one of my mysteries, a Mike Hammer mystery." The book had been not the poetry or philosophy of which MacDonald's sister had said he was so fond, but *Kiss Me Deadly,* by Mickey Spillane.

"What time did Colette come home?"

"It was a little late. Usually she'd come home about ten after nine. I think it was about twenty-five to ten, or something. I don't know. She had to drop off a—one of the girls in the class or something. I'm not—"

"Were the girls still up?"

"No, I think they'd just gone to bed. It's late, I know, but Kimmy—Kimmy stayed up late sometimes with me."

"So what happened? What transpired on this evening?"

"Nothing spectacular. I mean, she came home and probably had a—usually my wife would have a—a little brandy or—or one—one liqueur or something while we sat there. You know, it was our time of the day, sort of, and we just usually sat there and watched TV or read or something in the living room together. That's all I remember. I mean, I don't—nothing spectacular happened."

"Did you have a drink that night?"

"I don't remember, honestly. I don't—I usually didn't by myself. I might have had a liqueur with her but I don't remember."

"Do you know what time this happened? This is what I want, to build events here if I can. Now, she came home at twenty-five to ten?"

"Right. Roughly then."

"And the kids were in bed?"

"Right. I remember she came home a little late because she had missed half of—half of the show that's—the show that's on at 9 o'clock. It isn't Tom Jones. It's some show that's on Monday night at 9 o'clock."

"Glen Campbell?"

"We either watch Glen Campbell or Tom Jones or Johnny Cash. Those three shows during the week, so one of those three, whichever is on Monday night. I remember telling her she had missed the best part of it, and she said she had to drop someone off or something, 'I stopped at the 7-11' or something, and that was it. We didn't do anything unusual."

"Did you watch any of the late shows?"

"Ah, probably not. I think just up to the news. I turned it off. I usually don't watch TV except the sports or those three shows I was telling you."

"Well, try to think. Try to think about this. Did you watch the Johnny—"

"Oh, yeah. I was watching Johnny Carson."

"Johnny Carson?"

"That's right."

"Did you watch it?"

"Yeah, I was watching Johnny Carson. That's right."

"Was Colette there with you?"

"No. She started with me. That's—that's right. She started it with me and she went to bed. She didn't finish. I finished watching the Johnny Carson show and then—she was already in bed by the time it was over. She just watched the beginning."

"Any particular reason why she didn't stay there with you?"

"She was pregnant and she—she's getting more sleepy—more sleep when she's pregnant."

"Okay, well, she went to bed. What time did she go to bed?"

"Well, probably 11:30—no, 12 o'clock, 'cause I remember she started watching Johnny—now that you mention it—the Johnny Carson show with me."

"Now, had she changed clothes prior to going to bed?"

"Yeah. She always comes out and sits around with me in—in her pajamas. I mean, I say, 'yeah.' I—you know, this is just 'cause she did it every night. I don't remember her walking in and changing clothes, 'cause I was sitting there reading. Like all husbands do—they forget to notice a lot of things, but she always came out and sat down in her pajamas and had—usually had a liqueur and then go to bed. That was her routine."

"So she was in bed by midnight. Did you finish watching the Johnny Carson show?"

"Right."

"And then what did you do?"

"I read my Mike Hammer mystery."

"What else did you do?"

"Nothing."

"Did you wash dishes?"

"Yeah, I did. I washed the dishes for her."

"Okay. I'm not sharpshooting you now."

"No, no, no, I understand that. But that's right, I did. I did the dishes. I—once in a while—she hated dishes. The only thing she hated more was ironing, and if she left them she'd feel terrible the next day 'cause she'd left them. And she usually leaves them again until night and they'd just pile up. So, every once in a while, when I'm feeling good, I do them for her and she thinks I'm a big hero the next morning."

Gradually, almost imperceptibly, the tenor of the questioning sharpened.

"I'd like to get down to some other things," Shaw said, "that might be a little bit more close to home. I'm sorry, but I have to ask you about them. And that's these."

He took out photographs of the weapons that had been found at 544 Castle Drive. "Okay," he said. "Now this knife you took out of your wife's chest is curve-bladed. I think it was curved because somebody used it to pry something open or stepped on it or something along that line. Does this seem like something you might have had around the house? A paring knife?"

"With a curved blade?"

"Yeah. A bent blade."

"No. I mean, not—not that I know of, no. I didn't know of anything like that. I don't, ah—you know, my wife had some paring knives. I don't recognize this one in particular. Especially, that would have been—I know we didn't have one lying around because, you know, I would throw something like that out. I wouldn't, ah—geez, my wife would keep it forever, but I wouldn't. And if we had a knife with a bent blade I didn't know about it. I didn't see it and I don't recognize this."

"You say your wife had some around?"

"Well, sure. She would—you know, she'd cook in the kitchen and she had plenty of knives laying around."

"How many—how many paring knives did she have?"

"I don't know, quite honestly, because one of her drawers she just kept all full of junk. Usually—I usually went and used a steak knife. I could never find a paring knife."

"There was another one that we found," Shaw said. "That would be this one here. You see, now that's pretty distinctive. It says 'Old Hickory' on there."

"I don't know this one. I'd have seen the 'Old Hickory' sign if we had that around. I don't know that one."

"Can you specifically say that it is not from your house?"

"Yeah, unless she got a new knife or something that I didn't know about, but I don't think—I never saw that. And usually I had a rough idea of what was there, and I—I would have seen a knife with 'Old Hickory' on it. I didn't see that. I never saw that. So I can say that that's not from my house."

"You did some building around there, didn't you?"

"Right."

"Some shelves and that sort of thing?"

"You saw my abortions."

"You had some scrap lumber around there."

"Right."

"Well, we think that this club that you originally thought was a baseball bat might have come from around the house. In fact, I'll show it to you. I don't know if pieces of wood will mean anything to you from a photograph, but, well, there's paint on it. In fact, we had the idea that you might have used this around the house."

"I never saw it."

"People use pieces of wood to pry open doors—"

"Right."

"—and windows—"

"Right."

"—and for one thing and another."

"I don't recognize this. Now, I had—I always had some extra lumber laying around outside the back of my house, but I don't—how long is that? It's about three feet?"

"Yes, about three feet."

"Not specifically, no. I don't recognize this."

"Did you make the shelving in Kimmy's closet?"

"Right."

"There's a piece of wood there very similar to this. Very similar."

"Maybe it was around. I—I—you know, don't specifically recognize it from this—you know, from the photograph."

"Did you have an icepick?"

"I don't think I had any two-by-twos, and this is a two-by-two. I—I know I didn't have any two-by-twos specifically cut that way. There was four-by-fours, I think, in scraps."

"Did you have an icepick around the house?" Shaw repeated, showing MacDonald another photograph. "Is that your icepick?"

"No, I didn't have an icepick."

"You did not have an icepick around the house?"

"Not that I know of, no."

There was a brief pause. Then Ivory picked up the questioning, his own mind focused on the drops of Jeffrey MacDonald's blood that had been found in front of the kitchen sink.

"Did you go into the drawers with the silverware that morning?" Ivory asked.

"Any time during the morning? Oh, you mean the morning that it happened?"

"Yes."

"Not that I remember."

"Did you clean yourself up in the sink there—the kitchen sink?"

"I don't think so. I remember washing my hands off, you know, in my compulsive manner. But I—I thought it was in the bathroom. I don't think I used the kitchen sink at all. I used the phone in there, and maybe when I was talking on the phone—"

"What is the deepest you went into the kitchen?"

"Christ, I don't know. I was just—I probably just stayed there to talk on the phone. I—that's all I remember, just talking oh the phone."

"If we can drift back again," Ivory said, "you say during the initial assault you heard screams. Were they just screams or were they—"

"Words?"

"Yeah."

"Yeah."

"Like what?"

"Ah, my wife was, ah, saying ah—" He cleared his throat. " 'Jeff, why are they doing this to me?' "

"Were you still on the couch then?"

"Right."

"Did these screams continue, or did they cut out?"

"I, ah—I don't know, they asked me in the hospital and I don't, ah—I can't, you know—I don't remember any cutoff time specifically. They could or could not have continued, you know, while I was wrestling. I really don't remember, once this—really, the struggle was on. I remember sitting up and hearing them. I remember hearing my wife say, you know, 'Jeff, Jeff, why are they doing this to me? Help me.' I heard her screaming and I think I heard Kristy—Kimmy, the older girl, said, 'Daddy'—saying, 'Daddy, Daddy, Daddy.' "

"You fought your way to the entrance to the hallway?"

"Yeah, you asked me that fifteen times. Right."

"Could you see down the hallway? Did you see anything going on down at the end of the hallway?"

"No."

"What lights were on in the house?" Shaw asked. "Kitchen light?"

"Kitchen light was on. I left that on. And usually, we

left the—the bathroom light on—the big bathroom in the hallway, so it's shining—so the hallway was a little lit for the kids. And that was—I think that was on, too—when they woke up in the night, and—"

"You said when you woke up you could see your wife," Shaw said.

"Well, I could see—yeah."

"You could see in there?"

"Right."

"You could see your wife. Was that because the light was on in there?"

"Well, I—I didn't say that I could see my wife when I woke up."

"Well, again, I'm not—I'm not—"

"No."

"—sharpshooting. I just want to know."

"When I woke up, the first thing I thought of was—you know, I'm ashamed to say—myself. I mean, when I woke up I said, 'Christ, I'm going into shock.' And then I realized that everything was quiet and I started—you know, I started to remember that I heard screaming, so I was—I really didn't even like look ahead. I—I went into the bedroom and then I saw my wife.

"In other words, I didn't lay on the floor and look up, if that's what you mean, and see her. I remember, as I got up—I was lying there and I was thinking, 'Christ, I'm going into shock.' And—see, that's the first thing that hits—hits me when I was chilling. You know, my teeth were actually—literally chattering. And the light was on, and—it isn't real bright when just the bathroom light is on.

"Now, at the hospital they told me these shakes and chills—they weren't from shock. So it must have been from the temperature. It must have cooled off, that's all

I can tell you. You know, when I go over it in my own mind, it must have taken a long time for me to get the shakes and chills. My teeth were chattering, and that's a real chill, you know, in contrast to people when they say they're chilly. So if I wasn't in shock, the only thing I can say is—I have worked it over six million times—is that it must have been cold in that hall there and I was just cold from the cold."

"You think it was from the door being open?" Shaw asked.

"Right. That's what I mean."

"It was real warm when we got there," Shaw remarked.

"Oh," MacDonald said. "Jesus, I don't—well, the heat's always on. We just turn some of the radiators off if it gets too hot."

"Okay, this is the point," Shaw said. "You woke up, Captain MacDonald, while you were still on your living room couch, and you saw four people and you heard your wife somewhere."

"Right."

"You heard your daughter, right?"

"Right. This is what I, ah—this is what I can't figure out. Now, I've gone over this hundreds of times in my own mind, you know. Literally, all night long, many nights, and I—I don't—there's so many unanswered questions to me. If they—I assume they came in that back door. They had to come through there. You know, through my wife's bedroom—our bedroom. And I don't understand why, you know, by the time they got to me, that I still heard screaming. Or were there more people involved than four?"

"Four people are a lot of people," Shaw said. "Four strangers—"

"I know."

"—in a house your size are a lot of people."

"I know."

"There should be—"

"I know." MacDonald laughed.

Shaw did not laugh. "In my experience," he said, "and in his experience," pointing to Grebner, "and his," pointing to Ivory, "there should be a mess in your house. Not—"

"Right."

"There should be busted furniture and broken mirrors and bashed-in walls, and—"

"Oh, well—you people have more experience than I have," MacDonald said, "but I wouldn't normally—I mean, I wouldn't necessarily expect that. If someone is attacked when they're sleeping, I—you know, you might not get broken—"

"There aren't things out of place."

"Well, I don't know. What—"

"Does this suggest anything to you? Like maybe this group of people—"

"Knew the inside of the house? Or, yeah, were being careful, sure."

"Can you give us any better description of these people that you saw?" Shaw continued.

"I wish I had a Polaroid. You know, this—all I can say is everyone seemed moderate height. You know, this is ridiculous, I know, to you, but everyone seemed normal height. I don't really remember anything distinctive. I don't remember long hair on these people, and this is a little hard for me to figure out. If they were on, you know, LSD, or something, they're supposed to be hippies. They're not always. I mean, I've seen a lot of clean-cut Special Forces guys."

"How do hippies react?" Shaw asked. "Not hippies but people. How do people react when they are under the influence of LSD?"

"Well, anybody—"

"Are they capable of carrying out something like this? Coming to your house, out of all these other houses—"

"Well, now you're getting—now, see, you're getting to why they came to my house. If they—"

"Well, I'm not interested in why they came to your house, just for the moment. Let's say it was a matter of fate, okay?"

"All right."

"It had to be some house."

"Right."

"Why not yours? Why not—"

"Right. Okay. All right. In other words, can they do this?"

"Can they carry this out, all this business?"

"I've seen many patients that I felt were—now, you don't always know what they've taken."

"Well, let's say LSD for the moment."

"Okay. Well, again, now a person will come in the emergency room and say he's taken LSD, and he's having an acute anxiety reaction, paranoid, and he's, you know, seeing people that he's afraid of, or anything. That could be LSD, it could be speed, it could be mesc—you know, any of the—any of this amphetamine-type things—or mescaline. And very often the kids don't know what they've taken, so you have no way of knowing. But they always say LSD.

"Like I treated one two nights ago at Cape Fear and this guy was—not two nights ago—last week, and this guy was capable of anything, I'm sure. He was extremely agitated and wild, and all you had to do was move and, you know, he'd jump up and he was very paranoid. You know, people were attacking him and he had to defend himself."

"Do most—okay, let's branch away from that for just a minute," Shaw said. "The people that are taking amphetamines, uppers—"

"Right."

"We've got four of them now that we know about in your house. They're on something, we think. This girl was talking about acid—"

"Right, LSD, right."

"It could be, as you say, anything. Could be even peyote buttons, for all we know, right?"

"Right. Well, I don't know what that means. They'll—yeah, I've heard about them."

"They're excited, they're doing something that's emotionally exciting to them. They'd be jumping around wild, wouldn't they? There'd be a lot of hyperaction here. Is this correct?"

"Yeah, you—most of the—I agree with you. Most of the people I've seen on these drugs, you know, they don't—they're not steady and cool by any means. Usually, they're paranoid and anxious and—"

"When they do something, it's sort of in a frenzied kind of way, isn't it?"

"Well, I don't know. That's kind of a—I don't know."

"The other problem I have," Shaw said, "is a motive."

"Right."

"We've got to establish a motive for this thing and I don't see one. There's nothing even missing from your house—not even vandalism."

"Right."

"Captain MacDonald, there's nothing missing. You

have a lot of things in your home that people would like to steal."

"They were nice. I know."

"You have a lot of—a lot of drugs in your house."

"I know."

"Why?"

"Oh, I just got something of everything in case anyone ever asks me. Johnny-on-the-spot, you know. Very often I'd suture people, and I took care of half the neighborhood, you know, and—nothing there was controlled. I was careful about that. I didn't have any controlled drugs or anything like that. Everything was stuff there wouldn't be any problem with and no one should be after for any reason. And I just had—like, for instance, if we were going to go on a camping trip, I was all ready to make up a nice little kit with—you know, all the possibilities involved. But that was the only reason.

"All this came about when the Third Special Forces disbanded, and they had boxes and boxes of stuff they were just going to burn. And I thought that was stupid, so I just took a couple bottles of everything and was going to make up my own aid kit, you know, for my car, and camping and stuff. But I know it looked a little—a little excessive, I'm sure."

"It looked more than a little excessive," Shaw said, glancing at a list which showed that, among many other drugs, syringes, and disposable scalpel blades, MacDonald's hall closet had contained eighteen fifty-milligram vials of liquid Thorazine—an anti-psychotic drug often used to sedate unruly mental patients. "It looked real excessive, frankly. I'm being frank with you as you're being frank with me, I hope."

"Yeah, well—"

"Were you sending these things to people?"

"Just my mother, my in-laws. Diet pills, thyroid medicine, blood pressure pills."

"Okay, were you sending anything to anybody around here that would suggest—"

"Huh-uh," shaking his head to mean no.

"Can you give us any help along this line at all?"

"Geez, I wish I could. I just can't imagine that I've ever offended anyone enough—unless they're psychotic."

"And then that one person commits at least three others to his cause."

"At least. Right, right. Other people, and to—and to have no—no one break down, you know, no one come forth and feel bad or read the newspapers and say, 'Jesus, I know of,' you know, 'I know some people and I saw them Tuesday morning and they were all bloody,' or something. So I agree with you. I don't know. I'd sleep a little easier, I'll tell you that."

"Captain MacDonald," Shaw continued, having decided to further quicken the inquiry's pace, "there are some other things we found in the house. Some other questioning we have. We'll present them to you, and if you can explain them, fine. If you can't, we'll just have to worry about that. But I want to get with you on this thing because this is—this like money in the bank to you. This is real important to you.

"For example, let's start with one thing. This pajama top you were wearing, okay? We've taken this thing and we've examined it under laboratory conditions. We know what it's made of. We know what kind of fiber is in it. We know what kind of threads are in it."

"Right."

"Okay. Now, we have found fibers and threads in various places in the house. And one of the most puzzling things to me personally is that we found fibers from this jacket under Colette's body. Strung out under her body. And I'm interested in how they came to be there."

"Shaken off? Or—I don't know. Maybe—do these things shed? Are they laying all around the house? I mean, I don't know. You mean they're big fibers?"

"Yeah."

"Not—"

"Not microscopic."

"Not a fuzz," Ivory interjected.

"Not a fuzz?"

"No," Shaw said. "Fibers and threads."

"I don't know. I can't answer that."

"All right," Shaw said, "moving along a little bit further with this thing, how does it happen that the pocket from this pajama top has a little bit of your wife's blood on it—very, very minute amount—but it's laying in the bedroom. The rest of it—the jacket—is soaked with her blood—"

"I laid it—laid it over her."

"And with Kimmy's blood. Now, how does that happen?"

"Well, I'm sure I had blood all over my hands from everyone, when I was checking for pulses and stuff."

"Yeah."

"And, ah, when I went back to see my wife, I—I don't know how much, ah—Jesus, I don't know. If I had blood on my hands and I went back and touched, ah, this—this, ah, pajama top, could it have gotten on it from that way? I mean, I had blood all over me, you know. I mean I checked—I know I checked carotid pulses in everyone and I'm sure I got some blood on me from everyone. And I went back in to see my wife again."

"Like I say, this is important to you," Shaw said, "and I want you to understand what we're talking about. We've got your pocket in one location and it had a couple of spots of blood on it—Colette's blood. The rest of the pajama top, including the area beneath where the pocket had been, is drenched with blood. But the pocket was way over in another part of the bedroom, away from Colette."

"Could it have been torn off me, I mean in the struggle, and someone else dropped it?"

"That's what we think—that it was torn off during the struggle. But we have to find a way to get it to the bedroom."

"I don't know. Maybe someone, ah—maybe it was hanging on and when I walked in, it fell off. You know, I mean, I just, ah—there's a couple of ways I could picture it. Ummm, either—say that, when we were struggling, it was torn off—"

"Okay, we'll say that."

"—and the person on the way out the door dropped it. Is that possible?"

"Well, anything is possible," Shaw said.

"Right. Okay."

"Some things are less possible."

There was a short pause. Then Shaw said, "In addition, we found fibers from this jacket in Kristy's room and in Kimmy's room—both."

"Holy Christ."

"Again, I'm not sharpshooting you now—"

"No, I know."

"—but you told us that you took this off in the master bedroom."

"Right, well, now, how about my hands and stuff? Could it—could they be coming from my hands as I was taking it off and walking down the hall? I don't know. You know, when I—I mean, couldn't it have been attached to the hairs on my arm or something and, you know, ripped in the—in the struggle and fall off?"

"Well," Ivory said, "we're not talking about a, say, stray thread or a fiber here and there. We're talking about a profusion."

"Well, it doesn't make sense to me. A profusion, I don't know. All I can say is that—I don't know what this—you know, how ripped this jacket looks. I don't even remember it, to tell you the truth. I just remember taking it—taking it off my hands.

"But if it was ripped up, it seems to me that threads could be on them and on me. It could have fallen on them. That's all I can honestly say."

"Now, in addition to all this," Shaw said, confusing the names of MacDonald's two daughters, "we found a fiber from that jacket under Kimmy's fingernail, and it had blood on it, which would indicate somewhere she—"

"Under Kimmy's?"

"—she got her—"

"I don't know. It's pretty obvious what you're ah—" MacDonald laughed. "I don't know."

"Well," Shaw said, "this is why, Captain MacDonald, we've got these specific things we've got to talk about—"

"Right."

"—because you are the only person who knows what happened in that house."

"Listen, I know all about that, and, ah—look, ah, all—Jesus Christ. All I can say is that it seems to me these fibers in a struggle could have gotten on everyone, and I don't know. I—I mean, obviously, I wish—I can't give you the answers specifically. All I can do is make conjectures."

Abruptly, Shaw shifted direction. "At any point during the night," he said, "during this checking of your family before the military police arrived, did you wear a pair of gloves?"

"Did I wear a pair of gloves?"

"Yeah. You."

"Oh, yeah, to do the dishes."

"What kind of gloves were they?"

"She usually had two pairs laying there. A yellow, thick dish glove and—and a pair of my surgeon's gloves. I don't know which ones I used. I don't remember."

"But did you use gloves to wash the dishes?"

"Yeah."

"Okay. After you realized—after you had been attacked yourself and you woke up and you realized that there had been harm done in this house did you wear gloves at any time?"

"No."

"Not to take pulses or anything like that?"

"No."

"Okay. Well, we have a—we have a lack of blood in some places where there should be, Captain MacDonald, a lot of blood. There should be a lot of blood on the telephone in your bedroom and there should be a lot of blood on the telephone in your kitchen, but there isn't. The phone is down, it's off the hook, where's the blood? Did you wipe your hands off someplace?"

"Maybe on my wife's nightgown or something. Or when I was checking the pulses, I was—what are my pajama bottoms like? I—you know, I don't remember. Maybe my hands were relatively dry when I picked up the phone, but I don't—not before the first call, unless it was on the rugs or, ah—you know, ah, my wife—on the nightgown and stuff, you know. But I don't know."

"You've worked in the emergency room a lot," Shaw said.

"Right."

"It's your profession. And you don't get your hands full of blood and wipe them off and—and not contaminate what you touch. You get blood on what you touch."

"Right—unless it's dry. I mean, you know, if—now when—you know, when I woke up on the floor, if I had been there for a while, it could have been dry and not leave too much."

"It wasn't dry when we got there."

"Okay, that shoots that down. I don't know."

"You know," Shaw continued, "I've also been thinking about this big wet urine spot there on the bed. Was there a lot—"

"This happened all the time," MacDonald interrupted. "That—that's not unusual, you know. Every night, Kristy was in there—just about every night. I tried to tell my wife that the way to do it is to keep her in her bed one night, even though she cries. We did it with Kimmy and it worked. She never again came in, and there was no problem.

"But Colette, you know, said it was worth—worth getting up for one minute every night, rather than to have to go through two or three nights of yelling and screaming. So, she usually always came in. She was two and a half and still had a bottle, you know."

"That's kind of unusual, isn't it?"

"We were real easygoing. And if Kristy wanted a bottle, well, we decided, let her have a bottle. No big deal. Kimmy had a bottle a long time and she was fine. I mean there didn't seem to be any harm, and she was happy. She was a good kid, didn't have any problems."

"Kristy was pretty well taken care of, it seems like."

"Well, they were both taken care of. There was—I don't think either of them were really favored. They were totally different. Kimmy was real, you know, effeminate, and real—a real female. And Kristy was a tomboy, you know. They were both totally different, but I don't think either of them—you know, we loved them both for, you know, for different—for different things. Equally, I'm sure.

"You could yell at Kristy more because it didn't affect her. You couldn't yell at Kimmy. I mean, she got very upset if she thought, you know, you were disapproving of her."

"What kind of class was Colette in?" Shaw asked.

"What the heck was the latest one? I don't know. Something literature. I mean, I really don't know. She had just gotten an A in her Seventeenth-Century English—I don't know. It was a—it was—she was an English major and it was some kind of literature course."

"Was she after her degree?"

"Yeah, in English. She was going to end up—when I got to Yale, she's going to—she was going to try to, you know, get into Yale or a college nearby. Yale is accepting girls now, and she only needed about a year more. She had two years at Skidmore and a whole lot of courses since we've been married, different places. And she was going to try to get a, you know, a bachelor's in English."

"To what end?"

"I don't know. I suppose that she would—would have liked to have ended up being some kind of an instructor—preferably in a college atmosphere, you know, wherever I was. I was probably going to stay at a university to practice, and she would just piddle. You know, be an instructor, kind of a part-time thing.

"I didn't want her working, with the kids. And she

didn't want to work very much. And it was nice, you know, having her around, taking care of the kids and taking care of me."

Shaw intruded upon this reverie. "Kimmy was in your bedroom," he said, "and she got hurt in there."

"She got hurt?"

"Yes."

"You mean that night?"

"That's what I'm saying."

"Unless she went in—now, she hardly ever did anymore. Very rarely would she leave her bed. She was, you know, at the point now where she slept in her own bed and stayed there. You know, very rarely would she go in with Colette and myself. That was like once a month that occurred."

"If she had heard something," Shaw asked, "and been awakened, was she the type of child that would go and investigate to see what was going on?"

"Well, Kristy would. Even at two and a half, probably. But I'm not sure about Kimmy. Kimmy was like a—you know, she got bucked off the new pony I just got them once and she wasn't—it took her a while to get back on, you know what I mean? She wasn't a take-charge, and that—I don't know, that's conjecture, but Kimmy was—she was real effeminate and real soft and gentle and I—I don't—I don't know.

"But if she had a nightmare, for instance—the only parable [*sic*] I can draw—if she'd wake up crying from a nightmare, she'd just sit there and yell until Colette came in, whereas Kristy would come charging into the bedroom and dive into the bed.

"You know, a whole different—different way of doing something. If—if Kimberly heard screaming, I would doubt if she would—if she would—if she would go and investigate that. She's bright and curious, but she's also a very dependent-type child, you know."

"You don't think she would?"

"Well, she might have. How can you tell, really, what a five-year-old girl would do? If you had said to me, what would I expect?—Kristy, yes. Kristy would go charging anywhere, partially because she's young enough so she doesn't have any fear yet. But—but Kimmy—Kimmy was always different.

"She was always—you know, you had to take her by the hand, except in—except in academic things. I mean, she was the one that came home and knew how to read and write way too early and stuff like that, but like she would—she'd get pushed around by other kids, whereas Kristy—Kristy would defend her, believe it or not.

"Kimmy would come home crying and Kristy would run over and crack someone. So—geez—that's the first time I heard that. I—I didn't—I hadn't heard anything about—about Kimberly's being injured in the master bedroom. Umph."

There was a long pause.

"Now I did hear them both screaming," MacDonald said, "so I think I'm positive it was Kimmy. Definitely, it was Colette, because she's the only one who would call me Jeff and I know her voice. I'm sure the other one was Kimberly. See—you know—but—I didn't know that—what you just said."

"Don't read anything into this," Shaw said, "but if it comes to this, are you willing to take a polygraph in reference to what we've talked about this morning?"

"Sure. Absolutely."

"Well, that's fine. We wanted to get that out in the open. You realize you don't have to."

"Sure, that's fine with me."

"We might ask you to. Just to clear the air here."

It was by now 11:20 A.M. "How would you like to have a cup of coffee?" Shaw asked.

"I would. We've talked a long time."

"Bill, will you take care of that?" Shaw said to Ivory. "Show the captain where the coffee is."

The Voice of Jeffrey MacDonald

Fort Sam Houston became kind of a fun time, to my surprise. I thought it would be fairly difficult at first, but it ended that we were assigned to motel rooms rather than barracks, and I met this doctor from Williams College who's now an orthopedic surgeon on Maui, and he and I ended up sort of hanging around together for the six weeks of training at Fort Sam Houston.

We had a very different lifestyle than I initially thought. We started working out together—along with a veterinarian whose name I totally forget—which had always been my custom, even through medical school and internship, to try to get some running in at least several times a week and some exercise, occasional handball or basketball.

Fairly early on, they had this sort of Careers Day, where they put all of us in an auditorium and brought in different specialists from branches of the service and tried to get you to sign up. And I remember these mostly turkeys came across the stage and gave their little talk and there was really nothing very exciting.

And then a full colonel, a bird colonel, came out with his Green Beret on and his dress uniform with jump boots and all his medals over his left chest and his wings on and he gave about a two-minute talk.

Basically, what he said was, "Well, you guys can just join up and treat a fifty-yard-long line of malingering GIs who don't want to be there and who hate the war, and half of them just have V.D. and the other half don't have anything, or you can spend two years doing something really valuable: you can join up, learn how to jump out of planes, become airborne, a paratrooper, and then work with the best troops on earth, the United States Green Berets." He said, "If you have any guts for that kind of thing, see me," and he walked off the stage.

Well, this friend from Williams and I, we kind of looked at each other and said, "Jesus, that sounds pretty neat, we never even thought of that," and we both laughed and said, "Let's go," and, needless to say, we were the only two out of about four hundred people who went to see him.

This colonel, Colonel Himma, his first name was Einar, he had escaped, I think, from Germany in World War II. He may have been Norwegian or Swede, but I think he was German and he escaped during World War II and came to the Allied side and ended up going back to medical school in the forties or fifties and ended up in the Green Berets.

In any case, he was a tall German with a German accent and he still had this old Prussian way of dealing with officers and men and we were impressed with him and with the drama and the possibilities of jumping out of planes and being a Green Beret. This really turned both my friend and I on and we went away and, as I remember, we went out and worked out—it was about a hundred and six degrees in San Antonio in July but we ran a couple of miles together and did our chin-ups and push-ups and sit-ups and whatnot and felt pretty good about the possibility of becoming Green Berets, and I remember I called Colette later that night or the next day and sort of announced rather than asked that I'd been offered this chance to go airborne and go to paratrooper school and join the Green Berets.

And I remember there was a little silence at the other end of the phone. My mom was there at the other end, too, I believe. She was with Colette or Colette came next door to see my mom as soon as I called. In any case, I remember there was a little silence and then Colette's next question was, "Well, why in the world would you want to jump out of airplanes and be a Green Beret?"

And I must have been a little, you know, excited or up about it, but I was very enthusiastic and told her that they were the best troops in the world and we'd learn different things as well as doing the medical work—we would learn patrolling and long-range reconnaissance and jumping out of airplanes and demolitions and small weapons fire and all this stuff. And I explained to her how, instead of wasting two years in a sick-call line treating not very sick people, this way I had a chance to work with these incredible troops and if I went to Vietnam I might even go as a Green Beret physician.

Colette was uncomfortable about my becoming a Green Beret but she also respected me, you know, for making a firm decision—and she sort of, you know, she put her faith and her trust in me.

Also, to be honest, this colonel had told us that if we passed the physical test and signed the right papers and were willing to go to Airborne school, we could have our orders changed from Vietnam to Fort Benning, Georgia, and we would get orders from Fort Benning probably to JFK Center at Fort Bragg for Green Beret status.

And this was the thing she sort of latched on to, and I then sort of used as the trump card, I guess—that I was being taken off orders for Vietnam. And I then sort of realized how—that was the first time that I ever really understood that Colette was upset that I might be going to Vietnam. I had always been kind of casual about it and a little cavalier, but at that point that phone call brought me to a realization that Colette—and therefore probably my Mom and Dad were—I'm sorry, not my Dad but my Mom—were upset about me going to Vietnam.

So therefore that became the topic of conversation: that joining the Green Berets was getting me *off* orders to Vietnam, but that was not at all my intention in joining. As a matter of fact, I fully expected to go to Vietnam as soon as I got the Green Beret. And later on, as a matter of fact, I talked to two of my commanding officers and asked to go to Vietnam, on two different occasions, neither of which were fully discussed with Colette. At the time, it wasn't, I felt, appropriate. Now, in retrospect, of course, that's a decision I probably should have shared a little more widely with her. But I saw it as part duty and part something I wanted to do.

So we were down in Fort Sam Houston, which was clear and sunny and hot and dry, and we had these few little physical tests. I went and eventually took my test after working out for I think about another week with my friend from Williams, really hard every day. We went and took the test in our fatigues and boots, and we both passed with flying colors.

*   *   *

At Fort Benning, during my paratroop training, I was proud of working toward earning my wings. And of course my first jump is something I will never forget.

I remember very clearly going out the door—I was definitely, you know, scared, but as I got closer to the door my fear seemed to decrease; they didn't have to push me—and getting a sense of confusion as the air hit me and you spun around. I remember that the feeling of being tossed and turned was much more than I was prepared for, but I also remember what an incredible rush it was as you looked up and saw your open chute above you. It was sort of like, you know, your heart had stopped for a minute and then started beating again. Relief floods through you, this incredible relief, and next an exhilaration that you've actually done it— you've jumped.

A lot of guys gave out a tremendous whoop as we were heading on down towards the earth. The sky was full of new paratroopers and you could hear the yells of exhilaration up and down, guys giving Geronimos and war whoops and "I made it!" and, you know, even picking up on some of the yells that the instructors had us screaming while we were running all through Airborne school about going to kill some Charlie Cong. I'll never forget that exhilaration.

The day after my Airborne graduation I flew out of Fort Benning. I believe I had a couple of days and I flew to New York and I remember how neat it was to get off the plane at JFK and have jump wings on my dress Army greens. Still had a regular Army hat—officer-style hat— but I had jump wings now. And the casual Army hat, the soft Army hat, had a different patch on it now because I was Airborne. And I remember how neat I felt.

*   *   *

Now, arriving at Fort Bragg—it was actually the best time of the year for weather. The fall at Fort Bragg is clear and pretty, the sky is blue and the pine trees are all nice and there's a lot of green grass that still hasn't turned brown for the winter. And Fort Bragg was the home of the Airborne—the 18th Airborne Corps and the 82nd Airborne—as well as the JFK Center for Special Warfare—the Green Berets. So it was, you know, an elite base with a lot of elite troops, the 82nd Airborne being better than most of the ground troops and the Green Berets being allegedly the best of all.

In addition, fairly soon after I got there I was able to arrange for the housing at 544 Castle Drive and Freddy drove Colette and the kids down and we moved into the house.

Moving in, you know—moving, I think, is always traumatic—but it went very well. Colette was happy to have had some time with Freddy, I think, and the kids were—it was gonna be a super setup for us because the school was on post and was good and we would have no trouble getting babysitters and we had an income and a reasonable-sized house . . . each of the kids had their own bedroom, we had our own bedroom, it *was* officer's quarters, and to us it was great.

Also, being together again. You know, despite the bachelor atmosphere at Fort Sam Houston and a little bit in Fort Benning, it was really nice to be back with Colette and the kids.

My job seemed relatively easy and lots of fun. I was getting in a lot of jumps and learning some neat things. I was able to get my workouts in—right after Thanksgiving I started working out with the boxing team—and still have this great time to be with the kids and Colette. Also, I was not on orders for Vietnam and Colette was very relieved about that.

Once we were settled, though, I went to see my commanding officer, Colonel Kingston, and told him that I didn't mind going to Vietnam and that, as a matter of fact, I kind of wanted to go.

Bob Kingston was the guy who was in charge of the Third Special Forces when I first got to Fort Bragg and he made me his group surgeon one or two weeks after I arrived. In other words, I was the main doctor under Colonel Kingston.

I had heard all the legends about him. He's a guy who was behind the lines in North Korea, he was a Raider and he was behind the lines, apparently, for like thirteen months, which is really awesome when you think about it: he was probably five or six inches taller and thirty or forty pounds heavier than every other normal male in North Korea and yet he was behind enemy lines for thirteen months.

He also captured a pirate North Korean junk during the Korean War, on which he found a couple million dollars' worth of gold bullion. He was on special assignment to the CIA at the time, and he brought back his couple million dollars' worth of gold bullion and turned it over to the CIA and I'll never forget, his wife never forgave him for not shaving off a little piece. He had a lovely wife, British wife, Jo Kingston, and a gorgeous daughter, Leslie.

Kingston was the kind of guy that you would jump on a helicopter with or jump out of a helicopter with, or go into battle with. You sort of implicitly gave him your, you know, your life to hold for a while. And he gloried in it, to be honest. He was a real soldier. I mean a soldier who got his hands dirty. He was a man's man, no question about it.

And it was at this time—when I told him I would like

to serve in Vietnam—that Colonel Kingston told me that he really liked my style, that I was his type of doc, and that if and when he went back to Vietnam, which he felt would be within a year, he was fully planning on taking me with him as his group surgeon, and of course I jumped at that.

I remember leaving his second-story, second-floor office flushed with pride that this hard-core Green Beret who later became a general who ran the Green Berets, and, much later, who was named the first commander of the new Rapid Deployment Force, had given me such high praise.

And I remember going home and telling Colette how pleased I was with this evaluation from Colonel Kingston, and she was enthralled—or, actually, not enthralled, but she was proud.

Her eyes always sparkled this beautiful luminous brown when I got excited, especially if it was something that, you know, I had done or accomplished. Sometimes I know she felt it was a little silly or boyish or mannish or whatever that such a thing would excite a grown man. But I remember coming back from this and her being—or appearing to be—very proud about the fact that Colonel Kingston found me such a good officer.

I remember another time I took Colette to a retreat one Saturday morning early in our experience at Fort Bragg. I had just been given my Green Beret that I could wear with a training patch but couldn't yet wear with full insignia because I hadn't finished my Green Beret training, but I was proud of being able to wear my Green Beret, I remember, and I went to this retreat in my Green Beret and jump boots and dress uniform and it was one of those really impact moments that stand out and I'll never forget it and Colette never forgot it either.

It was like in late September or early October and we went to this retreat and we were standing in this clearing near the JFK Center for Special Warfare, having the review, and the flags, you know, were held by the troops and the troops were lined up smartly in their jump boots and Green Berets and Colonel Kingston gave about a five- or six-minute speech and it was one of those things that really did give you chills.

He, ah, there was fog rolling in and you could hardly see the end of the little parade grounds and he used a couple of anecdotes to remind us that he had been other times, other places, where the fog was rolling in and he'd had good troops with him and he'd lost most of those troops and that some of those men now had Medals of Honor and Silver, you know, Stars, or whatever the hell they are, and that we were, you know, we were Green Berets and we were to do our best.

It was a time of a lot of upheaval on Fort Bragg, of course. The beginnings of the antiwar movement were beginning and Jane Fonda was, within months, to descend on Fort Bragg, but Colonel Kingston gave this six- or seven-minute talk that was really sort of chilling in its beauty and its patriotism and I never forgot that and Colette was there and she was stunned by it also.

And I remember when we went back to the house that we both talked about it a little bit and how impressive a guy he was, and I repeated to her at that time some of the legends about Bob Kingston.

I went on one really exciting training exercise, down on Vieques, an island off Puerto Rico. There was Navy involvement. SEAL [Sea, Air and Land personnel of the Navy] involvement, submarine warfare expert involvement, and the Green Berets.

We had large scenarios written up in which we were gonna go into cities in Puerto Rico and set up these sort of dummy teams that would be watching students' revolts—student, you know, student-fomented demonstrations—and pick out the leaders and prepare scenarios on how they would be assassinated if it was in the best interest of, allegedly, their country and our country to do so.

And that's what we were doing down in the Caribbean: a mixture of Green Beret and SEAL teams, and of course they were in tremendous competition with each other, the Green Berets thinking the SEALs were dead on land and the SEALs thinking the Green Berets were pansies in the water. In fact, they were both good at both. They were both incredible sort of warrior-type people.

My job was chief medical officer for Kingston and part of my duties, of course, involved checking out local prostitutes in Puerto Rico near our base, and that's where the famous episode occurred where I was sitting at a bar with a master sergeant and he picked up one of the girls in the bar and then there was this horrendous battle and these paper-thin walls and the door was flying off and the walls were smashing down and it turned out that the girl he had picked up wasn't a girl at all but a guy in drag.

It was a female impersonator and he had been making out with this person for like ten minutes until he finally reached down between her legs and felt a hard-on, and went just crazy, he almost killed this person. I had to help pull the sergeant off this guy and then of course hush up the whole incident for the good of the Army . . .

The sad thing, of course, that happened on that trip was that I got called to go help Jay. Everything was hunky-dory, or so I thought. I was down being a Green

Beret and Colette was back at Fort Bragg, reasonably happily ensconced there, waiting for me, beginning the schooling that she was so proud to get back to each time, and the kids were in good schools—Kristy was in, like, a sort of a, basically a babysitting school, and Kimmy was, I believe, I guess, in kindergarten at the time. Yeah, she must have been in kindergarten. So we thought everything was fine and I got this telegram, the TWX, on the island of Vieques, that there was a family emergency.

So I remember still being in battle fatigues, and, you know, jungle gear, and getting onto an Army transport and Colette had been warned by the Army that I was on my way and she had a bag packed for me, and I changed into my dress Army uniform—I was wearing, you know, the Green Beret and paratrooper boots at this time and took, I believe, a commercial flight to JFK and that's the time when this priest who was sitting next to me began telling me how much he admired men in uniform and the next thing I know he's got his hand on my thigh.

Anyway, to make a long story short, that's the time Jay flipped out. He had this apparently psychotic break. It turns out later he admitted to being on amphetamines for a period of weeks, if not months.

He had been tending bar in Greenwhich Village and had just moved out of one apartment and was living with a merchant seaman, I believe, and apparently the stress of tending bar, drinking too much, taking amphetamines to stay up all night and party and then taking some LSD flipped him out, and he had this raging psychotic break including breaking away from my mother—inadvertently, apparently, knocking her down one time—policemen finally getting ahold of him and there being a struggle with the police, straitjacket, handcuffs, brought to the state mental hospital on Long Island and tried to dive through a window from the second story. This really horrendous episode. Finally sedated with Thorazine. And, now, several days later, I was arriving on emergency leave.

I went to this mental hospital with my mom, you know, this incredibly depressing place with the raging psychotics in their zombie-like Thorazine trances, and found my brother overweight, disheveled, with a psychotic thought process, and was, you know, absolutely stunned by the whole thing.

I could understand taking some amphetamines. After all, they weren't so bad, just stay up a little bit and party. But I couldn't understand the LSD, and Jay, of course, assured me that it was given to him unknown to himself. All the rest of the people around him were the bad guys and that if only I could get him out of the hospital he would be fine.

Well, he clearly wasn't fine. There's no question he had been sort of a fringe Mafia player for a while. All the people he was dealing with were those fringe types that go on junkets to Las Vegas—they all have businesses that are legitimate in New York, but they all go to the track and they bet a lot of money and they gamble with bookies, and—some of the businesses are not quite so legitimate, like Jerry the Drug Man, a guy who apparently buys up drug samples from drug salesmen and then wholesales them illegally to pharmacies.

And Jay would run up gambling debts on some of these Las Vegas junkets apparently, when he was taking amphetamines and feeling good, sort of in a manic phase, and he ended up at one time owing about $15,000 and my Mom had to cough up when some people came to visit her. She called me in Fort Bragg asking me what to do, and I said, "Well, if you have the money you're gonna have to pay 'em," because I didn't know what else to do. I certainly didn't want my mother's arms and legs broken, so there was a major amount of money that she took out of, I think, the life insurance policy from my Dad's death, that was used to pay off some loan sharks.

So when he had this schizophrenic break, ah, his main focus was on this Mafia-type personality. There was a lot of element of realism here, but when he had the psychotic break of course it became totally unreal, and *The Godfather* became sort of his Bible, he would walk around holding it, believing that he was a character in the book or that the book had become real and that people were really out to get him.

And I have to tell you that seeing someone in a state hospital is an incredibly awesome event. It's just shattering, the type of care that I know they get and having gone through medical school and taken a period of training at an institute like this and knowing all the scare stories. Seeing your own brother—who was always sort of an All-American hero—truly psychotic, was a very frightening thing. A tremendous, scary, vacant, desolate feeling about Jay and how he looked and the unbelievable turmoil that my mother was in from this.

So I went in and checked out his apartment in New York and that's when I went down to the bar he worked at and found a guy who may or may not have given him some of the drugs, but I thought he did, and he was the local supplier for some of the bartenders, and we had a little altercation—I sort of punched him out. Then I had to go back to Fort Bragg.

But the overriding feeling that immediately comes to mind about Fort Bragg was the sense of ease that Colette and I finally had and the new togetherness that really developed nicely.

Colette was getting out of, you know, a reasonably tough situation because she had been forced to live with my mom on Long Island and not really have control over her own life for a while, so there was the relief of getting together again and building our house again and her being able to go back to school, and having the cheap shopping available and the steady income.

So we were becoming really reacquainted and it was kind of fun because there was no pressure on me. It was low-key. I could be around, play with the kids, and there weren't other contributing things. There were no other women, I wasn't dating any nurses, I wasn't seeing people on the side. We were really recommitting ourselves to each other and it was a nice feeling.

I think emotionally, without any question, our relationship was getting stronger. I think the trust was building. I think some of the more obvious past escapades were beginning to fade. The little things that I did, the little affairs and the motel trips and stuff like that, that was nothing. It just meant absolutely nothing except it was a guy away from home, and it didn't make any difference one way or the other. Colette had never been happier. I think the kids were growing by leaps and bounds and were extremely happy and essentially oblivious to any problems at all between us.

So the Army remembrances are of, you know, for the first time in five years, a reasonably easy life and enough money coming in and new enjoyment with the kids.

It was really a flowering of the fatherhood and childhood times. It was Kimmy developing and running and playing and reading and becoming bright and inquisitive and us realizing that we had a super-bright daughter, and Kristen just beginning to be a little tomboy and running around the neighborhood and protecting Kimmy, and

being a little more aggressive than Kimmy, and us realizing that we had a beauty on the way up, also bright and
cheery and nonstop, and that we had a, you know, a
good future ahead.

The kids were basically past, you know, the real diaper
stage. Kristy still wore diapers but it wasn't like she was a
little infant anymore. She was beginning to grow and,
you know, talk and everything.

Specifically, each day I remember like breakfast with
the kids was so nice. I hadn't had that really, that luxury
of sitting and enjoying the kids at breakfast, and it *was* an
enjoyment; it wasn't a chore.

Sunday morning, especially, was a beautiful, beautiful
time. We always had a late breakfast. Very often, either
Colette or I would get up and sneak out while the other
one was sleeping and go down to the bakery and get
some baked goods. We even tried to do this in Chicago
and Bergenfield—get bagels and lox or something like
that, which wasn't very available at Fort Bragg.

But we—very often one of us would get up and do
that, and begin breakfast and then come back to bed
when the kids got up and fool around for a while. Um,
and this was like a big thing, this was a reattachment of
our entire family because we were having the time and I
wasn't tired and I didn't have to rush off to work and I
hadn't worked all night the night before and Colette was
the most relaxed she'd ever been, and we were making
love with, I think, more abandon than we ever had before.

Lovemaking with Colette was always a love thing. It
wasn't just getting laid or making out or, getting, you
know, getting fucked or whatever you want to say. It was
always a much prettier thing than that.

Colette never, like, openly demanded love from me

physically. She never sort of really grabbed me or she never said, ah, "I want you to fuck me tonight," or something like that. We never—it was never that kind of a thing between us. It was not like the incredible physical sex that I had had with Penny Wells. It was definitely lovemaking rather than pure sex. There's no question or comparison at all.

Our lovemaking had a very gentle quality to it that was exciting to us both, I think. And it took us a long time for new things to happen—new positions, new techniques. It always seemed that we were gentle and considerate to each other in our lovemaking and that each effort sufficed. We didn't have to do the next major position or change, or—we didn't go through these things violently or passionately, we went through them sort of quietly.

As a matter of fact, Colette was scared. I thought initially she was just a little vulnerable and a little naive, but it turned out that she had a real fear. You never really could pin down what it was from—whether it, sort of the unasked question: had she made love with her high school boyfriend, Dean Chamberlain, and had not been successful? Which was quite possible, because, to be honest, Dean was a jerk as far as I was concerned. I always thought he was a nitwit.

Or had the Purdue sophomore traumatized her? Or was it, in fact, that she was a virgin and had never really made love and was terrified of it and had, you know, quote, successfully, unquote, held off both Dean and the Purdue sophomore, and I was the first man she ever slept with—I don't know.

But it took many, many, many, many months—in fact, years—before Colette was able to really lose her inhibitions in our lovemaking. It wasn't until, I think, maybe the middle years of medical school that she was really comfortable walking around naked in front of me, and she never really got over it totally—it was always a little bit of concern, and that, of course, was basically a turn-on. She was always feminine and a little bit naive and a little bit vulnerable and it was a very exciting thing.

I don't mean to sound the music and roll the drums, but at Fort Bragg, finally, with more time alone with each other and me in certainly a better mood than I had been in for at least the prior year at Bergenfield and maybe even better than a lot of times in medical school, we could be more relaxed with each other, and we made time for each other and took a lot of time, and each person's—the other person's—satisfaction was important to us.

And we were beginning to realize that the outside world, the civilian world, offered limitless opportunities to us, and that we would have this great, you know, sort of dream come true without too much effort from here on in.

We also came to the realization that there was a world out there that we could conquer. I'd be at Yale for my residency and later probably teaching at Yale and practicing surgery and we'd have the farm, we'd have the horses, we'd have a boat, we had beautiful kids and a third on the way, and Colette was looking forward to the future with real glee and anticipation and Colette and I were very much in love again.

10

Instead of simply having a cup of coffee in a corridor, Jeffrey MacDonald had left CID headquarters for ninety minutes. When he returned, at 1 P.M., the radio had been turned off. Franz Joseph Grebner began to speak.

"I have been sitting here most of the morning," Grebner said, "not saying very much, just listening to your story, and I have been an investigator for a long time, and if you were a Pfc.—a young, uneducated person—I might try to bring you in here and bluff you. But you are a very well-educated man—doctor, captain— and I'm going to be fair with you.

"Your story doesn't ring true. There's too many discrepancies. For instance, take a look at that picture over there." Grebner gestured toward a photograph of the living room of 544 Castle Drive.

"Do you see anything odd about that scene?"

"No."

"It is the first thing I saw when I came into the house that morning. Notice the flowerpot?"

"It's standing up."

"Yes. Notice the magazines?"

"Yeah."

"Notice the edge of the table right there?"

"I don't understand the significance of it."

"Okay. The lab technicians, myself, Mr. Ivory, and Mr. Shaw, and any number of other people have tipped that table over. It never lands like that. It is top-heavy and it goes over all the way, even pushes the chair next to it out of the way. The magazines don't land under the leading edge of that table, either. They land out on the floor."

"Couldn't this table have been pushed around during the struggle?"

"It could have been, but it would have been upside down when it stopped. And the plant and the pot always go straight out and they stay together in all instances."

"Well, what—what are you trying to say?"

"That this is a staged scene."

"You mean that I staged the scene?"

"That's what I think."

"Do you think that I would stand the pot up if I staged the scene?"

"Somebody stood it up like that."

"Well, I don't see the reasoning behind that. You just told me I was college-educated and very intelligent."

"I believe you are."

"Well, why do you think I would—I don't understand why you think I would stage it that way if I was going to stage it."

"And your glasses, which are over there underneath the drapery. They could have gotten there, but you weren't wearing your glasses when you went into the bedrooms. And they are lying with the outer edge of the lens down on the floor, yet on the face of that lens there's blood."

"Maybe someone knocked them over."

"But how did they get the blood on them?"

"I assume from the person who knocked them over."

"Another feature here. There's an *Esquire* magazine laying there. There's a box laying on top of it. And on this edge, right underneath the box, there's blood on the edges of the pages. This whole thing here was staged."

"That's a pretty powerful statement. Changes things around, doesn't it?"

"Yes, it does."

"Well, I can't help you," MacDonald said. "What do you want me to say? You are telling me that—that I staged the scene and that's it. It is a little ludicrous."

"You must understand," Grebner said, "that I am looking at this from the point of an investigator, past experience."

"I understand that."

Grebner gestured toward another photograph. "Notice the rug right there?"

"Right."

"It slips and slides and rolls up very easily. In the position it is in, that's where you would have been having this struggle, pushing against three men."

"Well, at the edge of the bed [*sic*] and on the end of the hallway." (This was the third time MacDonald had said "bed" when he had apparently intended to say "couch.")

"This rug was undisturbed," Grebner said.

"Well, what do you want me to say? I don't—I'm not an investigator. You are telling me that—that I staged the scene and I—I'm telling you that things happened the way I told you."

"You know," Grebner continued, "you as a doctor and I as an investigator have seen many people come into emergency rooms and they are pretty badly hurt."

"Right."

"I've seen people who were shot directly in the heart with a .38 run over a hundred yards. You had one icepick wound—apparently from an icepick—punctured your lung to the point that it collapsed 20 percent. You had one small bump on your head."

"No, correction, I had two."

"Two? Okay, two. Not apparently wounds or bumps that would have been caused by this type of club that we have in this instance if anyone was swinging with any force."

"Well, I can't agree with you there, medically. I have treated patients who have died and there's nothing but a little abrasion on their forehead."

"That's probably true, but here you are. You've been hit twice by now. This didn't knock you out. This is according to your story. You're at a point here where the old adrenaline is pumping into your system—you are fighting for yourself and your children—and yet you pass out here, according to your story, at the end of the hallway."

"It wasn't exactly passing out, Mr. Grebner. I was hit on the head a couple of times."

"But that didn't knock you out. You were still pushing and fighting against these people and—"

"Well, apparently it did knock me out, though."

"—for an unexplained reason you passed out."

"No, no, I didn't pass out. Apparently I was knocked unconscious."

"By a third blow?"

"I don't—I don't know how many blows."

"But this weapon was used on Colette and Kim. It is a brutal weapon. We had three people here that are over-killed, almost. And yet they leave you alive. While you were laying there in the hallway, why not give you a good lick or two from behind the head with that club and finish you off?"

"Well, maybe I was—"

"You saw them eye to eye. They don't know that you wouldn't be able to identify them at a later date. Why leave you there alive?"

"I don't know. Maybe they assumed that—that I was dead, and the frenzy got worse and worse. I—I don't know. I've thought about this. I've spent many sleepless nights in the last six weeks, you know."

"Then we have the fibers from your pajama top directly under your wife's body."

"Sir, I told you I can't—I can't explain some of those fibers. That's—that's beyond my capabilities. I just told you the only thing I know and obviously the implication is real bad for me, but I can't—how can I explain that? I don't know."

"And as we enter the bedroom we have Kimberly's blood on that rug. To the right of the door we have the top sheet and the spread from your bed, and on the sheet are both Colette's blood and Kimberly's. And on the bedspread it's Colette's blood—large quantities. Now, hippies don't—they let bodies fall where they may."

"Right, I agree with you."

"So it is another staged scene, probably. Kimberly was returned to her bed—it's a possibility—carried in that sheet. And there was absolutely no evidence that could be found—even though we had technicians in there for five days—of an alien being in that house. You get that many people in a house that small, you're going to have evidence of it."

"I don't know what you expect me to say here."

"That club," Grebner continued. "You said you had

never seen that before? Do you know there is paint on it that is the same as paint on the sidewalk in back of the house?"

"Look, ah—"

"It is the same as the paint on scraps of wood which you have in your locked storage room. It is the same as the paint on a pair of surgical gloves that were in the locked storage room. That piece of wood came from the house."

"It might have," MacDonald said. "I haven't seen the piece of wood. I didn't recognize it from the picture. Jesus Christ, this is getting—what's this called? Circumstantial evidence? Yeah, well, go ahead," MacDonald said sarcastically, "what else do you have?"

"I was just throwing out things for you to consider."

"What you are doing is you are sitting here telling me that I killed my wife and kids! That's un—that's unbelievable. Christ's sakes, what's my motive? What'd I do that for?"

"We can conjecture a lot of reasons perhaps."

"You think I wasn't happily married?"

"I'm happily married, too. Sometimes I get pretty mad at my wife. Particularly when I was younger and more easily angered."

"You think I could get mad enough at someone to do that?"

"I have known it to happen before."

"Holy Christ! I'll tell you what it looks like to me. It looks like you've run out of ideas, and—and you are picking out someone—the easiest one. You've got to solve it by the end of the fiscal year so when the report goes in there's a one hundred percent solved rate."

"No," Grebner said. "I've been at this for twenty years and I'm going to stick one more. So I'm not in any hurry. It is just that we have all this business here that would tend to indicate that you were involved in this rather than people who came in from the outside and picked 544 Castle Drive and went up there and were lucky enough to find your door open. I've spent many a night out on this post and I know one thing: with the number of dogs we have around, you don't go rattling doors here to find one that's open so you can come in and for no apparent reason knock off three people. At that hour of the morning, the patrols we have around, there wouldn't have been four or five people—a group like that—wandering through the housing area—"

"Oh, that's a lot of baloney," MacDonald interrupted.

"—or driving through."

"I've never seen a patrol there at night and I've been here since August."

"Well, I can assure you, they are there. You probably weren't looking for them."

There was a pause.

"Well, where do we go from here?" MacDonald said.

"It's up to you."

"It's not up to me. I told you what I—what I know. You put some pictures in front of me, tell—tell me they are staged and that I did it."

"Let me tell you something," Shaw said. "I don't want to step out of line here, and if I am, I'm sorry. I don't know that you did it, Captain MacDonald. I don't know it at all. But my experience tells me that what you say isn't right."

"You mean because it is an unusual, bizarre crime?" MacDonald said.

"No, no. By the physical evidence that is in this house."

"And the lack of physical evidence," Ivory added.

There was another, longer pause. Jeffrey MacDonald whispered, "Wow." Then he said, "Step one, you lose your family. Step two, you get blamed for it, huh? That's terrific. Great."

"You are the only one that was left alive there," Grebner said.

"Oh, well," MacDonald said, the sarcasm now heavy in his voice, "that's—that's pretty significant."

"It sure is from the way the others were taken care of."

"How was I supposed to have gotten my wounds?"

"You could get these wounds, the ones you had, the puncture—you could have done it yourself."

"A couple of blows on the head and a lot of little puncture wounds and a little cut on the abdomen and a couple of stab marks in the arm and—and a puncture wound in the lung. That's reasonable. Or else I paid someone—that's another way.

"Well, I don't know what you men want me to say. I don't have much to lose, do I? I lost everything else. You men are making an awful lot out of this circumstantial evidence that can probably be explained, I can tell you that."

"That's why I'm bringing it up," Grebner said. "To see if you can explain."

"I mean I can't—I can't explain the scene. It just seems to me that in a struggle anything would be possible, you know what I mean?" There was a pause. "Jesus Christ," MacDonald said, "when did you people start thinking like this?"

"The scene in the living room," Grebner said, "I questioned when it first came up. I thought it was very odd."

"But it took—but it took—but it took—but it took your office *six weeks* to question me about these things?

Oh, man," MacDonald said softly. "Jesus Christ. This is a nightmare. This is like Edgar Allan Poe."

There was a pause. He whispered, "Wow."

There was another pause. "Apparently," he said, "you don't know much about my family and myself, I'll tell you that, to come up with that conclusion. Or me, for that matter," MacDonald said.

"What kind of man are you, Captain?" Shaw asked. "You say we don't know much about you. What kind of man are you?"

"Well, I'm bright, aggressive, I work hard, and I had a terrific family and I loved my wife very much. And this is the most asinine thing I've ever heard in my whole life. It's almost as bad as the next morning, thinking about this and thinking it was a dream."

Suddenly, he started to sob. "Jesus Christ . . . you can ask any patient I've ever treated. I go way out of my way. I've spent my whole—you know, my whole medical career—it isn't that long, but to date I've never had a problem with a patient. Always gone out of my way, always worked extra hours, always helped people.

"I loved my wife more than any couple I know. I've never known a couple that's—that's as happy as our family, and you come up with this shit. Goddamn it!"

He paused and began to cry. Almost a full minute passed before he spoke again.

"Goddamn it, how do you come up with that? We even had plans for a farm in Connecticut."

There was another long pause while MacDonald sobbed audibly.

Then he said angrily, "Well, that's a load of bullshit, I'll tell you. Goddamn it!"

"Jeff," Grebner said, "I have to go on what evidence is available to me."

"Yeah, bull*shit*. Looking at some circumstantial things and making a mountain out of a molehill."

"During an investigation," Grebner said, "we have to look at the circumstantial evidence—the real evidence. And we try not to make mountains out of molehills."

MacDonald continued to sob. Then he said, "What—what—no one ever had as good a life as I had. What the hell would I try to wreck it for? Christ, I was a doctor. Jesus, I had a beautiful wife who loved me and two kids who were great. We were just over all the hard things. It just doesn't—it just doesn't make any sense." He broke off again and continued to cry.

Then, with his voice once again under control, and looking the CID chief directly in the eye for the first and only time all day, he said, "Look, Mr. Grebner, what I told you is what I remember from that night, and that's the truth. All I can say to you is that, ah, you know, maybe things weren't exactly as I said, simply because of the excitement, but I told you what I know. In other words, there—there are some minor details that maybe are a little hazy and confused. But the gist of what happened is what I told you to—to the best of my abilities, and that's all I can say. I mean, I don't—I don't know any more. And the rest of it is pure bullshit."

There was another extended silence in the room—broken, once more, by Jeffrey MacDonald.

"What—what possibly could I have gained from this? I mean, what—Jesus Christ, what would I have gained by doing this?"

Slowly, Franz Joseph Grebner reached into his desk and took out an envelope containing additional photographs. He opened the envelope and handed MacDonald pictures of an Army nurse named Tina Carlucci.

There was another long pause. When MacDonald finally spoke, his voice was dull.

"She looks familiar, but—Tina. The nose looks familiar. She looks familiar, but I don't know who she is. Oh, I—let me see that. It looks like a girl I knew in San Antonio. I was with her one night, did not have intercourse, no big deal. She wrote me one letter and I ripped it up and threw it away. That's her."

There was a short pause.

"You are more thorough than I thought," MacDonald said, almost inaudibly.

"What?"

"You guys are more thorough than I thought."

On March 20, a Women's Army Corps private had told the Fort Bragg CID that while stationed at Fort Sam Houston, Texas, the previous December, she and a friend named Tina Carlucci had been approached at a post drinking establishment by two Green Beret officers, who had invited them to a party at the Westerner Motel in San Antonio. The officers had said they were at Fort Sam Houston only for the weekend, participating in a Special Forces parachute jump. One of them—the one whom her friend, Tina, had accompanied—had been Captain Jeffrey MacDonald.

Tina Carlucci had been located at Fort Leonard Wood, Missouri, in early April. She remembered the occasion very clearly. The date had been Saturday, December 6. She and MacDonald had spent the afternoon watching the Arkansas–Texas football game on television. That evening, as part of a larger group, they had gone to dinner at a restaurant called Valerio's. MacDonald had immediately taken charge, "ordering wine and the whole bit." He had seemed "very intelligent and well-mannered," and "right at home with a strange woman, very much at ease."

He had mentioned that every time he went on a trip he went out with other women. His wife, he said, knew all about these adventures. She had never told him she knew but he simply "knew" she was aware. He made particular reference to a party that had been held at the Sheraton Hotel in San Antonio the previous summer, when he had been at Fort Sam Houston, attending the physician's basic training course.

Nurse Carlucci recalled that when the group had returned to the motel after dinner, MacDonald had called his wife.

"He told her he would be home the next evening. Told her he missed her and that he loved her. Then he asked about her pregnancy check. He wanted to know if it was positive or negative. She told him she was definitely pregnant."

Later in the evening, while MacDonald was taking a shower, one of the other guests at the party took a picture of Tina on the motel bed, wearing MacDonald's Green Beret.

"I was sick that night," she said. "I had a bad cold and didn't feel like doing much of anything. He tried to make love to me once and I told him I didn't feel like it. He didn't try to force himself on me. We took our clothes off and fondled each other but there was no intercourse. We were together until 6 A.M. Sunday when he left for the parachute jump. He gave me some tetracycline and suggested I go on sick call Monday morning."

After seeing the photograph of Tina Carlucci, Jeffrey MacDonald was not quite so certain that he wanted to take a polygraph examination.

"Well, let me ask *you* a few questions here, men. Ah, you guys have been posing all the questions. What's the—what's the fallibility of this polygraph thing? You know, you guys with your circumstantial evidence here, you know—ah, what happens with normal emotion?"

"That's taken into consideration, of course. When people are challenged, there's a little more nervous tension than usual."

"Absolutely," Grebner said. "Murder is much more serious than stealing an M-16 or something."

"I'm just trying to, ah, prevent, ah, any more things like this, that's all. I can see what's going to happen if there is a little jig in the line. You and the provost marshal are going to jump and say ah-hah! We found our man."

"The provost marshal won't be reading the charts, and neither will I. We will call a polygraph operator who is not involved in the case. Operators can be obtained—probably come out of Washington—and are very competent and is a disinterested party. He won't care how it comes out."

"What does the polygraph tell you?" MacDonald asked.

"It tells basically what a person believes to be true."

"How infallible is it?"

"Well, the instrument itself just measures physiological changes."

"I know that, I understand that—that's what I mean."

"The percentage figures they have had on it is that it's less than one percent they have ever made a mistake on," Grebner said. "I mean, these are verified cases. This is on thousands and thousands of cases. These are the statistics that I have. I would say human error is involved in about four-tenths of one percent."

"Sounds pretty good," MacDonald said. "Now what happens if this test—what is your strongest evidence? What if the polygraph backs up everything I've said, and you still have all this bullshit lying around. Then what happens?"

"I will be the first guy to shake you by the hand and say I'm sorry."

"And if it comes up wrong? If I'm one of the ones who has a little, ah, a little more sweating than usual, then I immediately go to Leavenworth without a trial."

"No. In the first place, polygraph can't be used against you."

"It can't?"

"No. It is an investigative tool, Captain. We believe it."

"You mean it is not admitted in court? Why not?"

"There are several reasons. But mainly because with a jury they wouldn't know how to evaluate this type of evidence as compared to other evidence. If you went to most juries and said, well, there was deception indicated during the polygraph examination, they would over-weigh that evidence—and there's always that four-tenths of one percent."

"So if I take this polygraph test and it comes out okay, then I can, ah—you people will feel real nice towards me then? Right?"

"As I said, if it comes out no deception indicated, I'll say I'm sorry I bothered you."

"Sounds pretty good to me," MacDonald said.

"So, if you are willing to take it," Grebner said, "I will call and make the arrangements."

"Why not? When is this going to be done?"

"Well, I'd have to call them. Within the next day or two."

"You mean someone is going to fly down here to do this?"

"Probably tonight." Grebner left the office to call CID headquarters in Washington. William Ivory also departed, leaving MacDonald alone in the room with Robert Shaw.

"Christ," MacDonald said. "This will be in the newspaper within eight hours. I'll have my mother down here again, and my in-laws. I'll tell you what, this is a lot different from what I had in mind. I don't like this. You see, ah—Jesus, this scares me."

Shaw did not reply.

"You mean to tell me that this thing is never wrong?" MacDonald said. "I find that hard to believe, just from any instrument. And I just, ah—I don't like the, ah—so much emphasis placed on what look to me like pretty superficial things. That's the only thing I'm scared of, to be perfectly honest with you. I mean, it seems to me that you guys have gone on some pretty wild stuff in calling me a family murderer. I'm not asking, you know—it's just—ah, my own feelings in the matter right now are that it looks a little dangerous to me, because that, ah—ah—Jesus, that looks—ah, like pretty minor stuff, and ah, in my own mind I can explain it very easily, you know, and not feel bad about it, if you know what I mean."

Still, Shaw did not respond.

"I mean," MacDonald continued, "if I was investigating, I would say, Jesus, so the table—so the table is top-heavy. What if her knee was against it when it went over? You know, it just—it doesn't seem to me to be, ah—that, ah—you can call a person in and, ah—take what's left from him on something like that. It just doesn't—doesn't hold any water. And there's not much left. I mean—Jesus Christ."

"Well," said Shaw, "as you know, there's been a lot of work. We've had every major CID office in the continental United States doing work for us. We've had most FBI·offices doing work for us. Everything. Every aspect. And it's just not there, Captain MacDonald. Those people you saw just can't be found anywhere. People like them? Yes. There's been—I won't say arrests, but there have been thousands of detentions all over the country."

"Okay, two possibilities," MacDonald said. "One, they haven't been found yet. And two, they've already been questioned and have answered the questions satisfactorily. Now, isn't that possible? I mean, certainly—certainly in a lot of cases your best team wasn't on every person, if you know what I mean. I'm not implying or anything about individuals, but—"

"That's true."

"If you had every office in the country working, and every FBI, it is perfectly conceivable that these people have already been questioned and what's needed now is a break, a lucky thing. You know, a lady says, ah—geez, I used to know a girl, and she always said things like that when she came home looking funny when she was staying at that boardinghouse. You know, something like that.

"You know what I mean? You luck into it. And maybe I'm just, you know, I'm hoping for, ah—for a miracle, but it just seems to me that, ah—"

"It isn't inconceivable," Shaw said.

"Yeah. I mean, I've—I've—you know, I've read things where, ah—you have questioned people many times, and it comes back at the end that they questioned him once and he gave satisfactory answers and that was it.

"I mean, you know—they had a place or a time or, ah,

no motive whatever, and, ah—it's a big country, and a lot of people in it."

"That's right," Shaw said.

"As you know better than I do, trying to find some-one—"

"I hope this thing comes out like that," Shaw said. "I really do."

"So do I," MacDonald said.

Grebner returned to the office to say that the polygraph operator would be arriving that night and that the test would be administered either the next day or the day after that.

"Okay," MacDonald said. "Is that it?"

"Yup."

"Okay."

Jeffrey MacDonald left CID headquarters at 3:30 P.M. Ten minutes later he called to say that he had changed his mind: he would not take a polygraph test after all.

Grebner decided to have the operator come anyway and to talk to MacDonald again in the morning. Then he notified the provost marshal that MacDonald had finally been questioned. Then Grebner left for the Officers' Club, where he often met his wife after work.

The day had not gone badly, Grebner reflected. Given the night to brood about the fact that the CID was convinced he was a murderer, MacDonald might yet confess. That, Grebner felt, would certainly be preferable to trying to court-martial a Green Beret doctor from Princeton on charges of triple homicide in a case based entirely on circumstantial evidence.

At least MacDonald had not refused to answer questions. Given his detailed account of the attack and his ensuing movements—and the many conflicts between it and the physical evidence—the case against him was much stronger now than it would have been had he simply exercised his constitutional right not to talk.

The goal from this point forward, Grebner felt, was to keep him talking. To take advantage of the fact that he obviously considered himself so much smarter than anyone else. Much would depend on the next twenty-four hours, Grebner believed. The one thing he did not want was for MacDonald suddenly to demand an attorney and decline to answer any further questions.

Grebner stepped up to the Officers' Club bar and ordered his drink. Even before it was delivered, an acquaintance called out: "Congratulations!"

Puzzled, Grebner asked what the occasion was.

"Why, MacDonald, of course. They just broadcast the provost marshal's statement on the radio."

"What statement?" Grebner asked in alarm. They were still in the midst of interrogation. There was not to have been any statement.

"That you guys finally decided MacDonald did it after all."

Leaving his drink untouched, Grebner rushed back to his office. It was true. The provost marshal had felt that for public relations purposes it was necessary to inform the press that, "After six weeks of careful investigation, and examination of all evidence, we have been prompted to consider Dr. MacDonald a suspect." The statement had added that while formal charges had not yet been filed, MacDonald had been relieved of his duties and placed under restriction, pending further disposition of the case.

As a public relations gesture, the statement had the

desired effect: it even made the CBS *Evening News* with Walter Cronkite.

Franz Joseph Grebner, however, knew immediately that he would never again have the chance to ask Jeffrey MacDonald any questions.

The Voice of Jeffrey MacDonald

I went back to my office that afternoon and I got there shortly before closing and the office was like very, very expectant, because everyone, of course, knew where I had been.

Everyone watched me when I came in. And I tried to hold my most professional air. My buttons were lined up and my belt was at the right, you know, position, lining up with my fly and the buttons above. And I walked directly into my office and closed the door.

Then, at about five o'clock, I decided that what I would do was, instead of going out that night to eat in a normal restaurant or something, I would just go over to the officers' mess, the single officers' mess.

And I did do that. I was by myself. I went to the officers' mess right in the middle of the Special Forces area and I got on a cafeteria line and got a tray of food which I wasn't hungry for. And I remember standing in line, and they had a loudspeaker, you know, a speaker system with music, and I'll never forget this.

I was standing in line getting food, and I had just gotten through the cash register area and was beginning to sit down, when they had a news bulletin that Captain Jeffrey MacDonald, the Green Beret officer from Fort Bragg who six weeks earlier had claimed that his wife and children were brutally beaten and stabbed by four hippies, was himself today named chief suspect.

And I remember that truly—I don't mean to use clichés, but I don't know how else to explain it—the room was spinning again.

I was—it was an incredibly strange feeling to be in this room with a tray of food, beginning to sit down, and like the room stopped and everyone was looking at me and pointing, and, sort of, most of them trying to be unobtrusive.

And the bulletin was going on and on that the doctor, who had been treated at the hospital for multiple wounds, in a statement released just moments earlier by the Fort Bragg Public Information Office, was named as the chief suspect in the case, and that he would be confined to quarters or something like that.

So I remember sitting there and thinking, well now what do I do? Here I was listening to a newscast about myself, and there were probably, oh, a hundred to two hundred people in the room sort of semi-watching me, and I certainly wasn't confined to quarters or anything. And yet the whole thing was incredibly bizarre.

And I also was angry because I sort of had just left the CID and there was no mention of this type of thing, a press release of an actual statement that I was *the* suspect. I had been left with the impression that they hadn't solved the case and they were looking at everyone again, and they needed some answers from me because the nitwits had never talked to me.

So I didn't finish eating. I sort of got up and put the

tray where it belonged and went out, and started driving back to my BOQ. And I got back to the BOQ and there were MPs, there were several, like five, around the building, and one inside the building in front of my door.

That night was a very bad night. An absolutely bone-chilling, unbelievable and indescribable feeling of depression and nothingness, and it's—the best thing I can say is it seems to me that it's death, it must be what death is like, although death must be a little more peaceful than this. This was a turmoil that's beyond belief, a mental turmoil with images and with the weight of a depression adding to it that you're really unable to describe.

But I remember thinking for what seemed an eternity about suicide, and actually looking up and measuring visually the height of the pipes that were hanging from the ceiling in my room, and whether or not I could commit suicide using a sheet, or belts or something, and feeling that it seemed ludicrous, it seemed melodramatic, it seemed like it, again, wouldn't change anything and it would probably fail. It was probably gonna be a nothing-type attempt, and I could just see the guard outside the door rushing in and reviving me and then being this incredibly ludicrous situation of a failed suicide attempt the day you've been called the chief suspect in the murder of your family, which of course everyone would immediately take to mean that, well, he did it and that's why he was trying to commit suicide, and in fact that wasn't it at all: it was the incredible obtuseness and meaninglessness of, first, the loss, and, second, these accusations.

So that night was spent, you know, alone, looking at the ceiling, the desk light was on most of the night, I think all of the night. The paint in the room was a crummy paint, as a matter of fact it was light green. The ceiling was white but it was now an off-white, a gray white, really, from dirt. And the paint was peeling, the pipes were peeling, and I remember thinking that if I looped my belt over it there was gonna be paint chips all over everything.

I thought a lot that night—specifically, on purpose—about Colette and Kim and Kristy. And—this sounds silly and it's sort of even embarrassing to say—but I remember I kept thinking how, like, Colette would be angry. She would be very, almost self-righteous if she were able to hear what these nitwits were now saying I was a suspect in.

And I was like, having a conversation with Colette and she was saying, *I know you tried, and, believe me, that's all I ask*. And I was, you know, telling her I was sorry. And she's saying, *But you couldn't help it, it happened, and what's worse now is these jerks are now saying that you did it*. She said, *I could tell them otherwise*, and, you know, *Kimmy and Kristy and I know differently, so don't worry about it*.

And so, at about that time, when I was really in solitude and in this deepest of depressions and trying to wrestle with what, you know, what was happening, and why it was happening and what to do, dawn came up. It was a feeling of rebirth that I've had many times before, like when I used to work all night on Fire Island driving a cab. And when dawn came up you were charged with this new energy, despite being sleepless for like twenty-four hours.

That's what happened here: the dawn came up and all of a sudden a lot of the super-depression and gloom and suicide thoughts just absolutely melted away. The light of the day truly brought a new dawn, and what it brought me was an anger. It was almost like the sun was firing me and infused me with an energy to fight.

And I remember saying—and I even have a recollection that it may have been out loud—it may have been thinking, but I have this feeling that I almost said this one thing out loud, after this long, long night, and that was: "Fuck them! They're not gonna get me. They're not gonna make me commit suicide, and they're not gonna convict me of something that I didn't do, this outrageous thing."

And I said, "Fuck 'em. I will fight." And around 8:15 or 8:30, in fresh-pressed khakis and my jump boots, with my little satchel briefcase under my arm, I went over to the Judge Advocate General's office, and I walked in and the office was a long, thin office with multiple people at different desks, typing, and I walked in and there was a female secretary at the front, and I said, "I'm Captain MacDonald and I'm here to see about getting a lawyer."

And the whole world stopped in that room. Like, every typewriter stopped and every head turned to me, and there was this moment of suspended animation.

And I remember being a little imperious about it— imperial, I guess, is a better word—I sort of stood taller than before. And I said, "Maybe you didn't hear. I'm Captain MacDonald and I'm here to see about an attorney."

PART TWO

THE HOPE OF THE HYPOCRITE

For what is the hope of the hypocrite,
though he hath gained,
when God taketh away his soul?

—Job 27:8

1

Five minutes after Jeffrey MacDonald's mother got home from work on the evening of Monday, April 6, 1970—her first day back since Monday, February 16—she received a phone call from a captain at Fort Bragg informing her that her son was being held under armed guard in his BOQ room, a suspect in the murder of his family.

Within half an hour, Bob Stern called from New Hope, having just heard the news from Walter Cronkite. He told Dorothy MacDonald to hire a civilian lawyer immediately. She said she didn't know any lawyers. He said he would call his corporate attorney and ask him to recommend someone who specialized in criminal work. Half an hour later, he called back to say that Bernard L. Segal of Philadelphia would meet with them at 10 o'clock the next morning.

At thirty-eight, Bernie Segal was balding and slightly rotund. The hair he did have was thick and curly and flowed back from the center of his head, down his neck, almost to the level of his shoulders. Away from the office, he sometimes wore it in a ponytail. In rimless glasses, he bore more than a passing resemblance to the middle-aged Benjamin Franklin, which, for a lawyer in Philadelphia, was not necessarily a disadvantage.

Segal had been born and raised in Philadelphia. His father had owned a men's and boys' clothing store. He had attended the Philadelphia public schools, Temple University, and the law school of the University of Pennsylvania.

In the early 1960s, working with the American Civil Liberties Union, he had been active in black voter registration projects in the South and spoke often of how he had once spent three days in the Pascagoula, Mississippi, jail.

More recently, Segal had become well known (some would have said notorious) for his defense of war protesters, draft resisters, and military deserters. In addition, he had made something of a specialty of representing persons charged with violations of narcotics laws. He was, in fact, a staunch defender of the very types for whom Jeffrey MacDonald reserved the most scorn.

Politically, his leanings were toward the Left. Socially, his sympathies lay with the counterculture. Married, with three young children of his own, Segal seemed at first an odd choice as defense counsel for a Green Beret officer who had been accused of murdering his own family and who had blamed drug abusers for the crime. Jeffrey MacDonald's mother, however, was acting on short notice, under great pressure, with guidance from only one friend.

On the surface, it seemed no less odd that Segal would have been willing to take the case. The four intruders—had they been arrested and charged—would have been far more typical clients for Bernie Segal than was a Princeton-educated Green Beret doctor—the personification of the establishment ideal which Segal had so frequently challenged.

Bernie Segal, however, in addition to his other characteristics, possessed a forceful, flamboyant personality and considered the practice of criminal law to be at least as much theatrical art as judicial science. The limelight energized him. He did not shun publicity. He was at ease with an entourage and he had always been at his best on center stage. The lure of a case which had already made national headlines was powerful.

Besides, like so many others who had first read or heard the horrid details back in February, Bernie Segal had been affected on a personal level by the MacDonald murders.

"From the start," he said, "the story evoked a whole rush of very painful feelings. I can remember actually shuddering when I read about it the first time. My own children were only a little older than Jeff's—twin daughters, seven, and a son, five, at the time—so of course I responded as a father to the very special tragedy of the death of a child: that there was so much that they now would never have a chance to experience.

"Then there was the ugliness of the Manson syndrome. Here it was again, six months later. From working with many of my clients I was extremely familiar with LSD, and I remember saying, 'Goddamn the acid. Goddamn the acid'—a drug that could unleash that sort of evil.

"Not long afterwards, I saw a little squib in the Philadelphia *Bulletin* about the Alabama State Police stopping two men and a woman in a van on suspicion of involvement in the MacDonald killings, and I then began feeling, 'Oh, God, now they're going to stop every freak and long-haired American traveling in a group of more than one.' I began to feel resentment that this would open the door to even more repressive police behavior in America at a time when I was fighting against that sort of thing every day."

Then, on the evening of April 6, Bernie Segal received a call from a former ACLU colleague named John Ballard, of the Philadelphia law firm of Drinker Biddle and Reath. "A conservative, Quaker-oriented business law firm," Segal said, "but one with a social conscience."

As general counsel to the University of Pennsylvania, Ballard had referred a case to Segal two years earlier— that one also a triple homicide, involving a Penn student who, having been ejected from a fraternity Christmas party, had drunkenly poured gasoline on a papier-mâché snowman and had set the fraternity house ablaze. Three students had died, but Segal had succeeded in having the charge reduced to manslaughter, and his client had served only a short prison sentence.

Now, John Ballard said, he was calling on behalf of a corporate client from New Hope, one Robert Stern, whose "godson" (this was not technically true, but the close relationship implied by such a term had existed since Jeffrey MacDonald's early childhood) was the Green Beret officer who had just been held as a suspect in the murders of his wife and daughters at Fort Bragg.

Bernie Segal said yes, of course he would try to be of service.

"You must understand," Segal said, "prior to my meeting with his mother on April 7—in fact, during the meeting and even after the meeting—I had every reason to believe that Jeffrey MacDonald was guilty of those murders.

"The police only arrest the obviously guilty. They don't know how to catch the others. That's why the solution rate on major crimes is so low. So my thinking, all through that initial period, was 'He probably did it.'

"But you must remember also that at the start of any criminal case, the call comes in and it's like the alarm going off at the firehouse. At first, you're just running to the fire. You're responding to an emergency. Feelings about guilt or innocence—about the client as an individual—come later, if they're going to come at all.

"I must say, at the meeting on April 7, I was very impressed by Mrs. MacDonald. She was, quite obviously, upset, but she showed a remarkable sense of poise and presence. She was handling the crisis beautifully. I liked her very much right away. And of course I agreed to see what I could do."

The first thing Segal did was to call Fort Bragg. He was able to speak to Jeffrey MacDonald early on the afternoon of April 7. He explained how he had come to be involved.

MacDonald said he already had been assigned a military lawyer, a tall, slow-talking Virginian.

"Are his shoes shined?" Bernie Segal asked over the phone.

"What?!" MacDonald sounded incredulous. Here he was, all but accused of having murdered his own wife and children, and in his very first conversation with the Philadelphia lawyer who presumably had been hired to set things right, the first question the lawyer asks is about the condition of his other lawyer's shoes.

Segal repeated the question. "And this time," he said later, "I could almost hear Jeff smiling over the phone. That was when I first knew I had a client who was not only intelligent but who caught on very quickly. He said, no, as a matter of fact, the military lawyer's shoes were kind of scruffy. I said, 'Okay, in that case, trust him. Co-operate with him until I can get down there myself.' The point being, you see, that if an Army lawyer keeps his shoes shined, it means he's trying to impress the system. And if he was trying to impress the system in that situation—the system being one which had already de-clared a vested interest, just by public announcement of suspicion, in seeing his client convicted—then he wasn't going to do Jeff any good. The unshined shoes meant maybe he cared more about being a lawyer."

On Friday, April 10, Bernie Segal flew to Fort Bragg—where his long hair, he said, made him "an object of con-siderable, and not friendly, curiosity"—and had his first meeting with Jeffrey MacDonald.

"I was surprised by the way he looked," Segal said. "I'm not sure what I had been expecting, but he had a nice face. A very nice, open face. I liked the man I saw. I liked his immediate, strong handshake and the forthright style with which he presented himself. He seemed bright and alert. A man whom it would be a pleasure to know and to work with."

Not much of substance—other than fee—was dis-cussed at the first meeting. "I was there mainly to let him know the Marines had landed," Segal said. "Someone was going to help him. Affirmative steps would be taken."

Flying north that night, on the last plane out of Raleigh—after a seventy-five-mile drive from Fort Bragg—Segal formulated the first of those steps.

"Number one," he said, "the Army had to have some evidence. Otherwise they would never have made their announcement. Number two, a high percentage of persons killed are killed by members of their own family, so despite the favorable impression he'd made on me, I remained aware that his guilt was a real possibility. And, number three, if he had done it—given the nature of the crime—he had to be a very sick person. So I decided that was the first area I ought to explore.

"I didn't explain it in quite that way to him, of course. I believe the way I phrased it when I called him over the weekend was: 'Number one, whoever committed these crimes was a very sick person. Number two, I would like to show that it could not have been you because you are free of mental illness or defect; so, number three, I'd like you to come up here for psychiatric examination as soon as I can arrange it, because, frankly, your freedom from mental illness is going to be a very positive element in your defense.'

"Privately, of course, I was thinking at that point that I was probably going to have to employ an insanity defense."

On Tuesday, April 14, Jeffrey MacDonald wrote to Colette's mother and stepfather, Mildred and Alfred Kassab.

This is unreal. This seems like Edgar Allan Poe, or at least Alfred Hitchcock. I keep waiting to either (1) awaken, or (2) have someone come in and tell me it's all been a mistake and I can go.

The whole idea behind it is so incredible—I loved them so much I get sick when I think about them. I would gladly go to jail if that would bring them back—even if I could only spend one day with Colette, Kim, and Kristy again. But for them to come up with me as the villain is beyond my comprehension.

Apparently, I made several mistakes—first, I fool-

ishly thought that only people who did something wrong need lawyers—then I insulted the idiots when they questioned me on Monday 6 April—(never insult small-minded men in positions of power).

When I lost my family I didn't care about much at first. Then I gradually began to work again and just wanted to get back into medicine. Now this—I suppose it will pass and the truth will eventually come out, even if they make the mistake of forcing it through a trial. It no longer matters to me, because what little I had left (medicine) is pretty much destroyed by the Monday 6 April news conf. But it of course drags both my mother and you people down again—on top of everything else you've had to undergo. I'm so sorry for that—I wish I could spare you all of this mess.

I'm still confined to quarters—they shut off my phone & I have to be escorted to meals. I guess I'm guilty until proven innocent, and I haven't even been charged with anything.

Hope Mildred is getting out more. Trust you are all beginning to get back on your feet. Let me know when the pool no longer has ice on it.

I will keep in touch. Thank you, more than you know, for your support. You are wonderful people. I loved the girls (your girl—my girls) more than you can imagine.

Love,
Jeff

On April 18, Mildred wrote back.

Thank you for letting us hear from you. I have just returned from taking fresh flowers to the cemetery.

Kim's 6th birthday. When you go there and see the names in bronze it is still unbelievable. All of them! Just like using an eraser on a blackboard.

The waste, me rearing Colette with constant joy in her, bearing first Kim, then Kristy, in so much pain, your work together under such financial difficulties, to make a home, get your career, all for nothing.

The infuriating thing is the stupidity of the powers that be—letting two months pass, all chance of catching those monsters go by, and fastening on you.

Jeff, please know that Freddy and I have never wavered for an instant in knowing how idiotic that conclusion is. Good heavens! If anyone ever adored his family, you did. And they loved and trusted you implicitly, as we do. The horror of your position can at least help you from thinking too constantly of them.

Meanwhile, the guilty persons can leave the country if they choose. They must be caught! Someone must pay, and with their lives, for this awful thing they have done.

Freddy is extremely eager to do anything to get at the real people responsible. He loved Colette and the kids even more than he realized. He neither eats nor sleeps. We all wander around the house during the night eating sleeping pills and waiting for morning.

Know that we are constantly thinking of you and telling everyone of your love for your family. If your lawyer makes the right moves, he can get you completely vindicated and your future once more assured.

All of our love comes to you, Jeff. We know you.

On Monday, April 20, Jeffrey MacDonald, accompanied by an armed escort officer, presented himself in Bernie Segal's Philadelphia office. There, for the first time, he spoke to his lawyer in detail about the events of February 17.

To Segal, the most notable aspect of MacDonald's presentation was his almost total lack of affect—of any semblance of feeling or emotion—as he described the weekend leading up to the murders and the events of Monday, February 16, and then proceeded, with no change of emphasis, intensity, or tone, to describe how he had been awakened by the screams of his wife and older daughter, how he had fought unsuccessfully with the intruders, how he had fallen unconscious in the hallway, and then how he had made his way from the master bedroom to the bedroom of his older daughter, discovering the bodies of Colette and Kimberly and trying to breathe life back into them.

"It suddenly struck me," Segal said, " 'Jesus Christ—this guy is telling this story rather dispassionately. What am I dealing with here?' But just at that point he began to talk about the baby. About Kristen. And, as he did—it was an almost imperceptible thing—there was a catch in his voice. Just for a moment, and then he went on past it, but it was there—that little catch in the voice when he talked about going into the baby's room.

"And that's when I had my second level of response: 'Son of a bitch, I know what he's doing: as he's talking to me, he's not focusing on the horror. He's describing how *he dealt with* the situation. Describing how he was treating these people. He isn't really looking at the event head-on, because, obviously, that would be too painful. His focus is just a little bit off center—talking about the bodies as bodies. Not as his own wife and children but as people that, as a doctor, in an emergency situation, he was trying to save. Because the personal pain was too great to confront, he was describing his actions in a professional, clinical way. It was the only way he could tell the story at all.

"And, you know, it was perfectly understandable. It was how I might later describe to someone how I responded to an accident involving one of my own children: this was an emergency which required action; here are the actions I took. By keeping the focus steadily on that aspect, he was able to look past his own pain.

"This was very reassuring to me. I felt I now understood his apparent lack of affect. His response seemed genuine. Especially when I recalled that little catch in his voice when he talked about going into the baby's room. To me, that was the first real tip-off.

"This is not to say," Segal continued, "that I was suddenly overjoyed. It did not immediately convince me of his innocence. Remember, I still had only the vaguest idea of what the so-called evidence against him was. But by the end of that meeting, my mind was much more open to the possibility of his innocence, and I remember thinking, 'Well, I'll be interested to hear what the psychiatrist, Bob Sadoff, has to say.'"

On Tuesday, April 21, MacDonald was examined for three hours by Dr. Sadoff. He told the psychiatrist that he was innocent and that he knew he was innocent. He said the evidence against him was flimsy and that he knew he would ultimately be cleared. He said his friends and in-laws had been immensely supportive and that "everyone" was on his side, although maybe "the gods" were against him.

In notes of the interview which would later be presented to a federal grand jury, Dr. Sadoff reported that MacDonald said, repeatedly, that he was not paranoid, "even though people do whisper, 'There he goes,' when he goes to chow or when they see him on the street."

MacDonald added that he was the subject of many rumors—one being that he'd been having a homosexual relationship with Ron Harrison and that Harrison, in a fit of jealousy, had murdered Colette and the children. This was, MacDonald said, ridiculous.

He denied ever smoking marijuana or taking any drugs other than "ten diet pills in his whole life." He told the psychiatrist he had lost 12 pounds prior to February 17 as a result of directing the weight-control program for his Green Beret unit. He said he had weighed 198 pounds but that his average was 186 which, because of his weight lifting, was "mostly muscle."

In describing to Dr. Sadoff the events that had preceded the murder he said, as he had to the CID on April 6, that his wife had attended a class in "literature."

According to Dr. Sadoff's notes, he also described how his older brother, Jay, had "in a weird coincidence," suffered a psychotic breakdown on the night of the murders. He said that Jay was "on the fringe of the Mafia" and had fallen deeply in debt to Mafia loan sharks through drug purchases and gambling debts and that the attack upon himself and his family might have been intended as retaliation against his brother but that it did not seem like "a Mafia-type job."

He said that of the "four or five" attackers, one might have been a girl with blond hair and a floppy hat, but might also have been a long-haired male. During the struggle, he said, he had felt a sharp pain in his chest and had seen blood and then had felt his pajama top being ripped over his head. He told Dr. Sadoff that he had sustained fourteen lacerations in his chest.

MacDonald also complained to Dr. Sadoff that people

seemed to expect him to break down and show more emotion and that when he did not they assumed he was "cold-hearted." He said he got mad at people who expected him to cry in front of them.

He admitted to a feeling of relief that his wife and children were "gone" but said he was ashamed of that feeling. He said he sometimes missed the children more than he did his wife. He described Kristen as having been a "tough girl" and said Kimberly was more like Colette— "soft and feminine."

"He spoke in poignant terms," Dr. Sadoff said later, "about his preparing himself, his being a hero, his being all kinds of things: good-looking, bright, quote, 'a lover,' who had had a lot of girlfriends; being in an Ivy League school—he said he was the first member of his high school class in twenty-two years to attend an Ivy League school— getting through early, being a doctor, being the strong, brave Green Beret, and constantly doing such things as being boxing team doctor, lifting weights, and getting by on only three or four hours of sleep a night.

"Living up to this image of himself—this super-masculine striving, the fantasy of being a hero—was very important to him, yet when it came time to save his family, he was unable to do so.

"I think he did have some unresolved masculine strivings with, possibly, some latent homosexual conflicts. I wouldn't call it latent homosexuality, or even fear of it, but the need to overachieve in a supermasculine way is usually meant to compensate for or to mask any areas of inadequacy that he may have noted in himself, that others may never have seen.

"So he had a—a—an Achilles' heel, let's say, in this area of masculinity or virility, and some narcissistic need to be famous, or infamous.

"He told me that he had gotten a lot of publicity from the case and had received four hundred letters from all over the country, some of them marriage proposals, but usually just suggestions that girls come and stay with him. He told me he enjoyed getting the mail.

"As I saw him, here was a man who had lived according to certain expectations, going along with stereotypes, and in this kind of situation, even though it might have been devastating for the average individual, he had to prove to himself and to others that he was supernormal. That he was above the average and would be able to take it, no matter what the blow.

"Based on my examination, I was fairly certain that he was not directly involved in the killings of his family, but that he did feel guilty because he had not been able to save them."

The next day MacDonald traveled to the Norristown State Hospital outside Philadelphia and underwent six hours of psychological testing. He took the Shipley intelligence test; the Minnesota Multiphasic Personality Index, which provides a general profile of an individual's overall personality adjustment; and the Rorschach and Thematic Apperception Tests, which are designed to elicit information about aspects of personality that a subject might be making a conscious effort to conceal.

Over the weekend, with MacDonald having been escorted back to Fort Bragg, Bernie Segal—too impatient to wait for the submission of a written report—called Dr. Sadoff, whom he knew well and with whom he had worked often in the past.

"I said, 'How did the interview go?' And he said—I

remember this with perfect clarity—'I don't think your client killed his family.'

"It was a Saturday morning and I was alone in the office, and I remember for a moment I was breathless. Bob said, 'He does not appear to be mentally ill. In fact, he seems rather well balanced and healthy.' At this point I let out a long whistle. For what had seemed a long time, I had suspended my own judgment about this man. Now, for the first time, I had been given reason to actively, affirmatively think that he had not committed the crime.

"I still, of course, was not persuaded one hundred percent, but having come into the case carrying with me the presumption of guilt, and thinking defensively, I could now go on the offense.

"While I still believed that the Army would not have charged Jeff—or gone public with him as a suspect—unless they had some facts that pointed toward him, I could now approach the case from the point of view that their facts had led them to the wrong conclusion. The task now was *not* to prepare an insanity defense, but to plunge into the investigation of the case, and to go get the rest of the facts."

Segal's belief that he was representing an innocent man was strengthened further within the next few days when he received the results of the psychological testing.

"Captain MacDonald's adjustment certainly falls within normal limits," the psychologist informed Bernie Segal. "There is no sign of either psychosis or psychopathic tendencies that would lead him to commit a crime of violence. To what extent he can be successfully hiding actual guilt cannot be completely answered on the basis of psychological evaluation, but the nature of the crime is such that it was probably committed by either a psychotic or a criminal psychopath and it is clear that Captain MacDonald does not fit such a description."

Bernie Segal forwarded to the Army summaries of both the psychiatric and psychological evaluations in the hope that authorities could be persuaded that MacDonald lacked the capacity to have committed the crime. The hope proved naive.

At 1 P.M. on May 1, Freddy Kassab called a press conference in New York City to protest the fact that the Army had kept his stepson-in-law under restriction for more than three weeks without having actually accused him of any crime. "I was under the impression that it was only in Communist countries a person could be held in this way," Kassab said.

At 4 P.M. the Army announced that Jeffrey MacDonald had been formally charged with three counts of murder.

That evening, in Philadelphia, Bernie Segal told the press that his client was "very shaken and confused" by the development. "He cannot believe this has happened," Segal said.

On Long Island, Mildred Kassab said, "The entire United States Army must have gone stark raving mad."

Five days later, MacDonald wrote again to the Kassabs.

I'm just getting over the shock of actually being charged—even with the preparation and forewarning it was quite a jolt for this insanity to progress so far.

*I'm sure by now you're aware that the Army ig-
nored the results of tests done on me in Philly two
weeks ago before charging me. Typical Army—they
used a lot of mumbo jumbo, but the end result was
they refused to look at the results of the tests—evidence
that proves I'm innocent. Apparently even if I was
having communion in Rome with the Pope that
night, the Army would have suppressed that and
charged me.*

*My lawyer warned me of this from the beginning.
He said they will never admit they were wrong. He
very bluntly told me my innocence was very unimportant at this point—more important are things
like Army careers, publicity, egos, and incompetent
investigators.*

*Of course, in my innocence, I always held out hope
that someone would come, release me, and say, 'Sorry
for the mistake—you're free to go and experience the
grief of losing that which (whom) you love most.'*

*I am worldly about many things, but now I really
confess to a naivete about how people are prosecuted
for alleged crimes. Fortunately, it's OK with me if
they want to look into the past. I have nothing to hide,
and they can call anyone they want to the witness
stand to testify as to our family, the relations among
my family, or my personal or professional character.
Let them just 'drive on' because they will never find
anything but love in my family. I think they are the
ones who need psychiatric testing.*

*If there is a heaven, as Colette and Kim always
felt, I'm sure that Colette, Kim, Kristy and our un-
born son are there now—what must they be saying as
they look down on this insanity? Does their new status
give them infinite patience and understanding of*

*mere mortals' errors & procedures? Or are they as
sick of all this as I am. I wish I was with them right
now, wherever it might be.*

This time, almost a month passed before Mildred
Kassab could bring herself to respond.

Dear Jeff,

*How the days drag! Every day I look at a stack of
letters, yours on top, and say, today! The last time I
was going to write was on Mother's Day & Colette's
birthday. I started a letter and the damn tears kept
spilling on the paper, so I quit. I hope someday I will
stop weeping; it's a terrible weakness, I know, but it's
such a shame, such a pity.*

*Do you realize that it is just ten years this month
that we attended yours & Colette's high school graduation? You started out to beat the world and all of
the plans for the future—blasted by those killing
rats.*

*I am constantly thinking of how I can get someone
to find the sick sadists who killed my darlings. I will
never rest until these people—or should I say
animals—are caught and punished. There isn't a fit-
ting punishment any more, since we have become so
humanized.*

*I have many of Colette's letters and I read them
over and over. It almost makes me feel that it never
happened. But it did.*

*The swimming pool looks beautiful, all aqua and
white, with cement walls, patio, and new green sod.
The plantings are blooming and the whole thing looks*

like Hollywood. I hate it. We didn't do it for ourselves.

We love you and do wish so much for you, Jeff. If we could only make everything nice and tidied up again. It's just too big, though, and when you are all through you still have nothing.

2

Article 32 of the Uniform Code of Military Justice, which governs legal procedures applicable to members of the U.S. armed forces, requires that, subsequent to the lodging of a criminal charge by military authorities, an Investigating Officer be appointed to inquire "as to the truth of the matter set forth in the charges," and to make a recommendation, "as to the disposition of the case."

Col. Warren V. Rock, an infantry officer with thirty years' experience who was serving as director of psychological operations at the John F. Kennedy Institute of Military Assistance at Fort Bragg, was assigned to conduct the Article 32 inquiry into the murder charges against Jeffrey MacDonald.

Were he to find that the charges had merit, Colonel Rock could recommend that MacDonald be court-martialed. Should he find them to be without substance, it was within his power to recommend that they be dismissed.

It had become standard practice within the military to treat an Article 32 hearing as merely a formality, at which the prosecution—often unopposed by the defense—did no more than outline its case, presenting just enough evidence to persuade an Investigating Officer already inclined in that direction that the charges were worthy of referral to court-martial.

Bernie Segal, however, did not intend to follow standard practice. His past experience with the military legal system had led him to believe that once a case had advanced to the court-martial level—at which the defendant's fate was determined by a "jury" composed of officers chosen by the very military authorities who had brought the prosecution—it became almost impossible to win. At that stage the prosecution simply had too much control, and for too many of those involved—career officers, for example, concerned with their own chances for promotion—there was simply too much at stake: too much to be lost and too little to be gained from the embarrassment of a "not guilty" verdict.

Segal decided to mount a full-scale defense at the Article 32 hearing.

The proceeding was convened on the morning of Monday, July 6, well attended by the public and press. The lieutenant who had been in charge of the military police at 544 Castle Drive during the first hectic hours following the discovery of the bodies testified.

Under cross-examination by Bernie Segal, he admitted that he did not know how many military policemen had been inside the apartment; that he had never attempted to compile a list of names; that he had left no one in charge, to make sure that evidence was not disturbed, when he himself had left the apartment to call for an ambulance and to notify the provost marshal of the crime; that, in fact, one of his men had picked up the receiver that was dangling from the bedroom telephone in order to notify headquarters that the MPs had arrived at the scene; that even after hearing MacDonald's description of the four assailants, he had failed to order the establishment of roadblocks at exits from the post, despite suggestions from several of his men that he do so; and that soon after his arrival at 544 Castle Drive he had noticed wet grass, tracked in from outside, at various locations throughout the apartment, but that he did not know if this debris had been brought in, unknowingly, by his own men—at least a dozen of whom had been running up and down the dark and narrow hallway of the apartment, some on the verge of hysteria as a result of what they had seen—or, perhaps half an hour earlier, by the four intruders who had murdered Jeffrey MacDonald's wife and children.

Military officials in attendance were apparently taken aback by the sharp focus and aggressiveness of Segal's cross-examination. The realization that there was the potential here for unfavorable publicity quickly penetrated the upper levels of the chain of command. Following the lunch recess, it was announced that the remainder of the hearing would be closed to press and public.

Freddy Kassab went immediately to Washington and held a press conference. He said, "I am here today for the sole purpose of attempting, in my small way, to set the scales of justice at a normal balance.

"What I ask is not partiality, not anything illegal, not anything unusual: I simply ask that my son-in-law Captain Jeffrey MacDonald, be afforded the same right as any other American citizen, and that is a public hearing.

"I ask that the command influence that was used to close these hearings after they were open for a few brief hours be overruled by a higher authority. Surely, in this

great country of ours, there must be a way for a man—
even though he is in the Army—to receive fair and equi-
table treatment.

"My wife and I have a right to show to the whole
country that the charges against Captain MacDonald are
false.

"My wife and I have three graves to visit, and when
we do we want to feel that we are doing everything we
can to protect from any wrong the one that was most
dear to them."

Despite a Jack Anderson column harshly critical of the
Army for having barred the public from the proceedings,
the hearing continued behind closed doors.

The only spectator permitted to attend was Jeffrey
MacDonald's mother, who was allowed in after a wire-
service photograph showed her seated on the steps outside the locked hearing room, and an accompanying
story quoted her as saying that as a sign of her belief in
her son's innocence she would remain there each day
that the hearing was in session, or until the military police dragged her away.

Behind the closed doors, Bernie Segal was discovering—
to his amazement and to his client's delight—just how
confused, disorganized, and riddled with procedural error the Army's case against MacDonald really was. Segal's
vigorous and exhaustive cross-examination of prosecution witnesses unearthed a series of investigative blunders
far more extensive and significant than he would have ever
dared hope.

From the earliest moments at the crime scene, when
the military police sergeant had picked up the dangling
telephone, to the later laboratory ineptitude which had
resulted in the loss of the blue fiber from beneath Kris-

ten's fingernail and the piece of skin from beneath the fingernail of Colette, the Army had been, as Franz Joseph Grebner had known since February, grossly incompetent.

It turned out, for example, that the flowerpot whose upright position had so aroused Grebner's suspicions had actually been set aright by an ambulance driver who had ignored all instructions to leave the crime scene untouched. The same driver, according to the testimony of a military policeman who had observed him, had managed to steal Jeffrey MacDonald's wallet from a desk—all while the crime scene supposedly was being preserved.

The doctor who had been called to 544 Castle Drive to pronounce death testified that he had rolled Colette MacDonald onto her side in order to check for wounds in her back, and that in so doing he had removed the blue pajama top from her chest. He said he did not remember where he had placed it, but would not rule out the possibility that fibers from it might have fallen within the body outline on the floor.

The pathologists who had performed the autopsies had neglected to take either fingerprints or hair samples from the bodies, and, when a laboratory technician was later dispatched to the funeral home for the purpose of obtaining fingerprints, he found Kimberly and Kristen, already embalmed, "looking like two little angels lying there," and he could not bring himself to disturb them further. Thus, the children's fingerprints were never obtained, leaving many more "unidentified" fingerprints on the premises than might otherwise have been the case.

The CID had not realized that hair samples were lacking until after the bodies were buried. For "known hair samples" to match against the blond hair found in the palm of Colette's hand, the CID chemist was forced to rely upon hairs taken from her coat collar, not from her head. The efficacy of this procedure was severely undermined when it was determined—much to the prosecution's chagrin—that a "known hair sample" obtained from a sweatshirt of Jeffrey MacDonald turned out to be not his hair at all, but a strand of hair from his pony.

Each day's testimony—even during the prosecution's portion of the case—seemed to produce less evidence linking MacDonald to the crimes than it did new examples of CID bungling. The discarded pajama bottoms, the emptied garbage, the flushed toilets, the destroyed footprint which, superficially at least, had appeared to match a test print taken of the left foot of Jeffrey MacDonald—the string of errors would have been highly comical had their consequences not been so serious.

Segal learned, for example, that following Ron Harrison's February 19 press conference, investigators and technicians alike had rushed to read the *Esquire* magazine found in the MacDonald living room. By the time the blood smear across the top of the pages was finally noticed and the magazine dusted for fingerprints, the only ones found were those of CID personnel and military policemen.

Back at Fort Gordon, when the fingerprint technician developed the film on which he had photographed prints found inside the apartment, he discovered that more than fifty of the pictures were so blurred as to be useless. Perhaps, he theorized, trucks passing by or firing from a nearby artillery range had caused his camera to vibrate. Whatever the cause, when he returned to 544 Castle Drive to rephotograph the prints in question, he found that moisture had penetrated the protective tape he had placed over them and that more than forty had been obliterated and would thus remain forever unidentified—

markedly decreasing the certainty with which the prosecution could claim that there was no evidence of intruders inside 544 Castle Drive.

As the toll of blunders mounted, Bernie Segal suggested ever more pointedly to the hearing officer, Colonel Rock, that irreparable damage had obviously been done to the crime scene and that this damage had rendered useless—indeed, had thrust into the realm of wild conjecture—any inferences which might otherwise have been drawn from the so-called physical evidence.

Each day, as the hearing recessed, Segal would emerge from the room to regale eager reporters with tales of the latest fiasco. With Army prosecutors under strict orders not to comment in any way, Segal's accounts—which did not tend to minimize the significance of the mistakes— provided the sole basis for news reports on the progress of the hearing.

Thus, as the days passed and the Army was made to appear ever more foolish and incompetent, the original cynicism with which most reporters had viewed Mac-Donald's account—an attitude that, in the wake of the formal accusation, had hardened into open disbelief— began to give way to a sense that, in light of such gross investigative malfeasance, the handsome Ivy League, Green Beret doctor just might, after all, be telling the truth.

Public belief in the possibility of MacDonald's innocence increased dramatically when, in August, Segal actually began to put on his defense. He called to the stand a military policeman named Kenneth Mica, one of the first to have arrived at the scene. Mica testified that, en route, at an intersection approximately half a mile from Castle Drive, he had observed a young woman standing in shadow. It had seemed to him most unusual for anyone to be standing alone at such an intersection at 3:50 on a cold and rainy February morning, and, had he not been responding to a radio call he would have stopped to question her.

A few minutes later, Mica testified, it had come to seem more than unusual: it had seemed to be of crucial importance. For the woman standing on the corner had been wearing, in addition to a raincoat, a floppy hat.

As soon as Mica had heard MacDonald's description of the female intruder, he had informed the MP lieutenant of what he had just seen. He had urged the lieutenant to dispatch a patrol immediately, to bring the woman into custody for questioning. The lieutenant, however, had failed to respond to the suggestion (at the hearing he testified that he had not heard what Mica said), and the woman on the corner was never found.

Moreover, when Mica eventually had told military prosecutors about the woman in the floppy hat, he was instructed not to mention it in his direct testimony at the hearing. Only after the prosecution phase had been completed, with his conscience continuing to nag at him, had Mica chosen to approach the defense and inform them of what the prosecutors had urged him to suppress.

Having thus introduced not only a further extraordinary example of military police incompetence (and a glaring display of prosecutorial misconduct) but the first independent corroboration—however indirect—of Jeffrey MacDonald's story, Segal next concentrated on constructing a portrait of his client as the sort of man utterly incapable of having committed the crimes with which he had been charged.

Segal called to the stand a series of witnesses who had known Jeffrey and Colette MacDonald at various stages of their lives, and who, without exception, were convinced that MacDonald was a noble and honorable man who had deeply loved his wife and children and had been deeply loved in return.

A doctor from Columbia Presbyterian who had supervised MacDonald's internship spoke of his "stamina and equilibrium," and his extraordinary ability to "stand up under stress."

A classmate from Northwestern described the MacDonald marriage as "ideal" and added that he'd spoken to Colette by phone in early February and she had told him that their months at Fort Bragg had been "the happiest time in their marriage."

A Green Beret colleague described MacDonald as having had a "rare" level of communication with Colette and an "extraordinary" interest in his children.

MacDonald's next-door neighbor on Castle Drive said that as far as he could tell the relationship between Jeff and Colette had been "just great."

MacDonald's former commanding officer at Fort Bragg, Robert Kingston, was contacted in Hawaii where he was enjoying a short respite from his tour of duty in Vietnam. By telephone, Kingston, who, as a general, would be named in 1981 to head the newly created Rapid Deployment Force of the U.S. armed services, described MacDonald as "one of the finest, most upright, most outstanding young soldiers" he'd ever seen, and said MacDonald had also been, "very close, very devoted, to both his wife and children."

Robert Kingston's wife also spoke. She said she had come to know the MacDonalds unusually well because her own daughter was about their age and would occasionally double-date with Jeff and Colette. She said that MacDonald had been a "very loving father," and that both he and Colette had been looking forward joyously to the expected third child. Once, in fact, she had even said to her own daughter, "I hope you have a marriage like that." She was not asked about the valentine she had sent, nor did she volunteer information about it.

Perhaps most telling—and certainly most emotional—was the testimony of Freddy Kassab, who said he had known Jeffrey MacDonald from the age of twelve, had watched him grow to manhood, and believed him to be as fine a human being as he'd ever known.

From the first day of their marriage, Kassab said, Jeff and Colette had been as happy as "pigs on ice." MacDonald also had been deeply attached to his daughters. "Every time you turned around," Kassab said, "he had one of the girls, playing with her."

At Fort Bragg, Kassab said, "They were the happiest I'd ever seen them. They had less financial problems, Jeff came home most nights, which he'd never been able to do before. He had more time to be with the children, more time to devote to Colette. She was ecstatic about it." She was also "ecstatic," Kassab said, about the prospect of having a third child.

He then described, in overwhelmingly powerful and evocative detail, the scene Christmas morning when Jeff had taken Colette and the girls to see the pony.

Kassab was weeping openly as he prepared to step down from the witness stand. As an afterthought, he turned to Colonel Rock and asked, "Sir, may I add one thing?"

"Of course."

"If I ever had another daughter," Freddy Kassab said, "I'd still want the same son-in-law."

Leaving the hearing room, Kassab told the press that, "We know full well that Jeffrey MacDonald is innocent beyond any shadow of a doubt, as does everyone who ever knew him. I charge that the Army has never made an effort to look for the real murderers and that they know Captain MacDonald is innocent of *any* crime except trying to serve his country."

He then announced that he and his wife were offering a $5,000 reward for information leading to the arrest of the real killers.

Segal completed the character-witness phase of his defense by calling Robert Sadoff, the Philadelphia psychiatrist who had examined MacDonald in April. "Based on my examination and all the data that I have," Dr. Sadoff said, "I feel that Captain MacDonald does not possess the type of personality or emotional configuration that would be capable of this type of killing with the resultant behavior that we now see.

"In other words," Dr. Sadoff said, "I don't think he could have done this." He then added: "I rarely think about a person personally when they are patients. But if I allow myself that indulgence today—I found working with Captain MacDonald a great deal more pleasurable than working with many of the people I have to. He is a very warm person, and very gracious, and one whom—I must admit—I like."

At this point in the proceedings there occurred one of those dramatic strokes of good fortune which a defense attorney could go through an entire career without experiencing.

Bernie Segal was staying at the Heart of Fayetteville motel. There, one morning in August, he was approached by a deliveryman for the linen service which supplied sheets and towels to the motel. The deliveryman's name was William Posey, he was twenty-two years old, and he lived in the Haymount section of Fayetteville, which had become notorious as the city's hippie district.

Recognizing Segal from his picture in the newspapers—and aware of the fact that Freddy and Mildred Kassab had offered a $5,000 reward for information leading to the arrest and conviction of the killers—Posey told Segal about a former neighbor of his, whom he knew only by her first name, Helena.

In February, Posey said, he had been living on Clark Street, next to Helena. He knew her to be a drug addict, drug dealer, and member of a witchcraft cult. She was, according to Posey, approximately seventeen years old, and she frequently wore high boots, a blond wig, and a floppy hat.

At approximately 4 o'clock on the morning of February 17, Posey said, he had got up to go to the bathroom. Looking out his bathroom window he had seen a car pull "real fast" into the driveway that separated the house in which his apartment was located from that in which Helena and two female roommates resided.

There had been at least two, possibly three males in the car. They were making a lot of noise, Posey said: laughing and giggling. Then he had seen Helena emerge and walk "faster than she usually walks" into her house, as the car had pulled out of the driveway and had sped away down the street.

Posey had not seen Helena again until the day of the MacDonald funerals. On that day, he said, she had dressed in black and had hung funeral wreaths from the porch of her apartment. Acting as if she were in mourning, she had refused to speak to him when he approached. Subsequent to February 17, Posey said, Helena had ceased to wear her boots, blond wig, and floppy hat.

About two weeks later. Posey said, she had mentioned to him in a casual conversation that she was going to have to leave Fayetteville because the police had been "hassling" her about her possible involvement in the murders. Her problem, she said, was that she had been so stoned on LSD and mescaline that she was unable to remember where she had been, or whom she had been with, throughout that night.

She had left Fayetteville shortly thereafter and Posey had not seen her again until August. At that time, with the Article 32 hearing receiving front-page coverage in the Fayetteville papers, Posey had asked her whether she thought she'd been involved in the murders.

She had told him, he said, "I don't remember what I did that night." But she had also said when he'd asked her how she and her boyfriend were getting along, "Well, we can't get married until we go out and kill some more people."

Following Posey's startling testimony at the hearing, William Ivory located Helena and questioned her. Her full name, he said, was Helena Stoeckley. She was the daughter of a retired lieutenant colonel who had been stationed at Fort Bragg, and she was well known to the Fayetteville police, for whom she had worked as a drug informant. She had, in fact, been questioned about the killings in February, as had many dozens of other Fayetteville hippies.

Stoeckley could provide no useful information whatsoever, Ivory testified. She remembered only that she had been out for a ride that night, alone in a car, but she did not remember where she'd been or what she'd done.

It was obvious, from Ivory's sullen, unresponsive answers to Bernie Segal's questions, that he considered the entire matter of Helena Stoeckley a waste of time at best, and, at worst, a false trail that had the potential of diluting the strength of the case against Jeffrey MacDonald.

No less obvious was the contempt which Bernie Segal had for William Ivory. He considered Helena Stoeckley the key to his case. Here at last, he felt, was undeniable corroboration of the story his client had told; a drug addict who dabbled in witchcraft and who wore clothing that matched the description MacDonald had given and who had been observed in the presence of male companions shortly after the murders, and who could not account for her whereabouts during the time the murders had been committed, and *who had dressed in black on the day of the funerals and had hung funeral wreaths outside her apartment,* and who had then disappeared from Fayetteville because she feared the police suspected her involvement and *who had spoken of the need to kill again!*

And what had the CID done with her? They had sent Ivory down to chat with her—after Posey's testimony had made such a step a necessity—and the agent had returned to say only that she could not shed any light on the matter.

Never before had Bernie Segal cross-examined with such a striking combination of sarcasm and incredulity.

"Mr. Ivory," he said, "I'm not sure I understand. When she said she was alone in this car, did she indicate to you that she was the person who drove it?"

"Yes, she did say that."

"I see. And who did she tell you was the owner of this car?"

"She knew the owner by first name only. She did not know the last name. It was an acquaintance of hers."

"And what was the first name?"

"Bruce."

"Bruce?" Segal paused. Then he asked, "Did you make notes of your interview with Miss Stoeckley?"

"No, I did not."

"Is there any reason *why* you didn't make notes?"

"No particular reason, no."

"Isn't it standard operating procedure when you are conducting an interview that's related to an inquiry into a triple homicide to make notes of interviews?"

Ivory remained silent.

"Mr. Ivory, why were no notes taken of the interview with Miss Stoeckley?"

"I did have a notebook with me," Ivory said, "and I started to take notes but she got very nervous so I put my pen and notebook away."

"Did you make any notes at all in your notebook?"

"I believe I wrote her name down at the top of the page."

"And what did she do or say to indicate that she was objecting to your making notes of what she was saying?"

"She said something to the effect of, 'What are you doing? What are you writing?'"

"And what did you say?"

"I said, 'Nothing. I'm not writing anything,' and I just put it down."

"Did you ask her whether she objected to your making notes of the interview?"

"No, I did not."

"Why not?"

"I was concerned with getting over with the interview, rather than making her so nervous that she would not answer me at all."

"What was so terrible about making her nervous about asking her about her whereabouts on the morning of the 17th of February?"

"I don't know. That's why I put the notebook away. So I could find out."

"Did you find out where she was between the hours of 2 and 4 A.M. on February 17th?"

"No, I did not."

"Did you ask her where she was?"

"I did."

"What, if anything, did she say?"

"She said she could not recall, she could not remember."

"Did she indicate any reason why she was unable to recall?"

"Yes sir, she did."

"And what was the reason?"

"She said that she had been out on marijuana."

"On marijuana?"

"Yes, sir."

"Are those her words—that she was 'out on marijuana'?"

"That's correct."

"Mr. Ivory, you—was she telling you that she couldn't remember where she was because she'd been using marijuana?"

"That's correct."

"Mr. Ivory, you've had occasion to investigate cases in which cannabis sativa has been used, haven't you?"

"Yes, I have."

"To your knowledge, is that a medically recognized result of smoking marijuana—to lose memory?"

"Not to my knowledge."

"Not to your knowledge. Were you told by anyone that Mr. Posey had previously said that Miss Stoeckley said that she had been taking—one time she said LSD, another time she said mescaline. No one ever told you that?"

"She told me in the interview she was taking marijuana."

"Well, I want to know, were you armed with the information—"

"No, I was not."

"Now, did you ask Miss Stoeckley why she was not able to recall where she was, since marijuana is not known to have the effect of impairing one's memory?"

"Yes, I did."

"And she said what?"

"She said she didn't know. She just couldn't remember."

"Did you ask her about a blond wig?"

"Yes, I did."

"And did she admit to having owned a blond wig up until about February 17th?"

"She said she had worn one occasionally, but it was not here—that it belonged to a girlfriend and that she did not have it."

"And did she say when she returned or disposed of that blond wig?"

"No, she did not."

"Did anybody ask her whether it had been shortly after February 17th, 1970?"

"It was subsequent to that date, but the exact date she couldn't recall."

"And did she give you the name of the girl?"

"No, she did not."

"Did you ask for the name?"

"Yes, I did."

"Did she refuse to give you that name?"

"No, she said she just couldn't recall which of the girls it belonged to."

"Did she tell you where it was that she had effected

the return of the wig? The street or the apartment where the other girl lived?"

"No, she did not."

"Did you ask her?"

"No, I did not."

"Did you ask her whether she'd ever owned a large floppy hat?"

"Yes, I did."

"What, if anything, did she say about that?"

"She said yes, she did."

"Did she indicate where that hat is now?"

"She indicated she gave it to someone, but she could not recall the name of the person she gave it to."

"And did she indicate whether that episode of giving the hat away took place shortly after February 17, 1970?"

"She did not indicate the day, nor did I ask."

"Was there any reason why you didn't ask her when she stopped wearing, or got rid of, the hat?"

"No particular reason."

"Did you ask her whether she owned boots of any sort?"

"Yes, I did."

"And what did she say?"

"She said yes, she did."

"Did she indicate that she had given away or disposed of any pair of boots about the middle of February 1970?"

"Yes, she did."

"And what did she say in that regard?"

"She said she threw them away."

"And did she know where she threw them away?"

"Yes, she threw—she indicated that the heel was worn or broken and she discarded them in a trash can."

"Now, did you ask Miss Stoeckley whether she would

be willing to come here to this inquiry and tell us what she knows about her whereabouts on February 17, 1970?"

"Yes, I did."

"And what, if anything, did she say?"

"She said no, she would not come."

"Did you ask her why she could not come?"

"She indicated that she didn't want to become involved."

Because it was classified as an investigative proceeding, the preliminary hearing—unlike a court-martial—did not confer the power to subpoena unwilling witnesses.

"Did she give you the name of the other young ladies with whom she lived in the building next door to Mr. Posey?" Segal asked.

"No, she did not. She said she did not remember the girls' names."

"Did you ask Miss Stoeckley anything about who her male associates were?" Segal continued.

"Yes, I did."

"Were the answers as vague as all the other answers? First names?"

"First names, yes, sir."

"Did she tell you what is the last thing she can remember doing prior to 4 A.M. on February 17th?"

"Yes, leaving the house she was living in, alone, and driving in the car. Just driving aimlessly, she said."

"Did she have any idea about what time it was she left the house?"

"Sometime—midnight or after."

"Did she indicate how she fixed the time when she left the house?"

"No, just knew in her mind that it was midnight or after."

"You mean she knew in her mind, or that's all she chose to tell?"

"Well, that's what she told me."

"Did you ask her for a description of the owner of the car she was driving?"

"Yes, I did."

"And what, if anything, did she tell you in that regard?"

"He was a white male, former enlisted man in the Army, and she couldn't go into more specific details. I asked her to describe the man to me as best she could and she said he was twenty or under and a white male, dark hair."

"But did you ask her for any specific points of identification?"

"Yes, she could just give me a general description."

"When you say, 'she could just give' you—you mean she could, or that's all she *chose* to give you?"

"I couldn't read her mind. That's what she gave me."

"How about her demeanor?" Segal asked. "Did she strike you as being frank, candid, and open?"

"Yes, she struck me as being frank."

"Candid and open, is that right?" Segal asked, his voice rising.

"Right."

"And you thought a person who did not know the names of the persons she lived with was being frank, candid, and open?"

"Yes."

"And you thought that her inability to tell you the last name of the owner of the automobile she used for the evening was also frank, candid, and open?"

"Yes."

"And you thought that her telling you that she could

not remember where she was for approximately four hours because she was smoking marijuana, is a frank, candid, and open answer?"

"That's the answer she gave me, and I couldn't get anything else. I could only take it at face value."

"Well, the face value of that statement is a lie, since you know that marijuana doesn't have that effect on persons."

"I've never tried it. I do not know."

"I didn't suggest that. I said, based upon your experience as an investigator, you still felt that she was being frank, candid, and open when she told you she couldn't remember her whereabouts when she was smoking marijuana."

"What else could I say?"

"You could say she was a liar and ask her to be more specific about what she was doing and where she was."

"I possibly could have."

"But you did not, sir?"

"No, I did not."

"Did you make any attempt to find the car she talked about?"

"She said the man's now out of the Army and left the area."

Segal paused and stared at the witness. "You know, Mr. Ivory," he said, "I really find it very difficult to accept the idea that you just listened to this lady's statements point-blank and said, 'Well, that's it,' and wrote her off as a suspect in this case. It just defies all sensibility to think that this is the way investigations are handled. That it is just standard to take a series of very vague explanations and say, 'Oh, well, that's the end of it. We won't be able to check this person out in a triple murder case.'

"In my career I have been involved in over five hundred murder cases. I've represented seven thousand defendants in thirteen years and I have never heard of a true suspect being handled this way. Did you go back to the address next to Mr. Posey's house to make any inquiries?"

"I have never been there myself."

"Has anybody made any inquiries as to who are the persons who are on the lease in the apartment in which this girl lived?"

"I'm sure they have, sir."

"Well, now, why are you sure it has been done?"

"It seems like a rather elementary thing to do."

"I agree, but what I ask you is—"

"I don't know from my own personal knowledge."

"You *don't* know, then, whether anybody has attempted to find out who is on the lease for the apartment in which this girl used to live?"

"Of my own personal knowledge, no sir."

"Now did you talk to any of the other residents of that building or in the immediately adjoining buildings to see if someone might know something about her whereabouts or her activities?"

"I conducted no background investigation in that area."

"I don't mean a background investigation. What I am saying is, what did you do to cross-check her story by checking with neighbors or people who lived in that building or the adjoining building?"

"I have done nothing."

"Is there any reason why not?"

"Well, time. Some other things."

"Has anybody checked the electric bill, gas bill, and telephone bill for the particular apartment in which this lady lived?"

"Of my own personal knowledge, I do not know."

"A telephone bill might reveal long-distance or toll calls which would be of some interest in regard to who the person is calling, would it not?"

"Correct."

"To your knowledge, that has not been done."

"That's correct."

"Mr. Ivory, you really can't say to us that Miss Stoeckley was being frank, open, and candid. She was following her rules, which are not to tell outsiders who her friends and associates are."

"She said to me she only knew them by their first names."

"Of course the telephone company, gas company, and electric company and landlords don't generally function on the basis of just first names, do they?"

"That's correct."

"That avenue of investigation might produce last names, might it not?"

"That's correct."

"Is it fair to say that on the basis of what has been done up to now it could not be considered that the investigation of Miss Stoeckley's whereabouts on February 17 is complete?"

"It is not complete."

"Did you talk to her about her interest in witchcraft?"

"The subject came up, yes."

"Well, what was she asked to explain or to tell?"

"Well, when was she explaining the type of dress that she wore—sometimes black, sometimes purple—she said, 'Yes, I dress like that because I—the people there consider me a benevolent witch.'"

"Did you ask her what she meant by that?"

"Yes, she said a good witch as opposed to the witch-ing practices of black magic. I asked her if she was serious about this and she said, 'No, I'm really not a witch. It's just what people say.'"

"That's just what people say about her?"

"Yes."

"And she modestly declined to determine whether she was a witch or not?"

"Yes."

"Does that strike you as a rather unusual conversation you were having with her?"

"No."

"It was not?"

"No."

"Normal kind of freaky conversation you have with hippies, right?"

"That's right."

"Hippies are particularly trustworthy, truthful people?"

"Some are. Some are not very."

"Did you ask Miss Stoeckley why she sat on her front porch the day of the MacDonald family funerals wearing black clothes and with a wreath on her front porch?"

"There was no mention made of a wreath. She said she was dressed in black simply because she sometimes dressed in black. She attached no significance or no relationship between the two."

"Well, how did she happen to remember that she was wearing black on the day of the MacDonald family funerals?"

"I believe she said she read a newspaper article about it, or she heard it on TV or radio."

"Mr. Ivory, did you ask Miss Stoeckley whether she was in the MacDonald house on February 17th, 1970?"

"Yes, I did."

"And what did she say?"

"She said no."

"Did you ask her how she knew she wasn't there if she could not account for her whereabouts between midnight and 4 A.M.?"

"She said she does not know where the house was, she does not know Captain MacDonald, she knew nothing about it, and she's sure if she had been there she would have known it."

"Could she explain to you why she was sure that she would remember being there since she couldn't remember where she was at all?"

"I imagine she thought if she was involved in what happened there she would most assuredly remember it."

"She *felt* that she would remember? Is that right?"

"That's what I said."

"That's what *she* said."

"That's what I said she said."

"Where does she live today?"

"I have no idea where she is right now."

Toward the end of the Article 32 inquiry, at Colonel Rock's request, Jeffrey MacDonald was examined by a panel of military psychiatrists at Walter Reed Hospital in Washington, D.C.

The chief of the panel then testified at the hearing. He said that while he did not believe it to be within the proper realm of the psychiatric expert to try to assess whether a particular individual was capable of committing a specific act of violence, he had found no evidence in Jeffrey MacDonald of "mental disease, defect or derangement," and he did not have the impression that MacDonald had "fabricated or contrived" his account of the murders, leaving the distinct impression that he considered it most unlikely that MacDonald had committed the crimes. The psychiatrist added that he had found the defendant to be a "warm, engaging, personable young man."

MacDonald himself testified for three days. There were several new details in the story he told, and some slight variations from what he had said on April 6.

He now recalled, for example, that on the afternoon of Monday, February 16, he had spoken to the coach of the Fort Bragg boxing team concerning a trip to Russia that the squad would soon be taking. MacDonald had been working out with the team, he said, and had been asked to serve as team physician. It was possible that upon Colette's return from her class on Monday night he had mentioned to her the possibility that he would accompany the team on the trip.

He also said he now remembered that the course she had been taking was not "something literature" as he had said on April 6, but child psychology, and that during that Monday night class she might have mentioned to her instructor the problem they were having with Kristen's bed-wetting and the child's recent tendency to want to sleep in her parents' bed.

"This kind of thing occurred, oh, once a week," Mac-Donald testified. "Several times a week she would come into bed with us, but she would only wet the bed about once a week, once every two weeks.

"We were relaxed about it. One of us would get up and leave the bed, or else we'd put Kristy back. Occasionally, we'd wind up playing musical beds. I would move first, and then Kristy would go back to her own bed and I'd go back to my bed. Something along that line. Not the same thing happened every night.

"My wife and I had slightly different feelings about how to handle it. She said she didn't mind getting up and putting Kristy back in her own bed, or giving her an extra bottle. I suggested that we do the same thing we had done with Kimmy—she went through that phase for a matter of weeks and we put her back in bed and she cried for about three hours one night but she stayed in her bed and that ended the problem.

"Colette said it wasn't worth the effort. She said she would bring it up in her child psychology class and see what—you know, your own family would never believe your word as a physician—she said she would bring it up with her professor at the university.

"I didn't object to that because I knew he was going to say what I said, and I believe that night when she came back she might have said something like, 'We were talking about bed-wetting tonight,' and I said, 'Terrific, what did you learn?' Something like that. I'm not trying to be facetious. It's just so unimportant to me.

"Actually, I don't remember what we talked about. Really nothing significant. Really nothing stands out at all. It was just a routine evening. We enjoyed the time together. It was just—well, we did discuss the—the possibility that I was going to Russia with the boxing team, as team physician."

In describing the attack by the intruders, MacDonald said that after the black man had hit him with the club for the first time, he "literally saw stars and was knocked back flat on the couch." Later, as he struggled back to a sitting position, he had felt "a rain of blows" on his chest, shoulders, neck, and forehead and had noticed the glint of a blade. "Now, sometime during this," he said, "my hands were sort of bound up in my pajama top, and

I honestly don't know if it was ripped or if it had been pulled over my head."

Contrary to his April 6 assertion that he had not moved the body of his wife, MacDonald now said that when he first saw her, "she was a little bit propped up against a chair and I just sort of laid her flat."

He described entering the hall bathroom to check the extent of his own injuries and said, "Oh, yeah, I also rinsed off my hands. I don't know why. Your guess is as good as mine. I guess it's because I'm a surgeon at heart."

Most significantly, he now said that after picking up the kitchen telephone to repeat his call for help he might have washed his hands again in the kitchen sink.

"I know it sounds ridiculous," he said, "and I've been questioned extensively about it, and I don't know. I just—I have the feeling that either before or after the phone call I was rinsing off my hands for some reason.

"I know that on April 6 I said I did not think I washed my hands in the kitchen, but the next day my lawyer said the easiest way for a witness to remember something is to have to write it, and I spent the next several days writing out every single thing I could remember, and I think the logical sequence of events is clearer to me now. I would have to say I remember more now than I did then."

He remembered, for example, that while examining himself in the hospital either late on the afternoon of February 17 or at some point on February 18, he had noticed—in addition to the wounds observed by the physicians who had attended him—two bumps on the *back* of his head, two or three puncture wounds in his upper left chest ("I would have guessed them to be ice-pick wounds"), three puncture wounds in his upper left bicep ("which I would take to be icepick wounds"), and a series of "approximately ten" icepick wounds across his abdomen, all of which had already healed without treatment and none of which had penetrated the abdominal wall. Since the wounds did not require medical attention, he had seen no reason to mention them to anyone.

He said that upon his discharge from the hospital he had been so afraid for his own safety that he had borrowed a pistol and had slept with it under his pillow every night until after the armed guards had been posted at his door, following the announcement that he was a suspect.

He said he was "absolutely certain" that neither of the two paring knives nor the icepick had come from his house, though the club might have come from a pile of scrap lumber he had kept in the backyard. He repeated that he had never owned an icepick.

He said he had enlisted in the Army because he wanted to serve his country in Vietnam and that he had wanted so much to become a Green Beret that he had "told less than the truth" about a back injury suffered while playing high school football because he feared it might prevent his acceptance.

He said that, "very, very infrequently" he'd had a sexual encounter with a woman other than his wife. The only two times he could recall were the night in San Antonio with the Army nurse named Tina, and once, earlier that year, with a different woman, when he had been at Fort Sam Houston for his physician's basic training course. He said Colette had not known about either of these instances.

Tearfully, MacDonald concluded his testimony by

saying he had loved his wife "more than anything in the world," and that their time together at Fort Bragg had been "by far" the happiest, least stressful period of their married life.

Colonel Rock was quite obviously impressed by Jeffrey MacDonald: by his military bearing, his obvious sincerity, and by the sense of loss and sorrow that he communicated so effectively.

In a report filed on October 14, 1970—slightly more than a month after the conclusion of the hearing—the Investigating Officer wrote: "After listening to the lengthy testimony of the accused and closely observing his actions and manner of answering questions, it is [my] opinion that he was telling the truth."

Colonel Rock also wrote: "A significantly large number of character witnesses testified in behalf of the accused, covering a life span from age 12 through high school, college, medical school, internship, and military service. They testified to qualities [that made him seem] what can best be described as, 'The All American Boy.'

"Considering all known facts about the life and previous history of the accused, no logical motive was established. Because of the manner in which the victims were murdered, it is reasonable to conclude that the crimes were committed by persons who were either insane or under the influence of drugs.

"The accused was subjected to two separate psychiatric evaluations. Although there is a four-month time span between the two, there is a striking similarity in the conclusions. Basically, they believe he is now sane and was sane on 16–17 February. Both feel that the accused was not trying to hide any facts from them and that had he been they would have been able to detect it. The accused's psychiatrist stated, in addition, that the accused was not capable of committing the crimes. . . .

"Explanations for any discrepancies [in MacDonald's story] are logical, based on the testimony of the psychiatric experts, the time factor, his natural attempts to forget the horrible sights of 17 February, normal human failure to remember routine actions, and the confusion following the blow to his head."

Taking into account also the testimony in regard to Helena Stoeckley, the inadequate preservation of the crime scene, and the abundance of investigatory mistakes, Colonel Rock concluded his report with two recommendations:

1. That all charges and specifications against Captain Jeffrey MacDonald be dismissed because the matters set forth . . . are not true.
2. That appropriate civilian authorities be requested to investigate the alibi of Helena Stoeckley, Fayetteville, North Carolina, reference her activities and whereabouts during the early morning hours of 17 February 1970.

Two weeks later, choosing not to make public Colonel Rock's recommendations, the Army announced simply that the charges against MacDonald had been dismissed due to "insufficient evidence."

Jeffrey MacDonald immediately applied for an honorable discharge. He said he felt "bittersweet." He said, "This is no victory. My beautiful family is gone and their killers are still at large. I'd like to get those people.

I can't understand why the Army didn't try harder. I plan to do a lot of investigating. I think they should get the death penalty if they are caught. They made their decision when they killed my family. They should pay for it."

3

The murder of three members of a family does not, in all cases, bring about a heightened and sustained degree of interest in the survivor. But when the survivor is an intelligent, physically attractive, Princeton-educated physician who happens also to be a Green Beret officer and who tells the world, less than six months after the Charles Manson murders, that the violence done to himself and his loved ones was wreaked by drug-crazed hippies in an apparent replication of the Manson cult homicides, it is inevitable that he will become, for a time, the focal point of a certain amount of public attention.

That this happened to Jeffrey MacDonald was not surprising. That he found himself gratified and titillated rather than repelled by the phenomenon may also have been unsurprising, but in the months and years which were to follow the Army's announcement that the charges against him had been dismissed, it proved by no means insignificant.

Even before the Article 32 hearing began, MacDonald seemed entranced by the newspaper and television publicity he was receiving and decided that, eventually, he would like to have someone write a book about the case. Handled properly, such a book could make him not only famous but rich. He, after all, had a story, and nobody simply "told" a story anymore. People with stories sold the rights to them, something Bernie Segal repeatedly assured MacDonald that he would someday have the chance to do.

To that end, MacDonald began to compile what he would later call a "diary" but what was, in fact, a reconstructed account of his version of the events which had led up to and had flowed from those terrible early morning hours of February 17.

Thinking that someday this material could be turned over to an author whom he would come to employ, MacDonald, alone in his BOQ room in the evenings, began to write:

Saturday, 14 Feb 1970. Went to PX and bought Valentine's cards and candy for my three girls— Colette, Kimberly and Kristy. . . . I'm sure we made love that night, because we almost always did, given an evening together without others or without my work.

Monday, 16 Feb 1970. Routine day at work. Heard from boxing club coach who said I would probably hear within several days about the proposed 30-day trip to Russia as physician for the team. Colette is almost as happy as I am about the possibility of my going—although we both wish she could go. . . .

Later, there would be occasional mention of memories of his wife and children, such as: "The kids especially

in my thoughts today—tried to read Rod McKuen poetry but everything reminded me of the kids or Colette
and I had to quit," but the diary's dominant theme,
other than concern about the progress of the legal proceedings against him, soon came to be publicity.

> Friday, 22 May . . . The news today had the
> story of the $5,000 reward—it sounded very good
> on TV.

> Tuesday, 16 June—The publicity, I forgot to
> mention . . . was very good. Page One in the Sun-
> day Raleigh *News and Observer* and was a good hu-
> man interest story except we are sorry they used a
> picture of me in my convertible—it makes light of
> a very serious situation. It would have been better
> not to use that particular picture.

> Tuesday, 7 July—Yesterday's press fairly good to
> me. . . . Evening TV coverage excellent.

> Thursday, 9 July—It is apparent that the press is
> strongly behind me. . . .

There then had occurred an incident in which CID
agents, in an attempt to obtain a hair sample which Mac-
Donald had refused to provide voluntarily, forced off the
road a car in which he and his attorneys were riding. After a scuffle during which both Segal and an assistant,
Dennis Eisman, fell to the ground, the CID agents forcibly removed MacDonald to a site where the hair sample
was obtained.

Having sensed that a confrontation on this issue was
about to erupt, Segal had arranged to have a car full of

reporters and photographers trailing the vehicle in which MacDonald was riding. The incident was, therefore, widely reported. In his diary MacDonald noted:

> The news was out immediately—it appears to be the biggest story in weeks. Headlines all over, TV, radio, and countless phone calls. Rep. Pike, Sen. Javits, Jack Anderson's column in Washington—everyone is interested. The AP and UPI wire services told Freddy in Long Island that it is world wide, not just national.

The day after the incident, he wrote:

> More pictures today, taking some advantage of the neck brace worn by Denny, and involving AP, UPI, and local. The press conference in New York tomorrow [at which the Kassabs and Jeffrey MacDonald's mother planned to renew their demand that the hearing be reopened to the public] sounds like it will be well-attended.

The following day, he reported:

> The news conference was attended by two major TV stations, multiple radio stations, AP, UPI, local newspapers. Freddy just told me it went beautifully. No mention here yet, but it was on the 6 PM news in New York. . . . Dennis is wearing his brace, and there has been extensive TV coverage of same.

The publicity he was receiving, in addition to fueling his desire for more, also had the effect of attracting to his cause certain of those "beautiful people" to whose ranks MacDonald was drawn.

He got a letter from the Countess Christina Paolozzi, the New York socialite and fashion model who was at that time the wife of a Park Avenue plastic surgeon named Howard Bellin—a man whose friendship Mac-Donald had cultivated during his internship year at Columbia Presbyterian.

The Countess informed him that she and her husband had agreed to lend their names to a fund-raising effort in his behalf, and that Dr. Bellin had already written a letter seeking contributions to the "Jeff MacDonald Defense League."

She further assured him that, "If all goes well and they drop these ridiculous charges, we will give you a fund-raising party where you'll come in person. We've got a lot of guest rooms in this eighteen-room apartment on Park Avenue. You've got a room here when you get free, and we will show you how the rest of the world is living during this year of monetary crisis. . . . Oh! My Jeff, I have tears in my eyes for you darling. It is the waste. I do not understand. But only a few men get a chance to find out how much their friends would do for them. And how many people really honestly care. And maybe you are privileged that way."

The Countess's letter prompted an assistant of Bernie Segal's to announce to the press that, "The 'Jet Set' is joining the defense," and that letters requesting contributions had been sent to "all the big people—the ultra-rich."

To Jeffrey MacDonald, who had used grit, brains, and charm to climb from blue-collar Patchogue to the Ivy League and then to the threshold of an immensely promising career in medicine—but who now sat under armed guard in a bachelor officer's room at Fort Bragg, accused of murder—the allure of such a promised land was powerful. If celebrity was to be a by-product of his tragedy, he would not fight it.

The lack of aversion to publicity was a quality which MacDonald shared with his attorney, Bernie Segal. Not content with giving daily briefings to the local press (and hoping to spark interest in a book), Segal arranged for MacDonald to grant a lengthy and exclusive interview to the Long Island newspaper *Newsday*. It was the first time that MacDonald had spoken publicly, in detail, about the events of February 17. He had hitherto described them, even to his closest friends and family, as simply "too painful to talk about."

Though the interview occurred weeks before he would testify at the Article 32 hearing, MacDonald was far from reticent, describing in detail the attack and its aftermath (stating that he had sustained twelve icepick wounds across the abdomen and three icepick wounds on the left arm, one stab wound in the left arm, two stab wounds in the abdomen, and a stab wound in the right chest, and that at Womack Hospital he had been treated for shock) and even going so far as to discuss his contemplation of suicide on the night of April 6 ("I was laying in bed, looking at the pipe running across the barracks, an exposed pipe with all that dirty green chipped paint, and looking at my belt and saying to myself, 'If I jump off my desk with a belt, will it work?'") and to draw stick-figure diagrams which illustrated the locations of the bodies of his wife and children inside the apartment.

MacDonald also told the interviewer that "My whole image of myself has been changed drastically. It's been the hardest thing for me to accept—that I failed my family when I was needed most. You can put in all kinds of rationalizations—there were four people against one, you were hit on the head, you were unconscious—but the fact remains I did not defend my family and they are dead. This is what keeps me awake nights. In my mind I feel that I have let them down, and I have to live with that and that's been a crushing blow for me to face up to."

An even more crushing blow, he said, was the sudden realization, on April 6, that the CID suspected him of having committed the murders.

"In the prior six weeks, there was absolutely no hint that I was a suspect. As a matter of fact, on multiple occasions the provost marshal had personally assured the press that I was indeed not a suspect, that there was no evidence against me, and my wounds were multiple and serious and I could not have inflicted those wounds on myself.

"It's funny how long it took me to get the idea that some people, in fact, did not believe me. You know, it didn't normally occur to me—since I had witnessed four people and I had seen my kids and my wife in this condition—that this wouldn't seem reasonable.

"First of all, you know, you'd either have to be on drugs or be psychotic, there's no two ways about it. What was done in that house was not done by normal people.

"But apparently some people were bothered by the fact that I did survive my injuries, which, while serious at the time, are not as serious as the rest of my family's. Although in number I had just as many stab wounds, they weren't as deep because I was defending myself."

MacDonald then talked about April 6. "I walked in," he said, "and Mr. Shaw, and Mr. Ivory came in behind me, and Mr. Grebner said, 'Sit down, Captain MacDonald, we want to talk to you.' I mean it was a very somber act that I walked into. There were three men in business suits with guns on, staring at me, you know, and he said, 'We have a few questions to ask you,' and I said, 'Fire away,' and he said, 'First, before I do, let me read you your rights.'

"So I waived my right to counsel and they began questioning me, and there were very minor inconsistencies—nothing at all in, you know, the heat of the questioning, or as far as even they were concerned.

"But then, after a little over two hours of interview, they started asking me questions that were obviously indicative that they felt that the scene was staged, and my reaction at that was incredulous.

"I got mad at them. I was swearing at them, as a matter of fact. I said, 'You guys are out of your goddamn heads.' I said, 'What do you mean, staging? Six weeks after the crime is committed, you calmly assume it's staged by me?'

"And I said, 'First of all, you've shown me a tremendous lack of investigatory ability. You've had—you've been really incompetent from the beginning, both on the investigation and on your public relations. My wallet was taken from your custody. It's taken you six weeks to figure out that the scene was staged, and now you're telling me that I murdered my family and you have absolutely no evidence. And furthermore, what motive do you think I had?'

"At which point he pulled out a photograph of this girl from San Antonio, and he passed it to me and said, 'Do you know this girl?' And I looked at it and I said, 'Yes, it's a girl I knew in San Antonio.' And he said, 'How long did you know her?' And I said, 'One day—one afternoon and evening,' and he said, 'What happened?' and I said, 'Nothing. I took her out.' And he said, 'Did she know you were married?' And I said, 'She knew I was married and had two kids, and I told her so before we even decided on a date that evening.'

"He said, 'Did your wife know?' I said, 'No, I was away from home and it was a one-night date—pickup—and nothing happened, and there was absolutely no letters, no phone calls, no follow-up, no before, nothing.'

"I said, 'If you'd like to question the girl about that, feel free,' and they said, 'We have.' And I said, 'Terrific—then you know I'm not lying to you.' And they didn't say anything. They put the photograph away—put it in a folder.

"This was all done in a—in a tremendously Dick Tracy–like atmosphere. You know, they had a light shining in my face and two guys were facing me and one guy stood behind me and, like, every fourth or fifth question was from the guy behind me, and in order to see him and his reaction to either the question or any answer that I would give, I'd have to turn to face him. It was really juvenile.

"And I did not know that this was being tape-recorded, by the way. They didn't tell me that. They were just interviewing me. I never saw a tape recorder or a microphone or anything like that.

"Then Mr. Grebner left the room and Mr. Shaw, who had taken the hard approach—he had been the one saying, 'You murdered your wife, you staged the scene'—he left the room and they left Mr. Ivory.

"He was silent for about two minutes, and then he tried what is called in the Special Forces the Mutt-and-Jeff approach. He walked over and sat on the desk, and he leaned forward and he was very friendly and he said, 'Captain MacDonald, there have been a lot of allegations thrown around here today. Personally, I have no feelings on the matter except I don't like the way some of my, er, fellow workers do things. I don't like the way they approach the problem, and furthermore I don't really believe a lot of the things they have alleged here.'

"And I looked at him and I said, 'Mr. Ivory,' I said, 'Really, now, this is very juvenile.' I said, 'I'm sure you're the other half of the Mutt-and-Jeff team, and you expect by putting your arm around me and patting my shoulder I am supposed to break down and confess.' I said, 'Let me set you straight: I have nothing to confess to. I have never done anything.'

"Later, Mr. Shaw said to me, 'Would you take a lie detector test?' and I said, 'Absolutely.' I said, 'Without any question I'll take a lie detector test right now.' And there was stunned silence in the room. I was amazed at their reaction. They were stunned. They just sat there and looked at me, and about a minute later Mr. Grebner said, 'You will?' And I said, 'Absolutely. I haven't lied to you.' I said, 'I'll take a lie detector test.' I said, 'Let's take one.'

"And they looked at each other, and they said, 'We can't give it to you now.' And I said, 'Why not? You guys have made a lot of allegations. Let's take a lie detector test.' And Mr. Grebner said, 'Well, we have to get him from Washington.' And I said, 'Well, get him from Washington. I'll take a lie detector test.' And at that point he said, 'That will be all,' and I got up and left the office.

"Then, at 4 o'clock I got a phone call to report to my commanding officer, and he said, 'It's my unfortunate duty to tell you that you have been named as a suspect in the murder of your family.' And then he said, 'I better also tell you that they're having a news conference with AP and UPI in about half an hour,' and I was just completely stunned."

Later MacDonald was afraid that he might have given away too much for nothing. This concern was illustrated by his diary entry for Saturday, July 25, the day after the Army prosecutors had rested their case against him.

The *Newsday* reporter, he wrote, "has been here for days now, going through files in the office. I'm a little ticked off at Bernie—he won't tell me anything about the financial arrangements, but he has given away much valuable material. If I now want to see another author about the story, this guy has most of the best info, with no guarantee that I get anything."

Two days later, MacDonald wrote:

> *Newsday* reporter going home today. Had long conversation with him about the article. He assures me I will do well financially by him at the right time, just to trust him and Bernie.

Despite the fact that when the interview appeared, MacDonald found "very good response—it's being carried in Raleigh, possibly LA *Times* and *Chicago Sun-Times*," he was not content to leave such a vital matter as future publicity solely in the hands of Bernie Segal, nor to trust the *Newsday* reporter to do right by him financially. In October, even as he awaited the Army's decision on whether to dismiss the murder charges against him, MacDonald began to act as his own agent.

He wrote to John Sack, then of *Esquire* magazine:

> *Dear Mr. Sack,*
>
> *I am a 27 year old Green Beret physician currently awaiting the result (officially) of an Art. 32 investigation into the murder of my wife and two*

little girls. . . . This letter is being written to you for the purpose of interesting you in writing a major article and/or book regarding the events of the last 9 months. The Army has attempted to cover up a bungled investigation by charging me with the crimes, in spite of the fact that my story fits the facts. . . . We have complete files documenting the case and the Army screw-ups. . . .

The case has received nation-wide publicity on several occasions, as well as continuous local news in the NY and North Carolina areas. Several politicians have had some association with the case (Goodell, Pike, Ervin, Javits) and the Pentagon is intimately involved. Public opinion has changed so that it is now almost 100% on my side (at least from the mail I get). The case certainly has all the emotional impact any case could have, and in addition has some interesting sidelights, such as a fund-raising drive by a prominent NY socialite (Dr. Howard Bellin and his wife, Countess Christina Paolozzi). . . .

My lawyers are currently in contact with Look *magazine regarding a possible article, but I am more partial to your style and they will agree with any decision I make about the author. I would appreciate hearing from you as soon as possible. . . .*

On the same day, he wrote to Jack Nelson of the *Los Angeles Times:*

I have recently read of your exploits in the world of expose, as chronicled by Time *magazine—it occurs to me that you are well-suited to write a major article on my case, and I thought I would write directly to you and attempt to elicit your interest. My*

lawyers are currently in some first-stage talks with
Look *and* Esquire, *but nothing has been firmed up,*
and they will agree on whoever I choose to write the
story. . . .

He also wrote to a reporter named Jack Bass, of the
Charlotte, North Carolina, *Observer:*

I have recently read of your exploits in the world of
expose, as chronicled by Time *magazine—it occurs to*
me that you are well suited to write a major article
and/or book on my case. . . . My lawyers are currently
in some first-stage talks with Look *and* Esquire *but*
nothing has been firmed up. . . .

In both these letters, MacDonald mentioned that
among the "several interesting sidelights" was the fund-
raising drive being run by "NY Dr. Howard Bellin, M.D.
and his jet-set type wife, the Countess Christina
Paolozzi," that at least six senators were "involved intimately in the case," that there had already been extensive
publicity, and that "I now have full public support."
After John Sack declined to participate, MacDonald
wrote to author Robert Sherrill:

I am well aware of your interest in military jus-
tice. In addition, Mr. John Sack of Esquire *suggested*
to me recently that I contact you. This letter is an at-
tempt to stimulate your interest in writing a major
article and/or book regarding my case. My lawyers
are having some very preliminary-type discussions
with Look *regarding the case, but nothing is final-*
ized. They will agree with me on whomever I choose to
write the article/book, and I like your style, so I hope

you respond to this letter, either way, as soon as possible. . . .

He added that "people appear to be about 9–1 for me." During the same week, the editiors of *Time* magazine received a letter.

Dear Sir,

This letter is not a crank letter—all the facts in it can be verified by contacting the indicated people. My name is not signed because I am an active duty captain in the US Army and the Army has ways of making things unpleasant for people who speak out against the system.

I have recently been an escort officer for Capt. Jeffrey R. MacDonald, M.D., a Green Beret physician who stands accused by the Army of the 17 Feb. slaying of his wife, Colette, 26, and his two girls, Kim, 5, and Kristine [sic], 2, in their Ft. Bragg Apt. Let me review a few pertinent facts with you and let you decide if this is a news story or not. . . .

The letter continued for six pages, describing how MacDonald had been found "semi-comatose" in his apartment and had been rushed to Womack Hospital where he was found to be suffering from "several stab wounds (about 5)." It further stated that MacDonald had been "placed in intensive care, and he required two chest tubes to be inserted . . . to prevent death."

The letter continued, "almost every thinking person on post is behind Captain MacDonald," and its author stated, "I know for a fact that Senators Goodell and Javits and Rep. Otis Pike are looking into the Army's role."

Despite the fact that Captain MacDonald "remains in isolation," the letter said, "he seems to have maintained his cool, and his sense of humor, how only God can say. . . . His mother visits him frequently. . . ."

After urging that *Time* do a story on "this gross injustice," the letter suggested that reporters might want to contact Freddy and Mildred Kassab, "for a heartbreaking story of Capt. MacDonald's family life—how he bought his children a pony for Christmas."

The "jet set Countess" Christina Paolozzi was mentioned, as was the fact that "Cpt. MacDonald has received hundreds to thousands of letters, all favorable except about 10, he says. He has received them from all over the U.S., Canada, and from other countries, including Russia, Poland, England, Peru, Brazil, and Italy, all favorable to him."

In conclusion, the anonymous author wrote, "I sincerely hope you act on this letter. . . . Please try to set some of these facts before the public. It will be the truth and it will help to correct some of these terrible ills in the military justice system and it will force the military to release an innocent, grieving man. I'm so sorry I cannot sign my name."

The letter was written with a typewriter and on stationery which appeared remarkably similar to those used in the writing of the letters to which Jeffrey MacDonald *had* signed his name.

Time eventually did print an extremely sympathetic four-column article in its "Law" section under the heading, CAPTAIN MACDONALD'S ORDEAL (referring to him as an "All-American achiever who had always had his merit rewarded"), and the Jack Anderson column—never reluctant to pounce on an example of military malfeasance—ran a story which accused the Army of having tried to "railroad" MacDonald, a man whose friends "swore he was incapable of such a hideous crime." *The Washington Post* printed the column under the headline GUILTY IN BERET KILLING STILL AT LARGE.

Bernie Segal's negotiations with *Look*, however, failed to come to fruition, and none of the reporters or authors whom MacDonald had contacted agreed to tell the story he wanted told.

Several years later, before a federal grand jury, a newspaper reporter who had covered the Article 32 hearing and who had interviewed MacDonald in his quarters on the morning that the charges were dismissed would recall his strong interest in the attendant publicity. "He was elated, of course, and phone calls were coming in. He'd run out and come back in and fuss with his uniform and say to me, 'Well, what do you think I ought to do? Do you think I should wear a khaki uniform or put on my greens?' And I said, 'I don't know. You're talking about for pictures?' And he said, 'Yeah, for pictures, what do you think? The guys will be coming by twelve. Television and all that.' And I said, 'Well, I think you look great in your greens.' So he put on his greens and he laid them out and was really concerned about that.

"In the meantime, I was asking him things like, 'Well, now they've let you go. What are you going to do? How do you feel? And he said, 'I don't know. I can't tell you.' Then he says, 'The coffee will be ready in a minute.' And I start asking about revenge and he says, 'The natural feeling of grief was sometimes replaced with a helpless feeling of rage.'

"Well, at that point I was thinking to myself, you know, the guy says, 'I'm filled with a sense of rage' and yet he wants to know how his uniform should look for the photographers.

"I kept pushing at the revenge thing because I wanted to know what he was going to do—I knew what I would have done—and he said, 'Yeah, I'd like to get these people. I think they ought to get the death penalty if they are caught.' But then he started talking about going to a party in Philadelphia that night. And, like, he made a remark about the telephone operator that he'd just talked to on one of these calls that was coming in. It was really an off-color remark. And all this in between these very profound statements about how he wants revenge, and how he wants to kill people, to have the death penalty, and he's enraged, and then he says, 'Hey, that's a really sharp-sounding gal. I could do something with that.' And I said, 'My God, this guy is really flicking back and forth.'

"I got a short note from him about five days after my story came out. He said, 'That was a really good piece. The best one you've done on me so far. How about getting me some copies of those pictures. They were just great. Signed, Jeff.' "

Allard Lowenstein—by now a true and impassioned believer in his cause—arranged for MacDonald to be interviewed by Bob Schieffer of CBS. Within a week of his discharge the result appeared—as had the news, nine months earlier, that he was considered a suspect—on the CBS *Evening News* with Walter Cronkite.

"Captain Jeffrey MacDonald is a man under a cloud," Cronkite intoned. "He's lost his family under horrible circumstances and now he's fighting for his honor." During the interview which followed, MacDonald said he had suffered "approximately nineteen" stab wounds during the attack. Having then described the agony of the false accusation and subsequent legal proceeding, MacDonald charged that the Army was refusing to renew its search for the killers, "because they now see how totally incompetent their own investigation was and it would do nothing but hurt their image for the investigation to be reopened. I think it's as simple as that. They are just afraid of being shown up as the incompetent team of investigators they are."

Concluding the interview, correspondent Schieffer said that the House Armed Services Committee had asked the Pentagon for a full report on the case. "But still unanswered is, who did it?" Schieffer said. "MacDonald feels that it's about time someone tried to find out."

Four nights later, MacDonald appeared on the Dick Cavett show. Dressed in a new civilian suit and fashionably wide necktie, and with his hair longer and the beginnings of sideburns apparent, MacDonald walked onstage to be greeted by a surge of applause: no longer just a viewer of Johnny Carson, but—for one night at least—a competitor.

A sympathetic Cavett referred to the "baffling story" which included "incredible bungling on the Army's part," and which was, essentially, "just a nightmare that this man lived through, and still is."

Cavett then, saying, "I hope this isn't too painful for you—I feel like the journalist who asks the gory question," asked MacDonald to describe the night of the murders.

"I can skim through it briefly," MacDonald said. "To get deep into it does produce a lot of emotion on my part." He told how Colette had gone to her evening class, how he had put the children to bed, how later ("even though I am a Green Beret") he had washed the dinner dishes, and how, "my wife came home and we had a before-bedtime drink and watched the beginning of a late-night talk show."

He paused here, and a smile flickered across his face. The audience—aware of the Cavett–Carson rivalry—responded with generous, if slightly uneasy laughter.

Later, MacDonald said he had sustained twenty-three wounds in the attack, "some of which were potentially fatal." He said, "I could have died very easily. I was in an intensive care unit for several days, and had surgery—you know, chest tubes in my chest."

"Did this seem like a nightmare at the time?" Cavett asked. "It is always easy to say, 'He went through a nightmarish experience.' Did it—did you know that it was real, that it was actually happening, or did it seem like a dream?"

"Yes, it still at times seems like a dream. Nightmare really is a very mild term for that night. And what's happened since has gotten so unbelievable. I mean it just kept getting worse and worse and worse and you run out of words to describe it. Unbelievable kind of says it, but then you keep saying that and it doesn't mean anything after a while."

"Yes."

"There were no facts against me, as Colonel Rock's very beautiful report illustrates. He was appointed as the Investigating Officer, and he was—actually acted as judge and jury for this three-month hearing. And I was fortunate in getting a very intelligent, strong man who could withstand some of the pressures that the Army was bringing to bear. There are people in the Army who wanted a court-martial regardless of any evidence. I mean, I've watched these men. I've seen them testify and I've seen perjury."

"Could that be because they had to find somebody?"

"Yes. That was a very large part of it, I think. Absolutely. They had done really nothing. They had performed very incompetently and they realized that they had to do something. So they charged me."

"Yes," Cavett said. "We have a message, then we'll be right back."

Following the commercial, Cavett asked, "What's this done to you? Do people look at you and say, ah, how do we know he didn't do it?"

"Well, yes, right. That's ah—most people to my—you know, face-to-face meetings have been very nice. I must say that. But I don't think I'm being paranoid when I say that there is certainly a flavor of suspicion in a lot of people's minds, and, ah, it comes out in various ways. Some people pat you on the back as if to say, 'Well, we know you did it but it's okay anyway.' Other people say, 'Well, it's going to be very hard to have patients come and visit you in the future, isn't it?' And, ah, I was accepted for my residency in orthopedic surgery at your alma mater, Yale, two years ago, and now it's being reviewed by the board of trustees."

"Did—did—did the idea of psychiatric examination ever come into play?"

"Yes, we did that because my lawyer thought it was an extremely valuable tool. When he first met me he said, 'The first thing we have to do is have you examined by a competent man, and if he comes up with wrong findings, I'm not going to defend you.' He was very blatant. He was very honest with me and I appreciated that.

"So we went through a very long, arduous examination and he testified later to the effect that I was perfectly sane and normal and it was his opinion that I was not the personality type, or had any of the characteristics of people who would commit a crime of violence, especially on those close to him. Six months later, a team of Army psychiatrists came up with the same findings."

"What about the fact that you were a Green Beret? Does that color it in some people's minds because they say, 'These guys are trained to kill,' and so forth?"

"Well, I must say I would have expected that, but surprisingly enough I think my mail—I would read my mail as saying that the fact that I am a Green Beret gave me more support, I would guess. A lot of people wrote to me because I *was* a Green Beret, I think. And they said very nice things, like, 'I once knew a Green Beret and he couldn't possibly have done it.'"

"Dr. Jeffrey MacDonald, we have very little time left. What do you want to come of all this? What's going to happen next?"

"Well, I think Congress is looking into things. We hope that they get into it in a big way and reopen the old investigation."

"Congressman Lowenstein is helping you in some way?"

"Allard Lowenstein from Long Island, right. He's doing a magnificent job and he's just a great person."

"Ah, this must have cost you a fortune," Cavett was saying, "aside from all the other—"

"Right, well, aside from my family and whatnot, and the nine months, somewhere in excess of thirty thousand dollars."

"Not to mention," Cavet said—since MacDonald, to that point, had not—"that the ah, perpetrators of the crime are still free."

"Absolutely. There are at least four people running around who have, ah, murdered three people."

"It's just unbelievable," Cavett said. "Does it seem like your life was, in a sense, ended at one point and started again in a Kafka short story?"

"That's exactly the feeling that you get. And you still get the feeling when you—when I wake up in the morning, you know—that it really didn't happen and my wife's still here, and what not. It's been a hard year."

"Boy, it's a fantastic story. I don't know what to say about it. It'll be fascinating to see what happens. Good luck to you. After this message, we'll be right back."

And Jeffrey MacDonald exited to music and applause.

PART THREE

THE CONTEMPT OF FAMILIES

If I covered my transgressions as Adam,
by hiding mine iniquity in my bosom:
Did I fear a great multitude,
or did the contempt of families terrify me . . . ?

—Job 31:33–34

1

For Freddy and Mildred Kassab, the summer of 1970, like the spring, and like the last month of winter, had been a time of unrelieved torment.

In spring, her compulsion to bake having waned, Mildred had begun to plant roses, more roses, hundreds of roses, digging feverishly into the soil around her house, as if somehow, by sheer dint of spadework, she could force it to yield up to her that which she wanted so desperately—those whom it had forever claimed.

In summer, she had started to swim. Each evening, having completed her labor in the garden, she would place stereo speakers in her living room windows, facing outward, and fill the night air with the music of Chopin, Debussy, Schumann, Mozart, Beethoven and then immerse herself in the pool that had been built for Colette and the children.

"The passion and pain of the old masters," she wrote in a journal, "unleashing my own inner turmoil. Swimming in the night, up and down, up and down, for hours, the pool filled with music, until finally exhausted enough to go to sleep."

Her husband, as if sleepwalking, had eventually returned to work. Each day was a void, however, which would end only in a new night of sorrow. The only activity which energized him was his battle to clear his son-in-law's name. The only emotion which fueled him was rage—rage now not only against the nameless, faceless, vanished killers, but against the obdurate and merciless military bureaucracy which, with its false and sadistic accusation, seemed determined to compound the original tragedy.

Occasionally, Freddy Kassab would have a minor, tactical disagreement with Jeffrey MacDonald. If they offered him a lie detector test, Freddy wondered, why not take it? If they wanted hair samples, why not give them?

MacDonald, however, or occasionally his lawyer, Bernie Segal, would at such times remind Kassab that matters had passed beyond the point where cooperation with the investigators could be of value. The Army no longer had any interest in solving the crime: its only goal was to make the charge against MacDonald stick. It was on that—not on the arrest of the four intruders—that promotions were riding. The Army had committed itself: its goal was to destroy Jeffrey MacDonald. Under such circumstances, both Segal and MacDonald insisted, you gave them nothing. You fought them, with tenacity and savagery, on every point. This was war.

Kassab understood about war. He had lost a wife and child to one, long ago. Now, having lost also the last family that he would ever have, he was not about to interfere in Segal's attempt to win dismissal of the charges against MacDonald.

What did frustrate him, however, was his lack of

knowledge. Given MacDonald's refusal ever to describe the events of February 17, and given the Army's decision to bar the public from the Article 32 hearing, Kassab's only sources of information were the occasional newspaper stories based on briefings given to the press by Bernie Segal, or the phone calls from MacDonald in which he would gleefully describe the defense's uncovering of the latest example of the CID's negligence and ineptitude.

It was not until the *Newsday* interview appeared in late July that the Kassabs received their first account of what had actually happened to Colette, Kimberly, and Kristen. And it was vaguely disturbing to them that MacDonald had been so ready to share with a newspaper reporter those intimate and anguishing details which he had withheld from all others for so long, but the primary effect of the information contained in the *Newsday* story was to whet the Kassabs' appetite for more. The details of the slaughter provided only the coldest, most numbing sort of comfort, yet information—any information—relating to the deaths seemed all that could fill even a minuscule portion of the void.

As a first step toward the acquisition of knowledge, Kassab, during a telephone call in early October, asked MacDonald to provide him with the transcript of the Article 32 hearing. (As he would continue to do for several years, Kassab was—without the knowledge of the party to whom he was speaking—tape-recording all telephone conversations which were in any way related to the case.)

"How heavy are those volumes you've got down there?" Kassab asked.

"It's, ah, thirteen volumes, each about an inch and a half thick."

" 'Cause I was gonna say, you know, if your mother

can bring them back I can run them off on my big machine in the office."

"Aaah, geez . . . I—she just asked me for an extra suitcase 'cause she's overflowing because she's bought some clothes down here. I don't know. I'll see if we can—if I can arrange it."

"Yeah, because if she brings them up I can run them off on my big machine in the office. I'll run down on a Sunday."

"Well, Freddy, you've got—you have no idea what this entails. This is not, you know, like running off a letter."

"No, I know, Jeff. I realize it will take me a few rolls of paper, but—"

"This is well over two thousand pages."

"I know. I know it is. But what the hell, I'll buy the paper and I'll go down to the office on a Sunday and run them off."

"Yeah, well, I'll tell you what. Let me see what I can work out with a smaller suitcase and then see how much we can get in. I might have to do it in sections, and then mail the rest."

MacDonald, however, sent none of the transcript, telling Kassab a few days later that Bernie Segal had instructed him that it would be inappropriate to release the material before Colonel Rock had filed his report.

Having lost all else, the Kassabs now asked very little of life: only that Jeff, who had so deeply loved Colette, be cleared of the charges against him; that, however painful the knowledge would be, they eventually learn what had happened at 544 Castle Drive, and that those responsible for such a monstrous, evil act be brought to justice.

By the end of October, with the charges against Mac-

Donald finally dismissed, it was this last desire which began to obsess the Kassabs. They had assumed that within twenty-four hours of the dropping of the charges, the FBI would be back in the case, assuming control of the investigation.

But then a week passed. And then another. Nine months had now elapsed since the murders, and as far as the Kassabs could tell, no effort to find the killers was being made by anyone. The Army was apparently so embarrassed by the entire affair that it seemed unwilling to investigate any further, while the FBI—in response to a phone call from Kassab—declared that it had no plans to reenter a case in which, months before, it had been deprived of primary jurisdiction.

Fred Kassab's anger was immense. The killers were out there—scot free—and *no one was even trying to find them!* He did not stay idle for long. While MacDonald remained at Fort Bragg, awaiting his honorable discharge, Kassab contacted dozens of public officials demanding a renewed investigation.

Most receptive seemed Allard Lowenstein, the Long Island congressman and antiwar activist who did not need to be convinced that the Army was capable of both stupidity and injustice. Lowenstein, however, was only one man. Moreover, he had just lost a bid for reelection. By the end of January, he would not even be a member of Congress. Kassab, therefore, drafted a letter to all 500 U.S. senators and congressmen, requesting not only a hearing into the Army's mishandling of the case, but a congressionally mandated reinvestigation of the crimes.

After specifying twenty-nine counts of misfeasance and malfeasance by the Army—allegations which were based upon information supplied him by Jeffrey MacDonald and Bernie Segal—Kassab wrote, "An effort must be made by some body other than the Army's Criminal Investigation Division to find the murderers who are still running loose, maybe to kill again."

In his conversations with members of Congress—or, more often, with their administrative assistants—Kassab had begun to learn that when trying to prompt a public figure to take action—publicity (either the threat of it or promise of it) could be an extremely useful tool.

By mid-November then—though their motives did not entirely coincide—both MacDonald and Kassab were devoting considerable time and energy to the task of building the MacDonald case into a national issue.

Unaware of Bernie Segal's prior effort—during which the payment of a fee to Jeffrey MacDonald had been requested—Kassab arranged a meeting with a senior editor at *Look* magazine. The editor, himself unaware of Segal's original approach, expressed considerable interest.

Excited by what he considered a potential breakthrough, Kassab called MacDonald at Fort Bragg.

"I just had a two-hour meeting with the editor of *Look* magazine," he said.

"Oh, really?"

"And they are extremely interested in splitting this thing wide open. I told him I had three purposes: one, a complete investigation so that we can see if we can catch the people that did this—"

"Right."

"—two, I want you cleared *one hundred* percent"—something which, in Kassab's eyes, an announcement that the charges had been dropped for "insufficient evidence" had not accomplished—"and, three, to try and prevent this from ever happening to anyone else again."

"Uh huh."

"And they are definitely very interested. He says they have two investigating reporters who would make FBI agents look like school kids."

"Really?"

"He says the problem is you'll be sick of these people. They'll just about live with you. They'll look into every sneeze and what-have-you and wherefore, and it will take three months."

"Three months?"

"That's what he says."

"All right. Did you tell him how much material I have?"

"I sure did. By the way, have you still got that transcript?"

"Yeah."

"I'll tell you why, Jeff. We got to talking about that and he said, 'For God's sake, get that material out of there. And not only that—when you get it where you're taking it, make a copy and one copy must be in a safe in a *bank*.'"

"Yeah."

"So I think I'm gonna come down."

"Oh, don't come down."

"No, I'm not taking any chances, Jeff. For a hundred and fifty dollars' airfare it's not worth it. The minute you don't have that thing anymore they could still spit right in your eye."

"Aaah, listen. Don't—that's silly, to come down. I'll mail it up."

"No. I don't trust the mail. And the editor doesn't either. I spoke to him about it. I'll just come down and pick it up and meanwhile we can visit a little."

"All right," MacDonald said, a notable lack of enthusiasm in his voice.

Ten minutes later, MacDonald called back.

"Hi, Freddy? Listen, I was sleeping when you called before. Would you go over that once more, fast, for me? I mean, I thought that—you know, it was all about a story, and you're coming down tomorrow and everything, but, ah, I haven't been feeling well, I have the flu, and I was sleeping and I'm not sure I got all of it."

Kassab repeated his account of the meeting with the magazine editor.

"Was this *Look* or *Life?*" MacDonald asked.

"Look."

"And they're interested?"

"Oh, God, yes. He said that they were definitely very interested."

"Okay. Now what was this about a three-month-type thing?"

"He said it would take that long to do a complete investigation. They'll look into every sneeze, and—I mean, he said these two fellows that they've got make most FBI men look like public school kids."

"Oh, great. That's terrific."

"In other words, they'll do an *in-depth* investigation."

"Right. Now did they, ah, discuss—I'm sure finances never came up, huh?"

"What?"

"Finances never came up?"

"No, no, no, no. I never even thought of it."

"Yeah, well, see, that's got to pay for some of my expenses, that's the thing."

A few minutes later, Kassab received a call from an aide to Bernie Segal, instructing him not to proceed any further in discussions with any magazines because that was an area Segal wanted to supervise personally, to assure that "Jeff's interests are protected."

Within the hour, Kassab received another phone call

from MacDonald, who said this time that his lawyers had instructed him not to give Kassab a copy of the transcript because to do so would be to risk court-martial for release of classified information.

This news so angered Kassab that he inadvertently disconnected his electronic recording device.

The next morning, MacDonald's mother called. "Freddy," she said. "I just wanted to call because Jeff said you sounded very upset last night and he was upset. He sounded hysterical on the phone to me when he said, 'I understand Freddy's position very well but I am in danger of being court-martialed.' In other words, that kind of information cannot be released."

"I am upset," Kassab said. "The thing that upsets me is that they've come to the conclusion that this transcript is going to be a money-making scheme. Well, ah, I don't go along with that and for them to tell Jeff that he can't give me a copy of the transcript because somebody's going to court-martial him is a lot of nonsense, and I know it and they know it."

"Well, I don't know what the technicalities are, Freddy. I really don't."

"First of all, nobody has given an order to Jeff that he cannot release that transcript."

"Well, Jeff said to me last night—and I can only tell you what I heard from him—that there is that outside possibility."

"As far as I'm concerned," Kassab said, "this is just Bernie's way of scaring Jeff, which I think is a terrible thing to do because under no circumstances—there is no possible way—"

"Look, Freddy, everybody wants action. We all want to get the real killers, all right? By the same token, at this particular moment perhaps is not the time when the transcript essentially can be freed. Right now he is still in the grip of the Army."

Jeffrey MacDonald's mother then urged Kassab to relax a little bit, to try to unwind, perhaps to take Mildred away for a few days, maybe to Cape Cod, from which she herself had just returned. The Cape was beautiful in the fall, she said. Very restorative.

Kassab told her he would never take a vacation—he would not even take a weekend off—until the real killers had been caught.

Despite the fact that Freddy Kassab had been, from the start, Jeffrey MacDonald's most outspoken supporter, he had always made MacDonald slightly nervous. As Bernie Segal put it, "Freddy's a zealot, and there's no telling when a zealot might get dangerous."

As early as Sunday, June 14, MacDonald had written in his diary:

> Freddy called today—they are coming down to see me on Thursday or Friday. I have mixed feelings. I'm uneasy about seeing them. The last time I saw them, I was in the hospital, recovering from the tragedy and my wounds—now, I'm charged with the murders, and have to face the parents of my wife. Granted, they have been terrific in their support, but, like everyone else, they can't help but wonder. Besides, we have been a little worried about Freddy's statements that 'only a full court martial will clear my name,' which is a lot of bullshit. I just have to get out of this mess.

Five days later, after the Kassabs had arrived, MacDonald noted:

Today was not too bad. We had a very nice dinner at the Officer's club and they were really nice
about reaffirming their support for me.

There was, however, one point which concerned him:

Freddy wants a complete transcript of the Art.
32 hearing, but I don't think he should get it—I
don't see the reason for that.

Now that it was November and the charges had already been dismissed, MacDonald saw even less reason
for it. The case against him was closed. There was no
need for Freddy to stay involved. Let law enforcement
authorities renew their search for the four intruders.
MacDonald himself—once he was safely discharged—
would launch his public attack against the incompetence
and malevolence of the military bureaucracy which had
put him through so much needless torture, but there
was no cause for Kassab to start probing into the details
of the case. No good could possibly come of that.

Kassab—undeniably a zealot, at least insofar as the
murder of Colette and her children was concerned—
would not, however, wait passively for action that might
never be taken. He himself would act: prodding, goad-
ing, and cajoling others—particularly those in positions
of influence—to join him.

To act effectively, however, he needed to be fully in-
formed. To be informed, he needed the transcript of the
Article 32 hearing. To be told by an assistant to Bernie
Segal that he could not have a copy infuriated him.

If MacDonald was made nervous by Kassab when Kassab
was an unswerving supporter, he was considerably more

jittery about the prospect of Kassab's becoming alienated from him in any way. What Freddy wanted most was to have the killers caught. Perhaps if he learned that something along those lines had occurred, he would be able to relax a bit.

It was, thus, in an attempt to pacify his father-in-law that Jeffrey MacDonald—on the night of Sunday, November 18—called Kassab from his BOQ room and said, "There's something happened down here that I can't tell you about on the phone."

"Yeah?"

"Ah, all I can say on this phone is one down, three to go."

There was a brief silence.

"Did you get what I mean?"

"Yeah, I got what you meant."

"But that's for real."

"Yeah. Good. Good, good."

"I don't know," MacDonald sighed. "It doesn't really change anything."

"Yeah, I know what you mean. Well, nothing's going to change anything, Jeff."

"I think, ah, that ah, our friend Miss Helena Stoeckley is really gone," MacDonald said, "because I would have found out—there's no question that I would have been told had she still been in town. And, ah, he claimed that, ah, she wasn't around. And there's no question he was willing to say anything he knew."

There was another brief pause. Kassab, believing that MacDonald's own telephone might be tapped, remained deliberately unresponsive.

"So, ah, things are happening," MacDonald continued, "but, ah, like I said, it's—again, it's a very depress-

ing type of thing because nothing changes. I mean, ah,
still, Colette and Kim and Kristy are gone."

"I know."

"But, ah, it's necessary."

"Yeah. Well, give me a call when you can from some
other phone and give me a blow-by-blow or something."

"Well, I don't even like to talk on yours, that's the
problem. What I'll do is I'll send off a note from another
post office."

"Yeah. Or I'll be in the office tomorrow. In the morning, anyway."

"All right."

"You got my office phone number?"

"Yeah."

MacDonald called Kassab at his office the next day and
elaborated on his cryptic announcement. He said that on
the preceding Friday night he and some Green Beret friends
had tracked down one of the four intruders—the larger of
the two white males, the one without the mustache. After
beating him until he'd told them all he knew, they had
killed him. "He's six feet under," MacDonald said, adding
that he would continue to press the hunt for the other
three. Apparently he felt that this would be enough to satisfy Kassab's desire to see the killers apprehended.

Later that day, he wrote to Kassab:

> *I am beginning work on my speech for a news con-*
> *ference the day I get my discharge. I think here is best,*
> *but I'm not sure. AP & UPI seem to do a good job*
> *getting it out—we can deliver mimeos of speech &*
> *photos if necessary to Newsday, Post, L.I. Advance,*
> *and Times the morning I hold the conference.*

> *Or I can hold it up there, but then the area down*
> *here refuses to cover it well. Vice versa is not true for*
> *some reason. I feel quite satisfied the media is still in-*
> *terested enough to cover it. Don't jump the gun.*
> *(Only you know what I'm planning)—the time will*
> *come and it will only take one day's coordination of*
> *effort to get maximum exposure.*
>
> *I will deny our phone conversation of today if any-*
> *one ever asks. I'm sure you can figure out why. What*
> *must be done must be done.*

Within days of his arrival in New York in December of
1970—it was, in fact, on a weekday, and Freddy Kassab
was at work—Jeffrey MacDonald went to the Kassab
home on Long Island to deliver some pictures of Colette
and the children that Mildred Kassab had requested.

Ever since hearing, from her husband, that MacDonald had tracked down and killed one of the intruders,
Mildred had felt herself beset by a variety of conflicting
emotions: satisfaction that at least partial revenge had
been obtained, concern that Jeff's action might cause
him new legal problems, and frustration at the thought
that, by having killed the one person who might have
been able to lead him to the others, he had made it more
difficult for any fresh investigation to succeed.

Her rage at those whom she believed to have been the
murderers of her daughter was so intense that she felt no
qualms over Jeff's private admission that he now was a
murderer himself: so strongly did she believe that the
Army was not interested in seeking justice that she did
not begrudge him the act of having obtained some measure himself, however unorthodox and distasteful the
means.

But most of all Mildred Kassab felt curiosity. Who had

it been? What had he said? What had been the motive? Where were the others? What did Jeff intend to do next? If his purpose in telling the tale had been to defuse the Kassabs' interest in the case, it was obvious that he had badly miscalculated.

As Jeff sat at her kitchen table eating pie and drinking coffee, and looking everywhere around the room except directly at her, Mildred let ten minutes pass, waiting for him to say something. When he did not, and when it became apparent that he did not intend to, she herself brought up the subject which had dominated her thoughts for the past three weeks.

"Jeff, I know you don't want to talk about it, but I must know. What did you do? What did he say? Tell me."

MacDonald continued to glance around the kitchen, his eyes still not meeting hers.

"Oh, this guy," he said, "he's a complete idiot. He doesn't know what he's doing at all."

Immediately, it struck her as strange that he was speaking in the present tense, not the past. In addition, the more she had thought about it, the more foolish it had come to seem that he had eliminated the one person who could have definitively established his innocence. But even these notions were subordinated to her burning curiosity. Jeff's victim had been, after all, a man who had participated in the murder of her daughter.

"What did you learn?" she asked. "Did he tell you anything?"

"By the time we got through with him," MacDonald said, "he would have told on his own mother. He said he remembers being in the house, he remembers the shouting, but he doesn't know why he was there. He was so far gone on drugs he didn't know what happened."

"How about the girl? Did he know who she was?"

MacDonald was shifting ever more uneasily in his chair. He had finished his coffee and pie, and it was obvious that he was eager to leave.

"Yeah," he said, "her name was Willie the Witch, and she went away with the fellow with the mustache. They're both away."

Then Mildred mentioned her fear that Jeff's action might be discovered.

"Don't worry," he told her. "He's six feet under now." He added that they had arranged it to look like a robbery. Then he said he really had to leave.

"He was terribly uncomfortable talking to me about it," Mildred would later recall. "He wouldn't look at me. He just kept gazing all around the room, and eventually I started to feel that maybe he wasn't telling the truth."

Freddy Kassab did not appear on network television in December, but he did travel to Washington with two bulging suitcases that contained 500 copies of his eleven-page letter to members of Congress. He had decided it would be more effective to deliver them in person instead of mailing them.

For four days he trudged through the halls of the House and Senate office buildings, hand-delivering a copy to every office: a Willy Loman peddling his plea for justice.

Often, he would get only as far as the front desk. Occasionally, an administrative assistant would spend a few minutes with him. Everybody was very sympathetic. Nobody promised a thing.

He returned home, worn and weary, on the night of December 15. He turned on the television. He saw Jeffrey MacDonald on the Dick Cavett show. He was infuriated by MacDonald's performance.

Given an opportunity, on network television, to reach within minutes millions of the constituents of the political figures Kassab had spent four days vainly attempting to see, and to demand, through that medium, that the killers of his wife and daughters be pursued, MacDonald instead had focused almost solely on the injustices that had been done to him.

Equally galling was his playing off the audience for laughs. Amusement had passed from the lives of Freddy and Mildred Kassab ten months before, and it seemed to them profoundly inappropriate that the aftermath of February 17 should be presented, by Jeffrey MacDonald, as entertainment.

Perhaps most troubling, however—although it did not at the time seem to have the significance that it would later acquire—had been MacDonald's assertion that he had sustained twenty-three wounds in the attack and the implication that he himself had almost died.

Both Freddy and Mildred Kassab had seen Jeffrey MacDonald at Womack Hospital on the afternoon of February 17. "There wasn't so much as a Band-Aid on him," Mildred recalled. "Not even Mercurochrome." Freddy Kassab had returned to the hospital that evening and had found MacDonald "sitting up in bed and eating dinner with apparent enjoyment."

Perhaps, the Kassabs told one another, it was simply a lingering sense of defensiveness—the result of the false accusation—that had made their former son-in-law so grossly exaggerate the extent of his own injuries.

Kassab called MacDonald the day after the Cavett appearance. He informed him of his displeasure. At the same time, he renewed his insistence upon access to a copy of the transcript.

Now that he was out of the Army there was no plausible reason for MacDonald to object. Though he himself, in the wake of the story he had told them, seemed increasingly reluctant to be in the presence of the Kassabs, MacDonald had his mother deliver a copy of the transcript. She arrived—bearing thirteen manila-bound volumes—on Christmas Eve. She said, however, that they could only keep the transcript for a week. Then Jeff would need it back in order to prepare the lawsuit he was planning to file against the Army.

The Kassabs read in silence throughout Christmas Day. It was their first Christmas together without Colette. The transcript was the only gift they had received.

They read quickly. There was much to absorb, a great deal of it obscured by legal wrangling. Eventually, through the verbiage, the picture began to come into focus. The transcript provided the Kassabs with their first glimpse of the murder scene: their first close-up view of Colette's torn and battered body awash in blood on the bedroom floor; their first look, through the eyes of military policemen, doctors, and investigators, at the damage that had been inflicted upon Kimberly and Kristen. It was also their first exposure to Jeffrey MacDonald's detailed account of what had occurred.

Pausing only to try to sleep—or when tears so blurred their vision that they could no longer distinguish the words on the page—the Kassabs read until New Year's Day. So overwhelmed were they by the horror, so numbed by the excruciating detail, that they gave no thought whatsoever to analysis.

There was, however, one point that Freddy Kassab did find puzzling. It was MacDonald's statement that for more than six weeks he had slept with a pistol under his pillow because he so feared for his life.

Kassab recalled the detailed account in *Newsday* of

MacDonald's contemplation of suicide. The exposed pipes, the chipped paint, the logistics of trying to hang oneself with one's own belt, the conclusion that the attempt would be likely to end in failure. Why, wondered Freddy Kassab, if a man was lying in bed with a pistol under his pillow, would he be so concerned about whether or not he would be able to take his own life with his belt?

Kassab returned the transcript to MacDonald. He wrote to the Army, asking for a copy for himself. Familiar, by now, with Kassab's outspokenness and tenaciousness, the Army agreed to supply him with one if MacDonald would sign an authorization. MacDonald signed. Again, there was no plausible reason to refuse. Kassab received a copy in February. The same week, he also received a visit from two CID investigators.

In December, in response to congressional inquiries prompted by Kassab's hand-delivered letter—and by MacDonald's nationally televised accusations—the CID command in Washington had begun an internal investigation to determine the extent to which the Fort Bragg CID and laboratory technicians at Fort Gordon had been guilty of dereliction of duty.

The conclusion reached, as expressed in a letter sent to members of Congress by the Army's chief of legislative liaison, was that while the investigation had not been "a model of its kind," neither had it been "the amalgamation of incompetence, perjury, and malicious prosecution which Mr. Kassab envisioned."

On January 19, 1971, Col. Jack Pruett—the CID's director of internal affairs—was instructed to shift his attention to the murders themselves. He was given office space in the Federal Building in downtown Fayetteville. A task force of eight agents was assigned to him, under the supervision of warrant officer Peter Kearns. He was told to take as much time as he needed. He was told all necessary resources would be available. He was told he was expected to be thorough. He was told also that it was expected that this investigation would produce evidence sufficient to bring about the indictment of the killer or killers of Colette, Kimberly, and Kristen Mac-Donald.

Pruett and Kearns came to Long Island on February 11 to inform Freddy Kassab that the new investigation had begun. At the same time, they informed him that his son-in-law was still considered a suspect.

2

Jeffrey MacDonald had moved from Long Island to the Upper East Side of Manhattan in January of 1971. He took an apartment at 321 East 69th Street and found employment as an emergency physician at the World Trade Center construction site.

He also found part-time work as the assistant to a West Side physician known colloquially as "Dr. Broadway"—a man whose specialty it was to cater to the particular needs of persons affiliated with show business. In this role, MacDonald told friends, it was not uncommon for him to make 4 A.M. house calls bearing tranquilizers for agitated actresses.

In his free time, MacDonald was entertained by such friends as Dr. Howard Bellin and his wife, the Countess Christina Paolozzi. At one party, he said, he met the actor Hugh O'Brian. At another—he was almost certain—he had actually been introduced to Walter Cronkite. In addition, he began to date a woman who worked as a secretary for Joe Namath's lawyer.

MacDonald failed to keep a Washington appointment

with Allard Lowenstein. Talk of finding the real killers receded. He was speaking, instead, by early 1971, of the need to build a new life. Rather a rude shock it was, then, to receive a phone call from Freddy Kassab, informing him that at that very moment two CID agents were in the Kassab home describing him as a suspect still under active investigation.

MacDonald drove immediately to Patchogue, arriving at the Kassab house just as Pruett and Kearns were preparing to leave.

"He wanted to know what we were doing there," Kearns said. "He was somewhat put out. Angry at us. Not to the point of fisticuffs or anything. He was just angry. We advised him he was a suspect and therefore we couldn't discuss anything with him—we couldn't even talk to him—unless he had his lawyer present."

Arrangements were made promptly, however, and on February 19, in the library of the Philadelphia Bar Association, in the presence of Bernie Segal, Jeffrey MacDonald was interviewed by Pruett and Kearns.

After three hours of questioning, the agents showed MacDonald a picture of Helena Stoeckley and asked him if he could identify her as having been one of the assailants.

"I probably sound like I am avoiding the issue," MacDonald said, "but not from the photograph. I can't do that. I just can't do that. There are a number of reasons. Assuming, just for the sake of argument, that she was there, the conditions and the shortness of my being there, she was least likely for me to be able to identify. I would say that out of the four I saw—the four people— she is the least likely. I said this at the hearing. You know, it was really very quick. It is hard to—it is really hard to get across how quick this occurs and how little I saw of her. This is not a case of looking at someone's face like I am looking at you and thinking of her. It was just like that. That's all it was. I know I was seeing blond hair. For instance, it really does, when you look at the face—I would say probably not from this—the nose looks really prominent here. It looks like you would remember the nose right away. I just have the impression that I was looking at a much smaller, narrower nose. This is very bulbous. It looks very prominent. But I get a weird feeling. I get an uncomfortable feeling looking at her face. I just don't know."

Pruett and Kearns had a second interview with MacDonald in March. At the conclusion of this session they asked whether he might now be willing to take a polygraph test. He declined. He also refused to undergo a sodium amytal interview, a technique whereby an individual is questioned while under the influence of a memory-enhancing drug. It was explained to the two CID agents that his psychiatrist, Dr. Sadoff, felt that such a procedure might be injurious to MacDonald's overall mental health, in that it would cause him to reexperience, rather than simply to recall, the events of February 17.

"We felt sure we were going to have another interview," Kearns said. "We hadn't covered nearly all the area we wanted. But after that they turned down all our requests. In fact, after that second meeting in Philadelphia, Mr. Segal told us, 'Until I see your investigation taking a different course—that you're not channeling it towards Dr. MacDonald—you can expect no further cooperation.'"

Pruett and Kearns, however, were delving into other aspects of the case. In particular, they were looking into the matter of Helena Stoeckley.

One of the first people to whom they spoke was P. E. Beasley, a detective assigned to the narcotics squad of the Fayetteville police department. Prince Edward Beasley had known Stoeckley since 1968, when she was sixteen years old. By February of 1970 he had come to consider her the most reliable drug informant he'd ever used.

She was a graduate of Terry Sanford High School in Fayetteville, where she had been a member of the dramatics club, the chorus, the Future Teachers of America, the Girls' Athletic Association, the French club, and the Latin club. Known for her fine singing voice, she had played intramural volleyball and basketball and had been a contestant, one year, in the high school beauty pageant. She had also worked as a Candy Stripe volunteer at Fayetteville hospitals and had expressed interest in a nursing career.

Despite this wide range of activities, she was remembered by classmates as "much quieter than average," and as a person who shared very few of her feelings. A tenth-grade teacher recalled her as "a rather sad little girl who was not much in touch with reality."

Helena Stoeckley had always liked to make up stories. "Fabricating," many of her acquaintances said, was one of the things she did best. A teacher recalled the day she had come to school wearing a Duke University class ring and telling everyone that she had become engaged to a student at the Duke medical school. "The tale was completely made up and she had no boyfriend at all, except in her mind," the teacher said.

Following her graduation in June 1969, Stoeckley had begun to work in the Haymount section and to associate with what was generally considered to be the hippie element of Fayetteville. Her use of drugs, which had begun during high school, increased to the point that, in the fall of 1969, her parents told her that she was no longer welcome to live with them.

To P. E. Beasley, Stoeckley appeared to be "starving for attention," and was so eager for praise from him that—in order to please him—she turned in some of her best friends for dealing in narcotics. "Helena would do anything to get me to pat her on the back and act proud of her," Beasley said.

By January of 1970, Stoeckley was living in a trailer with two Fort Bragg soldiers named Greg Mitchell and Don Harris. Two weeks later, she had taken up residence on Clark Street, with two male civilians. Within days, she had moved next door to live with two young women from New Jersey. "We all hung around together," explained one of them, "and it really didn't make any difference where we slept." Stoeckley's drug addiction had by now worsened to the point that she was using marijuana, LSD, mescaline, and heroin—and beginning to take the heroin intravenously.

At 2 A.M. on February 17, 1970, Prince Edward Beasley completed what had been almost a twenty-four-hour shift and went home. Five hours later he was awakened by a phone call from headquarters and informed of the MacDonald murders. His first thought—he would say some years later—was that the description MacDonald had given, vague as it was, resembled Helena Stoeckley and her friends. He had known her to wear a floppy hat, boots, and a blond wig. He also recalled having seen her in the company of males, both black and white, who wore Army fatigue jackets—not in itself extraordinary, since much of the Fayetteville hippie contingent was composed of soldiers either recently discharged or AWOL from Fort Bragg.

Beasley got out of bed and drove to the trailer where he had known Stoeckley to be living with Mitchell and Harris. Finding it empty, he looked for her in several other locations. Then he went back home to bed. Late that night, he drove to Clark Street and waited outside her apartment. At about 3 A.M. a car containing Stoeckley and several male companions pulled into the driveway. Beasley approached her.

"Well, Helena," he had said—according to his later recollection—"You and these people you are with fit the description that was given of the MacDonald murderers. Now, I am going to ask you straight out: I know you and you know me. I want you to tell me the truth."

Stoeckley—who was not wearing a floppy hat, blond wig, or high boots—at first appeared to Beasley to be in a "joyful" mood. "She joked about her icepick," he said. "Then I told her this was a serious matter and not to act that way."

At this point, he said, Stoeckley took a step backward and lowered her head. "In my mind," he recalled her as saying, "it seems that I saw this thing happen." But then adding, "I was heavy on mescaline."

Beasley would later say that he had radioed the Fort Bragg CID and told them that he had suspects in custody. He waited for an hour and a half, he said, but when no one from the CID either called him back or came to Clark Street by 4:30 he felt he could not hold Stoeckley's companions any longer, and so he released them. Except for Helena, he said, he never saw any of them again.

Stoeckley herself, however—like hundreds of other Fayetteville area hippies—was questioned several times by authorities in the days immediately following the murders.

"Every time I go out they pull me in," she complained to a newspaper reporter. "The reason they're hassling me is I don't have an alibi. The night it happened, nobody saw me." Her comments were printed in a Fayetteville paper.

Eventually, Stoeckley was questioned by William Ivory of the CID. Already convinced that MacDonald was the killer, Ivory had conducted this first interview in even more perfunctory fashion than he did the one which followed Posey's testimony. By the end of February, despite her attempts to draw attention to herself, nobody was taking Helena Stoeckley seriously as a possible suspect.

On April 13, 1970, Stoeckley—whose own parents described her as "a girl who was always seeking constant attention"—was admitted to Womack Hospital, suffering from a pain in her right side and symptoms of drug addiction. The next day, she and her father were interviewed by a military psychiatrist.

"She admitted to drug abuse," the psychiatrist said. "Using Seconal, heroin, and many other drugs. She said she would shoot up almost constantly. She said this had been going on for almost two years."

The psychiatrist concluded that "currently, she feels terribly worthless and unwanted, and states that no one is sincere and no one really cares about her. She is extremely rebellious and sets up situations where she asks for help and then makes sure that you can't give it to her." He recommended that she be hospitalized at the University of North Carolina Medical Center in Chapel Hill for "long term psychotherapy."

She was admitted there on April 17 and placed on a methadone withdrawal schedule. She told the admitting psychiatrist that she had been taking "everything available, including heroin, opium, LSD, cocaine, methadone and barbiturates." She said that in February she had begun to feel "depressed and reclusive," and had increased her heroin consumption to eight or nine doses per day.

The psychiatrist noted that at the time of her admission, "she was oriented to person and place, but thought that the date was April 26 when it was actually April 17." She told him that two days earlier she had felt "outside" herself, and at times had felt that "someone was standing over her with a knife, about to kill her."

Having completed the methadone treatment, Stoeckley was discharged on May 11. It was noted that throughout her hospitalization she had "remained extremely reclusive and mistrustful." The final diagnosis was "narcotics addiction in a schizoid personality," and the psychiatrist wrote that "the prognosis of this patient seems poor."

Less than a month later, Stoeckley was readmitted to Womack Hospital, complaining of abdominal tenderness. She remained there until June 26, having been diagnosed as suffering from serum hepatitis and a history of drug abuse. Her liver was enlarged and needle tracks were observed along her veins.

In August, William Posey had seen Stoeckley in the Haymount district and had told Bernie Segal his story about her. Posey's testimony of the Article 32 hearing received extensive publicity—thanks to Segal and his assistant, Dennis Eisman—and soon after Ivory had reinterviewed her, Stoeckley decided to leave Fayetteville.

On September 11, she wrote to one of her former female roommates from Clark Street saying that the MacDonald case was causing problems for her:

> I am in deep deep trouble with the CID. Remember how I didn't have an alibi for the night of

*the murder? Well, our dear next door neighbor
stepped up and pinned the blame on me once again. I
know I did mescaline that night and borrowed somebody's blue Mustang—do you remember who owned
the car? All I remember is I took off and came back
about 4:30. . . . they have enough circumstantial evidence against MacDonald to try him for murder, but
first they have to rebuke Posey's testimony. He saw me
leave in that car but I sure don't know where I
was. . . .*

Stoeckley moved to Nashville and took up residence
in a small white house on the corner of Belmont and
Portland avenues. Among those with whom she became
acquainted was a freelance artist named Jane Zillioux.

"Helena's house was—a lot of hippies lived there,"
Jane said. "I lived across the street. At first I thought she
was a runaway. She seemed very young to me. I didn't
know how old she was. I never asked her. She just looked
too young to be away from home.

"She was sick. She had hepatitis. A lot of the time,
when I would see her, she would be yellow. Even her
eyeballs would be yellow. One day, when I hadn't seen
her for a few days, I thought, 'Well, I better check on
her.' I didn't know if those hippies were feeding her or
not. So I went over there. It was in the evening, sometime before Thanksgiving.

"I knocked on the door and I said, 'Helena, are you
there?' And she said, 'Yes,' and I went into her room.
She was weak and shaky and she sat down on the bed
and I sat beside her and I asked her if she was all right.

"She said, 'I've been sick,' and I said, 'Well, Helena,
why don't you go home?' You know, 'Why don't you go
home to your family and let them take care of you?' And

she said, 'I can't. I can't ever go home again. I was involved in some murders. My family don't want me around.'

"I didn't say anything. I was just too shocked. You know, I expected a teenage confession, like, 'I hate my mother,' or 'I'm a runaway.' I didn't expect that. I was horrified. But finally I said, 'Well, did you do it?'

"And she said, 'I don't know whether I did or not. I've been a heavy drug user and when you are on drugs you do funny things. When you're on drugs, you do things that you don't think you did. And other things that you think happened really didn't. So I don't know. I can't remember.'

"But then she said, 'When I came to myself—when I came to myself I was in the rain. It was raining and I was terrified.' Then she took her arms and wrapped them around herself and hunched her body over. The tears were running down her face and the mucus was dripping from her nose, and she was just hysterical. She flipped her hands up and said, 'So much blood, so much blood. I couldn't see or think of anything except blood.'

"I was trying to calm her down, but I wanted to get out of there, too. I didn't know if she was on drugs right then or not but I wanted to get out of her apartment. I didn't want to be there. I didn't want to hear that.

"So I said, 'Well, who were you with?' And she said, 'Three boys. I didn't know them. I was with them for the drugs.' She also told me it had been a woman and two small children that they'd killed and that she had been wearing her blond wig and white boots. I know they were white plastic-leather boots because before that when we were in a store once she pointed out a pair and she said, 'I had a pair of boots like these, and I loved them but I had to get rid of them.'

"Anyway, she just got all blubbery and incoherent—sobbing and crying, you know—and then she grabbed hold of my arm and said, 'You won't tell, will you?' And I said, 'No, I won't,' and just as quickly as I could I got out of there.'"

Three days later, Jane Zillioux did call the FBI office in Nashville to report the conversation and to give them Helena's name and address and to say that she believed it had something to do with the MacDonald murders at Fort Bragg. The FBI, however, simply thanked her politely and did nothing.

In early December, another acquaintance of Stoeckley's, Red Underhill, approached her apartment and heard the sound of crying from within. As he entered, she began to scream hysterically: "They killed her and the two children! They killed the two children and her!"

Not long afterward, Stoeckley returned to Fayetteville. On December 29 and 30, she was interviewed by CID agents who were just beginning the new investigation. She repeated to them her story of taking mescaline, getting into an automobile, and driving off alone. "Because of the drug use," one of the agents reported, "she couldn't remember anything that happened after that."

In January, Stoeckley returned to Nashville. She wrote to Prince Edward Beasley on January 20:

> Beasley, what does the CID want of me? I didn't murder anyone?!! Are they going to keep hassling me? Is there any way I can take a polygraph to find out whether I was at MacDonald's house or not the night of the murders, without the CID finding out the results? . . . Are they still suspicious of me or can I come out of hiding now? . . . I'm living in constant para-

noia. . . . Please let me know anything and please
don't give the CID my address.

Beasley, however, was cooperating fully with the CID.
Not only did he provide them with Stoeckley's Nashville
address, but on February 27, he accompanied a CID
agent to Nashville and participated in further questioning of her.

"She said she did not remember anything that had
happened on the night of the murders," he later recalled,
"except getting into a blue car she thought was a Mustang and that it belonged to a Bruce Fowler, who was in
the Army at the time. She said she remembered starting
the car and backing out of the driveway and after that she
remembers nothing.

"She said the last person she knew to see her on the
night of February 16 was Greg Mitchell, her boyfriend at
the time, and that he was the one who gave her the mescaline.

"When I told her that this type of narcotic would not
cause her to black out, and, if it did, she would not stay
blacked out for that long, she said she knew this and was
afraid she had a mental block that must have been caused
by some awful thing that she had seen that night."

The following day, Beasley asked her if she would
agree to be fingerprinted and to have her hair samples
taken. She refused. He asked her why. She said she was
afraid she might have witnessed the murders and might
know the people involved. She told him she'd been having dreams during the past few weeks which indicated to
her that she might know something about the case.

"I asked her what type of dreams," Beasley said, "and
she said she had dreamed of seeing people struggling
and violence and a lot of blood. Then she said she

thought MacDonald might have had something to do with the murders but she didn't know. Then she told me again that she did not know for sure what had happened but she had a suspicion that she was in some way connected to the incident."

On March 25, 1971, a tall, dark, and handsome Nashville narcotics squad detective named Jim Gaddis participated in a raid on the house in which Helena Stoeckley was living.

Stoeckley, who was not arrested, approached Gaddis and asked to speak to him privately. She asked if he knew anything about the MacDonald murders in North Carolina. She said she was a suspect in the case and wondered if he could find out whether she was still "wanted." She also told Gaddis that she had been a police informant in Fayetteville and would like to work with him in that capacity.

Gaddis met her on a street corner an hour later and, as they drove around town, she pointed out five different locations where narcotics were sold and identified the dealers. When raids the next day resulted in two arrests for heroin possession, Gaddis came to believe that Stoeckley could be useful—particularly when she agreed to let Nashville police place electronic surveillance equipment in her apartment.

Stoeckley continued to talk about the MacDonald murders. "She told me a lot of things about the case," Gaddis said. "She also contradicted herself several times about things she had previously told me.

"Some of the things she told me are that on the night of the murders she had taken some LSD but she said it had no effect on her. Later that night, she said, a boy named Greg gave her a large dose of mescaline. After that, she claimed she remembered nothing about where she was until sometime early in the morning. She told me she remembered coming home in a blue Mustang. She remembered getting in the car sometime around midnight and she remembered getting out of the car at her apartment but she couldn't remember if she was with anyone or where she went.

"On one occasion she told me that she definitely knew who had killed the MacDonald family but she didn't give any names. On another occasion she told me that she only had suspicions about who the killers were. On one occasion she even told me that Dr. MacDonald did it himself."

On April 23, a CID agent returned to Nashville accompanied by an Army polygraph operator. Stoeckley agreed to take a polygraph test in regard to her possible involvement. First, however, she had another discussion with Jim Gaddis.

"She again told me she wasn't involved in the murders but that she knew who the killers were. She wouldn't tell me who they were. When I asked her why, she said, 'Those people are suffering enough.' She did not tell me the reason the MacDonald family was murdered but said something to the effect, 'Some people would do anything for a fix.' She then said she had been there and had witnessed the murders, but she wouldn't give me any details. She also mentioned that Dr. MacDonald had once refused to give one of her addicted friends any methadone, but she wouldn't say who the friend was."

Stoeckley's first polygraph examination lasted from 6:15 until 10:30 P.M. "During the interview," the operator said, "Miss Stoeckley repeatedly acknowledged knowing the identity of the persons who committed the murders."

The next day she told Gaddis that the killers had made one previous attempt on Jeffrey MacDonald's life but had failed. "She didn't explain this any further," Gaddis said. "She kept telling me things but not explaining them any further when I would ask questions about what she said."

Later that day, she underwent further polygraph testing, during which she stated that in the previous three or four months her dreams had frequently placed her on the couch in Jeffrey MacDonald's living room and that MacDonald had stood over her, pointing at her with one hand while, in the other, he held an icepick which was dripping blood.

She also said that she knew the identity of the people who had committed the murders and that if the Army would grant her immunity from prosecution she would make the names available and would explain the circumstances surrounding the killings.

Refused immunity, she said she had already "talked too much," and retracted her earlier statement about knowing the names of the killers. Later in the interview, she reiterated her statement that MacDonald had killed his family himself.

That night, Gaddis took Helena Stoeckley out to dinner. He ordered wine for the two of them. At the end of the meal, he surreptitiously wrapped her wine glass in a napkin and put it in his pocket. The next day, fingerprints were lifted from the glass. After dinner, Gaddis drove Stoeckley to one of Nashville's lovers' lanes and embraced her. In the process—while running his hands through her hair—he was able to obtain a hair sample.

Laboratory analysis revealed that neither the hair nor the fingerprints matched any hair or fingerprints found inside 544 Castle Drive.

On the morning of April 26, Stoeckley, arriving for a third day of polygraph examination, announced that she would henceforth refuse to answer any questions and that she wanted to consult an attorney. She asked to be excused to go to the ladies' room and did not return.

The next day, she sent Gaddis a note:

> Please *believe I was* not *in that house!!!! I really and truly don't know anything about the whole mess. I'm sorry I had to leave but I couldn't listen to them lie any more, especially with you there. I'm only begging you to believe me. I'm telling the truth. Thank you for the meal. I'm sorry I let you down. Don't let them arrest me—please."*
>
> *Thanks & love,*
> *Helena*

In his written report, the polygraph operator concluded that, "Due to Miss Stoeckley's state of mind and excessive drug use during the period of the homicides, a conclusion could not be reached as to whether or not she knew who committed the homicides or whether she was present at the scene."

In the weeks that followed, CID agents located, interviewed, and gave polygraph examinations to all the people whom Stoeckley had named, at various times, as being possible participants in the crime. All denied any involvement and in each case the denial was supported not only by the cross-checking of stories but by the re-sults of the polygraph tests.

Agents also spoke to the two young women from New Jersey with whom Stoeckley had been sharing her Clark Street apartment. One said Stoeckley had not re-turned to the apartment at 4:30 on the morning of the murders but had been away until much later in the day—thus casting doubt on Posey's recollection. This room-mate also said that Stoeckley had enjoyed being mentioned in newspaper stories about the killings.

William Posey was found in Birmingham, Alabama, in June of 1971. One of seven children of a career Army man, Posey—the CID had learned—had been arrested for housebreaking in 1968 and on four separate occa-sions in 1969 had been arrested for drunk and disorderly conduct.

A polygraph examination indicated that Posey's testi-mony at the Article 32 hearing had not been truthful. When confronted with this result, Posey admitted that he had not seen Stoeckley get out of an automobile on the morning of February 17, 1970, but had only seen her walking from an automobile to her apartment. He also said he did not know that the car had been a Mus-tang. He said that a month or two after the murders he'd had a dream in which a Mustang had appeared, and for that reason he had testified that this was the car from which Stoeckley had alighted.

He further said that he was no longer positive that the morning he'd seen Stoeckley had been the morning of February 17, and that it had not occurred to him that she might have been involved until at least a week after the murders, and that the opinion he had formed at that time was the result of Stoeckley's telling him that she had been on drugs the night of the killings and could not remember what she had done.

Having absorbed all of this information, Pruett and Kearns discounted Helena Stoeckley as a suspect and began to probe more deeply into the background of Jeffrey and Colette MacDonald.

3

From mid-November through March of his sophomore year of high school, Jeffrey MacDonald had been absent from Patchogue. With no advance word to teachers or friends, he had abruptly departed for Baytown, Texas, to live with a family named Andrews—friends of the Stern family of New Hope, Pennsylvania, but people whom MacDonald himself had met only briefly and casually.

As they deepened their probe into MacDonald's background, Pruett and Kearns were struck by this event. It seemed odd to them that an outstanding student and athlete who was having no disciplinary problem of any kind should suddenly be removed from his high school and be sent more than 1,500 miles away, to remain away—through both Thanksgiving and Christmas—for almost four months.

Their questioning of former teachers and acquaintances did not turn up a definitive explanation but there were recurrent rumors of difficulty within the MacDonald family—including one to the effect that Jeffrey had been banished by his father in the aftermath of a brutal fight in which he had badly injured his older brother, Jay. One family friend even remarked that MacDonald's mother had often said, "One of Jeff's goals in life is to flatten Jay," so great was his envy over favoritism shown his older brother said to be.

Whatever its cause, the unexplained and prolonged absence from home was considered worthy of attention by Pruett and Kearns, for it was the first hint that a more turbulent level of emotion might have lain beneath the tranquil "all-American" surface of the MacDonald family.

Years later, Jack Andrews, Jr., a contemporary of Jeffrey MacDonald's and the son of the man who had extended the invitation to Baytown (and in whose home MacDonald resided during his stay) would recall that, "He never mentioned his family. It became apparent rather quickly that this was something he did not want to talk about.

"The story was that my father had just invited him down for a visit. But I knew there must have been some other reason behind it. At first, he was just supposed to stay for a couple of weeks. Then—I don't know quite how it happened—after he'd been here those couple of weeks it was just sort of decided that he was going to stay on.

"It wasn't my doing. Frankly, he and I did not get along well at all. Right from the start, he was always stepping on my toes. A couple of times it even led to some pushing and shoving. Once, I remember, was kind of serious—we got into a real tussle, right in our family living room. It wasn't too long after that that he went home.

"The thing I remember most clearly about Jeff is that he was always striving to be the center of attention. And not just in the normal way: you know, the new kid in town, showing off. With Jeff it was like a crusade—he had to try to look the best at everything.

"The first week or two after somebody would meet him, they'd always be tremendously impressed. But then—with guys, especially—it would eventually end up in a clash. Mostly because of the way Jeff had of insisting that every little detail always be just his way."

Jack Andrews, Sr., the Humble Oil engineer who had extended the invitation, had later died in an automobile accident, but his ex-wife, Mary C. Andrews, was able to recall certain details surrounding the event.

Her husband, she said, had met the MacDonald family through his friend and business associate Bob Stern, while on an extended trip to the Northeast. In the fall of 1958, she had joined him in New York for a time. One evening, she remembered, her husband had invited the MacDonald boys—Jay and Jeff—to come into New York City for dinner.

Unaccompanied by their parents, the two teenaged boys had ridden in from Patchogue on the train and had dined with the Andrews couple in Greenwich Village. The occasion had proved so festive that after dinner the foursome had gone to "a couple of clubs," at one of which a photographer employed by the establishment had taken a commemorative picture.

Soon afterward Mary Andrews had flown back to Baytown. Within a couple of weeks she was informed by her husband that when he returned he would be bringing young Jeff MacDonald with him for a visit.

The two of them—Jack Andrews, Sr., and the high school sophomore, Jeffrey MacDonald—left New York on November 11 and drove cross-country to Baytown, which is on the Gulf Coast of Texas. When later asked what had led to this sudden venture, Mary Andrews replied, "I think my husband Jack was just attracted to the boy."

MacDonald's stay in Baytown continued long enough for him to be enrolled in the Robert E. Lee High School there. "He stayed right through Christmas, I'm sure," Mary Andrews said. "I even remember the present he gave me. He knew I liked glass bottles so he bought me this tall, thin, blue glass bottle for Christmas. It really was very pretty."

Mrs. Andrews said she had the feeling that "Jeff never felt appreciated at home." That "he was someone who was really trying very hard to please all the time but that he felt he just didn't fit in his own family. That everyone liked his brother Jay the best."

She said she had never discussed it with either of Jeffrey's parents, but "frankly it seemed real strange to me that the family would just let him come down to stay for so long with people they scarcely knew. In fact, *I* had never met the parents at all—just the boys that one night at dinner."

Mrs. Andrews added that she could not remember precisely what had led to MacDonald's departure but that by March his presence in her home had become "a strain." She said, "It just got to be an uncomfortable situation."

The relationship between Jay and Jeff, however, was referred to by many acquaintances of the MacDonald family with whom the two agents spoke, including one woman who, since childhood, had been a particularly close friend of Colette's.

"I always thought Jeff and Jay were close," she said. "They had like a real close family type. The mother always gave the impression that, you know, they were really the ultimate as far as scholastics, sports, and everything. They were really tops in everything, and they gave that impression to a lot of people. You speak to people in town and they will tell you the same thing. They were really right up there as far as everything was concerned. You know, one was right after the other.

"But then, Jay—in high school he was the big man, right? And then he kind of just went to the other end. He was more or less like the flop out of the family, getting involved with the wrong type of people. Now he's a bum. He hasn't a very good reputation, between his drug use and in and out of different type jobs.

"Now, Jeff—he was a domineering type person as far as, you know, Colette and stuff. She seemed to be very devoted to him. But I knew through the grapevine that, like most guys, he wasn't so, you know, devoted back.

"Jeff was very well liked in school. He was voted Most Popular and stuff. He had his hang-ups. Everybody does. But I don't think he was an embittered, hateful person. They had arguments, yes. Nastiness from him a couple of times, but nothing violent.

"Just one time, I remember, he hit Colette. It was such a long time ago. We were maybe seventeen, sixteen. I think it was at my house—my mother's house at the time—and I just remember him reaching out and giving her a slap, and she was crying and got all upset over it and stuff, but that—it's so blank. It's not that vivid that I can say what they were talking about, but it sticks in my mind, the fact that he did.

"Colette, you know, she was very intelligent, extremely bright, very active—a good swimmer, and stuff like that—but she wasn't the type of person to spill her feelings to anybody. When she lost her father she became very inward and she very rarely expressed her innermost feelings. When her father committed suicide, she kept it all in."

As an adult, the friend said, Colette was "not much for housekeeping but lots of time for the kids. The last letter I got from her was about a month before the incident. It was a very newsy type letter. She said they were finally together as a family and Jeff was making extra money moonlighting. Financially, I think, they had really struggled because, of course, he was working while he was going to school.

"She was really delighted about being pregnant again. She said she was so happy. She said she just hoped and prayed that it would be a boy, for Jeff's sake. She said then the family would be complete.

"The only thing—she said she really hoped he would not go with this team—the boxing team?—on some kind of a trip. She really hoped he wouldn't go because she would be due around that time, but he was supposed to go and he kind of had his mind set on it and that was it."

Agents spoke also to the wife of Colette MacDonald's older brother. She said, "Colette was an extraordinarily sensitive person. I don't think she ever hurt another human being's feelings. She didn't make enemies. She was never a competitor in terms of feminine wiles. She just wanted to be with her man and that was it.

"She always loved Jeff. She was just crazy about him. And she was always into getting married and having babies. Like the thing of going to Skidmore. Her mother wanted her to go to Skidmore, but Colette would have been happy to just get married and have babies.

"She was great with her kids. She wanted a big family, lots of babies, but she had a very tough time having them and that cut it back.

"She lived with her brother and me one summer while she was at Skidmore—after her freshman year—and she and I used to sit down and she used to talk about Jeff a lot, and ask me if she should start going out with him again, and I said 'Yeah, go ahead,' because I knew where she was at. She was crazy about him. She was very much into Jeff. That was just where it was at with her.

"After they were married, I didn't see her as much. Just once in a while—when Jeff was at Columbia I saw her once or twice at Mildred's. Jeff was always working and Colette would go and be with her parents in order not to be alone, because Jeff worked these screwy hours all the time.

"The last real contact I had with her was when Jeff got his thing saying he had to go into the service the day he finished his internship. I was on the phone with her then for a few days because she was very upset—that he was going to have to go away, that he was probably going to have to go to Vietnam.

"Then Jeff called her from Texas and said he had enlisted in the Green Berets, and so he did not have to go to Vietnam. I don't think she was too thrilled about the Green Berets. She knew she could talk to me about it because I am anti any kind of violence and war and she knew that and she felt that way also.

"She was very antiwar—the Green Berets and the connotation and whatnot. She was very anti violence. Their father, you know, he died a horrible death. He hung himself. I don't know if Colette saw him or not, but my husband did. He was fourteen at the time. She was eleven. And after their father died, forget it. That was the end of the world.

"After that, she and her brother just started keeping things inside. They have always been people to hide the bad things. They both found it very difficult to express their emotions. Like I remember one time they sat down and discussed, you know, their father's death, and they both got very upset and there was too much emotion. It was too much of a hassle to remember all the bad times and they would stop it. Shut it down and drink coffee. That's the way they did it. Mildred is that way, too. She was that way about her husband, and now she's that way about Colette. She doesn't talk to anybody, she doesn't see anybody, doesn't talk to anybody about it. This is the way the whole family is emotionally. They stay very much to themselves.

"The MacDonalds were just the opposite. Their house was always full of people and the door was always open. There were six people coming in the front door and four people going out the back, and Colette was very excited about this—being with a family and lots of people—so she spent a lot of time over at the MacDonalds' because she did not have that at home. Holidays were a big thing in that house and she liked to be there.

"Mr. MacDonald—Mac—he was a big rapper. Oh, I loved him. He would sit around and bullshit, you know, and she liked this. He was a nice kind of a guy and she liked him, and Jeff was everybody's friend. Even at their wedding, Jeff was the kind of guy that always had people around him, lots of buddies and so on.

"Jeff was very uptight about hippies, from what I could see. Jeff was very straight. He didn't drink, he didn't smoke. Colette smoked, and he made her stop. Colette herself was very straight and stable and always wore little shirts buttoned up to the top and a straight skirt, but she didn't have that kind of prejudice.

"I don't imagine she and Jeff ever argued because, you know, she just—'I don't want to discuss it. It's a hassle.' She would be hurt more. She was easily hurt, but she would be hurt rather than angry. If somebody said something to her, to cut her, instead of coming back in a slandering fashion, you know, she would feel hurt, and she would withdraw and back out. She was never a pot-thrower or anything.

"When she was growing up, there were no fights in her house, no arguments. She was never struck. She was not disciplined by Freddy or by Mildred. You know, she didn't have anything of that nature in her life. Everybody was very protective of her. Colette was a very protected child. Her relationship with her mother was a real mother-daughter kind of thing. Colette and her mother were very close, and Mildred shielded her from all kinds of things. She was just smiling and happy and up and if something was bothering her, she kept it to herself.

"Her letters were about the good things, always about the good things. She said she had it good at Fort Bragg. Everybody had a bedroom and she was going to have another baby and the sun shined a lot and the kids had a pony and it was the nicest thing they had done together. It was the first break, in terms of normalcy—her first chance to settle down.

"I got a Christmas card from her, said she was very happy and she was making a baby. It was just a very up kind of card. Mildred and Freddy went down to visit, and Mildred said when she came back that she was so pleased how Colette was cooking, and, you know, cleaning house, and that she seemed very happy. She was excited that Jeff surprised everybody with a pony. It apparently surprised Colette, too. They wanted to have a farm and that pony was the first thing toward that farm.

"Of course, Colette was the kind of person that would

always make everything seem very right. She would never expose a problem or unhappiness that would reflect on Jeff or that would reflect on their marriage. She would do everything to make sure that everybody saw that they had a very good relationship. She didn't confide in me in terms of things like that. I don't even know if she did with her mother, because she was always very protective of Jeff and their private relationship."

Pruett and Kearns then talked to Colette's brother, who worked as a sales representative for a computer company.

"They were both very conservative people," he said. "For example, Jeff was highly—he disapproved of anything to do with drugs on any level. This was very absolute. And Colette, in terms of being contrasted with me, was always drastically more conservative, in my eyes sometimes to the point that her eyes were not open to enough things. Colette was very content to be a housewife and a mother. Many women today, they seem to want just about everything, but she was, from an early age—wanted babies and just wanted to strive toward motherhood.

"I think of Jeff as a very greatly controlled person. His temperament I find to be very even. I remember at a party, for example—this was for his mother's fiftieth birthday, in the spring of 1969—there was a guy at the table and he was the kind of guy who grew up as a tough. All the time he would pick up cement blocks and people and throw them around at random, and I forget whether—it was something to do with my wife, I think— and this guy could have picked me up and broken me over his knee and I wouldn't have been able to do a thing, and he came across the floor at Jeff's house and picked me right up off my feet against the wall and Jeff's response was one that I thought gave me a lot of insight into him.

"He immediately responded to help me and defend me yet it was with just the right amount of control. His anger was there to show the man that he had totally misbehaved at his home and was treating one of his guests poorly, and yet he didn't step over the bounds. He wouldn't just run up and belt somebody in the mouth. He had a lot of control, whether it be in statements or actions.

"Now, Jay—Jay was a tough guy. Jay is not the kind of guy you mess with. You don't go up to Jay and give him a hard time. Jay is a rough, tough guy and he would just pop you in the mouth.

"Jeff and Jay and their sister, Judy, were always close, and they did everything—for instance, their father was dying and they went out on a limb, the three of them, to buy him a boat. The whole family, from what I understand, it was kind of like all for one and one for all, everybody tried to help each other.

"In fact, the kind of people that Jeff's family was, I think, had a large amount of influence on their marital relationship. The MacDonalds were a very gregarious people. The kind who would invite a stranger in off the street for Thanksgiving dinner. They were very accustomed to doing that kind of thing. They were a very socially active clan and there was always something happening, and if there wasn't something happening, they created it. It was the warmest social environment I have ever been in.

"I personally couldn't have that much social life and have any kind of personal life. You know, for me that was too much one way, but it seemed to make Colette very secure and very happy.

"Colette was more or less adopted by them. We didn't have, in the Stevenson household, a lot of close family life. It wasn't the kind of family where you had a lot of big gatherings, and Colette always wanted this, and as a result, when she was so totally taken into the MacDonald family, it was a very warm, very good experience for her."

Of even greater interest to the two reinvestigators was a written report filed by a CID agent who had interviewed MacDonald's sister in Schenectady, New York, on May 7, 1970, as part of the original investigation.

According to the agent, the sister had described Mac-Donald as "a perfectionist who insisted that things in the home be maintained to his standards by his wife. This caused some arguments," the agent wrote, "and on occasion he would have outbursts of temper if things were not as he desired."

The last paragraph stated: "At one point in the interview, she was asked if she thought her brother Jeffrey was capable of killing someone. She hesitated and after some thought responded that although she does not believe he did kill his family she felt he was capable of killing if he were provoked."

Kearns reinterviewed MacDonald's sister. She told him in the spring of 1971 that all she had meant to imply was that anyone was capable of murder, not that she had meant to suggest that her brother had any particular predisposition in that direction. The agent who had conducted the original interview, however, insisted that the context had been clear and that her response had been quite specific.

An area of MacDonald's life that Pruett and Kearns placed under particularly close scrutiny was the time he had spent at Fort Sam Houston, Texas, just after his induction into the Army. MacDonald had not lived on post but at the Sheraton Motor Inn on Austin Road in San Antonio. Kearns spoke to a doctor who had shared the motel room with MacDonald.

"About the only thing that sticks out in my mind," the doctor said, "is the party we had the weekend after arriving in San Antonio. The party was held in a room directly under ours, occupied by two Army nurses.

"There were about six or seven nurses and eight or nine men, including members of a band that was playing at the motel. Everybody was drinking Gold Duck and I got bombed out. The party lasted all afternoon and well into the night. One of the nurses spent a lot of time with Jeff and seemed to get to know him quite well.

"Jeff dated her for a couple of weeks after the party and one night he must have asked me if I would sleep somewhere else so he could have the room. I don't remember him asking me but he must have because I stayed downstairs in the nurses' room with the same nurse who had been dating Jeff.

"I don't know who Jeff had in our room that night. The nurse who had been dating Jeff appeared to be hurt because she liked him.

"Then Jeff somehow became friendly with the manager of the motel and used to go out a lot with that gang. This manager was supposedly married to a model in New York and he really lived an incredible life, throwing wild parties and things like that.

"Jeff met a divorcée who worked as a stewardess for American Airlines, and they spent a lot of time together. She had a really outstanding body but was not terribly good-looking.

"After the course was over and Jeff had gone, I was

there a few days longer. One day I met the stewardess at the pool. I got the impression that she really liked Jeff and was very sad because she was never going to see him again. I reminded her that a lot of guys who attended school there were married and liked to have a good time but then they had to go back to their families. I got the distinct impression that she might even have planned on packing up and following Jeff."

An agent then interviewed the nurse who had dated MacDonald early in the summer. "I knew he was married," the nurse said. "He never told me, but after two weeks—after I knew him—I just finally asked how his wife was. He said fine and that was it. He did not talk about his wife, but he did mention his two children. He told me all the cute little things that kids do that wives like to tell husbands and husbands like to spread around. The only problem he ever mentioned was that his older daughter wet the bed and he was hoping that the younger one would not start, too."

The nurse added that as the summer progressed, "Jeff sort of split off from the group of friends he first had and began running with the manager of the motel, and some other guy who seemed to be one of the local nouveau riche fops. Do you know what I mean? One of these sleazy-looking people who has made it big all of a sudden. I don't remember what his name was. He was sort of repulsive.

"I could not see how Jeff could run around with them. Jeff was the perfect gentleman at all times. He was always sophisticated. I guess that was the attraction I had to him. The manager was repulsive. He was squalid, but he thought money would give him anything. It seemed that he and Jeff were, personality-wise, diametric opposites, and I could not see how they could get along.

"Oh, and there was also a little guy who lived about four or five doors down from me. He was thin, black hair, small thin face with a little pointed chin and he used to double-date with Jeff and his stewardess along toward the end of the course. This guy tried to attack me while I was asleep one night and I told Jeff about it the next day and Jeff almost duked him out. But nothing permanent happened to their relationship. They continued double-dating these stewardesses."

A sergeant who had been working as an undercover narcotics agent and who had infiltrated several parties at the motel during the time of MacDonald's residence reported that MacDonald had also dated a "blonde with a beautiful body" named Mary and a Swedish exchange student from a San Antonio college, who, according to "authorities at the college," was a "very uninhibited, promiscuous girl who might be a good prospect for any man desiring sexual relations."

"During the month of June," the agent reported, "a party was held at this motel at which the Special Forces were the hosts. During this party things got out of hand and the police were called. The personnel at the party were in the swimming pool nude and just about everything imaginable was happening.

"It was also learned that at the Jump Parties there was performed what is called a 'Special Forces wedding.' This was explained as being what they called a 'sandwich' wherein a girl performed oral sodomy on a man while a man performed anal sodomy on a girl.

"There are pictures of this scene but they had gone underground," the agent reported, "when it was learned this investigator was in the area. It was apparent that these parties turn into regular orgies where anything and everything goes, from drugs to any sexual act."

Jeffrey MacDonald, of course, had not been at the Sheraton Motor Inn in June but he had attended a Jump Party in December, and to Pruett and Kearns it was beginning to seem clear that he had been less than candid when he testified at the Article 32 hearing that only "very, very infrequently" had he had a sexual relationship with a woman other than his wife.

The reinvestigators then began to turn their attention to the life the MacDonald family had appeared to be living at Fort Bragg—a time which MacDonald would later recall as being filled with "a sense of ease" and a "new togetherness." Many of the MacDonalds' acquaintances offered support for this contention, but, bit by bit, Pruett and Kearns began to collect pieces of information which indicated that a more complicated range of emotion may have lain not far beneath the surface.

One Green Beret friend recalled "a minor argument one afternoon. MacDonald and I had gone to his house for lunch on a work day and Colette appeared a little irritable. MacDonald said he knew what it was all about. He said she had probably taken a diet pill. Colette said that was right—she seemed concerned because she'd had difficulty wearing a new pair of slacks."

A friend of Colette's recalled that she had, indeed, been taking diet pills prior to her pregnancy but that she'd stopped because of the "wild mood swings" brought on by the medication.

The wife of the warrant officer who had lived next door to 544 Castle Drive told investigators about one particular outburst of temper. "Colette was painting outside," the former neighbor said, "and the telephone rang and she went in, and when she came back she said, 'Did you hear me screaming at Jeff?' Then she went on to explain that he was downtown and he had just bought this new stereo set for $700, or something like that. She said she blew up over the telephone and told him with all the bills they had to pay, she couldn't see spending the money." Another neighbor reported that Colette had said she could "kill Jeff" because of the purchase.

As MacDonald's closest friend at Fort Bragg—and as the last person to have seen the family alive—Ron Harrison was someone to whom the investigators spoke at length. He told them, as he had always told everyone, that the marriage had seemed to him to be one filled with love and affection. The only signs of discord he'd ever noted, he said, were along the lines of Jeff saying to Colette: "Hey, what are you watching this for? The ball game's on." Or, "Ronald's out of beer, Colette." Or, "Ron needs some chow." At times like that, Harrison said, "She'd jump right up and take care of it. She was really number one and so were the kids."

MacDonald himself, however, according to Harrison, had been bitterly disappointed when Colonel Kingston, whom he had so idolized, was transferred to Vietnam and MacDonald's Special Forces group was disbanded. MacDonald had been reassigned to a different group and given a lesser position: preventive medical officer instead of group surgeon. According to Harrison, this development had annoyed him and he had begun to speak of his desire to get to Vietnam.

"Jeff was an impatient guy," Harrison said. "He was eager to do something. He wanted to go to the Nam, to Africa, to South America." To anywhere—it came to seem to Pruett and Kearns—other than 544 Castle Drive.

On post, however, MacDonald had continued the tradition—begun at Princeton and carried on through medical school—of entertaining large groups of friends. Harrison, who himself visited the MacDonald home "two or three nights a week," recalled particularly a large party at Thanksgiving when MacDonald's mother was down from Long Island for a visit.

Another guest remembered: "There were a lot of people there. Colette had done a tremendous amount of work. I never saw so much food. Jeff spent most of his time taking care of his guests. They had a new color television set, and a lot of the men were watching the football game. Jeff's mother and Colette spent most of the time in the kitchen. I recall they served Cold Duck champagne with the meal because one bottle sprayed all over the ceiling when it was opened."

For the Cold Duck, there was no need of a corkscrew, but Ron Harrison quite clearly remembered an extended discussion about an icepick. "There was a plastic bag of ice in the kitchen and the ice was all stuck together. As I recall, Jeff asked somebody—Colette maybe?—'Where's the icepick?' He was looking all around for it—in the kitchen drawers and everywhere. He was the host and couldn't find it. He even went out back to look. He said, 'Maybe it's with the stuff out there, the barbecue stuff in the shed.' So he went outside and looked around, but he came back without it because we finally had to use a screwdriver and the end of my knife—I had a pocketknife—to pry the ice apart and chip it away."

Another frequent dinner guest—following her husband's departure for Vietnam—was Josephine Kingston. "I saw Jeff and Colette twice a week, three times a week for a couple of months," she said. "I recall we drank Cold Duck, a sort of wine, with our dinners." Mrs. Kingston also recalled that "one of the children would often wet the bed and would then go to the master bedroom and get in Colette's bed."

There had been occasions, Mrs. Kingston said, on which she had seen Jeffrey MacDonald at her residence, alone. At such times, she said, the two of them had talked. When asked what they had talked about, she replied, "Oh, just everything." She recalled specifically that "he mentioned having a brother with some problems and he was sort of unhappy about that" and that "he wanted to go to Vietnam. He was very envious of my husband for his trip."

Mrs. Kingston also said, "I don't think, truthfully, that Jeffrey wanted more children." She said he had been "disappointed" upon learning of Colette's pregnancy. "It seemed they had just gotten to a stage in their life where they could leave the children with a babysitter and now another was on the way."

Eventually, the reinvestigators brought up the subject of the Valentine that Mrs. Kingston had sent to Mac-Donald from Honolulu.

"I know it was a silly thing to do," she said. "At the time, I thought it was just a gesture of friendship. When I left for Hawaii several weeks after my husband had been transferred to Vietnam, Jeff and Colette saw us off at the airport and I gave him a kiss. I remember telling him that this was the first time I had ever kissed him since I'd known him. Sending the card was just one of those indiscriminate things, absolutely no deep feelings involved."

She was asked why she had sent the card to his office and not his home.

"Oh, the whole thing was just a joke," she said.

Mrs. Kingston was then shown a copy of the Joan

Didion column, "A Problem in Making Connections," found in the same envelope that contained the Valentine. The column read, in part:

> I am a 34 year old woman with long straight hair and an old bikini bathing suit and bad nerves, sitting on an island in the middle of the Pacific watching for a tidal wave that will not come. . . .
>
> My husband switches off the TV and stares out the window. I avoid his eyes and brush the baby's hair. In the absence of a natural disaster we are left again to our own uneasy devices. . . .
>
> We are each the model of consideration, tact, restraint at the very edge of the precipice. He refrains from noticing when I am staring at nothing and frightened of the void. . . .
>
> At the end of the week I tell him that I am going to try harder to make things matter. He says he has heard that before, but . . . there is no rancor in his voice. Maybe it can be all right, I say. Maybe, he says.

Mrs. Kingston was asked if she'd ever seen the article before. "I don't know," she said. "I may have. It might be something my daughter would send to Jeff. I don't recall sending it. My daughter was writing on my behalf and she does things like that—sends clippings from magazines whenever she runs out of things to write about."

Colonel Kingston's daughter, who was twenty-two years old, said, when asked about the card, "That is an embarrassing thing. At the time I never thought anything about it. I was in Hawaii getting cards for several friends in the States when I ran across that card. It reminded me of the time at the airport when mother gave each of the MacDonald family a kiss on the cheek, even the children.

"Jeff laughed about it and teased her. I suggested to mother that we send him the card as a kind of joke about the kiss at the airport. If I had known that anything like this was going to happen, I would certainly never have sent it."

In regard to the clipping, she said, "I never sent that. Definitely not. I've never even seen it before. I wouldn't send Jeff something like this. It is kind of coincidental, isn't it?"

In addition to socializing with the wife of his former commanding officer and "becoming really acquainted" with his own wife, and making the acquaintance of nurse Tina Carlucci at Fort Sam Houston in early December, Jeffrey MacDonald, in the fall of 1969, was acquainting himself also with a number of other young women.

He was, Ron Harrison said, doing some "counseling" for the red-haired wife of a Special Forces sergeant who was having marital problems. He was also, apparently, teaching the nineteen-year-old daughter of another colleague how to drive. Harrison recalled stopping by the MacDonald apartment one evening just as MacDonald and the young woman—whose name was Carla and who lived only a few houses away on Castle Drive—were on their way out for a lesson. MacDonald told Harrison to make himself at home and have a beer, saying he would be back in about forty-five minutes.

So frequent did these driving lessons become that Carla's mother eventually came to suspect a deeper—possibly intimate—level of involvement. She told investigators that she considered MacDonald's attentions to her daughter to be "excessive" and said, "He took her out many places and seemed to be a little friendlier than an ordinary neighbor would have been."

Even the sixteen-year-old babysitter who lived upstairs came in for her share of attention. She told investigators that "He made one comment about if he had known girls like me when he was sixteen, he'd like to still be in school." Given the manner in which the remark had been made, the young woman said, she had considered it offensive.

By January of 1970, however, changes in MacDonald's manner were being noted. "I remember seeing Jeff looking very white and very tired and very serious," one neighbor said. "He wasn't his usual jolly self—you know, friendly and outgoing. He was moonlighting—holding down two jobs besides his Army job—and he just looked so tired."

The sixteen-year-old babysitter also noticed a change in both Jeffrey MacDonald and his wife. "After January," she said, "Colette hardly ever even said 'Hi' when I went over to babysit. She never smiled and Jeff wasn't too friendly either. When I saw them together, I just sensed they weren't happy. They didn't yell at each other, but now I look back and they never really smiled."

Colette, of course, was certain by now that she was pregnant. And though, to some friends, she had expressed enthusiasm at the prospect of having a third child, there were others who developed a different perception. One Fort Bragg acquaintance said, "I don't know how the subject came up, but she told me she had sort of gotten pregnant by mistake because she had forgotten to take one birth control pill. You know, at the time, I laughed. I sort of said, 'The joke's on you,' type of thing. She laughed, too, but I didn't get the feeling that she was overjoyed about it.'"

Also, by January, of course—according to what Mac-Donald himself had told Pruett and Kearns in one of the Philadelphia interviews—he was moonlighting at Cape Fear Valley Hospital "every night." In addition, he had made arrangements to begin a second moonlighting position at Hamlet Hospital on weekends. And he had also begun to work out with the Fort Bragg boxing team.

"He came into the arena on January 4," the boxing coach said, "saying that he wanted to work out and lose some weight. I saw him thereafter on January 6, 8, 9, 11, 12, and 20. There might have been a couple of days during that period when he came in which are not reflected in my logbook but those dates reflect the majority of his visits. As far as I can determine, January 20 was the last workout he participated in.

"When he came in the first time, the team members were going through a five-minute heavy bag drill. This is exceedingly strength-sapping and it generally takes months to build up the endurance to punch for the full five minutes. Captain MacDonald, however, during his first workout, participated in this drill and lasted the five minutes. Although he was winded at the end he did not seem to show the effects. I thought this was an outstanding performance for someone who had not been participating in any type of boxing program on a regular basis.

"Captain MacDonald was much stronger than the average individual and in much better physical condition when he started the program than the average soldier would be. He also had a considerable amount of drive and determination. After only a very few workouts he sparred with our middleweight champion and held his own during the minutes he was in the ring.

"He was very well accepted by the members of the team and very well liked. In fact, after his first few work-outs, I asked him if he would like to become the team physician. As I remember, he accepted without much persuasion.

"I don't recall exactly when I told him, but I did inform him of our upcoming road trips, starting on or about February 20 through to the last of April or the first of May. For the boxing staff this would be continuous traveling. We would go to Fort Jackson, South Carolina, for the U.S. Army trials, then to Fort Dix, New Jersey, for the Inter-Service matches, and then on to Trenton, New Jersey, for the National AAU matches.

"On the 12th or 13th of February, I called Washington and requested that Captain MacDonald be considered for acceptance as team physician. The colonel I spoke to said he would look into it and if Captain Mac-Donald's unit did not object, he would be so assigned. As I recall, that same evening, I called Captain MacDonald at his quarters and told him of my conversation with the colonel. I cannot recall his exact comment but as I remember he seemed pleased."

Colette, however—contrary to MacDonald's assertion in his "diary"—apparently had not been pleased. Not only had she mentioned her apprehensiveness to her mother and to the Long Island friend to whom she wrote in January, but she spoke of it to the friend who had begun to accompany her to the child psychology class in early February. "She told me that when her husband first was in the Army she'd had to stay home while he had gone down for his training and she didn't like being away from him. She sort of dreaded the thought of being separated again, but he was going somewhere with the boxing team."

The "somewhere"—Jeff had told Colette—was Russia. Not Fort Dix; not Trenton, New Jersey. The team coach, however, informed the CID reinvestigators that no trip to Russia had ever been planned or even discussed. "There was nothing scheduled for the Bragg or Army teams regarding Russia," the coach said. "The National AAU team had gone to Russia, departing on or about the first of February, but I had no conversation with Captain MacDonald regarding his desires to go with them and there was no travel scheduled for the Army team after the national championships in New Jersey."

Gradually, Pruett and Kearns drew closer to the time of the murders. MacDonald had said repeatedly that despite having worked a twenty-four-hour shift at Hamlet Hospital and having put in a full day at his office and having then played basketball for an hour, he had not been overtired on the night of Monday, February 16.

The woman whom Colette had driven to class, however, recalled Colette's commenting that Jeff had seemed totally exhausted. "She said—I forget if he was sleeping, or laying on the couch when she left. But she said he was really tired because he had worked all night the night before and then he had to go to work at Fort Bragg all day."

Having had, at the most, a half-hour nap on the living room floor before Kimberly had awakened him to watch *Laugh-In*, MacDonald had become so revivified during his wife's absence that upon her return he not only stayed up watching television with her until 11 but even after she went to bed he stayed up—to watch more television, to finish *Kiss Me Deadly*, and even to wash the dinner dishes at 2 A.M.

Like the unexplained sojourn to Texas and the nonexistent trip to Russia, this sudden infusion of energy puzzled Pruett and Kearns. With MacDonald no longer willing to talk to them, however, these did not seem matters which they could pursue. Instead, they focused on Colette's child psychology class.

Normally, she was not an active participant in class discussions, but on the evening of Monday, February 16, she posed a question.

"She raised the question," her friend said, "about her youngest child coming into bed with her and her husband in the night. She wondered whether they should allow the little girl to stay the night or if they should put her back to bed or what kind of solution they should try. It seems to me she said her husband felt that the little girl should stay in bed with him and, you know, that she should go and sleep on the couch."

Another member of the class recalled that "Mrs. MacDonald outlined the situation as one in which a little girl crawls in bed with her parents and pushes her mother out of bed. This was done by the child crowding the mother so far to the edge of the bed that she was no longer comfortable.

"The instructor asked Mrs. MacDonald if it was her child. She replied that it was. The instructor then asked if the child knew that Mrs. MacDonald was pregnant. She said yes. The instructor than asked the child's age. I think she told him two or three. The instructor then asked what she did about the child. Mrs. MacDonald told him that she had to go to sleep on the couch.

"The instructor asked Mrs. MacDonald what her husband thought of her sleeping on the couch. She replied that it was her husband's decision that the child stay in their bed and that she sleep on the couch. The instructor asked how often this happened. Mrs. MacDonald said a few times in the last two months.

"There was a general discussion about the problem, and the consensus was that after a short time the child should be taken to its own bed and made to understand that that's where it belonged. I remember Mrs. Mac-Donald sitting there smiling and nodding, apparently happy with the decision of the class. It was about this time that class ended. About five minutes later, I saw her at the Shopette. The next day I learned that she and her two children had been killed."

Colette had begun the course at the North Carolina State University extension at Fort Bragg on February 4—a course not in "something literature," as Jeffrey MacDonald had told the CID when first asked, and had repeated to the psychiatrist, Dr. Sadoff, but a course in child psychology, designed to give a basic overview of the relationship between childhood event and adult behavior.

Pruett and Kearns looked closely at Colette's class notebook. On her first night she had made notes concerning two basic personality types: "Sadistic authoritative—the personality that wants to make other person his dependent" and "passive dependent—relinquishes self-esteem to the other person."

The class met again four days later to consider the oral, anal, and phallic stages of pregenital development, "in which the libido," Colette noted, was "all directed toward self (narcissistic)," creating a "megalomaniacal attitude" in the child, who believed himself to be "omnipotent." Eventually, the normal child would pass beyond this stage to the point where "ego develops as some libido energy is directed toward other people."

A note on "ways of coping with anxiety" such as "regression" wherein the "individual reverts to more infantile behavior" was followed by a description of the phallic stage in the three- to four-year-old male:

a. identification with father up to this point
b. at this point father becomes a rival
c. little boy wants Mommy all to himself
d. Oedipus complex—kill father, marry mother
e. castration fear that father will take away his penis
f. this stage seems to set the stage for determination of homosexual or not—can he identify with father or not—most critical period of life for child.

Whether Colette might have come home from these classes eager to share with her husband some of the new knowledge she was acquiring could only be grounds for speculation, but the possibility that at least some portion of the final few hours of her life had been devoted to conversation with the man suspected of having killed her about either a specific problem concerning one of her children or the more general subject of the psychosexual development of the human being caused her notes from Monday, February 16, to be read with particular care.

The class had begun with a continuation of the earlier discussion of human defense mechanisms, such as:

fixation on earlier stage of development . . .

insulation: withdrawal into a shell of passivity and isolation . . .

compensation: covering up of weakness by over-compensating in another area

and

acting out—reducing anxiety concerning forbidden desires by allowing their expression.

Colette had written that such defense mechanisms were "denials, distortions or falsifications of reality," and "functions which occur in the ego's attempt to deal with infantile anxieties," and that they "always operate unconsciously."

There were later notes under the heading "Psychosexual Development and Psychopathology," including a paraphrase of Theodor Reik's description of the father in Western society as one (Colette wrote) "who feels unconscious guilt for impregnating his wife and also unconsciously wants her to go through the pains of childbearing. He . . . goes through the tortures of hell when she is in labor to punish himself for these feelings."

The last words she would ever write dealt with psychological disorders which manifested themselves in the genital stage of development.

Her final notes included references to such categories as:

Obsessive Compulsive—obsessive collecting or neatness . . .

Melancholic—feel guilty about aggressive impulses . . .

Paranoid Schizo—have high I.Q. . . . .

Manic—megalomaniacal psychotic. Everyone likes them, they think. The world is great. Very busy, hyperactive.

Then she bought some milk for the morning and went home.

As they pressed forward, Pruett and Kearns turned up a hitherto undisclosed fact regarding Jeffrey MacDonald's conduct *after* the crimes. During the Article 32 hearing—as he'd stood accused of the murder of his wife and children—MacDonald, while confined to Bachelor Officers' Quarters, had entered into a sexual relationship with Bonnie Wood, a young civilian woman employed at Fort Bragg.

Aware of who he was—as was virtually everyone else at Fort Bragg—she had frequently seen him sunning himself on his front porch during lunch breaks. One day she offered him a tuna fish sandwich and sat with him in the sun. Soon, he was able to persuade the MPs assigned to guard his quarters to permit her access to his room.

When questioned, Miss Wood said she had been "frankly attracted" to MacDonald. "He's handsome, he has a great body, and he was the most exciting thing around."

She said she had visited him in his room throughout the summer and fall, and that the relationship "certainly wasn't a secret." After the charges against him were dropped, she said, he even took her out to dinner once, double-dating with one of his former escort officers.

"Probably," she said, "if you had asked me at the time, I would have said I was in love with him." She said she could not recall specifically how many times they'd had sex, but that it was more than once and less than "dozens of times."

Other than being a violation of the terms of his restriction, this conduct could not be construed as criminal on MacDonald's part, but, to Pruett and Kearns, given the circumstances, it did indicate a certain lack of sensitivity.

The reinvestigation, of course, involved more than just character evaluation. The physical evidence which had from the start been at the core of the case against MacDonald, but which, in Colonel Rock's opinion, had been insufficient to bring him to court-martial, was thoroughly reevaluated, and the quest for new evidence was renewed.

William Ivory lay on the floor beneath Kimberly MacDonald's bed, within the still-sealed premises of 544 Castle Drive. As he looked up at the underside of the mattress, he noticed that it was supported by slats. He removed the slats and sent them to the CID laboratory at Fort Gordon, where a microscopic examination of the wood proved conclusively that the club used in the murder of Colette and Kimberly had been sawed from one end of a piece of wood that had been used to make one of the mattress slats.

Pruett and Kearns sent other portions of the physical evidence to the FBI laboratory in Washington. Paul Stombaugh, chief of the chemistry division, put Jeffrey MacDonald's blue pajama top under a microscope. He examined the icepick holes in the garment. Altogether, there were forty-eight. Each was cylindrical and smooth-edged.

To Stombaugh this indicated that the holes had been made while the pajama top was stationary. There were no ragged edges, and none of the tearing that would have resulted had the icepick been thrust through the garment while it was in motion, as it would have been if it had been wrapped around the wrists of a man who was using it as a shield to ward off thrusts from an icepick during a struggle.

Stombaugh also discovered that the two paring knives—the Geneva Forge knife with the bent blade that had been found on the master bedroom floor (and that MacDonald had said he'd removed from his wife's chest) and the Old Hickory knife with the straight blade that had been found next to the icepick under the bush twenty feet from the back door—made distinctly different types of cuts in fabric.

The blade of the Geneva Forge knife was dull and made ragged cuts.

The blade of the Old Hickory knife was sharp and made smooth, clean cuts.

Microscopic examination of the cuts in the clothing worn by Colette, Kimberly, and Kristen MacDonald—as well as a study of the autopsy photographs which showed the knife wounds in the bodies—proved, to Stombaugh's satisfaction, that all three victims had been stabbed with the Old Hickory knife and none with the Geneva Forge knife.

In other words, the knife Jeffrey MacDonald claimed to have removed from the chest of his wife had never been in her chest. The only cuts consistent with the blade of the Geneva Forge knife were those in MacDonald's own pajama top, leading Pruett and Kearns to deduce that MacDonald might have used that knife to inflict at least the superficial wounds on himself, and that he had then fabricated the story of removing it from his wife's chest in case his fingerprints were found on the handle.

As for the wound which had caused the partial collapse of MacDonald's right lung—this was consistent
with the type of cut that could have been made by one of
the many disposable scalpel blades which MacDonald
had kept in his medical supply closet just outside the hall
bathroom—the bathroom in which drops of his blood
were found on the right side of the sink.

But it was Paul Stombaugh's third finding which was
the most significant of all: the single piece of circumstantial evidence which, in 1971, most clearly seemed to
contradict the story—or stories—that Jeffrey MacDonald had told.

When Stombaugh realigned the sections of the torn
blue pajama top to restore it to its original shape, certain
of the bloodstains on the garment—stains made with
Type A blood of Colette MacDonald—formed a perfect,
contiguous whole.

To Stombaugh, and to Pruett and Kearns, this proved
that at least some of Colette MacDonald's blood had
been on her husband's pajama top *before* it was torn.

This could not have happened if the top had been
torn either during MacDonald's struggle with four intruders in the living room, or when he had removed it
from his wrists after discovering his wife's bloody body
on the master bedroom floor.

It could have occurred, however, if MacDonald, while
wearing the still untorn blue pajama top, had struck his
wife—perhaps during an altercation in the master bedroom—causing her blood to stain it before she reached
out, in anger or self-defense or some combination of the
two, and ripped the garment down the front, tearing
loose the pocket and showering the rug with dozens of
fibers.

As the fight had worsened, the pajama top could have

become more heavily stained with Colette's blood. And it could have been to account for the presence of her blood in such quantity on his pajama top that MacDonald had laid it across her bloody chest prior to the arrival of the military police at 544 Castle Drive.

By the middle of March 1971, Pruett and Kearns began to receive support from a source they considered almost as unlikely as MacDonald himself: his father-in-law and staunchest defender, Freddy Kassab.

Upon receiving his copy of the Article 32 transcript in early February, Kassab had been transformed. The transcript became for him a universe. At times he seemed its sole inhabitant. He read by day, he read by night. He read with the pure and ferocious attention that a biblical scholar might bring to a first encounter with the Dead Sea Scrolls. For a full month he did little but read.

As he read, Kassab began to underline, then to make notes in the margin. Most of these notes were on the pages containing Jeffrey MacDonald's testimony. By mid-March, Kassab had read these pages a dozen times. His marginal notes had spilled beyond the borders of the transcript and had grown into lists compiled on separate sheets of paper—lists of inconsistencies, of contradictions, of elements of MacDonald's story which Kassab either knew from direct experience to be false or which, simply as a matter of logic, he found impossible to believe.

He then went back to the beginning and drew up an indexed summary of every statement contained in the 153 pages of MacDonald's testimony. Next to each which he disputed he made a note.

Page 8. He volunteered to go into the Army. *Jeff told Colette he had been drafted.*

Page 24. He got a blanket and went to sleep in the living room. *Jeff normally slept with a pillow. Why did he not have one on the living room couch?*

Page 25. He heard Colette scream, then say, "Help, help, Jeff. Why are they doing this to me?" and then repeated it at least once. *Colette could not have cried out after the severe stab wounds to her neck—the trachea was cut.*

Page 26. He heard Kimmy screaming, "Daddy, Daddy," over and over. *Going on the assumption that Colette and the children were attacked first, Kimmy sustained several severe skull fractures and according to medical testimony these were inflicted prior to the knife wounds. It would have been impossible for her to cry out as Jeff says she did after the massive blow which caused the severe skull fracture. Also, at the time he says he heard her cry out, the club with which she was attacked was in the living room.*

Page 29. He says he literally saw stars and was knocked back flat on the couch. He felt like he was blacking out. *The account of this first blow with the club would certainly lead one to believe that Jeff was temporarily stunned. If so, why did the assailants not pounce on him? Why wait for him to recuperate and start to sit up again? Also, the blunt trauma wounds to Colette and Kimmy were very severe, yet Jeff received only a slight blow to the forehead, in spite of the fact that he had just come out of a sound sleep and was in a semi-sitting position.*

Page 30. He described a "rain of blows" on his head, neck, and shoulders. *Yet he received only one wound that was over ¼ inch deep. It is very strange that Jeff did not receive any knife wounds to his head, neck & shoulders, since his attackers were standing over him, swinging. Also, a person cannot be stabbed 10–12 times in the abdomen while in a seated position & especially leaning forward, if the person stabbing him is standing. Furthermore, not one drop of his blood was found in the living room from any of the approximately 23 incised wounds he claims to have sustained. Also, with the profusion of blood in those bedrooms, if there were assailants they would have gotten much blood on their hands and clothing. Why then was there no blood in the living room, where the struggle was supposed to have occurred?*

Page 31. During the struggle, his hands were bound up in the pajama top. *How did the pajama top get pulled over his head or torn from the back so that it would end up around his arms and hands when there was no one behind him, and when the pajama top was torn down the front?*

Page 38. From master bedroom he went to Kim's room. He did not put lights on. *Why would a father—especially a doctor—going into a room where his child was so brutally injured not put the lights on to try to treat her?* He could see her chest and neck. *How could he when she was covered to the neck with a blanket?* He stopped mouth-to-mouth breathing because air was coming out of her chest. *Kim had no chest wounds. Also, how did Kimmy's blood get on Jeff's pj top since he did not have it on when he examined her in her bedroom? And why were both children found lying on their sides if Jeff gave them mouth-to-mouth?*

Page 51. He claims four blunt trauma injuries to his head. *The doctor who examined his head saw only the one contusion over his left eyebrow. That is the only one I saw at the hospital at approximately 2 p.m.*

Page 83. He thinks he wore gloves to wash dishes. *To the best of my memory, I have never seen Jeff wash a dish. Even if he did he is not the type who would put on rubber gloves to do them.*

Page 84. He gave Kristen a bottle. She cried while

Johnny Carson was on. He turned set down when he heard her crying. *Why didn't Colette hear her? On p. 90 he says Colette, not he, responded to cries from children 95% of time. Why not this time, especially since Kris cried loud enough for him to hear over TV?*

Page 104. *His description of his exact position on hall floor upon regaining consciousness is remarkable. Also, how do you fall up the stairs and around a corner? Also, there was no blood found on floor. Also, the attackers did not panic and run after attacking Jeff. They carried Kimmy back to her room in a sheet, put her in bed, covered her up, then took the sheet back to the master bedroom. They even took the time to write on the headboard. Why then was the attack on Jeff not more severe? Why was he not reattacked as he lay on the hall floor?*

Page 121. He said he was at the kitchen sink either before or after he used the kitchen phone. *If it was before, why was no blood found in the sink? If after, why was there no blood on the phone?*

Page 124. He didn't call the neighbors for help because "I didn't know them that well." *How well does one have to know someone to call for help when your whole family has been murdered? Besides, he knew them well enough to invite them for cocktails when we visited at Christmas.*

Page 140. Denies ever seeing the icepick and says it couldn't have come from his kitchen. *Mildred saw an icepick and used it during our Christmas visit.*

On a new sheet of paper, Kassab began to jot additional questions and notes as they occurred, often in the middle of the night, as he lay awake, going over in his mind what he had read.

One knife and the icepick were found side by side just outside the back door and the club just a few feet away. As-

sailants running from the scene of a crime could not all together at one time in the same place drop their weapons. . . .

The rubber gloves that were used were never found except for a few small pieces. They were either flushed down the toilet or taken away. Why would the assailants do this, if they left their weapons behind? . . .

How did Kim's blood get on the bathmat that was covering Colette?

Jeff's blood on the kitchen floor is very odd, since some time passed between the attack on him and the time he went into the kitchen. . . .

It was proven conclusively that Kimmy was first attacked in her mother's bedroom, which means she heard her mother scream, woke up and ran into the bedroom. Why then did Jeff not hear Colette's screams when his head and the sofa were only a few feet from Kimmy's head? . . .

With a minimum of 6 persons (Colette, Kim & 4 assailants) fighting in the master bedroom in the dark, how is it that nothing is disturbed?

It was no single thing; it was everything. By the third week of March, against his will—for, given the spontaneity and consistency of his support, what could he have been less willing to believe?—Freddy Kassab, like Grebner and Ivory and Shaw a year earlier and now Pruett and Kearns as well, began to understand why Jeffrey MacDonald was a suspect. He began to see why MacDonald had been accused. He began, even, to think the unthinkable: that for all its mistakes, the CID might have been right; and he, in his blind faith and ignorance, might have been as wrong as a man can be.

Kassab placed a call to Colonel Pruett. He described the doubts—the torments—caused by his study of the transcript. He said there were two things he would like to do.

First, he wanted to travel to Fayetteville to check for himself every newspaper file, hospital record, and police report that might support Jeffrey MacDonald's claim that on Friday, November 16, 1970, he had participated in the killing of one of the people responsible for the murder of his family.

Second, Kassab said, he wanted access to the MacDonald apartment. In the company of authorized investigators, he wanted to test for himself the words of Jeffrey MacDonald against the physical reality of 544 Castle Drive.

Kassab flew to Fayetteville on March 27. He was met by Pruett and Kearns. On the first day, they established to their own satisfaction—through a check of police and hospital records—that neither Jeffrey MacDonald nor any of his Green Beret friends had killed a young white hippie without a mustache—or anyone else—anywhere in Cumberland County, North Carolina, at any time during November of 1970.

On the second day, they went into the apartment.

Thirteen months earlier, Freddy Kassab had sat alone in the driver's seat of Jeffrey MacDonald's white convertible, staring at the exterior of 544 Castle Drive, watching a neighbor come out to the front steps in his pajamas to pick up his Sunday newspaper.

He now stepped through the front door for the first time since Christmas of 1969. As a crime scene under continuing investigation, the premises had remained sealed.

Kassab was not maudlin. He did not express horror.

He did not display symptoms of grief. Those responses were by now months behind him. He was at Fort Bragg, he felt, as a technician, with certain tasks to perform.

All day, Kassab made measurements. He took notes. He paced off distances, referring again and again to the lists he had brought with him and to photographs of the crime scene provided by Pruett and Kearns (refusing to look at only those which depicted the bodies still in place) and to the copy of Jeffrey MacDonald's Article 32 testimony which he kept securely tucked under his arm.

The club used in the murders was 31 inches long. Kassab was 5'10", the same height as the black intruder MacDonald had described. Standing between the coffee table and the couch, Kassab tried to raise a 31-inch stick over his head, as MacDonald had said the intruder had done with the club. It was not possible. The living room ceiling was too low.

MacDonald had said that between 3:40 and 3:42 A.M. on February 17, 1970—between his first and second phone calls, in other words—he had looked out the back door in an attempt to detect any signs of the intruders, had gone to the hall bathroom to check his own wounds and wash his hands, had looked into the hall closet for medical supplies, had returned to the master bedroom to check his wife again for signs of life, had administered mouth-to-mouth resuscitation, and had checked for pulses at various points on the bodies of both his daughters, and had then, possibly even crawling for a time, gone to the kitchen, possibly even washing his hands again at the kitchen sink.

Kassab first walked through, then walked through more quickly, then ran through the actions MacDonald had said he'd performed. No matter how cursory the checks for signs of life, no matter how perfunctory the look out the back door and the washing of hands, it was not possible. No one could have performed those functions within a two-minute time span.

In the afternoon, Kassab went upstairs. With the permission of the current tenants, he lay on a bed in what had been the bedroom of the sixteen-year-old babysitter, directly above the MacDonald living room. Pruett and Kearns carried on a conversation in normal tones. Kassab could clearly hear the sounds. How likely, then, was it that a sixteen-year-old girl would have remained asleep through the sounds of a struggle between a Green Beret officer and at least four intruders, in which the officer was wounded twenty-three times by club, knife, and ice-pick? No more likely, Kassab believed, than it would have been for greeting cards on the dining area table to have remained standing through it all.

As he stood on the steps that led from the hallway to the living room, Kassab stamped his foot. Greeting cards on the table fell down.

In the evening, Kassab went with Pruett and Kearns to eat dinner at the Fort Bragg Officers' Club. Then the three men returned to the apartment. Some of his work, Kassab knew, could only be done in the dark.

He turned on lights only in the kitchen and hall bathroom. According to MacDonald, these had been the only two lights lit at the time of the attack.

Kassab then lay down on the couch. His head was toward the front door and his feet were toward the hall, just as MacDonald's would have been.

Pruett and Kearns stood above him, crowding between the couch and coffee table. Kassab looked up.

Wide awake and already well acquainted with the two men, he could scarcely tell who they were.

In that light, Jeffrey MacDonald, who needed glasses to read or drive a car, and who would have been just emerging from sound sleep, could not possibly have seen sergeant's stripes on the sleeve of a black man's jacket, or a mustache on a white man's upper lip, or the glint of a blade, or the color of boots, or a flash of knee, or the color or length of anyone's hair.

Next, Kassab stood in the doorway to Kristen's bedroom. Except for the section of floor that had been removed in a futile attempt to preserve the bloody footprint, and except for the absence of the bloody sheets, the room was exactly as it had been when the two-year-old girl had bled to death from stab wounds in her heart on February 17, 1970.

The room was dark. Absolutely dark. It received no illumination whatsoever from the light in the hall bathroom adjacent to it.

Jeffrey MacDonald could not have stood in this doorway with this room in darkness and seen his younger daughter on the bed, covered in blood.

Yet MacDonald had insisted—against all logic—that he had not turned on the light. Kassab thought he now understood why: by his own account, MacDonald's hands would have been covered with blood as he had entered this room. He already had handled the bodies of Colette and Kimberly and he had not yet gone to the bathroom to wash. But no blood had been found near the light switch. In reconstructing a story which would fit the physical evidence as he had then understood it, MacDonald had had no choice but to say that he had allowed the room to remain in darkness.

Freddy Kassab stepped to the edge of the bed in

which Kristen MacDonald had died. He leaned over, just as Jeffrey MacDonald had said he'd leaned over in order to administer mouth-to-mouth resuscitation. Kassab still could see almost nothing. Just as, in the darkness, thirteen months earlier, Jeffrey MacDonald could not have seen blood bubbling from his younger daughter's chest.

Kassab remained in the apartment until midnight. By the time he emerged he was not only thinking the unthinkable, he was convinced.

With the conviction there came a strange, icy calm. At last, Kassab knew who his enemy was. The anguish, rage, and frustration that had consumed him for more than a year began to fuse into a new and quite different emotion: a commitment so powerful, so concentrated, that its essence would sustain him for the next decade and more as he carried forward a single-minded, obsessive, and often solitary crusade to see Jeffrey MacDonald convicted of murder and imprisoned.

"It won't be easy," Pruett told him as they stood on the front steps of 544 Castle Drive.

It was, Pruett explained, an entirely circumstantial case, and to make it more difficult, serious mistakes—as Kassab was well aware—had been made in the original investigation. The Army's own Investigating Officer had found the charges to be not even worthy of presentation at court-martial.

With Jeffrey MacDonald now a civilian, a new prosecution could be initiated only by the Justice Department, which, given the complexity of the case and the time that had already elapsed and the mistakes that had already been made, was not likely to give the matter a high priority. There was too much chance for failure, too little chance for success, no matter how persuasive Pruett's evidence might prove to be.

"It could be a long haul," the CID colonel said.

"That's all right," Kassab said, staring into the darkness. "I'm only fifty-two years old. Besides, I've got the patience of Job."

4

To Mildred Kassab, the shock that accompanied her acceptance of the probability that Jeffrey MacDonald had killed her daughter and grandchildren was not much less devastating than the initial trauma of their deaths.

At first, she had not wanted to listen to her husband when he had begun to speak of his suspicions. She had been through so much already. *This* would be too much to bear.

Even when he finally made her listen, she refused to believe. He would show her his underlinings and his marginal notes and his pages of questions and comments. He would sit for hours and attempt to explain what he considered the undeniable logic of it all. But still Mildred would not allow herself to be convinced.

She did, however, recall with an uneasiness that grew slowly into terror, the minutes that MacDonald had spent in her kitchen the previous December, glancing nervously about the room as he piled improbable detail upon detail during his recitation of his tale of revenge.

Thus, when Fred Kassab called from North Carolina

the first time in late March—to say that Jeff's story of killing one of the intruders was a lie—Mildred felt herself begin to waver.

When he called again the next day—having spent his somber hours inside 544 Castle Drive—to say that the truth was no longer in question, Mildred felt the full horror begin to overtake her.

"The first doubts," she wrote in her journal. "The refusal to believe. Too awful to contemplate. Colette's love for him and death at his hands. Alone with her hurt and pain and keeping it secret. . . . The guilt—not to have known her unhappiness. To have been selfishly going about my own affairs while she was alone and fearful. . . . Their last moments, filled with such pain and terror. I said, 'Wait until spring.' With the last blow he crushed her head like an eggshell."

In May, Jeffrey MacDonald took a vacation trip to Barbados. He sent a postcard to Freddy and Mildred Kassab.

"It's nice," he wrote. "Great to get out of NYC. But it's lonely."

The Kassabs did not reply.

In June, having not been offered a residency at the Yale University Medical Center and having found that his New York celebrity was starting to fade—and aware, also, that he was a prime suspect in a continuing murder investigation (though this was an awareness which he kept very much to himself)—MacDonald moved to California and took a job in the emergency room of St. Mary's Hospital in Long Beach, a job offered by a former Green Beret physician from Fort Bragg.

Soon after his arrival, he sent his former in-laws a change-of-address card.

"Super busy," he scrawled at the bottom. "No news. Will write."

Once convinced of the Kassabs' willingness to accept the results of the reinvestigation, Pruett and Kearns began to share information with them. The worst day, for Mildred, was the Saturday in June when Pruett and Kearns arrived at the Kassab home to inform them that Helena Stoeckley had been effectively eliminated as a suspect.

While swimming in the backyard pool that Colette had never seen, Pruett and Kearns also told the Kassabs of Jeffrey MacDonald's series of infidelities.

For Mildred, especially, this news carried a special sting. "Because then," she said, "I knew that not only had he killed her: he hadn't even been a decent husband to her while she was alive."

Now that they were receptive to information which cast an unflattering light upon their former son-in-law, the Kassabs found that there was no shortage of it about. Most had to do with infidelity. Acquaintances informed them that during the summer of 1964—the first summer after the birth of Kimberly—MacDonald, while spending the week at his construction job on Montauk Point, had engaged in an affair with a secretary at the company by which he was employed.

Even more distressing to the Kassabs were stories that MacDonald had maintained a relationship with his former high school girlfriend, Penny Wells, even after his marriage to Colette.

Mildred now recalled an evening during June of 1969—just weeks before MacDonald had left for Fort Sam Houston. He and his brother and sister were giving a party to celebrate their mother's fiftieth birthday, and the Kassabs had stopped by briefly to pay their respects.

"Penny Wells had been invited," Mildred wrote in her journal. "Colette pointed her out to me and asked if I thought she was pretty. After we left, all the gifts were piled up and Jeff's mother asked Penny to open them and read off the cards. Colette stood by, and one of her friends later told me that she later went inside and cried in embarrassment and hurt."

An acquaintance told the Kassabs that several months later, Jeff, in full Green Beret uniform, had been observed embracing Penny Wells on the Patchogue train station platform. This was in November of 1969—a time that coincided with MacDonald's emergency home leave.

If this were true, and if it were true also—as Pruett and Kearns found it to be—that by February of 1970, Miss Wells had taken an apartment in New York City, then MacDonald's sudden desire to accompany the Fort Bragg boxing team on its trip, not to Russia, as he had told Colette (though having her think he was incommunicado behind the Iron Curtain would both relieve him of any responsibility for maintaining contact with her, and make the venture seem more of a "once-in-a-lifetime" opportunity than would have been a trip to Trenton, New Jersey), but to tournament sites that would put him within easy striking distance of his old high school flame, became much more understandable.

At home, in silence, and with even sharper, more insightful pain, Mildred Kassab read and reread the dozens of letters that Colette had written to her. In particular, she focused on the letters Colette had written from Chicago during Jeff's years at medical school—years that had apparently been filled with hope and joy.

Oh, by the way, I forgot to mention it on the phone but if Freddy really meant it about letting Jeff use his jacket this winter, it would really come in handy, I think. I have spoken to some natives and they say that it gets unbearably cold . . .

Kim's favorite game right now is really adorable. You know the way Jeff and I blow on her stomach and make that sound? Well, she has learned to do it now, too. Not on me, but on Jeff because he has his shirt off. She stands on his lap and leans down and blows on his chest and makes a little teeny sound and then looks up and laughs . . .

Poor Jeff has so much work. Yesterday he had an exam for which he had been staying up until 4 A.M. every morning. Unfortunately, it was not a hard test the way it was promised to be and he wasn't able to show what he really knew . . .

Freddy, I'm really sorry that I didn't get to speak to you on the phone but wait until we get home for Christmas—you won't be able to shut me up. And wait until Kim sits on your lap and pulls herself up by your ears. That will be only the beginning . . .

As you can guess, things are pretty rough right now, financially. We haven't paid our January rent yet so Jeff went looking for part-time jobs the other day. I really hate to see him work when he needs the

time for studying, but other than money problems ev-
erything is fine. Luckily, our dispositions are still
good. I guess because we feel that it isn't always going
to be this way . . .

Colette's last letter from Chicago had been written in
February of 1968, at the start of her husband's final semester in medical school and two years before she and
her children would be murdered.

Now that Jeff is almost a doctor, he has to wear his
white jacket to class and to the hospital. You should
see him, he looks really great—very handsome and
very professional.

Tomorrow he gives his first examination to a pa-
tient. The patient is told only that a doctor will be in
to see him and Jeff introduces himself as Dr. Mac-
Donald and is on his own from there on. Of course,
he has been practicing on me for a week, and I have
been percussed (when they thump you to find out
where and how large your organs are) and palpated
for masses and to find rigidity of muscles, symmetry
of the two sides, etc. and auscultated (listened to) un-
til I am sore. I'm really glad I'm not taking classes
this semester because it is a full time job being a pa-
tient!

Yesterday, we took Kim to the zoo. What an expe-
rience! As you can imagine, she was terrifically ex-
cited. I got a little worried because she was so excited
that she could hardly breathe (and I'm not exagger-
ating). She spent most of the time sitting on Jeff's
shoulders—or I should say jumping on his shoulders.
She was all exclamations and panting and jumping
and pointing. We took some bread along with us to

feed the animals and she almost went crazy with delight when she was able to feed the giraffe and the deer. The giraffe was the biggest thrill of all. Jeff held her up and the giraffe held out her tongue until Kim put it on and then ate it. (We took a few pictures of that!) . . .

Meanwhile, your grandchild Kristen is a DEVIL!! As you know, she didn't have any teeth . . . up until last week when she got 2 together. We were all up for 3 nights to get her through the trauma. Now she is a toughy and goes growling around the house like a baby panther.

She and Kim have been having so much fun playing together lately. They both play peek-a-boo and then they roll across the floor trying to catch each other. It's really a great feeling hearing your own kids laughing and having fun with each other.

*   *   *

During the summer of 1971, Mildred Kassab became aware of a lump in her breast. She told no one about it and did not seek medical attention, not even when it began to grow.

She referred, in her journal, to her "final acceptance of the truth and subsequent desire to just die. Stop hurting. Stop feeling. Hugging my growing cancer to myself, keeping it secret for my release."

But then, as she watched her husband grow stronger and more determined day by day, she realized the selfishness of her desire. She came to recognize, she wrote, "the need for action and retaliation." Colette had been her only daughter. It seemed not so much to expect of herself that she would assist her husband on his relentless quest for justice.

In October, she underwent surgery and began a series

of radiation treatments. In November, Jeffrey MacDonald returned from California for a brief visit to family and friends. He did not pay a social call on the Kassabs. Since the change of address card, they'd had no communication of any kind with him.

Freddy, in particular, had been growing increasingly restive through the fall. Believing what he now believed—and witnessing, daily, the agonies that his wife was enduring—it galled him immeasurably to think of MacDonald as a free man, enjoying the fruits of his new bachelor life in Southern California.

Aware that the investigation was still in progress, Kassab had vowed to himself that he would not do or say anything that would indicate prematurely to MacDonald just how much evidence the CID was assembling, but upon learning of the Eastern trip, Kassab was unable to contain his irritation entirely. He broke silence long enough to write MacDonald a letter: ·

> We have just been told by a friend that you were here on Long Island a few weeks ago. If this is so, I think you should be thoroughly ashamed of yourself for not at least calling us on the telephone.
>
> For one solid year we called you almost daily and did everything human beings can do to help you. In return, we received a total of two phone calls from you, one to stop me from coming to Fort Bragg to get a copy of the transcript.
>
> I have just inquired from both the Army and the FBI and find that you have never asked for any information on the progress of the investigation to find the murderers. Perhaps you would like to push the whole thing behind you. We can't & won't until whoever did this is punished.

As vague as that wording was, it seemed to make Jeffrey MacDonald uneasy. His tale of having killed one of the intruders obviously had not sufficed. The Kassabs *still* were not willing to forget. He replied to Kassab's letter immediately, and with considerable indignation:

I am answering your incredibly rude, illogical and factually wrong letter because I know deep down that the only reason you wrote it was because you did love Colette, Kim and Kristy (& hopefully me) so much. That love would not be apparent from your letter and I can only hope it is your frustration at not seeing justice done that propels you to write such trash.

I was in LI several weeks ago for 2 days (half day traveling to & from airport, half day at the graves, one day with mother/family/supposed friends and relatives).

I have been in LI on several occasions in the last 3 months, usually not to see my family but to continue work on finding 3 (or possible 4, 1 more might be added according to current stories in hippie family #2 in N.C.) fugitives. I find I accomplish more when less people know I'm around.

I must say, your apparent faith in Army investigators is puzzling, to say the least, when it is apparent to even the most casual observer that 1) usually they are incompetent if not criminal in nature, and 2) if not incompetent they are carefully picked to follow the Army line.

This is true in every case currently in the public eye, just as it was in our case. They are either incredibly inept or they are out to protect the Army. I have come to my final decision in this matter—to believe anything else is sheer refusal to face facts.

I am sorry I didn't call or see you this last visit. I truly tried, but every time I tried to leave my mother's apt. some other idiot would arrive. I didn't call because I felt you would be annoyed/hurt, if I called but didn't have time to come over.

If you want me to be blatantly honest, another reason I have hesitated seeing you more frequently is because I live/relive/re-relive the case day & night. I have to consciously try to think of other things to maintain my sanity. At times, free time is almost worse than being guarded in my room—in my room I would bitch more directly about the Army, but free I run around in circles, always thinking of the case & trying to do several things at once.

I find being with you and Mildred, as the most direct links to Colette, the most painful experience I have except reviewing my pictures & slides. It destroys me for several days and I've found it better to keep my own defenses up by being alone.

I cannot discuss Colette & Kim & Kris easily or well because they were everything to me, and when I am with you I find myself trying to do that. Do you see what I am trying to say?

As for the FBI & Army, that is an absolute lie that I haven't asked for information. I have been turned down on numerous occasions by both the FBI/CID (including those investigators you liked so well last spring) and Justice Dept. for any info on the case.

It is obvious the only way for justice to be met is for me to do it. I am doing it, have been doing it (4 trips to N.C. & Florida in last three months) and will continue to do it as long as my strength holds up (broken hand last trip, $2,000 spent).

The only legit help I foresee is private eye type, most

of which I have found is no more competent than lo-
cal cops. My next major goal is a large sum of money
(via an advance from a publisher for this purpose).
The first chapter of my book has been written, the out-
line is done, and still we are only dickering with pub-
lishers. They just won't come across fast.

I would like to push the whole thing behind me—
wouldn't anyone? I'd give anything to wake up and
find it all a bad dream and have my life & house
filled again with Colette, Kim & Kristy.

The only difference between you and I is that I
don't think you see the fact that justice will not bring
back my family. I want revenge, preferably brutal re-
venge—I don't care about justice any more. There is
no justice, in case you haven't noticed. You act as
though you are on a noble cause. I think the cause is
ugly, brutal, but necessary. I will do it—I have done
some (one-fourth or one-fifth of it). Don't try to
bullshit me about not caring. Our aim is the same—
don't let frustration drive you down. I have been so
frustrated at times in the last year you wouldn't be-
lieve it.

I'm sorry if this letter is too honest—just remember
it is honest. I care not for people's feelings any more.
If and when revenge becomes complete, I foresee such
pain at the full realization that it was all useless be-
cause my 3 girls are not back that life will not be
worthwhile. Meanwhile, try to remember the loss is,
for me, at least as great as your loss.

The Kassabs had not seen Jeffrey MacDonald's
mother since April of 1971 when she had come by their
house to deliver some slides of Colette and the children
which they had requested, and to tell them that Jeff was

no longer able to visit the cemetery: it was simply too upsetting for him.

Early on the evening of February 15, 1972, however, she paid them a surprise visit. She brought with her a small floral arrangement and said she had just heard that Mildred had undergone surgery.

"She was her usual buoyant, bouncy self," Mildred would later recall. "You know, 'Hey, kid, how are you? You're looking great!' That sort of thing. Actually, I looked pretty horrible at the time."

The Kassabs offered her a drink, which she accepted. Then Freddy found himself unable to contain his true feelings. He felt compelled, as he put it later, "to give her a few facts of life."

For the next two hours, Kassab explained, in explicit and extensive detail, what it was he had become convinced of and what it was that had led him to his conclusion—the conclusion being that Dorothy MacDonald's son had murdered his own wife and children.

"She didn't say a word," Kassab recalled later. "Not one word. For two hours she just sat there in silence with that one drink in front of her. She didn't get mad, she didn't get angry, she didn't dispute anything I said—and believe me, I said it all—she just sat there. When I had finished she stood up and said, 'Well, I think I'll go home.' That was it. That was the last time we ever spoke to her."

Months later—it was in fact in early summer—the Kassabs found notes on the graves of Colette, Kimberly, and Kristen. The notes were in the handwriting of Dorothy MacDonald. They said:

> *Dearest Colette—You were every inch a woman. God forgive me for not telling you this but I always respected you. All my love, Mom.*

*Dearest Kim—You were more precious to me than
life itself. God keep you from any more pain. I love
you, Nana.*

*Dearest Kristy—You were always the toughie.
May your spirit endure. Love you, Nana.*

The Kassabs turned the notes over to Pruett and
Kearns. Eventually, Dorothy MacDonald moved to
Southern California, where she bought a small house
only ten minutes from her son's condominium.

Having pursued leads in 32 states, Vietnam, Okinawa,
Germany, the Canal Zone, and Puerto Rico, and having
conducted dozens of new tests at the crime scene, and
having obtained and analyzed 34 additional laboratory
reports, and having interviewed 699 people, and having
obtained sworn statements from 151, and having administered polygraph tests to everyone whose testimony was
considered directly relevant—except Jeffrey MacDonald,
who refused to undergo such an examination—Colonel
Pruett's reinvestigation team completed its inquiry into
the MacDonald murders on December 6, 1971.

5

In early 1972, as CID agent Kearns worked on a report of the reinvestigation designed for submission to the Justice Department, other members of his organization kept Jeffrey MacDonald under surveillance.

A report filed on January 17 stated that "MacDonald enjoys the reputation of being a very professional doctor. He is constantly observed with latest medical journals and other associated literature, apparently for purposes of keeping abreast of all latest medical findings and techniques. His professional attitude toward his patients, both adult and minors, is above reproach.

"MacDonald is a conservatively 'mod' dresser. Although he has attended a few known social gatherings with a female acquaintance, he has not given any indication of being seriously involved with any particular woman. He is considered a moderate drinker and not a real 'swinger.'

"MacDonald has indicated he is interested in outdoor sports, fishing, hunting, skin diving, and strenuous body contact sports such as football.

"The apartment occupied by MacDonald is located in an exclusive area of Huntington Beach. Due to the covert nature of the surveillance, no direct inquiry could be made as to the monthly rental. The physical layout of the condominium is such that a surveillance of the apartment occupied by MacDonald is impossible without renting or otherwise occupying an adjoining apartment.

"Efforts to establish credit rating and bank account balance were halted when it was learned that recent court rulings in the state of California require that the individual concerned will be notified when an investigative agency has made an inquiry, and the agency must be identified to the concerned individual.

"In accordance with original instructions, no direct inquiries were made. The major portion of information obtained was the result of indirect inquiry made through various police agencies in this area. This was done to prevent insofar as possible revealing the US Army CID's interest in MacDonald's activities since his arrival in this area, and to preclude any publicity which might reflect unfavorably on the US Army."

On June 1, 1972, the 3,000-page CID reinvestigation report was delivered to the Department of Justice. Its conclusions were that all evidence compiled pointed clearly toward the guilt of Jeffrey MacDonald.

For thirty days, a group of Justice Department attorneys reviewed the report. It was then sent to Warren H. Coolidge, U.S. Attorney for the Eastern District of North Carolina. In early August, Freddy Kassab called Coolidge to inquire about the status of the prosecution. He did not tape the telephone call, but was sufficiently disturbed by Coolidge's attitude to write to him on August 9.

Since our phone conversation on Monday, I have been quite worried that you would decide not to proceed with the MacDonald case.

It has always been my impression that everyone connected with the case, both in the Army and the Justice Dept., was firmly convinced that Jeff MacDonald was guilty, including yourself. I do not understand what has been deducted from the case in the last two years. My understanding is that evidence (circumstantial as it may be) has been added.

I feel that I must be frank and straightforward with you and tell you of my plans should you decide not to proceed with the case. I intend to swear out a complaint against Jeff and have a Federal judge issue a warrant for his arrest, charging three counts of murder.

Our lives (my wife's and mine) ended on the day that our daughter and grandchildren were murdered and neither of us would allow the man we think committed the crime to walk around free. That would be asking too much of us.

The most important factor in this case is that everyone who has looked at it is firmly convinced that Jeff is guilty. Therefore, regardless of the outcome, the case must come to trial.

On September 8, however, Coolidge notified the Justice Department that having completed his consideration of the CID report, he had decided not to recommend prosecution. (There had been too many mistakes made in the original investigation; the evidence, much stronger now than it had been at the Article 32 hearing, remained circumstantial; the chances for obtaining a conviction appeared too slim to justify the effort and expense of proceeding.) The MacDonald file was returned to Washington.

On September 25, Kassab wrote to Assistant Attorney General Henry Petersen asking what future action was intended, and requesting a meeting. On October 6, he was notified by Carl W. Belcher, chief of the general crimes section of the Justice Department, that while the department intended to "thoroughly review this entire record in an effort to arrive at a proper prosecutive judgement thereon," it was felt that a meeting with Kassab would serve no useful purpose.

On October 14, Kassab responded with a passionate argument for prosecution which he concluded by saying:

> *My wife and I have only one purpose in life and that is to see a successful prosecution. . . .*
>
> *No one has studied this case as much as I have. I live with it night and day. No one was as convinced of MacDonald's innocence as I until I read the transcript of the pretrial hearing. . . . After two years and eight months of investigation and reviews we don't think we are being unreasonable in wanting that the case now go forward. This is what we want done, what must be done, and the guilty party punished.*

On October 25, Kassab wrote to inform Belcher that he had conducted interviews with four people in Patchogue in regard to Jeffrey MacDonald's extramarital involvement with Penny Wells and that he had forwarded tapes of those interviews to the CID in Washington. "The material," he wrote, "although not startling in nature, shows that there is a definite basis for this particular lead and does add considerable information."

Belcher replied on November 7 that, "we share your

concern over this matter and it is receiving the special attention here that all agree it merits."

On December 4, Kassab wrote again to Henry Petersen, this time, after noting the continued lack of action, stating that if the Justice Department refused to resolve the case the Kassabs would go to the media and "expose the whole sordid story."

The Kassabs did not receive an immediate reply, but they did receive a Christmas card from Jeffrey MacDonald. The printed message said:

> It is a time
> for memories and nostalgia
> a time for being touched
> by that spirit of love
> that is above us all
>
> A time for remembering
> the people and things
> that carry us through
> the hard times
> and the sadness
>
> A time
>   for remembering
>   one such as you . . .

Enclosed with the card was a handwritten note:

Dear Folks—

I try to get through these vacations by working hard—it helps somewhat but it is a difficult time. I

*hope you are well. I'm sure you don't want to hear
senseless chatter about my job, etc. so I will just say
I'm getting by. California is a better place for me
than NY.*

My best to all and I hope the New Year is better.

MacDonald had sent that card shortly after returning
from Tahiti, where he had taken a new girlfriend on vacation.

On January 30, 1973, Freddy Kassab wrote to the Attorney General of the United States stating that, in light
of the Justice Department's unwillingness to initiate a
prosecution, he intended to take the case against Mac-
Donald to the public.

The next day, Kassab granted an extensive interview
to a *Newsday* reporter named Bob Keeler. On Friday,
February 2, Keeler's story appeared under the headline
PARENTS LIVE TO SEE A KILLER CAUGHT.

"For Freddy and Mildred Kassab," Keeler wrote, "life
has narrowed to two purposes: keeping fresh flowers on
the graves of their daughter and grandchildren and pushing the government to find out who killed them.

"From the moment MacDonald was named as a suspect in the case, Kassab was his staunchest supporter. . . .
But now, after months of carefully reading and rereading
the 2,000-page transcript of a lengthy Army hearing and
after an eight-hour visit to the still-sealed house at Fort
Bragg, Kassab has doubts."

The story described the Army's reinvestigation of the
case and Kassab's futile efforts to persuade the Justice
Department to prosecute.

"We live this," Kassab had told Keeler. "This comes
to me before eating, before making a living, before any-

396   *JOE McGINNISS*

thing else. I'm having a hard time making a living because I can't concentrate on my work. We have one
object in mind and that is to bring this case to fruition. It
has to be brought to trial."

Mildred Kassab was quoted as saying, "We haven't
had any guests in the house since this happened. We
don't entertain. We don't go out anywhere. What do
you talk about? Do you pretend to enjoy a card game?
There isn't anything in the world that interests me other
than getting whoever killed her. As long as this is unsolved, they're dead, but it's living yet. It's living just as
much as it did the day after."

From his Huntington Beach condominium, Jeffrey
MacDonald said, "I really don't want to make any comments. Life has been hard enough to reestablish without
getting back into the papers. Freddy is upset because
there hasn't been anyone brought to justice. He's kind
of at his wits' end. There's no one who's more upset
than I am."

On February 15, Carl W. Belcher wrote to Kassab, saying, "The problem remains one of insuring that when
and if we initiate a prosecution, the jury will receive sufficient facts to render an informed and just verdict. In
fairness to those immediately concerned and to the public, we must and will be as thorough and objective as
possible in arriving at a prosecutive judgment on the
matter."

To Kassab, this still seemed an inadequate response,
and in early March he supplied information to the New
York *Daily News* which resulted in a March 16 story
headlined REOPEN MURDER CASE INVOLVING EX-ARMY
DOC.

The *Daily News* story, quoting "highly placed sources

in the Justice Department," said "new evidence has been uncovered in the case and a decision on whether to submit the matter to a federal grand jury will be made within two to five weeks."

That story—inaccurate though it turned out to be—prompted a flurry of action from a number of quarters. First, Jeffrey MacDonald tried to reach former congressman and former supporter Allard Lowenstein, with whom he had broken off contact two years earlier. Lowenstein, without returning MacDonald's call, contacted Freddy Kassab, at whose request he had first become involved in the case. Kassab recorded the conversation.

"I think it might be helpful if we could talk for a few minutes," Lowenstein said, "because I had a call the other day from Jeff, and I'm—I've sort of felt reluctant to be involved in things for the past year, and before I did or didn't do anything about this call I wanted to find out what your thinking was."

For the next several minutes Kassab described the process by which he had gone from believing in MacDonald's innocence to having become convinced of his guilt.

"All right," Lowenstein said. "Then you ended up a year later where I ended up a year before, when I got out of it."

"Yeah." This news was a total surprise to Freddy. He had no idea that the congressman had considered Jeff anything but the victim of a miscarriage of justice.

"You see," Lowenstein continued, "as I looked further into this and discovered things, my decision was a very tough one. I decided I could not press further in line with the original reason that you had come to see me. And I had a very tough soul-searching with, who had appointed me God to go beyond that? And I finally decided that I would simply get out of it entirely, and that's why you haven't heard from me in a long time."

"What you do is your business," Kassab said, "but I would strongly advise not being involved at this point. I don't have much doubt that there's going to be an indictment."

"Well," Lowenstein said, "I came to that conclusion two years ago. The problem I had at that point was the question of what, if anything, could be done, with the Army being as inept as it was. But then I had a further very difficult problem, which was that I was in a lawyer-client relationship with Jeff—if I was in any relationship—since I was no longer in Congress by then. I had to view an ethical problem from that end.

"So I decided at that point that the best thing I could do was to pull out, which I did.

"Now what's brought the whole thing up again is that Jeff called me. I guess you knew that."

"No. Well, I would assume he would have called a lot of people," Freddy replied.

"I guess there's no need to tell you a lot of the things that were brought to my attention which led me to my conclusion. Because, you see, I reached my conclusion independently of the people that you're talking about, and I did so on the basis of—I suppose cerebration is the only thing I can say: that is, using my head as I got pieces put together—questions that I raised and places that I went to.

"But I still am conflicted in one moral situation, and that is that if—and I don't know how to say this without sounding so unsure of the direction I should go as to make myself sound like Hamlet, but I—he's entitled to a lawyer."

"Absolutely."

"I don't know what I would do if it went back to his wanting me to be his lawyer. That's one reason I'm unsure I should even discuss this thing with anybody. But I've decided in my own mind that I don't want to be his lawyer. Of course, he hasn't asked me, but he told me at one point—of course he tells anybody anything, so I don't know what it meant—but he was very negative about Segal.

"I mean, this was at the point when I was involved in it, which is when we were trying to get him out of the Army and all the rest of that stuff."

"Yeah, I was embarrassed, though," Kassab said, "the way he was treating you when, you know, when you were waiting to see him in Washington and he didn't make it until two weeks later—he had other things to do, and things like that."

"Oh, it was bad," Lowenstein said. "But at the time we assumed it was disorientation. You know, you give the benefit of the doubt. And after a while you discover that it's not that—it is orientation, not disorientation. Which is a very different business.

"Well, when you learn that, of course, that also computes into what you do, and, ah—anyway, later, I put him in touch with two guys from North Carolina, Wade and Roger Smith, who are very close friends of mine and are the best lawyers in the state for this kind of a case. And those two guys and I—we sat down and went over this whole thing together. And—this conversation now—I really want this conversation to remain between us, so it's the type of situation where no one even knows we had this conversation—but when I talked to the Smiths I said, 'I want to be honest with you.' I said, 'My feeling about the situation is they tried to frame him and the whole thing was handled so badly and so outrageously that everything I've done and said about it so far I stand by.

"'But I also want to tell you that if we go into it any further you should understand that it's my view that—handled correctly—it's not a question of innocence. It's a question of, ah, establishing a defense, which is a very different business.'

"I said, 'I don't know if you're interested in doing that. I don't know if I am. I got into this out of the sense of injustice being done to him. Whether now I want to get into this in a game of criminal defense, I don't know.'

"So we talked about this and from the beginning I was very honest with them about it, and they decided that from their point of view they would be willing to proceed, but that they wanted to be sure they were dealt with honestly by him. In other words, that's their standard of ethics, and of course in part why they're as good as they are.

"At that point I told Jeff about them and about myself. I said, 'The decision as to whether you want us to proceed and how you want us to proceed depends on what you feel.' And I said, 'I think you should understand at this point I'm no longer—I certainly can't go around screaming that you've been treated unfairly. That's now finished.'

"And I said, 'As far as I'm concerned, if you want help in this situation then I want to talk to you about what happened and I want to talk to you about why, and I want to talk to you about all the things I've got to talk to you about and make a decision on how to proceed from there. There may be circumstances,' and so forth and so on.

"I didn't say to him I thought he was guilty, but it was certainly clear from that conversation that I was no longer saying, well, what I first—well—when you and I first talked.

"Now at that point he decided it would be better for him if the thing was not handled by any of us, which of course was the option I'd given him. So he at that point withdrew. When I said I withdrew, it was reciprocal.

"Now what puzzles me is why he called the other day, because—knowing what he knows about what I felt two years ago—I mean, I don't know why he's calling me and I have not returned his call yet."

"Well," said Kassab, "he's calling you for information. Basically, what he's looking for, I would assume, is to find out if you know anything that's going on in Washington. He called you because he's worried, and this was my purpose in doing what I did. He knows I'm behind it because he knows how adamant I am. I mean, I'm a milksop, basically, about almost anything in the world. I've always been. Except when I get my back to the wall, like in this case, where Colette, who was as dear to me as—aah, I'll never rest. Never. This thing has got to be brought to some kind of a termination."

"Sure," said Lowenstein. "Well, okay, we're clear then. And it's a relief to know that we arrived at the same thing, even if not at the same time."

Lowenstein did not return MacDonald's call.

Two days later, Jeffrey MacDonald called Kassab. It was the first time the two men had spoken since MacDonald had moved to California. Kassab's recording device was working imperfectly, but it did pick up the sound of a raised voice, and MacDonald's voice was raised frequently, particularly when Kassab mentioned his awareness of the fact that MacDonald had enjoyed sexual relations in his BOQ room during the Article 32 hearing.

"You believe that, Fred?" MacDonald shouted. "Because the CID told you it was true?"

"Absolutely."

"Is that what you're telling me?!" There was a quality of raw fury in MacDonald's voice that Kassab had never heard before.

"I'm telling you, Jeff. I've got a copy here of an affidavit from the girl."

"Oh, Fred. I'm really disgusted. You'll believe anything. You'll grasp at any straw. You could have affidavits from *fourteen* people. Do you know how many telephone calls I got while I was at Fort Bragg, Fred? I got them from Minnesota and Chicago and Los Angeles and everywhere else on earth. Every person in the world called me. If you think that affidavit means anything, you're crazy! I have no idea who you're talking about, Freddy, or what you're talking about, but if you're telling me I slept with a girl in my room every night that's just the most absurd, insane comment—*I hope you put that out, Fred!*" MacDonald screamed. "I hope you put that out sometime! I just hope you bring that out! Because if you have the—the *audacity* to believe something like that, then you deserve everything you get!"

"Jeff, I talked to the girl."

"*I don't care, Freddy!* I talk to a lot of people! I can get an affidavit from anyone, saying almost anything, if you put a little pressure and money in the right place.

"You talked to the girl," MacDonald continued, his voice dripping with scorn. "*What the hell does that mean?!* I got *marriage proposals* while I was being held in my room, the supposed murderer of my family. Now what kind of people do you think there are in the world?

"You know, for a year you tell me that you have undying backing for me, and what not. And all of a sudden I turn around and while I'm still trying to recover—"

"Do you think for one minute," Kassab interrupted, "that you hurt more than Mildred does?"

"Ah, yeah! I think I do, Fred. You know, I don't have to take this anymore! If you think I'm going to bare my soul to people like you after what I have gone through, you've got another think coming. But you ought to make sure of your facts first, because your facts are wrong. You're hurting innocent people. You're making yourself into a martyr, Freddy. You just won't let go."

"Time will tell, Jeff," Kassab said.

"Time *will* tell!" MacDonald shouted. "But you ought to have a little more compassion for the one who's suffered the most!"

The next day—March 22, 1973—aware, perhaps, that his telephone call had further alienated a person who was capable of doing him serious harm, MacDonald wrote, for the last time, to Mildred Kassab:

> *I am sorry to be writing to you under such distress-ing circumstances (again)—needless to say the recent press, TV and radio inquiries have again ruined any chance I had for some small measure of privacy and/ or sanity. Knowing the source of the publicity (NY Daily News, of all cheap places, via Freddy of course) only adds to my distress.*
>
> *I don't wish to re-discuss the whole case again and again—I live it all the time—but please let me say several things to you—they are true, I mean them, and I hope you reflect upon them.*
>
> *The first is that I was a good husband and father. Colette and I shared a love that was truly great—few*

people ever have the fun and contentment we had to-gether.

The second thing is that I did not commit any crimes (or sins)—that is, I did not have any part in the murders on Fort Bragg. Believe what you will, but that is the only truth—I loved Colette, Kim and Kris with all my heart. The garbage and crap that keeps coming up does not mean that I was involved in the killings.

There are some confusing aspects to the case—none are as confused as me when you ask, "Why?"—but please don't decide that because there are confusing things that I must be guilty.

I did tell Fred some things after I left the Army that were not 100% true—it (these things) were partly true—I magnified them to (I guess) help my own feelings of inadequacy and also I hoped to isolate myself with those comments and allow my mental status to clear.

Unfortunately, Fred has misread the importance of those comments—he is striking out in any direction, willing to hurt anyone & everyone with no thought of what is important and what is not important.

I tried to find solutions, could not, and also discovered that no matter what happened Colette was not coming back. So I moved out here and began working for a living, giving up the career Colette and I had hoped for at Yale.

Mildred—I was going to go on & on, but I don't think it is any use. The letter doesn't read well—I guess I never do communicate well, except in medicine.

I truly hope those absurd tales Fred told me on the

*phone about "girls" are daydreams—they certainly
are not true facts—I never lied to you about extramarital affairs—I never had an affair, but I did see
(date, sleep with) a very rare girl away from home—
the rest is complete garbage. No one else ever mattered to me except Colette.*

*I was going to write to Fred tonight also but it
seems extraneous. My mind is really in a turmoil
again. Please take care of yourself. I do love you—I
know I don't exhibit it well but even my mother com-
plains of that.*

*I love Fred also—I do feel extremely tense and
anxious and more than mildly hurt about him showing transcripts and letters and phone calls to any
creep who will listen—we all express our grief in different ways, and I think Fred feels I'm wrong because
I don't show it exactly like him.*

*If there was a legitimate point to be gained, fine,
but the record is clear now—the 2nd (CID again, if
you remember) investigation nicely dovetailed with
the first fiasco, except it made it even clearer that I
was not involved in the crimes.*

*Do I now have to spend another year in purgatory
for 50 or 100 thousand dollars, to finally be left with
memories of my departed family?* What price do I
have to pay to be left to exist?

*Try to tell Fred that I'm in agony also. I just don't
think shouting at the press will solve* anything *at this
stage. I hope your health is good.*

Love,
Jeff

The hopes of Freddy Kassab and the fears of Jeffrey
MacDonald notwithstanding, the Justice Department

was not about to convene a grand jury. The only action that was taken in April of 1973 was that the entire case file was sent back to Raleigh, North Carolina, for review by the new U.S. Attorney for the Eastern District, Thomas MacNamara.

Kassab returned to his typewriter and for the next nine months peppered Henry Petersen, Carl Belcher, and the Attorney General himself with letters, refusing to be placated by replies which assured him that work was continuing but that the case was a difficult one. Finally, on January 10, 1974, Carl Belcher wrote to Kassab. He said:

> *We have completed an independent review of the investigatory files in this case and have concluded that the evidence currently available is insufficient to warrant prosecution at this time. However, I have requested the Criminal Investigation Command of the United States Army to conduct additional investigation in an effort to develop further evidence. We will reassess our position regarding the feasibility of prosecution upon the receipt and evaluation of any additional evidence.*
>
> *I hope you appreciate that the Department of Justice shares your interest in this case and that we seek only to serve the interests of justice.*

Thus, a year and a half after having received the CID's report of its year-long reinvestigation of a case that had originally been investigated in the late winter and spring of 1970, the Department of Justice in 1974 was saying that it had decided to send the case back to the Army for further investigation.

By February 25, 1974, William Saxbe had become

Attorney General of the United States. Freddy Kassab wrote him a letter. After reviewing the history of the case, Kassab stated:

> The decision has been made by Mr. Petersen not to prosecute. He has advised me that he has referred the case back to the U.S. Army CID Command "for further investigation." A completely illegal move in my estimation, since *the one and only* suspect is a civilian.
>
> I have asked Mr. Petersen under what legal authority he is using the U.S. Army to investigate a civilian murder case. Instead of answering my inquiry, he has referred it to the U.S. Army, "for consideration."
>
> Mr. Petersen is attempting to pass the buck in this case. However, there is no way that the U.S. Army can or will legally continue to investigate a civilian. Nor will I allow this situation to continue. I intend to pursue this matter into the courts.
>
> I have not asked the Dept. of Justice to prosecute someone *they* do not think is guilty. I have not asked them to prosecute someone without evidence, nor have I asked that they proceed with a case where a *legitimate* indictment is not a certainty.
>
> I have been frustrated at every turn, however I still seek a legal solution and will continue to do so until I feel that no more can be done by one man against as formidable an entity as the Justice Dept. I swear to you that I will not allow the murderer of my daughter and two granddaughters to get away with those brutal murders.
>
> If you have any doubts about my intentions, I

suggest you consult the U.S. Army's CID command and Judge Advocate General's office for confirmation of the fact that I usually do what I say I am going to do. This case was closed once before for all intents and purposes in October of 1970 and at that time I paid a personal visit to the office of every Congressman and Senator in this country with the result that the case was reopened. I can do this again if it becomes necessary. . . .

On March 4, Kassab wrote to the commanding officer of the U.S. Army Criminal Investigation Division, asking him to put in writing a statement to the effect that, "in the opinion of your command it was Dr. Jeffrey MacDonald who committed the murders," and that "in the opinion of your legal department there exists sufficient evidence to show probable cause sufficient for an indictment and prosecution."

The Army—if not the Justice Department—shared Kassab's sense of frustration and was most willing to cooperate. Within two weeks, an Army legal officer wrote to say that, "Taken as a whole, the evidence makes it most unlikely that there were intruders at 544 Castle Drive, Fort Bragg, on the night of 16–17 February, 1970. The investigation also determined that the statements of several persons in the Fayetteville area who purported to have direct knowledge of the crime were absolutely groundless. An exhaustive analysis of the facts and the relevant law leads us to conclude that the investigation establishes a *prima facie* case."

On April 30, 1974—the eve of the fourth anniversary of the Army's original accusation against MacDonald— Freddy and Mildred Kassab, armed with this letter, and with a sworn affidavit regarding the facts of the case from Peter Kearns, appeared in the Raleigh, North Carolina, chambers of the Honorable Algernon T. Butler, chief judge of the federal district court for the Eastern District of North Carolina, to file a citizens' complaint charging their former son-in-law with three counts of murder.

The Kassabs asked that Judge Butler obtain copies of Kearns's 3,000-page summary of the reinvestigation, which had recommended prosecution in June of 1972, and of a memorandum written by U.S. Attorney Thomas MacNamara (and ignored by his superiors in Washington), which had recommended prosecution in July of 1973.

They asked further that if, on the basis of his study of these documents, the judge found probable cause to believe that MacDonald had committed the crimes, he either issue a warrant for the doctor's arrest or order the convening of a grand jury, even without the consent of the Justice Department.

Judge Butler did not accept the complaint for filing, but said he would take the matter under consideration and agreed to "submit appropriate inquiries to the United States Attorney and Department of Justice to determine their attitude with respect to the institution and prosecution of the charges."

Fearing that, despite the publicity generated by the filing of the complaint (MACDONALD ACCUSED AGAIN said the headline in *Newsday*), matters might once again grind to a halt, Kassab also sent a thirteen-page plea to all members of the House and Senate Judiciary Committees, in which he informed them of the events (and nonevents) of the preceding four years, and urged that they, too, seek from the Justice Department—at the very least—a coherent justification for its refusal to act.

The chairman of the House Judiciary Committee was Rep. Peter Rodino, who, the year before, had chaired the committee's pre-impeachment inquiry into the Watergate affair that had ultimately led to the resignation of Richard Nixon.

Assistant Attorney General Henry Petersen was even more intimately acquainted with Rodino than he was with Freddy Kassab and had no desire for further struggles—public or private—with Rodino's committee. Thus, the combination of a personal expression of interest by Rodino and a formal inquiry from the chief judge of a federal district court persuaded Petersen that the MacDonald case could not yet safely be laid to rest.

On June 21, Petersen wrote to Judge Butler to say that the department was "reconsidering" the case and had, in fact, assigned it for review to one of its "most experienced trial attorneys."

Petersen further stated that the department would present the case to a grand jury if, in the opinion of this "most experienced" trial attorney, the evidence appeared strong enough "to survive a motion for judgment of acquittal" at the close of the government's case in a jury trial.

The buck, in other words, that had been passed for two years within the Justice Department had finally come to rest on someone's desk.

The desk was that of Victor Woerheide, a sixty-two-year-old Justice Department attorney whose career had encompassed prosecutions ranging from that of Axis Sally during World War II to the recent indictment and conviction of former Illinois Governor Otto Kerner on bribery and conspiracy charges.

Woerheide functioned primarily as a troubleshooter within the Justice Department, taking on cases of unusual complexity or significance, generally after other department attorneys had failed to make sufficient headway.

Within the department hierarchy, he was responsible directly to the Attorney General himself, rather than to the chief of any section. In the MacDonald case, the authority vested in him by Henry Petersen was absolute. If, in Woerheide's opinion, the case was worthy of prosecution, it would be prosecuted. If, on the other hand, he did not feel it was of sufficient merit, then, as one department attorney later put it, "Freddy Kassab could have set himself on fire in the department courtyard and Henry Petersen wouldn't have stood up to look out the window."

For Freddy and Mildred Kassab, then, Victor Woerheide was a one-man court of last resort.

On a fine, sunny morning in early June, a mail cart laden with satchels, each of which was stuffed with thousands of pieces of paper—transcripts, witness statements, lab reports, photographs, diagrams, memorandums—was wheeled into Victor Woerheide's office.

He was a large man, six feet two inches tall and weighing more than 200 pounds. "And looking," an associate said, "as if he'd been that height and weight since he was about seven years old." He smoked cigars, he had silver gray hair which fell continually down over his forehead, and he had a very red face which seemed locked into a perpetual scowl.

Woerheide, in fact, suffered from a painful angina condition and until the MacDonald case had been presented to him—or, more precisely, thrust upon him—he had been giving serious consideration, in the wake of his triumph in the Kerner prosecution, to retiring from the Justice Department in order to divide his remaining years between his horse farm in Virginia and his villa on the Costa del Sol.

Approximately two weeks after Woerheide had begun his review of the case, he received a phone call from a twenty-seven-year-old military attorney named Brian Murtagh, who was attached to the CID command in Washington and who had been involved in the processing of paperwork relating to the MacDonald case since the completion of the CID reinvestigation in December of 1971.

As he had processed, Murtagh had read; and as he had read, he had formed the opinion that Jeffrey MacDonald was indeed guilty of the crimes with which the Army had charged him.

Once he had come to that conclusion, Murtagh found it difficult to accept that Justice Department attorneys—who had made it clear to him that they were equally convinced of MacDonald's guilt—could decide, for what they claimed were pragmatic reasons, that prosecution should not even be attempted.

"It seemed to me," Murtagh would say years later, "that the gravity of the crime was such that it was the duty of anybody who believed MacDonald guilty—and there was no one I talked to who didn't—to take all available steps to attempt to bring him to trial, no matter how unlikely conviction seemed. As far as I was concerned, that was the social contract. That was the duty of the people who held those positions." The holders of those positions, however, did not appear to agree.

The core of the problem, as Murtagh perceived it, was that no one with the power to make a decision had ever directly exposed himself to the minutiae of the case—the details of the physical evidence which, Murtagh believed, so clearly marked Jeffrey MacDonald as the killer.

Always, an assistant would be instructed to review the massive file, and he in turn would delegate to another assistant the task of doing the actual reading and that would lead to the compilation of a condensed report based upon which the first assistant would write a memorandum which would then be presented to the official who had first been asked to consider the question.

By the time a redrafted memorandum, designed to satisfy a superior who lacked the time to deal with raw material, reached a desk at the level at which decisions were made, it was as devoid of emotional content as a stock analyst's buy, sell, or hold recommendation.

Also, the recommendation was always the same: do not prosecute. From a cost-effectiveness standpoint, the MacDonald case was considered a loser. Whether he was guilty or not was irrelevant: without a history of similar actions, without a confession, without any witnesses, and with no apparent motive—even if the original investigation had not been so badly mishandled—the attempt to convict him was so unlikely to succeed as to render unjustifiable the resources that would have to be expended. It was as if Colette and Kimberly and Kristen MacDonald were and always had been mere abstractions.

Brian Murtagh, however, did not think of the case in those terms. He thought of the slashed and battered bodies of the pregnant woman and the two little girls, awash in blood in their own bedrooms during the darkest hours of a raw and misty night. For him, the prosecution of Jeffrey MacDonald was not simply a function of his professional life but a compelling moral issue. Murtagh eventually came to see himself not only as an employee of the U.S. government, but as a lawyer—the only lawyer—representing the interests of Jeffrey MacDonald's dead wife and daughters.

Brian Murtagh had become almost as preoccupied by the case as had Freddy and Mildred Kassab. For two years he had sought—in meetings and in memorandums—to convey his sense of moral urgency to the seemingly endless teams of Justice Department attorneys who had been given responsibility for reviewing the evidence. For two years, he had failed. He was, after all, only a twenty-seven-year-old Army captain. He wasn't even a member of the Justice Department.

"For two years," Murtagh said, "I couldn't get anybody to *feel*."

Murtagh had grown up in the Forest Hills section of Queens in New York City. He had graduated from Georgetown University. He was five feet seven, wore horn-rimmed glasses, and weighed 130 pounds. He owned neither sports car nor yacht, and neither countesses nor airline stewardesses sought his company.

One afternoon in the last week of June, having learned that the case was now in the hands of one of the Justice Department's "most experienced trial attorneys," he called Victor Woerheide to explain the depth of his commitment to the investigation and to offer to be of assistance. He expected to be told—and perhaps not very politely—that if Woerheide, or anyone else in the department, felt in need of help from a twenty-seven-year-old Army captain, he would ask for it. Instead, Woerheide said, "Pick me up on the corner of 10th and Constitution in half an hour."

Victor Woerheide spent that afternoon at CID headquarters in Washington, listening to the tape of Jeffrey MacDonald's April 6, 1970, interview. Victor Woerheide looked at the pictures. Victor Woerheide flew to Fort Bragg and, in the company of Brian Murtagh, spent hours inside 544 Castle Drive. He learned the fine points of blood and fiber analysis. Working seven days a week and up to sixteen hours a day, he studied reports of the investigation and of the reinvestigation. He also had Brian Murtagh reassigned to serve as his aide at the Justice Department. And, in perhaps his most radical departure from bureaucratic tradition, Victor Woerheide even asked to see Freddy Kassab.

For two years, to Kassab, the Justice Department had been a fortress he'd been unable to breach—a bastion of inaction fiercely guarded by an interlocking network of signatures, all of which appeared at the bottom of letters saying that the case was undergoing internal review.

Now, on July 18, 1974, for Freddy Kassab, the Justice Department was Victor Woerheide—hulking, red-faced, and scowling—sitting behind a desk which was littered with hundreds of unanswered phone messages, some of them dating back months, as well as pieces of a partly disassembled outboard motor.

Woerheide had one bare foot draped over the edge of the desk and was clipping his toenails into a wastepaper basket when Kassab arrived. He did not get up. He did not even put on his sock. But he did say to Freddy Kassab—whose commitment and perseverance he was already in awe of, and with whom, being a grandfather himself, he had developed a great empathy—that he believed Jeffrey MacDonald to be guilty of murder and that he was going to order the convening of a federal grand jury in the Eastern District of North Carolina.

The grand jury was impaneled in late July. The first person called to testify was Jeffrey MacDonald.

"We have no expectation that this grand jury is going to indict Dr. MacDonald," Bernie Segal told the press upon his arrival in Raleigh, North Carolina, with his client. "He's being called as one of about fifty people who have got bits and pieces of information to give."

At one o'clock on the afternoon of Monday, August 12, 1974, Jeffrey MacDonald entered the grand jury room. He was alone. In accordance with grand jury procedure, not even his own lawyer was permitted to be present. There were no cameras. There was no music. There was no applause. For an audience, there was only Victor Woerheide, an assistant from the U.S. Attorney's office in Raleigh, a court reporter, and the twenty-three citizens of North Carolina who had been chosen at random to serve as grand jurors.

It was a long way, indeed, from Dick Cavett.

PART FOUR

THE DAYS OF AFFLICTION

And now my soul is poured out upon me;
The days of affliction have taken hold . . .

—Job 30:16

The Voice of Jeffrey MacDonald

For me, for my own personal head, the move from New York to California, I think, was really what allowed me to survive. To come back from—you know, from February 17th.

It gave me space. It got me away from the people I knew and were around and all the things that constantly reminded me of Colette and the kids, and from Freddy and Mildred, and the concentration in the East on getting back into the case and either writing a book or continuing the pursuit with Congress, or, ah, continuing the pursuit of the assailants.

All of that was suddenly broken and I was out on the West Coast, working very hard by normal standards, but not hard by my standards—working sixty or seventy or eighty hours a week—becoming well known in medicine, writing papers, writing articles, chapters in textbooks, teaching a whole lot—I became a well-known instructor in cardiopulmonary resuscitation, I was one of the first instructor-trainers for the whole California Heart Association and then was made a member of the national committee for American Heart and began to teach CPR all over the country, and after about six months they made me director of the emergency room at St. Mary's.

I was making excellent money, building a new circle of friends, and after a while I really got into the lifestyle.

In the condo, I had this heavy, Spanish-style furniture and I bought first just a twelve-foot rowboat from Sears with an outboard motor and then I bought a twenty-eight-foot yacht and later of course traded that in for an even bigger boat.

I sold the Chevy and bought a four-passenger Mercedes convertible, two tone. It was really a gorgeous car. It was a movie star's, I can't remember his name . . . Dana Andrews. It was Dana Andrews's car, this very lovely two-tone brown, light brown over dark brown, with rolled red leather interior and the hand-rubbed dash made out of some kind of gnarled wood, and it was really fun, it was a beautiful car.

I had it for several years. The problem with it, it had no power going up hills and it was old enough and had enough miles on it and was underpowered enough that it was constantly breaking down and it got to the point where literally it was in the shop a week a month or two weeks a month, usually just waiting for parts, and I got a little tired of it, so I eventually went to the auto show in Los Angeles and got a—just on the spur of the moment, by myself one day, went to the auto show and was looking around and, to make a long story short, saw this Citroën SM—thought, on the first pass, that it was the ugliest car I'd ever seen, went back a couple hours later and thought that it was kind of a good-looking car—it was more unusual than anything else at the show—and went back about two hours later—now I'd been at the show about six or eight hours—and realized that it was really kind of a handsome car and it was four-passenger and it was kind of luxurious, but it was sporty, and, ah, I started thinking about it and two days later I started looking in earnest and called this dealer whose literature I had picked up and eventually he sold me one, a brown one with the JRM-MD license plates.

Seventy-two and seventy-three were really the fun times. They were very good years. I was beginning to put my life back together. I was becoming a successful doctor, and the rest of my life was made up of boating and working out and seeing Joy. We had a really tremendous relationship, both socially and emotionally and certainly sexually—she being the most sensual woman I'd ever seen—and me becoming very successful professionally.

Joy was this gorgeous receptionist who worked for one of the yacht dealers in the area, and I remember very clearly the first time I saw her. She had on a camel-colored suit and looked very prim and proper, had her hair up, and there was no real hint except in her eyes of this incredible beauty and tremendous sensuality that was to unfold.

But I remember I walked into the showroom and she looked at me and did a double-take and I looked at her and did a double-take and she stared at me and I stared at her, and basically our fates were sealed from that moment on, as silly and romantic as it sounded.

We spent a whole lot of time together—I'd say every weekend from Friday night until Monday morning and sometimes a night or two during the week, and certainly all of our going-out time was together. We really never went anywhere without the other person. All trips, all of my medical meetings that I went to, I always brought

Joy. We did a lot of little trips to Las Vegas, some trips to Lake Tahoe, and a lot of meetings, medical meetings.

Joy recognized in me my extreme competitiveness and also she fed, you know, my ego. She understood that I loved sports and football and basketball and baseball, and sort of always wanted to do the best possible in it, and she encouraged it. She would throw down the gauntlet on how far I could run or whether I'd be able to work all night and then play a big football game against the police. And she enjoyed watching me do it almost as much as I enjoyed doing it, if not as much. She was very flushed with the thrill of victory and the agony of defeat, just as I was. And we would have all these intense experiences together, very often with her needling me and then being very proud in whatever accomplishments I did make.

We had some just unbelievable vacations. I took her to Tahiti, as a matter of fact. I told her—asked her what she wanted for Christmas and she said, oh, just have a nice dinner somewhere, and I told her, well, I'll tell you what, instead of for Christmas—her birthday is December 9th—I told her that for her birthday before Christmas I would take her out to dinner, to the restaurant of her choice.

And she said fine, and she was, you know, thinking up neat restaurants in Beverly Hills and Las Vegas and San Francisco, and I said, "Why don't I just take you to Tahiti?" And she said okay, and just kind of giggled and the next day I went down and got the tickets and came back and gave them to her and she just couldn't believe it.

We had ten days on Tahiti, three days on Bora Bora, and seven days on another island. That was a fantastic vacation.

I'd say by springtime of '72 Joy and I were, you know,

really getting it on, so to speak, to use a lousy California expression. We had fabulous times together. In particular, we had some incredible times on the boat that are all-timers, in which the two of us—occasionally my mother was along—but frequently Joy and I went by ourselves and had these great weekends over at Catalina, swimming and sunning and fishing and diving and making love.

When Joy and I were alone, making love was a large proportion of our time, including out in the sun on the top of the boat, on the engine hatch and down below on the bunk and every conceivable place in between, and we were sort of shameless, you know—it was a shameless abandon.

It was two sort of passionate people, neither of which had had a very smooth life to that point—certainly mine had been much more tumultuous and traumatic—but it was two adults basically at play, trying to please each other and please ourselves, and we both understood that.

We wanted to experience everything, like, as fast as we could. We always tried to do the most with the best, the flashiest, the most fun, the highest flight and the longest trip and the deepest dive, and um, um, we had an absolutely fabulous sex life together. It was almost nonstop. It was—Jesus—sometimes day and night.

We went to Las Vegas one time and made love at least five times, didn't ever really get to the casino that first night, and the next morning took right up where we left off. And finally realized we had to get out of the room and go see Vegas a little bit. And we would stop at noon and stop late in the afternoon and then go out to dinner and then come back and make love and go out and gamble a little, come back and make love.

There was a need for a lot of release, a lot of immediate gratification. We did not, either of us, want to dwell on the past. We lived each day for that day, with a small bit of our eye on the future.

But I wouldn't let myself admit openly and in a repetitive fashion to her that I loved her. I wouldn't let her burrow into my soul, so to speak.

I was trying to explain to her that, look, we're in a funny situation. I am facing a background investigation in a triple homicide on which I had been charged once and found innocent, but this was now the civilian people. But she pooh-poohed—not the seriousness of the situation, but she had never considered that there would actually be a grand jury investigation, much less the publicity of an indictment.

I kept saying, look, we have to hold things off and be as reasonable as possible, because I can't expect you to stand by me should the worst occur. But her said and unsaid feelings came tumbling out, of course, that she wanted to be by me, that she loved me, and that that was to be part of the relationship: she would take me with any warts.

1

En route to his grand jury appearance, Jeffrey MacDonald had made some notes to himself in a Rite-Nice Wide Ruled Theme Book which he had purchased for 59 cents.

The first notes concerned the opening statement he wanted to make.

"Soberness," he wrote at the top of the page. "Willingness to cooperate."

Then he wrote: "Memory—will try hard to get details, but painful experience. Painful because birthdays, anniversary dates, anniversay of Feb. 17, sleeplessness and *Pain*—once being accused, then exonerated totally and now (?) accused because of *Army* reinvestigation."

On the next page, he wrote: "Not easy to talk about it," and what was, apparently, a line he intended to deliver: "Bear with me while I try my best."

MacDonald made it plain from the start that he was not pleased to have been summoned, but the tone of anguish which he had wanted to project somehow became twisted into something much closer to hostility.

"This is not easy, for me to appear here," he said. "You know, this is my family that I lost. I get accused of it. They don't even interview me. They don't even interview me for six weeks. Although I go to their office and ask, 'Don't you have any questions? Don't you want to talk to me?' No, no, no, we have suspects in custody. Six weeks go by. Fourteen MPs tramping through the house. Then I have to spend four years reliving this and now I'm back here in 1974."

"Captain MacDonald," Victor Woerheide said, "you have complained—"

"*Doctor* MacDonald, Mr. Woerheide."

"Doctor MacDonald, you have complained—"

"I asked for a civilian reinvestigation in 1970. The Army reinvestigated itself. You could never reconstruct the initial hour of that crime scene."

"Doctor MacDonald, we are going to do the best we can, and all I am asking you is your voluntary cooperation."

"I am here to cooperate, sir. I have never refused to talk to anyone. I have never pleaded the Fifth Amendment. Until my lawyers got to me, I offered to give a polygraph examination."

"At this time," Woerheide asked, "in aid of the present grand jury investigation, will you agree to submit to a polygraph examination?"

"Let me talk about that with my attorney."

"And another thing, while we are discussing examinations, I understand at the time that your psychiatrist examined you in 1970 and the Army doctors examined you, there was some consideration given to asking you to take sodium amytal—truth serum—and submit to an examination under the influence of this truth serum. So I am going to ask you to consider and discuss with your attorney cooperating with the grand jury to the extent of taking both the polygraph and the sodium amytal examinations."

"Let me make a comment about the sodium amytal interview," MacDonald said. "This was discussed with my psychiatrist and it was his recommendation that unless there was an overriding need for sodium amytal— unless there were facts, and I repeat the word *facts*—that an amytal interview recreates . . ." MacDonald paused.

"May I assist you," Woerheide said, "by saying that it causes you to relive the experience concerning which you are being examined and that would constitute a painful ordeal for you. And in his opinion, at that time, you should be spared the experience?"

"Right."

"Doctor MacDonald, the event happened four years ago. I think you will agree it is high time that this matter was resolved."

"But resolved in what fashion, sir? To cover up the CID investigation again?"

"I am not trying to cover up the CID investigation."

"The second Army investigation was finished a year and a half ago. This is unbelievable."

"We are going to go into that," Woerheide said. "That is one of the reasons you are here."

For five days in August, Jeffrey MacDonald testified before the federal grand jury. Looming over him throughout was Victor Woerheide—his voice, even at normal pitch, sounding in the confines of a courtroom like the blast of an ocean liner's horn.

It was Woerheide's objective, at the start of the inquiry, to get MacDonald on record in as much detail as possible. He then planned to bring forward witnesses who would contradict the testimony that MacDonald had given. The final step would be to recall MacDonald to the stand and to confront him with each and every contradiction.

Woerheide paced himself, working slowly through the hot August days, aware that at any time MacDonald could invoke his constitutional rights against self-incrimination and refuse to answer any further questions. He did not want MacDonald to consider him—just yet—merely an extension of Grebner, Shaw and Ivory, Pruett and Kearns. The longer he was able to project an air of impartiality, the more likely MacDonald would be to keep talking, and, in the end, Woerheide was convinced, it was MacDonald's own words which would incriminate him.

"Have you always had a good family relationship with your father, your mother, your brother, and your sister?"

"Yes."

"Have there been any problems?"

"Sure."

"Have there been any family crises?"

"Yes, there have been family crises."

"Have these family crises had any effect on you and your life?"

"Yes. I lost my family at Fort Bragg. That affected my life."

"I am referring," Woerheide said placidly, "to your family consisting of your father, your mother, your brother, and your sister."

"Sure. My father died at the age of forty-eight when I was in my sophomore year at medical school. That affected my mother and affected us. My brother used drugs and that affected us. My sister is mildly anxious, a young married female and has her crises and calls in the middle of the night, but nothing spectacular."

Woerheide then asked MacDonald to describe his trip north from Puerto Rico in the fall of 1969, at the time of his brother's hospitalization, only three months before the murders.

"I received notification of a need for emergency leave," MacDonald said. "I was just told that my brother was hospitalized. I subsequently found out that he was in a state hospital. He had a bad reaction to drugs and apparently beat up some policemen or was put in a strait-jacket and was taken to the hospital with handcuffs on. I think he had a broken wrist or something and then he dove through the window of the state hospital. I arrived there like a day and a half later."

"How long were you there?"

"Two and a half, three days."

"Did you visit with any friends while you were in Patchogue at that time?"

"Not that I remember."

"You don't recall seeing any friends at all?"

"Friends of my mother's probably would have stopped by the house, but I don't think that—"

"Well, this is a name that has cropped up and I am going to throw it out to you at this time. How about Penny Wells?"

"No."

"Do you know who I mean?"

"She is an old girlfriend of mine."

"And you didn't see her on that occasion?"

"No, sir."

Woerheide paused to look through some papers. Then he resumed.

"Now, I know there has been some talk about this famous Jump Party down in Texas. I won't go into that at this time—"

"Feel free, sir," MacDonald said sarcastically.

"No, I'll save that for a later point," Woerheide said. "But I just want to know whether there were any social activities during other Green Beret training missions that were comparable to the so-called Jump Party."

"No, sir."

Woerheide shuffled some more papers. "Now, going back to the occasion when you took the emergency leave and traveled to Patchogue, did you at that time go to a certain bar which apparently your brother frequented?"

"The Shortstop Bar."

"The Shortstop Bar. Where is that located?"

"I don't remember. I have been into a lot of bars to bail my brother out. This was either in New York, in Greenwich Village—I think that's where it is, actually."

"So while you were there you went down to New York, Greenwich Village, and you went to this bar?"

"Right."

"What was the purpose of going to this bar?"

"To find out who had been selling my brother drugs."

"What drugs was your brother using?"

"He said he had been taking amphetamines, uppers. And then the night of this bad trip, he told me that someone had given him two capsules—typical drug abuser comment. And I said, 'What were they?' and he said he didn't know. He presumed they were mescaline or LSD.

"Actually, I presumed that, because he was in this tremendous hallucinatory state. He was having wild hallucinations, but when I questioned him it was apparent that he had been speeding—taking amphetamines—for a long time that I hadn't been aware of. And on reflection, some of his prior actions seemed a lot more in tune with his speeding.

"For instance, he used to drive from New York to Chicago nonstop. And I used to wonder how the hell anyone can do that. It's a long drive. And he used to stay up all the time. He used to party day and night. It never occurred to me that my brother would be taking amphetamines."

"All right, now you went to this bar?"

"Yes."

"Well, describe to us the people you saw in the Shortstop Bar."

"They were just bums. A bunch of guys that don't work for a living. A lot of my brother's friends are that way. They're just bums. They sit and drink all night and now I find out they were taking a lot of drugs. So I had an argument in the Shortstop Bar with a couple of guys who said they knew Jay. I had been told that the bartender was one of the guys supplying Jay with speed. So I guess I got a little pushy with them and there was a little scuffle and I hit the guy or something like that."

"There was a little pushing and shoving?"

"I went up to him, and I said, 'Do you know Jay MacDonald?' 'Yeah, I know Jay.' I said, 'Do you know he is in the state hospital?' words to that effect. And the guy said, 'Well, no, I didn't know that.' I said, 'Yeah, he had a bad reaction to some pills someone gave him.' And he said, 'Oh,' or something. And I said, 'Yeah,' and I probably told him he was an asshole. And I heard he had given him the pills. And he said he didn't. You know, who the hell did I think I was sitting in a public bar accusing him of that. So the words got a little heated and I pushed him and he pushed me and I hit him."

That questioning had been designed to make only one point and it had succeeded: Jeffrey MacDonald was a man with a quick temper and no stranger to physical violence.

Seeming to skip almost at random from subject to subject—none of them directly connected with the murders—Woerheide kept MacDonald off balance.

"All right, sir," Woerheide said, brandishing a newspaper clipping, "I have here a *Newsday* article that was published October 20, 1970. The headline says BERET FREED IN FAMILY DEATHS, and it says in part, "MacDonald and his attorneys expect to conduct their own investigation. 'The Army has never followed up on some of the leads that we turned up,' MacDonald said. 'I plan to do a lot of writing and investigating. We hope to get either the appropriate civilian agency or to get our own investigators so we can find the real killers.' Did you, in fact, hire your own investigators?"

"I never hired investigators, no. My lawyers cost me up to thirty thousand dollars at that point. My mother had to sell her home to pay for it. Plus, I was trying to rebuild a life and it became a little—it became a little bizarre. And— no, I didn't. That's one of my great sins, apparently."

"Were you personally seeking out the perpetrators?"

"Only in a very ineffectual manner."

"That's not being very definite. Be explicit."

"It was the same type of thing as, you know, when you—you went into bars, you talked to some people. I tried to track down Helena Stoeckley. It just isn't like *Kojak*. It doesn't work that way."

"But you were making an effort?"

"Yes."

"On your own?"

"Yes, but I'm talking about a—you know, it was very difficult at that time for me to walk into a bar in Fayetteville and play undercover agent. This thing had been on the front pages for six months. There were hundreds of reporters around. You know, they were all over the place at the time."

"Well, you had friends. Were they helping you?"

"Not specifically. No."

"Were they helping you in a nonspecific way?"

"Yes. My lawyers still got leads. We still got phone calls. We still had things like that. Nothing great. No."

"Well, when you went into these bars around Fayetteville were you alone or did you have someone with you?"

"I believe usually I was alone. I probably had some Army friends with me occasionally."

"Can you recall the names of any of these Army friends?"

"Not at this time, no."

"But you were looking for the people who might be the perpetrators you described?"

"Right."

"What leads did you have?"

"Look, Mr. Woerheide, I can't come in here four years later and make it sound like I was some sort of avenging hero going through Fayetteville. That isn't what happened. You know, I went to bars. I questioned people. I asked some things. There were, you know, probably occasional little pushing matches. This isn't a big deal, this thing."

"What do you mean by 'pushing matches'?"

"Well, you know, I would get upset. You know, with some doper."

"And then what would happen?"

"Usually nothing."

"When something did happen, what would happen?"

"You mean you want me to recount every little fist-fight? Is that what you want?"

"If you can recall, yes. When you say, 'every little fist-fight,' how many were there?"

"A couple. I mean, you know, I—I was a very visible person in the community at that time. I could walk into a bar and fifty people would stop and say, 'Hey, that's Captain MacDonald!' You don't really get much information that way unless someone wants to come to you and give you information."

"How does the situation develop that would result in a fistfight?"

"I was sitting in a bar watching these kids buy little bags of pills right out in the open. They weren't even making any attempt to hide it. So I went over and sat down next to them. On reflection, it's really stupid."

"What happened then?"

"I asked some questions about Helena Stoeckley."

"What happened then?"

"People would say, 'It's none of your business.'"

"What happened then?"

"I said, 'The hell it isn't my business!' And I kicked his chair out."

"And there was a little scuffling?"

"Yes. You leave before the MPs get there."

"This happened several times?"

"Yes."

"Doctor MacDonald, over what period of time did you engage in this investigative activity?"

"I don't specifically remember. It was a period of, I guess, weeks to months. I don't specifically remember dates."

"Tell us when you initiated it and when you finally gave up on it."

"When I was released in custody in October until I got out of the Army in December."

"After that, when you were living in New York, did you continue this activity?"

"No, I did not."

"Subsequently you moved to California. Did you continue the activity while you were there?"

"No."

"In 1970, what was your personal relationship with your wife's stepfather, Alfred Kassab?"

"It was very good. It's not so good now."

"Did he visit you from time to time?"

"During the Article 32 but not after the Article 32 ended."

"Would you call him up and talk to him from time to time?"

"Surely."

"Would he call you up and talk to you?"

"Sure would."

"How frequently did you have these conversations?"

"It seemed to me fairly frequently."

"And were you holding anything back from him?"

"No. Unfortunately, I made some things up."

"What did you make up?"

"The extent of my own investigation."

"All right, tell the grand jury now what it was you made up."

"Let me just say that I was trying to rebuild my life and I was doing—I was trying to get out of the Army. We—my attorneys and my mother and myself—had begun to feel a little uneasy about Freddy—Mr. Kassab. He kind of took over the Article 32 hearing and a lot of the publicity surrounding it. He would hold news conferences up at La Guardia Airport. He was writing letters and firing off telegrams to anyone that would listen."

"Was this public officials?"

"Anyone who would listen. *New York Times, Newsweek,* magazines, radio, whoever he could talk to. And it was all in regards I was the greatest guy that had ever lived, the Army was absolutely hosing me, giving me a bad deal."

"You didn't disagree with that, did you?"

"No. That in fact is what happened."

"All right. Go ahead."

"What I was leading up to was there was a—really, a sense of uneasiness. Freddy became a media freak, if you want me to be honest. And he started talking to me frequently and writing to me frequently and it was always in reference to when we got our private investigation going.

"So then I said—well, I told him, 'Well, I've been in some bars, and you know, I've got some leads.' Critical mistake in my life, telling him that I got some leads. That started it. And then it was incessant. 'What do you have? Who have you found?'

"And I'd lost my family and I'd been through the hearing, I'd been wrongfully accused. Colonel Rock's statement at the end of a five-month grand jury is: the charges are not true. He didn't say there was a lack of evidence. He said the charges are not true. Right? So I'm trying to get out of the Army. I'm trying to figure out what's going to happen. And what do I do? Do I drift? Do I get into my residency? Do I spend the rest of my life prowling around looking for these people? And Freddy's hammering away, you know, about this investigation that we're going to—and then the authors started calling. 'When are we going to do a book on this?' 'I can hook you up with a great publisher in New York.' Lawyers from Long Island say, 'I have a good friend who is a writer.' And it became this unbelievable public thing.

Day and night phone calls. Not day and night literally, but frequent communications.

"So I sat down and talked to my lawyers and said, 'What do I do?' And they said, 'Do formal things. Do what you can. You're a physician. Go to Washington.'

"So when I got out of the Army I went to Washington. Allard Lowenstein takes me around and introduced me to Sam Ervin. Can you imagine going to a cocktail party and talking about a homicide? Congressmen and lawyers advised me to go on TV talk shows. So I got on the TV talk show. I got sick to my stomach. After that I said I wasn't going to do it anymore. They didn't have a right.

"Meanwhile, Freddy's driving me crazy. 'What have you found out?' So I told him I'd found other people. So he asked me—to make a long story short, I implied that I killed the person. Absolute insanity. So his wife wants to know the details. Did they scream? Were they in agony?"

"What did you say?"

"I told him, 'I can't talk about it.' So I left for California. What the hell was I supposed to do? But I still played along with this stupid game with Freddy.

"Freddy was an ex-intelligence officer in the Canadian secret service, or so he says, and he lives this day and night. He was in bars all through World War II listening to secret conversations. He was in D-Day. He was on the battleship on it. He was everything at all times. So I played this game. And finally I gave it up and wrote a ten-page, fifteen-page letter, and I said, 'Freddy, I didn't do it. I didn't do this.'"

"When did you write this letter?"

"I don't know. When I got to California. It was crazy."

"How long did you play the game?"

"I don't know. Months, verbally, with him. It was always the one incident. It was always the same thing. Mildred wanted to hear the details. Did they scream? Were they in agony?"

"Mildred is Colette's mother?"

"So-called mother. She's been bizarre for a long time. So I made this tremendous mistake, this fantastic error. I tried to be a doctor. I tried to rebuild my life. And I moved away. That's my three crimes. I was keeping Freddy happy. He's crazy. He's—this is absolute insanity. The man is a fanatic. He's an alcoholic fanatic. He has sat in that house and reread every single thing on this case for four years. That's a bizarre reaction to a tragedy. They haven't seen a friend. Friends come over to their house and try to take them out to dinner and they slam the door in their face. The guy is a fanatic."

"What was your purpose," Woerheide asked, "in making the statement in a letter dated November 9, 1971— that's approximately a year later—that you had made four trips to North Carolina and Florida in the preceding three months and that you were going to continue and that you had broken a hand on the last trip?"

"That was all part of this. I didn't have a broken hand."

"And it cost you two thousand dollars?"

"I was telling Freddy this great detective story. That I was doing all this work on the case because that's what he said he was doing. This is really just continuing that stupid game until I got up enough nerve finally to write him a letter and tell him the truth."

"Well, why all this explicit detail and color, like the broken hand? Were you implying you broke your hand slapping somebody?"-

"I suppose. You know, Mr. Woerheide, my actions during that period of time—I apologize for them. Jesus, that doesn't mean I murdered my wife and kids. It was stupid. I've regretted it every single day since I wrote the letter to Freddy. I regretted it the day I started it."

"You talked in the letter about writing a book. At that time were you involved in the writing of a book?"

"It's never been written. There were a lot of interviews with authors and publishers. All these supposedly helpful friends of mine wanted me to write a book. I didn't want to write a book. So you keep putting them off, you know? Several people wrote beginning chapters, like, and tried to get front money. When it became apparent that I was going to have to sit down with a person for a period of months and go over the whole thing and sort of live with an author, I said screw it. I'm not going to do it. I was trying to rebuild a life. And that's when I decided I've got to clear this up. So I wrote Freddy a letter and I said: 'Freddy, what I told you in the past is not true.'"

Woerheide resumed his reading of the letter that MacDonald had written to Freddy Kassab. "In the next paragraph you say, 'The one difference between you and I is that I don't think that justice will bring back my family. I want revenge. Preferably brutal revenge, and don't care about justice any more. There is no justice, in case you haven't noticed. You act as though you were on a noble cause. I think the cause is ugly, brutal, but necessary. I will do it. I have done some. One fourth or fifth of it.' Now let's talk about that statement."

"What I was trying to tell Freddy is that he was on a soapbox all the time. He made it sound like this was some sort of glorious thing to do. He didn't understand. I never heard Freddy and Mildred say, 'I want Colette back.' Never! They said they wanted to see someone hurt. What the hell does that do?"

Woerheide then read from a copy of the letter that MacDonald had written to Mildred Kassab in March of 1973 after his angry telephone conversation with her husband.

"Is this the letter you were referring to when you said you'd sent it to Freddy?"

"No."

Woerheide then read the paragraph in which MacDonald had admitted that some of the things he had told Kassab were not 100 percent true.

"Does that refresh your recollection as to whether or not this is the letter you are referring to?"

"I thought I addressed it to Freddy and Mildred, and, I believe, Colette's Aunt Helen. I'm sure I addressed it to all three. Helen was living with them."

Woerheide then read the portion of the letter in which MacDonald had said he'd never had an affair but that he had seen, dated, or slept with a "very rare" girl other than Colette.

"That's true. That's what I said to her."

"All right. Now why were you saying that at this time in this letter?"

"There had been a phone call from Freddy. He had called me up. He was drunk. It was the middle of the night and he was ranting and raving that he had—maybe I'm exaggerating, okay, but I recollected him as saying that he had just come from Fort Bragg and he had fifteen affidavits that the MPs were supplying me with girls while I was locked up in my BOQ room. So I said, 'Freddy, that's the most ludicrous comment I've ever heard in my life. It's obscene, perverse, and it's incredible.' He said—I don't know. He said he had sworn affidavits from fifteen girls in Fayetteville that the MPs or the CID or someone was supplying me with females while I was locked in my BOQ. I said, 'Freddy, you're crazy.'"

"Did you have any females in your BOQ?"

"After I was released from custody, sure."

"While you were in custody?"

"While I was in custody? Females in my BOQ room?"

"Yes."

"You mean other than friends and relatives?"

"I mean, was there a girl who would come in and have sexual relationships with you during the period that you were in custody in your BOQ?"

"No. Afterwards."

"During this time period there was no such girl?"

"There was a girl that used to—I used to sit outside with the MP guard and do some reading outside and she was a clerk or something, and it started out she walked by and she said, 'Hi! Aren't you Captain MacDonald?' And I'm standing there with an MP guard behind me, so I said, 'Yes, I'm Captain MacDonald.' And it started out—then like a month later she'd come by and give me a tuna fish sandwich while I'm sitting out there. And after—I dated her after I—you know, I took her out on a double date with one of my escort officers, as a matter of fact."

"While you were in the BOQ under escort and guard?"

"No. One of my escort officers who became sort of a friend after I was released from custody. She got another girl and we went on a double date. We went to a movie and had dinner or something."

"What was his name?"

"I don't know."

"What was the girl's name?"

"I don't know."

"You don't remember her name?"

"No."

"Does the name Bonnie Wood mean anything to you?"

"Bonnie Wood, right."

"How frequently did you see her?"

"I probably dated her several times after—before I left, before December."

"And you say Freddy purported to have affidavits from fifteen girls?"

"That's the sense of the conversation. Fifteen."

"You say that is completely erroneous?"

"Erroneous?"

"There were not fifteen girls? Will you say there were no girls?"

"You mean in regard to having sexual relations in my BOQ room while I'm under guard with an MP outside the door?"

"Yes."

"Yes, I would say that is erroneous." (It was, in fact, not erroneous at all, as the CID's reinvestigation had revealed.)

As the week progressed, Woerheide asked MacDonald to try to recall the names of anyone to whom, in the first days following the murders, he might have given any account, however fragmentary, of the events of the early hours of February 17. Eventually, MacDonald mentioned his attorneys, saying one of his military lawyers "gave me a yellow legal pad and told me to write down whatever I remembered whenever I remembered it. 'If you wake up in the middle of the night and remember something, write it down.' And this went on. This went on for a month."

"Do you remember how long this statement was, or this compilation of data, this narrative?"

"No."

"Have you seen that statement lately?"

"I've seen it. I haven't read it."

"Can you tell me who has possession and control of it?"

"My attorneys."

"Do you know of any reasons why that should not be shown or made available to the grand jury? Is there anything in there that you think might be harmful or detrimental to yourself?"

"I doubt it. It would reflect severely upon the CID."

"I am going to request that you make available to us these notes that you compiled."

"With all the irrelevancies and meaningless comments?"

"Yes."

"As I understand it, that's an attorney-client product."

"It is privileged," Woerheide agreed, "and you are at liberty to refuse to make it available."

"The statement itself has nothing in it except what I recollect."

"I'm telling you that it is a privileged communication to your counsel. You can, if you wish, waive the privilege and make this information available to the grand jury."

"Mr. Woerheide, are you setting me up as a fall guy?"

"No, I'm not."

"I've got instructions from an attorney that gets five hundred dollars a day and he says, 'You will not ever divulge attorney-client relationships.' And here I am divulging them."

"I have not asked you question one."

"I understand that. But the implication is—"

"I'm asking you to consult with him and give us an answer as to whether or not you are willing to give us this statement either in whole or in part. If you wish to Xerox it and excise portions of it, you are free to do so."

"The problem is, the unfairness is, if I respond in a negative fashion through attorney—"

"We'll be aware that you are doing it on the advice of counsel and you might not necessarily agree with the answer," Woerheide said. "But it's your decision, not your counsel's decision. You can accept his advice or reject his advice."

Woerheide shuffled some more papers. "Let me ask you this," he said. "In April of 1970, when you went up to Philadelphia, you were examined by a forensic psychiatrist. I assume this examination extended over several days?"

"It did. I don't know the dates."

"Now, besides seeing the psychiatrist, did you also see a psychologist who gave you certain tests?"

"Yes, I did. But I think we're going to have to stop talking about attorney-client relationships."

"I'm not asking you what you said to him."

"Yes, you are."

"I'm not asking what the psychologist said to you. I'm just asking were you examined by a psychologist who gave you certain tests?"

"Yes."

"Well, how long did you spend with the psychiatrist as opposed to the psychologist who gave you the tests?"

"I don't remember."

"Was it part of one day or more than one day?"

"Oh, it was more."

"How many days?"

"I don't remember. I honestly don't remember."

"Could it have been more than three days?"

"I would say that would be the upper limit. It was parts of two or three days." In fact, there had been only a single, three-hour interview.

"Now, between the interview by your own psychiatrist at the end of April and the Walter Reed examinations made in August, did you talk to anyone concerning the incident of February 16th and 17th?"

"No one except reporters."

"Who were the reporters?"

"I really don't remember, sir. There were hundreds of them. You know, they were all over the place all the time."

"Did you give a full description of the matter to any of these reporters?"

"I gave a long statement to one from *Newsday*."

"Was this with the knowledge of your attorneys?"

"Certainly."

"Was it tape-recorded?"

"I believe it was."

"Do you have any objection to our obtaining a copy of that tape?"

"It's not my property."

"Would you personally have any objection?"

"Only that—that my experience in the past with government prosecutors has not been very good. And you would have to view the tape with the understanding that that was a statement to a reporter."

"I understand that you were not under oath."

"It isn't even that. It's—this was a duty for me to, you know, to try to sort of equalize all the bad things my family had to read up on Long Island and stuff. And the Kassabs at that time. My in-laws."

"Well, let me ask you this. Is there anything that you

said in that statement that you feel at this time you would like to retract?"

"I'd have to reread it."

"I'll get a copy. I'll give it to you. I'll afford you an opportunity to reread it tonight. I'd like to know—"

"Sir, in other words, what you're saying is that you're viewing the statement as a statement of fact from me— otherwise you wouldn't be interested in it."

"Well, it is a statement by you recounting your recollections of the events of February 16th and 17th."

"You know, this wasn't even really with thought. This is just talking to a reporter. It's not at all like—you know, I should turn this around and say, do you want me to bring the provost marshal's news clippings, what he said in the press."

"I'm not interested in what the provost marshal said."

"Well, you should be."

"I'm interested in what you, as a witness, having knowledge of certain facts, have to say."

"But the newspaper isn't facts. That's the thing. And this was an interview sort of arranged by high-powered defense attorneys who want a story told publicly. You know, if I'd had it my way, I wouldn't even have given the interview. That's not a legitimate thing to me."

"Well, it is a statement you made for the benefit of anybody who chose to read it, and the statement is attributed directly to you."

"Sir, I think there is a much fuller, better account of this in the Article 32 investigation, taken under oath."

"But this was prior to the Article 32. You were not under any pressure. You were not under any strain."

"I beg to differ with you."

"It was done voluntarily and purports to cover the same territory."

"To imply that I wasn't under pressure at that time in my life is outrageous! I was under tremendous—"

"Did the reporter put you under pressure?"

"The interview was to me, yes."

"You were tense?"

"Yes, I was tense, Mr. Woerheide."

"You think you said anything you should not have said?"

"I don't know. I'd have to reread it. I don't reread newspaper clippings."

The next day, Woerheide said, "Doctor MacDonald, I gave you a copy of the statement that was published in *Newsday*, and I asked you to review it and inform us today whether there was anything that you felt should be explained or modified."

"The answer is essentially what I said yesterday. This is not a statement under oath. It's a statement to a reporter for a news story, and I think it should be viewed as such. There are a lot of things in here that now, if I looked critically at it, aren't exactly correct. But I don't see what relevancy that has."

"I see questions which purport to be verbatim transcript of questions asked of you and I see answers which I think purport to be verbatim transcript of responses that you gave."

"Sir, if you took what was quoted as verbatim in a newspaper—for instance, the Justice Department six months ago stating that this case would never be prosecuted. This is totally irrelevant. A news interview by a reporter."

"Did he ask you those questions, and did you give those answers?"

"I don't remember each one specifically. I get a general feeling as I read it that it's essentially, generally, the interview I had."

"Would you say it has been doctored in any way?"

"As I remember it, there are things that don't sound like me at all in here. I can't imagine me saying it. I don't know if it's been doctored or if I said it. Do you follow me? I don't remember stating some of the things he had me stating."

"I notice on page seven," Woerheide said, "and I don't want to get into the details of this right now, there is a—"

"Sir, may I say this? If this is going to be discussed, is the grand jury going to see it? I mean they should see this if we're going to discuss it."

"At this point," Woerheide continued, "I just wanted to ask you, did you furnish this drawing that's set forth here?"

Woerheide pointed to the diagram of the interior of 544 Castle Drive on which MacDonald had drawn stick figures to represent himself on the living room couch and the bodies of his wife and children in the locations in which he said he had found them. In his handwriting there were identifications of the various rooms, such as "Kristy's," "Kim's," "L.R."

"No, sir," MacDonald said. "I believe this was a drawing furnished the news media by the provost marshal."

"So that doesn't represent your work product in any way?"

"That's correct," MacDonald said, despite the fact that the drawings had been made by his own hand.

"All right. I have here also a transcript of a CBS interview of Captain MacDonald given on 11 December 1970. Can you tell us how this came about?"

"No, I cannot. I don't remember which interview you're talking about."

"This is a CBS interview which was part of a Walter

Cronkite news broadcast. The person who interviewed you is Bob Schieffer."

"Was that interview on Fort Bragg, sir?"

"Well, Schieffer states at one point here, 'We talked with Captain MacDonald in the office of New York Congressman Allard Lowenstein.'"

"I honestly don't remember that, being in an office in New York for an interview. There were hundreds of interviews like this during that time, sir. I honestly don't remember a CBS interview with Bob Schieffer."

"Do you recall who arranged this interview that took place in Mr. Lowenstein's office?"

"Sir, I honestly don't remember an interview in an office. It may have occurred, but I really don't remember it. Most of these interviews were done on the phone. There were a lot of interviews at Fort Bragg where they brought TV crews to the BOQ. But on December 11 that wouldn't have been the case."

"You don't remember being in Congressman Allard Lowenstein's office, Bob Schieffer being there, and, I assume, cameramen and technicians?"

"Sir, that was not an unusual occurrence at the time. Honestly. I mean, this was happening all the time."

"All right. I have here a somewhat more lengthy transcript captioned 'Jeffrey MacDonald's appearance on Dick Cavett show, 15 December 1970.' Do you remember that occasion, sir?"

"Yes, I do."

"How did that come about?"

"I believe that was Lowenstein's bright idea. To push along the congressional investigation that we were asking for—civilian type, not CID reinvestigating itself. But his feeling was that pressure should be brought to bear from any number of quarters. That was the last—that was when I finally said, this thing was too much and I wasn't going to do any more."

"All right. Now here you refer to the April 6 interrogation of you by military personnel. You say, 'It's really an interrogation, you know. They turn the light up in front of your face and have all these little tricks.' Now tell us about this business of staring into the light and the little tricks that were—"

"Sir, I don't want to make implications that aren't true. I didn't really ever—there was some sort of a desk lamp and someone reached over and adjusted something, and I realized from then on I was annoyed because this thing was shining in my face. That's all. That's all it amounted to."

"Where was the light located?"

"Somewhere on the desk, it seemed to me."

"Was it on the far side of the desk?"

"Sir, it wasn't important to me at the time."

"Well, it's become important by the fact that this reference to the light occurs so frequently in these news accounts that I read."

"Sir, we're not here to discuss news accounts. I have testified for three days. We haven't talked about anything that's factual."

"We're here to discuss misconduct on the part of the CID," Woerheide said. "Now you say, little tricks. What are you referring to?"

"Oh, the little—what's called the Mutt-and-Jeff approach that I'm sure you're aware of, where someone badgers you for about an hour or two and then he leaves the room, and the other guy sort of puts his arm around you and says, 'I'm really a nice guy and you can kind of lean on me and we'll get this all squared away.' It's a common interrogation technique."

"Later, here, you state that the CID man, a technician, I presume, destroyed fifty fingerprints. Now is that
an accurate statement, sir?"

"That may have been what I said. The numbers are
apparently not accurate. There were a lot of fingerprints
destroyed. I don't to this day know how many."

"So when you said fifty fingerprints were destroyed,
you now say that this was not accurate?"

"That was a common statement at the time, sir. It
was—that figure was being used a lot. It was just kind of
a common thing in talking about it."

"All right. Now, do you recall appearing before a
body of approximately a hundred law students in Philadelphia, Pennsylvania, on or about February 11, 1971?"

"I remember the appearance. I don't remember the
date."

"Who arranged that, Doctor MacDonald?"

"Mr. Segal. He is a professor of law at the University
of Pennsylvania and it was one of his classes, and there
was some discussion about the MacDonald case at Fort
Bragg, and he asked me if I would mind answering some
questions from his law students."

"Well, I have an article from the *Daily Pennsylva-
nian*—I assume that's a newspaper at the University of
Pennsylvania—and it says that 'Captain Jeffrey MacDonald charged that both the military investigators and FBI
agents falsified and destroyed evidence in an attempt to
railroad him into a conviction.' Can you tell us about the
FBI, and can you elaborate a little bit on this falsifying
and destruction of evidence?"

"First of all, your propensity to use newspapers as evidence mystifies me. Second of all, I don't actually remember ever saying that."

"Well, all right, moving ahead, do you remember a

letter from Fred Kassab on November 6, 1971, in which
he rebuked you because you were in the area and had
not called or visited him? And in response you said, 'I
have been in Long Island on several occasions in the last
three months to continue work on finding three—
possibly four, more might be added, according to current stories in hippie family number two in North
Carolina—fugitives'?"

"This is in reference to what we talked about yesterday," MacDonald said. "This is my trying to keep Freddy
at bay. You know, you are taking it out of context. You
should have read the whole letter. You probably did, but
you don't want the grand jury to hear it."

"We'll make it available to the grand jury," Woerheide
said.

At the start of the fourth day, Woerheide again asked
MacDonald if he would submit to either the polygraph
or sodium amytal examinations.

In response MacDonald read a statement that had
been prepared by his attorneys, both Segal and Michael
Malley, a former Princeton roommate who had worked
for the defense during the Article 32 hearing and who
had remained involved in the intervening years. The first
part of the statement maintained that no useful purpose
could be served by a polygraph examination because the
technique lacked scientific validity and because the results were inadmissible as evidence in a majority of state
and federal courts.

MacDonald continued to read: "Sodium amytal. Mr.
Malley has called to my attention as part of his advice
that he has known me for twelve years. That we were in
the same class at Princeton. That we were roommates
prior to my marriage to Colette. And we have talked at

length about my feelings, my emotional well-being, and—" He paused. He was beginning to weep as he read the prepared material. "—my ability to cope with the memories in my life after these murders."

It was with apparent difficulty that he continued. "He believes he knows me as well as he knows anyone and to the extent it is possible for one man ever to understand another, he believes he understands my feelings towards myself and my life.

"In his professional opinion, it would be prohibitively dangerous for me to undergo a sodium amytal examination. This is a drug which causes a person to essentially relive the episode. It is not simply recalling, as most of us recall the past, but it is a complete reliving with most or all of the emotional feelings—anguish, fear, and grief— to go with the experience."

So overwhelming, apparently, was the intensity of these feelings that MacDonald was once more overcome by emotion simply by reading about them. He sobbed audibly, unable to continue.

"Take your time, Doctor. Take your time," Woerheide said.

In a moment he pressed on. "After the session, this experience is remembered, and the person has the same reactions as if he had actually relived what was discussed."

Once more his sobs prevented him from continuing.

"Doctor MacDonald, you are reading that. Would you prefer to have it marked as an exhibit and placed in the grand jury record that way?"

MacDonald waged an apparently successful battle to regain a measure of self-control. "I think I'm over that part," he said in a firmer voice. "I'll just finish if it's okay."

"All right."

"After the session, this experience is remembered and the person has the same reactions as if he actually relived what was discussed. Because Mr. Malley knows me so well and knows the murders of my family are the most unspeakably difficult thing I've ever faced, he believes that I cannot recall to this day or describe them without the constant problem of breaking down.

"I function normally because I try so hard to avoid having to recall, to retell, and to relive. I usually am successful in avoiding to have to confront these memories in direct detail, but this success is a day-to-day battle.

"Mr. Malley believes, as does Mr. Segal, that if I were to undergo the sodium amytal session, the reliving the murders would be so emotionally upsetting that I would not thereafter be able to pick up my life.

"They believe that a drug-induced flashback would be so painful that my normal and largely successful-to-date attempts to live with this grief would be destroyed, either permanently or for a long time, so as to make me incapable of living under the circumstances as a normal person in a professional life as is now possible.

"Accordingly, they do not feel the extreme and dangerous resort of the sodium amytal is warranted. Both Mr. Malley and Mr. Segal are friends and lawyers charged with representing my best interests, and they cannot recommend that I undergo it. My advice from them in the strongest possible terms is not to undergo such a potentially debilitating experience."

"Well, that certainly is your privilege, sir," Woerheide said, "and no one will make any inferences on the grounds that you have not agreed to subject yourself to these tests. Now, we had one other request in regard to the notes you kept of your recollections in 1970."

"Let me give you an answer to that this afternoon,"

MacDonald said. "I mentioned it once and Mr. Segal spiraled through the roof, stating that was obviously attorney-client stuff."

Woerheide moved on to ask MacDonald about his association with the Fort Bragg boxing team.

"Did you work out with them?"

"Yes, for a short period of time."

"You've always had an interest in boxing, I take it?"

"Right."

"And in college were you on a boxing team?"

"It was a very loose club. We had a club at Princeton and I worked out with them. We never had any matches."

"Now, at Fort Bragg, was there any talk between you and the coach about being the team physician?"

"Right, he said they needed a physician and I had just come into the gym and I was watching the boxers work out one day and we started talking and he said, why don't you work out with us, and I started working out with them and then he mentioned the field trips— matches at other posts—they needed a physician. So, I thought that was a great idea. So I said, well, if it were possible I would like to do that. And he mentioned specifically there was a long trip to Russia coming up that he would like to have a physician on board for."

"When was that trip to be made?"

"Sometime in the spring."

"Do you remember when you talked about this Russian trip?"

"No. It came up on several occasions."

"Well, we're getting into the area very close to February 16, 17. Did you, on that day, meet the coach and discuss this Russian trip?"

"I don't remember whether I did or not, sir. I've been

asked that several times. And in the middle of summer, when my lawyers were questioning me about the events, that was really the first time that it ever clicked that that may have been the day—that there may have been a discussion on that day. But I'm not sure. I honestly don't recall that."

(Though in his "diary" for February 16, 1970, he had written: *Heard from boxing club coach who said I would probably hear within several days about the proposed 30-day trip to Russia. . . . Colette is almost as happy as I am. . . .*)

"During your growing-up period," Woerheide asked, "did you ever live away from home for any extended period of time?"

"Yes, I did."

"Will you tell us about that?"

"I went to Texas when I was a sophomore in high school. I lived down in Baytown for, I believe it was Thanksgiving to Easter of that year."

"With whom were you living?"

"Friends of Bob and Marian Stern. I don't know if they were really friends. They were business acquaintances."

"And the Sterns were friends of your family?"

"Right."

"What did you say the name of these friends was?"

"Jack Andrews."

"Was he, you might say, a contemporary of the Sterns and your father?"

"I believe he was a little younger. He was a young engineer for Humble Oil at the time. My father and Bob were older."

"Did he have a family?"

"He sure did."

"A wife and kids?"

"A wife and a boy, Jack."

"A boy, Jack? Was he about your age?"

"Same age. That's why I went down."

"What was the reason for your leaving home and living in Texas for this period of time?"

"Well, we just met them. Jack Andrews was kind of a free-spending type Texan who at least talked big. And he asked me at one time if I would like to come down and meet his son and spend a couple of weeks. So I asked my parents and they talked it over with Bob and Jack and came back to me and said, if you want to go, fine. And so I left at the end of our football season."

"Did you transfer to a school in Texas?"

"Not initially, because I was just going to stay a couple of weeks. But around Christmas time they asked me to stay. They thought it would be interesting. And I did, too. I was having a blast. So I called home or wrote home and they said, sure. So I entered the Robert E. Lee school in Baytown, Texas."

"Were there any family problems which resulted in your living away from your family for this rather extended period of time?"

"Not that I'm aware of," MacDonald said.

"Now I take it," Woerheide said, "being a doctor, you collected medical supplies?"

"Sure did."

"Did you have any pills, and I have no idea what sort of medication it is, that some people refer to as uppers or downers? I think those are things that have a tendency to stimulate your bodily functions or relax your bodily functions one way or another."

"There was a bottle of Eskatrol diet pills which had some amphetamines in it."

Having seen the CID report which stated that testing of MacDonald's blood "did not reveal the presence of any dangerous drugs," Woerheide did not pursue that line of questioning, and MacDonald volunteered no further information.

Slowly, Victor Woerheide, though still keeping his distance, began to circle closer to the events of February 17, 1970.

"I know you've been asked this question before," he said, "and I believe I can anticipate what your answer is going to be, but I believe the grand jury should have the benefit of hearing it. Did you have any problems of any type—specifically between you and Colette—regarding anything?"

"We didn't have any problems," MacDonald said. "That, as a matter of fact, has been overlooked in the past."

"There were no quarrels or disputes?"

"Nothing major."

"Were there any minor quarrels or disputes?"

"Yes, I'm sure there were."

"Do you recall any?"

"No, quite frankly."

"Well, did Colette complain about such things as spending money without you consulting her as to what you were spending money for?"

"Absolutely not."

"I complain to my wife when she does that."

"Absolutely not."

"You bought a stereo down there, didn't you?"

"That's right."

"How much did that cost?"

"I don't know. It was a package deal with the color TV and it was on time. Like two years of payments or something and the total was seven or eight hundred dollars for the two together, stereo and TV."

"Did she get upset about that?"

"No, she liked it. It was the first time we had had nice possessions."

"So, I take it, your testimony is that your marriage was serene, was calm, and there were no problems of any concern."

"That's right."

"Nothing that troubled the still waters of your marriage."

"That's right."

"How about the kids? Any problems with the kids?"

"Absolutely not."

"In some of the material I saw, it indicated that Colette was somewhat concerned about bed-wetting. Would you consider bed-wetting a problem?"

"No, and she didn't consider it a problem either. The only one that considered that a problem was the CID agent."

"Was this something you discussed with one another?"

"Sure."

"But these discussions didn't result in any arguments or disputes?"

"Absolutely not."

"Or misunderstandings?"

"Absolutely not. The problem was that Kristy still had a bottle at two and a half years of age and I thought Colette should take the bottle away when she goes to sleep. Colette said she didn't mind getting up and getting her a

bottle. That doesn't sound like a very big problem."
Neither did it sound like the situation Colette had described to her child psychology class on the last night of her life.

"How about Kimberly? Was she a bed-wetter?"

"No."

"She had long since outgrown that?"

"Right." This, of course, was contrary to what the nurse from San Antonio had said to the CID reinvestigators.

Woerheide moved to close range, asking Jeffrey MacDonald to describe the events of February 17 and the days immediately preceding.

"I guess Valentine's Day was Friday," MacDonald said, "and on Saturday Ron Harrison came over in the afternoon." (In fact, Valentine's Day had been Saturday, and Ron Harrison had come over that night.) MacDonald described the discussion of the contents of the *Esquire* magazine. "We thumbed through the magazine," he said, "and that was it. That's all there ever was, and for some reason this has become a tremendously important thing in my life."

He continued: "I don't know if Ron ate dinner with us or not. I don't even remember what we did that night. I presume we stayed home because I had to work the next morning."

He described driving to Hamlet, eating a steak for breakfast, and passing a quiet day in the emergency room. "I had several meals during the day," he said. "I took a nap or two, probably in the morning right after breakfast I went back to my room and slept for an hour or two. Did some reading. And I probably had about five and a half or six hours of sleep Sunday night, from roughly midnight on." (During the April 6, 1970, interview, MacDonald had said, "Now, when I'm at work I—I hardly ever sleep. I mean, the nurses can tell you that. They just call me and, you know—I'm there like that.")

Now, in 1974, he described driving back to Fort Bragg, eating breakfast, and going to work. "I did office work, mainly," he said. "My title was preventive medical officer, which the newspapers took to be, you know, counseling a lot of people on drug abuse when it was in fact keeping latrines clean.

"I presume that I was at my office most of the day. I may have run over either on the way home for lunch or sometime during the day to see this sergeant on the boxing team. I don't really recall that. This was kind of suggested to me, and it seems like a reasonable possibility. Really, nothing stands out at all, you know, about that day, except I believe we played basketball for a short period of time starting around 4:30.

"Most of the officers, we either played—I tried to get them to play either volleyball or basketball. The guys were always out of shape and they didn't like to run the mile or the number of laps but they'd play competitively, so I think I got the whole office to go over and play basketball for a while that day.

"Then I believe I went home, picked up both the children, and went down to feed the Shetland pony. And we had dinner at home and Colette split for class. So I probably, you know, cleared off the table—normal procedure—and got the kids in their pajamas. And relatively soon Kristy would go to bed. You know, I'd put her to bed.

"Kimberly stayed up with me. Sometime shortly there after dinner I think I probably—I was probably on the floor with Kimmy and had a nap. We were waiting for *Laugh-In*. We watched *Laugh-In* together. She liked the little guy who used to ride a bicycle and hit a telephone pole and fall over."

He described Colette's return home from class and said, "After Johnny Carson came on, she went to bed. I was still up. I was in the middle of a—reading something. I believe it was a mystery at the time. I read a lot of mysteries. I started reading after Kimmy, you know, went to bed. I had the TV on and I was reading something or something like that. I usually just leaf through something, or was reading while the TV was on. I didn't just sit and watch TV.

"I think Johnny Carson was a good show that night or something, and I watched it. There was somebody interesting on or something, so I watched most of that. And when that was over, I did the dishes and finished reading, or something. There was something like twenty pages or something in whatever I was reading, and I finished it.

"And sometime in here Kristy had started crying. So I went in and got her a bottle, which—you know—she didn't cry anymore. This was, you know, the thing the CID thought was so critical that Colette and I disagreed about. So I got her a bottle, and gave her a bottle because we had not yet decided not to give her a bottle if she woke up in the middle of the night. That's all."

"Did Kristen wake up crying often?"

"No. No, a couple of times a week."

"It wasn't a nightly routine?"

"No."

"Do you know of any particular reason she woke up crying that night?"

"No."

"As opposed to any other night?"

"No."

"Did you ask her?"

"No. It didn't seem unusual at all. It just seemed like something kids do sometimes."

"Did you ask her if she had a bad dream or something like that? What was wrong?"

"Oh, I probably did. I probably said, 'Everything's okay, Kris.' And she said she wanted a bottle, so I gave her a bottle."

"But you have no specific recollection?"

"No. Really what I recollect is she was crying and I went in, and we sort of talked or something and I got her a bottle."

"Do you remember what you talked about?"

"No."

MacDonald resumed his recitation.

"And then after I finished the dishes and finished reading this book, paperback style, I went in to go to bed. And Kristy was in bed with my wife and she had wet the bed, you know, on my half of the bed.

"I don't know, really, honestly, if she, you know—or if she did not have a bottle. I presume if she did have a bottle there with her I would keep it with her, and brought her to her own bed and put her in bed.

"She was two and a half years old. She wasn't diapered. She had, you know—the bed-wetting was a relatively infrequent thing. You know, she didn't wet her bed every night or every other night or even like that.

"It was kind of an infrequent thing or a weekly thing by now and she didn't wear diapers, and I didn't change her diapers. She had a—you know—wet thing, and she had her bottle and was going to sleep the rest of the night, so I just let her go to sleep.

"So I pushed back the covers to let the bed dry where she had been and I got a blanket and went to sleep on the couch. Big deal.

"And the next—you know, there was some lights on in the house. There was a light on in the kitchen and there was a light on in the main bathroom. So the next thing I remembered was I heard my wife screaming, and she said, 'Help, Jeff!' And at the same time I heard Kristy—Kimberly—I'm sorry, it wasn't Kristy, it was Kimberly. She was screaming, 'Daddy!'

"Colette said, 'Help, Jeff, why are they doing this to me?' And it sounded very loud to me. It still sounds loud. Kimberly said, 'Daddy, Daddy, Daddy, Daddy, Daddy, help!'

"And I started to sit up, and there was some people at the end of the couch the CID said was never in my house. And they couldn't find any evidence of fourteen investigators and three medics and the CID and MPs and doctors, and because they couldn't find evidence of these people, I'm guilty.

"The CID can't even fingerprint a phone that an MP has used and get his fingerprints, and they tell me they have no evidence of these people and that's why I'm here today. That's why.

"It is the most preposterous—they had no evidence that Ron Harrison was in my house, they had no evidence that my mother was in my house, no evidence the Kassabs were there, no evidence my brother was there, no evidence that anyone I ever knew was in my house except me, so I'm guilty.

"That's crazy! That's like something out of a TV show.

"I never said I saw hippies," MacDonald said. "I never said that. The provost marshal said I saw hippies. I said I saw people. I saw a person with long blond hair and a floppy hat on, and there was a light on her.

"And I never said I saw candles either. It was a light on her face, and I had the impression that there was something—you know, a wavering thing of an intermittent light or something, but I still think it was like candlelight—you know, it was an impression.

"It was in the midst of a dark room and over a period of ten to twenty to thirty seconds, and I never really saw her. I saw hair, I saw a face outline, and a hat, and that was it. That was all I saw, and while this was happening, Colette was screaming and Kimberly was screaming, 'Daddy,' and this guy hit me with something I thought was a baseball bat."

MacDonald continued his description of the fight, saying, "I couldn't use my hands well, because my pajama top was all around my hands. And I've been asked fifty million times, how did the pajama top get around your hands? I don't remember that. It could have been pulled over my head as I was struggling and let go of the guy's arm. It could have been ripped around my back. I just don't know. I just had—it was around my arms all of a sudden, and I was trying to push and I couldn't get my arms out of my jacket. Like when you see in a hockey fight when a guy pulls a shirt over the other hockey player—you know—I couldn't do anything.

"And the next thing I remember I was falling and I saw a glimpse of a knee, and that's the extent of all these allegations made by the provost marshal in the newspaper about fringed boots and white boots and black boots and muddy boots.

"What I saw was a glimpse of a knee in the top of what I thought was a boot and, you know, it seemed—what I really remember, it seemed shiny. So when they asked me was it wet, I said, yeah, it seemed like it was wet or was vinyl leather or shiny leather, that kind of thing.

"I never said to anyone that I know of that there were muddy boots, or anything like that, and all these things get taken—well, you'll get to that.

"So the next thing, I was lying on the floor. And I absolutely, distinctly remember I was lying there and my teeth were chattering, and there was absolute silence and I was laying sort of on my stomach with my arms under me, wrapped up in this pajama top.

"And I remember laying there, and then I remember thinking—Jesus, I heard all these screams, and it's silent, and I got up and walked down the hall to the bedroom."

He described discovering Colette, Kimberly, and Kristen, then returning to the master bedroom and dialing the operator, only to be told that if he was calling from on post, he would have to contact the military police himself.

"I don't know if I said anything or not, but I dropped the phone. I couldn't figure out what the hell she was talking about. So I checked Colette again— sometime in here I had covered her with my pajama top that I think was still on my arms as I was coming in the room—coming in—and first—you know—as I was coming in the room the first time, I took it off and Colonel Rock was very interested in whether I dropped it or threw it.

"Shit, I don't know if I dropped it or threw it. I think I threw it away. And then I had picked it up again and I covered Colette with it, covered her chest. And sometime in here I picked it up and looked at the wound again, I guess to see if it really—if I'd really seen what I'd seen. And I put it back on her, and I remember trying to cover her. I think that there was some clothes in the chair across from her, and I reached across and I was pulling things. I remember that.

"I don't remember a white towel that the CID is so interested in. I don't know if I covered her with a white towel or not. I may have. I may not have. I was covering her. And I checked her pulses. And when I'd come back from the phone I—I—it seemed to me that the back door was open. And I walked over to the back door and looked out. And I didn't see anything. But I remember thinking all this time how silent it was compared to how it had sounded.

"So I—I went back to Kimberly and I think now that I gave her mouth-to-mouth breathing, and it seemed to me that the air was coming out of her chest. So the CID said, 'Ah-hah! She didn't have any wounds in her chest.' She had wounds in her neck and chest area—the upper—the lower neck and chest, and all I can remember is it was bubbling. I don't specifically remember, you know, thinking to myself it was neck or chest. I remember that the air I was breathing into her mouth was now bubbling. And so I went to check Kristy, and sometime in here—really silly—it really sounds stupid—one of the times that I was coming out of the kids' rooms, I reached up or something like that and I felt my head and when my hand came away it had some blood on it, and I remember I was thinking to myself, my head really hurts—you know, I thought to myself—I wasn't even really—you know, making any sense to myself.

"I guess my thought was that it was blood from me, and I went in the bathroom and looked in the mirror. The bathroom is right there. It's like one step. It's not like a long voyage. It's one step.

"And I stepped into the bathroom, and I—you know,

I really can't put that in there. You know, it's put in—in narratives. It's put into testimony.

"So now, you know, if you really have to pin me down and force me to say so, I think that I went into the bathroom the first time that I came out of Kristy's room before I went in and saw Colette the second time.

"But if you knew how—you know, what do you say when you mean recollections? What I see is my wife and my kids, and I see bubbles coming out of their chests, and I remember them asking for help.

"And there's this dumb-ass operator, and I remember that I was talking on the kitchen phone and I was saying this is Captain MacDonald, I need help, I'm at 544 Castle Drive, and she said, 'Is this Captain MacDonald?' and I said, 'You dumb idiot, I just told you that!' Or something like that. I thought I was yelling at her. She testified it was very faint. Seemed to me that I was yelling at her.

"And then there were some clicks and buzzes and all kinds of sounds on the phone, and then a male voice said this is Sergeant something or other, and I said, "There are people who are dying here. We need medics and MPs,' and I heard in the background—'Tell Womack ASAP!' and I don't—really don't remember anything else.

"In the April 6 interview there—they made all kinds of inferences at the Article 32 that I said I remembered going back down the hallway to my wife. What I recollect—what I really recollect—is I remember the end of the phone conversation. And the next specific recollection I have is I was fighting with an MP and he was saying relax and I was saying, 'Relax?! Shit, will you look at my wife?! Jesus Christ, look at my wife!' And people were running by and shouting and screaming, and I heard, 'Put that down! Don't touch her! Don't move her!' And they were saying, 'Who did it? Who did it?' and people were struggling with me and pushing me and I was looking up, and all I could see was MP helmets, shiny helmets, all around me.

"And I remember I was fighting with these MPs or medics in the hallway, right between the two bedrooms. I was on a stretcher and they were fighting with me and strapping me down or something like that, and then I remember I was in an ambulance and I said, 'Get my wife and kids to the hospital.' And the next thing I remember is I was arguing with this nurse about my Social Security number. She kept asking me, said, 'What's your Social Security number?' And I said, 'Fuck you!' I said, 'What do you care what my Social Security number is?' I said, 'I want my wife and my kids,' and she said, 'They're all okay,' and I was sitting up or trying to sit up on the stretcher and I kept looking around and I said, 'Where are they? Bring them in!' And she said, 'They're all okay,' and I said, 'What the hell do you want my Social Security number for?'"

On the morning of the fifth day, Woerheide asked Mac-Donald about his wounds. "Now, I've never really said this before," MacDonald said, "because obviously I was the accused and it sounds ridiculous for you to testify about your own medical wounds, but if the exam I had in the emergency room were done anywhere other than in the Army it wouldn't be any good.

"It was a totally inadequate medical record of an examination from any physician's viewpoint. It's the first time I've ever said that, but it's true. And it's, you know, one of the two or three major reasons this case is still going on and I'm here: because of the medical record.

"I was never reexamined after the emergency room. No one ever came in and looked at me. And I don't care what anyone thinks anymore. That's shitty. That is inadequate medical care.

"So when I talk about the wounds I had, a lot of them aren't listed in the medical report. But that medical report is not a routine medical report by any means. There is no doctor that would be proud of that medical report. There were four contusions to the head, there was a much larger contusion to my left shoulder, there were three stab wounds, and then as far as puncture wounds there were roughly three, six, nine, and eight—about seventeen."

On the afternoon of the fifth day, Woerheide asked Mac-Donald if he would care to make a statement to the grand jury before concluding his testimony. He said he would.

"I'm sure it's going to occur to the grand jury," Mac-Donald began, "that if what I'm saying is true, how did this incredible sort of prosecution ever get going? And I'd just like one sentence to sort of give my theory, if I'm allowed that.

"It just seemed to me that Mr. Grebner and Mr. Shaw and Ivory made very, very critical errors on the morning of the 17th, never checked them, had the interview with me six weeks later, and from that point on they were set up sort of for a prosecution.

"It sounds absurd. Sounds absolutely ridiculous. But Mr. Grebner has testified under oath that he walked into the house, made a decision that the living room was staged and we asked him why and he said because of the flowerpot.

"All he had to do was ask an MP. All he had to was

line the MPs up and say, has anyone seen anyone touch anything? He never did. The first time the MPs were questioned was six months later. Now, that's unbelievable police work. So, you know, to come to a rational theory as to why what I am saying may be true or may not be true, how could the CID—why would the CID do this to Captain MacDonald?

"It wasn't any malevolent sort of thing with a nasty colonel in the background to ride down Captain MacDonald. It was, initially, stupid mistakes made. But then they acted on those mistakes. They never checked them, and they—they acted on those mistakes.

"Look, I'm here, obviously, defending myself, so what weight does my word carry? But to say that they found no evidence of other people in that house when they had the back door open and the front door open, and people walking in and out at random, with no guard at Kimmy's room and no guard at Kris's room and no guard at the master bedroom, preserving the crime scene—all you have to do is read the lieutenant's testimony. He had no idea how many men he had under his control. He didn't know their names. He didn't give them any orders except don't touch anything. That's all he said! He didn't station guards at the doors. There were unknown numbers of people walking through that house, including someone in dungarees who sat on the couch.

"To reconstruct that initial hour after they arrived is going to be impossible. That crime work that morning was destroyed. But I suggest to you, sir, that that doesn't make me guilty of homicide.

"And it just seems unusual to me that the CID would make a lot out of some bloodstains in the master bedroom which were five to seven in number with the largest being as big as a quarter when my remembrance of the house was that the whole house was covered with blood.

"And it seems to me when they picked me up and put me on a stretcher and take me down the hall and then bring another stretcher in the hall for the kids and what not, before these critical spots are identified—you know, to incriminate me on that basis is absurd. I find it really insane, actually, at this point of my life.

"They take a wheeled stretcher with me on it, struggling, and wheel it down the hall and out the living room. Then they take photographs and state to me that I staged the crime scene."

MacDonald's tone, as he continued, became increasingly aggrieved: what he seemed to want most to communicate to the grand jurors was the *unfairness* of it all.

"They also never bothered to ask the doctor if he had moved anyone, because—because to—apparently to them very important fibers wound up under the body of my wife. Fibers that they say belonged to my pajama top. Well, apparently we're never going to know if they could have belonged to my pajama bottoms either. But the fact is they never asked the doctor and the doctor stated he picked her up and looked at her back, and that the cloth could have fallen off her onto the floor at that point. In addition, I moved her. Apparently they failed to take that into consideration.

"I know it's going to be very difficult for twenty-three normal people to say, 'Well, Jesus, how can we believe this guy when the Army and all these investigators and the FBI spent all this money and time and they didn't find anything.'

"They never set up any roadblocks! And then the CID implicated me because a group of assailants that were in my house that night were never found. I suggest that they weren't found because of that initial couple of hours where unbelievably bad decisions were made.

"And I also suggest that later on when they got information about at least what sounds like good potential leads—I'm not saying that the leads pan out or anything; I'm not saying Helena Stoeckley is guilty—I'm not saying that. I'm saying that that indicates the type and the scope and the way that investigation went on.

"I don't mean to harangue the grand jury, I honestly don't, but some of the stories of the handling of this case are so bizarre that it is beyond belief. *They never set up any roadblocks!*

"Well, I'm on the stand. I'm not going to—I mean my life is—was shattered like, you know—you can't conceive of what was going on in my mind or anything. And it doesn't make any sense.

"But I do suggest to you that I'm a little confused about the line of questioning about the girl in the BOQ. This is half a year later, after I've been through an unbelievable thing. And for someone to visit me in the BOQ—even if it did occur before my release from custody, which I don't think it did—is totally meaningless.

"Well. I hope I'm getting my point across. To say that I committed homicide and murdered my wife and kids because they couldn't find any grass or mud in the house is the most atrocious, insane reasoning. And for me to be here today is crazy. This is insanity! The Army reinvestigation was done a year and a half ago—two million dollars and ten thousand pages, three thousand pages, or whatever it came to—making sure that we can't prove that the CID makes mistakes. That's what they did.

"If you add it all up, it sounds terrific. They've had

two Army investigations—in their words, the biggest investigation the Army has ever had. And they can't find the group of four assailants so therefore I'm guilty.

"All I'd like to say, sir, is, you know, you haven't asked me, but, you know, I didn't murder my wife and kids."

2

Jeffrey MacDonald returned to California, but the grand jury remained in session until January of 1975. More than seventy-five witnesses testified.

Gradually, a picture of Jeffrey MacDonald began to emerge: a context into which the grand jurors could place the man they had seen and the story they had heard during MacDonald's week on the witness stand.

Benjamin Klein, the surgical resident who had examined MacDonald in the emergency room in 1970, said, "I didn't feel he was in any great danger, medically. He was not suffering from shock and his wounds were not bleeding very much. He was able to sit up by himself and to talk without being short of breath."

Merrill Bronstein, who had been staff surgeon on call in 1970, said, "He was clinically stable. He didn't have a lot of things besides the pneumothorax and even with that he was not having any difficulty breathing and there was no change in his pulse, blood pressure, or other vital signs.

"He had the bruise on his left forehead, the superficial stab wound of the left upper arm, the stab wound in the left upper abdomen, and the stab wound in the right chest." This last Bronstein described as being a "clean, small, sharp" incision. It was only one centimeter in length.

"He had no other stab wounds on his body," Bronstein said.

"Would you say he did or did not have fourteen icepick wounds around his belly button?" Woerheide asked.

"He absolutely did not have any icepick wounds anywhere, and I saw his entire body because while I was there his pajamas were removed and I examined him from head to toe."

"Were you concerned about, let's say, his ability to survive the effects of the injuries?" Woerheide asked.

"No. I was concerned about his emotional status. That was the thing that affected me most, the thing that impressed me most, the thing that I had the greatest difficulty, as a physician, in dealing with. If he had had more medical problems, then I could have dealt with him clinically and gotten my mind off the situation."

"In your opinion, it was not an emergency?"

"No, sir. The most remarkable thing to me was that he was so upset."

Bronstein added that MacDonald had been transferred out of intensive care to a private room the next day. "I would stop by and ask how he was and chat for a few minutes. I certainly saw him every day he was in the hospital."

"Did he have visitors?"

"Yes, sir. His mother stayed with him a lot. She was up quite a bit. And I met a friend of his named Ron Harrison, whom he introduced me to in his room."

"Tell us about Ron Harrison."

"He was an unusual person. I never knew many people like Ron Harrison. He impressed me as being—and this is a surgical opinion, I'm a surgeon, I'm not a psychiatrist—he impressed me as being disturbed.

"I was worried when I met Ron Harrison. He told me that he was a killer. And he told me that he was going to kill the people who were responsible for this crime.

"He was a paranoid person. He was always worried about people being around. He said, 'Jeff wants me to find them and kill them.' And from him I took this seriously. I mean, I really did.

"He was in every day for sure. And I saw him after that. I was out with my wife one night, and he was in the same restaurant and he frightened my wife. It was just the way he appeared—the things he said. He said things that—my wife is a very gentle person. She would never think of killing anyone. She would not think of harming anyone. And he was talking about that.

"I have friends—or I had friends—who were in Special Forces, and I had friends who were not physicians in Special Forces, people that I socialized with, who I was in their homes and they were in mine. But they certainly, you know, would not choose as a topic of conversation or point of discussion with me, killing and death. They certainly would never discuss it in the presence of my family."

In fact, Bronstein said, it was the apparent closeness of the relationship with Ron Harrison which first caused him to doubt MacDonald's innocence. "Overall," he said, "I think I could have accepted Jeff's story without too much trouble. But I was worried after I met Ron Harrison. He was a frightening guy. I mean, he physically frightened me. I just didn't know how he could be Jeff's friend."

*   *   *

MacDonald's next-door neighbor, the wife of the war-rant officer and the mother of the sixteen-year-old baby-sitter who had heard no sounds of struggle, testified.

"He was the boss," she said. "He was the king of the castle and he was—when he told her to do something, she did it willingly and obligingly, a very good wife. She was a very obedient wife." Until, the woman said, the early morning hours of Tuesday, February 17, 1970. "I came out of a deep sleep and I heard Colette's voice," she said, "and it woke me up. The voice I heard was mad enough to kill."

"Could you distinguish the words?"

"No, but I got the gist of it, and I would swear on the Bible that it—that what—what it was like she was saying was, 'What do you think I'm going to be doing while you are doing all of this? Do you think I am going to be standing here doing nothing? If you touch one hair of those children's head or my head, I'll kill you!'"

The sixteen-year-old babysitter herself—now a young woman of twenty-one—also testified. Asked to describe her impression of the relationship between Jeffrey and Colette MacDonald, she said, "At the time I thought they were pretty happy because they didn't yell at each other. But now I look back and they never really smiled. Colette never smiled and Jeff wasn't too friendly after about January. Now that I look back, after January, Co-lette hardly even said 'Hi,' when I went over to babysit. I don't know. When I saw them together they weren't—I just sensed that they weren't happy."

In regard to the children's sleeping arrangements, the former babysitter said, "Sometimes Kim would ask Kris to come into her bedroom. Sometimes Kim would want to go into her parents' bed. I'd let them sleep wherever they wanted to. Kristen usually had a second bottle at night, and she would wake up and cry for it. Kim would wake up and cry, too. I'd have to go in and talk to her. She would just cry, I think Colette's name: 'Mommy.' She would hardly say anything when I went in there. I'd just tell her her mother and father would be home. She just listened to me."

"Did Kimberly ever wet the bed that you know of?"

"I think once."

"How about Kristen?"

"She would wet the bed pretty often."

The former babysitter also testified—after first saying she had no recollection—that the MacDonalds did, indeed, have an icepick. That, in fact, it was usually kept on top of the refrigerator and that she would use it, on occasion, to chip away ice in the freezer in order to take out popsicles or ice cream for the children.

The newspaper reporter who had covered the Article 32 hearing and who had interviewed MacDonald on the morning the charges against him were dropped also agreed to testify.

"You have to understand what it was like to cover that case," he said. "For anybody who was an attorney or newsman or investigator, anybody who was connected with it—it began to pretty well dominate your thoughts.

"I was there every day for eight hours, ten hours a day, and it sort of dwells on your mind after a while and you start to wonder when you go home at night. You say, 'Gee, I wonder what the facts are.' And it really eats you up.

"I think almost anybody that has been involved with this since its beginnings is almost overly interested in the outcome. I am. I can't let it go. I keep thinking about it.

"I spent a great deal of time discussing ten thousand theories about why he would have done it, if he did it, or how he could have done it, or whether these four people existed at all, and if they did, where did they come from.

"And it's never left me, the feeling of wanting to know what happened. I'm just as much involved right now, and feel just as much a part of this now as I did then. You know, no matter what I'd be doing—if I was selling hot dogs, I'd still feel like I was part of this.

"So all I can tell you is what I saw, what I felt, and what I perceived through that whole thing and since.

"First, I should say that I never met anybody who knew Jeffrey MacDonald on a social basis who didn't think he was totally innocent of these crimes. Who wouldn't back him a hundred percent and said he was just a number one guy. They supported him fully and said he was incapable of committing these crimes. And at the beginning I felt pretty much the same way.

"It was kind of strange, because we were fed spoon-fuls of his personality throughout a lot of the proceedings, and you spend five months with anybody and you start to get to know them and you develop whether you like them or don't like them. I happened to like Jeff MacDonald very much. That's what caused the great emotional turmoil.

"You know, Jeffrey MacDonald was just unbelievable. Here was this guy who was handsome, and all-American, and a doctor, and a Green Beret, and all these things and, you know, he was always very sunny in his disposition, and—the whole thing was just unbelievable.

"I mean, one thing was, Segal and his assistant—the civilian assistant—were a couple of clowns. One day the assistant brought his kids down from Philadelphia. He had this really cute kid, and somebody went in the PX and bought one of those little fatigue suits—you know, a Green Beret—a total Green Beret uniform with a real green beret and a major general's insignia on it, and of course everybody took pictures of him, and it went out on the wire services all over the place, and so that was—you have to understand the carnival atmosphere that was going on down there. It was just a really strange thing. There was no sense of reality to it.

"What we had here was an investigation into three brutal murders, and if you ever started thinking that way, it really got to you. It would happen to me at night sometimes. I'd go home after clowning around with these people and I'd think, geez, we've got three dead people here and somebody's going to have to answer for it, and that will kind of get to you after a while because that wasn't what was going on during the day. It was kind of a light, frivolous thing.

"Anyway, once it was over I did a lot of in-depth investigation of the drug culture in the Fayetteville area. I grew a beard and hair and everything and was living in the Haymount section for months, and for one thing, that's a very small community and the word moves through it like wildfire, and you know, if those four people came from Fayetteville and if they were hippies and they were drug people, somebody would have known it, somebody would have known something, somebody would have heard something.

"And another thing was, the terminology was just not right. 'Acid is groovy. Kill the pigs.' People who lived in the drug culture—they call themselves heads—and I can't think of a head that would be so uncool as to say that. 'Acid is groovy,' which was an old word even then, because even then *groovy* was not a cool thing to say.

"And also, four people who are doing acid couldn't

organize a trip to the toilet, let alone organize a murder of three people. Besides, LSD normally doesn't make people violent. The only drug that I can think of that causes that kind of reaction in people is an amphetamine of some kind."

The grand jurors learned a bit more of what had happened—if not on February 17, 1970, itself, then at least during some of the months before and after—when they heard testimony from Jeffrey MacDonald's former girlfriend, Penny Wells.

She began by describing Jeffrey MacDonald as having been, in high school, an "all-American, fantastic person," whom she had dated and with whom she had been physically intimate during their junior and senior years.

"Now, at the end of high school, do you recall Jeff taking a job?" Woerheide asked.

"I guess that's when he started over at Fire Island."

"Will you tell the grand jurors what Fire Island is? What sort of place it is and what peculiar features it may have? And what Jeff was doing over there?"

"It is a place where people from New York City go on weekends. And there are a lot of gay people in certain communities. I don't know which section Jeff was working in, so I really don't know. They party all the time. Jeff was driving a beach taxi over there."

Miss Wells said that at the end of the summer of 1962—the summer after Jeffrey MacDonald's freshman year at Princeton—the relationship ended, because she'd learned that he had been "apparently dating or living with someone over there."

"Another girl?"

"Right."

"And this disturbed you?"

"Yes. I approached him and I told him what I had heard. And he denied it. And I left."

"I take it you didn't believe him?"

"No."

"When was the next time you saw him?"

"It was somewhere around Thanksgiving of that year. I heard he was in town, somebody warned me that he was in town looking for me. I was in a restaurant with a girlfriend of mine and I saw him walking in so I walked out the other door. He saw me and came over to me and I just ignored him. I just ignored him and took off."

"When was the next time you saw him after that?"

"The day before he and Colette got married he came into the office where I was working and said he was getting married the next day. When I went out to my car there was a note. And it said something about receiving a gift."

"Something about your receiving a gift?"

"Right."

"And in whose handwriting was the note?"

"It was in Jeff's handwriting and it was signed with his initials."

"Did you in fact receive a gift?"

"It was left in my car. It was a negligee. It was red and black."

"Red and black. Were those your high school colors?"

"Yes, they were."

"Do you recall Jeff having made any remark concerning your dressing in red and black?"

"Yes, he did. He liked me in red and black."

"With the negligee, was there a note?"

"Yes, there was a little saying printed on the note."

"Sort of a rhyme or verse?"

"Something to refer to the negligee."

"Now, let's go to April of 1964. Colette is in the hospital. She's just given birth to Kimberly. Do you recall hearing from Jeff, or seeing him?"

"Yes, I believe it was a phone call that I got and he asked me to meet him for lunch, that he was in the area. So I said okay. We had lunch. And he knew I liked clothes and he asked me about a suede coat, about me wanting one, and I said, 'No, thanks, I can buy my own.' It was only a short lunch and that was it. I don't really recall what we talked about."

"Did he talk about you or did he talk about himself?"

"Probably about himself."

"And when was the next time you saw him?"

"I attended a birthday party for his mother, I think it was in June 1969. I had dated his brother, Jay, a few times, and he had asked me to his mother's party. I had no idea that Jeff and Colette were going to be there. And it was a little embarrassing. I was in one section of the yard and they stayed over at the other side. Mrs. MacDonald finally sat down to open her gifts and I was sitting right across the way from her and I think I handed the gifts to her to open."

"Now, directing your attention to the fall of 1969," said Woerheide, "do you recall seeing or meeting or hearing from, directly or indirectly, or having any contact with Jeffrey MacDonald?"

"No. I had never seen him." Not on the Patchogue train station platform, she said, nor anywhere else.

"Was he on your Christmas card list?" Woerheide asked.

"I doubt it."

"Well, during this period, the fall of 1969, were you occasionally seeing Jay?"

"Yes. Occasionally."

"Did he ever give you any news of Jeff?"

"No. Never talked about him."

"Do you recall Jay having any problems?"

"I considered him a problem. He was just a changed person from high school. His looks, his weight, his personality."

"Do you have any reason to believe that he had some involvement in the drug culture?"

"It's possible."

"What do you predicate this on?"

"Stories, rumors."

"Now, getting on to February of 1970, how did you become aware of the murders?"

"It was in the *Daily News.* I saw the name Jeffrey MacDonald and I said, 'Gee, I wonder if that's the same person.' I didn't know he was in Fort Bragg. So I went further and I saw 'Colette.' And I said, 'Well, it has to be.' "

"Now, as an old girlfriend of Jeff and as a friend of the family, what did you do?"

"I sent a sympathy card."

"Did you receive a response?"

"Yes. It must have been about two or three weeks after I had sent the card. It was just a very, very short note asking me if I had been contacted by the FBI, and to let him know if I was."

"Did you respond to this inquiry?"

"No. I held on to the letter for about three or four days and then I tore it up."

Penny Wells had moved to San Diego in November of 1970. In February of 1971 her parents sent her a newspaper story which mentioned that MacDonald was considering a move to Long Beach.

"I wrote him a letter, a very short note, and said if you

are ever in San Diego, give me a call. A very short time after that he called me from New York and said he may possibly get out to California and that he would call.

"Then, I guess it was around the end of May, he called and said he was coming out in June. I said I would pick him up at the airport. And I did. And he stayed with me for a while."

"Tell us about that."

"I was very disappointed in, I guess, his looks, first of all. Physically, he looked quite a bit different. He was a lot thinner. I don't think he was as good-looking as I had remembered him. And I guess I just got older and wiser and he wasn't what—well, I had no interest in him at all. We had just gone our own separate ways and there was just nothing. I think it was appearance at first and then after a short conversation I just had nothing in common with him. He wasn't as outgoing as he usually is."

"Did he show any interest in you?"

"I would say no. Not that he had a chance."

"You were just the landlady? A convenient place to put up with—"

"Without putting out."

"But back in the days when you were dating him, what sort of fellow was he then?"

"A fantastic person. Fantastic personality. Always was out to help somebody else. In fact he used to even study with me."

"What was your last contact with him?"

"Just a change-of-address card after he had moved to Huntington Beach. And at the bottom it just said: 'Super busy. Will call.' And that was the last I ever heard."

Thus, by the time Penny Wells had completed her testimony, the grand jurors knew not only that it had been she, not MacDonald, who had brought their relationship to a halt during his freshman year at Princeton, but that he had attempted to revive her interest in him both on the day before he married Colette and on the day after Kimberly was born.

Whether he had also seen her in the fall of 1969—on the Patchogue train station platform or anywhere else—and whether he had planned, or even desired, to see her while accompanying the Fort Bragg boxing team to New Jersey in the spring of 1970 (with Colette thinking that he was in Russia) could not be determined.

What had been determined, however, was that Mac-Donald himself, even as he lay in his hospital bed recovering from the wounds inflicted on February 17, was sufficiently concerned about how others might perceive the relationship to have responded to Penny Wells's sympathy note with a query asking if the FBI had been in touch with her.

And what had also been determined was that—however short-lived and unsatisfying the renewal of the relationship turned out to be—it had been Penny Wells who had met MacDonald at the airport when he flew to California in 1971 to take up residence there.

As the weeks passed, Victor Woerheide began to try to give the grand jurors a deeper level of insight into the character and personality of Jeffrey MacDonald by presenting testimony both from the various psychiatrists and psychologists who had dealt with him professionally and from members of the MacDonald and Kassab families.

Mildred Kassab said, "I called Colette on Thanksgiving and she said, 'Well, you can tell Freddy he can cut my throat because I think I'm pregnant.' His joke around the house was that if she became pregnant again he'd cut her throat because she'd had two very difficult deliveries by Cesarean section and in fact almost died from internal bleeding after the second.

"I asked how she felt about it and she said, 'Well, I don't know. I'm a little unhappy about it but everyone here is very happy.' And she mentioned that they had fourteen for dinner, and Jeff's mother was there. She said, 'Everyone is very happy about it except me.'

"Then we went down to visit them for Christmas, and Jeff was short-tempered in testy little ways, such as going into a little storm over, 'I told you, why didn't you pick up my suit?' Little things that were a tempest in a teapot. And Colette never answered and often I would think, why didn't she say something. But she never did, and therefore there were never any arguments when I was present.

"There were many little things here and there that made me unhappy without saying anything, and Colette would never tell me, she kept her problems very much to herself, but I recall—my sister bought a car for Colette because they didn't have a car and Jeff used it to go to the hospital and to work all the time—this was back in New Jersey or Chicago—and Colette walked with a wagon to do her shopping, carry her laundry, things like that.

"And one day Jeff stumbled over some bottles and said something about taking the bottles—why didn't she take the bottles back to the store? And she said she would get them back next week or something. I said to her after, 'Colette, he has the car. Why don't you tell him to take them back himself?' She said, 'Mommy, don't ever say anything to Jeff because he cannot stand criticism.' And I never did say anything to Jeff except the time we were down there for Christmas.

Murderer or Victim? Former Green Beret Jeffrey R. MacDonald in the yard of the Federal Correctional Institution at Bastrop, Texas, where he is serving three consecutive life terms for the murders of his wife, Colette, and two young daughters, Kimberly and Kristen. PHOTO BY ROBERT F. KEELER/Courtesy of *Newsday*

Alfred Kassab leads stepdaughter Colette Stevenson down the aisle in a Greenwich Village church in September 1963. At first MacDonald's strongest supporter, Kassab would ultimately become his staunchest accuser.

Colette and Jeffrey MacDonald after taking their wedding vows. She was pregnant with their first child, Kimberly.

Kimberly, 5 (left), and Kristen MacDonald, 2, in the summer of 1969.

Kimberly.

Kimberly (left) and Kristen dressed up for Halloween, less than four months before their grisly deaths. This photo was used by MacDonald's lawyer to elicit emotion from his client while testifying in Federal Court on August 23, 1979.

The scene of the triple massacre: 544 Castle Drive in Fort Bragg, North Carolina (right side of building), which remained sealed for over nine years until the case was finally closed. Although MacDonald's nearest neighbors were just a door away, they heard little evidence of a violent struggle on that fatal night.
EXHIBITS: U.S.A. *vs.* JEFFREY R. MACDONALD

The MacDonald's living room, as found by the military police on the rainy morning of February 17, 1970. Under the lower right corner of the overturned table lies the issue of *Esquire*, in which the murder spree by followers of cult leader Charles Manson was detailed. The afghan on the couch (left) was removed from the hallway steps for removal of the bodies. EXHIBIT: U.S.A. VS. JEFFREY R. MACDONALD

(Clockwise from upper left): Bernard Segal, MacDonald's attorney; Brian Murtagh, prosecutor; James Blackburn, prosecutor; Jeffrey MacDonald, defendant. AP/WIDE WORLD PHOTOS

Caskets containing the bodies of Colette (left) and one of her daughters are carried into the John F. Kennedy Center Chapel in Fort Bragg for funeral services February 21, 1970. The third casket is already in the church. AP/WIDE WORLD PHOTOS

A handcuffed MacDonald is led away from Federal Court August 29, 1979 after a jury found him guilty of first-degree murder in the death of his two-year-old daughter, Kristen, and of second-degree murder in the deaths of his twenty-six-year-old wife, Colette, and five-year-old daughter, Kimberly.
AP/WIDE WORLD PHOTOS

MacDonald and Segal (left) leave the Supreme Court building in Washington December 7, 1981, after the high court was urged to reinstate MacDonald's murder conviction, which was over-turned by a federal appeals court on the basis that he did not receive a speedy trial.
AP/WIDE WORLD PHOTOS

At the request of MacDonald, author Joe McGinniss (above
lived with the accused in a fraternity house on the North Carc
lina State University campus during the 1979 trial to gather ir
formation for a book. It was during the three years followin
the guilty verdict that McGinniss studied every aspect of th
case and formulated his own opinions. PHOTO BY NANCY DOHERT

"The atmosphere was very tense for some reason. I didn't realize it at first because Colette—usually she and Kimmy would sit outside and wait for us when we were coming, whether it was Chicago or Bergenfield—if we were coming they would be waiting on the corner for us.

"And this day as we were arriving we called at twelve o'clock and said we would be there in an hour. Then we had a blowout and had to shop for a tire and we didn't get there until after three. And she and Kimmy were still sitting on the corner, waiting for us. And I thought she seemed rather sad, but I thought it was because she was disappointed.

"We went in and she had the tree up. I said I was pleased to see it was the first house she'd had a chance to put draperies up, and that it looked nice, but she just didn't respond that much. She was very tense. I don't know why. I suppose it was because of her pregnancy. But there wasn't any laughter or the usual bubbly happiness that you run into when you come down to see one another on Christmas.

"We went to bed early that night and the next day was Christmas and Jeff took us—at eight o'clock he said he had a surprise. And we went down and there was the pony. And of course I was joyful and the children were. And I said, 'Oh, Colette, this is the beginning for your farm in Connecticut,' because she always spoke of someday having a big old-fashioned house with horses, cows, dogs, et cetera.

"And I said, 'This is the first live thing for your farm,' and she began to weep. I just thought she was awfully touched at the idea of the pony but since then I've decided perhaps she felt there wasn't going to be that happiness in the future.

"Then Christmas Day, after that, we were only four

people and the children, and as a rule it was the custom in Jeff's family to have a lot of people in. So he suggested calling the next-door neighbors—the people from up-stairs—and this was about four in the afternoon. And Colette was preparing dinner and very much into Julia Child's cooking at the time, a very ambitious dinner. Everyone does it once in a while. Chooses too many things that you can't do all at once. So I was helping her and she said, 'Oh, no, don't ask them down because they'll stay and stay, and dinner is started and they'll stay until eight o'clock,' and we had ducks in the oven.

"But Jeff was impatient about it and called them down anyhow. Well, we were busy in the kitchen, but we took turns going in to sit down. We made drinks and served them. I made eggnog and we sat with them a few minutes at a time.

"And it did get to be eight o'clock and the ducks were dried up. No one said anything, though. And after they left we put the things on the table, and I didn't realize anything was wrong until I realized the silence and looked up and saw the children were not saying anything and Colette wasn't saying anything. And I said, 'What's wrong?' And Jeff said, 'Oh, she's always that way when I want someone around. It's just darn bad manners to stay out in the kitchen and not come in.'

"I said, 'Well, Jeff, she told you we were busy.' Colette had told him in advance that she didn't think I would like it, really, because I hadn't come to visit those neighbors and she didn't think they were my type, exactly, and after all since we drove down to see them, why have someone else? I explained that to him but he just pushed his chair away and left the table.

"The children said nothing and Colette had a couple of little tears and no one said any more about it. I told him I thought he was acting very childish and he just flung out of the room.

"I think perhaps why things were so tense at Christmas was because this was possibly a time when they were getting along badly and she didn't want anything to erupt before us because she wouldn't want us to know anything was wrong. She would never confide in me if she felt that Jeff was unfaithful. She never would because I had been—too often when we are safe ourselves we become very complacent and we are ready to throw stones, and I was always quite noisy about men who chased around and whose wives were submissive."

"Do you recall," Victor Woerheide asked, "whether there was an icepick in the house?"

"Yes, I do. When I was working at the refrigerator—I had brought some little puff pastry hors d'oeuvres and things down with me for her for the holidays, and they had to go directly into the freezer and it was already loaded and I couldn't move the ice trays. So I got the icepick out, jabbed around until I got the ice trays loose and could use one of them for the pastry. So I know I used the icepick."

After Christmas, Mildred Kassab said, "my husband felt that Colette might be a little bit angry with him for something because her voice was different when he called her on the phone. He would call her frequently from his office because he had a trunk line, and she had always been very fond of him, since her father died when she was quite young.

"But after Christmas she didn't sound the same. I would like to mention also that Colette never forgot a birthday, anniversary, Easter, Mother's Day, and all that sort of thing. There were always cards.

"But January 19th was Freddy's birthday and it was

the first time in sixteen years that he didn't get a card from Colette—the first time she ever forgot. She'd always sent Valentines, too, and let the children put their little mark on and we didn't receive any Valentines. We thought about that afterwards. She must have been upset."

"Do you remember the last time you spoke to her?"

"Yes, I called her on—it was the day after a big snowstorm, right around the 14th of February, and she said she was alone. Jeff was working.

"She said they had taken someone to the airport a day or two before, and she said she was wishing she could have gotten on the plane. And Kimmy had asked, 'When can we go to Grandma's again?' And she said they would like so much to be able to come home.

"And I said, 'Well, the snow is very deep and it's covering the pool.' There was just a light cover of plastic on the pool and I was afraid at that time because there was no indication of where the pool was, and we had just put it in. The children wouldn't know where it was, and I said, 'Wait until spring.'

"So then she told me Jeff might have to go to Russia with the boxing team and if he did he would go in April and he wouldn't be back until the end of July, and he would be in Russia, so therefore there would be—no one would be able to communicate with him, and she would be alone when she had the baby and would I surely be there on the 18th of July? She really believed that he might forcibly be sent away without asking. In other words, he would have to go. I think she was becoming increasingly worried about the pregnancy. She hadn't been to a doctor yet, and she had already put on twenty pounds, she said, and she was worried about whether it was going to be a very large child.

"I said, 'I will be there. Regardless of anything in the world, I'll be there.'"

The former chief of psychiatry from Walter Reed Army Hospital testified. He was the same doctor who had testified at the Article 32 hearing, but the grand jury setting—with its privacy and absence of cross-examination—permitted him far greater latitude.

"The initial question that was put to me," he said, "was that a civilian psychiatrist had evaluated Captain MacDonald and had stated that he was incapable of committing such an act, and so I was asked if I would evaluate him and testify as to my own opinion as to that issue.

"The first contact I had was with Captain MacDonald's military attorney, who briefed me for about an hour and a half without Captain MacDonald being present, sort of giving his side of the story.

"Later that afternoon I was approached by the military prosecutors and by Mr. Ivory, the CID man. They arrived around four o'clock and I was exposed to pictures of the house and the bodies. I considered it a bombardment, and I used that word. Frankly it was rather disturbing to me, having six children of my own. I got out of my office about 6:30. I had a thirty-five-minute drive home and I trembled as I drove. I lived out in Galesville, Maryland, and when I drove home it was getting dark. I trembled and I did not sleep that night.

"The next day, I saw Dr. MacDonald. I met him at the door and shook hands with him.

"He was a very cordial, smiling, cooperative, warm person. He expressed his feelings of being upset at having to go through all of this procedure, upset that he was accused, but at the same time he created an impression of being a very engaging sort of person who was very facile in his ability to talk.

"I deliberately, in my first interview with him, did not discuss February 17 at all. I did the past history. He gave me a very bland past history, of what he considered to be a relatively normal family upbringing. Said that it was a happy family.

"We talked about his father dying of pulmonary fibrosis. He described his father as a leader, as a very masculine type of person; described his father in an interesting way: as a man who was constantly at battle with the world when he didn't need to be. And he described his father as feeling that women—I've got a quote here: 'That women had taken over the country.'

"I had the impression that between him and his father, in terms of emotional closeness, there was not much. He described his mother as a very calm, quiet, strong person. He talked about his brother, Jay. Everyone liked Jay, he said. Described Jay as a failure who'd had some fifteen to twenty jobs, who was on amphetamines, who'd had a paranoid schizophrenic break.

"He talked about Judy, his sister. And I got the flavor that somehow, even though his mother was described as a strong person, that somehow, within the family, women were put down.

"I asked him about himself. He described himself as a striving person, making the point that he would never have achieved what he had achieved or gotten where he had gotten if he had not been a striving person. That he was good at athletics. He made a point of never having cheated.

"Usually, when I ask that kind of question, I'll say, 'Okay, those are some of your good points. Can you tell me some of your bad points?'

"He described himself as compulsive. And here was the first time that any feeling, or what he called 'affect' came out. He became sad, almost tearful. Said that he was not accepting of his own family. Said not as accepting as a good father should be. He volunteered that he saw that as strange in himself because he was never annoyed by patients. He always could take all the crap that any patient could give him.

"He talked about what could have been if his family had not been killed. Said he could have had a closer relationship with Colette. He could have had a better relationship with the children. He described his wife as being the best mother in the world: warm, understood the kids completely.

"He talked about knowing her since eighth grade and dating since eighth grade. They had broken off a couple of times. I did not ask why. I asked him more how he reacted to these breaking-ups. He said that he would feel hurt and he would sulk. That she would cry and that that would hurt him.

"I obtained a sexual history. He said he'd had his first sexual encounter with the mother of one of his friends when he was fourteen years old.

"He talked about Kimberly, who was a very feminine child. He talked about Kristy as being a tiger. There was very little affect at this time. I was impressed with his coolness in giving me this information. He talked about his feelings about the Army, the implication being that he had a lot of anger toward the Army.

"He talked about his family's approach to Jay. He said his parents had been more casual toward Jay's accomplishments. He said that he, Jeff, had gotten more recognition than Jay. He felt bad about that. He felt that somehow that might be responsible for Jay's becoming a bum.

"I got into his use of alcohol. He talked about using it socially, judiciously, minimally really. He said he used medication, and, in fact, his wife had taken diet pills for some period of time in order to lose weight, and he, himself, had taken diet pills to lose weight when he was on the boxing team in college. He said that he was a fighter. His nose was broken four times while he was in high school. And that, essentially, was my first interview with him, which I deliberately kept relatively bland.

"I initiated the second interview by talking with him about his father. Apparently, there was a lot of feeling in the family about the father's death. He talked about his mother crying when he, Jeff, was around. He created the impression that he was sort of the person who carried the family through the father's death. He added at that time that Colette's father had committed suicide. I asked him if he could tell me any more about it, but he couldn't.

"I was not aware until he told me that Colette was pregnant at the time they got married. He made a point of the fact that they had intended to get married later anyway.

"He discussed entering service. All doctors, when they enter, go to Fort Sam Houston for a basic officer's indoctrination course, and while he was there his thought was that he was going to end up in Vietnam, which was the expectation of most young doctors if they went into the service at that time.

"He spoke of a colonel coming down and giving a talk to the group about Special Forces. He was extremely impressed by the physical appearance of this man. He really was very impressed. There was a lot of feeling expressed about this man. It was almost as if the appearance and the presentation of the man, more than a judicious discussion of what would be involved in going into Special Forces—it was almost as if his impression of the man was more important.

"He volunteered further sexual history in terms of having an affair with an airline stewardess. I began to get a, you know, a question in my head in terms of whether— I didn't pull this out of him—whether he volunteered this to impress me, or what. I don't know. They apparently—she spent a weekend with him in Texas, and this was apparently a second-time encounter that he had had.

"We talked more about his brother. He made the point that he was the only one in the family that could really handle his brother. He expressed that he didn't really understand his brother and his family didn't understand his brother, and he talked about his brother's potential for violence. He was very upset that his mother had to see this violent behavior that the brother displayed. He expressed this with an affect of anger and shame. He said he was ashamed of his brother.

"Then we got to the night of the 16th and the morning of the 17th. He talked about having come home from work, having gone with the kids to feed Trooper, the pony he had bought.

"He talked at some length about having purchased the pony very secretively. That it was a big surprise to the family. He talked with some pride about having worked with the man whom he bought the horse from or whose property he was going to keep the horse on and how the two of them had—he would make up stories about where he was going, and he would go over and they built the shed the horse would stay in. He made quite a big deal of it.

"I was aware that one of the points the prosecution was making had to do with some conflict between Captain MacDonald and his wife over the handling of the children in terms of bedwetting and in terms of the children climbing into bed with them.

"I had not raised it yet, but somehow at that point in the interview it came up. His wife that night had discussed it with her psychology teacher.

"I have in the back of my mind—it's characteristic of doctors—it seems true in my family that my wife never takes my advice. I can treat my kids' colds but when it comes to medical opinions, you know, I'm low man on the totem pole. I'm not sure that isn't true in a lot of physicians' families. But I think there was a flavor of that there, and I began to probe and try to feel for areas of conflict between him and Colette. Because, again, the point had been made so strongly to me by the prosecutors that they saw this as a potential motive.

"I didn't get a degree of reaction like that from him. He said, in fact, that he wasn't upset that she had discussed it with the professor. I think I would have been, but he said he wasn't. The professor, he said, advised a firm hand, which is exactly what he had advised.

"He said, 'Colette could take less crying than I, and that's probably why Colette tolerated it more'—that is, she couldn't tolerate putting Kris back in her own bed and making her stay there.

"He mentioned that his wife was four and a half months pregnant. He also mentioned that he was reading a novel by Mickey Spillane called *Kiss Me Deadly* that night. He described his wife coming home from the course. He talked about having a friendly conversation with his wife. He was interested in what the professor had had to say and so forth.

"He later described how he went to bed, and Kris was in bed on his side and had wet the bed. He picked her up and put her back into her room. There were periods here when he would become emotional, become tearful, but he recovered quickly.

"I recognized that he had been interrogated previously, and so I allowed him the lack of affect that I would have expected from a person describing these things about his family. I did not get much feeling from him at that time. It was matter-of-fact, but I gave him the benefit of the doubt, because he had gone through this story so many times.

"As the interview progressed, I was becoming a little more probing. Kristy was wet. Why didn't he change her? If she had wet the bed enough to make it so wet that he didn't want to sleep in it, I figure that would be a pretty wet diaper. He said that it wasn't. She was not very wet. She was asleep and there was just a small amount of urine on her pants, and he didn't want to disturb her, didn't want to wake her, so he just put her to bed.

"I didn't buy that. But that was it. Then we talked about him falling asleep on the couch. He decided not to disturb Colette and make the bed or cover up the wet spot and go to sleep with Colette. He said this again in a very matter-of-fact way. Then we went through the arrival of the people in the house. He was awakened by screaming, and these people were around him. He related this again in a fairly matter-of-fact way.

"Later, he talked about running into Colette first, giving her mouth-to-mouth resuscitation, feeling her pulses, running into the children's rooms, feeling for pulses, giving mouth-to-mouth resuscitation. Finally knowing that they had been stabbed because when he would breathe in, the air would come out of the chest. He talked about coming back down the hall, talked about making the phone call, all of this again without much feeling. More of a clinical thing.

"Then he became angry. He said he was put in an ambulance. Some son of a bitch wanted to know his serial number. He was yelling. He was swearing. There was affect then. Feelings expressed.

"I asked him what he was going to do when this was all over. And he said something fairly insightful, in the sense—I, by now, which is after about a total of four hours of interviewing him—I had the impression that he was depressed. That what I was seeing as being clinical, as being matter-of-fact, was interpreted, by me anyway, as being controlled, very controlled, very—I hope you understand what I mean by controlled: in terms of controlling his feelings, not allowing his feelings to well up.

"He substantiated that a bit in the sense of—he said he didn't know what was going to happen when this was all over. He said that what was keeping him going was that he was fighting and that he was a fighter and had been a fighter all his life—a fighter in the sense of defending himself.

"We talked about his mother having sold her house in order to help pay the legal fees. He said he didn't care about the money. He felt that he would recover—that he would go back to being a doctor.

"Then he got a very quizzical look on his face, almost wanting me to empathize with him, and he said, 'You know, those bastards want to have a victory party when this is all over.' He was talking mainly about his lawyers. And he said, 'I don't want to have a victory party. I mean, this is a fight but I don't feel there is any victory. I've lost my family and I just—and I will be relieved, that's all.'

"And that's the essence of my two interviews with him. As I have expressed before, I had a fairly strong impression that Dr. MacDonald is a pretty controlled guy. He is capable of maintaining control, but he also has this device of going into some kind of tirade to avoid allowing emotion to become expressed. That is, the emotion may be sadness but he turns it into anger about what they are doing to him.

"An impression that I began to get also was that he seemed extremely dependent on what other people thought of him. For all of us, how other people respond to us affects how we feel about ourselves, but that can go to an extreme and I think it did for this man. He needs much, much more than the average person in terms of reassurance from other people that he's a good guy.

"I think that partly explains what we saw initially as a kind of naivete, openness, honesty. I'm talking about a matter of degree. I'm not trying to put a label on him or say this is sick. I'm talking about it more as a way he operates."

"All right," Victor Woerheide said. "Now could you put this all together and tell us what your psychological evaluation of Jeffrey MacDonald is? What makes him tick?"

"Well, I see this man—who was twenty-six at the time I examined him—as the sort of person who uses—probably his primary mechanism of defense, his primary mechanism of handling stress, is denial.

"I think that explains, for example, his not putting a story together for himself until April 6—or at least he says he didn't. He didn't think about it. It's sort of inconceivable to me that someone wouldn't be ruminating and thinking about it and trying to put it together. I think he's capable of just blocking it out.

"I think he used other mechanisms—action. I think I described earlier that he talked with some sense of grief about not relating as well with his family as he thought he ought to, and yet being able to relate to patients easily. I think to wear his doctor's coat was easier for him than to be a man. I think that's his orientation. I think that's probably why he is oriented to the kind of work that he is doing—emergency medicine: because he knows what to do.

"In talking to other people about him, I've used the word *hysteric*. I don't mean hysterical in the sense of histrionic, blowing-your-cool kind of thing. By hysterical what I mean, as a professional, is a person who is extremely effective at using denial. If presented with twenty pieces of data, he is capable of seeing only three or four and drawing his conclusions from those. I see him as that kind of person.

"I was very struck by how his story seemed almost as if it were reconstructed. I don't like to use the word *canned* because that can be misinterpreted or distorted. But the story—even about the 17th, let alone his life history—was told in a way, not so much rehearsed, but with very little feeling. That's what I mean by reconstructed.

"And that is part of the characteristic of the hysteric type of person. I'm not going to apply a label to him. I don't feel he is pathologically ill. But all of us have personality types, all of us have lifestyles, and I'm trying to describe his type.

"Part of it is impulsiveness—example, buying the pony, I suppose. Example: responding to the colonel and the impression he made by joining the Special Forces.

"Also, tremendous dependence, again, on what other people think of him. And creating a good impression: the tremendous importance of creating a good impression. The tremendous importance of not letting other people see him break down and cry. As he put it, almost in a paranoid way—if you'll pardon my use of a clinical term—'*They* get benefit out of my crying. I don't get any benefit out of it.'

"And the importance of being an achiever. The importance of being a fighter."

"All right," Woerheide said, "I take it your conclusion was, as far as mental disease, he must be classified generally within the normal range?"

"Yes, sir."

"Do you agree that he is a man with basic inner feelings of inadequacy—a possible lack of manliness, by his own definition of the term?"

"I hope I've conveyed that. He needs to compensate. He needs to achieve. He needs to volunteer for jump training. He, in fact, had to lie. He had to lie in order to get into jump training, because on the physical exam, on the questionnaire—'Have you ever had back trouble?'— he checks no. Because if he had had any history of lumbar disc disease, the result of his high school football injury, they would never have let him into the paratroopers. But he needed to do that. So, yes, I see him as—well, having to work against a feeling of inadequacy."

"Having these feelings of inadequacy and having to work so strenuously to overcome and compensate for them—maintaining the front, the facade, that he had to maintain—do you think it's appropriate to say he had some underlying pre-psychotic tendencies?"

"There, I have trouble."

"I'm just wondering if it's possible."

"I think it's possible."

"You've testified that under a situation of stress he tends to lash out verbally at others."

"Yes, sir."

"Let me ask you this: in a situation of stress, let's say extreme stress in a family atmosphere where you have a combination of, say, fatigue, a possible recent quarrel—where he might be accused of a lack of competency, a lack of adequacy, in the family situation—could he react in a violent way? In your presence he lashed out verbally. I'm talking about lashing out physically."

"I think he could. Yes, sir."

"And could he lash out physically with sufficient violence to kill members of his own family?"

"I believe he could. That's not to say he did. That doesn't say that at all. But, you see, interestingly, there are a lot of clichés thrown around. He was brought to us—to me, initially—as Jack Armstrong, the all-American boy. He had been, you know, just peachy-keen, achiever, super-wonderful all his life.

"He didn't come across to me as Jack Armstrong, the all-American boy. He came across to me as having lots of holes. I can't label that as pathology, but if you're talking about the realm of possibility in this man, yes, I think it does exist.

"We answered the standard questions in the sense that there was 'no evidence of mental disease, defect, or derangement,' which was the primary question.

"But was there defect such that, even knowing the difference between right and wrong, he could not adhere to the right? We said no. But there may have been. We did the best we could. We certainly used every device we could to try to uncover illness if it was there. Did we miss the boat? We may have.

"Again, in terms of what you described—of a man who could suddenly lash out—if I were *his* psychiatrist, I would certainly play that in terms of defense as much as I could."

"Temporary insanity?"

"Yes, sir. We had no evidence, but—I said we did everything we could. We didn't actually do everything we could. There were periods of the night of the 16th, morning of the 17th, about which he was very vague and hazy. And I offered to arrange for an amytal interview.

"It's frequently treated in newspapers as if it's truth serum, but it's really not that. I mean, it's not something that makes you tell the truth. What it does is, it's a procedure in which you use an anesthetic to a point where a person loses some degree of his conscious control of thought processes. And in a person who has a lack of memory, very frequently it can help. Lack of memory, by the way, very frequently is because of a need to not remember, rather than events just passing away.

"We offered to do an amytal interview, and quite frankly, our purpose was twofold. As I said, he was a warm, engaging person. We were concerned about him. We did not want to precipitate more of a depression, but we felt that if it was underlying, then we might as well surface it and treat it, rather than have him live with this tragedy for the rest of his life.

"But we also felt that it would—if he were innocent— it would help him be more clear in his description of the people and of the events. He refused that."

At this point, one of the grand jurors asked a question. "If you were in Dr. MacDonald's shoes, wouldn't you agree to take this test?"

"If I were in his shoes and I implicitly believed in my innocence?"

"That's right."

"I would certainly take the test. It could only help me."

"There is no way it could harm him—I mean, mentally?"

"As I said, we might have precipitated a greater depression, but then we could treat it. That would have been the only risk. But, yes, if I were in his shoes—and thank God I'm not—but if I were and it were offered to me, I would take the test."

"You added one element in your previous answer," Victor Woerheide said. "If you were in his shoes and you knew you were innocent, you wouldn't hesitate to take the test."

"That's right."

"But if you were in his shoes and you knew that you had done it, would you take the sodium amytal?"

"No, sir."

Jeffrey MacDonald's brother was called to testify. He had arrived in Raleigh with shoulder-length hair and a buckskin bag fastened by a large wooden peg. Six feet tall and weighing well over two hundred pounds, he was the only witness among seventy-five equal in physical stature to Victor Woerheide.

"Where do you live now, Mr. MacDonald?" Woerheide asked.

"Now?"

"Yes."

"Right here."

"Before you came here, where were you living?"

"Yesterday?"

"What's your address—your residence address?"

"I don't honestly know what you mean by residence. I've always been curious to know what that means."

"Let me ask you this: when did you come here?"

"What do you mean, 'come here'?"

"When did you come to Raleigh?"

"You mean arrived in Raleigh? I arrived last evening at about seven o'clock."

"And where did you come from when you came here?"

"I came here from the airport."

"The airport in Raleigh?"

"Right."

"How did you get to the airport in Raleigh?"

"Eastern Airlines flight number 738."

"And where did you embark on that flight?"

"Philadelphia."

"How did you get to the Philadelphia airport?"

"In a limousine from the George Washington Motor Lodge near Fort Washington."

"And how did you get to the Fort Washington Motor Lodge?"

"In one of my automobiles."

"And where did you start from when you went in one of your automobiles from wherever you were to—"

"From a house on 307 Aquetong Road in New Hope, Pennsylvania, on the planet Earth, where the subpoena was delivered to."

"Do you keep your personal belongings in that house?"

"I keep my personal belongings in that bag in that room where we just came from."

"But apart from those that you carry around, do you keep other personal belongings in that house?"

"Some."

"And you sleep there from time to time?"

"Sometimes."

"And you receive mail?"

"Only when it is imposed upon me."

"The U.S. Postal Service, however, occasionally delivers mail there for you? It's addressed to you at that address?"

"As I said before, only when it is imposed upon me."

"Do you have a business or an occupation of any sort?"

"I don't know what you mean by business or occupation."

"Well, do you have any means of livelihood?"

"I don't know what you mean by that."

"Do you have any means of self-support?"

"I don't know what you mean by that."

"Do you have a source of income?"

"I don't know what you mean by that."

"Do people ever pay you money for services performed?"

"Sometimes."

"What services do you perform?"

"I occasionally would deliver a load of firewood."

"Where do you operate this firewood delivery business?"

"Where I can. If the deal was right, I would take a load of firewood to Peking."

"If people want to get in touch with you to order a load of firewood to be sent to Peking or anyplace else, where do they get in touch with you?"

"Word of mouth. In other words—and not to break your chops, but when I'm unloading a load of wood someplace, somebody might come along and say, 'Hey, pal, where did you get that load of wood? I'd like to get one.' In which case I would make a deal with the guy, and I would deliver another load of wood."

"Let's say they don't see you unloading a load of wood, but they know that you are a source of supply for a load of wood and they want to get in touch with you?"

"I just told you how I operate—word of mouth."

"Where do they come to find you?"

"Where they see me unloading the wood."

"That's the only place they can contact you?"

"Yes. That's the only place they could contact me—that's the only place that I have been contacted."

"I see. Then you don't operate a store, or shop, or let's say, an established business?"

"A shop—meaning a permanent place of business in one location? No."

"Are you the brother of Jeffrey MacDonald?"

"Yes."

"And you're about a year older than he is?"

"About nineteen months."

"And you grew up together?"

"Yes, I guess so. Some would probably say that he matured a little more than I did."

"Will you, at this time, describe the sort of family life that you and your brother lived as you were growing up?"

"With all due respect, I don't understand what that question has to do with anything about the situation that I thought I was brought here for."

"Do you remember," Woerheide said, "when I spoke informally to you in another room prior to your coming in here, that your brother had requested that we call to testify a psychiatrist who had been retained by him? And do you recall that you were shown portions of the transcript in which your brother testified before this grand jury concerning the family situation, the interpersonal relationships within the family?"

"I recall that, and I recall that my response to that was that you could take all the psychiatrists and all the psychologists in the world, put them on an old troop transport, and you could tow that old warship into the middle of the ocean, and you could blow the fucking thing right out of the ocean and tomorrow the world would go on like nothing happened and nobody would miss nobody. That was my response to what we talked about in your office."

"Yes, but we did talk about the family relationships, too, did we not?"

"Yes."

"Will you please give the grand jury the benefit of your observations?"

"I don't understand what that has to do with the case."

"Let me say this. I don't want to waste a lot of time."

"You wasted four and a half years."

"Just listen to me!"

"I'm listening."

"You're here to answer questions and not to ask questions! If necessary, we can take you before a judge—"

"You can lock me up for twenty-five years. You can lock me up for a hundred years! You can throw me out the window. You can take me down the hall and shoot me, but don't tell me that I'm not here to ask questions also, pal! If you're going to ask a question, I'll ask a question."

"You are here as a witness—"

"I am here because I am commanded to be here by a piece of paper that was served to me in New Hope, Pennsylvania, and that's the only reason I am here. Because if I didn't appear, some Gestapo would come at gunpoint and take me away and bring me here to force me to try and answer questions. And if I refused to answer the questions, my ass would be locked up. Not yours. I understand that full well. And don't tell me that I am not going to ask a question if I am asked one. Now if you want to ask me a question, before I put my ass on the line I want to know why."

"I'm going to ask you the question once more," Woerheide said.

"You can ask me the question ten more times."

"Will you inform the grand jury of the interpersonal relationships in the MacDonald family, as you were growing up?"

"I don't understand the question."

Victor Woerheide paused. He walked back to his desk. He sat down. He conferred with an assistant. He began to look through a sheaf of papers. Sighing deeply, he stood again, with a new piece of paper in his hand.

"Do you recall a birthday party for your mother, which you planned and organized in June of 1969?"

"Yes."

"Do you recall that Colette and Jeffrey MacDonald were there?"

"Yes."

"Do you recall that Penny Wells was there?"

"No."

"Do you know Penny Wells?"

"Yes."

"Was she a girl that you were dating at that time?"

"At what time?"

"During the time frame within which fell the birthday party for your mother in June 1969."

"That is possible. In all the years that I've known that gal, I've gone out with her possibly ten or twelve times. At the time of that party, the main purpose in my mind was to satisfy a desire of pleasing my mother by giving her a fiftieth birthday party, since my father had been deceased for some time, and I felt that that was something to do. Now if I made a date with Penny Wells, it was purely an afterthought type of a situation so that I would have a companion for that particular day, or an escort, as it were."

"Well, do you remember whether or not your brother suggested that you bring Penny Wells to this party?"

"As I just said to you, I don't even know if Penny Wells was there that day. And as I said in your office before, I could have balled her that night and I still wouldn't remember if she was at that party. If she opened all the presents or handed out the presents to my mother at that party I am not aware of that. Now if I am not aware of all those things, there is no way I could truthfully say whether or not my brother asked me to ask Penny Wells to be at that party, with all due respect. I am not trying to break your chops. I am trying to help you. But I am answering that question to the best of my ability."

"Do you recall that Colette was at the party?"

"Yes."

"Do you have any recollection that Colette was offended because Penny Wells was there and was getting some special attention, let's say?"

"I don't know if Penny Wells was at the party or not. And if I don't know if she was there or not, then I really don't know if there was any tension between Colette and Penny."

"Well, in your observation, was Colette in any way jealous of Penny Wells?"

"I don't think there is a woman alive who could make Colette jealous in the sense of nastiness or vindictiveness."

"If she might have reason to believe, rightly or wrongly, that this other person was a threat to her marriage, how would she react?"

"I'm not sure I understand the question."

"Well, if she thought that Jeff were attracted to an-other woman, perhaps to another woman to whom he had been particularly close in the past, and that this at-traction on the part of Jeff constituted a threat to her marriage, in the sense that Jeff might leave her or have an affair with her or something of that sort—"

"Well, you're saying a lot there. When you're talking about threatening a marriage, there's a lot of room to play with. In other words, certainly gals' marriages would be threatened if their husbands were having an affair. I dare say there are certain marriages that are threatened if the man isn't having an affair."

"Well, how do you size it up in this situation? You knew Colette and you know Jeff."

"Yes, and if you're speaking about Jeff having an affair I don't think that would be a threat, in Colette's mind, to the marriage. Because I could very easily see Jeff hav-ing an affair and maybe ten affairs, but no romance to the extent of feeling involved, or a real true love sort of a situation."

"I take it Jeff was a man who was attracted to women, and women found him attractive?"

"There's an old family joke that when we were grow-ing up the girls used to pay Jeff to dance with them in grammar school—ten cents a dance."

"And I assume Jeff did have casual affairs with a num-ber of girls from time to time?"

"Well, that would be purely an assumption. I was never present at any of these alleged affairs. I don't have any films or tape recordings of those affairs. However, as far as my own opinion is concerned, and knowing Jeff quite well, I would say that he was capable of having many affairs."

"All right, tell us about Jeff," Woerheide said. "What sort of a guy is he? What makes him tick?"

"He's a highly energetic, ambitious person. Unfortunately for him, I am his older brother. And he has had to live in my shadow whether he wanted to or not. I am physically bigger than Jeff. We were brought up in a school system and a locality and by a set of parents who thought that football was good, and sports were good, and Boy Scouting, and participating in certain community situations where we, as children and students, were brought into the public eye, so to speak.

"And just by the very fact that Jeff was a year behind me he had to suffer the consequences of me getting the headlines in high school. I had no control over that. I had no control over the fact that when I was on the varsity, he was on the JV. My mother and father would come to the games on Friday night or Saturday and see me under the lights and it wouldn't matter if I caught one pass and we lost by a hundred points, I was still a hero in my parents' eyes.

"And not that they even went to his games, but even if they did go watch him play Monday, it was still a JV game. If Jeff scored nine touchdowns he was still a JV and I was still a varsity. He was still my younger brother.

"I am trying to give you some idea of what did shape his life, perhaps, a little bit. I mean, it had to have an effect on him. Like, I made it a point never to bring a book home from school no matter how much work I had, and I could always get by. He carried every book home from his locker every single night, plus he would go to the library and bring home an extra ten for security. Then he'd read them all and he'd be a straight-A student while I was getting by with a 70.

"Now, if you're asking me why he would do that, he

was, in his own way, trying to be better than me, without saying anything to me or to my mother or father. Because he had to live in my shadow forever. And I think he might even have resented me a little for getting by without bringing home all the books.

"It's very difficult for me to converse with my brother and really make any sense. In other words, I really can't get into a conversation with him anymore and really have an understanding at a certain level. I think, philosophically speaking, my thoughts go off in a totally different direction from his own. My value system is altogether different from his. Now why his value system developed the way it did—if it was just because of the position by nature that he was placed at—I don't know.

"I went into the Marine Corps. You know, like in the gung-ho sense, the rah-rah American-type situation, I think the only thing that could be better than that would be the Green Berets, and that's probably why, in my mind, he chose the Green Berets. Although if I said that to him, not only would it offend him, but he would deny it vehemently. But you tell me why he went in the Green Berets. You tell me why if I do a hundred sit-ups, he wants to do a hundred and one. If I drive five thousand miles in two days, he wants to drive six thousand. But not to beat me. Well, you tell me why.

"As far as what motivates Jeff, I think as he was growing up there was more of a sense of desperation on his part as to what the future held, or what was going to happen, because he was always following in my footsteps and they might not have been pleasant footsteps to follow.

"Like I always had a job and he could never get the same job. He'd have to take something a little bit less. When I was working as a stock clerk, he was delivering newspapers because I had already delivered newspapers. Then when he got to be a stock clerk I was working on the back of an asphalt truck. And when he was working on the back of an asphalt truck, I was driving the truck.

"He had to become a doctor because he knew that I wasn't a doctor. He was going to be a political scientist or whatever. He became a doctor. I don't know why, but I do know why, if you can understand what I'm saying. It's one of those unspoken things. I can't—I know why inside of me, and yet if I say it, that ruins everything and then—because it would be denied.

"I think he still is—he had a tremendous sense of loss when my father died. I called him about ten minutes after my father passed away, when he was living in Chicago, and I said, 'Jeff, I have some bad news. Daddy died.' And he instantly broke down on the telephone and cried.

"He really sensed a tremendous loss. I don't know if he ever really developed a—I think everybody needs a father of sorts. Somebody that they can talk to or lean on or cry on his shoulder once in a while. And I don't know who that person would be in my brother's case, after my father passed away. There was no one alive that would be an adequate substitute. If he was looking to me for guidance, he didn't see any, and so he went on his own.

"And, well, I think myself and my sister and my brother, we realized how much effort and how much of my own mother's and father's lives were literally given to us as children, in order for us to have things they never had. The things they had to give up in order for us just to go to school. My father would get two jobs so my brother could go to college. And my sister went to college and my mother had the job. Things like that.

"We never talked about it, but then you begin to

think, well, now, we can almost see the end of the tunnel and we'll be able to help them—meaning my mother and father, financially. Start to give them back the things they had to give up. But after you lose a parent, you can't repay those things. Now we can't repay anybody. You can buy a bigger headstone."

"Speaking in terms of Jeff, now," Woerheide asked, "would that leave him with a sense of guilt?"

"I don't see what that has to do with the case. Guilt could enter into the picture in the sense of an unfulfilled desire, or a disappointment, but if you are a reasonable person, and my brother was a truly reasonable person, you'd have to assume that he knows that he had no control over the fact that my father died."

Woerheide then asked Jay MacDonald about his brother's attitude toward Freddy and Mildred Kassab. First, Jay expressed his own opinion.

"Mildred—I wouldn't waste my time telling you what I think about her. If she had twelve cents in her pocketbook, she would go out and get a twenty-five-dollar hairdo just to keep herself on the chopping block.

"She marries Freddy and he treats her very well. Puts her in, you know, a five-hundred-dollar-a-month apartment that's not good enough for her. She wants a thousand dollars—living in the best place in New York, you know. They should have been living in a two-hundred-dollar-a-month place. They were living way over their heads.

"But Jeff, you know, sort of liked that kind of life. I think he saw in the way they were living that that's the way he would like to live someday. From the way we grew up as kids, in a house that was constantly under construction, with very poor parents, to see Freddy and Mildred living in these luxury apartments, I am sure that was the way he wanted to live. But Jeff was too much of a real person to do it on credit. He wanted to pay as he goes.

"Still, he admired Freddy. Like the day they were married we parked the cars in front of the apartment house and went upstairs to drop off some gifts, and we got back down and there were 'No Parking' stickers slapped on the windshield, that the doorman had put on the car.

"Well, Freddy ran downstairs, and I had never seen that done before. He chewed the guy out, berated him in front of everybody, made the guy get a bucket of water and a sponge and wash these things off the car. That made Jeff laugh. He said, 'Gee, I like the way he does things.'

"But, in other words, the guy didn't have a pot to piss in, and he was ordering people around, living in these big fancy places, and I guess Jeff just figured, because of the way he was brought up, that's the way he would like to live. In other words, Jeff is the kind of a guy who would sit down with Freddy and say, 'Freddy, you are a schmuck. You are really a phony son of a bitch, but I like you.' I mean, that's really where it's at with Jeff."

"Well, were the Kassabs supportive of Jeff and Colette?"

"Are you kidding? Jeff was going to be a doctor. He could have been blind, deaf, and dumb, and a four-legged nanny goat, and Mildred would have been happy that Colette was marrying him because he was going to be a doctor. She was just marrying off a daughter for the money angle. So if you are asking me did they back Jeff and Colette, yes. If that is what you call backing."

"Has there been any change in this relationship?"

"Well, I would daresay that Jeff probably has lost respect for the man since Freddy has done a 180-degree turn. Not because he's against my brother but because he was for him and now he's against him. He was totally for him through the whole pretrial hearing. Now, you know, after the whole thing's over and because somebody hasn't been brought to justice or to trial or whatever, he's willing to turn around and sacrifice somebody he'd really supported."

"Does Jeff talk to you about this?"

"If I talk to him on the phone, like he'll say, 'Freddy's making waves.' Meaning that the guy is—I mean my brother lost a wife and two kids and is at a loss for what to do. And he sort of gets to feeling that Freddy and Colette's mother think that they are the only people that lost somebody. And Colette's not even Freddy's own daughter."

"Let's go to February 17th," Victor Woerheide said. "When did you first hear about the fact that Jeff was in the hospital and Colette had been killed?"

"I was at a friend's apartment in Queens, and I heard a radio broadcast that said there had been a murder in North Carolina, that a Captain MacDonald had been wounded seriously and that he was in a hospital and that his wife and two children had been murdered."

"Did you make any arrangements to go to North Carolina?"

"No. I made arrangements to go back to the hospital."

"Well, did you subsequently go to North Carolina?"

"Yes."

"Did you stay very long?"

"I don't know how long we stayed. But we attended a ceremony at a Catholic shrine or one of the churches at Fort Bragg and there were three white coffins on the podium where the honcho stands, and my brother was in front of me.

"I remember him walking in very, very slowly. He was in uniform, but he seemed to be like—like he could hardly walk. He shuffled like an old man would shuffle.

"My brother's the kind of guy that would—he's always breaking something, breaking bones or getting hurt or something, but the kind of guy that, you know, two salt tablets and another mile. You know, never give up. And he wouldn't have showed that he was hurting unless he had to.

"And he was hurting when he walked into that church. The whole thing didn't last too long. And when we walked back outside, there was nothing to say. He stood in front of me and he was shaking because he was quite weak, plus he was emotionally drained. I knew that he was really hurting. I knew that he was hurting physically and I knew that he was hurting emotionally. And I was at a loss for words. For the first time in my life I didn't know what to say. I mean, I didn't even know how to console him—my brother. I didn't know what to say. He just stood in front of me and there was nothing I could say. Then he was put into one of the Army cars and taken back to the hospital."

"I'm not trying to pinpoint this as to time and place," Victor Woerheide said, "but sometime thereafter did you talk to your brother about what happened on February 17th?"

"Well, I know there was no conversation about it until he was charged by the Army. Then, like, a little seed was planted in the back of my mind as to, you know, thinking that the Army can never make a mistake—that if the Army would charge my brother, then quite possibly he might be guilty.

"So I felt that in order to live with myself, I had to make up my mind whether or not my brother was a murderer. It took me two years to decide that he wasn't, only because I never, ever wanted to ask him point-blank."

"I take it you did not point-blank ask him?"

"I never did. No."

"But you talked to him?"

"Right."

"What did he say to you?"

"He used to get so mad and upset that I had the audacity to ask him those kind of questions to the point where he would yell and scream at me—not yell and scream, but I mean, like, more or less tell me to mind my own business and how could I be so stupid as to ask a question like that."

"You said that ultimately you became satisfied in your own mind that Jeff did not, in fact, kill Colette, Kimberly, and Kristen. What was it that satisfied you?"

"We were on a long-distance telephone conversation, I believe between Pennsylvania and California. And this has been after like months and months, if not years, of talking back and forth on the phone and when we were together and me asking in my own stupid way about what happened.

"And as stupid as this sounds I don't remember what the question was, but the way my brother responded left no doubt in my mind that he was innocent."

"What was it he said? What was the clincher?"

"The clincher was there was nothing he could say. He was crying. He broke down over the telephone."

"He cried?"

"And cried. In other words, it was—the only other time that I ever heard him like that was when I called him and told him that Daddy died. Like I could hear him break down on the phone and there was silence for a long time. And that was what happened when I talked to him in California.

"What I was trying to do was to get him to break. I wanted him to yell at me and tell me to shut up or go fuck myself or get lost, or something like that which would cast a doubt in my mind, but when he broke down the way he did—as if: 'the government's against me, I lost my family, and now you, my own brother, are going to turn on me.'

"That was like the straw that broke the camel's back. I realized once and for all, come hell or high water, that my brother was absolutely, totally innocent of all charges.

"The embarrassing thing is I don't even remember the question I asked him, but because of the nature of his response—the emotional level—that was something that could never possibly be faked. There is no way to fake something like that."

"Did Jeff ever tell you, after the Article 32 was over, that he was going to get revenge?"

"He told me he had been out looking for these people in North Carolina."

"Did he tell you at any time that he had found one of the people?"

"I vaguely recollect hearing that. Now, I don't know whether Jeff told me or whether that's just part of my knowledge of the case."

"Did he tell you what he had done when he found this person?"

"No."

"Did he tell you that he had forced him to admit that he was one of the intruders and after forcing this admission from him, that he killed him?"

"No."

"Had he told you that, would you believe him?"

"Well, depending on the circumstances. In other words, if he told me that in a joking manner, I would take that as a joke."

"Let's say he told you over the telephone."

"It's not a joking matter."

"No, it's not a joking matter. Say he told it to you over the telephone, or he wrote you a letter. He says that if you tell anybody about what I've said over the phone I'll deny it. And he wrote you a couple more letters, and he says, 'I've gotten revenge as to one of them and I'm still looking for the others.' Would you believe it? Knowing Jeff the way you do?"

"Did that happen?"

"He said it happened."

"Where is the body?"

"You haven't answered my question."

"The stakes are getting high."

"Then he said he lied about it."

"Then he said he lied about it?"

"He said it was all a lie."

"Wait. First of all you're giving me what appears to be a hypothetical situation, although the situation, in fact, might be true. Then you're asking me to give an opinion about—"

"I'm trying to probe into what sort of person Jeffrey MacDonald is, that's all."

"Well, you'd have to give me a little more information, since my brother's involved and there's a lot of—in other words, what—why would he kill the person?"

"If he said this to you, would you believe him? That's my question."

"If he said it, I'd have to believe him."

"And if he said afterwards it's a lie, then you'd believe it was a lie?"

"Yes. But, I mean, if you want to get into something that heavy, I would certainly want more detail."

"Would you have a lingering doubt—if he said it was a lie—about having believed him the first time?"

"I'm not sure I quite understand what you're saying. If you're asking me if my brother is capable of committing murder, then I say, if his family had been murdered, yes, he's capable of murdering somebody. If his family wasn't murdered, then I say he's not capable of murder."

"You had a lingering doubt for two years—do you think he was capable of murdering his family?"

"No."

"Why?"

"He's too—he's too smart for that."

"It's not a matter of morals or ethics? It's just a matter of not getting himself in a bind like that?"

"Right. He's smart enough to know that there's a hundred alternatives."

"Is he smart enough to think he could beat it?"

"My brother is not the kind of person that would put himself in the position of having to beat something."

"Mr. MacDonald," Victor Woerheide said, "as you know we have three dead people. As you know, there are possible suspects. These suspects include your brother, since he was the only survivor left in the house that morning and the only information given came from him. His story may be believable or it may not be believable. But is there anything that you can think of, that you can tell this grand jury at this time that might throw some light on the matter?"

"If I thought it would do any good, I would be prepared right now to sit here for the next five years and on to infinity and continue talking. I'd read the Bible backwards, forwards, and sideways, and tear up phone books on my brother's behalf.

"He was cleared of all charges against him, and for him to be subjected to the same type of interrogation over and over again is beyond my comprehension. And it is beyond my sister's comprehension, my mother's comprehension, doctors that my brother is currently working with or has worked with in the past, people that he served with in the military, friends of the family, priests, lawyers, I could go on and on about what everybody seems to feel is the ridiculousness of the situation.

"In other words, how long can this go on? In other words, if he's found not guilty the second time, four years later somebody decides that my brother is supposed to be subjected to the same sort of thing and the whole process repeats itself again?"

"Mr. MacDonald, there hasn't been any trial of the ultimate issue in this case. To wit: who killed—"

"You say there hasn't been any trial! In the sense of how you or whatever are the law agencies of any particular state or nation defines trial. In other words a trial is, quote, such and such.

"But I firmly believe that my brother has been on trial, as have other members of our family. Because our ways of life have been interfered with. Our psychological advantages or disadvantages, if you will, have been interfered with to a great degree. Our whole course of activity has been greatly interfered with. If that isn't a trial of sorts, I couldn't begin to tell you what I think a trial is."

"Mr. MacDonald, you've been brought here to contribute any information that you can that will be helpful to the grand jury in resolving the matter, particularly any information that might be helpful or beneficial as far as the possible involvement of your brother is concerned. Do you have anything you wish to offer the grand jury?"

"Freddy was on my brother's side, and when the whole thing was over and done with and no scapegoat had been found, Freddy turned against my brother and used his influence with somebody in the State Department or in politics in Washington somewhere—turned the whole matter around and put the onus on my brother."

"If you feel that there has been anything wrong said or done at any time during the course of this investigation by anyone, including Freddy Kassab, and you feel you have something that would be helpful to the grand jury, and might be beneficial to your brother, now is the time to say it."

"What good would it do?"

"Do you want to say it or do you not? It's up to you."

"What can I say?"

"Whatever you have on your mind."

"This is absolutely incredible."

"You have nothing to say?"

"I have a lot to say."

"Say it."

"What good will it do? My telling you my brother is innocent, that doesn't help me, it doesn't help him—"

"You weren't there. You don't know what happened. I know that. But tell us whatever you want to tell us."

"My brother's getting a raw deal."

"Is that it?"

"This whole thing is a sham, a farce."

"Is that it?"

"This whole thing has reeked from the beginning."

"Is that it?"

"I understand full well the amount of bullshit that is involved in this whole thing."

"Is that it?"

"As far as you guys and all your investigators, I am on the twentieth floor and I think you are a pile of shit, and I didn't think they piled shit that high."

Another of the Army psychiatrists who had examined Jeffrey MacDonald at Walter Reed in 1970 testified.

"We began rather innocuously," he said. "I took a little past history, a general history of his childhood. He talked about his slipped disc and how it happened. There were four minutes to go in a varsity game, and the coach was keeping all the seniors in. Even though he had all this profound pain, he continued. I don't know whether they won the game or not. Then he talked about running the athletic program for the fraternity he was in at Northwestern medical school.

"I asked him what he did for fun as a child, and he talked about reading. He said he read more than most other kids. He read everything. He read all the Lassie books. Later, he liked to read history. He enjoyed reading to his own children. He now reads mystery books. And he said he deliberately will not try to figure out the end. He doesn't try to outguess Sherlock Holmes, he said. He's read all of James Bond, Mickey Spillane, John D. MacDonald.

"He said he liked his jump training at Benning. He liked challenges. 'It's like are you man enough?' he said. He lived through it, therefore he stood up to the challenge. The people around him liked his attitude and that was important to him.

"His decision to go into paratroopers was because they were 'hard-core.' He talked about calling his wife to tell her he had decided to go into Special Forces. 'She knows how I respond to these guys.'

"Out of four hundred thirty docs at Fort Sam, only two signed up for Special Forces. 'I'm kind of proud of you,' he said his wife told him. 'The fact that you take the hardest thing to do and you do it well.'

"He talked about enjoying his work—working with dedicated, real soldiers. He was interested in what really motivated those guys. It was exciting. It was patriotic. Not second-rate.

"Then I tried to go backwards," the psychiatrist said, "into various, what I thought were neutral, not-charged areas. I asked about his growing up and he talked to me about his dog, a collie named Lady, that had been poisoned.

"The way I conduct an interview is to try not to ask questions. I try to sit back and let the person talk. Then I try to go with the person wherever he moves to, because not only is the question important, but what he says and how he says it and what areas he moves to after are important.

"And he talked to me about his dog and his dog being poisoned by a neighbor lady and about his going away. He rode a bike five miles to a park and he sat there all day. And he felt the police had let him down because, I think, he asked them to perform an autopsy on the dog and they said they couldn't do that.

"And from there he moved—by his own volition—to talking about a pony that he had purchased for his children and his wife. And how he stabled the pony in a barn and that he would go with the children to feed the pony and care for it. He was talking rather glibly at this point.

"He said initially Colette didn't want to have the

pony. But that she now went out with them and would be with the children and the horse. And at that point—quite unexpectedly—his mood changed very dramatically. He started to cry. And I said, 'What are you crying about?' And he said he was crying about his family, and he really became quite upset, crying quite heavily. And he began to say that it's not right. That it shouldn't have happened—that he never did anything wrong, and it's just not right. It was very striking, the amount of feeling that was being expressed here. He said that he had taken care of some of the crummiest people in the world and how could such a thing happen—how could this possibly happen?

"Then he started talking about how wonderful his wife was—that she was one of the kindest persons he had ever known and that he still wakes up and expects her and the children to be there. And that he has to fight constantly to be cool and competent. And that he has a tremendous feeling of guilt about not being competent—not being able to handle the situation. Then he goes into tears again.

"I asked, at this point, about how he thought all this would come out. He said, 'These proceedings? I'll get out of these proceedings. I've got the most competent lawyer in the world. And he's got the best of all possible worlds—an innocent client.'

"And then he went on and became quite angry and began a long tirade about the incompetency of the Army investigators, which to me—I didn't know anything about what was going on. In fact, I had started by telling him I didn't want to hear about it. So they might have been incompetent, for all I knew. But he went into detail, saying, you know, first of all they didn't respond and then when they did respond they came in and destroyed the crime scene, and then they absolutely refused to go out and look for the people that did it. The FBI just ran away from the case—a whole list of tirades. He was really angry at the Army for their misconduct.

"And then he starts talking about them charging him—that, you know, it's a big thing at Fort Bragg. There are two camps: the Doc did it or the Doc didn't do it. Those were his words.

"And he was saying that they didn't understand why he was lying on the couch and he went into details about his being on the couch and those kinds of things which I didn't have any knowledge of and frankly it didn't make a lot of sense to me.

"So I asked him would he like to have some time to get himself back together. And he took that time and he composed himself. After that, we began talking about his feelings about the family, and he began telling me of the dreams he'd been having. Dreaming of waking up and hearing the children screaming. And he can still see his wife lying on the floor.

"But then he tells me that his dreams have changed— his anxiety dreams. Now he has anxiety dreams about Colonel Rock, the guy that's doing the investigation. He dreams of Colonel Rock looking at him and saying, 'Did you do it?' And he's saying no, but having this feeling that Colonel Rock couldn't hear him, and he's having to tell Colonel Rock over and over and over again, louder and louder.

"Then he began telling me again about hearing the screams in his dreams. And in spite of my letting him compose himself he's crying again. Then he says he now has nice dreams about his family. About riding the horse—about seeing Colette ride the horse. She was like a big kid. She loved surprises. Then he says he doesn't want to share those dreams, doesn't want to talk to people about them.

"He thinks all this—people asking him about him and his wife is really an invasion of his relationship with her. He thinks people are being kind of morbid in asking him about it again and again. And, actually, I hadn't asked him about this at all.

"Well, I was taping this interview and at that point the reel ran out and I had to turn it over and he began to compose himself more. He really did begin to get himself together. He said it's okay for women to cry, but men shouldn't cry, which is a fantasy that most Green Beret people have.

"Then he began to talk about his sexual history. That his first sexual experience was somewhat alarming to him, and—oh, yes, as a teenager he once had two girls offer to have sex with him at the same time and it really repulsed him. He said it wouldn't repulse him now. In fact, he described having one-night affairs with two women.

"I asked him about his immediate sexual life and he told me that some woman had offered to come and have relations with him, and he had refused because he didn't think that would be quite right, given the circumstances.

"Then he talked about as a child either wetting the bed, or masturbating and having wet dreams, and hiding the sheets. He can remember doing that—hiding the sheets from his mother.

"I asked him specifically had he ever been impotent and he said yes, he had at one time with a girl who was very attractive but very pushy. And he was concerned about that. Then he said, well, this could have been because he had been drinking some Cold Duck and he was too drunk to have relations.

"Then he talked to me about his sexual relations with his wife. Having relations three or four times a week. He immediately says that he was never impotent with his wife and that he and Colette were always able to have relations, but that at the time of her death their sex life was not all that great. She was five months pregnant and that bothered him. He didn't have much interest in sex with her.

"I asked him if his wife knew about his extramarital affairs, and he said no, and that's not important. Then he qualified that and said maybe she did know about the airline stewardess down in Texas, but they never talked about it.

"Then I went back and began in terms of homosexual experiences and I'm sure the question I asked was the standard question—have you ever had any homosexual experiences.

"He said he never had. He talked about his experiences with homosexuals on Fire Island while he was driving a taxi. He said he made extra money by fixing up homosexuals with other homosexuals. He kind of did whatever people would pay him to do. He said that sometimes the homosexuals would travel with a female companion, and he said after he fixed the guys up with other homosexual friends, he would take their girls out. There was a phrase he used: 'Two hundred dollars, plus playmates.' I think he was describing what his compensation would be for a weekend's work."

"Did you come to an assessment of your own," Victor Woerheide asked the psychiatrist, "as to his character and personality and what kind of man he is?"

"Yes. I see Dr. MacDonald as an individual who is striving constantly to be a superman. He's very bright and he's very, very talented, but he's constantly striving to be the best—to be a superman. To be a he-man, and going in the Green Berets and all of this business. Underneath that, in my opinion, is very definitely a defense against latent homosexual desires.

"By homosexual desires I don't mean he's a practicing homosexual. Far from it. But that he has that drive to be a homosexual which he doesn't act on. He's not a homosexual, but he has homosexual desires and also certain psychopathic tendencies: that is, telling me about his extramarital affairs. Again, almost being too much of a man.

"He is not a man without defect, which is essentially what his own psychiatrist was telling Colonel Rock. You know, 'Here's a guy who couldn't possibly do this.'

"What we were saying and what we continue to say is, whether or not he did it is not up to us. But we disagree very vehemently with his own psychiatrist's conclusions that he could not possibly have done it."

"Would you think," a grand juror asked, "that a questioning or challenging of his manliness would pose a threat of setting him off?"

"Challenging his manliness in the sense of Colette maybe not liking too much his having become turned off sexually as her pregnancy began to show itself and accusing him of, you know, not having it as a male and that's why he doesn't want to sleep with her, yes. This guy's a Green Beret tiger in black boots and I think that would be quite a challenge."

"An area where he would be particularly sensitive?" Victor Woerheide asked.

"Yes, sir. That's my opinion."

"And if some remark were made along this line: 'You're not a man. Let the kid sleep here and you sleep on the sofa' or something like that, that might be sufficient under conditions of stress, such as fatigue?"

"Right."

"The fatigue coming from not only the strain of being twenty-four hours on duty at a hospital, coming back home at six o'clock in the morning, spending a full day working and playing basketball—all of these things put together. Here is a man who should be tired, ready to go to bed at eleven o'clock when his wife goes to bed. But he's up. He's up until two o'clock in the morning reading a Mickey Spillane mystery."

"It's puzzling. I can't, as a professional, do any more with it than you can."

"But doesn't it indicate some stress? Some strain?" Woerheide asked.

"Sure."

"And this fatigue and stress, stemming from such conditions, making a man particularly subject—"

"That I can testify to. Yes. What stress does is it exaggerates those sort of basic personality qualities that we have. When you're exhausted is when those things that you perhaps don't like about yourself or that you would wish were different, and that you're normally able to maintain control over—under stress, that's when those things come out."

There was only one other question, this one from a grand juror. "At any time, during MacDonald's talking to you, when he was talking about Colette's kindness and gentleness, did he ever say to you that he loved her?"

"No."

"He never said that?"

"That word was not mentioned. That word was not used. I thought that was remarkable, too."

Jeffrey MacDonald's sister testified. She was asked first about seeing her brother in the hospital after the murders.

"I walked in and he was alone in the room. He was laying, looking out the window, and as I walked in he turned, and he said, 'Oh,' and I saw him and we both started to cry. I went over and started stroking his forehead and we both just started saying, 'Fuck, fuck, fuck,' and I came out with some insane statement like, 'Well, at least the time you had was good.'

"Then other people came in the room—all sorts of peripheral people were arriving, and we would go out into the hall and start making jokes about something. We'd start laughing and crying. I think everyone was hysterical, but instead of crying we were, like, laughing hysterically, or—I was."

"Did he talk at all about what happened?" Victor Woerheide asked.

"No."

"He told you nothing about it?"

"Someone had the TV on in the room, and what would happen is we'd go in and someone would turn the TV on and there'd be maybe eight people in the room staring at the TV and nobody was talking directly about what had happened.

"The only facts—my mother never discussed it. Jeff never discussed it. Freddy never told me anything. I just knew what I got from the paper. I would read a paper and I'd find out what had happened."

"All right, now since then it's been more than four years. Has he ever told you anything about it specifically in the intervening years?"

"No. The only thing I would do is I would point out to him that his personality is the type that elicits anger from other people. And that he should be careful. Hoping by what I said to him I would get the message through, so he would open up and tell me. Because I

wanted to know where this much hatred came from—
this much energy to destroy—if he was aware that he
created a lot of anger in a lot of people. But he didn't
think that."

"And he never opened up—"

"No."

"—and told you the story?"

"No."

Woerheide then asked about Colette.

"I think she liked her life. I think she liked, you know,
having a man, and having a baby, and having a closeness,
having a unit. I was involved in how many cool guys had
asked me out and, you know, that type of thing, a different world. So we really didn't communicate too much.

"She seemed to feel comfortable being a woman. She
was a very sophisticated and a nice person. She wasn't
any dum-dum. She was a fully developed human being.
She was a very strong person. I admired her. I sort of
modeled myself from her.

"They didn't have a lot of money and they didn't
have a lot of time together because Jeff worked hard, but
she always seemed to accept that and say it's okay because he's working toward something good. She didn't
seem to need instant gratification.

"She said, 'When Jeff's through his internship and his
residency, we'll have everything. We'll have time together and we'll have money. We'll have everything at
thirty-five that most people don't get in a lifetime.'"

"Tell us about Jeff now."

"I think he puts up a big front, you know, a big show
of being confident and the great rescuer. But I think inside he's a feeling, sensitive person. I have never seen
him be cruel. I've heard him be critical, but I've never
heard him be cruel.

"I've seen him selfish in the ability to, like go to Princeton, which was using quite a lot of money, say, from our family, and that made me feel—like, I would feel guilty if I had to do that. But he said, 'No, I'm working hard and I will become a wage earner and I certainly will help Mom and Dad out then. So I don't feel guilty about it.'

"But as far as selfishness when it came to harming someone, or degrading someone—when I say degrading, he would give information to someone that I would say the person could be degraded by. But, from his point of view, it was realistic information, like, 'You can't eat ten doughnuts and expect to lose weight.' And that was a fact. I would get insulted but it was a fact. But he would never say to me, 'You little fat thing!'

"And he didn't push people out of the way. And he never—he never—if you needed help, you needed to talk, he was never, say, too busy to listen. He'd listen and he'd usually find a good answer.

"I felt that he was very adult. I think that he and Colette were very adult with each other. In the setup of marriage with a guy like that, it would be very easy for a woman to become Little Bunnie Doe, and Colette wasn't Bunnie Doe. She was very adult. She was a very three-dimensional person, an extremely well-adjusted person, and very sensitive, a very deep person.

"When someone spoke to her, she didn't just hear what they said. She understood that they were coming from their life experience and who they were. She had a very good way to really understand what somebody was asking.

"And so it was very good, she with Jeff, because he would be sort of—come out with something, an immediate statement or something and she would say, 'Now,

Jeff.' And she'd, you know, usually push for more clarification.

"It was very nice because it was helpful. They supported each other. Their temperaments—they were a very—they were very—an ideal—well, not ideal—well, they were adults. They were grownups. They weren't like two little lost kids in the world. They knew what their responsibilities were. They had a child. They had educational requirements to meet. They did it and they didn't complain about it. They didn't act like martyrs. They really enjoyed—if they were, say, struggling as students at Princeton, they were very quick to point out that they also had Cosmo Iacavazzi or whatever having dinner with them or that they would attend a very good concert or they would be with Bill Bradley on the weekend. They would point out, no, it's really okay. This is really okay with us. We're enjoying it.

"And in Chicago she would point out to me that this living was temporary and that it was not—you know, money wasn't important at this particular stage of her life, or in Jeff's life. And the fact that he did compete— she said it was good because then when he came home he had things to share with her. He wasn't a husband who was just sitting at home watching TV, drinking beer."

"In your conversations with Colette, did she ever indicate that there were any little, let's say, irritants in the relationship?"

"Yes. There was one. My brother felt that people who smoked were not using their heads. Every time he came home from a party, even if it was raining, he hung his suit outside to get the smell of smoke out. It seemed funny to see them hanging out on the clothesline, and Colette thought it was very funny, because she and I used to sneak smokes in the bathroom or something and blow it out the window. But that was just something funny, very childlike. It wasn't, you know—it was just something amusing.

"The only other thing that got him upset was the way that people ate. Sloppy eaters—he always thought that was repulsive. That was the only time I can remember seeing him being a very heavy-type parent person. He was very judgmental when somebody ate sloppily."

"Did you know Penny Wells?"

"I never had much contact with Penny because I thought, compared to Colette, she was a ding-dong."

"Was there any, let's say, rivalry between Colette and Penny Wells as far as Jeff was concerned?"

"I don't think so, because I think Colette's opinion of Penny was comparable to mine: that she wasn't a serious contender for anything except maybe Playgirl of the Year."

"After February 17th, did the thought ever enter your mind that Jeff might have killed Colette?"

"No. When I found out that someone else had a suspicion, I was shocked. I was really shocked. But then I began to process it and think, well, is it possible? For my own sanity I had to know. I had to check out that possibility. And I thought about it, and the only conclusion I could come to was that you'd have to be crazy to stab someone thirty-seven times. And he wasn't crazy. I don't think there was anything in his nature that could justify destroying people like that."

"Do you think he's capable of an act of violence?"

"Well, the CID asked me that and I said, 'He's going to Vietnam, and if you're going to Vietnam, you have to accept the consequence that you could kill somebody. So in that sense, yes, because he was a Green Beret, but when you say violence, like, you know, he wasn't the type of person who had angry outbursts."

"When he went into the service, why did he opt for Special Forces?"

"Well, because of the adventure and to be the greatest. You know, to be the best. It was like when my brother Jay went. My father said, 'If you're going to do it, be the best. Be a Marine.' So Jay became a Marine and then realized that he wasn't exactly Marine on the inside.

"But, you know, it was stressed to be the best. It was stressed to achieve. And there was a stress within yourself. You know, you'd feel better—that you were half dead if you didn't achieve."

"Do you remember seeing him on the Dick Cavett show?"

"Yes. He called up and said make sure to watch and to call some people in the area and tell them to watch because he was going to be on. And I watched, and personally I don't agree with mass presentations of something. I don't like people who talk about tragedy in front of millions of viewers. I don't agree with that.

"But I also knew at that time that he was not a person that everyone would love to invite to a cocktail party—because people didn't know. I mean his case was dropped because of insufficient evidence, which was saying that this guy might have killed his family. And he's walking around the streets of New York as the guy who might have killed his family, and while I felt that it was inappropriate in regards to the feelings, you know, the horrible tragedy, the fact was that there was so much anger, too. There was so much helplessness. What could we do? How were we going to get some action? How were we going to get people to actually follow leads?

"So when I talked to him afterwards about it, he said

it was important that he do it, so people who didn't know could hear it from his side. They could hear from his point of view that he was okay, he was a person, he wasn't a monster. He felt this was a way to get rid of this leprosy he was walking around with—people not knowing whether to shake his hand or to walk away."

"Do you remember him saying anything about conducting an investigation on his own?"

"I wanted to get private investigators, and he said we'd get milked dry. He said the FBI were the best investigators in the world. Why should we hire some rinky-dink private eye when the FBI had all the information."

"Did he tell you about how he and some of his friends were conducting their own investigation of the bars and hippie hangouts in Fayetteville?"

"I just remember—now I wasn't, like, recording things in a very systematic way. There was something about a girl that had a candle and went into a bar in downtown Fayetteville with three guys and said, 'Acid is groovy, kill the pigs.' But I—I've never—I just felt it would be kind of crass on my part, you know, to ask him about things like that."

"And he never told you he had found one of the intruders?"

"We haven't discussed anything since that period."

Jeffrey MacDonald's sister was then asked if there was any additional information she had that she thought might be helpful to the grand jury.

"The only thing I have," she said, "is an opinion. And my opinion is that he's not capable of that type of violence. He's a healer. He chose to heal, and he is very aware of pain and the fact that people do live in pain. His intention in living is to help, to heal. And I don't think he lets his ego get in the way too often.

"I think when his ego, say, would get in the way it would be like in sports or something. To me anything competitive is a form of violence. So if you want me to say there's violence—maybe competition. But as far as being a striker or a person who had to go out and punch the world, you know, have this hatred—I really can't see it.

"I just think there are a lot of victims involved here. There were three lovely people who were victims, and I feel that my brother, my mother, and Mildred and Freddy Kassab are victims. And then there are peripheral victims like Jay and myself, people who really can't get about living until this thing is worked out.

"I think the thing—you know, everyone wants it solved. And maybe we can't accept the fact that we can't solve it. I think my brother has been like a puppet on a chain, at the whim of, you know, a new investigation.

"I think Freddy Kassab is a very nice, feeling human being. I just think he has dedicated his life to a bad dream. People who dwell on an incident that happened four years ago, and devote their lives to it, that is bizarre to me.

"And I get angry because I wonder are other avenues being explored. You know, I don't know what the overall thing is. I think my brother's sane. I think he's normal. And I think these acts were performed by people who were not normal.

"I think he and Colette had a very healthy relationship. I think that he was a very sensitive and gentle man, and I think that one of the reasons this case has gone on so long is because he is so gentle and so reasonable. I think if he had had more unreasonable reactions at the time, it would have pleased people who like carnivals.

"At the time this happened, the chaplain came down the hall and we were laughing. We were telling jokes—

absurd, horrendous jokes. And the chaplain said, 'Well, you people don't need any help. You're obviously taken care of. You're obviously okay.' And then he'd go in and talk to the Kassabs who were sobbing, you know, and in dark glasses and stuff.

"Well, I mean, there are lots of ways of handling something that nobody can handle. And, unfortunately we all have the attitude that we're not going to cave in. We're not going to say, you know, 'help.' Because we knew there was nobody who could help. The only thing we wanted was to see my brother live.

"I wish—I wish he had been more selfish. Because I think a lot of his pain would have been avoided if he'd just let himself be a burden, say, to my mother, to the Kassabs, and asked for help. Unfortunately, there are people who need those types of displays to believe in something.

"So I really wish my brother was a bullshit artist. If he was a bullshit artist, he would put on this big carnival affair of suffering and being a person who is completely wiped out.

"You see, everybody else imagines that they would be wiped out, and I am sure he probably is inside. He just doesn't go into an orgy in front of a lot of people about it. He feels that he has to go on and he has to live. And nobody can seem to accept the fact that a human being can go on and can struggle and keep on living.

"If people had a few carnival tears or a few carnival breakdowns, they might believe him. I really wish he was a bullshit artist."

The Army clinical psychologist who in August of 1970 had made his own analysis of the tests given to Jeffrey MacDonald in Philadelphia in April was called to testify.

He spoke first of the opinions he'd formed from his review of MacDonald's responses to the Minnesota Multiphasic Personality Inventory, a test consisting of 566 true-false questions ranging from "I like mechanics magazines" to "My father was a good man" and "At times I see things that other people do not see." The test is designed to provide a general profile of an individual's overall personality adjustment.

"I think the first impression I had that was remarkable," the psychologist said, "was that there was no indication from this particular test that there was any significant pathology existing.

"By that I mean I was asked to evaluate whether there was any indication that the gentleman who filled out the exams was either psychotic or psychopathic. In going over this particular test, I found no indication to support either one of these diagnoses.

"Secondly, the data from this test was remarkable in what was not there, rather than what was. I found an absence of anxiety, an absence of depression, an absence of agitation, and I expected there to be some there. I expected there to be a high level of anxiety indicated and what I found was low.

"Now, as part of this test there are what we refer to as validity keys. We rely on them to give us an overall impression of the attitude with which a person took the examination that allows us, roughly, to say, yes, this is a valid test and we can use this data; or, we should be cautious in using it because it may be invalid.

"I went ahead on the assumption that the material in this test was essentially valid. That was at that time. My experience in the intervening years would lead me to question that now. I now look at this test data on the MMPI, and I have a question in my mind as to its validity.

"My reservation is that the person who completed the questionnaire seems to have answered the questions in such a way as to present himself in the best light possible. That does not necessarily mean that he lied, but it at least indicates a certain awareness of the implications of some of the questions he was asked, and at least some attempt to present himself in the best light possible. That's why, today, I would want further examination.

"Typically, a person who has some awareness of himself—good points, bad points, or accepted and nonaccepted characteristics in our society—and who wanted to present himself in the best light possible would try to increase certain scores by answering questions in a positive way that would make him appear to be a very even-tempered, easygoing person without any particular things bothering him.

"Now the data, as we get it to analyze it, is presented in graph form. And on the graph there are three lines. The middle line is considered to be average, or normal. Anything below the lower line would be considered pathological and anything above the upper line would be considered pathological.

"So, a person without significant disturbances or conflicts, his scores would range between the upper and lower lines. But a person, also, who is trying to present himself in a good light—and not everybody is able to—would also range his scores within these areas. And this is the pattern we have in this case.

"But the reason I have some question about it is that the degree of guardedness or caution that is shown in the validity keys that I mentioned before is significant enough to make me question it—to say, well, all right, is this valid? Should we take it just as we have it, or should we pursue it further?

"Without pursuing it further, there is no significant pathological condition indicated. However, on one scale here—it happens to be the scale which tends to be most sensitive to picking up feelings of anger and anxiety—it's almost not plottable on the graph, according to this individual's responses.

"That means there is almost a total absence of any score. That means he did not describe himself in any way as having any anger or agitation, and I find that remarkable. It may, in fact, be true, but I find it rather unusual. In fact, in my experience, this was the first time I had ever seen it.

"In the report I wrote back in 1970, I said, 'The only explanation for this that I can offer is that the subject is able to muster massive denial or repression so that the impact of recent events in his life has been blunted.'

"At that time I had just been out of school a short time. I had academic training that was good and, I think, quite substantial. But since then I've had a few years' time where I've had to start dealing with people, and that's different from what you learn in school. Your view changes. You start to see things that maybe you didn't see. And in this case—it jiggles my mind a little bit. It makes me a little cynical about accepting that particular test form just as it is."

The second test about which the psychologist spoke was the Thematic Apperception Test, in which the subject views a series of nineteen pictures and one blank card and makes up a story about each.

As described by its developer, Dr. Henry A. Murray of the Harvard Psychological Clinic, who devised the test in the early 1940s, "The TAT is a method of revealing to the trained interpreter some of the dominant drives, emotions, sentiments, complexes, and conflicts of a personality. Special value resides in its power to expose the underlying, inhibited tendencies which the subject is not willing to admit, or cannot admit because he is unconscious of them.

"If the pictures are presented as a test of imagination, the subject's interest, together with his need for approval, can be so involved in the task that he forgets his sensitive self and the necessity of defending it against the probings of the examiner, and before he knows it, he has said things about an invented character that apply to himself, things which he would have been reluctant to confess in response to a direct question. As a rule, the subject leaves the test happily unaware that he has presented the psychologist with what amounts to an X ray picture of his inner self."

In analyzing MacDonald's TAT responses, the Walter Reed psychologist found evidence of several areas of inner conflict.

"One was dependence and independence," he said. "Others were sexuality, or lust, and intimacy; affection and strength; hostility and love. It seemed to me that in all of these conflicts there was a unifying theme. And that theme seemed to be power relationships—who's in control, who will control, who will be controlled, who has the influence, who has the clout.

"The other thing that seemed to be of significance was that the subject's view of life was one in which events are thrust upon people and they have to react to them. From these stories that he created to go with the pictures, it didn't seem to be that an individual is one who goes out and so much creates his own way and makes life what he wants it to be. Rather, it seemed to be that events are happening and you have to deal with them. You have to overcome them or surmount them.

"It's a reaction kind of orientation rather than an initiating kind of orientation. That in itself is not to be considered pathological, but that type of person might tend to see life as a series of problems which have to be overcome by himself, and therefore might be resentful and bitter. If it went to an extreme, this person would tend to see himself as victimized, perhaps, or perhaps somewhat of a martyr.

"This would put someone in a rather angry stance toward life, and, again, that's why I was surprised to see so little anger reflected in other areas.

"I mentioned also, in my 1970 report, that 'The subject appears to be quite concerned with the issue of the definition of manliness and the related topics of appropriate behaviors for men and women.'"

His analysis of MacDonald's Rorschach tests, the psychologist said, did not indicate "either schizophrenic or psychopathic thought processes operating." Rather, "the approach to situations that I picked up here was a mixture of both hysteroid and obsessive-compulsive features.

"By hysteroid I mean the tendency to exaggerate the emotional component. For example, what a person who is not hysterical might feel as sorrow, a hysteroid person would experience as grief. And what a non-hysterical person would experience as an agitation in life, a hysterical, or hysteroid-type, person would experience as a major trauma, a major problem to be dealt with.

"As to obsessive-compulsive features, I mean that the person is usually very, very careful to include in his thinking and in his planning all possible angles and all possible details of that particular situation, program, issue that he is dealing with.

"This type of person does not feel at ease saying, well, let's not worry about that. *Everything* needs to be worried about and everything needs to be accounted for. And this type of person gets ill at ease when all things are not accounted for.

"Now it's uncommon to have both of these characteristics presented by the same person, because, typically, we think of them as being opposing views. The hysterical type of person says, oh, what the heck, let's not worry about it at all, and the obsessive-compulsive type says, we've got to worry about every single detail.

"It is possible to have them both together, but when you do, usually the situation is that the person is under a great deal of stress, and his usual ways of handling situations are coming apart."

"Well," asked Victor Woerheide, "does that tend to indicate a pre-psychotic condition? An underlying paranoid condition?"

"Yes, the status when this is present is usually pre-psychotic. Specifically, a paranoid psychosis would most likely develop quickly if the stressful situation were not alleviated in some way."

"What is a paranoid-type psychosis?" Woerheide asked.

"The paranoid-type psychosis takes one of two forms. In either case, the individual becomes convinced that his particular view of reality is absolutely the only correct view, and that anybody that disagrees with it is completely out of synch.

"The two forms it usually takes are either persecution or grandiosity. In the classical forms, the persecution type is where the person feels that everybody is out to get them, or kill them, or do them in. The grandiose type that you hear about most often is the person who believes he's Napoleon or Jesus Christ. These are the most dramatic forms, the extremes. There are all kinds of gradations in between.

"My feeling was with Captain MacDonald, if he were to become psychotic, it would probably be more of the grandiose type."

"Let me ask you this question," Victor Woerheide said. "Under a very stressful situation that might occur suddenly, could you have a psychotic phase of short duration and then, let's say, a return to the pre-psychotic condition?"

"I believe so. Yes."

"And let's say, with a paranoid phase of brief duration, would a person with a tendency toward the grandiose type of psychosis, a paranoid condition, be liable to commit an irrational act of violence?"

"Well, that is possible. You used the term *liable*."

"I should have said *possible*."

"It is possible, yes. Being of that state of mind does not preclude violence. It makes it possible. But, if I may comment on that, I don't think it's necessary to say that the person who committed these murders must have been either psychotic or psychopathic. I feel that's narrowing things too much."

"Please explain that."

"Well, it's possible for a person who normally lives a very well-contained and controlled life to reach a breaking point where he has an explosion—an explosion of rage. Now, you expect some types of people to be prone to that more than others. The data that I was able to look at in this particular case lends itself to that possibility.

"I refer back now to what I said about hysteroid features and obsessive-compulsive features. The hysteroid features—if a person had those, first of all, he tends to overreact, or dramatize situations.

"The obsessive-compulsive feature has one thing of

particular interest to me, and that is that this type of person does not easily express anger. To my way of thinking, that's the main issue. This type of person would not usually exhibit anger by pounding his fist or something like that. He would not be threatening people, but he would still be angry.

"Now this hypothetical type of person would be likely to do a long, slow burn. But at some particular point that anger may just come out."

"Something triggers an explosion?"

"Yes. And you might then—with this type of person—you might then think about rage—if you could distinguish rage from anger—you might expect this person to be full of rage at some point."

"All right," Woerheide said, "now with respect to this person to whom these documents relate, can you think of some incident, occurrence, event, statement—some challenge that might trigger this explosion?"

"Well, it seems likely to me that one of the main themes or values in this person's life could be called manliness. It might be referred to as sexuality, but I think sexuality is a little too narrow. I would call it manliness, which would include sexual behavior, but would include more things, too, like status, power, influence, rank, prestige.

"It seems to me that if this person were to be seriously challenged in terms of his own concept of who he is and how other people see him, he is most vulnerable in this area of manliness. And that if he were pushed in this area—if he's going to explode—that's most likely, I think, where he would explode."

"Let's say, if a woman, his wife, and he have a quarrel, and she said, 'Oh, you're not a man,' or something more specific, could that do it?" Woerheide asked.

"If your question is, could that bring out a rage, I think yes."

"And could it bring out a rage that might be characterized as a temporary paranoid psychosis?"

"Well, I don't know, because that is an academic question, and you have many, many disagreements about that."

"All right. Let's put it in layman's terms. Under the circumstances that I have outlined, is the subject capable of a violent outburst?"

"I think so."

"Which he might very well regret a few minutes later?"

"Yes, yes. I think this type of person might be swept up in a rage."

"Well, let's say he had just killed his wife. Do you think he would go so far as to kill his children to cover up the fact that he killed his wife? Do you think he could go to an extreme like that in a rage?"

"I could only speculate about it, but I can imagine that a person like this might commit murder at a point of rage. And the rage might not be over in a period of just a minute. The rage may last for some time. If that occurs, then I'd say that maybe this is possible."

"The whole thing could basically be accomplished in, let's say, two or three minutes," Victor Woerheide said. "There's no problem about a period of rage extending that long, I take it?"

"No, I don't think so. Also, whether subsequent people—like the children in this case—would be murdered at the point of rage, I don't know, but I can imagine that the fear at that point might have been an overwhelming, extraordinary fear."

"Now in regard to this particular case," Woerheide

asked, "and the paranoid-type psychosis, might this be expressed by, say, in regard to the MPs who came to the house and found an emergency situation, the CID agents who conducted the investigation, the medics who came and gave first aid, the hospital personnel who treated him—taking the attitude they're all bunglers, they're idiots, they're stupid, they are jerks, they didn't do things right, they're incompetent—"

"Yes, it could be conveyed that way. Also, in reviewing the informal psychological data—that is, how did the subject relate to the examiner and to the testing situation, I might say that I felt there were several instances where I had to question—is this man's reality testing amiss somehow? Is there some psychotic process operating here?

"Because his behavior was quite inappropriate, given the data I had. And even if some of the comments and the asides that the subject made during the examination were explained away and therefore did not look psychotic or paranoid, there still remains an attitude conveyed by the subject which I would call 'paranoid-like.'

"It is the conveying of a contempt, of a disparagement towards the examination, towards the examiner, towards the whole process that was going on at that time.

"In my experience, I have found that to occur usually with people who have a long-standing paranoid orientation toward life. Either they feel they're being done in or persecuted a lot, or they feel that they are someone very special and have maybe special privileges and this sort of thing. More the grandiose type.

"I call it 'paranoid-like' because I had not enough data nor opportunity to pursue that further, but to me that's a legitimate question."

A grand juror then asked a question: "Does every individual have a certain amount of paranoia?"

"No," the psychologist said. "I disagree with that. There is a school of thought within psychology and psychiatry that would hold that everyone has a little bit of everything in them. But I don't hold to that myself. I think that that really makes our discipline somewhat ridiculous. Because to me it's on the order of saying, well, everything in the world is a shade of yellow, but if you're not yellow, that just means you're a different variety of yellow. I don't find that appealing at all."

"Then I conclude," the grand juror asked, "that everyone does not possess that point of rage which would push them into an act of brutal violence? Some people do not possess that point?"

"Well, I think theoretically it is possible to say that any one of us could become enraged. But, practically speaking, there are people that I'm sure all of us have known who never exhibit rage. And not necessarily because it's suppressed. It's that their world view is different, and so they don't get into that sort of thing. My feeling is that you cannot substantiate the idea that we all are this way and the circumstances simply haven't occurred to us."

The psychologist was then asked, as had been the other witnesses, if he had any further comments to make.

"Well," he said, "it is a little bit outside my area of training to answer the question of whether or not this person committed murder, but I do feel it within my area to say that it is possible that this person could have a rage reaction and might have become violent at that time. I think it is possible.

"And when I first wrote my report four years ago, I took care to state that I could not assess the probability of the subject's having committed murder. I have acquired some experience since 1970 which makes me change my opinion. I would now put more emphasis on the likelihood that it could happen."

Jeffrey MacDonald's mother came to Raleigh to testify.

"Mr. Woerheide," she said, "in our family we had three children, two boys and a girl, and it was a strongly masculine-oriented family. Jay, being the firstborn, was kind of a special person, naturally, to his father, and there was some sibling competitiveness in terms of Jay being the one who was reasonably successful in the early years. Jeff would, in a sense, emulate him. Like if one played football, then the other one became interested in playing football. They were like three-sport men in high school. They were both good. Jay happened to win an award as the All-Suffolk Lineman of the Year; Jeff was the quarterback on his team.

"Now with Jay, there was some difficulty when he reached junior high school. He would have highs and lows, like he would work hard and get good marks and then he would go into a slump and I would be called in and they would suggest that he was goofing off a little bit.

"When he left high school—because my husband's background, you see, he was an engineer at the Brookhaven National Labs, but he was a man who was slightly upset about the fact that although he is classified as an engineer, he was not a four-year college graduate and one of the things that troubled him was that although he was capable and respected by everybody and his judgment was used frequently, and he was always considered a top-notch man, still, essentially, among the college people he was not valued as high in his salary, monetarily, and as a result he felt it was very important for his children to receive college educations, and so it was in our minds that Jay would go to college.

"I realize now in looking back that one should really sit down and explore with the person whether or not that is what they wish to do. However, he really posed no objection and he was accepted at three colleges and he visited one and liked it very well—I believe it was the University of Virginia—and he visited another and didn't like it as much but his father insisted that he take the Northern choice rather than the Southern. With all due respect to the South, my husband just felt that the Northern education was something more akin to his background and so he went to St. Lawrence University in northern New York State."

"But he never finished college?" Woerheide asked.

"Excuse me, sir, you see, he really did, only it was like a hard way round. You see, St. Lawrence was ready to have him stay out for six months after his first semester because he took a girl after a prom back to Canada and then he came back and used very bad judgment again by speeding, being picked up, and because he was a St. Lawrence student it was reported to the college and because they had had three cases of similar nature, they sat in kind of harsh judgment on him perhaps. We got the notice that he was being held out of college for six months.

"Now I as a parent, and my husband, Mac, felt that if we let him not go to college for six months that he might not continue and because of that feeling in the family that he was capable we thought we might try more locally, and Jay seemed very satisfied with the idea of going to a college on Long Island where he could come home nights.

"And he did finish college at Adelphi by essentially

going nights, days, working in between, and always financially trying to help so that everybody could support their own weight along with what we as parents were contributing.

"As a personality, Jay looked like a leader and somehow because of the size of him and the quality of magnetism that he had, people assumed him to be one when in fact he tended to take on coloration from whoever he was with.

"Like for instance the time that both kids worked as taxi drivers. My kids really put forth a great deal of effort whether they were taxi drivers, construction men, supervisors of construction—Jay went on to become a million-dollar-a-year salesman in insurance after he had graduated from college but it seemed to me that in everything he did, his judgment wasn't too sound. In order to prove himself, he was spending more than he was literally earning and it got to a point where he really was heavily in debt, but I was not cognizant of that until I guess it was too late."

"He was on drugs?"

"Well, he had come into college in his freshman year at 175 pounds and by the time he had finished at the end of the first year he was close to his present weight of about 240. So I should have recognized that the signs of distress were there. That kind of ingestion of either alcohol or food to that extent in that short period of time I recognize as sort of an oral need for support and I should have perhaps been more alert.

"At any rate, in order to reduce, because he was a big man with a big appetite and loved big parties and did everything in a large and grand style—which was very much like my husband's attitude—like open the house, everyone is welcome—he probably tended to take on that aspect of my husband and he began apparently to take pills to reduce, to curb his appetite.

"I learned later from Jeff and Judy both that he was probably taking much too much Dexedrine and that they were both aware of it and they had worked with him verbally and tried to warn him that it would have devastating effects but they really were not telling me because they felt that I would be upset.

"This was right before he went down into the Village and became a bartender. He was a salesman and working with these men and so forth on the big construction jobs and I had the feeling then that he was living beyond his means, but he was always overwhelmed by the idea of, like, owning a Cadillac, things of that nature. He was a little grandiose in his dreams.

"But of course you must realize also that when he started working on the beach—on Fire Island—that became part of his life. He really enjoyed the beach and as a result, each year, the reason why his jobs never seemed to last too long was that he was perfectly willing and able to work, say, from September through May but the minute it was summertime, for some reason that terminated his employment.

"And you could see the pattern and we would all say to him, Jay, you really ought to think seriously about this and he would say, 'This is my way, and I like the beach, and I can make do at the beach.'

"So he would rent this large house and then rent parts of it to the 'groupies,' who were people who came in and took a room for the season. Even in this beach situation, he did a magnificent job in terms of providing. He would be the cook for these people plus their friends and sometimes would even set up like lobster things on the beach, but always in a big style. Almost too much. I realized somehow that a sense of proportion was kind of wrong.

"Then, apparently, they had started on marijuana at the beach, which I learned later because when he became ill, I learned through Mr. Hayes, who is Jay's friend, that they all had been smoking pot.

"What happened was, I was at work one day and the phone rang in the morning and I answered it and as I recall it was Jay and he said, 'Hi.' And I said, 'Hello, how are you? Nice that you should call in the middle of the day, it lends a nice note to the occasion.'

"And he said, 'I just called to tell you that I love you and that I love Judy and I love her husband and I love their kids and I love everybody, but Mom, my head is all mixed up.'

"And I said, 'Jay, where are you?' And he said, 'I am with Billy—he is here.' This was Mr. Hayes. And I said, 'May I speak to Billy, please?' And he put Billy on and I said, 'Billy, what is wrong?' And Billy said, 'I don't know, Mrs. Mac, but he really sounds like he is not all together. He has been driving around for a long time, he does not know how long. He has taken something that did not agree with him.'

"And I said, 'What are you saying, he has taken something!' And he said, 'Well, I think he has taken something that was sold to him. He said he took a lot of it and the next thing he remembers is that he woke up in the gutter somewhere, and anyway he is all confused.'

"And I said, 'Billy, where are you now?' And he said, 'I am at work.' And I said, 'How did Jay get there?' And he said, 'He drove here. He said that he followed the taillights of a truck and through God's providence it landed him here.' And I said, 'I am coming right over.'

"I got the directions—it was somewhere in Brooklyn.

He was a garment manufacturer. In fact, I had a tour of his plant while I was there. When I got there, Jay was sitting at a desk clutching a copy of *The Godfather,* which apparently he had read and for some strange reason had begun to identify with.

"In other words, all of the stories seemed to him like he was involved in that Mafia scene and he was really very withdrawn. He would answer if asked questions but they were not too cohesive. He looked frightened. When he did get up and move, he moved near the edge of a wall.

"So I said to Billy, 'The only thing I can do now is call a man who is a professional who can give me some help. He needs help.' I had a friend who was a school psychologist and I called him and asked if we might have an appointment and explained that it seems that my son had taken a heavy dose of something and seemed disjointed in his mind and I would like help.

"He said the only time he could see us would be the next day, and I asked, well, what could I do in the meantime? And he suggested that we stay with him, like talk him down, if possible, and that he would see him tomorrow.

"So Mr. Hayes and I took him to a nearby motel. We hired three rooms—Jay being in the middle—and we stayed with him all night. We constantly talked with him. All during the time you could see that he was panicked into the feeling that some impending doom was happening—something terrible or dreadful was happening.

"The next day he got in the car very willingly with me and we drove out to Long Island where this doctor was and the doctor took him inside and spoke with him for only twenty or thirty minutes. He then came out and said, 'Mrs. Mac, he is sick and should be hospitalized.'

"He then spoke to Jay and told him that his mother was going to take him to a place were they would help him, and Jay said, 'No thanks,' and got up and ran out of the building and down the street.

"And I looked at the doctor and I was crying and I said, 'I just don't know what to do at this point. I am really frightened for him.'

"And he said, 'Yes, in fact he should be picked up and I will have to call the police.' And I said, 'Well, if you feel that is wise,' and he said it is the only thing to do at this point.

"So he proceeded to call and explain and gave the description of Jay and said I could go to the police station if they picked him up and so forth, but I felt that I would like to go out and get him myself and I got into my car and started driving and I drove through a few of the main streets, up and down, and finally at an intersection I saw several cars stopped and I stopped my car because I recognized Jay.

"There were several cops around him and they had him in handcuffs and I walked over and of course a crowd was gathering and Jay was standing there trying to resist being arrested which seems understandable because he was really distressed and frightened out of his mind.

"So in order to try and quiet him I put my hands up on his chest and said, 'Jay, we are not trying to hurt you. You do need help, please understand that. We are your friends.'

"And at that point he took his handcuffed hands, broke out of the grip of the policemen, and came down and knocked my hands off his chest. And the police sort of stepped back and said, 'See that, he even hit his mother.'

"Then he was getting slightly more resistive so the police, after he had struck me, decided that he was a real rough one, and they were all wrestling with him with his hands behind his back in handcuffs.

"Now Jay was a very large person and he had very large hands and wrists so it was difficult for them and when they put the handcuffs on he was really upset.

"I asked the policemen if they would help me get him to the private psychiatric hospital and they said no way. They said once the police are involved he goes to a police station and a staff psychiatrist is called and examines the person and if he deems it necessary he goes to the state mental hospital in Central Islip.

"So they asked me to please follow them over to the police station and I did. And when he got there he was mute, he wasn't talking and he wasn't reacting anymore. And all of a sudden he rolled on the floor, like went off the side of the chair and kept saying, 'The handcuffs are killing me,' and then he started to cry and said, 'The reason is I am afraid of dying, I thought I was going to die.'

"Then one of the policemen said, 'My God, I used to go to school with him, Mrs. MacDonald. What happened to him?' At that point we waited for the psychiatrist and it was very quiet and I explained to him that he was not going to die. He was healthy and well and we were going to help him. We would have to go from here to a hospital and I asked him if he understood that and he said he did.

"We waited and the psychiatrist came and of course he had to be hospitalized, so they took him to Central Islip and it is probably now eleven or twelve o'clock at night.

"A psychiatrist began to talk to him there and said,

'Do we really need to keep the handcuffs on?' and the cops said, 'You don't know how strong he is—it took a lot of us to get him down to the ground.' But the doctor said, 'I trust him, he seems calm now, let's give it a go,' and they took the handcuffs off and then the doctor said to the cops, 'It's all right, we'll keep him, you can go.' And they left.

"And then we sat and talked and the psychiatrist probed with me into some of the background and I explained that the death of his father had been very disturbing to Jay and he had never, in a sense, shown in a way, like his deep emotional feeling, like he was, again, trying to hide it.

"It was difficult, perhaps, for him. Because in our household, like there was this bit about a stiff-upper-lip kind of thing that even I, perhaps, could not help him to be able to show his emotions.

"Now, when Mr. Hayes, Jay, and I were at the motel, I had phoned Jeff, realizing it was probably putting a burden on him, but I personally felt that I did not have a husband and I wanted to talk to somebody who had good sense and also because I knew that he would be concerned.

"I called Fort Bragg and when the phone was answered it was answered by Colette and I explained that I did not mean to upset her in any way, but that I called to speak to Jeff because we were having a little problem with Jay.

"And she said he was not there. He was on maneuvers or special detail down in Puerto Rico, but she wanted me to tell her about it so I said, 'Well, Colette, I think Jay has probably taken a bad dose of something and he seems a little out of his mind right now and I am getting professional help for him, but I just wanted to talk to Jeff because he had such a quiet, nice mind that what he can do is ease me a little bit. But it's not necessary and please don't burden him with it. And she said, 'You know Jeff—he loves Jay and he would be very concerned and I think he should know.'

"I learned later that Colette got permission to call through on the field telephone where he was on maneuvers. He then got special permission to leave Puerto Rico and come up. He arrived, to my recollection, the very next day."

"What was he dressed in?" Victor Woerheide asked.

"He was dressed in his full military garb. You know, a Green Beret wears his beret and he wears a uniform and he has boots on."

"Did he bring any other clothing with him?"

"Well, interestingly enough, I can only remember him in the uniform for the entire time he stayed there. In fact, even when we visited Jay at the hospital, which was several times—and Jeff spoke to the psychiatrist many times—he was always dressed in his military garb.

"Jeff told me that he reviewed with Jay how it happened, who gave it to him and the answer was always that it was just some guy who was selling the stuff. Then Jeff was discussing the fact that Jay was mostly concerned with impending death because he had watched his father die. He was with him during the last hour."

"Was Jeff there also?"

"No, Jeff was in Chicago. And the thing that distressed Jay was the absence of color in the body following death, plus the fact that there was excretion, probably semen or urine, which is a very natural thing, but to him it was frightening. He had never talked about this to anyone but he was able to relate it to Jeff, and Jeff explained the process of death to him.

"Now on the day following, Jeff asked the doctors how they thought Jay was doing, and they said they did not think he was psychotic, but that he'd had a very bad drug reaction, and he said, 'We think we should be able to release him tomorrow, but we must caution you that he is going to have bad flashbacks and we have him on Thorazine at this time and he should be maintained on Thorazine and he should get this kind of a dosage,' and so forth. 'And if he gets in trouble, occasionally, if he gets the same feelings—and we have discussed this with him—he should not panic, that it will probably pass. But he should be maintained on Thorazine.'

"At that point they told us we could come for him the next day and we took him home and Judy had prepared a lovely supper. She had things cheerful and nice. Jeff said it was time for him to go and what they would do was go back to New York and then Jeff would take off from New York to return back to his base. But he would see that Jay got back okay. He wanted to see where it was that he worked. And that was the last time I saw them as brothers together, when they left to return to New York."

"Was Jeff ever violent? Did he ever, in your presence, strike anybody?"

"No. I mean, as kids, he and his brother would wrestle occasionally. Things like that. But no. I think Jeff dislikes disorder or chaos or violence or disruption. He is by nature a lover of beauty and harmony and peace. I think most people find him to be a delightful person to know. I have never known him to be abusive. He likes to keep things serene.

"As a result his nature as a baby—he was, you know, the kind of kid that even when he woke up from his sleep he had a grin from ear to ear. I must confess that I thought he was kind of a little slow mentally at first because he was just so happy all the time.

"He had a wonderful, sunny disposition. And he was a very amenable child. Responded—like for instance at Christmas in order to make it look like you were getting a lot of things, you'd slip in things that were absolutely needed, such as a flannel shirt, or underwear or whatever, and when he opened his presents he was always very enthusiastic. You know, 'Just what I wanted!' And you'd laugh because it might be two sets of underwear. It was like a filler present, you know, but still he responded to it. He was always—he had joy and he brought joy to lots of other people."

Woerheide then asked about the relationship between Jeff and Colette.

"Like every couple," she said, "there were times when I'm sure they were a little hassled, but it didn't seem to be anything. They looked like they were truly very much in love."

"Now when you were visiting them at Thanksgiving in 1969, I take it Colette knew she was pregnant again?"

"Apparently."

"What was her—"

"Reaction? She seemed very pleased. Now, I was a little upset, I must tell you. I didn't say this to her, but I felt that because of the difficulty of her pregnancies, that you know, it was kind of, you know, maybe they ought to at least give her more time.

"But she always wanted a large house with a lot of children, dogs, and horses. I mean, it was sort of a dream of both of them to be able to live in a place—like they often talked about living in Vermont or someplace of that nature where they could enjoy, in a sense, a natural existence. You know, space, children, and animals.

"So when I embraced Colette and asked how she felt about it, she said, 'I am very happy. I know that it will be okay. It is probably a little soon, but it will be okay.'"

"When you visited at Thanksgiving, where did you sleep?"

"I slept with Kimberly."

"Was it Kim's idea that you sleep in bed with her?"

"Yes. We had kind of a special thing. Kim and I always—we kind of looked at each other and grinned. I can't describe it to you otherwise, but when I came it was always, 'Nana, you know you sleep with me.'"

Dorothy MacDonald then, for the first time, lost her composure to the extent that she began to sob.

When Victor Woerheide resumed his questioning—his inexorable, inevitable, unavoidable questioning—his voice was unusually soft.

"Was there any problem as far as bed-wetting was concerned?" he asked.

"I don't think Kimberly was bed-wetting any longer, but I'm not sure of that. I didn't live with them that long."

"When was the next time you went down there?"

"Just prior to New Year's."

"How were they getting along?"

"To me, it seemed very much the same."

"Any problems? Any tensions?"

"If there were tensions, they were not obvious. There was no overt fighting, the conversation was normal and routine. I remember what we did—New Year's Eve we went for dinner with a group of people, and I went home early and relieved the babysitter and they stayed out to dance. To my observation it looked like a normal, happy married couple who were having a New Year's Eve out with friends."

"Did you ever help around the kitchen at all?"

"Oh, yes. At Thanksgiving or even the next time, yes, I would always be helping. Either setting the table or helping with the meal. I remember, inadvertently, I had thrown away the makings of gravy for little meatballs that Colette was preparing for hors d'oeuvres, and I felt very badly about it.

"But I told her, 'Hey, kid, don't sweat it because I have a little secret recipe that I can sort of concoct.' And I got out some gravy mix and some onion soup and, well, you know, put together a gravy base and put the meatballs in it, and kiddingly I said to her, 'It'll be the hit of the show.' She said, 'Okay, I'm glad we were able to recover.' And so we put out all these hors d'oeuvres for the people, and it was satisfying and she laughed and said, 'You've done it again.' "

"Do you remember that they kept things like Popsicles in the freezer for the kids?"

"Oh, yes, that would be a common thing for them to do."

"Well, do you remember specifically any of the household utensils? Speaking of, for example, an icepick?"

"Sir, I've gone over in my mind a million times. May I answer that? I can't. I would not be able to identify anything."

"Well, in the freezer things have a tendency to frost up. Do you remember using an icepick—"

"I had no time—not no time, I had no occasion to use one, to my recall."

"Do you remember when they were preparing drinks, let's say, at Thanksgiving, that Jeff went around looking for an icepick? As a matter of fact, he went out into a shed in the back to look for an icepick."

"That could very well be true, sir. But I have no recalls [*sic*] of that."

"When you visited at Thanksgiving and New Year's, did Jeff say anything about having some connection with a boxing team, working out with a boxing team?"

"I think there was some discussion of it, but—it's not a strong memory of mine. In other words, I know that he was always involved in some kind of sport or other. He was also a trooper, a paratrooper. He was jumping. I went to see one of his jumps with Colette and the children and that kind of thing. You know, we spent time talking or watching him do things of this nature. He would play ball."

"Do you recall him saying anything about taking a trip with the boxing team?"

"There was some discussion. Yes, you're right. There was some discussion about that."

"Do you know where he was planning to go?"

"Oh, boy. Would Russia sound ridiculous?"

"No, it does not sound ridiculous."

"I just sort of had this mental flash, but it sounded like so far out."

"Did Colette have any comment to make on this proposed trip to Russia?"

"I think she was, again, like hoping that there wouldn't be a long absence. I must say probably there was some concern on her part because of course he had been absent a fair degree of the time because of his workload and his internship and so forth. But, by the same token, she understood that he had this, like, sort of desire to participate, and be, in a sense, an outstanding person. No matter what he did he was always trying to, you know, do a good job. That kind of thing."

"Did Colette have any reason to be jealous?"

"If she did she never mentioned it to me, sir. Okay? That's as fair as I can be with you. She might have been the type of woman that felt that way and would not discuss it with his parent. I do not know."

"Whether justified or not, did Colette think she had any reason to be jealous of Penny Wells?"

"Sir, you're asking me something that I have never heard discussed."

"Well, I'm going to ask you specifically: when Jeff was up there about September or October when Jay had this problem which caused him to be hospitalized, did Jeff have an occasion to look up Penny Wells, spend any time with her?"

"If he did, sir, it was without my knowledge."

"All right, now, on February 17 and in the days immediately thereafter, did you question your son in any way about any of the details of what had happened inside that apartment?"

"No, and may I emphasize that I was the mother of a young man whose wife and children were murdered and my concern was to give solace and to try and help him bear this agonizing burden. I did not question him."

"You stayed down there during that entire week?"

"Yes, sir, but my time was not always spent with Jeff. I had a few other things that I had to take care of."

"What things are you referring to?"

"Well, I got a telephone call from Mr. Hayes, and he said that Jay wanted to talk to me. And I spoke to Jay on the telephone and Jay sounded like he wasn't himself again, as though he might have been having one of those things that the doctors called a flashback.

"And he asked me, 'Mom, tell me what is happening?' And I told him and he sounded like he was a little disjointed, and I said to him, 'Where are you now?' And he said, 'I am with Billy.' And I asked Jay if he would be kind enough to let me speak to Billy, which he did, and I said to Billy, 'Jay sounds ill.' And Billy said, 'I am afraid to tell you, Mrs. MacDonald, that he really is not well again and I honestly don't know what to do.' And I said to Billy, 'You know the hospital that he went to before and my only request is that if you feel he is not manageable, perhaps they will be able to help. Undoubtedly, it is a flashback, or to your knowledge, has he done anything stupid, like taking drugs again?'

"And Billy said, 'It is possible, I don't know. But he is getting messages out of the TV again, which is one of the symptoms of his trouble before.'

"And I said, 'Well, the messages he is getting today from the TV are very real, but I am sure that he can't keep them in perspective.' So I said, 'Billy, I can't be in two places at the same time and right now I really feel as though I cannot leave North Carolina.'

"So I asked Billy, 'Can you talk to him and see if he will voluntarily go with you back to the hospital?' And Billy said, 'Okay, I will try, Mrs. Mac.' And I believe he called me back later that night to inform me that they had been successful in convincing Jay, not with ease, that he should return to the hospital.

"The next day, late that night after having visited Jeff, I got this message that I would have to call the hospital because something was wrong with Jay. So I called and they assured me—now this was probably close to midnight on the 18th, as I recall—that Jay was sound asleep. He had been tranquilized and he was fine.

"And I told the people on the phone that I was confused because the message indicated there had been some trouble. And they said, 'Well, Mrs. MacDonald, there was trouble earlier.' Apparently during the night he awoke and he did not know where he was, and he became very deranged and he put his fists through the window and said that he needed to get out and he had to get down to see what was going on. But they said they gave him heavy dosages of Thorazine, and it tended to quiet him down and now he was resting and in fact fast asleep."

"How long did Jay remain in the hospital? Isn't it true that he was at the funeral service?"

"Yes, that was because our family has this marvelous friend, Mr. Robert Stern, from New Hope, Pennsylvania, and when he heard Jay was in difficulty, he contacted a doctor in Bucks County and explained the situation and arranged for private, follow-up care, and for Jay to live with his family, because he had known Jay almost all his life, and the next day it was arranged for Jay to be released in his custody when it was decided that Jay was now manageable, and Mr. Stern took Jay from the hospital down into the Village to remove his clothing from the place where he was staying and took him back to Bucks County, to his own home.

"On the following day Mr. Stern felt it was imperative that Jay be present at the service, so that his presence would support the family and so there would be no conjecture as to why the brother was not there. So he flew down in his company plane, bringing Jay, and then went back on the plane to Bob's home.

"The day after the internment in Long Island, I drove to Bucks County and spent probably a good part of that day talking with the psychiatrist who Mr. Stern had arranged for, trying to establish some background and then I drove back on down to Fort Bragg."

"Now, after Jeffrey was released from the hospital, did you and he have occasion to take a short trip together?"

"Yes, as I recall the wife of his commanding officer met me one day in the lobby of the place where I was staying and suggested that I take him to the seashore for a bit, just for a few days' recovery.

"I asked Jeff if he would like to go and he said yes, and we did go. And he just walked the seashore and we picked up shells and had breakfast. And I remember just driving around seeing the countryside and trying to restore. But on my honor I never probed. I could not ask questions. I felt that other people had."

"You didn't probe and he didn't volunteer, right?"

"That's correct."

"Now, after the charges were dropped," Woerheide said, "why didn't your son remain on the East Coast? Doesn't he have connections on the East Coast?"

"Yes sir, in a sense, but they are almost all painful. His father is gone, his grandmother is gone, his wife and children—primary—are gone. Even his house is gone. There is nothing there."

"But isn't it strange that he moved from one edge of the continent all the way out to the other?"

"At the time, you must remember, he was working very hard to get his life together, and he did work in New York for six months. And believe me, when you see what it is like to live in New York City, I don't think it is the ideal situation. It isn't a spot that either he or even Colette would have wanted to be. In other words, it was not their lifestyle.

"So when Jeff and I discussed it, I encouraged him to go. 'This is something that if you think will help restore your spirits because the sun does shine, and if the people are kind, and if you can be engaged in the work of your interest—why not?' "

"Well, it seems to me he might want to stay around to occasionally visit the graves."

"Let me tell you something. I don't even visit those graves. I did very consistently in the very early years but I found that after a while—first of all, the memory of the children—and that includes Colette, because essentially she was my child—the memory is very pure and very good and I would like to keep it that way. I don't mind putting flowers on the graves, but I don't want to enter into a competition."

"What do you mean by that?"

"Mr. Woerheide, I am not casting aspersions, but it is true that Mr. and Mrs. Kassab keep those flowers fresh and there are multiple baskets of flowers and they are never left to wilt or die.

"Their visits there are continuous but by the same token it seems like a show and I will tell you why. Beside those bodies lies the body of her husband and there is no tombstone or name commemorating him. This may sound harsh, and I pass no judgment, but as you know I am sure that man committed suicide and Mildred could not ever forgive this. As a result she will not honor him by even putting his name there." (This, as it happens, was not true. There was, and is, a marker at the grave of Cowles Stevenson.)

"Please let me clear some of these things up right now. The fact that there was a great deal of attention paid to the girls' graves was pleasing at first, and then I realized that in a sense it was symbolic, as though they were keeping alive more than the memory of the death of the children: it was mostly for attention to be brought to this thing.

"Now for the loss of three lives attention must be paid, but it seems to me not in this showy way. So I feel that if that is how they spend their time and since I, for about a year and a half, have felt that it would be impossible for me to continue visiting or meeting them on the basis that their attitude toward Jeff had changed, then you will have to forgive me when I tell you that I prefer to have the thoughts of my children in my mind rather than in flowers placed on a grave where there are already too many placed."

"That is very interesting," Victor Woerheide said. "Tell me, Mrs. MacDonald, why do you think the Kassabs, who were so supportive of your son, suddenly changed their mind about him?"

"In the dynamics of human behavior one has to stop and wonder why attitudes change. Now let me start from the beginning, as I see it."

"By all means, do so."

"Frequently, I have heard the story over and over again from both Mildred and her sister Helen that Mildred was the youngest and the prettiest, and therefore a lot of attention was paid to making sure that Mildred's life was filled with gaiety and good things. She was given the opportunity that the older sisters and the parents worked towards giving her and she herself was almost prepared to sort of be onstage.

"In all sincerity, the woman has had a tough time because there have been tragedies in her life. But every time something happened, it always seemed to—you know, she is a little lady, but a very powerful lady and the power is in that she shuts out more. In other words, she has the power, I think, to change her temperament.

"Now what happens is that when her husband died— and this is foreign to my lifestyle—she was a lady who traveled in the more elite set in Patchogue. We were with other kinds of people. They were good people, from all walks of life, but Mildred was very selective about professional people.

"When her husband died, the concern in the family was for Mildred. So they gathered together and they sent her on a world tour of one year, and when she returned, they then established her in a hotel in New York for six months, and they gleefully talk about how she was set up in the best table in the dining room night after night to attract the attention of wealthier people, because obviously they would be in that vicinity.

"Now this is not hearsay. This is what is being told me over and over again. And eventually she did attract the attention of one Alfred Kassab, who is by all means a reasonably attractive man. His family was wealthy—he came from the South, as I understand—and he and Mildred were genuinely attracted to each other. I am not disputing that.

"And then they got married. And when they got married—and this was told me over and over again by that family—Freddy's mother was insane with rage and decided that she would cut him out of her will. And because of this, Mildred and Freddy—mostly Mildred—would talk incessantly to me about how they were going to work to declare his mother incompetent at the time of that will. Because they wanted their rightful share, and they were accustomed also, of course, to money.

"Again, this may sound a little too strong, but there were times, sir, in her conversation when everything looked very good and we were all together and there was no tragedy yet—there were times when my feeling was that their concern was much more for Jeff than for Colette.

"Mildred tended to apologize for Colette. I found her to be an entrancing girl. Sometimes she looked a little harassed, but it was mostly, I felt, that she felt she wasn't managing very well. I was aware of her faults and they made us understand each other better.

"But, by the same token, I really feel that one of the things that made everything okay in their eyes was the fact that Jeff was going to be a doctor. I have a feeling that they felt very well protected by the fact that there was going to be someone to lean on. Now that may sound severe, harsh, or whatever. But I honestly feel that when Jeff made the decision to move to California, that was the beginning of their disenchantment.

"Also, let me tell you that from day one, February 17th, when we arrived, Mr. Kassab made some really strong statements about how he was going to pursue this case down to the end of his days.

"And I realize that we all handle our grief and our anger in different ways, and this statement by itself is an understandable one, but by the same token he also feels he has to, like, prove this to his wife, who is the one behind him, like making the spitballs, and he is throwing them. I really think he has been pressured in this way."

"When was it that you first traveled to California and visited your son?" Woerheide asked.

"I went probably in August of the first year when he was there. I went again in February." (This would have been within days of February 15—the evening on which Freddy Kassab had spent two hours explaining to Dorothy MacDonald how he had come to believe her son guilty of murder.) "I felt that was probably going to be a bad time for him as it is for all of us always. Always Christmas and February are very bad."

"What is his lifestyle out there?"

"Well, he works very hard, and that has sort of been the story of his life. He does socialize. He entertains at home a great deal because that has always been a style of his life. He has always been a good host. He has a boat. I have enjoyed being on it. It is a very refreshing experience to be back on the water. That, again, was part of our lifestyle."

"So you feel he had adjusted well to California?"

"Yes, and I remember being very impressed by it myself. It was sunny, the people were kind, traffic seemed to flow in a nice way, and things seemed logical. Roads led somewhere. In other words, they have better—it just seemed to me that people were very nice. There was a calm approach to life, there was a joyfulness, people looked healthy. People seemed to be tan, brown, kind.

"I was depressed and it appealed to me. So I went back and actually looked for a little house and found one and felt that it would be nice to be able to retire here because you could pull in with a car to a station and you have a knock in your motor, the man would raise the hood and he'd fix it and you'd say how much do I owe you and he would say, 'For what? Fifteen minutes?' And I'd think this is a whole new way of life. It was really very pleasing."

"Well, since he's been in California, has he talked to you at all about the night of February 16 and 17 or does he put that out of his mind and talk about other things?"

"I think we talk about the pain of loss."

"But apart from the time when he testified before the Article 32 hearing, that's about the only time that he sat down in your presence—"

"—and told the whole story. That is correct, sir. And I've never probed. I'm sure that some people think that may be very strange. But I felt that there were enough people asking questions, and that I, in a sense, you know—"

"Since the FBI and the CID were asking questions, it was superfluous on your part?"

"It seemed to be that there were people who were asking questions."

"Mrs. MacDonald, before we close, do you have any comments that you wish to make to the grand jury? If there is something I haven't inquired into that you think should be brought to their attention?"

"No, except I am sorry that they have been imposed upon, because I feel that essentially we've been through a grand jury hearing before."

"Well, this is not an imposition, Mrs. MacDonald. There are three dead people."

"I understand that very well."

The Philadelphia psychologist who had administered the tests to Jeffrey MacDonald in 1970 and who had found "no sign of either psychosis or psychopathic tendencies" was called to testify.

Victor Woerheide first asked him how it had come about that he had been called upon to examine Mac-Donald.

"In a rather unusual way," the psychologist said. "The defense attorney, in an effort to help prepare a potential defense, requested that Captain MacDonald be examined by a forensic psychiatrist in Philadelphia with whom I had worked on previous occasions. The purpose, as I understood it, was to show that he was not mentally ill. The crime, apparently, was of such a nature, as it was explained to me, that it was highly likely that someone who was fairly disturbed would have committed it. And one line of reasoning that the defense was pursuing was to show that Captain Mac-Donald was not so disturbed.

"So I was not being asked to examine him to determine whether he was not guilty by reason of insanity or anything like that, but simply to see if there was any sign of emotional illness or maladjustment or what his potential for extreme violent behavior was."

"How many days did you see him?"

"Only on one day."

"Is this the ideal procedure?"

"I would prefer to see a subject over several days, but in this case I remember that there was a great hurry about getting the whole thing done, and the subject could not be provided over several days."

"I assume that in conducting the type of examination you conducted, you first have to establish a certain rapport with the subject?"

"Yes, and the difficulty in establishing rapport with someone like this is to initially convince him that you are indeed working for his defense. I mean, you have to reassure him that it is important he explain himself as frankly and openly as possible.

"It was particularly difficult in this case because Captain MacDonald was a very intellectualizing fellow. He thought things out a lot in his head and was always anticipating and worrying and concerned about what might happen next and what would be the results of what he would say. I suppose that's sort of an appropriate concern, but it stood in the way of getting him to open up, frankly.

"So I spent some time with him pointing out that what he told me he was telling me in confidence—that the information would be communicated only to his attorney and the psychiatrist employed by his attorney, and that it was very important that he discuss things with me as frankly and openly as possible.

"He was concerned because he said the incident was very much on his mind, and he was afraid that the fact that it was would influence his test results and might suggest that he had committed the crime.

"I said, on the contrary, if he attempted to keep such information out, it would certainly look as if he were being evasive. As we went into the examination it seemed fairly clear that he had taken my advice. His responses were quick. They did not suggest that he was being carefully reflective, thinking ahead of what he was going to say. He showed no indications, in other words, of planning ahead in what he was saying and trying to make himself look good. Instead, he seemed to be speaking quickly, openly, frankly, and without reserve."

"Now can you tell us what your general observations were with respect to Captain MacDonald?"

"Besides his concern that his preoccupation with what had happened might influence the test results, what struck me first was that he was the sort of person who initially comes across as very self-possessed. This is a man who doesn't turn to other people for help with his problems. This is a man who can work things out for himself.

"So he denies any emotional difficulties, any complaints. Many individuals, if you ask, 'Have you ever had any problems of getting along?' would say, 'Well, occasionally, yes.' Captain MacDonald tended not to do that. He seemed to be the sort of person if you came up to him on the street at any time he would tell you things are going fine.

"He seemed quite naive psychologically. Some people with no training or education are very sensitive and quick to think in psychological terms and know how people are thinking and feeling. He was not this sort of person. In spite of the fact that he had completed college and medical school, he was not an insightful—he was a very bright person but not a person who understood how the mind works and how people think. He was really quite dumb in that regard.

"He seemed to come across as a person who had very little understanding of his own behavior. And this made me feel that more than most people, Captain MacDonald would not be very good at subtly or cleverly or consistently hiding features about his personality. He was too naive to do that.

"You know, if you have any smarts psychologically and a psychologist asks you, 'Do you have any problems at all?' you know you are not supposed to say, 'Oh, no, Doc. No problems at all.' You're supposed to say, 'Well, yeah, you know, like anybody, I have occasionally.'

"He didn't have that kind of smarts. It made me feel that this was a person who was not going to have the sophistication to evade things cleverly.

"Once he actually began the tests his responses were very quick, almost impulsive. There was no indication whatsoever that he was trying to conceal or hide things that came up. In fact, in the actual content of his test responses, material came up that was clearly related to the incident. And so, overall, there was certainly no indication whatsoever that he was attempting to conceal his thoughts about the deaths or to convince me in any way of his innocence.

"And the overall results—just looking at the whole works—falls broadly within normal limits. In other words, there is no particular thing on any of the tests that jumps out at you as a strikingly abnormal finding.

"On the MMPI, for example, there is one scale that

approaches the abnormal range but doesn't quite get there. You and I probably have ones that approach the abnormal range and don't get there either. Might even have a few over it. Which may or may not mean anything.

"Actually, the fact that they are all within normal limits is in itself unusual. Of all the people that I have ever seen who have been accused of violent crimes, it's pretty unusual that—I suppose because in most instances, even on the cases where they've been found not guilty, they had an adjustment such that there was reason to believe that they might have done it. In other words, there were some abnormal features in their adjustment.

"Now, the main thing that came across about Captain MacDonald is that basically this guy—and if you talk to him you're going to find this hard to believe—basically this guy is a very passive, dependent guy with marked feelings of inadequacy.

"But this is all concealed by a surface where he presents himself as adequate, competent, in control, perfectly well adjusted, and always at ease and ready to handle whatever comes up.

"So there is this sort of shell of adequacy or competency, but inside, these marked feelings of not being assertive enough, not being adequate, having real doubts about himself.

"And all this is very much unconscious. Like, if you asked him, 'Well, underneath you really are sort of worried about yourself, huh?' you would really get him up in the air because he would say, 'What do you mean?'

"He might get threatened if he worried about you, but if you were a person that he could sort of put down, he would have no hesitation to say, 'What are you talking about?'

"So it's this contrast between the way he presents himself and what comes across unconsciously as you begin to spend time with him and test him and talk with him and work with him.

"For example, on the MMPI, the highest scale—the one that's approaching the abnormal range—is the masculinity-femininity scale. And he is scoring rather in the feminine direction, which doesn't mean homosexuality or anything like that, but men who score in the feminine direction are men who are usually somewhat passive, not terribly direct or assertive, people who, when they are angry or upset would express their feelings in somewhat more passive ways. They might, for example, be sarcastic rather than directly argumentative.

"To give you another example, here's a TAT story. He sees a picture of a boy looking at a violin, and he is asked to tell the story about it. Generally, on all the TAT stories you say, 'Tell me what led up to what is going on now, how it comes out, and how the people are thinking and feeling.'

"Okay. It's just a boy looking at a violin. It's purposely made so you can't say exactly what's going on. You have to make it up.

"Now, he says, 'This is a little boy who is getting ready to practice his violin.' He didn't have to say, 'little' boy. Why did he use the word *little*?

"'He's getting ready to practice his violin. He's a little annoyed.'

"Okay, now some of you probably would see this boy as annoyed; some of you might see him as pleased. But for Captain MacDonald the boy is a little annoyed. 'He'd rather be doing something else. He's had it a number of months and is barely adequate.'

"Now where is that coming from in this picture? *'He's*

had it a number of months and is barely adequate.' I'm trying to present this in a way that is pretty straightforward, you know. One can dwell on psychoanalytic interpretations of this material and see the violin as a symbol for the male sexual organ and all this sort of thing, but that's getting pretty hot and heavy. And I think the point gets across without getting into all of that.

" 'He'll give up other things to practice it.'

"Now what's going on here? He's annoyed. He's barely adequate. He isn't really liking it, but he will give up other things to practice it.

" 'After much discussion with the parents—one-sided from the parents' viewpoint—he practices it for a number of years and then gives it up. He thinks there are nicer things to do with his time than something that doesn't fit in with his idea of the role of a young male.'

"Now, the point about this story is there's nothing strikingly aberrant about it. He doesn't say that the boy is going to take the violin and set it on fire or anything like that. It's not wildly abnormal, but it does reveal certain things about his personality adjustment.

"He clearly attempts to present himself as a strong, competent man, but his underlying dependency needs require him to gain the approval of those in authority over him, an approval that he gains by conformity.

"So, on the one hand you've got a guy who wants to be strong, competent, and independent, but on the other he wants everybody to approve of what he does. Basically, he is this passive guy with doubts about his adequacy. But he wants to be seen as strong and competent. He is really worried about what people are going to think.

"In other words, despite his assertions of well-being and independence, these mutually contradictory needs of being independent and autonomous on one hand and gaining approval on the other can't lead him to any real independence. As long as he is caught in that bind he's never really going to become a completely mature individual.

"Now there are probably a lot of people in the world that, by this definition, are not completely mature individuals. So I don't mean to say that this constitutes some markedly abnormal feature. But the crux—the irony—of his situation is that to the extent that he gains this approval from authority that he needs by conforming, to the same extent he loses his sense of adequacy and strong masculine identity.

"In other words, if you've got any insight, you know that every time you submit and go along with what authorities are saying, you're losing that much of your own independence and integrity.

"How do you handle that? Well, he handles it by not having insight. Other people might handle it differently. Some people might develop tics or stomach pains: the key thing about Captain MacDonald is that he handles his conflicts by denying that they exist. He puts a little part of himself over here and a little part of himself over there and he never puts it all together. And as long as he doesn't put it together, it doesn't upset him.

"So, you or I might look at Captain MacDonald in a brief conversation and think, how can he hide from his feelings like that? Well, I'll tell you how. If he didn't hide from his feelings like that, he would be every day confronted with the fact that on one hand he's saying he's a strong, successful male and on the other hand he is bowing down to authority and giving in to people, and he wouldn't be able to handle it.

"As a result, he handles it by completely hiding from

his feelings. He is a guy who is simply not in touch with his feelings. It's a crucial part of his personality adjustment that he does not understand what's going on in him: he has no insight.

"In his interview with me, he said, 'You know, what bugs me about all this, people keep phoning and wanting to give me sympathy about what's happened, like they want me to cry on their shoulder. I'm not going to cry on anybody's shoulder.'

"Now, if you are going to be charged with a crime, you probably shouldn't have this kind of adjustment because it doesn't look good when people come around and you don't look upset. But there is no way in the world that a person with Captain MacDonald's personality adjustment is going to look upset in the presence of people. Because that would indicate that he has some feelings, it would indicate that he can understand what is going on inside himself, and that would open up all sorts of problems for a person with his adjustment.

"Now, another thing is, I think, really, as you begin to spend time with Captain MacDonald, you begin to see that he's got a nostalgic longing for his early childhood. All of this that we're talking about, of course, is pretty much pushed under consciousness, but when you hear him talk about his boyhood, he clearly seems to regret the loss of his early, dependent, conforming role.

"Then, he knew how to win approval and respect. He was a bright, good student. He was athletic. He knew how to do all kinds of things that would win approval and attention. You know, the glowing schoolboy. Perfect. That was it for him.

"Well, what do you do when you're this bright, accepting schoolboy? You conform. You do all the right things to win the adulation of your parents and teachers.

But what do you do when you grow up? How does a person with this image of himself as a young, successful, bright, student athlete handle becoming an adult?

"Let's look at another picture. It's a picture of a man climbing a rope. He says, 'A gymnast showing off, climbing the rope in gym to the delight of others. Jesus! How do you make a story out of this? He feels silly that he has to show off to amuse his friends.'

"You see, if you're a good, young, bright, athletic kid, you don't feel silly. But when you get to be an adult, other feelings start to creep in.

"He says, 'He'd rather have the attention in another way, but he is the center of the party and continues to do it to keep his large number of friends nearby laughing. Afterwards, he always feels foolish, but the next time the occasion arises he does the same thing again. He will continue to entertain people, each time feeling it really isn't him doing it. He'd rather sit down and talk to a friend than perform, but he will continue because of his fear of losing friends.'

"So he's stuck. The only way Captain MacDonald can handle it is not to consciously recognize this conformity and need for approval as a subjection of himself. And as long as he can do that, he can continue to view himself—particularly in regard to his professional competence as a doctor, as an incipient surgeon, and the esteem and approval that he gains by that, as an indication of his adequacy as a man."

"How would that affect his family situation so far as his wife and two children are concerned?" Victor Woerheide asked.

"He would be a guy who would lose himself in his work. His contact with any potentially intimate human relationships—particularly his wife and children—would be marked with reserve and handicapped by his conflicts about independence and dependence.

"This is a guy, for example, who would be appalled at the thought of woman's lib, because the authority—if so many people start questioning his authority, that's going to be a problem for him. That isn't unusual. There are a lot of people like that. But this is the way he is, too.

"He would probably be able to be most intimate with people where the lines of authority and structure are most clear. And of course that's only true in a marriage if your wife willingly subjugates herself to you.

"He was able to express what warmth he was able to express much more easily with his children than he was with his wife. And occasionally in the tests a sort of nostalgic quality would come out in regard to his children, as at one point he saw in the Rorschach—on Card Five—he saw the upper details as the head of a bunny rabbit.

"'I see a bunny rabbit,' he said. 'We gave one to Kimmy about a month before this occurred.'

"The whole idea of the bunny rabbit: this is sort of the softest, pleasantest type of response he gives on the tests. And even then he didn't make it as soft and pleasant as he could because he emphasized, 'It looks like the bunny rabbit because of the form, the ears coming up, the feet coming down.'

"He might have said, for example, it looked like a bunny rabbit because it looked soft and furry, which would be sort of a warmer, more affectionate type of response, but he didn't do that.

"So even at that level he can't let his defenses down that much. He instead sort of emphasized the hard line, the edge, the form that creates the perception of the bunny rabbit.

"You see, on the Rorschach, we show people a series

of these inkblots and the person tries to say what they are. And one of the ways we score the test is to go back over it once we've gone through all the cards and say, 'What about the blot made you see it that way?'

"People see different things for different reasons. Some will say, 'Well, it was just shaped like that,' or, 'Well, it has sort of a soft, textury quality that makes it look like that,' or, 'Well, it seemed like they were moving,' or, 'Well, the color made it look like that.'

"When you pull all these things together and add up the totals, one of the things we look at in scoring the Rorschach is the extent to which a person tends to use one or another determinant: color, texture, movement, shape, form, all of these things.

"And there is a tendency for certain sorts of mental states to be associated with the tendency to use certain sorts of determinants.

"For example, people who are intellectualizers will tend to use human movement often as a determinant of what they see. People who are very emotion-laden often tend to be much more responsive to the colors.

"Now, Dr. MacDonald showed a much greater tendency to respond to things like movement and form than he did to color. So this is another way we might get from the tests support for the hypothesis that he really doesn't utilize his emotional responses very effectively. Another thing we score is the tendency to look at whole concepts as opposed to relatively small, detailed aspects of the blot. Captain MacDonald was much more inclined to look at small, teeny details. On some of the blots he gave about ten responses, and almost none paid any attention to the blot as a whole: instead, he went around interpreting this little piece, that piece, a little piece here, a little piece there—a much more compulsive, detailed, precise, careful approach to things instead of a more global approach.

"So he comes across as a person who is quite organized and compulsive. He tends to avoid emotion, to deny and repress his feelings. He's quite organized and quite compulsive in his approach to problems, very systematic and detailed, and that helps a lot if you're the sort of person who wants to compartmentalize everything and put one feeling here and one feeling there. He can do it in a very efficient, organized, systematic way.

As a result, things don't overwhelm him. They don't interfere with his function. He's able to function, really, quite effectively. Particularly by choosing a profession that enables him to be a strong authority figure and that helps him escape from emotional responsibilities.

"He becomes a physician. Better yet, he becomes a surgeon, because a surgeon doesn't have to interact emotionally with people. He's God. He is the authority. Nobody questions him. In fact, he doesn't even have to talk to patients because they're under anesthesia during the whole procedure.

"I suspect if you brought in and examined a whole slew of surgeons, you would find most of them having emotional adjustments very much like Captain MacDonald's.

"What I'm trying to get across is that these characteristics in his personality are neither uncommon nor maladaptive for many purposes. They just don't make him into a very affectionate, warm, loving spouse. But there are a lot of people out in the world that are not affectionate, warm, loving spouses.

"In terms of his life history, however, and in keeping with his need to conform, as well as his need to be emotionally dependent on people—even though outwardly he doesn't acknowledge this—he married quite young and he married under circumstances where it wasn't altogether clear that many people would have married.

"He married young and set up a family and went through, in a way, still carrying on with the image of the golden boy. But his marriage was not a combination of two terribly mature or adequate individuals. It was, rather, a relationship where he would have the support and approval of his wife while he failed to become involved with her in an emotionally close or mutually cooperative relationship.

"In many ways, he resented and avoided the demands and responsibilities of being a father. And he was able to use his academic and professional career as a reasonably acceptable excuse to avoid involvement.

"You know, how can a wife complain that he's not spending enough time around the house when he's getting a medical degree, working hard to support the family, and buying presents and giving things to everybody.

"So what does the wife say? Well, the wife is saying things like, you know, 'Couldn't you just be around the house a little more, give us a little more love and affection, a little more of your time?'

"It's hard to just say no. Instead, what you say is, 'I've got to work.' You know, 'I've got to do all these things. I'm doing this for you.' So he chose a profession that took care of his time and in a sense took care of his responsibilities because it limited the extent to which he would have to emotionally and maturely communicate more effectively in the family situation.

"I hope there aren't too many doctors in the audience here. It works quite nicely, I might add.

"But in those situations—such as with the family—where there was less structure, he ran into problems.

Where he couldn't clearly be either the one on the bottom or the one on the top, there he gets into difficulty.

"Wanting the approval of society, and not wanting to do anything to disrupt a situation that was, in the outside world's eyes, very successful—a doctor, married, settled, children—he was caught in a dilemma.

"He was caught up in something that on his own he was not strong and assertive and aggressive enough to find his way out of, either by achieving a closer relationship with his wife or by getting a divorce.

"And he couldn't communicate openly about these feelings, either with himself or with his wife because he was so caught up in this stern, authoritarian image of himself.

"Look at this picture: it's sort of a 1930-ish picture of a man and a woman, and the man is sort of turned off to the side looking away, and the woman has her arms around him. People often see that the woman is pleading with the man in some way. Okay, now here's his story:

"'I'm trying to make out the expression on his face. This is a husband and wife. The husband feels strongly about something, and the wife is obviously showing pride and concern over her husband's anger and is trying to console him.'

"I mean, the husband is an angry, striving, aggressive, assertive beast and that makes the woman feel good. He goes on: 'He enjoys that she is responding so nicely to his show of concern. He'll be able to control his feelings through her urgings. They'll both feel fine. She showed her concern and love, and he gave in to her wishes in calming down. I suspect the inciting cause was an advance made to her by the milkman, or a slight to her by her boss. So he was going to protect her or keep other people away. She's calming him, but she really appreciates a show of affection.'

"So he is the sort of stern, taciturn, demanding, authoritarian figure, and she is pleading, don't do it, I know you're protecting me, but calm yourself—urging him to be happy and successful as a husband.

"But there's no real communication about his feelings or thoughts or ideas going on here. People are behaving according to images.

"In many ways, a person of his conformity might achieve a great deal through close relationships with older male figures. But he fears emotional closeness with males due to his fears of homosexual impulses in himself.

"Now, actually, he doesn't have any real, strong homosexual impulses, but he's afraid that he might. He has a fear of the possibility that these things might exist, and thus he's turned off from close relationships with males.

"Let me give you another example from the TAT. In this picture, one person is lying down and another is standing over them, bent, with the hand out. The person standing is usually seen as male. The person lying down—it's really sort of obscure, but probably it's more commonly seen as male.

He says: 'This is an old man and a boy. They're both hobo types traveling together. The old man has been traveling with the young man as a friend for the last two days, through Texas. The old man looks at the boy and thinks of his own son, and on this night he felt a sudden urge of affection and fatherly-type feeling for the boy while he's sleeping. He wanted to reach over and touch the boy—his shoulder or his hair. The boy is going to wake up and misunderstand and run away and break up a nice friendship. His misunderstanding prevented a lasting friendship from developing, the old man being much more hurt than the boy.'

"Now," said the psychologist, having no awareness of Jeffrey MacDonald's sudden departure for Texas at the age of fifteen and his automobile trip from New York in the company of Jack Andrews, Sr., "in a sense, here, I think that Captain MacDonald is identifying with both figures. He's the young boy who is afraid of the relationship with the older figure, but he's also the older figure who can't communicate his feelings to the boy.

"And there is really sort of a bittersweet quality about these feelings, that he simply doesn't know how to express or accept. He has in himself a longing and a need for these things, but no idea of how to get at them or how to communicate about them, so he stays isolated.

"An important element, you see, in his concept of the masculine role is that a man does not show emotion or weakness. To ask for help or understanding is a sign of inadequacy.

"Thus, his confident manner which initially gives the impression of strength, is, in fact, a rather rigid defense which doesn't permit him to become close to other people and doesn't allow him to ask for support even when it would be appropriate.

"If he were to bring his feelings out more consciously and openly, then all his conflicts about adequacy versus need for support would come out in the open, too, and make him much more anxious and upset and depressed.

"He can't tolerate that. So all these things are kept sealed over. I'm bringing them out from some of the test results but that doesn't mean he's consciously aware of them.

"Now when a person is concerned about their adequacy, about how successful they are, and that person happens to be an American man, one of the ways that this gets expressed is in terms of heterosexual behavior. How do they make it with women. And obviously this is going to come up with Captain MacDonald.

"But the problem is, he is confronted with not only his image of himself as a very adequate male, but his need to be socially conforming and get acceptance and approval.

"So what does he do? He has a whole series of affairs with women but never with a lot of satisfaction or success. And he is always overcome afterwards not by any deep internalized sense of guilt, but a sort of a feeling of shame. The difference that you might see in a young kid who has done something wrong and is caught by their parent and feels ashamed and blushes and turns red as opposed to the idea of guilt, where somebody does something wrong—they know it is wrong and internally they're bothered by it. It doesn't matter that nobody knows about it. Internally, they've got a sense of guilt.

"His behavior was more motivated out of this sort of shame because he was concerned about the approval of others.

"So, although to listen to him, he might present himself as sort of a stud—a very successful male in having sexual encounters, in fact he really is not. He is not comfortable with himself in this image. So he's not free to go out and be consistently, sexually aggressive.

"You know, a person who is completely liberated in this sense—although he might not approve of it—a person who is completely liberated in this sense might perfectly well be able to go out and have affairs and if the wife brought up any objection, you'd just say, 'If you don't like it, leave me.' You know, 'This is your problem. This is the way I run my life.'

"Okay. He couldn't do that at all. Another person

might be so bothered by guilt over having an affair that he might stop and not have any more. That would be another way of handling it. Instead, he had affairs but was never completely happy in having them and yet he couldn't completely stop them.

"So there was this sort of continually wanting the approval and affection and love of the women but also wanting the approval and affection and love of society.

"The fact is, he has a sort of unusual combination of defenses—unusual in the sense that psychologists like to type people into nice, neat little compartments. And that's great when we write textbooks, but unfortunately when we meet with a real person, they don't fit into such nice neat compartments.

"He has this funny combination of, on one hand, an obsessive approach, an intellectualizing approach. That's a fairly unusual combination of defenses, and I think it makes him particularly difficult to understand.

"Now, what does all this have to do with the actual crime that occurred? On the basis of a psychological examination, I don't think a psychologist can determine if a person is lying or not. I think I can with relative certainty describe his adjustment, describe what he was like, account for why he is reacting to what happened the way he did, but as to whether he could be lying about a specific detail or not, I can't read his mind.

"And I think in general it's very difficult to say who, and under what circumstances, can commit a murder. Give me a group of one hundred people and let me examine the group and I might predict out of that hundred what proportion might be likely to commit violent behavior, but you give me one person and ask me to predict, and boy, I'm not going to make any money. I'd rather bet on the horses.

"So, from my understanding of Captain MacDonald's adjustment, the two questions I would want to ask myself are, one, what sort of circumstances would be maximally stressful for him and might lead him to commit a violent crime, and, two, if he committed a violent crime, how would he go about it and how would he respond to it.

"Now, on the basis of his adjustment, it is my feeling that the most stressful type of circumstance would be one where a person not in authority over him and not under him, but a person he hasn't clearly got a structured role with—like a wife or a peer—would say something that would directly challenge his basic area of conflict: his sense of adequacy and masculine autonomy.

"So a taunt from his wife suggesting that he lacked confidence or he lacked virility, I think, would perhaps be the most upsetting thing to him—the thing that might lead him to become most angry, most likely to commit a violent act.

"I cannot think of a basis that would provide sufficient stress for him to commit a violent act against someone who was not in this clearly unstructured role to him. In other words, people way in authority over him, he would have no trouble submitting. That was his style of life. People way in authority under him, they're clearly under him, they wouldn't provide as much stress.

"Therefore, based on my knowledge of him, I could not conceive of emotionally stressful circumstances that would be such that would lead him to kill his children. But I could think of some that might lead him to be angry enough to do something to his wife.

"I have seen murderers who were essentially cold-blooded, psychopathic killers who killed without any particular concern for what they've done and maintained a perfect calm—not because they were defending against anything but just because they didn't care, and coldly and calculatedly went about their business and afterwards tried to handle and conceal evidence and save themselves.

"And I've seen people who have committed a murder in the midst of a psychotic episode. And I've seen people who were basically rather passive, dependent individuals that held their feelings inside of them, with adjustments like Captain MacDonald's—and like probably some of you—who have indeed committed a murder.

"Usually, the murder is of a spouse. The great majority of murders are the murders of spouses. But the way this sort of individual typically responds is immediately afterwards they break down.

"They frequently become amnesic for the whole event and pick up the phone and calmly say, 'I don't know what's happened. There's a knife in my hand. I think my wife, or husband, is dead. You'd better come quick and bring the police. And you come in and the children are sitting there crying and there's just one big mess. And then you go to interview them and they say, 'I don't know what happened.' They have blocked it completely from their minds. One study done in England estimated that in approximately 60 percent of the murders they studied, the person who was accused was amnesic for the event.

"Now, Dr. MacDonald is a person who does repress and deny and compartmentalize, and it's my feeling that were he to have committed such a crime, his response afterwards would most likely be that type of response."

"Can you generalize," Victor Woerheide asked, "about how long such an amnesic episode might last?"

"Sometimes they last indefinitely. Most of them persist for some time. It depends on the way you handle them, and of course it's always confused because some people that are apparently amnesic are actually concealing details of the crime.

"Incidentally, I want to make clear that when I use the words *denial* and *repression,* I do not mean a conscious attempt to, like, say, 'Oh, I'm not going to tell this.' It means that it is completely blocked out of the conscious mind: that the person does not have that information available to himself.

"And I am saying that in this case it is quite likely that had Captain MacDonald committed such a violent crime, he would have completely blocked the whole episode from his mind. In other words, he would not know how it happened and he would have run around trying to be the doctor and save everybody."

"But is it also likely," Woerheide asked, "that if he did block it out, let's say temporarily, that he might some moments afterwards become aware of the fact that there were dead people in the house and he is involved in their deaths, and being aware of that and being a highly intelligent man with quick responses, and being mindful from conversations he had in the recent past concerning the Sharon Tate case in a magazine article that was in his house, that he might be capable of creating a scene that might have some semblance of a similar crime being committed in his house by certain unknown intruders?"

"No, it doesn't make sense to me that if he had blocked it out of his mind by the unconscious motives we are talking about that he would then—having blocked it out—think, 'Oh, I must have blocked it out unconsciously and really I've done it, and therefore I've got to conceal the evidence.' Usually, people's minds don't work that way. I mean, that would be pretty strange—to act upon the basis of something you're not consciously aware of and then go ahead and try to conceal it.

"Also, in regard to what had happened to him, he was by no means totally unaware of the loss that he suffered, even though he was emotionally constricted in his expression of his sense of loss. He had begun, in talking with me, to verbalize some awareness of how little he had communicated his feelings to his wife and family. And, furthermore, he began to verbalize some of the feelings that he had had of feeling trapped in marriage and caught up in responsibilities he had assumed.

"And he was aware of the ironic quality that something that had happened—the loss of his wife and family—had both made him realize how little he had communicated to them of his feelings, and at the same time gave him a sense of shame because he was aware in some sense that what happened provided him with relief. And the most ironic aspect of all, from his point of view, was that his life was saved and his family was killed—from his expression of it—because he had failed to react aggressively. If he had been the man that he thought he was, the whole thing wouldn't have happened. The fact that he was alive was due to the fact that he was not the man he says he is. If he had been what he says he was, he would be dead because he would have withstood them, and either chased them away or been killed himself."

"Do I understand you to say," Victor Woerheide asked, "that with the death of his wife and children there was a sense of, let's say, release, a sense of liberation, a sense of relief?"

"Yes. That was part of his reaction to what had happened. I might add that the fact that he could reveal this to me was one of the things that impressed me with his relative sincerity and frankness."

When the psychologist resumed the stand after lunch, Victor Woerheide said to him, "The man you examined, Dr. MacDonald, testified for a period of five days before this grand jury. I want to outline some of the things that came out during his testimony and ask you how they fit within the framework of your conclusions with respect to his personality adjustment.

"During the Article 32 proceeding, and prior thereto, and for a period of time thereafter, Dr. MacDonald received very strong support from his in-laws, Colette's mother and stepfather, people by the name of Kassab.

"At the conclusion of the Article 32 proceeding, MacDonald made a number of statements to the press. He also appeared on TV. Among other things, he said he was going to conduct an independent investigation because he was not satisfied with the job the Army had done. They were bunglers and incompetents. He was going to find the people who committed this offense and he was going to get revenge.

"Later, in a telephone conversation with his father-in-law, he stated in substance: 'I've been conducting my investigation in the bars and hippie hangouts of Fayetteville. I have found one of the persons who was an intruder into my home. I took him out. I, in effect, beat him up. When I was through with him, he would have told on his own mother. Then I killed him. He's six foot under.'

"When MacDonald testified, he said, yes, I did tell this story to Kassab. On subsequent occasions, extending for a period of over a year, he wrote letters to the Kassabs saying that he was pursuing the investigation further. He already had gotten one of them. He still had at least three to go. He was making transcontinental trips. He broke his arm. It cost him four thousand dollars.

"Then, when he testified before the grand jury, he said, 'Yes, it's true. I wrote these letters. I had this telephone conversation. I said these things to Kassab. I used these terms. It was all a lie. But I was forced to do it. I was forced to do it by Kassab, by his pressing me to go forward.'

"Now, how does this fit into your analysis of Dr. MacDonald as a man?"

"I can answer some of that," the psychologist said. "I can't answer all of it. It would not be at all surprising for him to respond to what had happened with quick, impulsive, angry, vindictive outbursts, like, 'Those idiots, those imbeciles, those nincompoops.' And he might do this without thinking of the consequences for himself.

"In a way, if I were an attorney, I would hate to defend a guy like this because I would never be sure but what the minute he got out of my sight he was going to do something on his own that blows the whole defense, because he was convinced that, by God, he knew what to do and he knew it was the right thing.

"He's a very opinionated guy. So that's perfectly consistent. He's right and everybody else is an idiot: that's him all over.

"It might also be perfectly consistent for him to say, 'I'll get revenge. I'll work this out, those guys don't know how to do it. I can solve this.' But it would be very inconsistent for him to in fact conduct an investigation over the next couple of years and do it.

"I would expect he would make the quick, impulsive outburst and then quickly seal over all his feelings and go on to something else."

"But would he lie about it?" Woerheide asked. "And lie about it to the extent of saying, 'I found one of them. I tortured him. I killed him.'?"

"That certainly sounds like a strange sort of lie to make up. I'd have to look at it from this point of view: what would be the sort of thing that could make a person like Captain MacDonald lie? If he perceived he was being forced into something by somebody that he had respect for, and he saw as a stronger authority figure, he might go along superficially with things.

"In other words, I don't know his relationship with his father-in-law, but if his father-in-law was perceived as a strong, secure, authority figure, it might be that Captain MacDonald might have lied to go along with that, even though he himself was trying to put these things out of his mind and go about his business in his bland, denying way. That might provide some of the motivation.

"That is a rather grisly story to make up, however, and my explanation doesn't really do it justice. That's just one thing that comes to mind.

"Another is that MacDonald is a guy who likes to be right. He wants to be the authority himself, and it may be that if somebody were bugging him and trying to tell him that he wasn't doing the right thing, conceivably that might provide a motivation, where he in effect might just be saying, 'Get off, buddy,' telling him where to get off by making up something bizarre.

"For example, on some of the tests he did with me, he would occasionally make a remark interspersed in the test that really was sort of putting me down. You know, he would say, 'I guess that sounds a little hysterical.' Or, 'I see this area as a breast, but I'm a breast man. That's the reason I see breasts. I know you psychologists make a lot of things out of this,' which was sort of saying, 'I understand everything that you do, and it's a bunch of nonsense.' "

"All right," Woerheide said. "He gave an extensive interview to a newspaper reporter. This was taped and was published in serialized form over a period of days, setting forth verbatim questions and answers. When asked about this, he said he really didn't want to do it but he was forced to do it, he was compelled to do it by his lawyers."

"That may be the truth," the psychologist replied, "but regardless of what his lawyers told him, it's certainly true that Captain MacDonald would have gotten quite a charge out of trying to make the Army look stupid. To show that he was right and they were wrong. He would get a lot of enjoyment out of that, no question in my mind."

"Now, after the Article 32, he appeared on the Dick Cavett show. He was on Walter Cronkite's news program. And he gave a number of interviews. He called his sister, who lived out of town, and asked her to get everybody they knew to tune in the Dick Cavett show on the night he appeared.

"When asked about it here, he said, 'Well, I really didn't want to. I was forced to do it. This was because certain congressmen and Kassab were pushing me. I had to do it because they made me.'"

"My inclination, again, I think, is that probably he would get a great deal of enjoyment out of doing that. This is another example of his tendency to do things regardless of the effect on him when he thinks he is right.

"In other words, if a person wanted to act in the manner most helpful to himself, having gone through the Article 32 proceedings as he did, it seems to me there would be a couple of options.

"One, you might really have a firm, idealistic belief that you had been mistreated by the Army and that there's something wrong with the whole system and you're going to set out in a sort of messianic way to change the system.

"I don't see MacDonald as having that type of motivation. I don't think he is the type that would maintain a long-term, idealistically oriented campaign. I think he is too much concerned with his own gratification and sealing all of this over and getting out of it.

"Now, if you were going to be mature and responsible about this, and you were not so oriented, your next step would probably be to think, 'I'm out of this, by God, I'm going to get as far away from this and lay as low as possible.' You know, not to stir up the hornet's nest again.

"Well, here's an example, I think, where instead of behaving in his own best interests, he impulsively sounded off in a way that was neither dedicated towards idealistically reforming the situation nor towards keeping attention away from himself and letting things calm down.

"It is simply an index of his self-righteousness, and his need to appear strong and assertive, that would lead him to do things that actually work against him.

"You know, I can't think of anything better calculated to get the Army or somebody else back down on his back again, trying to hurt him."

"Just one final point, Doctor. His current lifestyle apparently involves working in an emergency room on the West Coast, he has a very nice apartment, he associates with attractive people, attractive girlfriends. He has an expensive sports car, he has a large boat. And he apparently is leading a lifestyle entirely different from the kind of life he had when he was married. Do you have any comment?"

"It strikes me," the psychologist said, "that the style of life you're describing is perhaps one of the few viable alternatives left for him, given his adjustment.

"That is to say, Captain MacDonald wanted to go into a residency in surgery. In view of what he went through, it seems to me very unlikely that he could be accepted for a residency in surgery. So his professional goals—the thing he had planned for a long time—were undoubtedly quite upset.

"Now, there are some people who would react to that in one way and others who would react in another. Again, from what I've said about Captain MacDonald, I would expect him to react to that by denying that it was an upsetting thing. To quickly reconstitute his defenses and set up a life where he was perfectly happy, content, relaxed, and appeared to be an adequate, competent man.

"What's available to him? To retreat to the golden-boy style of life he led in school? Now you can't be a golden boy by getting good grades or that sort of thing when you're not in school. But you can live in an open, relaxed, Southern California style: nice cars, women.

"That doesn't surprise me. It seems to me that's quite consistent with the way he might be expected to react to it."

"And by being a single swinger—"

"I don't think he would be a terribly effective swinger, by the way."

"Ostensibly the swinger, let's say."

"Yes. I think, again, it's quite superficial."

"But without a wife who would make demands on him?"

"Right."

"And without children who would make demands?"

"Exactly. I think, in fact, it's probably a very adaptive response for him. He's probably a lot better off living that style of life for the time being than trying to get married again."

When Freddy Kassab was called to testify, he said, "Jeff was a nice boy from all I ever saw. He used to come over on the weekends and cut the lawn. When he and Colette started going again, Mildred and I were very pleased. We liked Jeff. When Colette told us she was pregnant and that they wanted to get married, we tried to talk her out of it only because Jeff was going to medical school and she had only put in two years of college. But when Mrs. MacDonald came in and talked to us, we said, 'We don't have anything against it. They should go ahead and get married if that's what they want.' Which they did.

"My belief in his innocence was based on the fact that I knew the boy. However, I knew nothing about what occurred that night, nor did my wife. Nobody told us a thing. We were just going on the assumption that how could a man such as we knew do such a thing to his wife and baby children.

"And of course the worst thing of all, in a way, was to turn around and write in blood on the headboard of the bed. This is something that is just inconceivable. But when you sit down with the facts and you analyze them and you see that his whole story is a fabrication, you are left with only one conclusion.

"We knew prior to this of what we considered a failing he had, but we didn't put too much stock in it. But the fact is that Jeff has complete disdain for anyone and everyone that I have ever known him to know. He has contempt for everybody. Out of their sight, though. His disdain is not in their presence. In other words, the minute somebody walked out the door that's who he talked about. Jeff had a habit of doing this at all times. He is mentally, in *his* mind, superior to most people. This, you know, was the only thing we ever knew about him that we didn't care for. But what the heck. You know, we've all got our faults, so we just overlooked this.

"But he would never criticize anybody to their face. He never had the guts to do it. He never fought me to my face. He never came back when I started accusing him of all this stuff and confronted me with anything. Never. Never. And he knew about it, because I got to the point where I sat his mother down in my kitchen after he moved to California and I said, 'I think there are a few things you ought to know.' So he knew about my thoughts. But he never called me and said, 'What's this all about?' He just wrote me a couple of letters and said, you know, 'I'm out here doing fairly good.'"

Toward the end of his testimony, when asked if he had any theories about what might have precipitated the murders, Kassab said, "That area is a dark area. Something happened that caused an argument. I believe that it was an instantaneous thing. He may have socked her and she may have picked up the hairbrush and hit him back. And that just sent him into a blind fury, to be hit by a woman.

"But nobody will ever know, because I assure you, Jeff MacDonald will never tell you."

There was, however, one person who was willing to try to fit together the pieces of the puzzle: Paul Stombaugh, chief of the chemistry section of the FBI laboratory, who had first been shown evidence pertaining to the Mac-Donald case in 1971.

In the summer of 1974, Victor Woerheide and Brian

Murtagh had again presented Stombaugh with the physical evidence collected at the scene and had asked for a
more exhaustive analysis. Having obtained permission
from Freddy Kassab, who had legal title to the cemetery
plots in which Colette and Kimberly and Kristen Mac-
Donald were buried, they had also asked Stombaugh to
supervise exhumation and take hair samples from the
head of each body.

Having done so, and having made microscopic examinations, Stombaugh determined conclusively that the
blond hair found in the palm of Colette MacDonald's
hand had—without question—been her own, and not
that of a blond intruder.

Toward the end of the grand jury hearing—it was by
now, in fact, January 15, 1975—Paul Stombaugh was
summoned to Raleigh to report on his laboratory findings. He first summarized the results of his 1971 analysis:

—That there were forty-eight puncture holes in
Jeffrey MacDonald's blue pajama top that could
have been made by the icepick that had been found
outside the house. Further, that the holes had been
made when the top was stationary. None had the
tearing at the edges which would have resulted
from their having been made while the garment
was in motion. Similar icepick holes in Colette
MacDonald's pink pajama top had been made
while that garment was stationary.

—That some of Colette MacDonald's blood
had stained the pajama top before it was torn.

—That the cuts in all garments other than the
blue pajama top had been made by the Old Hickory knife, despite the fact that it was the Geneva

Forge knife MacDonald had said he'd pulled from his wife's chest.

Stombaugh then described the results of the more extensive analysis which he had just completed.

He had discovered, he said, that certain of the bloodstains on the Hilton hotel bathmat found on Colette's abdomen matched outlines of the Old Hickory paring knife and of the icepick, indicating that those two weapons, while bloody, had been laid temporarily—and perhaps even wiped—on that bathmat.

He had discovered also, he said, that certain of the bloodstains from the sheet found rumpled on the master bedroom floor matched the sleeves of Colette's pajama top, and that still others seemed to have been made by a pair of hands and by the bare left shoulder of an adult human being.

The implication, Stombaugh said—the inescapable implication—was that someone wearing Jeffrey MacDonald's blue pajama top (which had already been stained by Colette's blood) had covered Colette's body with that sheet and then had picked up her body and carried it.

Stombaugh stepped down from the witness stand and stepped to a slide projector. The room was darkened. A slide was displayed on a screen. In garish, awful color.

"Now, this is Kristen's room," Stombaugh said, his voice perfectly even and controlled. "And I'd like to direct your attention to this area right here, this is the top sheet on that bed, and it has a huge bloodstain on it. Yet there is no bloodstain underneath, on the bottom sheet.

"In reading the reports, it was reflected that the huge bloodstain on the top sheet in Kristen's room was Type A blood—is Colette's blood type. Kristen had Type O blood, and the rest of the blood in that room, the bulk of it, was Type O.

"Now, in examining this stain, it was not one that would have been put there just by somebody's hand. It's a huge stain, as you can see. An awful lot of blood flowed there. The only way you get staining such as this is from a steady flow right down onto it."

The lights came on, Stombaugh returned to the witness stand, and the multicolored bedspread, which also had been found rumpled on the master bedroom floor, was laid out before the grand jurors.

"At one time," Stombaugh said, "this had a very heavy flow of blood from a Type A person directly onto it. In fact, even today, there's a large cake of blood on this—a specimen of Type A blood.

"Now, if this bedspread had been placed down on the floor of Kristen's room, and Colette's body were lifted off the bed where she was bleeding, she would have bled directly on the spread. Then her body could have been covered with this sheet, and as the person lifted it up, he stepped on the blood in this bedspread.

"The spread, you see, is very heavy, and blood does not soak through it. It acts like a little bit of a well in there, and holds it. If he stepped in that and carried Colette's body out of this room, he would leave a bloody footprint."

There was a short silence in the grand jury room as this image lingered in the mind.

Then Victor Woerheide said, "In addition, you looked at Kristen's bedspread, didn't you?"

"Yes, sir, I did."

"That bedspread, it's been testified to, had marks of blood on it that were in the blood type of Kimberly. It's also been testified that there is Kimberly's blood type—

Type AB—on the club. Can you offer a possible explanation of how the AB blood might have gotten on that bedspread?"

"Yes. This stain is not a result of direct bleeding. It's been a transfer of blood. In other words, a very bloody object having AB blood on it was placed here. It could have occurred by resting the club, in a bloody condition, on the bedspread."

"All right," Victor Woerheide said. "Now from your observations and the evidence that you studied, is it reasonable to say that there was a struggle involving a person wearing the blue pajama top in the master bedroom at which time the blue pajama top was torn? And is it reasonable to say that Colette MacDonald, having suffered an injury and bleeding, was in a position on the bed of Kristen MacDonald over near the wall where she bled directly on the top sheet of Kristen MacDonald's bed?"

"Yes, sir, and I'd like to point out one other thing in that regard. If I can have the pajama bottoms?"

Victor Woerheide removed Colette MacDonald's pajama bottoms from a plastic bag and handed them to Paul Stombaugh, who displayed them to the grand jury.

"The only injuries Colette MacDonald suffered," he said, "were from her waist up. She had no injuries from her waist down. Now, what puzzled me was how her pajama bottoms—the front of them—got so much blood down on the legs. And according to the laboratory report this is all Type A blood, her own blood.

"It's direct bleeding and it's a lot of bleeding, and we have two places where we find this type of thing. One is the top sheet of Kristen's bed and one is on these.

"This would indicate to me—due to the fact that this bed is only thirty-six inches wide—that Colette Mac-

Donald was probably knocked across the bed, up against the wall, and fell forward, causing the blood to drip down onto the top sheet and onto the pajama bottoms."

Stombaugh moved on to the next order of business, removing a large photograph from an envelope.

"This," he said, "was a photograph taken at the time of autopsy, and it shows the damage to Colette Mac-Donald's chest. If you'll notice—I guess the people in the back can't see too well—we have twenty-one icepick wounds.

"According to the autopsy report she suffered twenty-one icepick wounds to the chest. They were deep and penetrating. In studying the wounds, we see a group of five in her right chest and a group of sixteen in her left chest area. Now, in studying the pictures of Colette as she was found on the floor, we see that she has this blue pajama top draped over her."

In refolding Jeffrey MacDonald's pajama top "exactly" as it appeared in the crime scene photographs, Stombaugh said, it was observed that the forty-eight icepick holes in it could have been made by twenty-one thrusts of an icepick and that those twenty-one thrusts seemed to be in alignment with the twenty-one icepick holes in Colette MacDonald's chest—sixteen on one side and five on the other—indicating strongly that she had been stabbed with the icepick after the blue pajama top had been laid across her chest.

"Now, we can't say positively this happened," Stombaugh said. "We're pointing out this is a possibility. It could have happened. Because all the holes are accounted for, and we did come up with the same number and the same locations."

"Now, Mr. Stombaugh," Woerheide said, "on the basis of your analysis of the physical evidence that you have referred to here today, have you developed any theory of how all these things fit together? What happened that night?"

"Some events," Stombaugh said, "I guess, we'll never know. But it would appear to me that the fight started in the master bedroom. I believe Dr. MacDonald probably struck his wife in the face with a fist, knocked her down. This would cause the blood to start flowing. She probably had a bloody nose, and through a struggle there, this is where her blood got onto his pajama top before it was torn.

"Kimberly might have awakened, due to the screaming, and come up and tried to help her mother. He might have pushed her aside, and—this is just supposition on my part, but I feel probably this club—I imagine it could have been kept in the utility room which is a very short distance from this bedroom.

"I sort of suspect, possibly, Colette might have picked this club up and socked Jeffrey with it, which could account for the bump on his head.

"He was a bruiser, so he took the club away from her and went to swing at her and probably—accidentally or on purpose—struck Kimberly on the side of the head with it, causing her to bleed, and this would account for the AB blood found near the entrance to the room.

"In the doorway here, in the rug, it had soaked through pretty much, indicating someone had lain here bleeding a good bit.

"When he did that, I think our little bent knife comes into play, because this is the type of knife that's very dull, and the type a lot of people, including myself, keep around for painting because it makes a good thing to scrape paint with when you drop some on the floor.

"I think this was near the club in the utility room and

I think Colette grabbed it and attacked Jeff with this thing, possibly causing the little cut in his left abdomen. That cut was slight and was made with a tearing action. A knife such as this would do that.

"And when she did that, he leveled her with this club. Then things, I think, sort of quieted down, because I believe Colette undoubtedly had to have been unconscious at that time.

"I think he picked Kim up, carried her into her bed, and, due to the AB blood spatters on the wall, I believe he hit her again with the club and killed her.

"While this was going on—or possibly before that—I think Colette came to, came into Kristen's room, to protect the only child that is not dead, and he caught up with her in there and really let her have it with the club again.

"This possibly is where both her arms were broken, because they're defense wounds, and she was knocked across to the wall, and we know that she was here at some time in order to have bled this much here.

"I guess he kind of got himself oriented, picked up the bedspread and the blue sheet from the master bedroom and carried them back into Kristen's room, reached over and picked up Colette.

"Now at this time his pajama top had been torn, but it probably wasn't too bloody, and I believe all the blood that's on the pajama top—the bulk of it—got on there when he reached across the bed and picked her up and put her down on this bedspread.

"Then he covered her with this sheet, and, having blood on him—fresh blood, wet blood—and also on his hands, he reached down, picked her up, carried her back into the master bedroom, where she eventually was found.

"After that, he probably went to the kitchen, and he could have been bleeding by this time from the cut in his abdomen, and he got the rubber gloves and picked up the Old Hickory knife, and went back in and did the job on the rest of them, and ended up with the icepick on Colette.

"I think when he put her body down is when he took his pajama top off and threw it across her body. Then, I believe, he put the bathmat down next to her and put each weapon down on the bathmat as he was finished using it, and then as he left, he put the bathmat on her body, and went out the back door, and threw the knife and icepick out."

"In regard to some of the specifics," Victor Woerheide said, "all we can do is speculate. And," he said to members of the grand jury, some of whom had begun to embellish or expand upon Stombaugh's theory, "your guess is as good or better than mine.

"But it seems to me there's no question there was a struggle. I do think that Colette, she was a healthy woman and not a weakling, and I think Colette did attempt to defend herself.

"I think it's consistent with her defending herself that she would pick up the club and swing it at him and hit him on the forehead with it. Not the sort of blow that was strong enough to break the skin or anything, but to raise a lump.

"At some point, I do think that Colette, in defending herself, did inflict some injury on him. And it seems to me the ones that are most likely to have been inflicted by Colette are the bruise on the forehead, and the cut in the abdomen. As to the other wounds, I think that they are most likely to be self-inflicted.

"All we can do at this juncture is speculate as to some

of the details, but the circumstances, it seems to me, lead to the inevitable conclusion that there was a struggle; that the struggle involved a man wearing that pajama top, and that serious injuries were inflicted on Colette and the girls, and Colette ended up bleeding very heavily in Kristen's room; and the club was swung there; and the club was swung in Kimberly's room; and somebody wearing those pajama tops and carrying Colette, whose pajamas had blood on them that was transferred to the sheet, carried her out of that room and made that footprint, and you have heard testimony saying that that's the footprint of Captain MacDonald."

"Did his pajama top match his pajama bottoms?" a grand juror asked.

"We don't have the bottoms of his pajamas," Woerheide said. "They were thrown away in the hospital and were burned. But if we did have the bottoms, I think I can predict—and I feel very confident and I think Mr. Stombaugh would agree with this—that you'd find a lot of Type O blood on the bottoms.

"You see, Kristen was stabbed in her front and she was stabbed in her back, and she was stabbed very deeply both front and back, and her body was down over the edge of the bed, and there's a pool of her blood on the floor, and I think he sat on the bed and he had her on his lap, across his lap, while he was stabbing her."

Dr. Robert Sadoff, the psychiatrist who had examined Jeffrey MacDonald in Philadelphia in the spring of 1970, and who had testified at the Article 32 hearing that he was incapable of having committed such a crime, was the last psychiatrist to be interviewed by Woerheide. Now, four and a half years later, he did not seem nearly so certain of his opinion.

In preparation for the interview, Woerheide had been provided with a copy of a report Dr. Sadoff had delivered to Bernie Segal in 1970. Inadvertently, however, an original, raw report—not the modified, edited version—had been delivered. In this initial report, the psychiatrist had referred to a polygraph test which had apparently been administered to MacDonald, with surprisingly unfavorable results. "There must be some distortion in the polygraph test," Dr. Sadoff had reported to Segal.

This was the first item about which Woerheide asked Dr. Sadoff.

"As I recall now," the psychiatrist said, "there was a polygraph test. And frankly, it looked as though he did not do well on the test, or the test results were equivocal. My recollection is that it was equivocal, and not as I would have expected it to be: that he would have passed with flying colors."

Knowing that polygraph evidence, in any event, would not be admissible in court, Woerheide did not pursue the matter further.

"In arriving at your conclusions in regard to Dr. MacDonald's capacity to commit this crime," he said instead, "I take it you relied on what Dr. MacDonald had told you personally?"

"Yes."

"You accepted his story at face value. You didn't question the veracity of any of the details that he recounted to you. Now, had you been furnished with additional information, which information, let's say, was scientifically reliable, and refuted what Dr. MacDonald had told you, do you think it would have caused you to modify your conclusions?"

"To the extent that I would have felt compelled to reexamine Dr. MacDonald and confront him with the evidence that I had, and the story that he told me, and find out why they were different. Based on what I found out from that confrontation, I would assume that I could have changed my conclusions, yes."

Woerheide then presented to Dr. Sadoff a summary of the testimony of Paul Stombaugh before the grand jury: the forty-eight icepick holes in MacDonald's pajama top corresponding to the twenty-one icepick holes in his wife's chest; the fabric impression on the sheet that indicated MacDonald had carried his wife's body from the bedroom of his younger daughter to the master bedroom where it was found. The analysis of fabric impressions, he said, had the same degree of scientific validity as did the identification of fingerprints.

"It is becoming increasingly confusing," the psychiatrist said. "There is a problem in dimensions here. One is, you're dealing in a fairly precise science with what you have. And you're talking to a psychiatrist who is dealing in a fairly broad arc, not so scientific. And I'm not sure how to judge the scientific evidence that you've got here. I am terribly impressed with what you have done. But I don't know how to—how to—all I can say is I found no serious psychiatric illness within him."

"Did you find any insecurity on his part so far as his masculine role was concerned?"

"There was, a—a—an Achilles' heel, let's say, in this area of masculinity or virility. But I have to find it very unlikely from a psychological standpoint that he could have committed this crime."

"On the basis of the information that was available to you at the time that you examined him."

"Yes, that's right."

"But it is possible that having further information made available to you, you might revise that?"

"There are a lot of things I'd have to go through. With the new information that I now have, I would have to discuss this with him.

"However, as I indicated, what you are talking about is the sledgehammer to my nail file, in a sense. In the face of the overwhelming amount of scientifically oriented material that you have presented here today, I am not so sure that a psychiatrist right now is the proper person to be talking to."

"Well, each of the other psychiatrists and psychologists who have examined and tested him have testified before the grand jury and they did discuss his personality traits and I don't think there was any disagreement among any of them.

"They all said, in fact, that he did have an Achilles' heel—his Achilles' heel being his masculinity, his fear of latent homosexuality, and that having the Achilles' heel, given certain special circumstances, such as fatigue, an argument about something like bed-wetting, differences of opinion about how to solve the problem, Colette seeking advice from somebody other than Jeffrey concerning how to deal with this thing, such as the professor of her psychology class, and him staying awake for a long period of time, not going to bed at the same time as his wife, when he comes to bed finally and finds the bed wet and so on and so forth, in an ensuing argument if Colette had said certain words, she could have triggered a violent reaction. Are you in agreement with that?"

"Well, I would say, with that having occurred and with his having an Achilles' heel—if someone hits the Achilles' heel at the wrong time, either during a time of fatigue or when he is under the influence of alcohol, I would say that it is possible he would be capable of striking a blow."

"And once the blow is struck, I assume that things could get out of control?"

"They could."

"There could be general chaos?"

"He could lose control," Dr. Sadoff said.

3

On January 21, 1975, Jeffrey MacDonald was called back to Raleigh to testify again before the grand jury. His degree of hostility and defensiveness had intensified greatly since August, and his sarcasm and anger were in evidence almost from the start.

"We have a few loose ends," Victor Woerheide said. "Let's go back to April of 1970 when you went to Philadelphia and you were interviewed by a psychiatrist and interviewed and tested by a psychologist. Now, were you interviewed or tested by anyone else during this period of time?"

"No," MacDonald said.

"Specifically, were you given a polygraph test?"

"We had some discussion about it, but the answer is no."

"I don't mean a polygraph test by a polygraph expert connected with the Army or connected with the government investigators, but a polygraph operator let's say privately retained to examine you?"

"No. I'd have to discuss any more answers on that with Mr. Segal."

"I see," Woerheide said. He moved on. "As you know, when you were here before we asked you about various girls or ladies that you knew and one of those was Penny Wells. In the course of the investigation we have contacted some of them. There is a name I don't think we have mentioned to you. That is Laura Talbot. Do you recall her?"

"No."

"Well, it's going very far back but do you remember being employed by Atlantic Construction, Inc.?"

"Yes, I do."

"And do you recall when that was?"

"No. It was summer employment one of my years in college, I think."

"Well, specifically, do you remember it was the year of 1964?"

"No, I don't."

"Well, do you remember where you worked in 1964?"

"No, I'm sure you know."

"Well, when I mentioned Atlantic Construction, does that refresh your recollection with respect to Laura Talbot?"

"Yeah, I think she was a secretary working there."

"Oh, and tell us what happened?"

"I balled the girl. Big deal, she was a secretary."

Among the findings made by Paul Stombaugh at the FBI laboratory in Washington was that the stain on the bed of Jeffrey and Colette MacDonald was consistent with the urine of a person having Type AB blood—the blood type of Kimberly MacDonald—as opposed to the Type O blood of Kristen. Woerheide now confronted Jeffrey with the contradiction between this fact and his statement that it had been Kristy who had wet the bed the night of the murders.

"In regards to the bed-wetting problem in the family," Woerheide asked, "you say Kimberly never wet the bed?"

"Well, not now. She was five years old. When she was a baby she wet the bed. I mean, every kid wets the bed."

"When did she stop wetting the bed?"

"Kimberly? I don't know. When she was about two, I suppose."

"And thereafter it was not a problem?"

"No."

"Doctor MacDonald, I'm sort of skipping around here. There was a bloody footprint in Kristen's room, and the footprint is your footprint. Now, can you tell us how you got blood on your foot in that room and how that footprint happened to be made?"

"I have no idea, sir."

"Well, when you were in the room did you feel any blood under your feet? Any slipperiness, or wetness on your feet?"

"No, I wasn't thinking about that. I'm sure you would have been."

"Well, when you were in the room, Kris was in the room?"

"That's right."

"Was there any other person in the room?"

"Not that I know of."

"Well, let me ask you this: did you see the bedspread or the sheet from the master bedroom in that room?"

"No, I didn't."

"When you were in Kris's room, did you have your pajama top on?"

"No."

"When you went from Kris's room the first time, did you carry anything with you?"

"No, not that I can remember."

"When you left Kris's room the second time, did you carry anything with you?"

"I don't believe so."

"Doctor MacDonald, we have been told that this bloody footprint that I have referred to—the impression it made on the floor indicated that you must have been carrying something because of the dimensions of the footprint itself."

"Who told you that, the Army?"

"That is the information we have."

"Well, it's very suspect information, Mr. Woerheide."

"Sir?"

"Very suspect information. They can't even take fingerprints much less make decisions about them."

"We're told that fibers and threads from your pajama top were found in Kris's room and in Kim's room. They were found on the beds, under the covers of the beds. Can you tell us how that happened?"

"No. I presume it would be contamination from me or from the other people who were in the house that night. If you'd stop trying to prove that it was just me you may think about some of the other choices."

"Well, we are trying to consider all the possibilities—"

"You're not trying to do anything."

"—and hoping you could be helpful to us—"

"No, you're doing the same thing."

Woerheide paused. He allowed thirty seconds to pass. The room was silent. Then he said, "I'm told some fibers were found under Kris's fingernails. Can you tell us how that happened?"

"No."

"You have no idea?"

"I have no idea."

"I'm told that when they recovered the sheet and the bedspread they found some fibers and threads and hairs and I'm told that among these was a hair from Colette's head that was twisted around a thread from your pajama top. Do you have any idea how that happened?"

"No, I don't. Was this before or after I was dragged across the floor and everyone was in and out of the house?"

"These were found when the things were examined."

"You mean after twenty people ran in and out of the house a couple of times and everyone moved everyone and this is the critical evidence?"

"Doctor MacDonald, I'm also told that on the top sheet of the bed in Kris's room they found a large amount of Colette's blood which indicated massive direct bleeding by Colette in that area. Do you have any idea how Colette's blood got in that location?"

"Nope. Unless it was from my hands."

"I am also told that the footprint going out of the room was in Colette's blood."

"I'm sure I had bloody feet," MacDonald said.

"How did they get bloody?"

"From blood on the floor."

"Well, I'm told there was none of Colette's blood on the floor there. The blood was Kristy's blood."

"Well, I had been in the master bedroom first, Mr. Woerheide."

"So you think you picked up Colette's blood in the master bedroom and you tracked that footprint on the floor going *out* of Kris's bedroom as a result of having blood from the master bedroom on your foot? Is that correct?"

"I don't know. You're asking me for explanations that I can't give. I don't know. Maybe it was a lab error. Maybe they mistyped the blood. With their record, I wouldn't see that as an unlikely possibility."

"Okay, where would you say you were when you started bleeding as a result of the injuries that you sustained, Doctor MacDonald?"

"I never noticed much blood on myself. I don't know."

"Well, you had all these injuries when you were lying on the floor in the hallway there, did you not?"

"Yes."

"Were you bleeding at that time?"

"I don't remember seeing any. I suppose I was."

"How heavily were you bleeding?"

"I just told you. Apparently you are not listening. I didn't see any blood. How can I then say I was bleeding heavily?"

"Well, at one point you went in the bathroom and looked at yourself in the mirror and saw that you had blood on you. Did you observe then that you were, in fact, bleeding?"

"No. I've told you that ten times."

"Well, I'm also told that splinters from the club were found in the master bedroom and in each of the children's bedrooms but none were found in the living room. Now, do you have any explanations as to that?"

"First of all, Mr. Woerheide, there's a lot of traffic up and down that hall, including a stretcher. The second, I have no idea. I can't answer that. Seems to me the club was used in the other rooms after it was used on me."

"Well, what would that signify now? Colette and Kimberly were screaming when you awoke. That's what woke you up. And yet, at the time they were screaming these four people were in the living room with the club striking at you. And yet it is the club that they were striking at you with whose splinters are found in all three bedrooms. Now do you have any theory that explains this?"

"Only that it sounds to me like the club went from where I was into the other rooms."

"When you were in the master bedroom, did you notice the word on the headboard—PIG?"

"No, I didn't."

"How close did you get to the headboard?"

"I don't specifically remember. The only thing I remember is being next to Colette."

"Well, the fibers from your pajama top were found behind the headboard, in the area where a person would be standing if he wrote the word PIG on the headboard."

"Hmmm. Maybe one of the assailants did it. Did you ever think of that?"

Unruffled by MacDonald's sarcasm, Woerheide proceeded. "Now in the area of the living room by the couch," he said, "a very close examination revealed no fibers or threads from your pajama top, but there are so many scattered across the master bedroom that you can still go into the house and check the rug and pick up almost as many as you want. Now, can you explain that?"

"No, except that when I took off my top, there's where I took it off. Picked it up and moved it a couple of times. The doctor who examined my wife testified that he moved it. Just seems to me that that's an explanation."

"Doctor MacDonald, when you were here before, I showed you a couple of knives and an icepick, and as I recall you said you didn't have an icepick and you didn't recall either one of those knives as being in your house."

"That's right."

"Witnesses have testified before the grand jury that they observed items that appeared to be the same as these in your house prior to February 17th."

"Uh-huh. Witnesses now, four years later. That's good. That's good police work. How much did you pay them? More than you paid the grave robbers?"

"Doctor MacDonald, in the master bedroom of your house fragments of a rubber glove were found and these fragments were found to be identical, so far as the material from which they were made, to the rubber surgical gloves that were kept under your kitchen sink. And your blood type was found in the area where the rubber gloves were kept. Can you tell us about that?"

"No. I have already testified that I may have gone to that sink. I have already testified that we had gloves in the house."

"Did you put on the gloves?"

"That night?"

"Yes."

"Not unless I put on gloves when I was doing the dishes."

"Well, there was blood on these fragments of rubber gloves I'm talking about."

"I didn't scatter fragments of rubber gloves around the master bedroom."

"Well, if you had the rubber gloves on while you were doing the dishes, how come some fingerprints were found on the dishes."

"I have no idea."

"Your fingerprints."

"I didn't say I had them on. You keep asking me if I had them on. I said I don't know. But it's logical I may have put them on."

FATAL VISION   631

"Wouldn't it surprise you if by—"

"Nothing would surprise me, Mr. Woerheide."

"Would it surprise you if I told you that by chemical process your print could be found on those rubber glove fragments?" (In this instance, Woerheide apparently was attempting to goad MacDonald into an intemperate reply—no such chemical process had been performed, nor, indeed, did such a process even exist.)

"Nothing would surprise me," MacDonald said. "I'm sure, at this date, you can do anything you want. That is why the whole thing is ridiculous."

Victor Woerheide removed from an envelope a photograph of Jeffrey MacDonald's blue pajama top. "Here are a number of icepick holes," he said. "One, two, three, four, five—it goes right up to seventeen in the back. You weren't stabbed in the back. You weren't injured in the back. Can you tell me how those icepick holes got there?"

"I presume it was around my arms."

"I see. While it was around your arms, they were stabbing at your arms? Is that it? They got in there then?"

"Yeah. We've talked about it at length, Mr. Woerheide."

Victor Woerheide removed the Hilton bathmat from a plastic bag. "Doctor MacDonald," he said, "this is a bathmat. I want to show you, when you take the Old Hickory knife and lay it down here it is a perfect match with the outline of this bloodstain. And this stain here is a perfect match for the icepick. Now, you said this bathmat may be one of the things you put over Colette's body. Is it possible that when you were handling this you also had a knife and an icepick in your hands?"

"No, I didn't."

"Well, where was it you found this bathmat?"

"I never said I found it, Mr. Woerheide. You made me reconstruct a story in which I may have pulled this from the green chair in the bedroom and put it over her. Why don't you stick to the facts for a change, Mr. Woerheide?"

Victor Woerheide held up a photograph of the blue sheet that had been found rumpled on the floor of the master bedroom. "This," he said, "shows the pattern of the blood on the sheet. There is a small amount of Kris's blood in one area and the rest of the sheet basically was soaked with Colette's blood. They didn't find any of your blood on the sheet." Woerheide's deep voice began to rise, like a strong wind preceding a storm.

"Now I am going to ask you again: did you handle that sheet that night? Did you touch it? Did you have anything to do with it?"

"Not that I remember."

Woerheide removed more photographs from an envelope. "Doctor MacDonald," he said more quietly, "I want to show you a few pictures. On the bottom here is a picture of the sheet and above it is a picture of a part of Colette's pajama top.

"An expert in making examinations of this type has testified before this grand jury that the pattern of Colette's pajama top and the bloodstains from Colette's pajama top were transferred from Colette's body to the sheet, and he was able to tell how this sheet was laid over Colette—the position she was in when the blood was transferred from her pajama top to the sheet.

"The same man has testified that your pajama top had blood on it; that it was blood of Colette's type, and that the pajama top was torn, and that the design of your pajama top, the textile design, the creases, the beading, and the design of the bloodstain on your pajama top were transferred to the same sheet.

"He's also testified it was your pajama top that was torn on the left side, leaving your left shoulder bare. And that there were marks indicating where your left shoulder transferred blood to the sheet. And this was Colette's blood."

Woerheide's voice had again been steadily rising, filling the grand jury room. Now, he was approaching a crescendo.

"Tell us!" he demanded, his face a deep crimson, his scowl severe, his words spaced evenly, like fence posts enclosing the territory that Jeffrey MacDonald had been occupying for five years: "Tell us—how—that—blood—from—your—body—and—from—Colette's—body—got—on—that—sheet!"

"I have no idea! I have no idea!" MacDonald shouted in response. "I don't even know what crap you're trying to feed me!"

"Doctor MacDonald: did you take Colette off the bed in Kris's room, lay her on top of the bedspread on the floor in Kris's room, cover her with this sheet, then pick her up and carry her out of the room?"

"No, I did not do that," MacDonald spat back.

"And lay her on the floor of the master bedroom?"

"No, I did not do that!"

"Your pajama top, Doctor MacDonald, transferred blood to that sheet at the same time that Colette's pajamas and Colette's body transferred blood to that sheet. And your footprint indicates that you were carrying something out of that room. And the footprint is in Colette's blood."

"None of that happened, to my—Jesus. Oh, would you—the answer to the question is no."

"All right. I have another question," Woerheide said. He held up another photograph. "This is Colette's chest.

It shows a total of twenty-one icepick stabbings that penetrated deep inside of her body, went straight in."

He held up three other pictures. "These show how Colette was covered by your pajama top when they found her. Mr. Stombaugh, of the FBI, by careful examination of these photographs was able to reconstruct the manner in which the pajama top was folded.

"He did reconstruct it. He found there were forty-eight icepick penetration marks on your pajama top. And when the pajama top was folded the same way it was folded on top of Colette's body, these icepick holes went through your pajama top and into her body. *Now—can—you—tell—us—how—that—happened?!*"

"No, because I don't believe it. It's a lot of bullshit."

"Take a look at the picture."

"You can do anything you want to with fifty holes in a pajama top is what I am trying to say, Mr. Woerheide. It's a bunch of crap. If this was a legitimate investigative technique, why wasn't it done four years ago?"

"Do you have any other comment?"

"No, except that by my being unable to explain blood spots you make me guilty of homicide of my family."

"Well, tell me this," Woerheide said, "did you ever at any time become enraged at Colette?"

"I can't remember being enraged, no. Angry, sure."

"Was there anything she could have said to you at any time that might set you in a state of rage?"

"No."

"If she had accused you of a lack of sexual competence, would that have—"

"Oh, my."

"—would that have set you in a state of rage? Or would it have had no effect whatsoever as far as you're concerned?"

"I can't imagine me being in a state of rage over that."

"How about accusing you of a lack of masculinity?"

"Colette? Accusing me of that?"

"Yes."

"No, I wouldn't be in a state of rage."

"Now, that night there was no argument or quarrel between you and Colette?"

"None whatsoever."

"And all of this evidence that I have told you about is fabricated?"

"I don't know what to make of it, Mr. Woerheide. It doesn't make any sense to me. I have told you what I know to the best of my ability."

"And so far as you know, Colette was not in contact with that sheet?"

"I don't remember seeing the sheet. I was lying against Colette."

"Doctor MacDonald, you say you came to in the hall, you went down to the master bedroom, you took the pajama top off from around your wrists, you threw it on the floor, and then you put it on Colette's body. And obviously Colette's body was bloody. And blood could have been transferred at that time to the pajama top.

"Now, until the time that you laid it on her body, was there any way you can explain how blood would have gotten on it?"

"How blood would have gotten on it?"

"Your pajama top. Her blood."

"Not unless there was blood from the assailants originally."

"In other words, they picked up blood from Colette and transferred it to your pajama top?"

"I'm just hypothesizing."

"Well, I want to make clear to you the information

that's available to this grand jury in this matter. One item of information is that Colette's blood was on your pajama top in a certain area that became torn. And the blood was there before it was torn."

"I have no idea what that means."

"Do you have any explanation for that?"

"Do I?"

"Right."

"I'm not a criminologist."

"Now, Doctor MacDonald, you have always said that it was Kristen who was wet. Kristen, who was in the bed with Colette and wet the bed."

"Right. It was."

"A test of the urine spot indicates it was Kimberly's urine and not Kristen's urine."

"Kristy was in the bed," MacDonald said. "Jesus Christ! What do you want me to say? Kristy was in the bed. She wet the bed and I put her back in her own bed. You people are crazy! I picked up Kristy and put her back in her bed."

"And it was not—"

"It was not Kimberly."

"It was not Kimberly who was in the bed?"

"Jesus Christ!"

"Well, do you have any reason for saying it was Kristen instead of Kimberly?"

MacDonald did not respond, but he sighed loudly enough for the sound to be picked up by the tape recorder used by the court reporter who was transcribing the proceedings.

"As I say," Woerheide continued, "scientific laboratory evidence indicates—"

"Scientific bullshit!"

"—it was Kimberly's urine—"

"*No!*"

"All right," Woerheide said. "Now the evidence indicates that Kimberly was injured in the master bedroom. That her blood is on the carpet and is in the vicinity of the door."

"So Mr. Shaw told me."

"Do you have any explanation for that?"

"No, not unless the blood was tracked in by other people."

"Well—"

"What if the blood dripped off weapons?"

"All right, when you first came in, Dr. MacDonald, I asked you about whether or not you had been given a polygraph in Philadelphia and you said you'd have to talk to Mr. Segal about that. So, as we break for lunch, I'm going to suggest that you do talk to Mr. Segal and then let us know what your answer is."

"Okay. Are we going to be finished today, Mr. Woerheide?"

"Yes."

Jeffrey MacDonald left the room. Victor Woerheide returned to his desk and examined some papers. "I think I'm just about through with him," he told the grand jurors. "There are one or two little items that we could ask him about but I think at this juncture it's scarcely worthwhile.

"I'll give you an example. He met a nurse, I think it was down in Texas, and they got acquainted and he was talking about his family and told her that they did have a problem with their older child, Kimberly—she had enuresis, which is a fancy word for bed-wetting.

"Now he comes up here, and he says, no problem at all with Kimmy as far as bed-wetting. Well, we could ask him, you know—we know from the girl who gave us the statement that she does know him, she had the conversation with him, and this is what he told her.

"But if I ask him about the conversation with the girl, I'm sure he's going to deny it. Well, this is just one of several instances. In any event, I was told by Mr. Segal when I was talking to him sometime back that Dr. Mac-Donald was planning to go to Europe to do some skiing in the Swiss Alps. I might ask him when he plans to leave." Woerheide paused. "And whether he plans to come back."

The grand jurors laughed.

"Another thing, the psychiatrist from Philadelphia, in his first report, refers to the polygraph which indicates a guilty reaction on the part of MacDonald, and he explained it away. Now, it's possible he has a copy of the polygraph report. Certainly, I think he knows the identity of the polygraph operator. I suppose we could subpoena the operator."

Having been in session since August, however, and with their minds apparently already made up the grand jurors displayed little enthusiasm at the prospect of still more witnesses. And Victor Woerheide, having worked incessantly at the case since early June, wanted to do no more than was necessary to obtain the indictment.

There was a delay at the start of the afternoon session. Woerheide explained that he had just had a conversation with Bernie Segal. "He came out from an inner room and he said will you give us another fifteen or twenty minutes, and I said all right.

"So, I think they're cooking something up, and they're gonna—MacDonald's gonna read some sort of a statement to you."

"We already figured that," one of the grand jurors said, to general laughter.

When Jeffrey MacDonald returned to the witness stand, he brought with him two prepared statements. In the first, Bernie Segal argued that Woerheide had violated attorney-client privilege by asking MacDonald if he had undergone a polygraph examination while in Philadelphia during the spring of 1970.

After MacDonald had finished reading it, Woerheide asked him if he had any further statement to make.

"You mean before we close?"

"Yes."

"Yeah, I have a few things," MacDonald said. "I think the grand jury ought to know how this case has been investigated. Since you like newspapers, Mr. Woerheide, I have here a clipping from December 1974 from *Newsday* about the graves of my wife and children. I'd like to let the grand jury take a look at it. It's indicative of how the case has been investigated from beginning to end, Mr. Woerheide.

"No one asked the husband or the father if these graves should be opened, or could they be opened. What you did was you son-of-a-bitches paid off six gravediggers fifty dollars apiece not to say anything.

"And I'd just like to put that in evidence because that's exactly how the whole goddamned case has been handled."

"Well," said Woerheide, taking the clipping, "we'll mark this as MacDonald Exhibit 31."

"I'd also like to say for the record that I don't appreciate you lying to and badgering my relatives in order to get some testimony from them. Specifically, I'd like to say that my sister was told that the only time Dr. MacDonald broke down and cried in August was discussing the sodium amytal interview."

"Who allegedly made this statement to her?" Woer-heide asked.

"That creep that works for you," MacDonald said, referring to Brian Murtagh. "That little viper. The little guy who doesn't have enough politeness to introduce himself. Or doesn't know any of the social amenities." (In August, at their first meeting, Murtagh had, in MacDonald's opinion, failed to identify himself adequately.)

MacDonald paused briefly.

"There's a lot I'd like to say. But what I'm going to do, if it's okay with you, so I'll make some sense instead of yelling and screaming like I did last time, I'd just like to sort of make my statement which I wrote on the plane.

"This, of course, was with the help of my attorneys. This is me, but they edited it and said you shouldn't say that and do say this—what they always waste lunch hours doing."

Jeffrey MacDonald began to read. "It's been five long years since my life collapsed when my family was murdered. I tried to start over—I'm reading this, this is obvious. I'm not going to speak off the cuff because I wanted to say too much."

He resumed his reading. "I tried to start over again in California. Some people—Mr. Woerheide, Colonel Pruett, my father-in-law—they don't seem to understand how hard it's been for me. They seem to feel that because I moved away from New York, away from the graves, somehow I don't love my family, and I don't miss them, and I faked everything about the murders.

"This means, of course, that I never cared for my family at all. And, of course, that leads to that I must have killed them.

"The last time I was here, in August, and this time, I tried to answer your questions. I have told you as much as I know except in regards to attorney work products that Mr. Segal says I shouldn't talk about.

"I wish I knew more of your questions, especially today. I wish I knew why it happened. And I wish I knew who killed Colette, Kristy, and Kimmy.

"I wish I could tell the grand jury the answers to all the questions Mr. Woerheide has been raising for five or six months. These are questions that I have had to live with for five years.

"I have had to accept that I may never know what happened. It is not easy to live with that, but it's really all I can do.

"What I wanted to tell you about is what my life has been like since the 17th of February. That seems to bother Mr. Kassab and Mr. Woerheide and everyone else. They all seem to think that I just walked away from Colette and Kimmy and Kristy. And that shows I couldn't have cared for them. They all seem to think that if I never cared for my girls I could have killed them.

"And then going out to California and bought a car and a boat and forgot all about it. Well, that's not true. People want to know why I don't spend all my time crying on other people's shoulders. Why don't I break down? 'Is he cold? Doesn't he have any feelings?' Wouldn't that show more of my love?

"Let's start with the newspaper interviews and the Dick Cavett show. My mother, my brother, and my sister all tell me that when they were here they were asked at length why I did those interviews, and yet why didn't I ever talk about the killings to anyone else, including my family.

"No one questioned me about it. I'm not going to

talk about it for no reason. And the reason I went on the Dick Cavett show is because a congressman called me and asked me to go on. And I also know that a lot of people don't believe me.

"I have a right to try to live and try to get this statement out once and for all. So, I did two things: I talked to *Time* magazine and I talked to the Dick Cavett show. You know, the upshot is I was trying not to have to spend the rest of my life explaining to everyone that meets me.

"In the confusion of the time, I thought that if I said it once loudly enough maybe I wouldn't have to continually, you know, reply to those questions.

"I don't find it easy to beg for sympathy. Every time I tell the story of February 17th, I—you know—I die a little bit. I'm ashamed that I couldn't help my family. But I tried.

"I'm the one that hears Colette and Kimmy. I can't keep talking about that. You expect me to talk about it over coffee to everyone that comes by or I'm not normal.

"The grand jury—except for my lawyers, the grand jury and Colonel Rock are the only people who ever heard the whole story. My lawyers never really heard the whole story until I was in front of Colonel Rock. I mean never in detail at once in one sitting.

"You make it sound like we are supposed to be sitting and talking about it constantly. The only one that I know that does that is Freddy.

"So, I don't spend a lot of time talking about it. I don't tell everyone I meet. I don't tell all my friends. I didn't tell anyone the whole story. That doesn't seem abnormal to me and yet you make it seem the other way. You make it sound like it's abnormal that I don't go around telling everyone. Saying, 'Hey, let me tell you about Fort Bragg, 1970.'

"That brings me to Freddy. He feels, I guess, that I never told him the full story. And I didn't. He also feels that I lied to him when I told him about these stupid, pathetic attempts to find the real killers.

"He's partially right but he's partially wrong, too. I never did sit down with him and tell him the whole story. But contrary to the implications that he keeps leaving, he was apprised of everything. We were in daily contact. He knew exactly what was being said all through the Article 32. And then I gave him a copy of the Article 32.

"And it isn't as though—later on, a couple of years later, geez, it sounds like he never knew what was going on and he never heard. He heard daily. He talked to Bernie and the other lawyers and myself all the time. He knew exactly what was going on. I never just decided to just go over to his house and sit down and start telling him again. He never asked, for one. My friends never asked. You know, my family has never asked me. My mother has never said to me, 'What happened?' It seems to be one of my major sins that I don't talk about it all the time.

"Freddy was a funny kind of friend. All through the Article 32 he was my devoted supporter. He was proclaiming my innocence the loudest. He said he would be the only one, or he would have been the first to know if anything was wrong between Colette and me, even if we never told him, because he was so close. He knew we were happy.

"Freddy was the hardest person for me to talk to later, because of that. I mean, he made a very dramatic and nice testimony for me at the Article 32. But then at the end, here I'm in this obligation to Freddy. I'm supposed to devote my whole life to the night of the 17th and spend the rest of my life foraging through North Carolina, one-man FBI.

"Well, I can't do it. And I knew I couldn't do it, and I lied to him. I told him that. I was ashamed that—well, I'm ashamed now I told him. I'm ashamed I didn't die that night. That sounds stupid to you, I know.

"So here I was, trying to prove, especially to Freddy, you know, that I would do the best I can. So I do this little fantasy bit. Well, that's over. We've talked about it. I tried to satisfy him."

MacDonald flipped through the pages of his statement. "Shit," he said, "it's not making sense even reading it. 'I'm sorry I told Freddy about it.' This doesn't make any sense."

Nevertheless, MacDonald continued his reading. "So now I'm up to the winter of 1970–71 and I'm in New York trying to practice medicine, waiting for my residency at Yale to start in June of '71, trying to carry on my life.

"But you've got to understand that this was a life that Colette and I had planned. Colette and I were supposed to go to Yale and get a farm and I was supposed to be a hotshot orthopedic surgeon and live on a farm with the kids.

"I can't—I mean, I can't keep that dream going without Colette and the kids. So I go out to California. So what? There's no crime in that.

"Essentially, to paraphrase all these pages that I'm turning, you know, I just had to change my life. So I go out there and work with a friend of mine from the Army, a different kind of life. I don't expect Brian Murtagh to understand that. Maybe the grand jury will.

"Right now, in California, I'm director of the emer-

gency department. After I left here in August they made
me director. Big deal, they called me in and they said,
'Despite what's happening, we still like you.' And I said,
'Big fucking deal, you don't have to like me.' And they
said, 'No, you're doing a good job and we want to make
you director. So I'm director now.'

"It's a busy emergency room." MacDonald's voice,
which had been firm, was beginning to quaver. "A lot of
car accidents, and heart attacks. And gunshots . . . and . . .
stabbings.

"I work very hard. And I work on purpose. I've got to
work. I stay busy, see a lot of people. I'm exhausted. I
work a twelve-hour shift. I make a lot of money. That's
not my goal in life. I make a lot of money so I spend a
lot. That's another crime.

"I—this really sounds trite—I like emergency medicine. You know, I help a lot of people. It makes me—
makes me feel a little useful." He paused momentarily,
sobbing.

"You know," he resumed, "I didn't do enough to
save my family. And then you come in here and you say
someone's folded the top of my pajama top and put little
probes through it and that means that I killed Colette.

"What can I say about that? These arguments about
other women are just—they are absurd. I've slept with a
lot of women. It doesn't mean anything to me, at all. It
never has meant anything to me. It's been very easy for
me my whole life. I haven't chased one girl in California
and I must have slept with thirty since I've been there.

"Because I didn't spend the rest of my life, you know,
praying on the graves, you tell me I don't love my family.
And that means I must have killed them. That's not
true!" Again, MacDonald began to sob.

"Oh, it's a lot of shit.

"I didn't kill Colette.

"And I didn't kill Kimmy and I didn't kill Kristy and I didn't move Colette and I didn't move Kimmy and I didn't move Kristy and I gave them mouth-to-mouth breathing and I loved them then and I love them now and you can shove all your fucking evidence right up your ass!"

Three days later, the grand jury returned an indictment charging Jeffrey MacDonald with three counts of murder.

PART FIVE

CRY ONE
FOR THEM

If, in the future, you should light a candle,
light one for them.
And if, in the future, you should say a prayer,
say one for them.
And if, in the future, you should cry a tear,
cry one for them.

> —from the closing argument to the jury
> delivered by Assistant U.S. Attorney
> James L. Blackburn in the
> trial of Jeffrey MacDonald

1

Jeffrey MacDonald flew back to California as soon as he had finished testifying. On Friday, January 24, 1975, he took Joy ("the most sensual woman I've ever seen") for a ride on his boat.

When they came back, in midafternoon, Jeff lifted weights and did sit-ups while Joy watched. His mother stopped by, which was not uncommon. She and Joy were sitting on the couch, chatting, while Jeff, in his underwear, was starting to flip through the day's mail, when there came a knock on the door.

He opened it to find three FBI men standing there. They told him the grand jury had just handed up the indictment. After dressing, he was taken, in handcuffs, to the Orange County jail, where he was held on $500,000 bail. A week later, following a hearing at which more than a dozen doctors, nurses, nuns, and policemen testified to his good character and professional skill—and at which, in open court, he was compared, not unfavorably, to Albert Schweitzer—bail was reduced to $100,000. This was immediately pledged by friends and colleagues, allowing him to resume his normal life.

The nuns who ran St. Mary's Hospital believed Jeff MacDonald to be a magnificent human being and saw no reason to allow this unfortunate misunderstanding with the Justice Department to interfere with his performance of professional duties. Despite the indictment, he was permitted to continue as director of emergency services. There seemed never the slightest doubt in the mind of anyone who knew him there: he was a tragic figure, almost heroic in his strength and tranquillity under duress. The indictment, it was widely believed at St. Mary's, was nothing more than a manifestation of how the judicial system could be perverted by the sick and evil whims of a single man—in this case, Jeff's ex-father-in-law, Freddy Kassab.

A trial, he told everyone, would of course demonstrate his innocence, but the indictment itself was such an outrage, so clearly unjust, invalid and unconstitutional, that the charges should never come to trial.

From San Francisco, where he had begun to teach law at an inner city school called Golden Gate University, Bernie Segal had assured his most favored and famous client that the indictment would be quickly dismissed.

Segal began to file motions, seeking dismissal on constitutional grounds. He argued, first, that the indictment constituted double jeopardy because MacDonald had already been cleared of the murder charges by the Army. Secondly, Segal contended that the indictment, coming almost five years after the original filing of charges, was a violation of MacDonald's right to a speedy trial, as guaranteed by the Sixth Amendment.

In Raleigh, North Carolina, Federal District Court Judge Franklin T. Dupree, Jr., denied both motions, ruling that, unlike a general court-martial, the Article 32 hearing had been merely an investigative proceeding and thus not the equivalent of the jury trial which would have made the principle of double jeopardy applicable.

Judge Dupree also declared the speedy trial claim invalid, finding that this right did not pertain until after a person had been "accused" of a crime, and that, "in this case [accusation] did not occur until the indictment had been returned."

After also denying a motion for change of venue, Judge Dupree set a trial date of August 18, 1975.

His new circumstances began to affect Jeffrey MacDonald's personal life. For months, his relationship with Joy had been deteriorating, and now the added pressures which arose in the wake of the indictment contributed to its total dissolution.

"We were at the point of starting to talk about seeing other people," MacDonald said, "and then when I wouldn't see her on a Friday night I'd go crazy and try to call her and try to find out where she'd been. She did date several people, one of them being someone who played on the Los Angeles Rams.

"We had gone to one of those big basketball games that I organized, in which the Long Beach Heart Association that I had become very prominent in, was putting on this charity basketball game; and our team was playing the Los Angeles Rams football team in basketball. We had this big crowd in Long Beach City College gym, and we had cheerleaders on both sides, and then we had rented a country club for a cocktail party afterwards that the Rams came to.

"Joy, of course, was this extravagantly sensual person with a tremendous body. And I was dancing with everyone at the party, and Joy just decided, well, she was gonna, too. What's good for the goose is good for the gander.

"And she ended up dancing with Jack Snow and Isaiah Robertson and I think Jack Youngblood and a bunch of others. And I remember that I was furious that she had the nerve to do that. And then I calmed down and realized that it was my decision, I had made that decision, and I would have to sort of control myself and understand that if I was gonna date other people and keep Joy at a distance, then she was probably gonna end up dating.

"She came up to me and said that she couldn't live this way. We had some long, teary episodes, sort of very painful, about six months. She clearly loved me, and I loved her, but I wasn't willing to give up my solitude, the grieving process, my bachelorhood, the occasional dates with other people.

"So we were in the midst of this breakup anyway, and the indictment dramatically accelerated it. She leaves town, says she can't be in the same town with me if we're not in love, and foolish me lets her go north. Then, you know, I'm doubly distraught: this thing, trying to protect myself, and, honestly—I'm not saying this to be a good guy—I think trying to protect Joy somewhat.

"I mean, in retrospect, I think Joy is probably the reason I had those years of real success and happiness in '72 and '73 and '74, just prior to the year of the new pain. I think Joy, for a lot of reasons, made those years possible.

"She was not Colette and she never tried to be Colette, and she would almost state that openly. She was defiant, she was rebellious, she was saucy, she was tantalizing on purpose, things that Colette never was.

"Joy—sometimes it seemed like her goal in life was to

turn on a hundred men at a big cocktail party and she did it without even trying. If she tried, it made it even worse. She was a staggering sensual person. And yet she, you know, she was gentle and loving and kind and she wrote me poetry and we shared so many incredible moments together. I mean, they were years that I think a lot of couples probably don't have that much passion and love and giving to each other over twenty-five or thirty or fifty or a hundred years, and we had it all in two or three.

"It was certainly a tumultuous love affair. We had passion enough for ten and I think love enough for at least five or six, and I wish we had gotten married, to tell you the truth. I think we probably could have had a nice life together."

On August 15, 1975, three days before the trial was to begin, the U.S. Court of Appeals for the Fourth Circuit, sitting in Richmond, Virginia, ordered a stay and agreed to hear Jeffrey MacDonald's appeal of Judge Dupree's original rulings.

Thus, rather than having to fly to Raleigh to stand trial on three counts of murder, MacDonald was able to continue living the life he had built for himself in California. Professionally, he had remained extremely active, aiding in the development of a national training program in cardiopulmonary resuscitation, in addition to continuing as director of the St. Mary's emergency room and the Long Beach paramedical squadron. In his personal life, too, he continued to evolve despite his regret over the departure of Joy. By August, he had begun to date a woman named Bobbi, who worked as a nurse in a Los Angeles hospital.

"Bobbi," MacDonald said, "was, and is, this very,

very gorgeous redhead—stunning appearance; tall and very sophisticated looking. A really lovely creature, taller than Joy, though not as busty, not nearly as sensual, especially in her impact in a room, but lovely in a more ethereal way, and I think as attractive to a lot of different people, although, like, the sap starts flowing in a group of men when Joy walks by, whereas with Bobbi, you know, there are raves about her beauty but it isn't quite the sensual beauty that Joy always had. In any case, I thought Bobbi was one of the prettiest girls I'd ever seen.

"The relationship blossomed very quickly, even under this stress at the time. It was funny, I always had said to myself and *did* say to myself all through the first year or so with Joy—I mean, with Bobbi, I was not gonna sort of just fall into a situation and have it happen; I was gonna be more in control of it. And I told Bobbi right from the word *go* that I wasn't looking to get married, that I had just had a long relationship with Joy and it ended kind of painfully, and I was in the midst of this thing, I still had the indictment over me. She understood completely and we started dating.

"But it's just like always: you date a person two or three times in a row and pretty soon that's all your friends can do is ask you two as a couple out; and whenever you want to have people over for dinner or go somewhere with a foursome or something, it's much easier to call a girl that you know instead of starting to play the singles game each time; and so Bobbi and I, as well as being very attracted to each other, sort of got into our one-on-one situation fairly quickly, even under the circumstances."

The relationship had, in fact, blossomed to the point that Jeffrey MacDonald and Bobbi were on vacation to-

gether in Hawaii when, in January of 1976, he received a
message to call Bernie Segal immediately.

Segal informed him that, by a 2-to-1 vote, a three-
judge panel from the Fourth Circuit Court of Appeals
had overruled Judge Dupree on the speedy trial question.

The panel majority found that the Army's filing of
charges on May 1, 1970, had been the "functional
equivalent of a civilian arrest warrant," and that, following the dismissal of the charges, the Justice Department's delay in seeking an indictment—due, at least in
part, the appeals court ruled, to bureaucratic "indifference, negligence, or ineptitude"—had violated MacDonald's constitutional rights. They ordered the indictment
dismissed.

The charges of indifference, negligence, and ineptitude
had been the very ones which Freddy Kassab had leveled
so often and so heatedly between 1972 and 1974. Now,
however—and it would be difficult to conceive of bitter
irony's coming in a purer form—the Fourth Circuit decision nullified the result which Kassab had sought so fer-
vently to obtain.

To Jeffrey MacDonald, however, there was nothing
either bitter or ironic about the result.

"We're in Hawaii," he said, "at this condominium on
Maui recommended by my accountant—having, incidentally, an incredibly romantic time: for sheer fun and
opulence, you know, doing nothing but lying in the sun
and making love, it was, I think, even the equal of the
trip I took with Joy to Tahiti—and got this call that I call
Bernie as an emergency and was told that the Fourth
Circuit had ruled in my favor, that the case was over, that
I had won.

"Well, the emotion—I was sort of speechless, it was like this unbelievable weight had been lifted off my shoulders. I wasn't, like, laughing, it was just, uh, it was almost, uh, sort of tears of relief rather than tears of joy. It wasn't a joyful time because I felt that the whole prior six years up to this had been a, you know, a charade, a nightmare, and not sort of like an athletic event that you're trying for the end of but a prison camp or some sort of survival that you had to get through. And it wasn't a matter for exultation to finally win; it was a matter of relief that it was over. And I didn't really feel that it was a great victory, I felt it should have happened in 1970, that it should never have happened, anything should never have happened.

"But in any case I had this new relief, called my mom from the same—I was standing by the, you know, this phone outdoors when I called Bernie, hung up, dialed my mom, then talked to someone at the hospital, and that was all I could get at the time. Got home to California and there was this big celebration back there that, you know, it was over for me."

The Justice Department, however, did not consider it over. Now that the great wheel of bureaucracy finally had been set in motion, its tendency was to continue rolling forward. In March, government lawyers asked the full Fourth Circuit Court to rehear the case. Six weeks later, the court split 3-to-3 on that request, thereby effectively denying it and leaving the Justice Department only one further option: a petition to the U.S. Supreme Court.

Such a petition was filed in June. A full year passed with no response.

Through that year, Jeffrey MacDonald's new romance continued to ripen. "Bobbi," he said, "was, of course, a whole different person than either Colette or Joy. But while it's clear that she had a *very* different approach to life and personality and style than Joy, she was not *that* different from Colette. And I wonder just how much—I don't think my initial infatuation with Bobbi had anything to do with Colette.

"I think that Bobbi was an alarmingly good-looking woman, really very chic and sophisticated-looking. Very attractive, wore the right clothes, didn't wear bras, had a nice body, knew how to dress, knew how to travel, was, *is,* extremely witty, very intelligent, easy to be with. That was all very attractive right from the beginning.

"But I think as we started seeing each other frequently, and, you know, falling in love and spending a couple of years together basically—the good times and the bad times—she got closer to Colette. By that I mean that Bobbi, I think in my mind, created some confusion over who I was in love with: was I in love with Bobbi or was I in love with, you know, an attempt to re-create Colette?"

On June 20, 1977, the Supreme Court announced that it would accept the Jeffrey MacDonald case for consideration. Briefs were filed in the fall and oral argument took place in January of 1978.

On May 1, in an 8-to-0 decision which did not deal with the merits of MacDonald's specific claim, but which was consistent with its previous rulings barring pretrial appeal in criminal cases, the Supreme Court declared that an appellate court cannot assume jurisdiction over a speedy trial claim prior to trial. To permit such a procedure, the Supreme Court said, would only "exacerbate pretrial delay."

Faced, once again, with the likelihood of having to

stand trial, MacDonald began to encounter difficulties in his relationship with Bobbi.

"I found that the closer and the deeper the case became—in other words, once the Supreme Court turned down the Fourth Circuit victory for me and now it looked like the case would clearly go to trial, and I was having to do recollections again for Bernie and for case preparation and read all the Article 32 files again and get my files in order—I found that reliving the past and the years of my marriage and Kimmy and Kris were again vibrant and back in my mind day and night.

"And I was having this terrible role confusion in which Bobbi was becoming Colette. If it happened once it happened fifty times: I turned and was just ready to say 'Colette,' when Bobbi was there, and I actually had to think to say 'Bobbi.' I remember being terrified, the many nights lying in bed or at a movie and turning suddenly to her and being frightened that I almost called her Colette.

"Besides, Bobbi was beginning to—this was, of course, two years into our relationship now—Bobbi was beginning to need more, just as the old cycle always occurs. Joy had needed more at two and a half or three years; now Bobbi needed more. Seven days a week was what she wanted. We had a nice relationship on a five-day-a-week basis, well, four-day-a-week basis, but it wasn't enough.

"There was this unease in Bobbi all the time and constant picking and a need to reinforce and be told that she was loved. Even stronger than Joy, to be honest; she's a more insecure person. She has a lot of great strengths, but on this particular point she was very insecure.

"She was making visible demands, both verbally and with body language, and we got into this absolute identical situation that Joy and I had gotten into, where we both loved each other—it wasn't this, again, tumultuous A-plus sensual love that Joy and I had, with quick ups and downs, and lots of sensual makings-up, and quick trips everywhere, and sort of living on the pleasure principle—it was a different kind of thing, more structured and more orderly, partially because Bobbi liked it that way, but certainly because my life was much more businesslike and professional than it had been, and more dedicated to work, plus paying Bernie and getting ready for the case.

"But in any case, I found that I could devote less emotional effort to Bobbi at this time than I could even to Joy before. And our relationship took on this same six-month downward spiral that Joy and I had undergone, and almost for the same reason: I couldn't give up enough time and verbal effort and emotional commitment to truly, you know, to be truly dedicated to that person. I just couldn't do it, it wasn't in me, I didn't have the strength, I had too many other things happening that I felt *were* important. And eventually we split."

In October of 1978, the Fourth Circuit Court of Appeals upheld Judge Dupree's denial of the double jeopardy claim, and, in March of 1979, the Supreme Court refused MacDonald's request that it review that decision, thereby clearing the way for trial.

Jeffrey MacDonald flew east during the second week of July. He might not have been on the "emotional high" that had been the goal of the friends who had arranged the fund-raising dinner and disco party in his behalf, but he was, at least, accompanied by Candy Kramer, who had replaced Bobbi in his affections the previous fall.

"Bobbi was either already gone or she was in the

midst of leaving, or something like that," he said, "and I walked into a restaurant one day for my normal brunch about nine or ten in the morning, and Candy walked through with a girlfriend of hers by the name of Laura, another super-fox.

"They both had on their, you know, California T-shirts and short shorts or something, and they walked through and I asked, 'Who the hell was that incredible blonde that just walked by?'

"About two weeks later, I saw her again in the same restaurant, and this time the cook introduced us. And Candy told me later that she fell in love as we met. I batted my eyes once and she was gone. She was twenty at the time, and I of course thought this was a lark, and took her out to take out a gorgeous blonde, basically. And we eventually had this relationship.

"She grew up in a lifestyle very different than the one I did, sort of a spoiled California kid without any real goals or direction or ability to work hard, or really think too much, other than maybe another trip to Europe, or, you know, a good party somewhere. By the same token, she's a super-good person with really a good heart and soul: warm, beautiful, fun to be with."

On that second weekend of July 1979, Jeff and Candy stayed at the Park Lane Hotel in New York City. They went for a horse-and-buggy ride through Central Park. They ate a lavish dinner at Maxwell's Plum. They saw a baseball game at Yankee Stadium. Then, when the weekend was over, Candy flew back to California, and Jeffrey MacDonald flew to Raleigh, alone, to stand trial for the murder of his wife and children—murders that had been committed almost nine and a half years before.

2

In early June, Bernie Segal had written Jeffrey MacDonald a letter.

> *Dear Jeff:*
>
> *I am a little concerned about your wardrobe for the trial. The most important matter is for you (1) not to convey a "southern California image," (too much sun tan, polyester and beachy colors); (2) that you not appear to be "too casual" about the whole matter (the world needs to see you looking somber, serious, burdened and even concerned about this trial); and (3) that you do appear to be (at least as to your looks) truthful, reliable and responsible. . . .*

Segal was also concerned about the jury. At a cost of $15,000, he employed a Duke University psychology professor to assemble a demographic profile of the "ideal juror." The professor's staff made more than nine hundred random phone calls, asking respondents such general questions as whether they believed people in military service were more likely to commit violent crimes than civilians, whether they felt doctors made too much money, and whether they accepted the notion that a person who has an extramarital affair is not necessarily a bad person.

In reference to the MacDonald case specifically, those contacted were asked whether they had heard of it (81 percent had) and whether they had formed an opinion about his guilt (6 percent said he was "certainly guilty"; 29 percent said "probably guilty"; 33 percent said "probably not guilty"; 5 percent said "certainly not guilty"; and 27 percent said they did not know).

The respondents were also asked a series of demographic questions pertaining to age, race, marital status, length of residence in the county, educational background, political affiliation, and regularity of church attendance.

A subsequent analysis of the demographic and attitudinal responses disclosed the combinations most closely associated with a predisposition toward belief in innocence. The professor had then weighted each of the factors, much as a horse player will do when analyzing a field of thoroughbreds, and had devised a mathematical formula that would enable Segal to evaluate each prospective juror quickly on the basis of responses to questions asked during the selection process.

The surprising result of the survey, the professor from Duke said, on the Friday before jury selection was to begin, was that the ideal jury would be composed mainly of conservative whites over the age of thirty-five—in most cases, just the kind of jury sought by the prosecution.

"It's true," the professor conceded in the temporary office Segal had acquired in downtown Raleigh. "What we want is the kind of typical 'good citizen' that the government is probably going to go after. They won't be able to figure out what we're doing. In fact, they may think we've gone a little crazy. You know, normally you see an American flag in the lapel, you get rid of the guy. Here, that's just the type we're looking for."

Jeffrey MacDonald, who was at the meeting, shook his head. "I hope you're as good as your reputation," he said, "because everything you're saying goes against my gut feeling."

"I know, I know," the professor said, "and I know that it's your life, not mine. But I'll tell you what," he continued, suddenly smiling. "If I'm wrong, I won't serve any time for you, but I promise I'll work for free on your appeal."

Jeffrey MacDonald glared at the man from Duke. Bernie Segal quickly interceded, employing his most soothing tone. "Jeff, Jeff, relax. There's not going to be any appeal. We're going to pick a jury that will not only acquit you but will come back and award punitive damages."

"I hope you're right," MacDonald said, getting up to leave the office. "Because, frankly, this scares the hell out of me."

Once the client had departed, the professor, who himself could be described as young and liberal, was able to speak with greater candor. "What Jeff doesn't understand," he said, gesturing toward his pile of statistical analysis, "is that it's my friends we want most to get rid of. They all think he's guilty as hell."

MacDonald was living in a small room at one end of the second floor of the Kappa Alpha fraternity house on the campus of North Carolina State University. The house was occupied also by MacDonald's mother, by Bernie

Segal, and by five other lawyers and legal assistants (including Mike Malley, the ex-Princeton roommate, now a corporate attorney in Phoenix, who had taken a leave of absence to work without pay in his old friend's behalf), as well as by four fraternity brothers who were remaining on campus for the summer. Segal felt that Jeff would have a better chance for privacy at the college than he would in a downtown motel.

The housing at Kappa Alpha had been arranged by Wade Smith, the local counsel whom Segal had retained to assist him. An accomplished bluegrass musician who had been, in the late 1950s, a starting halfback on the University of North Carolina football team, Smith was a senior partner of the respected Raleigh firm of Tharrington, Smith and Hargrove, and the same attorney who had been recommended to MacDonald by Allard Lowenstein in 1971, when Lowenstein had become convinced that MacDonald was not a victim of military injustice but, rather, a man in need of a good criminal lawyer.

A native of the small North Carolina town of Albemarle, Wade Smith was a sturdy, gracious, exuberant man and the father of two bright and attractive teenaged daughters who were just a bit older than Kimberly and Kristen MacDonald would have been had they lived. At forty-two—having recently retired undefeated from state politics after two terms in the legislature—Smith was, perhaps, the most renowned practitioner of his craft in the state. He also possessed, in uncommonly full measure, a combination of kindness and wit. "Wade's the golden boy," Bernie Segal had said. "He's the best of what they have down here."

It was neither Segal nor Smith, however, who was on Jeffrey MacDonald's mind when he reached the Kappa

Alpha house late Friday afternoon. It was the jury selection man from Duke.

MacDonald did not speak about it right away. He changed into a pair of red gym shorts and—despite the heat and humidity—went out to run five miles around the North Carolina State University track. When he returned, he lifted weights for twenty minutes. Then he showered and put on a pair of white slacks and a T-shirt that said, "California Breast Stroking Team—Stroker." Then he opened a can of beer and looked up at the wall of the Kappa Alpha dining room, where a picture of the fraternity's most distinguished graduate member, J. Edgar Hoover, was hanging.

"What worries me," MacDonald said, "is that by our figures *he* would be the ideal juror."

On Saturday morning, July 14, Jeffrey MacDonald and his mother drove twenty-five miles to Chapel Hill to be interviewed by a new psychiatrist Bernie Segal had hired.

Robert Sadoff, the Philadelphia psychiatrist who had examined MacDonald in 1970 and who had testified at both the Article 32 hearing and the grand jury proceedings, was prepared to do so again, but Segal, a Jew from the urban Northeast, did not want to go before a Southern jury—however carefully chosen it might be—with only a Jewish psychiatrist from the urban Northeast to explain that Jeffrey MacDonald could not possibly have killed his wife and children. He wanted a man from North Carolina to say the same thing. In Chapel Hill, at the University of North Carolina, he had located one with impeccable credentials. And the psychiatrist seemed willing to testify, pending his interview with the defendant and the defendant's mother.

Segal himself went on Saturday to the chambers of

Judge Franklin Dupree to argue a series of pretrial motions. His relationship with the judge was not good.
Since 1975, in fact, when Dupree had rejected Segal's
bid to have the indictment dismissed on constitutional
grounds and then had denied his request for a change of
venue, he had considered the judge an enemy.

"He is, in brief, an asshole," Segal said at breakfast at
the Kappa Alpha house on Saturday morning. "He is the
pits. A despicably low individual. The problem is that he
has all the proper mannerisms for a judge and manages
to communicate a totally spurious aura of fairness. He
may be a dummy, in other words, but he doesn't have a
style that makes him easy to hate."

Accompanied by Wade Smith, Segal returned from the
judge's chambers to the downtown office at 4 P.M. The
temperature was 92 degrees and the humidity was 90
percent. It had been that way in Raleigh for a week.

Segal took off his suit jacket (dark pinstripes), loos-
ened his tie, lit a cigar, opened a can of diet soda, and
stared glumly and silently out the window.

Wade Smith took a seat next to the desk.

"How did it go?" asked Mike Malley, who had been
working in the office all day.

"Well, we won a few things," Smith said. "Nothing
that would gladden anyone's heart, but it didn't go
nearly as badly as it could have. I think he's beginning to
understand that we're not bad guys. We didn't gain an
awful lot on some points, but we did manage to get his
attention. I had the feeling that the ice was melting just a
bit. I believe he's starting to come around."

Segal, wreathed in cigar smoke, his feet on his desk,
continued to stare out the window.

"It was not a day to feel elated about," Smith continued, managing a smile, "or even greatly encouraged by. But neither should we feel discouraged."

Bernie Segal put his feet down, removed the cigar from his mouth, and swung slowly around in his chair. "Actually," he said, "it was a disaster. We didn't get the sweat from his armpits today."

Judge Dupree had agreed that the jury could remain unsequestered and that prospective jurors could be questioned individually and not in groups—a point vital to the selection technique Segal intended to employ—but since the prosecution had not opposed either of these motions, Segal did not consider the judge's granting them to be a victory.

There had been, on the other hand, nothing ambiguous about Dupree's ruling on the motion that the defense be provided with a free copy of the daily trial transcript—something which otherwise would cost $1,000 per day. He had denied it. And when Segal had argued that his client could not afford to pay for daily transcript—while the prosecution, backed by a limitless, taxpayer-funded expense account, of course could—the judge had replied that Dr. MacDonald did not strike him as an indigent defendant, and that, in fact, he had recently received a newspaper clipping from California describing a "disco party" designed to raise funds, presumably for just such a purpose as this.

Even more ominous, from Segal's point of view, had been the judge's announcement that he was reserving decision on the admissibility of certain points Segal considered vital to the defense. These included references to the constitutional questions of speedy trial and double jeopardy, as well as mention of Helena Stoeckley's continuing admissions to others that she (whose whereabouts were currently unknown) believed herself to have been involved in the murders. Other points on which the judge had not yet made up his mind were whether the jury should be told of the report filed by Colonel Rock which had found the charges against MacDonald to be "not true," and whether they should be informed of Dr. Sadoff's 1970 testimony that Mac-Donald lacked the capacity to have committed the crimes. Indeed, the judge said, he was not at all certain that he would permit any psychiatrists to testify, since the question of insanity was not at issue and since he believed that conflicting expert testimony tended to confuse a jury needlessly.

Pending his later rulings on these matters, the judge had said, no mention of them would be permitted in the opening statement to be made by the defense.

"So what's the status of our opening statement?" Mike Malley asked.

"We don't have one," Bernie Segal said. He looked out the office window again, at the scorching summer sun and the stifling, humid air that hung heavily over the somnolent Southern city. He took another sip of his Tab and another puff of his cigar. He said, "I guess we can talk about the weather."

Soon, however, the three lawyers began to go to work. Whatever the judge's restrictions, an opening statement would have to be delivered within a week.

Segal's first decision was that Smith should be the person to deliver it. He wanted the jury's first impression to be of a familiar local presence. Segal believed they would find this reassuring. Even if they did not know Wade Smith personally, the jurors would be more likely to give credence to words spoken in a cadence and with an accent to which they were already well attuned. Later—particularly during the cross-examination of government witnesses—there would be a place for Segal's harshness and histrionics, but the folksy, gentle manner of the Raleigh lawyer, Segal believed, would provide the most effective possible introduction to the version of events that Segal wanted the jurors to accept.

"I think," Segal said to Smith, "that the first thing you'll want to suggest is that this is an unusual case. This is a crime that occurred more than nine years ago. We have to hit that theme constantly. Enough is enough. Too much time has gone by.

"Then, I think it's important to set the family scene. Here was a man twenty-six years old, who had just completed medical school, achieving the dream of a lifetime. But before he embarked upon his career, he wanted to do service for his country. So there he was, at Fort Bragg, with his wife—his childhood sweetheart.

"I think it's important to mention, incidentally, that he had a partial scholarship and had to work to get himself through Princeton. That he came from a poor family and that his mother and father both worked to help pay his way. Right from the start we want to offset this image of him as a rich doctor from Southern California."

Wade Smith was taking notes on a yellow legal pad. Mike Malley was sitting in silence. Working hard on his cigar, Segal continued to build the scenario. "He does so well at Princeton that after only three years he's accepted at medical school. He does so well there that he earns one of the top internships in the country. And at the end of *that* year he agrees to serve his country as a Green Beret—not because he's any sort of macho killer, but in order to help those who need help the most: the boys we sent to fight in Vietnam.

"Then you paint a picture of the peace and tranquillity they enjoyed at Fort Bragg. Take it right up to

Christmas, tell how he bought the pony for his daughters. And if that doesn't get somebody a little lumpy at that point, we've picked the wrong jury."

Segal paused for a moment. "You might also stress," he said then, "that at Fort Bragg, for the first time, they did not have to scrimp for money."

"And," Mike Malley added, "that for the first time in their married life they got to spend a lot of time together."

"I'm not sure, Mike," Segal said. "The cynical response to that is, 'Yeah, and they found out they didn't like it.' I don't think we ought to hit that note too hard. You see, the point is, as long as people do not see him as some California, hip, swinger—some money-grubbing doctor—he's halfway home to being acquitted."

Wade Smith was nodding. This was a language he understood well. "Humanize him," Smith said. "Make the jurors want to embrace him."

"Right," Segal said. "After all, who's the government got to embrace? Freddy Kassab?"

"And let's not leave out Colette," Segal continued. "She was growing as a person, too. Even on the evening of February 16—the last night of her life—she was going to a child psychology course, trying to better herself. Jeff stayed home and played with the kids, put them to bed— parenting by the father, you see. A real good evening, just like so many others they'd enjoyed.

"Then, 'You will hear from the last person who saw her alive—the woman to whom she gave a ride to class— how Colette MacDonald felt about her life, her husband, her marriage.' The human details. That loving scene between husband and wife as they have a drink, chat about the events of the day, enjoying the time that they considered their special time together. Then she goes to bed, he finishes the housework, reads a bit for relaxation, watches TV."

For a moment, Bernie Segal's eyes appeared to moisten. Then he said, "You might as well mention the bed-wetting here, that makes it less ominous if the government tries to use it as a motive. 'And what were his choices? Either to wake his pregnant wife in order to re-make the bed, or simply to go back to the couch so as not to disturb her as she slept, and to fall asleep on the couch himself, having no idea of what was about to befall him and the people he so dearly loved.' "

Wade Smith was nodding and writing fast. Without missing a beat, he picked up where Segal had paused. " 'You will learn of the intruders,' " he said. " 'You'll see them. You'll come face to face with them.' "

"Fine," Segal said. "Although I think you'll want to be synoptic about the details of the struggle."

" 'And then we'll show you how and why the government has been so consistently misled in this case.' "

" 'And you'll learn how Jeff has tried, over the years,' " Mike Malley said, " 'to rebuild his life, only to be dragged back to face this.' "

"Yes, yes," Segal said, getting up from behind his desk and starting to pace. "And the fact that he's never remarried. That's very important. And continue with how the government has kept this alive for *nine years*—keep coming back to the nine years. And I think it's really important that we promise to explain the errors that the government committed—what led them astray."

"At some point," Wade Smith said, looking up from his pad, "they're going to learn that Jeff told Freddy a lie. How do you want to deal with that?"

" 'He throws himself into his work as a means of forgetting,' " Segal said, beginning to gesture expansively with his cigar. " 'But all the while, one set of people will not let him forget. Will not let him rebuild. Will try to make him live in the past. Who is responsible? His *step*father-in-law, a fanatic, a man obsessed, a man named Alfred Kassab.

" 'A man who wanted to spend every weekend combing the bars of Fayetteville in search of the killers, doing what the Army, the CID, the FBI should have been doing.' "

" 'You will hear how Doctor MacDonald tried to escape from the trap of living with this obsession,' " Mike Malley said.

"I think *escape* might not be a good word," Segal said.

"All right. How he tried to free himself from this obsession."

"Incidentally," Smith asked, "how do we refer to him? As Doctor MacDonald?"

"As Jeff," Segal said. "We want to humanize him. We want them thinking of him as just plain Jeff, the kind of guy they'd like to have for a next-door neighbor. And we want to contrast that with the image of the wicked stepfather, Freddy Kassab."

"He'd be your next-door neighbor," Malley said, smiling, "if you happened to live in a waterfront condominium in Huntington Beach."

"We minimize that," Segal said. "What we emphasize is the fact that this trial represents an opportunity for the jury to put an end to nine years of suffering."

"That the system is finally going to work," Smith said.

"We want them thinking, 'Oh, the poor man,' " Segal said. "We want to put on them the full knowledge that they have the ability to relieve him of his suffering."

" 'And before this trial is over,' " Smith said, " 'you will see the full dimension of this man: decent, intelligent, hardworking, devoted to community service—capable of mistakes, like the rest of us, but, in 1970, not drunk, not on drugs, not mentally ill . . .'"

"We want them to feel a little sad at the end," Segal said. "A little sympathetic. But mostly a little cynical. Suspicious of the government's case."

"'Look at the man,'" Smith intoned. "'Look at the life that is supposed to have created this monstrous destruction.' And then we hold the government's feet to the fire. 'They cannot prove he *might* have done it. They cannot prove he *could* have done it. They must prove, beyond any shadow of a doubt and to a moral certainty, that he *did* it!'"

"We need to stress the gore," Segal said. "You've got to feel the blood on the floor. Paint the crime scene monstrously: knives, icepicks, clubs. Colette—both arms shattered. The children, five and two, beaten and stabbed and battered in the most horribly sick way. Paint it monstrous because we don't have a monstrous defendant. The jury will look at him and say, 'Did *he* do *that*?' And there's no way they'll believe it."

"I agree with you," Smith said, getting ready to leave. He was living not at the Kappa Alpha house but at home. "I'll present it as kind of a down-home discussion," he said. "We don't want to seem to be enjoying it, or in our glory. More that the sad moment has come, but now the jury has the opportunity to let Jeff return to California and live out the rest of his life in peace."

To which Segal did not respond, "Amen," but he did say, "Are you going to take Jeff to church with you tomorrow?"

"I think so," Smith said. "It can't hurt. It'll be restful, and maybe a little inspirational. At least it will give him a look at some of our people, and he can see that folks here are not all out to get him."

Smith departed. Segal and Malley moved to an outer office, where Segal's six assistants had been working all day. Ten minutes later, Jeffrey MacDonald and his mother arrived, just back from Chapel Hill.

"Well?" MacDonald said.

"Well, what?" Segal said.

"What happened?"

"Nothing happened."

"What do you mean, nothing happened? What happened with our motions? What happened with the judge?"

"Jeff, I just told you, nothing."

"Okay, Mike, your turn. What happened?"

"Like Bernie said, Jeff. Nothing happened."

"All right, how about any of the rest of you? Does anybody feel like telling me what the fuck is going on?"

None of Bernie Segal's assistants responded.

"Jesus Christ!" MacDonald said. "I'm paying for eleven fucking lawyers, you'd think one of them would have the courtesy to tell me something." He paused and looked around the room. Still, no one spoke.

"Oh, I get it," MacDonald said. "It's a joke. Like a surprise party. Any minute now you're going to tell me the judge threw the whole case out of court. It's all over. Case dismissed. I can go home. The champagne is coming up in the elevator, they're icing it now."

"No, Jeff," Segal said. "I'm afraid you're going to have to wait a few weeks for the champagne."

Then he took MacDonald into his private office and broke the bad news about the judge's rulings. After that—to get it all out at once—he went on to explain that Wade Smith was going to make the opening statement.

"You're not going to do the opening?" MacDonald said. "I can't believe it. You've had nine and a half years to get ready and now you tell me, two days before the trial starts, that you're not even going to make the opening statement? Bernie, I flew three thousand miles just to hear you. Come on, now, give me a break."

"Jeff, we have Wade, he's an asset, he has to be utilized. And his greatest strength is his personality. He doesn't know the case as I do, but he has the capacity to relate to people, and that's important. He'll be working from the scenario that I gave him. I walked it through for him this afternoon. Essentially, conceptually, it's mine. The only change is that Wade will deliver it instead of me."

Segal then outlined the essence of the statement for his client. Jeffrey MacDonald was still not pleased.

"That sounds flat, Bernie, very flat. There's no zingers in there. Not one zinger. I expected you to crucify them, not just tease them a little bit."

"Jeff, the opening is just setting a tone. That's all it is. We have the whole trial to get in our zingers. And believe me, the tone will be good. Very low key. Wade will be fine. He'll do it as well as it can be done."

"Sure, sure," MacDonald said. "Don't bother, I know the rest: if he screws up, he'll work for free on the appeal."

Bernie Segal's loud laughter broke the tension. "Jeff, go home, run five miles, have a beer. And take it from me, from the one person who has never misled you: there isn't going to be any appeal."

Jeffrey MacDonald stayed up late that night, watching *Saturday Night Live* on TV.

For 81 percent of the people contacted by the Duke psychology professor to have said yes, they had heard of the case involving Dr. Jeffrey MacDonald, was extraordinary. In such random samplings it is rare for 81 percent of those polled to be able even to identify the President of the United States.

It seemed likely that for the remaining 19 percent unawareness ended on Sunday morning, with the publication of a front-page story in the Raleigh *News and Observer.* The article was accompanied by pictures of Jeffrey MacDonald in the company of his "colorful, West Coast attorney," Bernie Segal, and by old pictures of Colette and Kimberly and Kristen, and by a photograph of the boarded-up exterior of 544 Castle Drive—the murder scene still sealed after nine and a half years, pending final adjudication of the case.

As the date for trial neared, the story said, more and more people had begun to drive slowly up and down Castle Drive, staring. The woman who now lived next door to what had been the MacDonald apartment was quoted as saying she "couldn't sleep for a week," after being informed of what had happened there.

An Associated Press story printed in the Sunday paper in nearby Durham portrayed Jeffrey MacDonald as a man who lived "the good California life," complete with posh condominium, stewardess, sports car, and boat. The story also quoted Bernie Segal as having said that he'd wanted the trial moved from Raleigh to a "hip, sophisticated community," because, "God knows how a redneck stands"—a remark which Segal denied having made.

A television crew was stationed outside the Kappa Alpha house, hoping to film a glimpse of MacDonald if he emerged. News broadcasts featured hourly reports on the impending trial, even though jury selection had not yet begun.

*   *   *

For a final review of selection procedures, the Duke professor arrived at Kappa Alpha early Sunday afternoon. Clearly, Jeffrey MacDonald was still concerned.

"The thing that keeps me awake nights," he said, "is how valid are our starting premises? Suppose we're wrong?"

Once again, Bernie Segal spoke with reassurance. This was science, this could not fail. "Besides," he said, beginning to chuckle as he lit a pipe, "I intend to provide you with the ultimate safeguard, at great sacrifice to every principle I hold most dear: I will wear a Confederate flag in my lapel."

The mood remained upbeat all afternoon. Some of the Kappa Alpha boys brought in a keg of beer and two dozen steaks and hosted an early evening barbecue. Wade Smith came over with his banjo. Songs were sung. Jokes were told. Jeffrey MacDonald basked in the attention. It felt more like the kickoff of a political campaign—with MacDonald, of course, as the candidate—than it did the eve of a trial for the murder of a pregnant woman and two little girls.

By late evening, MacDonald's mother had brought out an album of family snapshots and was showing people what Jeff had looked like, in California, when he'd grown a beard. As the keg of beer neared its bottom, giddiness began to prevail. Wade Smith could be overheard telling the Duke psychologist that he had neglected to ask the one most important question of all: "Have you ever been the victim of a homicide?"

It took three days to pick the jury. Seven men, five women, all but one of them white, all but one (the same one) with at least some college education. Half were over the age of forty. Included were two accountants, a chemist, the son of a socially prominent Raleigh physician, a former Green Beret sergeant from Fort Bragg, a former North Carolina state policeman, and a woman whose son, during the school year, resided at the Kappa Alpha house.

Midway through the process, Jeffrey MacDonald said, "Every time Bernie stands up to accept one of them I feel another nail being hammered into my coffin." Both Segal and the Duke psychologist, however, were delighted with the makeup of the jury.

"Take the former highway patrolman," Segal explained. "The prosecution wanted him because he used to be a cop. But we wanted him for a better reason: because we're going to show that the evidence in this case was so badly screwed up that no decent cop would want to be associated with it."

And even MacDonald was vastly relieved at the inclusion of a former Green Beret. "That tie is so strong you'd walk across water for one another," he said. "There is no stronger bond. So at the very worst"—here, he laughed nervously—"I know I've got at least a hung jury."

Freddy and Mildred Kassab were in the courtroom throughout the process of jury selection, sitting side by side in the second row on the right, across the aisle from (though not acknowledging the presence of) Jeffrey MacDonald's mother, just as they had sat across the aisle from her sixteen years earlier in that small Catholic church in Greenwich Village.

Kassab, stocky and florid, sat fanning himself with a prosecution floor plan of the interior of 544 Castle Drive. His wife, pinched and small, sat next to him, staring straight ahead in silence. Occasionally, Freddy, his arm around her, would lightly stroke her shoulder with his thumb.

Less than ten yards from the Kassabs—after all the years of being separated from them by 3,000 miles—sat Jeffrey MacDonald. He was, as instructed, wearing a conservative, well-tailored suit. For the most part he, too, stared straight ahead, his face impassive. From time to time, as a prospective juror was being questioned, and as the Duke professor was handing up a card with a final rating, he would bend to consult with his attorneys.

At the end of the third day, with the twelve jurors and four alternates finally seated, MacDonald, carrying a briefcase, walked down the center aisle toward the rear door.

Freddy Kassab had just stepped out into the lobby to speak to reporters. By sheer chance, MacDonald reached the door at the same moment as Mildred Kassab. For the first time in more than eight years, their eyes met. He glanced away immediately. They did not speak. Her gaze—in which both immense pain and raw hatred were apparent—followed him as he walked out the door.

Driving back to the Kappa Alpha house, MacDonald said that of course he had seen her and that he had been very tempted to speak to her. "I wanted to say something like, 'I hope you get through this okay,' but I was afraid she'd probably take it the wrong way."

In the next day's paper, Mildred was quoted as saying yes, she had seen him too. "The only thing I could think of," she said, "was Colette, clumsy with her five months' pregnancy, trying to get away from him." No, she said, she had not been tempted to speak. "What was I supposed to say—'Good luck'?"

3

Victor Woerheide had dropped dead of a heart attack while walking to a corner store to buy a bottle of Tabasco sauce in October of 1975. To prosecute the case in his stead, the Justice Department had chosen James L. Blackburn, an assistant U.S. Attorney from Raleigh.

Blackburn was a short, cordial, soft-spoken man whose silvery gray hair and open, boyish face seemed to blend wisdom and innocence. He, like Wade Smith, was a native of North Carolina. He had, in fact, grown up on the campus of Wake Forest University, where his father had served as Methodist chaplain and from which he himself had later graduated.

Blackburn's courtroom demeanor was not that of a bloodthirsty prosecutor seeking headlines, but of a quiet, country man with a sad but inevitable duty to perform. One could, without stretching the imagination unduly, picture Blackburn as a courteous young aide to General Lee at Appomattox.

Even Bernie Segal, whose contempt for both Judge Dupree and for Blackburn's Justice Department col-

league, Brian Murtagh, was boundless, admitted that
Blackburn struck him as a decent man. "Twisted and
wrong," Segal said, "but decent."

Blackburn was thirty-four years old, he had a two-
year-old son named Jeffrey and a daughter who was just
two months old. This was the first murder case he'd ever
prosecuted.

For four weeks, the prosecution presented its evidence
before Judge Franklin T. Dupree, Jr., a sixty-five-year-
old native of nearby Fuquay-Varina, North Carolina.
Much of the time was devoted to complex explanations
of the circumstantial links that bound MacDonald to the
commission of the crimes. Though he had Brian Murtagh, with all his knowledge, at his side, Blackburn's
early presentation seemed tentative and occasionally confused. At the end of the first week, in fact, a wire service
story reported that the case against MacDonald was off
to "a shaky start."

The testimony was sometimes gruesome (particularly
that of the pathologists, whose autopsy descriptions were
accompanied by slides of the bodies, designed to emphasize the severity of the injuries sustained). A great deal of
the evidence was highly technical, and every bit of it was
challenged, point by point, by Bernie Segal, who, with
waving arms and a voice by turns booming and coldly
sarcastic, went after prosecution witnesses like a German
shepherd mauling a jogger.

Just as in 1970, every investigative blunder was exposed. The jurors, who sat silently and attentively
through the long, draining days, learned—as had Colonel Rock in 1970—that the flowerpot had been stood up
by a military policeman, that Jeffrey MacDonald's wallet
had been stolen from under the eyes of the MPs, that the

lieutenant had failed to send a patrol to look for the
woman standing in the shadows, that the garbage had
been emptied, the *Esquire* magazine read, the bedroom
telephone handled, the bloody footprint destroyed, the
toilet flushed, the children's fingerprints never taken,
other fingerprints poorly photographed and inadvertently destroyed, Jeffrey MacDonald's pajama bottoms
thrown away, MacDonald himself interviewed at the
hospital while heavily sedated, and that a "known sample" of MacDonald's hair had actually come from a pony.

Nine and a half years later, Bernie Segal's imagery was
still intact. "They came in like a herd of circus elephants,"
he said of the MPs, implying strongly once again that no
valid inferences could be drawn from physical evidence
so poorly preserved.

Throughout this phase of the trial, the defense was
exultant. Each day, Wade Smith would leave the courtroom and, while declining to comment publicly, would
privately express an ever growing sense of confidence.

"I can see it on their faces," he would say. "The jury
can't believe that Jeff is even here . . .

"A wonderful day, we did nothing but gain . . .

"This is not going to be as hard as we thought . . ."

Even MacDonald himself grew so confident that he
began to give interviews to the press. He was aware, he
told one reporter, that some people found his apparent
lack of emotion disturbing. "There's no question," he
said, "it would be better for me if I were so distraught I
could hardly get to court every day. But I think the jury
will see the real me when I testify. I hope they understand that not everyone wears their heart on their
sleeve."

Still, it appeared to another interviewer that "Most of
his answers, even when asked about his feelings, are

given matter-of-factly, almost coldly, as if he were speaking about someone else."

Only when he began to discuss his tormentors did MacDonald show sparks of real feeling, and that feeling appeared to be anger. "It took them six months behind closed doors, without a defense, to get a grand jury to issue an indictment. If that doesn't tell a normal person something, that normal person isn't thinking. . . .

"I've testified whenever they've asked. I've given them whatever they've wanted. And here we are on trial on false charges nine years later because of the mindless, middle-level federal bureaucracy, with people like Brian Murtagh who run around without any controls."

A "competent superior," MacDonald said, would have halted the prosecution before it had even gone to a grand jury, much less to trial. "Sure, I'm bitter," he said. "They're building careers on my case. But the truth has to come out sometime. They can't keep lying forever."

MacDonald said he "could not conceive" of a conviction. "That," he said, "would be the Alfred Hitchcock ending to the horror story."

To some observers, however, there were indications that MacDonald was drawing at least as close to a pair of handcuffs as he was to a chilled bottle of celebratory champagne.

It was not possible to assess the impact of the government's presentation upon the jury (except to note that none of the jurors seemed entirely unmoved by the sheer horror and sadness of it all), but Judge Franklin Dupree was proving considerably more scrutable.

Judge Dupree, who had been appointed to the federal bench in 1971 by Richard Nixon, was possessed of an unusually mobile, expressive face, and from the earliest days of the trial the expression most often seen upon it as Bernie Segal conducted cross-examination was one of distaste.

Obviously alert, attentive, and sometimes even taking notes during Jim Blackburn's direct examination, the judge would lean back in his chair with his eyes closed, grimacing in exasperation or rubbing his temples as if his head ached during those periods when Segal was repetitively questioning a prosecution witness.

With even casual spectators openly remarking on the judge's expression, it seemed only logical to assume that it would, to some degree, indicate to the jurors where his sympathies (or lack of sympathy) lay, and possibly even suggest to some where their own belonged.

It was not by body language alone, however, that Judge Dupree seemed to be placing obstacles along Jeffrey MacDonald's path to freedom. His rulings on several major evidentiary motions did much to shape the course of the trial.

He ruled, for example (over Bernie Segal's spirited objections), that the prosecution would be permitted to read extensively from the March 1970 issue of *Esquire* magazine.

"The government," Segal argued to the judge at a bench conference, "has suggested that because there was an *Esquire* magazine in which an article appeared about the Sharon Tate murders, that therefore this placed some idea in the defendant's mind.

"Your honor, we only need to trot out all the newspaper clippings. I mean, you would have to be probably a three-toed sloth hanging upside down in a tree to have lived in America in 1969–70 and not heard of the Sharon Tate and La Bianca murders.

"I mean, that is not a fact that has any special inference to be drawn. You know, when I buy a subscription to *Harper's*, I take whatever junk they send me—the good and the bad. Am I supposed to have the inference that just because there is something in there, that I chose it? Not at all. You get that with a subscription. You get a magazine. You get a subscription to it. It comes in regularly. The government says, 'Ah, ha. From that fact we wish the jury to draw the conclusion that he read it'—that in fact he read all the things that they say: that in fact it was the source of information. It was the idea.

"There is just no conceivable way that makes logical sense. I mean, it imputes to the magazine some kind of compelling power, some kind of magic that the editors of this magazine and all others wish they had.

"It is just simply too remote to be sensibly put into this trial. I mean, it almost has the character of fantasy. Take an intelligent man. No one has to prove that MacDonald is intelligent, that he was literate, read newspapers, and knew what was going on in the world.

"And because he has a magazine subscription and they have chosen the article—what about all the other articles? Do we now get to introduce everything he had read in that last year? 'Love Thy Wife.' 'Be Kind to Thy Children.' 'How Happy It Is in America.' Can we introduce all that, your honor? Why not? Put that idea in his mind, too—to love his family and care for them. Why isn't that fair game?

"We will be reading *Esquire* magazine, your honor, for quite a while if the government is allowed to do this. We should also be entitled to show everything else he read within a reasonable time frame that would reflect on his state of mind. Why not all the chapters in the Bible that he read? Why not? That goes to his state of mind."

Without pointing out that it was *Kiss Me Deadly,* by

Mickey Spillane, and not the Bible, that MacDonald had been reading in the time frame that immediately preceded the murders, Jim Blackburn argued for the relevancy of the *Esquire* material.

"We have done an analysis of those articles," he said. "And we know also what the defendant has said these people said—'Acid and rain, groovy, kill the pigs.' A girl with long blond hair carrying a candle—this sort of thing.

"Now, if the government's theory is correct, there were no such individuals. If there were no such individuals, they had to be invented from somewhere. Because these magazine articles were read by the defendant—and that has been shown by some of the fingerprints that were found on those articles, and of course Ron Harrison has said in his grand jury testimony that MacDonald had read it and said it was wild, or something like that— it does show that MacDonald was aware of those articles.

"And I think that when you look at the articles and see that the word *acid,* the word *rain,* the word *pig,* a girl with long hair, and candles are in those articles—"

"*Groovy?*" the judge asked.

"I think so, sir," Blackburn replied.

"*Groovy*—what does that mean?" the judge asked.

"Far-out," Brian Murtagh interjected.

Then Blackburn continued: "I do think, your honor, that it is probative to the government's theory of the case and the fabrication of the story. I am not suggesting that he read it first, necessarily, and then got the idea. I would suggest that perhaps what happened is the killings took place and he remembered the article and used it. And that is where some of these words and things come from. The fabrication of the defendant's story could well have come from his having read the article a short time before these murders occurred."

"Mr. Segal says that everybody who knew anything, up to and including the three-toed sloth," the judge said, "used those same words, because every time you picked up a paper, there they were. I have no recollection of having read them, and I take four daily newspapers and have for about fifteen years. I remember something about the Manson case, but I don't read murder cases."

"The word *acid*, your honor, is part of our vernacular," Segal said. "It is found in dictionaries—"

"You are from California," the judge interrupted. "I am not sure the word *acid* is common parlance in Johnston County and Warren County and Harnett—the places where these jurors come from. Maybe some of them are sophisticated enough to have heard the term *LSD* and the use of *acid* as synonymous with it, but I am not so sure about that."

"In 1970," Segal said, "when this case was first brought, I was not from California. I was from Philadelphia, and even in Philadelphia we had heard of those things. And we were among the last to get the word on anything."

"Your honor," Brian Murtagh interposed, "the articles in the *Esquire* magazine are not limited solely to the Manson killings. There are additional articles which involve an interview by a reporter of a 'witch' in California. Apparently, they have such things in California. At least they did at that time."

"They don't have anything but pretty girls now," Judge Dupree said, "at least judging from the ones they bring here." This was a reference to one of Bernie Segal's young assistants, with whom the judge had recently enjoyed a game of tennis.

Her charms notwithstanding, he allowed the prosecution to read all that it wanted to of the March 1970 issue of *Esquire* magazine to the jury.

Segal's bitterest and most significant evidentiary struggle during this phase of the trial concerned the admissibility of Paul Stombaugh's work with the blue pajama top. It was Segal's contention that Stombaugh's work had been invalid and was unworthy of submission.

"The demonstration that he did in the laboratory did not replicate in any reasonable fashion the facts that were known," Segal argued. "The most transparent failure is that the demonstration does not bear any resemblance to the physical facts of the case. This was not an experiment designed by a forensic scientist to prove a point. It was a lawyer's idea of how to prove an argument. That is, can you make forty-eight holes in the blue pajama top fit into twenty-one holes in Mrs. MacDonald's chest?"

That Stombaugh had not included in his alignment the icepick holes in Colette's own pink pajama top was, Segal said, "a fatal flaw," since the icepick, as it penetrated her chest, would obviously have had to pass through that garment as well.

A second flaw, Segal charged, was that no evidence supported the contention that the pajama top, as re-folded in the FBI laboratory, was in the same position in which it had first been found at the crime scene.

"If there are no facts to prove that the garment was in this position," Segal said, "then the fact that you could make forty-eight holes go into twenty-one holes— ignoring, of course, the pink pajama top—proves what? It proves I can juggle two oranges. But what does that mean to this court? If two oranges being juggled have no relevance, the fact that I can do it has no place in the record of this case. It is a demonstration for the sake of a demonstration. It is not a demonstration for the sake of illuminating the proof of this case.

"You just can't say that everything in the world can be given to the jury. There are limits that the rules of evidence have placed even on the government's theory of the case, and I want to see those properly invoked. The potential for prejudice here is so substantial that it is unfair to the defendant to permit this."

In response, Brian Murtagh said, "We are not saying, and Mr. Stombaugh will not testify, that the top was in precisely the same position as it was found on her body."

The government, Jim Blackburn added, contended only that Stombaugh had refolded the garment "generally" the way it appeared in crime scene photographs—with the right sleeve folded inside out and the left panel, which contained no puncture holes, trailing off alongside the body.

At that, Bernie Segal erupted. "At the grand jury, Stombaugh said he folded it *exactly* as it appeared in the pictures. That is his word—*exact*. If you try to back away from it now, his skin will be flayed all over this courtroom!"

Ignoring the outburst, Blackburn calmly reiterated for Judge Dupree the government's view of the significance of the pajama top: there were three types of blood found on it, the majority the Type A blood of Colette; at least some of that blood was on it before it was torn; MacDonald had said he'd placed it on his wife's body; the top had forty-eight puncture holes in it; doctors had testified that MacDonald had no icepick wounds; Colette, however, had twenty-one puncture holes in her chest; a pathologist had testified that these had been inflicted while her body was in a stationary position; likewise, the absence of tearing around the circumferences of the holes indicated that they had been made while the garment was stationary.

"Now if the defendant himself didn't go to bed that night before with a pajama top with forty-eight holes in it," Blackburn said, "then how did those holes get in that pajama top?"

Colette's pink pajama top, Blackburn argued, had not been included in the reconstruction simply because it was not relevant. Of course there would have been holes in Colette's pajama top: she had been wearing it when she was stabbed. The point of Stombaugh's demonstration had been to determine whether the physical evidence would support the contention that the icepick holes had been made in the blue pajama top after Jeffrey MacDonald had placed it on the body of his wife.

"Because if we can show this," Blackburn said, "we show that it is totally and utterly inconsistent with his own story. Is it prejudicial? Yes, I would say it is. That is precisely why we seek to introduce it. I don't think it is erroneously prejudicial. I think it shows, frankly, that his story is wrong and that it is at variance with the facts as we know them today."

Judge Dupree agreed to let the jury hear Stombaugh's explanation of what he had done with the torn blue pajama top and to allow him to describe the conclusions to which his work had led him.

He took a less tolerant view, however, of the relevancy of Colonel Rock's report on the 1970 military hearing—the report which concluded that the charges against MacDonald were "not true."

"I am concerned about the confusion which may arise in the minds of the jurors if this kind of evidence is admitted," the judge said, during another bench conference. "Won't a jury say, 'How can this man be not guilty in the Army and be guilty in this court?' Won't an argument appeal to the jury that, 'In the Article 32 proceeding there was only required to be a finding of probable cause to prosecute. If a four-month trial there didn't result in even that marginal finding, then how on earth can we, the jury'—wouldn't they say?—'say on virtually the same evidence that this man is guilty beyond a reasonable doubt?'"

It was for precisely this reason, of course, that Segal wanted so badly to have the Rock report introduced as evidence. But to do so, Judge Dupree continued, would be to suggest to the jury that a valid judicial proceeding had already occurred and had led to a finding of not guilty. The entire trial, then, would be invalid under the constitutional protection against double jeopardy. Since, however, the double jeopardy argument had already been made, unsuccessfully, by the defense prior to trial, no suggestion that the charges against MacDonald had been "not true" in 1970 should be allowed to influence the jury's decision in 1979.

To admit the Rock report, Dupree concluded, would be to imply "that on this evidence no jury could find the defendant guilty beyond a reasonable doubt," and for that reason he excluded it.

An even more serious blow to the defense was dealt when Dupree ruled that no psychiatric testimony would be admitted at trial. In July, prior to trial, Bernie Segal had arranged for MacDonald to be questioned for six hours in the office of a Beverly Hills hypnotist. The entire session had been videotaped. Segal had then edited the videotape and had brought a ninety-minute version with him to Raleigh, hoping to be able to show it to the jury.

One evening at the Kappa Alpha house he screened it for a very small audience which included a forensic psychiatrist from the University of North Carolina. The psychiatrist had already examined MacDonald and had written a twenty-four-page report which he ended by saying:

> On the basis of my clinical experience as a psychiatrist and criminologist and on the basis of my knowledge of theories and research into the area of violence, I would conclude that there is only an extremely remote possibility that a person of his type would commit a crime of this type. Certainly, no one with Dr. MacDonald's personality organization has ever been known to commit such a crime.

It was Segal's intent to have both the Chapel Hill psychiatrist and Dr. Sadoff from Philadelphia testify regarding the improbability of Jeffrey MacDonald's having murdered his family, and then to have the jury watch the videotape of MacDonald, under hypnosis, actually *reliving* the night of the crimes.

The tape began with MacDonald giving a description of the intruders far more detailed than any he'd ever managed before. He described the black man as having a heavy, square face with "baby fat" on the cheeks; short, kinky hair; flared nostrils; thick lips; light brown skin; and a thick neck which would have taken a "sixteen and a half or seventeen" shirt collar.

The taller of the two white men had been stocky and muscular with a "tall" face, high forehead, short, clean, light brown hair, and a "muscular, weight-lifter's neck." His eyes had been "vacant," but he had been "good-looking" nonetheless. "A clean-looking guy," MacDonald said, with a "strong jaw" and a dimple in the center of his chin, "approximately three-eighths of an inch in length." In addition, he had worn a light tan windbreaker and a cross (about an inch and a half long) on a "fine chain" around his neck.

The shorter white man had been an Italian with greasy hair and a bad complexion. His face had been pie-shaped, he'd had a "thin, pencil mustache," "nasty, ferret, weasel" eyes, as well as a weak chin and skinny neck. He'd worn a gray sweatshirt with pockets in the front and had looked "wasted, like a doper."

The female, too, had been "weak-looking," with a "pointed chin," and "long, straggly, unkempt" blond hair. Her face had been "almond-shaped," her nose had had a bump on it, and she'd spoken in a "wasted, monotone" voice, with an "unpleasant, medium-high pitch." Her right eye had been shaded by a "light tan or off-white oyster color" hat which had been made of felt. The brim of the hat had been floppy and about "fifteen to twenty" inches across.

On the videotape, MacDonald then reenacted the attack. *"What are you doing here?"* he shouted to the intruders. *"What the hell is going on? What the fuck are you people doing here? What are you assholes doing in my house? . . . Get the fuck out of here, you assholes!"* Then, having heard his daughter scream, *"Daddy, Daddy, Daddy, Daddy, Daddy!"* he shouted: *"Kimmy, I'll help you!"*

His narration continued: *"I'm trying to push them away. They're pulling me to the end of the couch by my shirt. I'm all—I'm all bound up. . . . My arms are all wrapped up. I can't do anything. I'm still trying to kick the fucking blanket off my feet! I—I—I—can't do any-*

thing! My hands aren't free. I can't do anything well. . . .
They're punching me in the chest. My head hurts. . . . I've
got someone's hand. I saw a blade. The fucking pain isn't
a punch—I got stabbed. . . . My fucking pajama top is
wrapped all around. I can't free my arms! Fuck! Someone
hit me with a club. I don't know what to do. I've got to get
my hands free! I've got to keep them away. 'Acid is
groovy . . . Kill the pig!' It's all I hear. No sounds. 'Acid is
groovy . . . Kill the pig.' They're going to kill me! I can't
keep holding on. I can't keep holding on! I can't do it!
Fuck! I'm sliding forward. I see a knee—a bare knee. My
arms! They're so heavy. I can't get them up. I can't get
them up . . ."

Later, in a voice so distraught, so filled with pain and
desperation that even the forensic psychiatrist began to
cry, he recounted what had happened after he had regained consciousness. Giving mouth-to-mouth resuscitation to Colette (*"The air is coming out of her chest! It's*
not working!"), observing Kimberly in her bed (*"She looks*
bloody, too. She's my little girl. She looks funny. She looks
dead"), and then Kristen (*"Kristy, you'd better be okay. . . .*
She looks pale. She doesn't—doesn't look good. She doesn't
look like she is breathing").

Toward the end, he described his final circuit through
the house, returning first to Colette and lifting the pajama top he had earlier placed across her chest. *"I hugged*
her. I told her . . . the kids would be okay. I'm kneeling next
to her. I want to see if her chest looks as bad as I first saw it.
I put the pajama top back. I decide to check the kids one
more time. I've got to check Kimmy. Kimmy is my little
girl. I've got to go see her. . . . Kimmy is limp. Kimmy looks
terrible. I pick her up. My left hand is under her shoulder,
picking her up. My right arm is under her neck. I give
Kimmy mouth-to-mouth. It doesn't feel right. The air must

be escaping. I can't help her! I check her femoral pulse. There's no pulse. I pick up her bedclothes. And lay them on her. And go see Kristy. I have to see Kristy. Kristy has got to be okay. . . ."

The emotional impact of the tape, particularly on those not intimately familiar with the facts of the case against MacDonald, was overwhelming. "If he's guilty," the psychiatrist said, "he deserves an Academy Award."

To the immense chagrin of Bernie Segal, however, the jury never got to see the videotape. Indeed, the jury was not even permitted to hear from Dr. Sadoff or from the North Carolina psychiatrist, because of Judge Dupree's ruling—issued after MacDonald had submitted to examination by a psychiatrist and a psychologist employed by the prosecution—that such testimony was irrelevant in a case where the insanity defense was not being employed and, given the likelihood that the prosecution and defense psychiatrists would tend to contradict one another, that their testimony would be less than illuminating.

"The broad question of whether or not it is open to the defendant to bring in an expert opinion that his character is such that he probably would not have committed a crime such as this is a very, very close question," the judge said. "There is some good argument to be made on both sides.

"It is my own conviction," he added, "that to pit shrink versus shrink would simply tend to prolong the case and at best would prove something that would just tend to confuse the issues. The law on this, while certainly not settled by any stretch of the imagination, is not such as to allow this evidence to be admitted. And rather than let things run to Christmas, I would just as soon stop it now and wonder the rest of my life—which I would allot about three seconds to this—as to what they would have said."

During the fourth week of trial, however, the jurors did hear from Paul Stombaugh of the FBI laboratory. He was a fifty-two-year-old former football player from Furman College who had spent twenty-five years in the FBI before his retirement in 1976. For the last sixteen of those years he had worked in the FBI laboratory in Washington and had testified as an expert in hair, fiber, bloodstain, and fabric analysis in more than 300 criminal cases in forty-eight of the fifty states, and had appeared as an expert witness before the Warren Commission's investigation into the assassination of John F. Kennedy.

Unlike his grand jury appearance, at which he had been encouraged to articulate his theories, at the trial Stombaugh was restricted to fact.

Even so, his testimony was considered by many observers to be the most damaging to MacDonald of any given at the trial. It was through Stombaugh that the prosecution first informed the jurors of the following:

—that the cuts made in the pajamas worn by Colette, Kimberly, and Kristen MacDonald had been made by the sharp, straight Old Hickory knife and not the dull, bent Geneva Forge knife;

—that the cuts in Jeffrey MacDonald's torn blue pajama top had been made by the Geneva Forge knife;

—that no cut in the pajama top corresponded to the location of the chest wound which had caused the puncture of Jeffrey MacDonald's right lung;

—that the pajama top had been torn down the left front seam and down the left sleeve in a manner which indicated that someone standing in front of Jeffrey MacDonald had ripped it as he spun away, and not—as he had told investigators—that it had either been torn over his back as he had fought with intruders or that he had torn it from his wrists himself as he had entered the master bedroom;

—that the top had been stained by Colette MacDonald's blood in at least four locations *before* it had been torn;

—that the forty-eight puncture holes in the pajama top were perfectly round, with no tearing around the edges, indicating that they had been made while the top was stationary, and not while MacDonald was using it as a shield to fend off an icepick-wielding intruder;

—that bloodstains on the Hilton bathmat corresponded with the shape and dimensions of the Old Hickory knife and the icepick, indicating that someone had either rested them or attempted to wipe them on the bathmat before discarding them out the back door;

—that bloodstains on the sheet found on the master bedroom floor matched impressions made by the bloody sleeves and cuffs of both Jeffrey's and Colette's pajamas, indicating that persons wearing those garments had come into direct contact with the sheet while the garments were still wet with blood;

—that the sheet also contained bloody handprints and, in blood, the outline of a bare human shoulder;

—that "when the pajama top was folded as near as possible to the way it was folded on top of the body at the time the photographs were taken," twenty-one holes were discernible in the top layer of the garment, and that these fell into a grouping—sixteen on the left side and five on the right—which was consistent with the grouping of sixteen icepick holes on the left and five on the right side of Colette MacDonald's chest; and, further, that the remaining holes in the garment could be aligned with those top twenty-one in a manner which indicated that it would have been possible for someone to have made all forty-eight with twenty-one thrusts of an ice-pick—the same thrusts that had made the icepick holes in Colette's chest.

Understandably, Bernie Segal did not go quietly into the dark night toward which Stombaugh's testimony was leading. At a press conference called even before he began his cross-examination, Segal termed Stombaugh's conclusions "shocking" and "totally without foundation," and said, "excuse the pun, the biggest fabrication I have ever seen." Any scientific organization to which Stombaugh might have belonged, Segal said, should "throw him out" on the basis of his testimony at the trial.

Judge Dupree was less than charmed by Segal's outburst, particularly when, the next morning, Segal, at the bench, objected that the government was taking too much time to conclude Stombaugh's testimony, and, by repetitious questioning and use of charts and photographs to illustrate Stombaugh's words, improperly attempting to persuade the jury that Stombaugh's opinions had a scientific validity which he felt they lacked.

"They keep putting repeat copies of the same thing, so just in case, somehow in their closing arguments, they don't mention it fifty times, they will have mentioned it fifty-five. Now, your honor, you have repeatedly told me that I cannot argue with government witnesses. I cannot argue my case. Why is he being allowed to make argument—"

"Wait a minute," Judge Dupree said. "Are you insisting on a right to argue with the witness?"

"No, your honor."

"Or with counsel during the trial of the case in open court?"

"No, your honor, but what I ask for—"

"I just wanted to know if I had misunderstood the proprieties of the situation."

"The proprieties are, your honor—my feeling is that your honor has found that when I put questions to the government's witnesses, we are told it is improper to argue with the witnesses—that the time to argue my case would be at the end.

"Now, what the government does—they have ten photographs, exact duplicates of each other. They keep putting them up, attaching them to exhibits. They're showing the jury for the umpteenth time another copy of the same photo—that is duplicitous. It is repetitious. It has been in evidence more times than any of us can count. And I object. It is not fair to permit that. It is misleading. And I am saying there ought to be a limit at some point."

"Well, Mr. Segal," said Judge Dupree, "if the Lord lets me, I am going to treat both sides equally in this case. I am going to let both sides have a full and fair hearing, and develop their cases exactly like they want to. You are going to be fed out of the same spoon. That is the rule that obtains at all times in this court. I am going to give you all the time that you need. We have spent too much time in this case here now to be talking about duplicity.

"You spent forty-five minutes yesterday afternoon qualifying—or trying to disqualify—the witness here. And then you held a press conference, apparently, and expostulated further on his lack of requirements. And it appeared on the front page of the paper this morning.

"I am not complaining about that, but I am saying, as

far as giving you the full opportunity to develop whatever you want to do, I am doing that for you and I am doing that for him.

"And while I'm at it, for whatever it's worth—and I say this to both of you—when lawyers give interviews to the press, it has been my observation over the years that lawyers who are entirely confident of their position and who believe in the correctness of their cause, eschew that kind of thing. To me, it just telegraphs some weakness.

"As far as the jury is concerned, I am hoping that they are observing their oath and are not reading anything. There is always the possibility, though, that they will. Therefore, while I don't want to muzzle anybody, I don't see why we can't stick to our knitting here in the courtroom.

"I don't give a damn what appears in the paper, myself. But when it is on the front page, they can't escape it. They had on yesterday's front page verbatim quotations as to how the defense was going to destroy some witness—Stombaugh, probably, and all that stuff.

"Here again, I don't run lawsuits. I sat out there thirty-four years, and I saw a lot of judges that came to town and professed to know more about my case in two hours than I had been able to learn in three or four years of living with it. So I wouldn't do that. I will let you run your case.

"But for whatever it is worth, I'll say that I think talking to newspapers while the trial is in progress as to what you are going to do with your evidence and so forth—I think it may come very close to transgressing the rules of professional responsibility in ensuring a fair trial for both sides."

When Segal did begin his cross-examination, however, it was with a further attack upon Stombaugh's credentials.

He had subpoenaed Stombaugh's undergraduate records from Furman College. He asked Stombaugh if he had ever taken a physics course while in college. Stombaugh said that he had.

"And that was the course you got a D in, isn't it, Mr. Stombaugh!" Segal shouted.

As government attorneys loudly objected, Judge Dupree instructed the jury to disregard Segal's remark.

"Your honor," Segal said, spinning to face the judge, "this man has been qualified as some kind of pseudo-expert. I want to find out—"

"Objection!" Brian Murtagh shouted.

"I want to know whether he has any basis for making the statements he has made," Segal said.

"Now, wait a minute," said Judge Dupree. "If you have any arguments to make, you make them here at the bench."

"I will make them wherever your honor will decide they should be made," Segal said with an air of exaggerated politeness that bordered on insolence.

"Well, I just said right here at the bench." Judge Dupree then turned to address the jury. "Members of the jury," he said, "counsel has just made a statement to the effect that this witness has qualified as some kind of pseudo-expert. The court considers that that comment was improper. The court can understand that counsel—as I've told you before—may in the heat of battle sometimes say things that on further reflection they might not have said. I ask you, however, to disregard that comment. It will be for the jury to determine whether or not this witness is an expert. As the court has said, the evidence tends to show that he is. It will also be for the jury to determine what weight, if any, his testimony is to be accorded."

By now, Bernie Segal had reached the bench, where Judge Dupree told him, "I have apologized for you about all I am going to before this jury. I don't want your client to be prejudiced before this jury by outbursts such as this last one you made. I have an obligation to look after him as well as everybody else in this case. And I want to see that it is done. If you have got any outbursts to make, or if you want to make any argument, come up here."

Segal's cross-examination, however, continued in a bitter, sarcastic vein. Focusing on Stombaugh's assertion that one of the bloodstains on the sheet could have been made by a bare shoulder, Segal said, "As a matter of fact, don't almost all of us have some kind of very fine hair on our shoulders?"

"That is right."

"Did you find any hair lines on that smear?"

"No, sir."

"Did you look for any?"

"Yes, sir."

"How did you look for them?"

"With a magnifying glass."

"Ah!" said Segal, stepping backward and raising his eyes toward the ceiling, in mock astonishment. "We have a scientific instrument here."

"Objection!" shouted Jim Blackburn.

"All right," Segal said sharply, glaring toward Blackburn. "It's not a scientific instrument."

"Objection!"

"Members of the jury," Judge Dupree said wearily, "disregard the comment of counsel about the magnifying glass."

In regard to the bloodstains on the sheet that Stombaugh had said were made by the pajama cuffs, Segal said in accusatory fashion, "You just took the cuff and you took the bedsheet and you looked at them side by side. Is that what you did?"

"I did a little more than that, sir. I sat down and studied the stains for long periods of time."

"Did you say, 'study'?"

"Studied them, compared them, examined them, things of this nature. A direct comparison to locate the area on that cuff that corresponded with that stain."

"Studied," Segal said scornfully. "How did you 'study' it? By looking at it?"

"Looking at it," Stombaugh agreed.

"Compared—how did you do that. By looking at it?"

"Direct comparison. Yes, sir."

"Well," Segal said, his voice suddenly rising to a shout. "Every word that you've used—every adjective— that meant only that you looked at it and you looked at it and you looked at it! Is that right, Mr. Stombaugh?"

"That is correct."

"If the jury then gives these items the same attention, they will be able to do exactly what you were able to do, is that right, Mr. Stombaugh?"

"Perhaps."

"There is no secret scientific method that you used that they are not aware of, is there?! That you haven't told us about?!"

"No, sir."

"It is just looking!" Segal screamed. *"That is what your fabric impression testimony is about. Just looking!"*

"I believe that is what I have testified to," Stombaugh said.

It was, undeniably, far from what Victor Woerheide

had told Dr. Sadoff while the grand jury had been in session: that the field of fabric impressions study was the scientific equivalent of fingerprint analysis. But the jury would not be concerning itself with what Victor Woerheide had said four years earlier. The jurors would be interested only in whether—to them—the stains on the bedsheet appeared to have been made by the bloody cuffs of Jeffrey and Colette MacDonald's pajamas.

Toward the end of his cross-examination, Segal tried to invalidate the pajama top reconstruction.

"Now, you told us yesterday, Mr. Stombaugh, that you did not really do this little demonstration with the pajama top exactly the way it was on Mrs. MacDonald's body. Isn't that what you told us yesterday?"

"No, sir. We folded it—"

"Did you say that or did you not say it yesterday?" Segal interrupted sharply. "Then you can explain as long as you want."

"Object to comments of counsel," Brian Murtagh said.

"It is not a comment to tell a witness he can answer," Segal said. "Your honor, I resent that. It is not a comment to say that I will give him all the chance to answer a question. It interrupts cross-examination needlessly."

"All right, now," Judge Dupree said. "If you have some objection to make, the customary way to do it is to come up here. I will not take any lectures from counsel from either side. If there is an objection and you want to be heard, we will hear it at the bench."

"My response, your honor," Segal said, without taking as much as a single step toward the bench, "is I do not think I was making a comment when I said I would give the witness a chance to answer."

"There was an objection before the court. I was prepared to rule on it, but we had another lecture superimposed on the subject."

"I apologize," Segal said.

"That is what I am calling to your attention."

"I did not mean to do that."

"Restate your question and we will let the witness answer."

"Yes, your honor. Let me just regather my thoughts." After a short pause Segal continued.

"Do I recall you correctly," Segal continued, "as having told us yesterday that you did not fold the pajama top in the demonstration exactly the way it appeared in the photographs?"

"We folded the pajama top as close to it as we could."

"That is the most you are willing to say about the way you folded it for your demonstration?"

"And when we folded it that way, then we observed twenty-one holes in the top."

"Before we get to the holes, I just want to understand whether, when you finished folding it, you think you got a fairly good replica of the way the garment was laid over Mrs. MacDonald's body."

"Yes, sir. I feel we did the best we could."

"Well, doing the best you could—is that the same as being a pretty good replica?"

"I would say so."

"Is that the strongest statement you are willing to make in support of the way the garment was folded—that that, you think, is the best you could do with it?"

"Working with what we had, we did the best we could."

"Well, now, tell us some of the ways in which your experiment in folding is really different from the photographs."

"Mr. Segal, I have been answering your question—the same one over and over—the only way I can answer it. We folded the pajama top the way it appeared in the photographs. We found twenty-one holes in the surface. The question was: Could those twenty-one holes on top be lined up with the forty-eight holes? Could this be done? And we—"

"Didn't you just simply tell them, Mr. Stombaugh," Segal interrupted, "'Of course you can take any forty-eight holes and put them in twenty-one holes'? That that is not a scientific experiment! Did you ever tell them that?!"

"Objection!" Brian Murtagh said.

"Objection sustained," said Judge Dupree.

Sustained objections notwithstanding, Jeffrey MacDonald was exuberant by the time Segal had finished.

"Stombaugh's the reason I'm here," MacDonald said later that day. "Him and Brian Murtagh. And Bernie just absolutely destroyed him. You've just seen their smoking gun turn into a piece of shit. If the judge had any balls at all, he'd throw the whole case out right now. He wouldn't even make us put on our defense."

In private, Segal raged against the judge in the vilest terms imaginable. He raged against Republicans, of whom Judge Dupree was one. He raged against the South. He raged against the U.S. Army and the FBI and the U.S. Supreme Court: all those forces that had conspired to present Judge Dupree with this opportunity to exercise his malevolence.

Segal seemed to bear no less antipathy toward Brian Murtagh. While it was Jim Blackburn—that courtly young Southern gentleman—who had been presenting the bulk of the prosecution case, it was Murtagh, Segal's adversary from grand jury days and surrogate for and successor to the Grand Inquisitor, Victor Woerheide, who had been besting Segal in argument on the evidentiary points before Judge Dupree.

Early in the trial, Dupree had noted the depth of bitterness which seemed to exist between the two men and had called them both to the bench to issue a warning.

"The reason I want you both up here," he had said, "is because it has been apparent to me from the very first time that the two of you appeared in this court that there was a certain amount of friction and animosity between you.

"I quite understand. I sat out there for thirty-four years. In the dog days of August and during the third week of a trial you may spurt off something that you, on reflection, would not have done. You did that yesterday," he said to Segal. "You were just about to do it again today, and I must say—and this applies to both of you—I am not going to have it.

"The thing that I am apprehensive about is this: one or the other of you, if you show these displays of temper and hostility and animosity, are going to prejudice your client. I am here to see that this trial is conducted fairly, and I am not going to tolerate its being tried in a climate of hostility for either side. We are going to try it calmly.

"It ain't your case," he said to Segal, "and," turning to Murtagh, "it ain't yours. It belongs to the parties in the case and you are just here in a representative capacity—both of you—and I am expecting both of you to so conduct yourselves.

"The last thing I ever would do, if I could avoid it, would be to embarrass a lawyer in front of a jury and his client. But if I have to do it in order to maintain order in this court and conduct this trial like it is supposed to be, then that is what I am going to do."

Following that lecture, Segal, for at least a few days, seemed to keep his distaste for Murtagh under tighter control, at least within the confines of the courtroom.

But as Dupree ruled against him time and again, and as his bitterness and frustration grew, Segal, who had been described as "the picture of confidence" in one newspaper account only a few days earlier, began to vent spleen in the press; and since it would have been grossly inappropriate (and counterproductive) to make public some of the private opinions he held regarding the attitude of Judge Dupree, it was Brian Murtagh who became the focal point of Segal's public outrage.

"What I dislike with considerable intensity," he told one reporter, "is that Murtagh is an anonymous, faceless little man who, in the outside world, would be of very little consequence to anybody's life. But he, as a bureaucrat, is suddenly draped with the power of the whole United States government, and people act as if he is a person with the judgment, intelligence, and maturity to be taken seriously."

Murtagh at thirty-two was just as thin and sallow, his hair was just as lank, and his manner was just as acerbic as it had been five years earlier when Jeffrey MacDonald had called him a little creep and a viper who did not know any of the social graces. Murtagh's sense of moral outrage that MacDonald had not yet been convicted and imprisoned had grown even greater over the years. (He had accompanied Paul Stombaugh to the cemetery in September of 1974 and had gazed into the opened coffins at the physical remains of Colette and Kimberly and Kristen, and the memory of what they had been then, as compared to a vision of what they might have been had they been permitted to live, was not one which would ever fade.) He chose not to respond to Segal's attacks.

"I just don't deal with Bernie if I can avoid it," was all he said.

At a surprise party at the Kappa Alpha house—the occasion being Bernie Segal's forty-ninth birthday—the highlight was the presentation to Segal of a set of darts and an enlargement of a recent photograph of Brian Murtagh.

One by one, each member of the defense team took a turn throwing darts at the picture. Jeffrey MacDonald scored a direct hit. He cheered for himself as his attorneys and their assistants clapped and laughed. In high spirits, he seemed oblivious to the possibility that, under the circumstances, it might not have been appropriate for him to be propelling a sharp pointed object toward even the photographic representation of a human being.

MacDonald's buoyancy might have been lessened even further had he been aware of the private remarks which a criminologist, hired by the defense as an expert witness, had made to Bernie Segal after having learned of Paul Stombaugh's findings.

"This is very convincing evidence," the paid expert said, referring to Stombaugh's pajama top reconstruction. "Now I see why they got the indictment."

Segal attempted to be dismissive, discoursing at some length about how even the government's own theory of the crime offered no plausible explanation for why MacDonald would have placed his pajama top on his wife's chest *before* stabbing her with the icepick.

The criminologist simply shook his head. "You can raise all that, Bernie, but this is like a fingerprint. Holy Christmas! That's very convincing stuff. Bernie, I'm not

an attorney, but after seeing this my advice to you"—and
here he leaned forward and gave Segal an avuncular pat
on a pin-striped knee—"is to get as much as you can into
the record for appeal."

Over Segal's strenuous objections, the jury visited 544
Castle Drive. On a very hot and very sunny August
morning—a day as different from February 17, 1970, as
a day could be—the twelve somber, silent men and
women (and four alternates) filed through the musty,
cramped space in which Colette and Kimberly and Kristen MacDonald had been clubbed and stabbed to death.

Jeffrey MacDonald, wearing a dark, heavy pin-striped
suit despite the heat, also reentered the apartment for
the first time since he'd been carried out on a stretcher,
nine and a half years before. He had no role to play, no
function to perform, but Bernie Segal wanted to be sure
that the jurors were aware that no sense of guilt prevented MacDonald from returning to the scene of the
crime. Afterward, he stood outside in the company of
Segal and Wade Smith. A crowd of perhaps one hundred
had gathered behind barricades erected by the military
police.

As the jurors reentered the van that would carry them
back to Raleigh, and as MacDonald prepared to return
to Wade Smith's station wagon, he was surrounded by a
throng of excited housewives and smiling children who
called out words of encouragement. Some of the children even rushed forward to shake his hand.

Like a baseball player signing autographs on his way
out of a stadium, MacDonald worked his way slowly toward the car. It was the first time in nine and a half years
that he had made physical contact with a child on Castle
Drive. It was nice, he said, once he was inside and the air

conditioning had been turned on. He appreciated such signs of support. The children waved at him as he departed.

Back in court, the prosecution played a tape recording of the April 6, 1970, interview. This was an event which marked for more than one member of the jury the end of the presumption of innocence.

"Until I heard that," a juror would comment later, "there was no doubt in my mind about his innocence. All the evidence had just seemed confusing. But *hearing* him turned the whole thing around. I began to look at everything in a whole new way. There was something about the sound of his voice. A kind of hesitation. He just didn't sound like a man telling the truth. Besides, I don't think someone who just lost his wife the way he said he did would have sat there and complained that her kitchen drawers had been a mess."

"There was a cockiness," another said. "Arrogance when there should not have been arrogance. It was so different from what I think my own attitude would have been under the same circumstances that it just started me wondering what kind of man he really was. After the tape, I started to believe he *could* have done it. And once you start to believe that—with all the evidence the government had—it's not a big step to believing that he did it."

And then came the day on which Mildred Kassab testified. For a while she had attended every session of the trial. Then the judge had ruled that anyone who would later be called as a witness would not be permitted in the courtroom prior to testifying. After that, Mildred spent her days in a small apartment, just a few blocks from the courthouse, that she and her husband had rented for the duration of the trial. With the shades pulled low against the heat and the steady hum of air conditioning in the background, she resumed writing in the journal she had begun years before—forcing up the memories, even the worst of them, as a means of preparing herself to testify.

"March 18th, 1964—Jeff called us. Kimmy was born! Colette's narrow hips were not meant for babies. She was torn and exhausted before they did a Cesarean, but the moment I walked into her hospital room she lifted the infant from her breast and said, 'Here, Mom. Here is one of your lost little girls.'

"I had to leave Monday morning. I had an appointment made some weeks earlier to redecorate a funeral home (Kemp's—he buried them in 1970) and had to meet workmen there.

"Jeff took me to the train in Princeton. I said, 'Take care, I'll be back on the five o'clock train tomorrow.' He looked so proud standing there: a new father. (He only stood until the train pulled out and then drove into N.Y. to meet his girlfriend.) So, the great deception began . . ."

She wrote of her life after the murders.

"The hunt for her letters . . . Looking at movies and slides to hold on to our memories . . . The feverish planting of roses and more roses . . . The pictures losing their meaning and becoming only pictures . . . Holding on to a dream . . . Tiptoeing through the day to try to keep the dream alive—to no avail.

"The first couple of years—looking through the fence at the five year old and two year old children next door. Then finally 'borrowing' them for hours at a time: someone to shower with all that bottled up love. It didn't work, though. The two and five year olds became six and nine and fantasy ended . . .

"Keeping our lives separate from others because our grief contaminated those who were too close to us. Their lives must not be infected by our feelings . . .

"Freddy's company moving from New York to New Jersey but I could not think of moving, of leaving them behind. Living on with Freddy coming home weekends because I couldn't move away and leave them and all of the memories stored in the rooms of that house—they were still there.

"I wanted every stitch of clothing they ever owned, down to the last torn sneaker. No one else should get to wear those poor, shabby personal things. I kept every single thing, too, until 16 months ago when we moved to a smaller house. I still have a few things from each one that can recall a day or an event we shared. A doll of Kristy's. Kimmy's little purse from the jacket she wore last, with two dollars in it. A couple of colored shells . . .

"The beauties of the world they would never see, the music they would never hear. The sunsets and the mornings, watching the bird feeder through my binoculars and seeing a pair of courting blue jays strutting and posturing beneath the rhododendron bushes with the sun just rising through the trees . . . All so achingly beautiful, and they would never know.

"I think the reason I have kept my mind all these years is because my greatest grief has been for Colette and her poor, poor life with him. Forgetting my own pain in realizing hers. I pray she knows he is being given some punishment, however small and unbalanced it is."

The next day, from the witness stand, when asked on cross-examination by Bernie Segal if it were not true that she had become somewhat "preoccupied" by the subject of her daughter's murder, Mildred Kassab replied: "Of course. Wouldn't you be?"

She also said: "I devoted six years of pregnancy to having Colette. So I can certainly devote nine years to finding her killer."

From the first days at Kappa Alpha, Jeffrey MacDonald's own mother was a highly visible presence. The nine and a half years of sorrow and fear had rendered her high-strung and gaunt, but her energy and cordiality remained undiminished.

Whether her task for the day was to drive her son to court in the morning, to take his suits out for dry-cleaning, to aid (or sometimes supervise) Segal's student assistants in the downtown office, to replenish beer, wine, and snack food supplies, or simply to listen sympathetically to the defense's account of what sort of day it had been in court (like other witnesses scheduled to testify, she was prohibited from attending trial sessions), she performed with relentless vigor and a cheerfulness which, under the circumstances, seemed almost as remarkable as her son's expressed certainty that the case could not be lost.

When her time to testify did come, Dorothy Mac-Donald impressed all who saw her as a warm, gracious, and courageous human being—the same impression she had made on those who had known her in Patchogue when the MacDonald children were growing up, on those with whom she'd come in contact as a frequent companion to Jeff and Colette after their marriage, and upon all those—including Franz Joseph Grebner, Victor Woerheide, Brian Murtagh, and now Jim Blackburn—with whom her life had been at cross-purposes since her daughter-in-law and grandchildren had been murdered.

No witness—himself included—did more to help Jeffrey MacDonald's cause. Indeed, one juror even remarked after the verdict had been announced that, "I think she swayed many jurors," with her talk of the love that had existed between Jeff and Colette. "By the time she finished," this juror said, "I know that my mind had been changed."

In addition to Dorothy MacDonald, Segal called to the stand more than a dozen other character witnesses. Their composite testimony was that MacDonald was a peaceful, truthful, honorable man who not only had dearly loved his wife and children but who had turned out to be a skilled and compassionate emergency physician at St. Mary's Hospital in Long Beach.

Jim Blackburn did not dispute these assertions. Of most character witnesses, in fact, he asked only a single question: were you inside 544 Castle Drive between the hours of midnight and 4 A.M. on February 17, 1970?

As each replied in the negative, Blackburn nodded politely, turned away, and said, "I have no further questions, your honor."

Segal also called a "mystery witness"—a man from Roanoke, Virginia, who, in February of 1970 had lived within a hundred yards of Castle Drive and who said now, nine and one-half years later, that at about midnight on Monday, February 16, while sitting in his apartment gluing a model plane together (having recently returned from a tour of duty as a helicopter pilot in Vietnam), he had seen two white men and one white woman with long blond hair, all wearing sheets and all carrying candles, walking past his doorway toward Castle Drive.

There was no doubt that his story was intriguing. It

might have been considerably more serviceable, however, if he had told it to investigators on February 17, 1970, rather than waiting nine and a half years. The witness, whose name was James Milne, said the reason he had not mentioned it before was that no one had bothered to ask.

The prosecution did not seem unduly alarmed by Milne's highly publicized appearance. "I don't know that there weren't three such individuals," Brian Murtagh remarked. "They could have been coming home from choir practice."

His implication was clear. The essence of the case against MacDonald remained what it had been from the beginning: what was found inside—not who had been seen outside—544 Castle Drive.

In an attempt to combat this, Segal called a series of witnesses who qualified as experts in the field of criminology. Chief among these was John Thornton, a quiet, bearded, pipe-smoking professor from the University of California at Berkeley. Thornton had been ballyhooed to the press by the defense as "our Stombaugh," but his time on the stand turned out to be an unexpected bonus for the prosecution and also provided the center-stage highlight of the summer for Segal's nemesis, Brian Murtagh.

Thornton, as anticipated, disputed Paul Stombaugh's contention that bloodstains on the sheet found on the master bedroom floor formed the impression either of hands or of a bare human shoulder. Unexpectedly, however, he conceded that other impressions clearly *were* those of the cuffs of Jeffrey and Colette MacDonald's pajama tops.

Bernie Segal tried to explain to reporters that this admission had not been as damaging to the defense as it appeared. "No one can prove when those impressions were made," Segal said. "They're just another of the meaningless facts that exist in this type of complicated case."

When Thornton resumed his testimony, however, he provided the context for an incident, the implications of which no amount of explanation could neutralize.

Thornton's central contention was that Stombaugh had been incorrect in his assertion that the absence of tearing around the forty-eight holes in the pajama top indicated that the top had been stationary at the time the holes had been made.

To substantiate his claim, Thornton cited the result of a laboratory experiment he had performed in California, wrapping cloth identical in composition to the pajama top—65 percent polyester and 35 percent cotton—around "resilient material," then stabbing through the cloth with an icepick while an assistant jerked the resilient material back and forth. The resultant holes, Thornton said, had been perfectly cylindrical, with no elongated tearing around the edges.

Brian Murtagh was handling the cross-examination of Thornton. What, he asked, had been the "resilient material" around which Thornton had wrapped the experimental cloth?

"Ham," Thornton said.

Murtagh had neither the personality nor the courtroom experience to feign amazement in the histrionic manner of Bernie Segal. His astonishment was genuine.

"Ham?" he said. "You took a piece of *ham*? Like in a ham sandwich?"

Ham, Thornton explained, provided the closest possible replication of a human body in terms of its ability to absorb the impact of a thrust.

"Ham!" Murtagh repeated, walking away from the

witness, toward the prosecution table, shaking his head. Some of the jurors began to smile and even titter.

It had not been sliced ham, of course, but a whole ham. Still, ham is ham, and no matter how earnest and erudite John Thornton appeared from that point forward—and his credentials were impeccable, his intelligence above question, his reputation in his field beyond reproach—the image that lingered was of this bearded Californian, with utmost seriousness, wrapping a piece of cloth around a ham and calling that a scientific experiment. It was an image which cast a very slight shadow indeed upon the stark, expansive landscape of Paul Stombaugh's earlier testimony.

At the prosecution table, Murtagh opened a briefcase and took out a blue pajama top. It was not Jeffrey MacDonald's, but it was the same shade of blue and made of material similar to the top MacDonald had worn on the night of the murders. Wordlessly, Murtagh removed his suit jacket and wrapped the pajama top around his wrists, binding his hands.

He was standing directly in front of the jury. With almost catlike quickness, Jim Blackburn, who had sat silently throughout the entire cross-examination of Thornton, picked up the icepick that had been used in the MacDonald murders nine and a half years before.

With Bernie Segal apparently too astonished even to object, Blackburn lunged at Murtagh and began slashing at him with the icepick. Using the pajama top as a shield, Murtagh deflected the blows. That is, he deflected all but one. That one made a small cut in his right arm.

Now, Bernie Segal was on his feet. "Do you need a doctor, Mr. Murtagh?" he said, gesturing toward Jeffrey MacDonald. Murtagh declined the offer of medical aid, though a secretary was dispatched to find a Band-Aid.

When the laughter in the courtroom had subsided, Murtagh held up the pajama top. Many of the holes were elongated, ragged cuts—not perfectly cylindrical punctures.

Two persuasive points had been made. First, when a pajama top is wrapped around someone's wrists and used to fend off icepick blows, the resulting holes will not be round and clean. Second, even in a brief, restrained, courtroom demonstration, Jim Blackburn had been unable to avoid inflicting a puncture wound on Brian Murtagh's forearm.

Had it occurred to the jury to wonder why, in the course of a frenzied attack by intruders in a state of homicidal mania, no similar icepick wounds had been inflicted upon the forearms of Jeffrey MacDonald, though there had been forty-eight punctures in the pajama top which he said he'd had wrapped around his wrists, and which he said he had used as a shield?

John Thornton described the courtroom demonstration as "silly" and "rinky-dink," but John Thornton was not a member of the jury.

With his perimeter overrun and with even his inner lines of defense beginning to crumble, Bernie Segal recognized that the time had come to rush a real "mystery witness" into the breach. Helena Stoeckley had saved him—and Jeffrey MacDonald—once before, in 1970. Maybe she—or the invocation of her—could be made to do so again.

First, Segal subpoenaed Stoeckley's parents. Then Judge Dupree issued a bench warrant for Stoeckley herself on the grounds that she was a material witness in a homicide case.

Stoeckley's parents came to Raleigh and said they did

not know where their daughter was. The last time they had seen her was in early June, when she had come to Fayetteville for a brief visit from a drug rehabilitation center in Columbia, South Carolina. She had said then that she planned to move to the small South Carolina town of Walhalla, to live with a man whom she had met at the rehabilitation center. "I don't know her address," Stoeckley's mother said, "and I don't want to know."

In a private interview with defense attorneys, the mother also said that even if her daughter were found, it was not likely she could contribute much of value to the trial.

"She called up, must have been a year and a half ago, four o'clock in the morning, all befuddled. She said somebody was chasing her and had taken her car keys. Then it turned out she'd had a stroke. We got her home, she was like a vegetable. She couldn't talk, couldn't eat, her face quivered, saliva would run out of her mouth. We put her on a strict diet and let her rest and after about three weeks she was improved, but still she was not quite right."

She had left home again, this time for Daytona, Florida, where she said she planned to work in a hospital. The next thing her parents had heard was that she had been arrested for drunken driving.

"She's had her gallbladder removed," her mother said, "she's had three liver biopsies, and she's been spitting up blood and passing blood in her stools for years. She's not at all like she used to be. She's a physical and mental wreck. She's not even a human being anymore. You find her now, sure she'll talk. She'll always talk. But I'm telling you, she's gonna talk all kinds of nonsense."

Chain-smoking Virginia Slims cigarettes, Helena Stoeckley's mother described her daughter's original reaction to the murders. "It really hurt her. She was a very soft-hearted person and she especially loved little children. She said right away, 'Not a hippie around here would do a thing like that. Everybody's gonna pitch in and find out what happened. We've got to find out who did this.'

"I really believe it was Beasley who first put the idea in her head. Beasley was her Daddy image. He had a terrific amount of influence over her. She told me he had been up to talk to her right after it happened and then she said, 'Yeah, I've been thinking, and I don't really know where I was that night. I might have been there.' And I just knew right then that Daddy Beasley had talked her into it."

Obviously, it would not suit the defense's purposes to put Helena Stoeckley's mother on the witness stand, but Bernie Segal had assembled a cast of additional characters whose testimony seemed more likely to be useful: William Posey the laundry deliveryman, Jane Zillioux and another Nashville neighbor named Red Underhill, and Jim Gaddis of the Nashville police department, as well as the CID polygraph operator who had conducted the 1971 interview with Stoeckley, not to mention Prince Edward Beasley himself—now in retirement and eager to testify about how, nine and a half years earlier, Helena Stoeckley had joked to him about her icepick and had said that in her mind she thought she might have been at 544 Castle Drive while the murders were being committed.

Then word was received that Stoeckley herself had been located: hiding in the back of a trailer on the outskirts of Walhalla, South Carolina. She was immediately transported to Raleigh in the custody of federal agents.

*　　*　　*

At four minutes before ten o'clock on the morning of Thursday, August 16, 1979—exactly one month after the trial of Jeffrey MacDonald had begun, and nine and a half years, to the day, since Monday, February 16, 1970—a day which had ended with her taking mescaline in her driveway on Clark Street in Fayetteville—Helena Stoeckley, escorted by a U.S. marshal, walked into a small office on the ninth floor of the Federal Building in Raleigh, where Bernie Segal was waiting for her, hoping to persuade her to confess.

She was neatly, even demurely attired in white shoes and a floral print dress. Her hair was black, her complexion sallow. She was many pounds overweight. Her eyes were dull and her thin lips unexpressive. She spoke in a soft voice almost entirely devoid of affect. Her left arm was in a cast. It had been broken in Cincinnati, two weeks earlier, when someone had hit her with a tire iron during a dispute involving narcotics. Her fiancé, Ernest Davis, whom she had met in the drug rehabilitation center in Columbia, South Carolina, paced barefoot, unwashed, and unshaved in a small corridor outside the office.

For almost a decade, in Bernie Segal's mind, Helena Stoeckley had been a figure of near-mythic proportion. Now here she was, three feet from him, politely declining his offer of coffee and doughnuts. She would, she said, be grateful for a can of diet soda.

Segal began to speak in a voice so quiet and so gentle that it was as if Helena was sleeping and he did not want to risk awakening her. Yet there was an almost painful intensity to his tone. This woman, he believed, had the power to set Jeffrey MacDonald free and to provide Segal with the greatest triumph of his career. His first words were like surgical instruments. Utilized with the utmost skill and delicacy, they might enable him to stride forth from this room and announce to the judge and the jury—and the press—that there was no need to proceed further with the trial: one of the real killers had just confessed.

Segal had, at his side, an album containing photographs of the crime scene. He placed it on a table before Stoeckley. The first picture was not a particularly horrid one: all it showed was a portion of the kitchen of 544 Castle Drive. There was a calendar hanging on a wall. The top page of the calendar said February 1970.

"See that, Helena?" Segal said softly, leaning so close to her that he could have put his arm around her if he'd desired. "See that calendar? It has been there for nine years. Waiting. Waiting for somebody to tell us how this story should end."

She stared at the picture. There was absolutely no change of expression on her face. She took a sip of diet soda.

"I can't help you," she said tonelessly. "I wasn't in that house. I didn't have anything to do with any of this."

Bernie Segal began to shake his head. "No, Helena. That won't do. You can't get away with that anymore. It's got to end. We are at trial now. The time has come. I'm serious, Helena. You *were* in that house. I know it and you know it. Now let's talk about it. Don't go on punishing yourself."

She stared at the floor, shaking her head, still with no change of expression. "I don't know what you want to know. I was never in that house."

"Helena, believe me," Segal said. "If you talk to me here, if you tell me what happened, I can make this very short and painless. Helena, you can put it behind you

JOE McGINNISS

forever. Now, for your own conscience. And for the sake of that man in the courtroom. That man who has been made to suffer unjustly for nine years.

"And, Helena, you will not be prosecuted. Nothing will happen to you. That I can promise you. The statute of limitations has expired. This is the end, Helena. Right now. Right here. All you have to do is talk to me."

For the first time, Stoeckley looked directly at Bernie Segal. "I can't help you," she said. "I can't tell you things I don't remember."

For nearly two hours, Segal persisted. His tone changed from soothing and protective to harsh and demanding and back again. It made no difference. He might as well have been a morning quiz show. Stoeckley was tuned to his station but she was only a viewer, nothing more. There was nothing he could do or say to move her.

"Helena, people have gone to the electric chair for having said *one-tenth* of what you've said about this case! *I've got six witnesses!* People to whom you've already confessed! They're waiting in the next room. One after another, I'm going to put them on the stand and have them tell the jury what you've told them. Then, by law, I have to put you on the stand."

She looked at him coolly. In silence.

"Helena, the choice is yours."

"I can't help you."

"Helena, remember what you told Jane Zillioux? 'The blood . . . the blood . . . I remember the blood on my hands!'"

She shook her head. "I don't remember ever saying that."

"Do you think Jane Zillioux is lying?"

"I didn't say that. I just said I don't remember saying

that." Still, there was no inflection, no spark—not even of resentment—in her voice. "Do you realize how much drugs I've taken since that happened? I'm not gonna sit there and say yes to things I didn't say, or things I don't remember saying. Besides," she said, "how do you know he's not guilty?"

Segal returned to the albums of crime scene and autopsy photographs. He turned to a picture of Kimberly. A picture that showed the fracture of her skull and the piece of cheekbone protruding through the skin of her face.

"That was his flesh and blood, Helena. What kind of father could do that to his own flesh and blood?"

"Somebody on drugs could do something like that. Not acid. Maybe speed. Did they do blood tests on him right away?"

"Yes, Helena. They did blood tests. There were no drugs, there was no alcohol."

"Has he been given psychiatric evaluation and everything?"

"Yes, Helena, he has been given all of that." Segal flipped to a picture of Colette. "Look at his wife, Helena. Look at this picture. Her jaw was broken. Both of her arms were broken. Her skull was fractured right down the middle. She was stabbed—with a knife, with an icepick—dozens of times. Helena, that was the work of a repulsive, crazy person. Dr. MacDonald is a normal, decent human being. Even the Army psychiatrists who examined him agreed to that."

Segal turned to a picture of Kristen. A colored picture, taken before the body had been removed from the bed. The bright red of her blood filled the room.

"Only somebody crazy or whacked out on drugs could have done something like that," Stoeckley said. "I don't know what anybody else is capable of, but I know I'm not capable of that."

"Helena, no one is asking you to say that you did that. You will not be touched. I promise you. You will not be indicted, ever. All you have to say is you were there, holding the candle. Saying, 'Acid is groovy.' You don't remember hurting anybody. Then you ran out the back door."

He turned to another picture of Kimberly. "Helena, help us end it. I beg of you. Look at this child's face. For God's sake. To accuse the father of these babies of having done that to them . . . Helena, look at this! Look at this one. Smashed with a club. Come on, Helena, how much longer will that man have to sit there, accused of something so monstrous. You have it in your power, Helena, to end it. Right now. Otherwise, Helena, I guarantee you: I am going to take you into court."

"If I could remember," she told him, "I would say."

Segal stepped into an adjacent room, where his other witnesses had been waiting. One by one, like the ghosts of Christmas past, he brought them in to confront her with the things she had said to them years before. Beasley. Gaddis. Zillioux. Underhill. The polygraph man, whose name was Brisentine. And finally her ex-neighbor, Posey.

None of it mattered. She said hello. She said, nice to see you, how've you been? But whenever they asked her about the MacDonald case, she said "I don't remember any of that."

One by one, the witnesses trooped out of the room. Segal was admitting defeat. There would be no dramatic announcement. There would be no news bulletins on TV. No eight-column headlines across page one. There would just be a truculent, uncommunicative, apathetic witness—thirty pounds overweight and looking far less menacing than pathetic—telling the jury she didn't remember a thing.

Now, too late, Bernie Segal realized he would have been better off if she'd never been found. Much easier to have conjured up the image of a drug-crazed and murderous hippie from the distant and dangerous past and to have the jury seize upon that as an explanation than to present them with this burned-out woman and expect them to believe that she had ever stood over a couch on which Jeffrey MacDonald had been sleeping and had held a candle beneath her face while chanting, "Acid is groovy . . . Kill the pigs . . . Acid and rain . . ."

Segal left her, in the company of her fiancé, the barefoot and bedraggled Ernest Davis, while he went to inform the judge that he had completed his witness interview and that he was prepared for the trial to resume.

It was now lunchtime. Helena Stoeckley had been given a bologna sandwich. She sat quietly, placidly, chewing her food and slowly turning the pages of the crime scene and autopsy photo albums, as if she were browsing through a movie magazine.

On the witness stand, under oath, Helena Stoeckley denied that she had ever been found by a psychiatrist to be mentally ill or that she had ever been committed to a mental institution. This was, of course, untrue. She had been a psychiatric patient at the University of North Carolina medical center in the spring of 1971 and had been diagnosed as a paranoid schizophrenic, subject to delusions and hallucinations.

In describing her educational background, Stoeckley said she had attended Aquinas Junior College in Nashville during 1971 and 1972 and had studied police science there. In 1974, she said, she had taken a six-month operating room technician's course at a Fayetteville hospital. In 1975, at Daytona Beach Junior College, she said, she had taken nursing courses.

She then described the extent of her narcotics addiction during the early months of 1970. She had been injecting heroin and liquid opium intravenously six to seven times per day. She had also smoked marijuana and hashish on a daily basis; had consumed LSD "almost daily," and mescaline "about twice a week," in addition to using barbiturates and "angel dust."

On Monday, February 16, 1970, she had followed her usual partem of drug consumption, topping it off with the tablet of mescaline given to her in her driveway by a soldier from Fort Bragg named Greg. She recalled reentering her apartment after having consumed the mescaline but said she remembered nothing after that until her return to the apartment at about 4:30 or 5 A.M., in a blue car with "two or three" soldiers from Fort Bragg. She said she could recall neither the owner of the car nor any of the other passengers.

She said she did not recall ever telling anyone that she thought she might have been involved in the MacDonald murders—only that she could not remember where she had been during the time that the murders had taken place. She added: "All I said to the CID whenever I talked to them was I didn't know where I was at that time."

This was by no means the startling testimony for which Bernie Segal had been hoping. It seemed, in fact, actively harmful to his case. Segal lost further ground when, on cross-examination, Jim Blackburn extracted from Stoeckley the remark that she had worn her blond wig "infrequently," and that she had not been wearing it on the night of Monday, February 16, because Greg, who had given her the mescaline, did not like it.

She also said she had never been inside 544 Castle Drive and that she had never seen Jeffrey MacDonald until that very morning when she had entered the courtroom to testify.

As Blackburn's cross-examination continued, Stoeckley came to seem more like the star witness for the prosecution than for the defense.

"To your own knowledge," he asked her quietly, "did you participate in the killings of the MacDonald family?"

"No, sir."

"How do you feel toward children?"

"I love children."

"Of your own personal knowledge, did you kill Colette MacDonald?"

"No, sir."

"How about Kristen?"

"No, sir."

"How about Kimberly?"

"No, sir."

"Did you try to kill Dr. MacDonald?"

"No, sir."

"Do you know who did?"

"No, sir."

"Do you recall ever being in the MacDonald apartment carrying a candle?"

"No, sir."

She also said that the night of February 16–17, 1970, had been by no means either the first or the last night on which she could not recall her whereabouts or activities. Given the level of narcotics she had been consuming at the time, this remark seemed her most clearly credible statement of the day.

Flustered and frustrated, Bernie Segal knew that the jury would have to hear—as soon as possible—from those to whom Helena Stoeckley had told a different tale. It was time for the parade of the Stoeckley witnesses—a last, desperate attempt to reincarnate the spirit of evil hippies. The prosecution, however, had no intention of standing idly by, mere spectators at such a parade. They, in fact, sought to have the marching orders countermanded.

In a criminal trial, when a witness is called to testify, he is, in general, permitted to speak only of what he did or had done to him directly, or of what he personally observed.

Were Helena Stoeckley to have told the jury that she remembered standing over the couch in the living room of 544 Castle Drive holding a candle, there might have been some question about how much weight the jury would have been inclined to give her testimony, but no dispute whatsoever regarding her right to deliver it.

Whether it was equally proper for police officers Beasley or Gaddis or polygraph operator Brisentine or laundryman Posey, or ex-Nashville neighbors Zillioux and Underhill to relate what Stoeckley had told *them*, was a somewhat more complicated question.

Rule 804 (b) (3) of the Federal Rules of Evidence, which govern procedures in federal court, says, "A statement tending to expose the declarant to criminal liability and offered to exculpate the accused is not admissible unless corroborating circumstances clearly indicate the trustworthiness of the statement."

Out of the hearing of the jury, Judge Dupree heard the six "Stoeckley witnesses" describe what she had told them concerning her possible involvement. Having al-

ready heard Stoeckley say she had no recollections of
having participated in the murders, he had now to decide whether the jury should hear statements also from
those to whom she had been less unequivocal.

Understandably, the prosecution thought such "hearsay" evidence ought not to be admitted. Even more understandably, Bernie Segal believed the statements of
these witnesses to be crucial to his defense. At the Kappa
Alpha house, in light-hearted moments, he would hand
out pens that said, "Your Criminal Lawyer: A Reasonable
Doubt At A Price That's Right," and it was reasonable
doubt—not absolute proof of innocence—for which he
was striving now.

In conference with Judge Dupree, Brian Murtagh
said that the statements of the Stoeckley witnesses, "because of their inherent lack of credibility" and because
they were hearsay, ought not to be deemed admissible.

"We have no physical evidence whatsoever to tie her
to the crime scene," Murtagh said. "You know, you say,
'Well, why do you think you were there?' and she says,
'Because I think I was there.' You know, you go round in
circles on that."

Bernie Segal was reaching new heights of indignation.
"The fact that the government might want to attack her
statement," he told Judge Dupree, "does not deny the
defendant the right to introduce it. If it was the United
States prosecuting someone for murder and it had these
kinds of statements and so-called admissions by the defendant, would the court for a moment hesitate to let the
government introduce it?

"I find it difficult to believe that any court would hesitate to let the government put it in. The fact that someone is crying and weeping when they are talking about a
murder that is horrendous does not make it inadmissible.

"The fact that later on they say, 'I would like to pull it back and withdraw it,' can't affect admissibility. It goes to weight. That is the issue.

"We want everything that she said to come out. The fact that she both admits and denies, in my judgment and my experience, has never precluded a confession or admission from being put into evidence.

"Many a defendant has said, you know, to the police officer while being taken to the station, 'Yeah, I was involved.' Then he gets to the station and they get a formal statement. 'Oh, no, I will not admit that on paper,' the defendant screams. 'You cannot let that thing in. I mean, I said I didn't do it.' The court says, 'It's for the jury to decide which statements are admissible.'

"Why is the defendant here now being told that after he has done the job that should have been done by somebody else, he can't offer the evidence? It just seems to me that we have established beyond any reasonable argument the right to put this forward."

Responding, Brian Murtagh once again quoted that portion of Federal Rule 804 (b) (3) which pertained to trustworthiness of the statements. "Your honor," he said, "first of all, Ms. Stoeckley's statements are not clearly admissions of guilt. If anything, what they are is what has been brought out on direct and cross-examination: that the woman doesn't know where she was that night; that she was being constantly interrogated by the police; and that she began to have fears about not being able to account for where she was.

"And these statements cannot be taken out of that context and out of the context that the woman has been a drug addict, has had hepatitis, has been incoherent and—to use the description of one of the witnesses—hysterical. So it seems to me that these statements are not trustworthy, and they certainly are being offered to exculpate the accused."

Without commenting on whether or not her testimony at trial had seemed believable, Judge Dupree said, "I think her incompetency at the time she made at least some of the statements attributed to her has been more than adequately established."

"Your honor," Segal said, "I dare to disagree. As a matter of fact, there is a certain internal consistency that always has impressed me about what she has said. Now, while I truthfully do not think there is any evidence that Helena Stoeckley inflicted an injury, there is clearly evidence in my mind from all these witnesses that she carried a candle and was present."

Brian Murtagh would not budge. "Your honor," he said, "we are talking about whether a reasonable person making these statements at the time would so appreciate the gravity of the statements that they wouldn't make them unless they meant them.

"I don't think we have that in this case. What we are talking about here is somebody who is hysterical, perhaps hallucinating. Under those conditions, she makes various statements. Now, those statements are never of an unequivocal nature. It can all be drawn back to her lack of an alibi and the fact that she is constantly being interviewed, picked up, hassled by the police, and having to account for her whereabouts. I think you can't take it out of that context.

"And I still think, Judge, that the issue here is that the rule mandates that the statements should not be admitted unless there are corroborative circumstances which clearly indicate their trustworthiness. And I just don't see how Mr. Segal can argue that these various statements which are all over the lot are trustworthy or unequivocal."

"Your honor," Segal replied, "we are talking about the denial of the right of a defendant to show that there is evidence that could raise a reasonable doubt on his behalf, because it tends to show the involvement of someone else. Remember, that is all his burden is. And I think the fact that a great range of witnesses, coming from every side—police officers, people who do not know this person, people who wanted to help the person—this broad range of people coming forward to say that she has made statements which have the tendency to involve her in the crime are statements that deserve to be heard by the jury.

"And, as my last observation, your honor, I do say that these crimes were not committed by reasonable people. These acts are unreasonable. These acts are so consistent with the kind of culture, the kind of persons that Ms. Stoeckley was involved with, that they in themselves tend to be corroborative. I think we have a tendency—in our own sanity—to lose sight of the fact that we are dealing with, truly, acts of monstrous insanity."

"Your honor," said Brian Murtagh, "they've had Helena Stoeckley herself on the stand for the better part of the day. I think she was more than cooperative with both sides. The basic issue here is that the defendant has not been prejudiced by the exclusion of Helena Stoeckley's testimony. She was asked point-blank on the stand the sixty-four-dollar question about whether she was there or whether she did it. I think we have more than satisfied constitutional requirements in that regard. These further statements are not her statements, they are the statements of other witnesses, and I do not believe they meet the applicable standard of trustworthiness as specified in 804 (b) (3)."

It was four o'clock on Friday afternoon, the last hour

of the last day of the fifth week of the trial. Franklin T. Dupree said, "The Court will rule on this motion Monday morning at 10 A.M. Take a recess until that hour, please."

Helena Stoeckley spent the weekend in Raleigh, Bernie Segal still hoping that he might be able to turn her presence to advantage. Using Jeffrey MacDonald's money, he obtained a room for her and her fiancé at a motel called the Journey's End.

On Sunday morning, Segal received a phone call from the manager of the motel. She said that someone had just tried to drown Helena Stoeckley in the swimming pool. Segal immediately dispatched a female assistant—a San Francisco attorney named Wendy Rouder—to the scene.

Rouder was told that it had been Stoeckley's fiancé, Ernie Davis, who had been holding her head under water in the pool. In addition to her broken arm, Stoeckley, by Sunday morning, had a swollen and blackened eye where it appeared that someone had punched her. She told Rouder that this had occurred the day before when she had stepped into a hallway to buy a can of soda from a machine and a complete stranger had walked up to her and struck her.

Rouder, concerned that Ernie Davis, perhaps, was not reacting well to recent stresses, and fearing that he might have been the cause of the black eye as well as the "drowning" attempt, persuaded him to step into the motel corridor while she spoke privately to Stoeckley for a moment.

"Helena, do you want him to leave?" Rouder asked.

"Yes," Stoeckley said. "I want him to go." She immediately began placing his clothes and personal belongings in a suitcase, adding, as well, all the motel ashtrays she could find.

Red Underhill had accompanied Rouder to the Journey's End and was prepared to see Davis to the bus terminal and to give him twenty dollars (of Jeffrey MacDonald's money) for a one-way ticket out of town.

"Will you be all right?" Rouder asked. "Or would you like somebody to stay with you?"

Stoeckley said she would prefer to have a companion. "How about you?" she asked Rouder. "Could you stay?"

Rouder agreed to spend at least the afternoon with Helena Stoeckley, but left the room briefly to permit Stoeckley to inform her fiancé privately that his presence in Raleigh was no longer desired. Ten minutes later, the door swung open and Davis, bare-chested and carrying the suitcase, ran down the hall.

Reentering the room, Rouder and Red Underhill found Stoeckley in the bathroom, bleeding profusely from the nose. She said no, Davis had not hit her, she had simply walked into a door.

With Stoeckley holding towels to her nose and tilting her head back in an attempt to get the bleeding to stop, Wendy Rouder spent the afternoon with her in her motel room. As the bleeding gradually subsided, Stoeckley and Rouder began to talk. It was mostly small talk—Stoeckley described to Rouder how she had had, at one time, a magnificent singing voice, and how, had it not been for the stroke she had suffered, she might have had a career in opera.

Eventually, there came a lull in the conversation. Then Stoeckley said, "I still think I could have been there that night."

"What makes you think so?" Rouder asked.

"I don't know." There was another pause. Then

Stoeckley said, "That rocking horse. That rocking horse in Kristen's room." Seeing the toy horse depicted in one of the crime scene photographs had brought back to Stoeckley a flash—of memory? of imagination?—in which she had been sitting on the horse, trying to ride it, but had been unable to, because "the wheels were broken and it wouldn't roll." (The rocking horse, as it happened, had been on runners, not wheels.)

Then, after another pause, Stoeckley added, "You know, Kristen. Kristen Jean. Those pictures. When I looked at those pictures, I knew I had seen her somewhere before."

Rouder kept talking to Stoeckley throughout the afternoon, taking notes on the conversation. At one point, she asked if Stoeckley still felt guilt about her involvement.

"Of course," Stoeckley replied. "What do you think I have taken all these damn drugs for?"

"If MacDonald were convicted," Rouder asked, "do you think you could live with that guilt, too?"

"I don't think so."

"Isn't there anything you could do to get rid of the guilt?"

"Maybe sodium pentathol, or hypnosis, or something," Stoeckley said.

The conversation was interrupted by the manager of the Journey's End, who called to say that Stoeckley was no longer welcome at the motel.

A room was obtained for her at a nearby Hilton. Later in the afternoon, as Rouder and Stoeckley sat together in an automobile, en route from one motel to the other, Stoeckley again said, "I still think I was there in that house that night."

"Helena, is that a feeling you are having or a memory?" Rouder asked.

"It's a memory," Stoeckley said. "I remember stand-ing at the couch, holding a candle, only, you know, it wasn't dripping wax. It was dripping blood."

Punctual as always, Judge Dupree strode quickly into the courtroom Monday morning and immediately asked to see counsel for both sides at the bench.

"Since court adjourned on Friday afternoon," he said, "I have spent a substantial portion of my waking hours researching and deciding the rather interesting eviden-tiary question which was posed—the question being whether statements by the witness Stoeckley should be admissible through other witnesses—statements made outside of court in far distant times.

"I will rule," he continued, "that these proposed statements do not comply with the trustworthy requi-sites of 804 (b) (3). In fact, far from being clearly cor-roborated and trustworthy, they are about as unclearly trustworthy—or, clearly untrustworthy, let me say—as any statements that I have ever seen or heard.

"This witness, in her examination and cross-examination here in court, has been, to use the government counsel's terminology, 'all over the lot.' The statements which she has made out of court were 'all over the lot,' also, so it can't really be said that the hearing of those statements would lead to any different conclusion than what the ju-rors got while she was here in open court.

"This testimony, I think, has no trustworthiness at all. Here you have a girl who, when she made the state-ments, was, in most instances heavily drugged, if not hal-lucinating. And she has told us that herself. She has stated that in person. I think that this evidence would tend to confuse the issues, mislead the jury, cause undue delay, and be a waste of time. She has already told this jury everything that you proposed to show by these witnesses.

"And, Mr. Segal, let me say that I did not reach this decision lightly. I spent roughly seven hours on this thing on Saturday. I spent the entire day Sunday until 11:30 last night wrestling with this thing. And, as I do routinely in criminal cases—I lean over backwards to make sure that no criminal defendant is ever deprived of a defense.

"But I am thoroughly convinced in my own mind that your position is without merit with respect to this particular evidence. I have ruled on it, and as I say, I did not reach that lightly because I am risking a terrible lot of judge time and juror time down the road if I make an error and it has to be retried. But I am confident of my position on this one."

Even in the face of Dupree's decision, Bernie Segal clutched at one final straw: the weekend's events involving Stoeckley and his assistant, Wendy Rouder. Not only had Stoeckley implicated herself in the MacDonald murders the day after they had occurred in 1970, she had done so again *within the preceding twenty-four hours*. Surely the jury was entitled to hear from Wendy Rouder about Stoeckley's remarks, and, in particular, about her professed fear of testifying truthfully in open court.

"I would ask the court," Segal said, "to consider the circumstances under which these most recent statements were made. There is no indication of hysteria, no indication of drug abuse, no indication of anything other than the fact that these statements were made because they weighed heavily on the mind of this person.

"The statements were made at Ms. Stoeckley's initiative and it seems to me that they so clearly reflect upon her state of mind that they ought to be heard again now. I think that if this testimony is heard, the jury would be in a far better position to make a determination as to evaluating Ms. Stoeckley's testimony, which we all struggled so hard to get. I think that all the instincts that surround this case cry out—*Let us know what Helena Stoeckley has said.*"

It was Jim Blackburn who responded this time, repeating that, as Murtagh had argued Friday afternoon, "statements by Helena Stoeckley are not trustworthy. They simply are not credible. And I would also say to your honor, in regard to the question of 'reasonableness'— she stated that the candle was dripping not wax but dripping blood. Candles, of course, don't drip blood."

"I don't know," Judge Dupree said. "With Helena they may. I remain of the opinion," he continued, "that this Stoeckley girl is, I think, one of the most tragic figures that I have ever had appear in court. She is extremely paranoid about this particular thing, and what she tells here in court and what she tells witnesses, or lawyers in a motel room, simply cannot have attached to it any credibility at all in my opinion.

"And, incidentally, Mr. Segal, I'm glad you mentioned it because I had neglected to tell you—just completely overlooked it—but I want you to know that among others called by Helena, she called me twice on Saturday night stating that she was living in mortal dread of physical harm by Bernard Segal, counsel for the defendant, and that she wanted a lawyer to represent her.

"I think the jury has got as clear a picture of this particular witness as they will ever have, even if you brought in not just Friday's six witnesses or your new one today, or even a whole wagonload of people—everybody that you ever talked to about this thing.

"I will exclude the evidence. Let the jury come in."

And so the trial of Jeffrey MacDonald continued, with the focus now, in the sixth week, shifting directly to the defendant himself.

4

On the evening before he was to testify, Jeffrey MacDonald, as was his custom, ran five miles around the North Carolina State University track. Summer vacation was drawing to a close and the NC State football team had already progressed to that stage of preseason practice in which physical contact had begun. MacDonald joked that if the trial were to drag on much longer, he would have to treat his legal staff to season tickets to NC State football games.

Bernie Segal and Wade Smith were sitting in a small room, waiting for MacDonald. They had sent out for pizza an hour before and the oil was now beginning to seep through the bottom of the cardboard box and to congeal on the tops of the lukewarm slices.

"Close that door," Segal said, once MacDonald had entered the room. "Lock it. Put a DO NOT DISTURB sign on the door." This was, in Segal's mind, the most important night of the summer—the most important night of the past nine years—the night he prepared Jeffrey MacDonald to testify.

With MacDonald already edgy and impatient, Segal began to outline the tactic he intended to employ on direct examination. "Jeff, I know it is going to be extremely painful for you, but tomorrow I really want the jury to meet the victims. Tomorrow, I am going to bring Colette and Kimmy and Kristy into that courtroom as living, breathing human beings. I've got the pictures, Jeff. I've got them from your mother. Pictures of the girls dressed up to go trick-or-treating on Halloween. A picture of Kimmy sitting on your lap while you were studying for a medical exam. A picture of the girls on the pony with you standing right alongside. A picture of Colette in the backyard, just outside 544 Castle Drive, repainting a piece of furniture.

"I'm going to show you those pictures tomorrow, Jeff. I've got them in slide form and I'm going to show them on a screen so the jury will be able to see them, too. I want the jury to see not only the pictures, but also to see you seeing them.

"And then, Jeff, I'm going to make you look at some of the crime scene photographs. Some of what you saw in those first moments after the murders. Some of what you've been trying to forget for nine years."

"Terrific, Bernie," MacDonald said, sarcastically. "Jesus Christ! Why don't you just hire four people to club me and stab me while you're at it."

"Jeff, listen to me. You are the client. This is your life, not my life, at stake. If you really don't want to do it, I won't do it. But I need those pictures. I want that jury to see your family. I want them to see *people*, not just a collection of fibers and hairs and bloodstains.

"This case, Jeff, is unique. Normally, you want the jury to forget the victims. You want to ignore them during the defense. Here, our goal is just the opposite. We want them to go into that room to deliberate with one thought and one thought only on their minds: '*This* man did *that* to *those people?*'"

"Jesus, Bernie, after six weeks of telling me the prosecution case isn't worth shit, now it sounds like you're saying I've got to sit up there and prove my innocence."

"No, no, no," Segal said. "Don't misunderstand. I think we could rest right now and win. There is no case against you. There never was, there never will be. That is just as true now as it was the first day I said it. But I don't want that one holdout juror to make us go through all this again."

"Which one?" MacDonald said. "You mean the former state cop with that pinched mouth and nasty eyes, or that accountant with the purple splotches on his hands who's been looking at me for six weeks like he's a member of the KKK and I'm a nigger he just caught molesting his daughter, or do you mean that weepy woman in the first row who looks at Blackburn like she's praying he'll propose marriage to her every time he turns in her direction."

"Jeff, Jeff," Segal said. "We have wound up with exactly the jury we want. Our system has worked. There is absolutely no question about it. I understand that you're getting antsy. I understand it's been a long six weeks. But please don't start second-guessing our judgment now. It won't do us any good and it will only make the next few days even harder on yourself."

"What do you mean *now?* I've been telling you this from the start. I said it the very first day. Those weren't jurors you were choosing, they were twelve nails for my coffin."

"Listen, Jeff, we're not here tonight to talk about the jury. We're here to talk about you, and about what you're going to say tomorrow and about the way in which I want you to say it. And it's exactly this attitude you're displaying right now—the sarcasm, the bitterness, the snide remarks—that I want to be sure the jury never gets to see.

"So get it out of your system tonight. That's fine. Sharpshoot us. Only you'd better not do it on the stand when Blackburn starts to cross-examine you. You don't have to be Laurence Olivier. You don't have to sell them a bill of goods. Just be yourself and you'll be fine. But I want you to look *past* Blackburn—look *at* the jury. They're the ones you're talking to, not him."

"Blackburn," MacDonald muttered. "He's a chicken shit. He's got no guts at all."

"All right, Jeff, all right," Segal said. "The problem is, at the grand jury you came across as abrupt, cocky, chauvinistic, sarcastic, and callous about women. Here, you have to be a little humble. If the jury sees that you're getting impatient with Blackburn, they might feel that you could also have been impatient with your children, and that is an impression that we certainly don't want them to develop."

"So what happens when he asks me why I went into the Green Berets? You don't want me to tell him it's because I love to strangle people with piano wire?"

"No, Jeff," Segal said patiently. "I don't want you to talk about piano wire."

"And if he asks me if I've got any homosexual leanings, I'll say, 'Well, I have been noticing your nice, tight ass, Mr. Blackburn.'"

"Jeff, will you please listen!" Segal said. "For one last time—for the sake of the rest of your life—you will have to be patient with a prosecutor who has never experienced the loss of his own wife and children. We all know there is a lot of pain here. All we're trying to get across is that it should not come out as anger. As I said to you in the letter I wrote you in June, you want to convey feelings that are appropriate to the occasion. Just focus on the jury. Forget Blackburn. Forget Freddy. Forget how much Murtagh has gotten under your skin."

"Murtagh is a turd. I hate him."

"Yes, Jeff, but letting everybody in the courtroom recognize that is not what you want to do. You can't afford to come across as arrogant."

"Or as a homicidal psychopath, I suppose."

"Jeff, this is exactly what happened at the grand jury. The jury will not be sympathetic with someone who is overtly, and consistently, belligerent. That's how Woerheide pissed all over you at the grand jury."

"Woerheide! That Nazi."

"All right, Jeff. There's no point in belaboring this any further. I've known you for nine years and I know that you're smarter than you're acting right now. Just remember that you've got people on that jury who like you and who want to help you, and who are charged up to help you. Tomorrow, you've just got to give them the ammunition. On direct exam, I'm warning you, I'm going to go straight for your emotions. I'm going to reduce you to a slobbering mess. I'm going to show you every picture you've never wanted to see, and I'm going to ask you every question that you've never wanted to answer. I'm going to leave you with the jury in the palm of your hand. And all I want to tell you, before you leave here right now so that Wade and I can get to work on specifics, is that we want you to come out of the cross-exam sounding like the same person you were on direct. It's that consistency that will make you believable. You'll score no points with overt bitterness. Once you're ac-

quitted, I don't care what kind of names you call anybody at the press conference on the front steps of the
courthouse, but tomorrow, I implore you, for the sake of
the rest of your life, don't be snotty."

"All right," MacDonald said, standing up. "I appreciate all the advice. And I only have one piece of advice to
give you about how to handle the direct examination."

"What's that?" Segal asked.

"Go easy on the pony, Bernie. After all those character witnesses, if they hear about that pony one more time
they're gonna puke."

At 10:01 A.M. on Thursday, August 23, 1979, Jeffrey
MacDonald took the witness stand. For nine and a half
years, he had been telling his story—to the military police at 544 Castle Drive in the early morning hours of
February 17, 1970, to ambulance drivers, orderlies, and
doctors at Womack Hospital, to Ron Harrison and to
the CID and FBI later that morning, to his own mother
and to Freddy and Mildred Kassab that afternoon, to
Grebner, Shaw, and Ivory at CID headquarters on April
6, 1970, to the Philadelphia psychiatrist later that
month, to the reporter from *Newsday* later that summer,
to the Army psychiatrists at Walter Reed, to Colonel
Rock at the closed Article 32 hearing, to Dick Cavett
and a nationwide television audience shortly after his
discharge from the Army, to Pruett and Kearns in February and March of 1971, to the grand jury for a total of
six days in August of 1974 and January of 1975, and in
a hypnotist's office in Beverly Hills in early July—but
this was the first time he had ever told it in public, under
oath, and it was the time that could determine whether
he would spend the rest of his life as a free man, or as a
prisoner.

"Doctor MacDonald," Bernie Segal began, "where do you reside, please?"

"In Huntington Beach, California."

"Doctor MacDonald," Segal said softly, "are you married today?"

"No," MacDonald said, biting his lip and looking as if he were about to cry.

"Is there some reason why you are not married?"

With that, the sobs began to come from MacDonald's throat. "I can't forget my wife and children," he managed to say.

"Do you still have occasion to think about your family, even though it has been nine and a half years since they died?"

"Every day," he sobbed.

Segal's tone and manner were that of a funeral director, about to assist a grief-stricken widow to a limousine. "May I ask, Doctor MacDonald," he said, appearing embarrassed by the necessity of speaking at all, "what are your strongest or most consistent memories of your wife, Colette?"

Jeffrey MacDonald, who had been through it so many times, for so long, had to make himself go through it one more time. He rubbed his eyes with his hand, as if wiping away tears, and he began to glance helplessly around the courtroom, as if hoping that someone could come and save him from all this. Then the sobs came again, preventing him from answering immediately. It was demeanor quite different from that which he'd last displayed in a Raleigh courtroom, when, at the end of his grand jury testimony, he had told Victor Woerheide to shove all his fucking evidence right up his ass.

"Excuse me," MacDonald said, momentarily regaining his composure. "Colette was very beautiful and intelligent and warm. She was a great mother and wife."

"May I ask, Dr. MacDonald, what are your strongest memories of your daughter Kimberly?"

"Of her beauty and brightness," MacDonald said. "She was very inquisitive, I think exceptionally bright—a delightful person, and very loving."

"Can you share with us, please," Segal continued, "what are your memories of your daughter Kristen?"

"Well, she was the prettiest of all of us. She was a little ball of fire. She was a tomboy at two and a half and she was very loving also."

He covered his face with his hands, and his shoulders began to heave as sobbing sounds came from his throat. It was all that Bernie Segal could have wanted.

"What sort of things did you and your family—the four of you, including the children—what sort of things did you do together?"

"We lived together," MacDonald said. "We shared most everything. We had a good life. We were all friends. Colette and I shared the children growing up. We shared our life experience."

It went on that way for almost five hours, not including the morning recess, the break for lunch, and the afternoon recess. Segal had MacDonald read the printed message in the Valentine card that Colette had given him from Kimberly and Kristen ("To a Wonderful Daddy: Dad, there are millions of daddies in the world, it's true, but the nicest by far is you"), and he had MacDonald read the Valentine card that Kimberly had made for him in school ("I'll trim my little Valentine with hearts and ribbons gay, to tell you I love you, today and every day"), and he showed MacDonald a series of enlarged photographs—visible also to the jury—and asked him to identify each one. "This is Colette and I when we were getting married. . . . This is Colette and I when Colette was pregnant in Chicago. . . . That's me with Kimberly as a baby in Princeton. . . . That's Kimberly. . . . That's Kimberly and I on a couch in Chicago. . . . That's Colette playing with Kimmy. . . . That's Kimmy and I studying for an examination in medical school. . . . That's Kristy, probably about eighteen months old. . . . That's Colette and I at my mom's home. . . . That's Kimmy and I holding ice—I was playing in a football game the day before and had a bruise on my face, and Kimmy and I were both applying ice. . . . That's Colette and Kim swimming. . . . That's Colette and I at a Princeton football game. . . . That's Kimmy and I at the children's zoo in Chicago. . . . That's Kim and I playing at the beach—I was just covering her up with sand. . . . That's Colette, Kim, and Kristy. It is Christmastime. That is my family."

"About what year?" Segal asked.

"Nineteen sixty-nine."

"The last Christmas you and your family spent together?"

"Yes."

"Finally, I want to show you this photograph—the last of the series. Tell us what it depicts and what you know about it."

"That is Kim and Kris."

"Are the girls dressed up in some kind of costumes, Dr. MacDonald?" Segal asked, his own voice now seeming close to the breaking point.

MacDonald, sobbing again, was unable to answer. All he could do was nod.

"Would that be Halloween of 1969?"

"Yes."

"Do you see the clothing that Kristen MacDonald is wearing?"

"Yes."

"What is it, Dr. MacDonald?"

"Pajamas made up like a clown."

"The same pajamas that she was wearing on the night of February 17, 1970?"

"Apparently so."

"Your daughter Kimberly—is she wearing some kind of nightgown also?"

Again appearing unable to speak, MacDonald nodded.

"Can you tell us what it reads across the top of the nightgown, please?"

"Little Angel," MacDonald said, and then he, Segal, and a number of others in the courtroom, which was filled to capacity, began to cry openly.

Among those who did not cry were Freddy and Mildred Kassab, who were seated in the front row. Grinning sardonically, Kassab shook his head from side to side, and uttered the word *faker* loud enough so he could be heard across the aisle.

During the course of the morning and afternoon, MacDonald said, at various times, that Colette had been "ecstatic" at the news that he had decided to enlist in the Army ("She thought it was great"), that he had very much wanted their third child to be a boy, because "I thought it was fair that we had one boy," and that both he and Colette had felt that his proposed thirty-day trip to Russia with the boxing team "was an advantage and sort of a privilege, and a good time, and an honor. She was not reluctant in the least."

Segal did not question MacDonald in detail about the

apparent discrepancies between his account of February 17 and the physical evidence found inside the apartment. ("The government, like hounds to the fray, will leap at that tomorrow," he said later. "It was not part of what I wanted to do.") He did, however, elicit from his client the information that MacDonald was "not certain at all" about the exact details of what had transpired. "I have never been certain," MacDonald said. "I have never told anyone I was certain. It is extremely vague. There is a lot of confusing thoughts. There is a lot of sounds, and there is a lot of sights, and the recollection is hazy, at best."

Segal made MacDonald look at the crime scene photographs, and asked him if they were an accurate representation of what he had seen.

"All I remember is a lot of blood," he said, looking at a colored picture of Colette's battered body on the floor. "She looked bloodier than that to me."

When shown similar pictures of each of his daughters, MacDonald said, "That is Kimmy," and also identified Kristen—much as his neighbor, the warrant officer, had done nine and a half years before.

"What did you do there, in Kristen's room," Segal asked, "on this second trip?"

"I only recall doing one thing." MacDonald, throughout the day, had never been far from tears—or at least from the appearance of them—and now he was, once again, on the edge.

"What was that?" Segal asked softly.

"I patted her on the head and said she'd be okay." His voice trailed off into a sob.

"I'm sorry," Segal said. "I heard you say that you patted her on the head but did not hear the words."

"He said she'd be okay!" Franklin Dupree interjected

sharply, glaring at Segal with an expression of obvious distaste.

Later, Segal asked MacDonald to describe what his life had been like following the dismissal of charges against him and his honorable discharge from the Army.

"I don't really remember the last part of the month of December. It was kind of depressing with Christmas coming up. I was seeing friends and friends were trying to see me and we were also trying to reopen the investigation. We were making trips to Washington, D.C. I was having meetings with congressmen and senators and newspaper people and TV people. There were people trying to write a book about the case. It was a very confusing and depressing time."

"When you went to New York City, what were your plans for the future? What were you going to do with the rest of your life?"

"Well, I was trying to figure that out. The plans that Colette and I had always had, you know, they were shattered."

"Well, what were the factors that caused you to give up your goal of taking a residency at Yale and going to California instead?"

"There were a lot of reasons. I did not have the interest in becoming a great orthopedic surgeon teaching at Yale because it was part of Colette and the kids, and that was our dream. And with part of it gone, it did not make much sense, but I had other reasons also."

"Well, I would like you to share those with us, please."

"The East Coast had become a very sad place for me. I was uncomfortable. My friends were very supportive, and yet I was uncomfortable receiving their support. No one really knew what to say, and I didn't know what to say, and it was constantly there because it was constantly in the press; and the reinvestigation was now beginning."

"How did you arrive at the decision to go to California? What were the key factors that helped you make that decision?"

"Distance from Freddy. A new environment. Not so many people maybe worried about my welfare, my emotional makeup and constantly either—you know—trying to support me or to get me to do something like public appearances or to write a book or whatever. And I just—it was—once I arrived in California, I had this tremendous sense of relief."

"Now, when did you arrive in California?"

"July 5th, 1971."

"Where did you start working at that time?"

"St. Mary's Hospital in Long Beach."

"Where you still are employed today?"

"That is correct."

"What kind of life did you build for yourself between July of 1971, and, say, January of 1975? Just tell us about the kind of life you created for yourself up until that juncture."

"Well, I was working very hard. I developed a good position at the hospital. I was active in community affairs. Our group was becoming prominent in the area in emergency medicine. We were teaching at USC and later UCLA. I bought a house on the water—not a house—but a small two-bedroom condo which I still—that is where I live now. I bought a boat and lived on the water—working, I think, fairly hard."

"How many hours a week do you ordinarily work?"

"Eighty—seventy or eighty."

"Why do you choose to work that many hours, Dr. MacDonald?"

"It just seemed easier. Work was good for me."

"Easier than what?"

"Easier than sitting and thinking."

"About what?"

"My family."

There was a pause, as Jeffrey MacDonald, apparently once again overcome by emotion, lapsed into silence. Bernie Segal walked slowly toward a table on which lay a number of items which had been introduced into evidence.

"Dr. MacDonald," he said, "I want to show you the four instruments that we have come to hear so much about during this trial: the club, the bent-bladed knife, the straight knife, the icepick.

"I want you to look at those weapons, please, and I want you to now hear me and respond, if you will, to what the indictment has said."

Segal began to read. "In the First Count, it is charged: 'That on or about the 17th day of February, 1970, at Fort Bragg, North Carolina, upon lands acquired for the use of the United States and under the exclusive jurisdiction thereof, and within the Eastern District of North Carolina, Jeffrey R. MacDonald, with premeditation and malice aforethought, murdered Colette S. MacDonald by means of striking her with a club and stabbing her, in violation of the provisions of Title 18, United States Code, Section 1111.'"

Segal stared at Jeffrey MacDonald. "Did you stab your wife? Did you club your wife?"

"I did not."

"With those or any other weapons?"

"I never struck Colette."

"Dr. MacDonald, I want to read to you the Second Count of the same indictment, and again ask you the same question. In that count it is charged: 'That on or about the 17th day of February, 1970, at Fort Bragg, North Carolina, upon lands acquired for the use of the United States and under the exclusive jurisdiction thereof, and within the Eastern District of North Carolina, Jeffrey R. MacDonald, with premeditation and malice aforethought, murdered Kimberly K. MacDonald, by means of striking her with a club and stabbing her, in violation of the provisions of Title 18, United States Code, Section 1111.'"

Again Segal stared at MacDonald. "Is that true?"

"It is not true. I never harmed Kimberly."

"I will read you, Dr. MacDonald, the Third Count of the indictment, and ask you to respond again. 'That on or about the 17th day of February, 1970, at Fort Bragg, North Carolina, upon lands acquired for the use of the United States and under the exclusive jurisdiction thereof, and within the Eastern District of North Carolina, Jeffrey R. MacDonald, with premeditation and malice aforethought, murdered Kristen J. MacDonald by means of stabbing her, in violation of the provisions of Title 18, United States Code, Section 1111.'"

For the third time, the lawyer's eyes met those of his client. "Is that true, Dr. MacDonald?"

"It is not true."

Taking a deep breath, Segal approached the witness stand and handed Jeffrey MacDonald a piece of paper. "Finally, Dr. MacDonald, I would like for you to share with us all a letter addressed to you dated August the 26th, 1969, from your wife in Patchogue, Long Island, to you at Columbus, Georgia. If you would be good enough to read that to us, sir."

In a halting, stumbling voice, MacDonald began to read the last letter Colette had ever written him. "Sun-

day night. Darling Jeff, what a difference a day makes—
or even a few minutes—especially when you take me
from the . . ." His sobbing temporarily prevented him
from continuing. ". . . nadir of despair and return me to
that happy full of love and life feeling. Thank you sweetheart, you really know how to handle me.

"In case you're getting ready to jump out of an airplane and need a little material for pleasant daydreaming,
here are a few of my favorites: (1) Remember the night
you came to Skidmore in the snow for 'Happy Pappy
Weekend' and stayed in the Rip Van Dam, the fashionable watering place of the New York jet set. (2) The
night we came home from Paul and Kathy's and we decided to have something to eat in the city and we went to
Manana after walking around a bit. This is one of my favorites because I think we were definitely on the same
wavelength that night. (3) When you were in the Infir-
mary at Princeton because you had dropped the weights
on your chest, you wrote me an abstract story entitled
'The Cool Guy and the Warm Girl.' Do you remember
that at all? I do. It was beautiful. (4) New Year's Eve this
year—what could top that for a feeling of togetherness!
(5) Cutting up onions and peppers together and planning for our giant Champagne Brunch—and then, of
course, the brunch itself. (6) The first time you came to
Skidmore and the picnic we had in the woods. Four
kisses. Colette."

With trembling hands, Jeffrey MacDonald lowered
the letter to his lap. He looked five years older than he
had five hours earlier. He began to sob loudly, and, as he
did, Bernie Segal's own eyes filled with tears. Three
members of the jury were weeping openly and the sound
of sniffling and sobbing could be heard from all portions
of the courtroom, except the right front row, where

Freddy and Mildred Kassab sat, dry-eyed, staring un-flinchingly at MacDonald. The extended pause in the proceedings was punctuated by Freddy Kassab's short, sardonic laugh.

Then Judge Dupree declared a recess until the morning.

5

In approaching the question of how to conduct his cross-examination, Jim Blackburn kept one principle uppermost in mind: he did not want the trial—and eventual jury deliberation—to turn into a referendum on whether Jeffrey MacDonald was or was not a good guy, on whether he had contributed more or less to society than had Freddy Kassab.

It had been a careful analysis of the physical evidence and the physical evidence alone which had persuaded Blackburn, when he first was assigned to the case, that MacDonald was guilty beyond a reasonable doubt. And if that evidence—all of which he had managed to introduce, and most of which, despite Bernie Segal's attempts to taint and dilute it, still seemed to him to stand strong and true—had been sufficient to convince him that this case could be won, then that physical evidence, all by itself, ought to be enough to convince a jury.

The more that the jury's attention wandered from it, the more likelihood there might be that reasonable doubt might creep in. So, in the end, after many nights of lying awake next to his own wife, with his own son, Jeffrey, and infant daughter in nearby rooms, Jim Blackburn decided that when the moment for cross-examination came he would not attempt a character assassination. He was not seeking to convict MacDonald of perjury, or adultery, or of having told lies to Freddy Kassab: he was seeking to convict him of murder.

Despite all warnings—and even with his entire future hanging in the balance—Jeffrey MacDonald was unable to control the caustic, bitter strain that ran so deep within him. Even Jim Blackburn's softest, most inoffensive questions—and Blackburn's manner, in contrast to Victor Woerheide's booming intimidation of five years earlier sometimes bordered on the almost deferential—met with a cutting, acerbic response. This prickly, touchy, hostile witness—so easily irritated, so quick to flash to the point of anger—bore little resemblance to the broken, saddened, grieving survivor who had brought tears to the jurors' eyes the day before. Despite having had nine and a half years to prepare for the occasion, MacDonald seemingly could not prevent himself from adopting the one mode of behavior likely to do him most harm.

"Now I take it this is the pajama top you wore to bed that night?" Jim Blackburn asked, holding up the garment—torn and punctured, its bloodstains now faded to a rusty brown.

"I only have your say-so."

"Is it not the pajama top that you wore?"

"I have no knowledge."

"Have you ever seen it before?"

"Sure."

"Were you ever shown this pajama top by the grand jury?"

"I believe I was."

"Were you asked then whether or not this was the same one?"

"I was asked questions similar to yours just now."

"Well, were you ever asked whether or not this was the pajama top that you wore that night?"

"I am sure I was. I don't recall the question, but it must have been asked of me sometime."

"Well, I wasn't there. What was your answer then?"

"Assuming, you know, the normal chain of custody, that is probably my pajama top."

"I take it when you went to bed the night of the 16th and wore this blue pajama top, it was not ripped?"

"I don't believe so."

"Certainly not in this condition?"

"No."

"Was there any blood on it when you went to bed that night?"

"Not that I know of."

"Were any puncture holes in it?"

"Not that I know of."

"Do you know where it was ripped?"

"No."

"Did you rip it?"

"I may have."

"Did you ever hear any ripping sounds?"

"No, I do not recall ever hearing a ripping sound."

"How did these holes get in this pajama top?"

"From the assailants."

"Where was it when it got holes in it from the assailants?"

"My recollection is that it had to have been around my wrists."

"What were you doing with it?"

"I was fending off blows—trying to get my hands out."

"You don't know whether it was torn at that time?"

"I have no idea."

"You don't know whether it was pulled over your head?"

"I do not."

"But you were using this around your wrists or hands to fend off the blows of the intruders, is that correct?"

"That's correct."

"Was it between your hands?"

"Part of it must have been between my hands because my hands were not touching each other."

"And all forty-eight puncture holes got in here, in this pajama top, at that time?"

"That's what I would have to presume, yes."

"Can you tell us why those are circular, round holes and not tearing holes?"

"Can *I* tell *you* that?"

"Yes, sir."

"I was fending off blows that were coming straight at me, and I was pushing out against them. I see no reason why the fabric should be torn and not have circular holes. It was not at all like the demonstration that you showed the jury."

"Doctor MacDonald, you did not receive any icepick wounds in your hands or wrists or lower parts of your arms, did you?"

"None that I recall. Why I did not I cannot say."

"Now, when you say you took the pajama off of your wrists and threw it down, you don't recall where you threw it?"

"That is correct."

"You did not hear any ripping sounds at that time. Is that correct?"

"Mr. Blackburn, I was not listening for ripping sounds. I saw my wife covered with blood."

"I understand that, and I appreciate that. What I am asking is, did you hear any ripping sounds?"

"No," MacDonald said, with a very definite edge to his voice, "I do not recall hearing ripping sounds."

"You saw the knife in your wife's chest, right?"

"That is correct."

"And you pulled it out, right?"

"That is correct."

"Did you wipe the knife off?"

"I have absolutely no remembrance of that."

"Do you know whether the knife was bloody when you pulled it out of your wife's chest?"

"I have absolutely no remembrance. I saw it in my wife's chest and I took it out."

"So it could have been bloody or it could not have been bloody?"

"Well, I would assume that having been in her chest it was bloody."

"Well, how was it that no blood or very little blood was found on the knife?"

"I have no idea."

"Doctor MacDonald, can you tell me, sir, how two threads—two threads microscopically identical to threads in your pajama top—got on the club outside the door of the utility room area, when you stated that you never went outside that house?"

"I cannot."

"Did Colette bleed on your pajama top before it was torn?"

"Not to my knowledge."

"Did you struggle with Colette and did she tear your pajama top in the V-neck part of it?"

"She did not."

"Did you struggle with Colette in the pajama top?"

"I never struggled with Colette."

"Did you wear your surgical gloves that night?"

"I did not."

"Why did you put your pajama top on top of Colette's chest?"

"I guess it was an attempt to try to treat my wife— cover my wife."

"For possible shock?"

"It was sort of an attempt to do something, I guess. I can't really explain why I put it on her."

"That night, did you ever touch the bedsheet and the bedspread depicted in that photograph behind you?"

"I have no recollection at all."

"Are you saying you did or you didn't?"

"I am saying neither."

"Dr. MacDonald, if the jury should find from the evidence that there is a fabric impression or contact print matching the right cuff of your blue pajama top on it, do you have any explanation for that?"

"If the jury should find?"

"Uh-huh."

"No."

"If the jury should find from the evidence that there is a fabric impression or contact print of handprints and the left shoulder on that sheet, do you have any explanation for that?"

"It is hard to answer, because the evidence that you claim to be evidence has been disproven. You want me to make a supposition based on something that—"

"Well, suppose the jury disagrees with you, and does find that it has not been disproven, and finds what I said—do you have any explanation for that?"

"No."

"Suppose the jury finds from the evidence that in that bedspread there is a seam thread matching your blue pajama top entwined around a hair with blood on its shaft matching that of your wife Colette—do you have any explanation for that?"

"No."

"Suppose the jury should find from the evidence that pieces of rubber or latex are found in that bundle of bedding on the floor. Do you have any explanation for that?"

"I have none."

"Suppose the jury should find from the evidence that the word PIG on the headboard over where your wife slept was written in Type A blood with a gloved hand. Do you have an explanation for that?"

"I have no explanation for that."

"Doctor MacDonald, should the jury find from the evidence that on debris from the sheet of the bed in your master bedroom there are fifteen purple cotton sewing threads microscopically identical to those in your blue pajama top and seven blue polyester cotton yarns identical to the yarns of the blue pajama top—assuming that the jury should find evidence to be true, do you have any explanation for that?"

At this, Bernie Segal stood to object. "Your honor," he said, "I do not believe the defendant has to explain the government's case for them. I object to that. It is not proper to make a continued line of questioning on this. I object to the question. I suggest that it rises to the point of suggesting that the defendant has some burden to prove away facts that the government has raised in the first instance."

"I will overrule the objection," Judge Dupree said.

"May I ask your honor then," Segal retorted, "to give an appropriate instruction in regard as to what burden the defendant does or does not have? I would request that at this time."

"I will say to the jury," Dupree said, turning toward them, "as you have heard from time to time and as you heard during the course of your selection, the burden is always on the government to prove each essential element of the crime charged in the indictment by evidence convincing the jury beyond a reasonable doubt. That is the rule of law under which all criminal cases are tried in this court or courts of this country, and it is in full force and effect from the inception of the trial right on through to the final verdict."

The judge then permitted Blackburn to continue his cross-examination. "Doctor MacDonald, would you like for me to repeat the question?" Blackburn said.

"No."

"What is your answer?"

"Is this the sheet that Mr. Ivory scooped up and stuffed in the plastic bag?"

"No, sir."

"Which sheet are we talking about?"

"The one that was found on the bed."

"I have no answer for that."

"Assume, Doctor MacDonald—or suppose—that the jury should find from the evidence that in the master bedroom as a whole, there were sixty or more purple cotton sewing threads found which microscopically matched your blue pajama top and eighteen blue polyester cotton yarns which microscopically matched the pajama top and one blue-black sewing thread which matched your pajama top. Assume for a moment that the jury should find that evidence to be true, do you have, sir, any explanation for that?"

"With the understanding that they have not matched those fibers and threads against the pajama bottoms, no, I don't have any explanation for it."

"Assume for a moment that the jury should find from the evidence that no purple threads or blue polyester cotton yarns matching any of those found in your pajama top were found in the living room, do you have any explanation for that?"

"It would lead me to feel that the shirt was pulled over my head rather than ripped from around my back."

"Do you remember it being pulled over your head?"

"No; neither do I remember it being torn."

"Okay, when you left the master bedroom and Colette, you went then to Kimberly's room, is that correct?"

"That is correct."

"Were you wearing your pajama top at this particular time?"

"Not that I recall."

"What did you do; did you just sort of lean over and give her mouth-to-mouth, or check her?"

"I don't specifically recall."

"You didn't get on the bed with her?"

"Get on the bed with her?"

"Yes, sir."

"No."

"Well, suppose the jury should find from the evidence that on Kimberly's bed on top of the covers, and also inside under the covers and on the pillow closest to the wall that there were fourteen purple cotton sewing threads, microscopically identical to your pajama top; and approximately five blue polyester cotton yarns, microscopically identical to your pajama top—suppose the jury should find all of that from the evidence. Do you have any explanation for that?"

"Not unless they came from my arms. I can envision threads hanging on to my arm hairs and dropping off at some later time. That seems like a rational explanation."

"Suppose the jury should find, Doctor MacDonald, that Type AB blood, the same as that of your daughter Kimberly, was found on the blue pajama top; and that you were not wearing that pajama top when you went to see Kimberly. Do you have, sir, any explanation for that?"

"Pure conjecture."

"Is that your answer?"

"Pure conjecture that any of us can make."

"Well, is that—do I take it then that any answer that you give would just be, as you said, conjecture on your part?"

"That is correct."

"With respect to Kristen's room, suppose the jury should find from the evidence that there is a purple cotton sewing thread and a blue polyester yarn microscopically matching that of your blue pajama top on the bed in her room, do you have any explanation for that?"

"It's pure conjecture, again."

"Doctor MacDonald, suppose the jury would find from the evidence that splinters matching the club on the table over there were found in Kimberly's room and Kristen's room, do you have any explanation for that?"

"Do *I*?"

"Yes, sir."

"Nothing more than the obvious."

"Which is that they were struck in there with the club or someone struck them with the club?"

"Correct."

"With respect to Kristen's room, supposing the jury should find from the evidence that blood—Type A blood, Colette's blood type—is found on the wall over the bed in Kristen's room, and also that Type A blood is found, through direct bleeding, on the top sheet in Kristen's bed. Do you understand what I have said so far?"

"Sort of."

"Let me rephrase it. Suppose the jury should find from the evidence that Type A blood—Colette's blood type—is found on the top sheet of Kristen's bed in massive amounts and also on the wall over the side of the bed, splattered; do you, sir, have any explanation for that?"

"Making the very large assumption that the CID could type blood, no."

"Do you know your wife's blood type?"

"A."

"Do you know Kimberly's blood type?"

"We have been told here many times."

"Did you know it in 1970?"

"No."

"Kristen's?"

"No, I don't believe so. I don't believe I knew any of ours."

"Doctor MacDonald, suppose the jury should find from the evidence that all the blood on the floor in Kristen's room, with the exception of the footprint, is that of Type O—Kristen's type—and suppose further that the jury should find from the evidence that that is your footprint exiting that room, and suppose the jury should find further that that footprint is made in Type A blood—Colette's blood type. Do you have any explanation?"

"Well, I would probably agree that that was my footprint since I was there. As far as the blood-typing, again assuming the CID accurately typed the blood, I am not—you know—I have no explanation for the blood-typing and patterns, assuming they are correct."

At the lunch recess, Bernie Segal and Wade Smith worked with MacDonald as if they were seconds tending to a prizefighter between rounds.

"Your general tone is very good," Segal assured him. "Just don't piss on the CID anymore. And watch the facial stuff—it's getting bad. I know you're getting tired of playing Mr. Nice with him, but you've got to be more inert: less feeling revealed. You can't start with nonverbal communication because the jury will be very alert for that."

"Blackburn has lost you," Smith said. "This afternoon, he is going to be a desperate man. He will know he's only got an hour and a half to win the case. You're ahead. Way ahead."

"Just like in a fight," Segal said. "You are ahead on points, be like Muhammad Ali—keep backpedaling. You're in round eleven of fifteen. Just take him the last four. Yesterday, we poured our hearts out. Our blood is all over the floor. Today, we simply want you weary after nine and a half years. No anger, no sarcasm, but no more tears: after yesterday, they would seem anticlimactic."

"Doctor MacDonald," Jim Blackburn resumed quietly, "when we broke for lunch, as I recall, I had just asked you, and I think you answered the question about the footprint and the blood in Kristen's room. Now, again, sir, should the jury find from the evidence that that is your footprint as you indicated it probably is and that the blood in that footprint is Type A blood, can you tell us at all where you got that Type A blood from?"

"I have no idea." MacDonald's manner was openly hostile.

"Doctor MacDonald, did you take the bedspread and that sheet from the master bedroom off the floor, place Colette on the bedspread, step in blood on that bedspread, and pick Colette up and carry her out of that room?"

"I did not."

"Doctor MacDonald, with respect to the Hilton bathmat that you have seen in the courtroom, do you recognize that?"

"Yeah. Yes, I do."

"You all had a Hilton bathmat, I take it?" Blackburn's courtly Southern manner was standing out in bolder relief against MacDonald's sullenness as the day wore on.

"Apparently so."

"Well, do you recall where it was the night of the murders?"

"I do not."

"Did you place it on Colette?"

"I don't recall doing that."

"Could you have done that?"

"I could have done that."

"Should the jury find from the evidence that the blood on the Old Hickory knife was wiped off on that bathmat, and also that the icepick that was found outside the house was wiped on it, do you, sir, have any explanation for that?"

"Not unless the assailants did that."

"Doctor MacDonald, suppose the jury should find

from the evidence that the blood in the bathroom sink is Type B, your blood. Do you have any explanation for that?"

"No."

"Doctor MacDonald, at any time, did you in any way take a scalpel, or any instrument, and inflict any injury on yourself while at the bathroom sink?"

"I did not."

"Suppose, sir, that the jury should find, from the evidence that no Type B blood—your type blood—is found in the living room area where the struggle with the intruders allegedly occurred, and you were allegedly stabbed: do you have any explanation for that?"

"Nothing other than the obvious one. The wounds weren't bleeding very much."

"Suppose the jury finds from the evidence that you were stabbed and the wounds weren't bleeding very much, and that you did not go into the bathroom until you had passed through, by your own account, five other areas of the house and that B-type blood is found in the sink, do you have any explanation for that?"

"Your honor, I object to the form of the question," Bernie Segal said. "It is compound, confusing."

"Overruled," said Judge Dupree.

"Do I have an explanation why there was B-type blood on the sink?" MacDonald said, his edginess increasing. "Is that the question?"

"Let me ask you again, if you want me to," Blackburn said.

"Fine."

"Suppose the jury should find from the evidence that your blood is Type B, and that the reason that there is no B-type blood in the living room is because the wounds don't bleed very much, as you have stated, and that you do not go into the bathroom until your sixth stop, and that they find from the evidence that there is B-type blood on the inside of that sink: do you have any explanation for that?"

"Well, when I checked myself, I saw my own chest wound that was bubbling. That is the only obvious answer that I can give."

"Doctor MacDonald, suppose the jury should find from the evidence that there was no blood in sufficient quantity to be typed on either the telephone in the master bedroom or the kitchen, and that they should find from the evidence that you went there and used the phone as you have indicated: do you have any explanation for why there would be no blood?"

"No. There was blood on my hands. I used the phone. I have no explanation for that lack of finding."

"Doctor MacDonald, let me show you again the blue pajama top. Suppose that the jury should find from the evidence that, one, there are approximately seventeen puncture holes in the back of that pajama top, and secondly, that you have no injuries, puncture or otherwise, in your back. Do you have any explanation for that?"

"Well, I know why I don't have any puncture wounds in my back. I was being stabbed from the front."

"With respect to my question, sir, do you have any explanation for how those holes got in the back of that pajama top?"

"Just that it had to have been when it was around my wrists and hands and fending off blows."

"Would your answer be the same with respect to the number of holes—over thirty more in this right area of the pajama top?"

"That is correct."

"Doctor MacDonald, suppose the jury should find

from the evidence that Colette MacDonald was beaten and stabbed a multiple number of times, that Kristen was stabbed a number of times, and that Kimberly was stabbed and beaten a number of times.

"And suppose, sir, that the jury further finds that the injuries that you sustained were not consistent in degree of seriousness with those that they sustained, and that you are quite obviously still alive. Do you have any explanation for that?"

"Your honor," Bernie Segal shouted, "that is objected to as argumentative! That is not a question at all!"

"I will sustain the objection to that question," Judge Dupree said.

"Doctor MacDonald," Blackburn continued, still with the same gentle, almost apologetic manner, "should the jury find from the evidence that what has come to be known as the FBI reconstruction of the blue pajama top—suppose the jury with respect to that should find that the forty-eight puncture holes in your blue pajama top correspond or match up with the twenty-one puncture holes in Colette's chest: do you have any explanation for that?"

"No."

"Your honor," Blackburn said, turning away from MacDonald, "that concludes the government's cross-examination."

Bernie Segal and Wade Smith were exultant. "He stoned you with popcorn," Smith said gleefully, after court had recessed for the day.

MacDonald agreed. "Like I told you, Blackburn's chicken shit. I think he was really afraid of me."

6

When, on the morning of Tuesday, August 28, it came time for Jim Blackburn to make his closing argument to the jury (following an hour and forty-five minutes during which Brian Murtagh had summarized the physical evidence and its significance in detail), he began by stressing again the discrepancy between the injuries sustained by Jeffrey MacDonald and those inflicted upon the members of his family. As it had been throughout the seven weeks of trial, his tone was much more one of sorrow than of anger.

But he made his points: both of Colette's arms had been broken by the club as she had attempted to defend herself; her skull had been fractured; she had been stabbed over and over again with the knife—the Old Hickory knife, not the Geneva Forge knife that MacDonald had said he had found in her chest—and she had been stabbed twenty-one times in the chest with an icepick.

"Let's think about Kimberly MacDonald—the five-year-old," Blackburn said softly. "She also got hit by this club. It fractured her skull. The base of the skull—you saw that really just horrible picture of the back of her skull that was cracked in six to eight places. Her nose was broken and pushed off to the right."

It was obvious to jurors and spectators alike that it pained Jim Blackburn to have to talk about such evil, tragic matters; but it was obvious, too, that he felt a profound sense of duty—a moral as well as a legal, obligation—once again to focus the attention of the jurors—nice people, all of them, his manner said; the sort with whom he would be happy to be friends; the sort with whom he would much rather be discussing happier things—upon the grisly details of the murders committed at 544 Castle Drive nine and a half years before, because only by doing so might some measure of justice be achieved.

And so he reminded them once again of the stab wounds in Kimberly's neck, and of the knife and icepick wounds in the chest of the two-year-old, Kristen.

"She didn't get hit with the club," Blackburn said. "She was the only one that didn't, but she got hit a lot with the knife and a lot with an icepick. At least thirty-three times somebody raised a hand and came down in her body with both a knife and an icepick.

"You remember also that she had some cuts in her fingers. One, in particular, sort of long cut was in the nature of a defensive wound. You know what that suggests, ladies and gentlemen? It suggests that before Kristen MacDonald died, she knew—she knew what was going to happen, and she tried to fight back."

The eyes of several jurors shifted quickly from Blackburn to Jeffrey MacDonald and back again.

Blackburn held their attention as he summarized the testimony of those physicians at Womack Hospital who had examined and treated MacDonald: he reminded the jurors that the defendant had sustained only a bruise on the left side of his head, scratches down the left side of his chest, two knife cuts so superficial that they did not even require stitching, and the injury to the right side of the chest which had caused the pneumothorax.

"Well, I am not going to stand here today and argue for long, ladies and gentlemen, over whether a pneumothorax is or is not potentially life-threatening," Blackburn said. "That could go on all day long. But I do submit to you, ladies and gentlemen, even if the government concedes—which we do not—that that was a potentially life-threatening wound; even if we concede—which we do not—that point: how many—how many did he get compared and contrasted with the number his family got? One.

"How many icepick wounds did Dr. Bronstein say he saw in Jeffrey MacDonald's chest? None. How many icepick wounds did the emergency room orderly, the first person who washed up the defendant, say he saw in Mac-Donald's chest? None. How many icepick wounds did the chief of surgery say he saw? He said that he didn't observe any.

"Now, I am not trying to suggest by and in and of itself that because the defendant was not killed, he is, therefore, guilty of the slaughter of his family. I don't think that is sufficient evidence. I am not saying that. But I am saying that when you compare and contrast his injuries to their injuries, it certainly should raise in your mind the question as to why he was not hurt worse.

"And, ladies and gentlemen, let me ask you some other questions. Why, if these intruders had some particular grudge against the defendant, why didn't they kill him? Why, if they came there for wanton destruction, didn't they kill everybody? Why do you kill a two-and-a-half- and a five-year-old and don't kill the one who could identify you? Why? Why did the intruders leave the defendant alive?"

Blackburn then shifted his focus to the pajama top, holding it up, once again, in front of the jury. "Ladies and gentlemen, according to the testimony of Paul Stombaugh, this thing has forty-eight puncture holes in it. Is the defense saying that in a life-and-death struggle— *that in a life-and-death struggle*—you stand there with it in a stationary position while somebody comes at you with an icepick—I don't know how many times—and doesn't hit your wrists and doesn't hit your arms? Where are the icepick injuries to his hands? Where are the icepick injuries to his wrists and arms? By everyone's testimony on this subject, there were none. I submit that that story is not worthy of your belief.

"Ladies and gentlemen, I suggest that the evidence shows that there was, in fact, a life-and-death struggle in the house that night—there truly was.

"I suggest that there were at least two white people involved in it. I suggest the evidence shows that there wasn't a black person involved. There was only one white male and one white female. The white female was Colette MacDonald and the white male was her husband, Jeffrey MacDonald. I suggest to you that some of the injuries that Jeffrey MacDonald sustained could well have been inflicted by his wife, Colette. We know from the evidence, ladies and gentlemen, that she fought—she fought mighty hard before she died. You don't get both of your arms broken by standing there waiting to be killed. You don't get all the injuries she got just standing there waiting to be killed. You just don't do it.

"Ladies and gentlemen, the defendant's theory of defense in this case has sort of been like this: 'I tell a story and you are to trust me. I am telling the truth. I loved my family. I loved Colette. I loved Kimberly and Kristen. Trust me. I couldn't have done this. I could not have done this. There has been a lot of character testimony. They say I can't do this; and therefore, because I am not the type of person, I couldn't do that.'

"Ladies and gentlemen, if we convince you by the evidence that he *did* it, we don't have to show you that he is the sort of person that *could* have done it.

"The other part of their theory is to attack—attack the Kassabs, attack the CID, attack the Justice Department, and even attack the government prosecutor. What they really want to do, ladies and gentlemen, they want to create confusion.

"But I suggest to you, ladies and gentlemen, that if we prove to you that that was MacDonald's footprint in A-type blood, if we prove to you that Colette's blood got on that pajama top before and not after it was torn, then it doesn't make any difference if there were five thousand hippies outside Castle Drive at 4 o'clock in the morning screaming, 'Acid is groovy; kill the pigs!'

"Ladies and gentlemen, the defendant, by all the evidence, is an outstanding doctor. I don't think anybody could dispute that. In 1970, he had a lot to live for. His wife, Colette, had a lot to live for, too. She had a dream, according to his testimony, of a farm in Connecticut with five children, and cats and dogs and horses. The children had a dream, too. They wanted to grow up. They wanted to be alive. They didn't get that chance. The defendant did. And the defendant wanted to continue, I suggest, his career.

"If we are correct—if we are correct, and the defendant did what we claim he did—if he could murder his family, think for a moment what he would do on the witness stand to save his life and his career. Think, ladies and gentlemen, about that when you judge the testimony and credibility of all the witnesses and you put his to the same test to which you put Paul Stombaugh, or any of the others. I can only tell you from the physical evidence in this case that *things* do not lie. But I suggest that *people* can and do."

There was a fifteen-minute pause for the morning recess. In the suite of offices reserved for the defense, Jeffrey MacDonald expressed impatience at Blackburn for taking so much time with what was so patently a preposterous line of argument. The highlight of the trial, from MacDonald's point of view—the three hours that would almost make the whole nine and a half years seem worthwhile—was going to be Bernie Segal's closing argument, in which he would not only dismantle the government's physical evidence piece by piece but would say all the things that MacDonald himself so badly wanted to say—about how narrow-minded, vicious, power-hungry bureaucrats had inflicted almost a decade's worth of needless suffering upon a great and compassionate physician, thereby depriving him of the opportunity to try to recover from the most grievous personal loss a man can suffer.

The afternoon would bring Bernie Segal's finest hours ever in a courtroom—there was no doubt in MacDonald's mind about that—and he could scarcely contain his irritation at being made to sit, as if in a waiting room, while Blackburn nattered on about irrelevancies.

There was, however, in Blackburn's manner, when he resumed his closing argument at 11 A.M., a gravity and intensity which made it plain that no matter how Jeffrey

MacDonald might view it, he, Jim Blackburn—in the last hours now of the first murder case he'd ever tried—did not intend to fill the remainder of the morning with idle chatter.

"Ladies and gentlemen," he began, "when you take all seven weeks that you all have been here and all these charts and all this testimony and all the bench conferences and you pour them all out the window, you are left with two things on which I suggest that you have got to make a decision.

"One is the defendant's story and his credibility. If you believe it is true, if you believe everything he said, then your task is relatively simple. You will acquit him.

"If, on the other hand, you contrast that with the physical evidence and somehow it doesn't wash, it doesn't make sense, then you have got a little bit more of a difficult task and it might take you a little longer.

"I suggest that when you compare and contrast his story versus the government's story, you have got to come down on one side or the other, because I suggest to you that the evidence in this case—if it shows nothing else—shows that what he said and what the physical evidence says are not reconcilable. They are diametrically opposed.

"Ladies and gentlemen, I am not about to suggest that the burden of proof ever shifts to the defendant, because it doesn't. It stays with us.

"But you recall on cross-examination that we asked the defendant a lot of questions—that if the jury should find this and that, did he have an explanation. And you recall essentially his testimony: 'It would be pure conjecture,' or 'No,' or 'I can't recall.' Perhaps he does not have to explain, but think for a moment if you were on trial for your life and the only thing that made your story perhaps not believable was its inconsistency with the physical evidence.

"Don't you think if you *could* explain it, you *would*? Don't you think for one moment if you were on that stand and somebody asked you a question like I asked Dr. MacDonald and you could tell me, 'Mr. Blackburn, you are an idiot. Here is the answer. Bam': doesn't it make sense that you would do that? I suggest that it does.

"What about the blood—the Type A blood that Paul Stombaugh testified was on the pajama top before it was torn? Did you hear any defendant's experts say that there wasn't Type A blood on the pajama top before it was torn? Did you hear that? No, you didn't. And don't you know if they could have had an expert here from somewhere to say that they would have, because, ladies and gentlemen, the defendant's story is that he placed the pajama top on Colette after she was dead.

"All of the evidence, however, suggests that that pajama top was ripped before and not after it was placed on top of the chest of Colette MacDonald. Well, what does that suggest to you?

"It suggests, ladies and gentlemen, that Colette Mac-Donald bled on that pajama top before it was torn. We asked the defendant if he had an explanation for that, and he said not to his knowledge. Don't you know that if he could have explained it, he would have?

"We even know that Kimberly's AB blood type was on the pajama top. How did it get on there? Well, we know—if you believe the defendant's story—that on the first visit to the master bedroom—the first circuit—he took it off and put it on Colette's body and then he went to check Kimberly and then he perhaps got Kimberly's blood on it. But he did not see Kimberly until he had the pajama top off. How does the AB blood walk from Kimberly's room to the master bedroom and get on the pajama top? We asked him that question, and his response was, 'It would be pure conjecture.'

"We know, at least, that the pajama top was placed on Colette's chest. That is one thing about which the government and the defendant are in agreement. He said that he was in a state of confusion and that perhaps he put it on there to get her warm and protect her from shock, but he wasn't sure why. He was confused.

"I think that you can infer from this evidence that the reason the pajama top was placed on top of Colette's chest was because it already had Type A blood on it and he had to have an explanation that would sound reasonable as to why that Type A blood was on it.

"How did threads and yarns from the pajama top get on Kimberly's bed underneath the sheets? Fourteen of them, when the pajama top was already off? Now, we asked the defendant about that and as I recall, he said, well, they were sticking to his arms. If you believe that that is where they came from, fine. We suggest that they came from the blue pajama top itself as Kimberly MacDonald was carried back into that room with that torn pajama top and placed in that bed.

"What about Kristen? We know that at least one thread matching the pajama top and a splinter matching the club were found in her room. We know that Type A blood, from the evidence, was on the wall, splattered. We know from the evidence that Type A blood from direct bleeding was found in massive amounts on the top sheet. We know, ladies and gentlemen, that Colette MacDonald had no injuries on her legs, yet there was a lot of blood—her own blood—on the pajama bottoms. How did that blood get there?

"I suggest from the evidence that you can infer that it got there because the killer took this club and after Colette MacDonald went to Kristen's room, she was banged again with the club up against the wall and fell over and bled on the pajama bottoms."

Blackburn paused and began to pace slowly back and forth across the courtroom. "Ladies and gentlemen," he said, "we have heard a lot about fabric impressions and contact prints on the bed sheet. How did they get there? One fabric impression contact print matched the right cuff of the defendant's blue pajama top. What did the defendant say about the bed sheet? To his memory, he could not recall touching or coming in contact with that sheet.

"But you have got a massive amount of Type A blood in the center of that sheet. You have got two impressions matching the arms of Colette's pink pajama top there. And you have got MacDonald's blue cuff—the right cuff—on that sheet. How do you explain that? What is the explanation for that?

"And then the footprint. Even the defendant agrees the footprint was probably his. The intruders did not go barefooted. The left footprint that was exiting Kristen's bedroom was made in Type A blood. How was the footprint made? And how did the fabric impressions—the contact prints—get on the sheet?

"I submit that it is reasonable to infer from the evidence that after Colette MacDonald was struck with the club in Kristen's room, she came to rest on the floor. We suggest that that bedspread and that blue sheet from the master bedroom were then brought into Kristen's room. Colette was laid on it, and, ladies and gentlemen, she was picked up and carried back to the master bedroom. And we suggest that as the defendant did that, he stepped, unbeknownst to him, in a blood type that was not Kristen's and made that footprint as he exited that room."

Glancing briefly at handwritten notes, Blackburn moved on. "We know," he said, "that pieces of latex were found torn and some with Type A blood on them in the master bedroom. How did they get there? We asked the defendant about it, and he said, 'Not that I can recall,' 'No,' or 'No explanation.' Again, while he has no legal responsibility to explain, don't you know—don't you know that if he could have, he most certainly would have?

"We know that somebody wrote the words PIG in Type A blood on the headboard over where Colette MacDonald slept. We know that a blue thread matching the pajama top was found in that area. We know that there is a good possibility from the evidence that the surgical glove fragments found in the bedroom matched gloves found elsewhere in the house.

"And isn't it interesting, ladies and gentlemen, that droplets of Type B blood—that of the defendant—are found in the kitchen near the cabinet where surgical gloves are kept? According to his story, the kitchen was the thirteenth stop on his rounds—drops of blood at number thirteen, but at number one, where he was cut according to his story, there wasn't any.

"I think you can infer from the evidence, ladies and gentlemen, that this defendant with his medical knowledge—with his medical ability—knowing that MPs would soon be on the way—very likely inflicted one—not all, but one—injury in the bathroom, and that is where the B-type blood came from and that was close to the end and that is why B-type blood was not found until number thirteen in the kitchen.

"But, ladies and gentlemen, I believe that you could

throw the whole shooting match away except for two pieces of evidence. I think you could just hold on to two—this club and this pajama top." Blackburn held both in front of the jury.

"Why are they so important? Well, you remember, the defendant said that he hadn't seen this club until April 6th, and he didn't think this was the club that he was hit with. The club, the knives, and the icepick were outside the door. He didn't go outside the door, but he went to it. The club had A and AB blood on it and it had two little blue threads on it which matched identically the threads from this pajama top.

"That sounds sort of minor, really, until you think about something. How did they get there? If he never touched the club, if he never saw it, if the pajama top was not taken off his body until this club was already out the door, how in the name of all that is reasonable did they walk out the door and get on the club and stick to it?

"I suggest from the evidence that there is an explanation and that is that this club was not outside the back door until *after*—that pajama top dropped threads and yarns and blood to the floor, and as the club fell on the floor, it picked up the threads and picked up the yarns with the blood and then it was thrown out the door.

"Ladies and gentlemen, I have talked to you a long time about all this type of evidence. But what does it mean? How could this have happened?

"We know from the evidence that the defendant, as we have said before, was a good doctor. We know that his family loved him. We know that from the Valentine cards. We know from the card that he read from the witness stand shortly before the end of direct examination that Colette loved him very much.

"I suggest to you, however, that what the defense

tried to do was to prove the defendant's love and character through Colette and not through himself. We know that the defendant had been unfaithful in his marriage. We know that he had worked the weekend before; he was perhaps tired. We know from the evidence that there was a—maybe it is a minor problem—the problem of Kristen coming to the bed. We know that he, according to his story, went to bed late that night and found that the bed was wet.

"I am not by any stretch of the imagination suggesting that the slaughter took place over any one thing. I don't think so, but I think that you can infer from the evidence that a fight developed in the master bedroom between Colette and the defendant—a struggle—an altercation. We know that Colette was bruised—perhaps she was struck.

"You know those words—'Daddy, Daddy, Daddy, Daddy.' I believe those words were said, but not from fear of intruders. I think you can infer from the evidence that they were said as Kimberly came to the master bedroom to find out what was going on between her father and mother. We know that she was there. We know from the evidence that her blood was found on the sheet, on the floor, and in the hall.

"We suggest, perhaps, that Colette, in an attempt to save herself or to fight back, got the old dull Geneva Forge knife and perhaps struck the defendant.

"I suggest that the defendant, perhaps in a frenzy, perhaps mad, perhaps disgusted, perhaps exhausted—he knew that he was going to be away for thirty days in March, if he could, while his wife was six or seven months pregnant—the defendant in one tragic, brief moment—so brief—lost control and came back with that club, and as he did, he struck Kimberly and struck his wife.

"At that point, ladies and gentlemen, the future is at stake. It may be too late at that point to undo that which is done. You know how hard it is to unring the bell. You know the words, 'Jeff, Jeff, Jeff, why are they doing this to me?' Think how close that is to, 'Jeff, Jeff, Jeff, why are *you* doing this to me?'"

"After Kimberly was struck, we suggest that she was picked up and carried back to her room and struck with this club again and that Colette went to protect or to see what was happening to Kristen, and while she was in there, Colette was struck again and carried back to the master bedroom.

"Then, of course, things had simply gone beyond repair. You can't go back and make the family happy again, drink liqueur, and watch Johnny Carson. It has gone too far.

"An Old Hickory paring knife was located and that knife was taken and Colette MacDonald was stabbed sixteen times and Kimberly was stabbed in the neck at least eight to ten times.

"I think that you can infer from the evidence that— you know, you remember the *Esquire* magazine and the words in it: the Manson-type murders and a multiplicity of weapons equaling a multiplicity of people. An icepick was obtained. And Kristen was stabbed with the icepick after she had already been stabbed with the knife.

"You remember the testimony of the CID agent who interviewed the defendant in the hospital on the morning of the murders, and who said that he became incoherent and confused when he talked about Kristen. Kristen was so hard to talk about. Perhaps that was because it was the most cold to do—a defenseless little girl. Kimberly and Colette had perhaps been struck while he was angered, but not Kristen." Blackburn paused again, allowing the jury to think about that for a moment. Then he resumed.

"Well, you know, there is no such thing as perfect murder. The pajama top was probably already on Colette's chest. And I think you can find from the evidence that the defendant forgot it was there and made that terrible mistake of stabbing Colette with the icepick through that blue pajama top and that is how those holes got there.

"He didn't know at that time that four years later, the FBI would figure out that forty-eight can match twenty-one.

"I believe that the weapons—the Old Hickory knife and the icepick—were wiped off on the bathmat. Do irrational and irresponsible drug-crazed people wipe off weapons and then throw them outside to be found by investigators?

"Why did he say that the Geneva Forge knife was pulled out of the chest of Colette even though Paul Stombaugh testified that in his opinion that knife was dull and did not make any of the cuts in her clothing? Remember, he said, 'Don't forget that I pulled the knife out of her chest.' I suggest that you could find from the evidence that he did that because he didn't know what was on that knife and he had to have an explanation for why it was there—he forgot to throw that one out.

"I suggest that the Geneva Forge knife didn't kill anybody. If he pulled it out of her chest, why does the evidence suggest that there was no significant amount of blood on that knife? Perhaps, because it didn't go in that chest—it nicked the defendant's arm.

"I believe that the surgical gloves were then taken—I think you can find from the evidence—and used to write the word PIG on the headboard. The self-infliction of one injury was made, the story was concocted, the MPs were called, and he lay down next to his wife to wait for help."

Once more Jim Blackburn paused, and when he resumed his voice was even softer—his cadence slower—than before. "You know," he said, approaching the jurors now and looking directly at them, "the defendant had a lot of nice character testimony, and I am sure that each of you, if you were accused of a crime, would have the same."

Leaning forward, his voice almost a whisper, his regional accent thicker than it had been for seven weeks, he said, "But don't ever forget that perhaps the greatest crime of all was committed 2,000 years ago. And the night before Christ was betrayed, Judas Iscariot would have had twelve of the best character witnesses this world has ever known to have said he couldn't have done it. But you know that he did."

Every eye in the courtroom was on him now, every ear awaiting his next words. "Ladies and gentlemen," he said, "if in the future, after this case is over, you should think of it again, I ask you to think and to remember Colette, Kimberly, and Kristen.

"They have been dead for almost ten years. That is right now around 3,400 or 3,500 days and nights that you have had and I have had and the defendant has had that they haven't. They would have liked to have had those.

"And so if in the future you should say a prayer, say one for them. If in the future you should light a candle, light one for them. If in the future you should cry a tear, cry one for them."

The sadness in his tone, the sadness in the room, had a weight to it that was the culmination of nine and a half years of the grief and agony of all who had cared—and of all who had come to care—about Jeffrey MacDonald's pregnant wife and little girls.

"We ask for nothing in the name of persecution," Blackburn said. "We ask for nothing in the name of harassment. We ask for nothing in the name of what is wrong. Nothing. But, God, we ask for everything in the name of what is right and in the name of what is just. That is why we are here. We ask for everything in the name of truth.

"Ladies and gentlemen, this is horribly tragic and horribly sad, as you know, because you have seen Mrs. Kassab and you have seen Mrs. MacDonald and it is sad for both of them—both of them were grandmothers, not just one—and it is sad for the defendant.

"But it is sad most of all for those who paid the highest price of all—with their lives.

"And so we ask you, ladies and gentlemen, to return a verdict of guilty as to clubbing and stabbing Colette, guilty of clubbing and stabbing Kimberly, and guilty—perhaps most of all—of stabbing little Kristen.

"You remember—I am sure you have heard it many times—part of the third chapter of Ecclesiastes—'There is a time for everything under the heavens—a time to be born and a time to die.'

"Surely, God did not intend on the 17th of February, 1970, for Colette, Kimberly, and Kristen MacDonald to die.

"It is time, ladies and gentlemen. It is so late in the day. It is time that someone speak for justice and truth and return a verdict of guilty against this man."

7

The night before, Bernie Segal had spent hours preparing his closing argument. He continued to insist, even privately, that the jury would acquit MacDonald even if he, Segal, were to offer no closing remarks whatsoever, but he had waited more than nine years to purge himself of all the rage and frustration and anguish he felt on behalf of his most favored, most publicized client, and he had no intention of letting the moment pass.

In its closing days the MacDonald trial had come to attract the attention not only of the North Carolina press and of *Newsday* on Long Island, but of *The Washington Post, The New York Times,* the *Los Angeles Times,* the television networks, and the news magazines. *People,* to Segal's horror and to the astonishment and dismay of Jeffrey MacDonald, had just printed a feature story on Freddy Kassab and his long quest for justice, in which Kassab was pictured surrounded by law books, looking somber and determined, as if he were perhaps a new appointee to the U.S. Supreme Court, and in which he was quoted as saying, quite unjudicially, "If the courts of this country will not administer justice, then I most certainly will."

Of the three hours and fifteen minutes allotted to the defense for its presentation, Segal had decided that he would speak for the first two, focusing, in detail, on the inconsistencies in the government's circumstantial case. Then Wade Smith would speak for an hour, in the finest down-home, country-boy style he could muster, about what a wonderful human being Jeffrey MacDonald was, and about how much love he and his family had shared, and about how unthinkable it was that a man such as this could have performed deeds such as those with which he was charged.

Smith, it must be said, given free rein for an hour, had the ability not only to make each and every member of a Raleigh jury feel that he had known and loved them all since kindergarten, and that the opportunity to speak to them again, even under such unfortunate circumstances as these, was one of the greatest and rarest pleasures of his life, but that even so decent-appearing and kindly a man as Mr. Blackburn—while by no means duplicitous, or even manipulative—might be just the teeniest bit less worthy of their absolute faith and trust than he had hitherto seemed.

Then Segal was to return to the lectern once again for fifteen minutes of fire and brimstone—venting every bit of his and Jeffrey MacDonald's spleen at the way they had been treated throughout the whole sordid affair. He would attack the CID, the FBI, Victor Woerheide, Brian Murtagh, and each and every principle for which they stood, and by the time he was finished, the jury (he was convinced) would be worked up into such a frenzy of anger at this high-handed government mistreatment of a truly decent and noble human being that they would hardly be able to sit through Jim Blackburn's rebuttal, so eager would they be to bring to an end Jeffrey MacDonald's long personal nightmare.

It did not work out that way. Bernie Segal carried a wristwatch with him to the lectern, but he was so caught up in the moment that not once—until he was interrupted by the tapping of Franklin Dupree's pencil and a quiet reminder from the bench that "You have three hours and fifteen minutes and you have already used three hours and ten minutes of it"—did he look at it, nor did he, apparently, give any thought whatsoever to the passage of time.

After two hours of Segal's rambling, sometimes incoherent, often vituperative, and consistently repetitive harangue, Wade Smith had found himself faced with what he considered to be perhaps the most difficult decision of his legal career.

Should he leave the defense table, walk to the lectern and whisper to Segal that he was running well over the previously arranged time limit, and what's more, *he had not yet even begun to cover most of the specific points he had intended to include in his argument*—or should he, because, as had been made clear to him from the day Segal and his entourage had arrived in Raleigh, he was not, in fact co-counsel, but only another one of Segal's many assistants, just sit tight and let nature take its course?

Jeffrey MacDonald, the client, was sitting beside him. If MacDonald had so instructed him, Smith indeed would have made that long and embarrassing walk across the courtroom to tell the chief counsel that he was letting his last chance for even a hung jury, much less an acquittal, drown beneath the endless torrent of his words.

But MacDonald, though squirming uncomfortably in his seat from time to time, like each of the jurors and everyone else in the courtroom except Segal, did not issue any such instruction. So Wade Smith sat still and watched silently—and in professional horror—as Bernie Segal, like a runaway truck on a steep, icy hill, careened wildly out of control.

From the start, at 1 P.M., when Segal had said bitterly and sarcastically to the jury, "Yes, ladies and gentlemen, there has been a tragedy, but we haven't talked about the real tragedy in this case yet"—the real tragedy being, in Segal's mind, not the murders of Colette and Kimberly and Kristen, but the subsequent "destruction" of Jeffrey MacDonald's life by the American legal system, Segal's tone and style and content—particularly coming after Blackburn's quiet country elegance—had been not at all what the jury had been expecting, or wanting to hear.

By 4:10, when Judge Dupree finally and mercifully tapped his pencil, Segal was swinging wild roundhouse punches at the government, as if he were the prosecuting attorney and it was the Justice Department that was on trial.

". . . Again, the government makes fun," Segal was shouting. " 'Why did you come forward, Mr. Posey?' If you come forward at all, you get mocked! If you don't come forward because you think they don't need you, you get mocked! You can't win!"

Even after three hours and ten minutes, Segal had not yet gotten around to Helena Stoeckley. He was forced to squeeze her into the four minutes which followed the tapping of the pencil, leaving Wade Smith with exactly sixty seconds, rather than the prearranged sixty minutes, to convince the jury that Jeffrey MacDonald was such a decent man that he couldn't possibly have killed his wife and children, no matter what the physical evidence appeared to show.

A recess was declared by Judge Dupree, during which Smith went over to bargain with Jim Blackburn—to bargain the way two good old boys can, knowing that they will both be living and practicing in the same city long after Bernie Segal and Jeffrey MacDonald and all the out-of-town newspaper reporters have departed.

As a professional attorney—and in order to minimize the possibility that Judge Dupree might grant Smith his entire hour—Blackburn, who had forty minutes remaining to him for rebuttal, agreed to give Wade Smith ten minutes of that time.

There wasn't much Smith could do to repair the damage, but he tried. He picked up his tempo, the way he might have on his banjo, and played it hard and fast and as strong as he could.

"Let your insides talk to you for a minute about the case," Smith suggested. "What do you *feel*? Don't you wonder *why* when you think about this? *Why* did it happen? Don't you wonder, when you are thinking about whether Jeff did it, *why* would he have done it? Can you think of a reason why?

"Now, the prosecution is not under any obligation to furnish a motive. The law does not place that burden on them. Nevertheless, there is natural law. That is law that we feel inside of us—every one of us. And we feel that we can say to the prosecution, 'Tell us why. Tell us *why* this man would have destroyed his family.'

"Think about the photographs that you saw of Jeff with the family, Jeff with the children, Colette with the children, the children playing. It makes no sense. There is no motive. It is unbelievable. It is incredible. Don't you know that Jeffrey MacDonald could not have destroyed his children? Don't you know that that raises a reasonable doubt?

"If you look at the autopsy photographs of those little children and think about what it would take to cause someone to raise a knife and destroy them—to destroy Kristen—not just destroy her but absolutely mutilate her—just stab her to death, thrust after thrust after thrust. It can't be true."

Wade Smith paused. He looked across the courtroom at Jeffrey MacDonald, who was sitting perfectly still, eyes downcast, hands folded on the table in front of him. Smith turned back to the jurors.

"He needs peace," Wade Smith said softly. "He hasn't had it in a long time. You, as a jury, are immensely powerful because you can give him peace for the first time in years and years."

Months later, one of the jurors was to remark, "I don't know, I don't know. We wanted to believe. We really did. Maybe if Wade Smith had just talked to us a little longer . . ."

But he didn't—he couldn't—and Jim Blackburn did. He talked for the final twenty minutes. "You know," he said, "I couldn't help but think during the last ten minutes, listening to Wade talk about motive, you know, and the unbelievability of it all—and I suppose, in a way, it *is* unbelievable that a successful person might kill his family and that a person to whom his children cried 'Daddy' might raise his hand in anger or rage, or coolness, perhaps, and kill his family—but I can't help thinking back to what I said late this morning.

"We don't contend—we don't contend that Dr. Mac-Donald killed his family because Kristen wet the bed. We contend, ladies and gentlemen, that the defendant killed his family because events overtook themselves too fast.

"Think yourselves for a moment in your own daily lives if you have been angry at someone but not really meaning to be and you have raised your hand—maybe to your own child—but you would never, you know, follow through. You stopped short. You didn't do anything.

"Suppose when you are tired late in the night or early in the morning and you are worn out and things just aren't going right, that you do raise your hand and before you can regret it, you have done something that is irretrievable. Everything else, ladies and gentlemen, we say, in that crime scene, flowed from that moment.

"I don't say to you that the defendant, as I said this morning, has always been a bad person. I don't say to you that for the last nine years, he has been a bad person. But I do say to you that on the early morning of the 17th of February, time stopped in the MacDonald home for a flicker of a second, something happened which caused tragic events to unfold and the killing of the children was necessary for self-survival.

"Mr. Segal, in his presentation this afternoon, attacked again—he attacked us, he attacked the CID, he attacked Stombaugh. Anybody who has ever been with the government, as I recall, was attacked. He said that our case was like a house built on sand. I suggest to you, ladies and gentlemen, the only sand in this case is that which was perhaps attempted to be thrown into your eyes to keep you from seeing the evidence.

"You know, Wade Smith talked a minute ago about what you feel inside. Well, that is all right. But what is inside when the defendant takes the stand and does not attempt to explain the unexplainable? When he is asked questions and doesn't give an answer and relies on his counsel to answer for him?

"We rely, ladies and gentlemen, and ask you to rely on the law of common sense. I will repeat it again this afternoon because it makes a whole lot of sense to me. Don't you know if he *could* have, he *would* have?

"Mr. Segal said earlier that the physical evidence doesn't say anything—it doesn't speak. It is only attorneys speaking. I say to you that the physical evidence simply *cries out* an explanation. The fact that twenty-one thrusts through the pajama top can make forty-eight holes that line up with twenty-one holes in the vicim's chest is a singular, significant fact which, I tell you, proves to me beyond a reasonable doubt that Jeffrey MacDonald killed his wife, Colette, and it is a very short leap from that to say that he killed the other two as well.

"This is a difficult case, not because the evidence is difficult, but because of the people involved—the Kassabs, who have been injured and will be injured for the rest of their lives regardless of your verdict. Mrs. MacDonald, who has been injured and will be injured the rest of her life regardless of your verdict; their friends who will suffer the same fate, and, I guess, the defendant himself.

"You know, I am sure it is very sad for everybody who knew these people to look at those photographs. I think it is very sad for people who knew these people to look at pictures of the kids playing, of Halloween and Christmas. I wish more than you know that we could have shown you that kind of picture. I wish more than you know we weren't here. I wish more than you know that I did not think the evidence pointed to the defendant.

"I think the supreme tragedy in this whole thing really is, if our evidence is correct and the defendant did it, which we believe he did—think for a moment of the last minutes of Colette, Kimberly, and Kristen, when they realized that they were going to die and they realized for the first and the last time who it was that was going to make them die.

"You wouldn't think it. People have said that he is not that kind of guy, but, ladies and gentlemen, we think that he did.

"For that, we are sorry. For that, you have an awesome burden and responsibility. You have got to decide, beginning tomorrow, what the evidence is and what your verdict will be. We believe strongly—as strongly as we don't want to believe—that he did it, and that he is guilty of Count One of first-degree murder, of Count Two of first-degree murder, and Count Three of first-degree murder, and I ask you to so find."

Then Blackburn added a final word. He said, "Wade said that you might have the power to give the defendant peace. Well, we suggest, ladies and gentlemen, that regardless of your verdict—whether it is innocent, innocent, innocent, or guilty, guilty, guilty—you don't have the power to give this defendant peace."

And then, like a man leaving for the last time the bedside of a dying relative, Jim Blackburn slowly turned from the jurors and walked back to his chair.

The seven weeks of trial had exacted a steep price from all concerned, but there were few who could claim to have suffered more than the jurors. The extraordinary responsibility—having to decide whether to set free forever a man who had been under investigation and prosecution for almost a decade, or whether to condemn the same man to spend the remainder of his life in prison—

when combined with an unceasing awareness of the particularly horrid and profoundly depressing nature of the offense had combined to make the summer of 1979, for many, the most traumatic of their lives.

And, for seven weeks, through the gore and the shock and the sadness, this knowledge—that one day they would have to decide—had been growing inexorably almost in the manner of a malignant tumor.

The former state policeman who had scored so high on the Duke professor's selection chart (and who was to be chosen by his fellows as the foreman), had for weeks been awakened at night by the sound of a baby crying. There was not, however, any baby in the house. Coming awake in the darkness he would awaken his wife alongside him to ask her if she heard it, too. She never did. Some nights the cry lingered for so long in the air, even after he had come fully awake, that he would get out of bed to investigate—to be sure that there was not a crying baby in another room. There never was.

Another juror—a twenty-seven-year-old chemist, himself the father of a two-and-a-half-year-old son—had been unable to sleep at all the night before deliberations were to begin. Shortly after 1 A.M. he had tiptoed into the bedroom of his son and had stood for a long time, in silence, staring at the boy's sleeping form. "The thought that a father could stab his child through the heart thirteen times . . ." he said later. "It was almost too difficult to grasp."

Almost. As the Raleigh *Times* said in an editorial the day after the verdict was announced, "One of the jury's most difficult obstacles was its instinctive rejection of the idea that a well-educated, apparently civilized man like Dr. MacDonald, committed to healing and saving lives rather than to taking them, could have wrought this horror."

And, as another of the jurors was to say: "Everybody was sorry for Dr. MacDonald. We didn't want to convict him."

There was a party that night, just as there had been a party the night before the first day of trial. Wade Smith came with a guitar. For some time it was feared that Bernie Segal would not come at all, so despondent was he said to be in the wake of his closing argument.

Segal eventually did arrive, though, and there were beer and wine in moderation, as there had been the first night, and—as on the first night—Wade Smith eventually began to play music and to sing.

The room was filled with a spirit of camaraderie, touched with the first traces of nostalgia. Tension regarding the fact that on the morrow the jury would begin to deliberate the fate of Jeffrey MacDonald was, for at least a few hours, repressed. The mood seemed almost akin to the last night of summer camp: soon, whatever the outcome, all these people who had worked so hard and who had shared so much with such intensity would be scattered to various parts of the country, and the chapter of their lives titled "MacDonald Trial" would be closed, though for none of them soon forgotten.

Wade Smith, as was his custom, sang traditional favorites: familiar verses, with which it was easy to sing along. For the most part he kept the tempo upbeat. It was toward the end of the evening that he played and sang a more contemporary song: Bob Dylan's "I Shall Be Released." To many in the room the words to this were less familiar, and so there were fewer voices joined to Smith's, though no lack of attention to the lyric, by the time he reached the final verse:

Standing next to me in this lonely crowd,
Is a man who swears he's not to blame.
All day long I hear him shout so loud,
Crying out that he was framed. . . .

Shortly after 4 P.M. the next day, in the suite of defense offices located just down the hallway from the courtroom, Jeffrey MacDonald's secretary, who had flown in from California, was on the phone to New York making reservations for MacDonald and Candy Kramer to spend the following night at the Warwick Hotel in New York City. She had already made a dinner reservation at a West Side Italian restaurant named La Scala. She had also just sent off a check to Evergreen, Colorado, enrolling MacDonald in a wilderness photography workshop that would begin the following week.

In the background, there was talk of how to handle the press conference after the acquittal—who should speak first, Segal or MacDonald—and of whether to leave Raleigh by chartered plane immediately or to wait for a later commercial flight.

There was also some discussion about whether MacDonald should wear into the courtroom the bulletproof vest which a Long Beach policeman had flown east with—in case Freddy Kassab, in his moment of supreme and final frustration, might try to administer with a gun the "justice" he for so long had threatened—and talk also about whether the *Queen Mary* might be rented for the victory celebration which would be held upon MacDonald's triumphant return to California.

Only Wade Smith, who as the trial had progressed had drifted further and further from the core of the MacDonald group, remained detached and isolated. For long periods, he sat by himself at the defense table in the suddenly vacant courtroom, his hands clasped before him, staring alternately at the ceiling, the walls, and the floor. It was as if he were a lone worshiper come to an empty church, seeking a few midafternoon moments of solace and tranquillity. Indeed, he would say later that he *had* wanted to pass those final hours in silent contemplation, removed from the nervous, noisy, obtrusive optimism and forced gaiety of the defense suite. Wade Smith had tried many cases and he knew all too well when a big one was about to be lost.

MacDonald was just beginning to explain to a pert, young female assistant the intricacies of Las Vegas craps tables when a court clerk knocked on the door to say that—after only six and a half hours of deliberation—a verdict had been reached.

It took only a few minutes for the entire cast to reassemble. Then Judge Dupree nodded at a bailiff, who opened the door that led to the room in which the jury's deliberation had been conducted.

The first juror to walk through the door was the ex–Green Beret. His head was down and he was crying. He was followed, almost immediately, by the woman whose son was a member of Kappa Alpha. Her head was down and she was crying, too.

Then there was a pause, which seemed long—though maybe it was only ten or fifteen seconds—before the third juror came through the door. But it didn't matter. It would not have mattered if the pause had lasted an hour. Not only Jeffrey MacDonald and Bernie Segal and Wade Smith and MacDonald's mother, and his secretary and the friends who had flown in from California, but Jim Blackburn and Brian Murtagh and, in the first row of the right side of the aisle, Freddy and Mildred Kassab, knew what was coming. An ex–Green Be-

ret who has just voted to acquit another ex–Green Beret
of three murder charges does not walk into the courtroom in tears.

MacDonald was found guilty of second-degree murder
in the deaths of Colette and Kimberly, and guilty of murder in the first degree—because the jury believed it to
have been a calculated act, designed to support his cover
story—in the death of his younger daughter, Kristen.

MacDonald's mother rose from her seat and hurried
to a small private alcove just outside. From there, as
Judge Dupree prepared to pass sentence upon her son,
her keening wail of torment could be heard, above the
continuing weeping and sobbing of some of the jurors.
Not the ex–state policeman though: chosen as foreman,
he had announced the verdict dry-eyed and in a flat, un-
emotional voice.

Dupree asked the defendant if he had anything to say.
MacDonald stood. He was wearing his best pin-striped
suit. Jeff MacDonald: Most Popular, Most Likely to Succeed, Princeton, med school, the Green Berets, the
childhood sweetheart, the two little girls, the farm in
Connecticut, the medical career—even the boat and the
sports car and the condo and Candy Kramer—all ashes
now, as far as he was concerned. Dust and ashes.

He said only this, speaking in a loud, though slightly
husky voice: "Sir, I'm not guilty. I don't think the court
heard all the evidence."

Judge Dupree sentenced him to three life terms in
prison, to be served not concurrently, but consecutively.
It was the harshest sentence he could administer, the
death penalty not being applicable under federal law.

Then a U.S. marshal approached, carrying handcuffs,
and Jeffrey MacDonald—his face betraying no more

emotion than does the surface of a glacier—held his arms out in front of him, as requested.

With the handcuffs secured around his wrists, and with Bernie Segal's immediate motion for bail denied by Franklin T. Dupree, MacDonald was led out a rear door—a door through which he had never walked before. He did not look back. If he had, he would have seen Freddy and Mildred Kassab sitting side by side in silence, staring at his departing figure until it disappeared behind the door.

CONCLUSION

IF I HAVE WALKED WITH VANITY

If I have walked with vanity,
or if my foot hath hasted to deceit;
Let me be weighed in an even balance,
that God may know mine integrity.

—Job 31:5–6

1

I suppose from the start I had suspected that there must be more to the case against MacDonald than he had suggested to me on the day that I met him. The Justice Department does not try a man for murder nine and a half years after the crimes just because his father-in-law is mad at him. But certainly I had arrived in Raleigh bearing the same presumption of innocence which was to be required of the jurors. As the weeks passed, however, the doubts grew.

There were the fibers and the bloodstains and the footprint, and of course the blue pajama top whose forty-eight holes matched the twenty-one in Colette's chest. All this was new to me, and it began to grow rather unsettling as I rode to and from the courtroom with MacDonald and over to Chapel Hill with him on the weekends to browse through bookstores, and to Durham to stroll with him across the campus of Duke University, which he said reminded him so much of Princeton, and as I sat up late with him—and his mother—watching *Saturday Night Live*.

It was not the sort of thing one spoke about over the Kappa Alpha dinner table, but *he had not been badly hurt in 1970.* Those twenty-three stab wounds that he had referred to on the Dick Cavett show: they had never existed. A bump on the head, two slight cuts from a knife, some fingernail scratches (and this was long before I learned that a piece of skin had been found beneath one of Colette's fingernails) and a neat, clean incision, one centimeter long, between two ribs, just deep enough to cause the partial collapse of one lung. This was all that had resulted from his struggle against three armed attackers: a struggle during which he was aware—he said—that he was fighting for his own life and for the lives of his wife and children. ("He's either lying," Franz Joseph Grebner said in 1970, upon learning the limited extent of MacDonald's injuries, "or else he's the biggest pussy in the world.")

I had by now seen the pictures of his wife and children. I had seen too many pictures too many times. I had seen pictures that had been taken when the bodies were found, and I had seen pictures taken at the autopsy, after the blood had been washed off. The crack in Kimberly's skull looked like an aerial view of the Grand Canyon. She had been a five-year-old child. Kristen had been two and a half. She had been stabbed more than thirty times in her chest and back. I had seen slides showing the holes in her heart.

And Colette—pregnant Colette, the childhood sweetheart—her skull fractured, both arms broken as she had raised them in front of her to ward off blows, and her chest penetrated—not once, as had been the chest of her husband—but dozens of times, by both knife and ice-pick, weapons which had been thrust into her up to the hilt.

Jeffrey MacDonald had not needed a single stitch to close his wounds. "Not even Mercurochrome," as Mildred Kassab had said. For years he had been saying that he'd been knocked unconscious and had almost been killed by the attack upon him in his living room—yet not one drop of blood had been found there.

At the hospital, his vital signs had been normal, while back at the apartment the CID photographer had to leave because he was about to get sick to his stomach.

There were a lot of nights I did not sleep in Raleigh. It got worse toward the end, particularly after Helena Stoeckley had testified. It was not so much what she had said or hadn't said—it was Jeffrey MacDonald's absolute lack of reaction to her presence.

If his story were true, she was the woman who had participated in the slaughter of his family and here she was, after nine and a half years, twenty feet from him in the courtroom. Yet he showed no anger; no sorrow; not even curiosity. There was anger at the judge, of course, for not permitting the "Stoeckley witnesses" to testify; there was anger at Brian Murtagh and Paul Stombaugh and Mildred Kassab. But toward the woman who had—he said—destroyed the people he had loved most, and who had reduced his own life to dust and ashes, he displayed less emotion than he did while watching Gilda Radner perform on *Saturday Night Live*.

Two days after his conviction I drove with his mother and Candy Kramer to visit him at the Federal Correctional Institute at Butner, North Carolina, where he was being held temporarily, pending a decision on where he would be sent to serve his term.

In the visitors' lounge, which was not dissimilar to a

bus station cafeteria, MacDonald, wearing canvas slippers and shapeless, gray, prison-issue clothing, embraced first his mother, then Candy Kramer, then me.

We sat at a small, Formica-topped table. Candy, who had flown to Raleigh from New York after the verdict, had brought clippings from the previous day's *New York Times* and New York *Daily News*. Each paper had printed a front-page story about the conviction, accompanied by a picture of MacDonald, in pin-striped suit, being led from the courtroom in handcuffs.

He read the stories through from start to finish. When he was done he looked again at the pictures on page one. He had made the *Daily News* before, but this was the first time that a photograph of him had ever appeared on the front page of the *Times*.

When the visit was over, he gave the clippings to his mother, so she could file them in the scrapbooks which she had been maintaining for nine and a half years.

"If we can prove that he did it," Jim Blackburn had said, *"then we don't have to prove that he's the kind of guy who could have done it."*

They had, indeed, proved that he'd done it. Not to the satisfaction of his mother, or Candy Kramer, or his friends from Southern California, but his mother and Candy Kramer and his friends from Southern California—unlike the jurors—had not attended every session of the trial.

For Blackburn and the jurors it was over. But not for me. Having learned all I had learned during the summer, I now felt I needed to know more.

As I left MacDonald there, behind the bars and concrete walls and steel doors of Butner—having just had him tell me that he hoped I was a friend who would stand by him—it was not possible simply to accept the jury's verdict. I had to try to learn more about what kind of man he really was.

I flew home the next day and the day after that a letter arrived. MacDonald had written it even before I'd been to see him. He had written it on the morning of Thursday, August 30, 1970—the morning after his conviction.

Zero Hour + 18

I've got to write to you so I won't go crazy. I'm standing in my cell only because they don't allow chairs in solitary. I'm trying to fathom—trying to figure out what the fuck happened. Those words from the foreman's mouth crashed into my brain & I can't think straight. Just as I felt, "Finally—justice and maybe some peace down the road,"—he said "Guilty" of 2nd Degree murder. The room was spinning and I couldn't hear the rest. I remember the tears on many jurors' faces, and I remember the look of "Please, forgive me," on the faces of the black juror and the lady who cried so much—but I really can't remember the jury polling except how forceful the guy with the pinched face in the front row (3 in from the right, I think) said, "Guilty," 3 times. He really believed it. I can't understand how it happened—12 normal people heard a good portion of the "evidence" (not all of course) and bought the gov't line of bullshit. Was it just because the gov't said so? Were our jury selection people wrong?? I guess so— they were so right-wing, middle class, they couldn't believe the gov't would falsify evidence, or fake it, or redo it, or build an imaginary web of circumstances based on vicious Mildred Kassab now remembering, "Something was wrong in that house."

I am now a convict. Convicted of murder of my family. Colette and Kimmy and Kristy had come back so strong to me over the past three months it was like 1970. The 9 years had been swept away and I knew it would be a slow painful recovery for the next 1 to 2 years when the "not guilty" verdict came down. Now—I just don't know. My brain has never felt like this. In 1970 I was so numb with grief I just plodded through the motions. The night of April 6th 1970 was brutal—but I don't remember the pain like this.

The fucking walls are closing in. Every once in a while a warden or a shrink comes around and asks how I am. Someone in my voice answers, "OK—just taking it one day at a time." What I mean is that "I'm going crazy—I'm trying to hold on 1 sec. at a time." I wish the guards here were brutal—you could focus on some uniformed asshole and out-tough him (even if that meant not falling for the hint of a threat or an insult). Here the fucking guards are all "correctional officers" who went to at least 2 yrs. of college & discuss things like, "The first 24 hrs. are the worst," and "Keep a low profile"—Do you know those lectures?

Why the fuck am I in Solitary? The warden says for my benefit, so inmates won't test the new "Fast gun from the West." I don't really want to talk to inmates but a little more light in the cell and a window bigger than 8" by 8" looking at another solitary cell across the hall would help. If I don't run soon I'll go nuts.

Last night was the longest ever. The guard looked in my window with a flashlight every 15 min. for 12 hrs. (suicide watch). The few times I fell asleep a flashlight would immediately penetrate my eyeballs. I

*can't figure out what the fuck I'm supposed to kill
myself with. They only allow plastic spoons with the
meal, the guard sits right outside my cell, and checks
every 15 mins. I guess I'm supposed to have smuggled
something in, despite the 3 strip searches, the 6 gates
we went through, and my room, which is bare except
for a welded, one piece bed, a single piece toilet with
sink above it and a stand bolted to the floor (for food
and toiletries).*

*I want to see Bernie because I love him & he is
probably hurting beyond belief & wants to know he is
not to blame. I want to see my Mom because no matter how I look, by seeing me she will be better (and I
probably will be, too). I would also love to see my best
friends—including (I hope) you. But in all honesty
I'm crying too much today and do cry whenever I
think of my close friends. I feel dirty & soiled by the
decision & can't tell you why, and am ashamed. I
somehow don't feel that way with Bernie & Mom but
think today it would be difficult to look at you or
shake your hand—I know I'll cry and want to hug
you and yet the verdict stands there, screaming, "You
are guilty of the murder of your family!!" And I
don't know what to say to you except it is not true,
and I hope you know that and feel it and that you are
my friend.*

Jeffrey MacDonald remained in solitary confinement
at Butner for six days. He wrote me a letter every day,
sometimes more than one a day.

*I knew my Mom was strong but she surprises even
me. What an incredible person to pull it all together
and be so optimistic so soon after the crushing defeat.*

Someday when this is over I hope I can return just part of her love and caring. . . .

It's strange how 48 hrs. can alter your perspective so much. If you had asked me Wed. AM would I accept a victory through the court of appeals, I would have laughed at you. Now I am pleading for my lawyers to argue the best case ever in front of 4th Circuit in order that I may win a more hollow victory than anyone ever previously guessed I would accept. Like Lenny Bruce said—when it's your ass-hole they are pouring hot lead into, then tell them you'll withhold secrets from the enemy (& not before). Of course I'll accept a 4th Circuit victory. It will be more difficult to face my friends than it would have been with a victory last Wed at 4:45 p.m.—but I'll do it. I hope my friends accept it—and the rest of the world that thinks I got off on a technicality will have to wait for your book. If they won't read your book, fuck them. Then they are worse than the jury. I can't get my mind off the tear-stained faces. Why couldn't they have had the courage to vote the way I'm sure the majority felt in their gut—proof of guilt was not *beyond a reasonable doubt. . . .*

Have you ever been strip-searched? You strip naked and they look in your ears, armpits, mouth. The guard says 'Lift it up,' and you lift first your penis, then your scrotum. You then turn around, bend over & spread your cheeks. You then lift up each foot so the guard can see the bottoms of your feet. After they search your clothes, shoes, socks & underwear you put it all back on. It's always slightly sweaty because either you're on the way to a visit and are anticipating the pleasure/pain of it—or you are coming from a visit and are suffering from the new-each-time separation from the real world.

*I can now think of Colette & Kim and Kris and
not go crazy. And I can separate Colette from Bobbi.
And I can even squeeze Candy in there and not confuse it all. But 12 tear-stained faces keep intruding.
The foreman's voice keeps me awake. Couldn't the son
of a bitch have found 'reasonable doubt'? . . .*

In the first moments that followed the jury's announcement of its verdict, Franklin T. Dupree, Jr., had
denied Bernie Segal's plea that MacDonald be permitted
to remain free on bail pending appeal. The judge had
said, however, that he would consider a written motion
to that effect. Segal filed such a motion on September 4.

The next day, with Dupree not yet having ruled on
the request, the process of transferring MacDonald from
Butner to the Federal Correctional Institution at Terminal Island, California, was begun.

Despite the ominous sound of its name, Terminal Island was, under the circumstances, as desirable a destina-
tion as MacDonald could possibly have hoped for. A
low-security institution on the outskirts of Long Beach,
just fifteen minutes from St. Mary's Hospital and less
than half an hour from his Huntington Beach condominium, Terminal Island did not, as a rule, house individuals convicted of homicide. In fact, of the more than
five hundred inmates, MacDonald would be the only
one serving a life sentence.

It was not, then, Terminal Island itself that was objec-
tionable from Jeffrey MacDonald's point of view: it was
the means by which he would get there. Early on the
morning of September 5, MacDonald was placed aboard a
Bureau of Prisons bus to begin the long journey west. Unlike Greyhound or Trailways, the federal prison transport
system did not offer express service to the coast. A prisoner

would ride the bus to wherever its next stop happened to be. There, he would be held—for hours, days, or weeks—until the next leg of his journey could be scheduled.

MacDonald's first stop was the federal penitentiary at Atlanta. From there he wrote to me on Thursday, September 6, expressing (among other sentiments) his displeasure at his attorneys' decision to permit his transfer while the bail question was still under consideration by Judge Dupree.

> *Fucking lawyers are a pain in the ass. They charge you coming & going and for all their little expenses, lose goddamn cases when they shouldn't be lost, promise you the world all the while, and don't know shit about what they are doing. They operate like mail order physicians. The whole profession sucks. . . . Every prisoner along the way fell over laughing when they heard I could have stayed at Butner until the bail was settled. Everyone in the system knows the single worst thing about the prison system is the method used for cross-country transfer: up at 4 a.m., into bus at 5:30 a.m., chained & manacled (ankles, waist & wrists) & drive to next prison. It may take 4 hrs. or 14. No one cares. You stay in chains the whole time (ankles, wrists & waist) so if the bus overturns you can burn to death instead of escaping. The bus is caged, barred, partitioned & has 3 hacks (guards). You can't have anything. No shoelaces. No contact lenses. No books, magazines. If you want to pee, you struggle down the alley in chains, spend 10 minutes getting your fly open & pee down a big hole in the back of the bus. Holding tank, but no chemicals of course. The coffee runs out at noon, so from noon until 9:45 p.m. you get nothing. The sandwiches are bread*

& 1 (I mean one) slice of corned beef 1½" wide, or bologna. If the air conditioner breaks, tough. (No windows to open.) Each night you spend 2 hours getting photographed & fingerprinted at some Federal hovel, and then get put in Solitary. No possessions at all. No books, letters, watch, contacts, deodorant.

Every guard & prisoner at Atlanta knew I was coming. The prisoners were OK—every guard said. 'Keep your fucking back to the wall—Don't let anyone next to you. Some crazy mother-fucker will kill you here for a headline,' and on & on. By the time you get to Solitary you're begging for a single cell— and then you find out some inmates ('walk-arounds') have keys to the cells & walk in every once in a while to 'check things out.' You can't beat the son of a bitch to a pulp for scaring the shit out of you because you don't want Thorazine & a strait jacket. It's clear that you're being measured & if you're cool & handle yourself OK you suddenly get a bar of soap or a cup of (real) ice water through the foot slot. Or the dude across the hall tells you which hack to watch out for. Or someone says, 'He's the Green Beret who got screwed—leave him alone.'

I'm sitting in the VIP suite in Solitary. Some porno king just vacated it. I'm in a long line of celebrities to get this cell. I don't know what to make out of this insanity. Tomorrow at 4 a.m. I'll get awakened— I'm going to Texarkana jail, by bus. I was lucky, they said. Usually you have to wait at least a week for the Texarkana bus. The inmates say it takes up to 3 months to cross the country unless you're 'top priority celebrity' status. Can you dig it? A celebrity because I got railroaded by a N.C. judge & jury for something I didn't do 9½ years ago.

The next day, Judge Dupree reaffirmed his denial of bail, stating, "While it is true that this defendant is a well established professional man and has never heretofore failed to meet all court appearances, the situation with which he is now confronted is far different from that which has heretofore obtained. As a highly skilled physician, the defendant presumably would have no difficulty in finding employment in any one of the many countries of the world which do not have extradition treaties with the United States, and the temptation to seek refuge in another country would certainly be great indeed."

Not yet informed of Dupree's decision regarding bail, MacDonald wrote to me from Texarkana:

> *I'm going nuts waiting to hear about bail. No news in Atlanta and now nothing here for 2 days. You'd think that lawyers that spent $200,000 losing a case could spend $5 on a telegram to Texarkana with some news. IF I ever get out of jail, I hope to Fuck One of them gets shot or in a car accident & comes to my emergency room. We'll discuss fees first, then I'll disappear for a while and let them watch a clock on the wall for a while. Then I'll slowly institute treatment, stopping every now & then to wait for more money. Gradually, they'll realize that this could take years. Every time they get uptight, I'll give them the option offered me: continued flow of money for unknown treatments that are not necessary, or I can sign off the case and they are free to find another Dr. I'd love it.*

MacDonald remained in Texarkana for another ten days. Then he was bused to El Reno, Oklahoma, and then to El Paso, Texas, from where he was finally flown to the Long Beach airport, arriving on September 27, in chains. He wrote to me two days later from Terminal Island, terming it "reasonable—decent food, exercise, no harassment from guards & only subliminal violence. It's still prison. But bearable."

He then wrote: "It is very strange to sit on my bunk in prison (for Christ's sake!) and see Long Beach harbor. The ships, the sailboats, the breakwater—downtown Long Beach and the seagulls and pelicans. I see it all through (a) bars, (b) wire fence, (c) barbed wire with razor-type barbs. I am so near to my home, my friends, my work, but in truth light years away. . . ."

He continued: "I'm trying to get over some mild anterior shin splints from running on concrete in prison sneakers. My clothing box has arrived from home & I now have my Etonics. I'm also lifting weights. . . ."

He then mentioned—saying he would supply more detail later—"Notoriety upon arrival. Press attempts to see me. Everyone aware of my arrival." And continued:

> *Support continues to pour in & has really been phenomenal. I still am getting letters from N.C. citizens who apparently were/are outraged by the judge & jury's actions. People here in Long Beach have been just super. The job is still mine at the hospital. The staff is behind me, and hundreds of people from all over are offering money, time, letters, etc. etc. It makes me feel good. . . .*

On October 5, 1979, Bernie Segal asked the Fourth Circuit Court of Appeals in Richmond to overrule Judge Dupree's denial of bail.

On October 12—MacDonald's thirty-sixth birthday—friends and former colleagues from St. Mary's rented an airplane to fly over the prison, trailing a sign that said,

HAPPY BIRTHDAY ROCK—"Rock" being the nickname he had acquired in the emergency room in tribute to his coolness and steadiness under pressure.

Oral argument on his motion for bail took place before a three-judge panel of the Fourth Circuit court on November 6. Ten days later, the appeals court upheld Judge Dupree's denial. The following week I flew to California.

2

"In all the orthodox psychoses," Hervey Cleckley has written in *The Mask of Sanity,* "there is a more or less obvious alteration of reasoning process or of some other demonstrable personality feature. In the psychopath, this is not seen. The observer is confronted with a convincing mask of sanity. All the outward features of this mask are intact; it cannot be displaced or penetrated. . . . Examination reveals not merely an ordinary two-dimensional mask but what seems to be a solid and substantial structural image of the sane and rational personality. . . . The observer finds verbal and facial expressions, tones of voice, and all the other signs we have come to regard as implying conviction and emotion and the normal experiencing of life as we know it ourselves and as we assume it to be in others. . . .

"Only very slowly and by a complex estimation or judgment based on multitudinous small impressions does the conviction come upon us that, despite these intact rational processes, these normal emotional affirmations, and their consistent application in all directions, we are dealing here not with a complete man at all but with something that suggests a subtly constructed reflex machine which can mimic the human personality perfectly.

"So perfect is this reproduction of a whole and normal man that no one who examines him in a clinical setting can point out in scientific or objective terms why, or how, he is not real. And yet we eventually come to know or feel we know that reality, in the sense of full, healthy experiencing of life, is not here."

I rented a car at the Los Angeles airport and drove to Long Beach.

On that hot and cloudless Saturday morning in June, when I had driven down this same San Diego Freeway en route to my first meeting with Jeffrey MacDonald, I had been listening to an FM music station. Just as I had finally found his condominium and had located a parking space, a song ended. It was a song I had never heard before. The disc jockey, a woman, said, "I don't know why I decided to play that. It hadn't been programmed. Something just came over me and made me do it." As I was turning off the ignition, she gave the name of the song. It was "Psycho Killer, Qu'est-ce que c'est?" Those were the last words I had heard before meeting Jeffrey MacDonald for the first time. All summer long I had been telling myself it was only a coincidence, nothing more.

Now, in November, heading toward Long Beach on another warm and sunny afternoon, I turned on the radio. The first song I heard was from the new Eagles album, which had just been released. The song was called "Heartache Tonight," and it began:

Somebody's gonna hurt someone
Before the night is through.
Somebody's gonna come undone,
There's nothin' we can do . . .

I drove to St. Mary's Hospital and parked the car. I went inside and saw Jeffrey MacDonald's secretary. She gave me the keys to his condominium. She said he was holding up well. I would be living in the condominium during my stay. It was conveniently situated—less than half an hour's drive from Terminal Island—and it would provide me with easy access to the thousands of pages of material related to the case which Jeffrey MacDonald had accumulated over the years, and which he had agreed to make available to me in order that I might be better able to write my book.

Among those personality disorders upon which considerable psychiatric attention has been focused in the past decade is a condition known as pathological narcissism.

In his 1978 book, *The Culture of Narcissism*, Christopher Lasch has identified some of the character traits associated with this disorder as being "pseudo self-insight, calculating seductiveness, nervous, self-deprecatory humor, a dependence on the vicarious warmth provided by others combined with a fear of dependence, a sense of inner emptiness, and boundless repressed rage." Indeed, Lasch writes, the personality of the pathological narcissist consists "largely of defenses against this rage."

Unable to "acknowledge his own aggression, to experience guilt, or . . . to mourn for lost love objects, because of the intensity of his rage," the pathological narcissist, "while sexually promiscuous rather than repressed, and often pan-sexual as well," seeks to "avoid close involvements, which might release intense feelings of rage."

Instead, he "attempts to compensate himself for his experience of rage and envy with fantasies of wealth, beauty, and omnipotence."

Jeffrey MacDonald's condominium was quite comfortable, once I got used to all the mirrors.

In the mornings, I would sit on the deck for a while, enjoying the sun. The *Recovery Room* bobbed gently at anchor, only a few feet away. MacDonald's friends were continuing the payments on the boat and on the Citroën-Maserati and on the condominium itself, so everything would be waiting for him when he returned. They all felt—because he told them repeatedly that it was certain—that this would be only a matter of months. The Fourth Circuit Court of Appeals, despite its denial of bail, was sure either to dismiss the charges entirely on the same speedy-trial grounds it had invoked in 1975, or, at the very least, to order a new trial—so contaminated had the first one been by the malice and bias of Judge Dupree.

I would spend hours each day with MacDonald's files. Going box by box, drawer by drawer, folder by folder, through every piece of paper I could find. He had, of course, the complete transcript of the Article 32 hearing, and, in addition, he had copies of the grand jury testimony of each of his family members, as well as of all those witnesses who were later called by the government to testify at trial. I would read slowly through these volumes, taking notes, becoming aware for the first time of an enormous amount of detail that had not been presented at trial.

I found, for example, in the notes prepared at the request of his military attorney shortly after his interview with the CID on April 6, 1970, that MacDonald had written that on Monday, February 16—in addition to everything else he had done—he had "called a Maj. Sampson—he is a pediatrician at Womack. We discussed moonlighting at Lumberton Hosp. and I asked to be put on the staff. He said I could begin working there shortly."

Thus, in addition to having worked every night of January at Cape Fear Valley Hospital in Fayetteville, and having begun to work weekend shifts at Hamlet Hospital sixty miles away, MacDonald had—on the last afternoon before the murders—sought yet a third moonlighting job. This seemed hardly consistent with his assertion that the months at Fort Bragg had been "a reattachment of our entire family because we were having the time and I wasn't tired and I didn't have to rush off to work . . ."

In the same notes, he also had written: "One more thing—I think I got a call from the coach of the Fort Bragg boxing team. He had mentioned to me they needed a doctor to accompany the team for 30 days on a trip to Russia. I jumped at the chance, and offered myself. He called me on Monday, I think, to tell me the Dept. of the Army was trying to get me on orders for the trip, and I would probably hear from him in the next several days. Both Colette and I were very happy about this." This was consistent, perhaps, with his 1970 "diary" entry regarding the boxing trip, but hardly with what he had said under oath to Victor Woerheide: that "the first time that it ever clicked" that there might have been a discussion regarding a boxing team trip to Russia had been in midsummer, during the Article 32 hearing.

I also found it curious that later in these notes, while

describing the attack by the four assailants, MacDonald had written—as he had told Dr. Sandoff in Philadelphia in April of 1970—"I suppose it's possible 'she' [the female intruder] was a male with long hair. CID never asked me if it was possible she was male."

In late afternoon, I would drive to Terminal Island. I would sit with MacDonald for two or three hours each evening, in the visitors' lounge. Most nights, his mother was present. Occasionally, when her airline work schedule permitted, Candy Kramer would be there also. Often, friends and colleagues from St. Mary's came to call.

MacDonald would talk about the horrors of his cross-country bus trip, of the evil personified by such figures as Dupree, Murtagh, and the Kassabs, of the failure of the jury selection process and of Bernie Segal's closing argument, of how—despite it all—he could not understand how the jury could not have at least found reasonable doubt. When the visit was over, I would stop and get a bite to eat. Then I would return to the condominium.

He never came right out and asked me what I thought. And I never came right out and said. For him it must have seemed easier to assume that with me his innocence had never been in question. To ask directly would have been to risk getting an answer he did not want. For me, of course, it was easier to let him go right on believing whatever he cared to believe. At least it seemed so at the time. The more I learned the less easy any of it turned out to be.

There was no dearth of enlightening material in the files. One folder marked "Book" contained a copy of a letter that Joseph Wambaugh had written to MacDonald on

March 28, 1975, in response to an inquiry about whether
Wambaugh might be interested in writing a book about
the case. This was only two months after MacDonald
had been indicted.

> *You should understand that I would not think of*
> *writing your story. It would be my story. Just as* The
> Onion Field *was my story and* In Cold Blood *was*
> *Capote's story. We both had the living persons sign*
> *legal releases which authorized us to interpret, por-*
> *tray and characterize them as we saw fit, trusting us*
> *implicitly to be honest and faithful to the truth as we*
> *saw it, not as they saw it.*
>
> *With this release you can readily see that you*
> *would have no recourse at law if you didn't like my*
> *portrayal of you. Let's face another ugly possibility:*
> *what if I, after spending months of research and in-*
> *terviewing dozens of people and listening to hours of*
> *court trials, did not believe you innocent?*
>
> *I suspect that you may want a writer who would*
> *tell* your *story and indeed your version may very well*
> *be the truth as I would see it. But you'd have* no
> *guarantee, not with me. You'd have absolutely no*
> *editorial prerogative. You would not even see the book*
> *until publication. . . .*

The next day, MacDonald had sent a brief note to
Bernie Segal, along with a copy of Wambaugh's letter.

> *Enclosed is very interesting. What do you think?*
> *He sounds awfully arrogant to me but it will be an*
> *obvious best seller if he writes the book. Please get back*
> *to me ASAP.*

Wambaugh, of course, had not written the book, though his discussions with MacDonald and Bernie Segal had continued into the summer of 1979. Now, I was writing it. As would have been the case with Wambaugh, MacDonald had absolutely no editorial prerogative. And the "ugly possibility" to which Wambaugh had referred had now become a reality.

I found in the files a program from an athletic event: the Long Beach Heart Association's Second Annual Benefit Basketball Classic, April 11, 1975, played at the Long Beach City College Gymnasium.

The "classic" consisted of a game between a team composed of Los Angeles Rams football players and one which consisted of emergency room physicians and technicians from various Long Beach hospitals.

At guard, number 7, age thirty-one, height five feet, ten and a half inches, weight 185 pounds, was Jeffrey R. MacDonald, M.D. Beneath his name and picture in the program was a caption which he had written himself: "The Second Coming of 'Dr. J'—watch his hands!"

This had appeared just three and a half months after MacDonald had been indicted on charges of having murdered his pregnant wife and two daughters with his hands.

An extensive study of the narcissistic personality disorder has been made by psychoanalyst Otto Kernberg, who published many of his findings in a 1975 volume entitled *Borderline Conditions and Pathological Narcissism*.

"On the surface," Kernberg writes, pathologically narcissistic individuals "may not present seriously disturbed behavior; some of them may function socially very well." Many possess "the capacity for active, consistent work in some area which permits them partially to fulfill their ambition of greatness and of obtaining admiration and approval from other people."

Kernberg has observed "a curious apparent contradiction between a very inflated concept of themselves and an inordinate need for tribute from others. When narcissistic personalities are in a position of objective importance they love to surround themselves with admirers in whom they are interested as long as the admiration is new. They obtain very little enjoyment from life other than from the tributes they receive from others or from their own grandoise fantasies, and they feel restless and bored when external glitter wears off and no new sources feed their self-regard."

Kernberg considers the main characteristics of narcissistic personalities to be "grandiosity, extreme self-centeredness, and a remarkable absence of interest and empathy for others in spite of the fact that they are so very eager to obtain admiration and approval. . . . It is as if they feel they have the right to control and possess others and to exploit them without guilt feelings, and, behind a surface which very often is charming and engaging, one senses coldness and ruthlessness. These patients not only lack emotional depth, but fail to understand complex emotion in other people."

Kernberg has noted that "the pathological narcissist experiences other people as basically dishonest and unreliable. The greatest fear of these patients is to be dependent on anybody else, because to depend means to hate, envy, and expose themselves to the danger of being exploited, mistreated, and frustrated."

Conversely, however, such individuals experience "a remarkably intense envy of other people who seem to have things they do not have, or who simply seem to enjoy their lives."

Such a "devalued concept of self," Kernberg has observed, "can be seen especially in narcissistic patients who divide the world into famous, rich and great people on the one hand, and the despicable, worthless 'mediocrity,' on the other. Such patients are afraid of not belonging to the company of the great, rich and powerful, and of belonging instead to the 'mediocre,' by which they mean worthless and despicable, rather than 'average' in the ordinary sense of the term.

"Narcissistic patients," Kernberg continues, possess an "overriding necessity to feel great and important in order to cancel feelings of worthlessness and devaluation. At the very bottom of this dichotomy lies a still deeper image of the relationship with external objects, precisely the one against which the patient has erected all these other pathological structures. It is the image of an enraged, empty self—the hungry wolf out to kill, eat and survive—full of impotent anger at being frustrated, and fearful of a world—devoid of food and love—which seems as hateful and revengeful as the patient himself."

Kernberg cites the case of one patient who "fell in love with a woman whom he considered very beautiful, gifted, warm; in short, completely satisfying. He had a brief period of awareness of how much he hated her for being so perfect, just before she responded to him and decided to marry him. After their marriage, he felt bored with her and became completely indifferent toward her. . . . After that, the patient gradually developed strong hatred toward her for having all that he felt he did not have."

One evening at Terminal Island, MacDonald gave me a letter which he had just received from his brother.

At the risk of losing your eternal friendship, I am going to ask you point blank if you killed your wife & daughters, and if you don't want to answer the question then it's still all right with me, but the question is one that has been gnawing at me since 1971 & I feel that at least to ask the question would be to unburden my mind, but then of course I immediately lose your respect by even thinking of asking the question, but since you think that I have a mental problem, I think that one way of me helping myself is to unload those questions which I know have been bothering me.

(I have to assume that the answer is "No, I did not kill my wife or either of my daughters," and if such is the case then I can rest assuredly, but then the problem is, why are you there? If you're not guilty, then you don't belong in jail. If you don't belong in jail and are in jail then something is terribly wrong. If something is wrong, what & why, & how can we remedy the situation?)

I'm sorry to even consider asking the question, but since 1970 I've been answering questions from many people & I've always asked them—"Have you ever asked him (you)—did you kill your wife and/or daughters?" and no one ever said that they had asked you, so if anyone ever asks me again, I can say, "Yes, I asked him and he said":

a) Yes

b) No

c) Fifth Amendment

d) Other

e) ——————— (You fill it in.)

Jay had enclosed a stamped, self-addressed envelope for reply, but Jeff told me that of course he had no intention of replying. Laughing, he said this was just one more example of how mentally disturbed his brother continued to be.

Kernberg has found that the narcissist's "haughty, grandiose and controlling behavior—particularly, the excessive demandingness, the arrogant, and exploitative relationships these patients develop with women—is a defense against . . . the projection of rage."

Under most circumstances, Kernberg makes clear, "narcissistic character defenses protect the patient against the intensity of his rage." And, because of the narcissist's "superficially smooth and effective social adaptation, the serious distortion in his internal relationship with other people—may come as a real surprise."

Indeed, it has been Kernberg's observation that "the transformation of a previously bland, mostly indifferent, apparently well controlled narcissistic personality into an openly raging person may be quite striking." He notes also, however, that "aggressive outbursts—quick flareups and subsequent dispersal of emotion—" do occur, particularly under conditions when the narcissist feels "superior to or in control of those against whom [his] rage is directed."

At the condominium, I came across an article entitled "Dangerousness, Diagnosis and Disposition," written in 1968 by a Philadelphia psychiatrist named Melvin S. Heller and presented to a conference of trial judges. There was nothing to indicate why MacDonald had acquired a copy of the article or why he had retained it for so long, but certain passages did not seem entirely irrelevant.

"Violence may be meted out in a controlled, measured fashion," Dr. Heller wrote, "or in an uncontrolled blind rage, in which event the instinctual discharge of primitive aggressive impulses is prominent." Further on, calling attention to man's "genius for deception," he stated: "In view of man's capacity for inappropriate and unexpected violence, especially when planned behind the camouflage of smiles and flattery, the prognosis of dangerousness . . . requires sophisticated judgment, clinical experience, and an intimate knowledge of the individual and his milieu. . . ."

I then found the one document which, during trial, Bernie Segal had not permitted me to see: the report of the prosecution psychiatric team, based upon their examination of MacDonald in August. Though he had not permitted psychiatric testimony at the trial, Judge Dupree had made reference to this report in his denial of bail, writing that it "tends to indicate that the defendant does indeed possess those traits of character which are consistent with his commission of the crimes with which he is charged and that he possesses other traits which tend to cast serious doubt on the credibility of his explanation of how the crimes occurred."

Their first look at the report had left Segal shaken and MacDonald angrier than he had been at any other time during the trial. Reading it now, three months later, with the sun shimmering on the water beyond the sliding glass doors, I could see why.

The report, signed by the examining psychologist, Hirsch Lazaar Silverman of South Orange, New Jersey, began by describing MacDonald as "a man unhappily confused about his own masculinity," and said, "His thought processes are distinctly marked with unconscious feelings of considerable inadequacy, in great part consciously and deliberately concealed by a facade of assertiveness, which he confuses with manliness."

It said, "There seems to be an absence in him of deep emotional response, coupled with an inability to profit from experience. He is the kind of individual who is subject to committing asocial acts with impunity. He lacks a sense of guilt, he seems bereft of a strong conscience, and he appears incapable of emotionally close or mutually cooperative relationships with women.

"Derivatively, he apparently avoided, even resented, the demands on him to fulfill the responsibilities of having been a husband and a father of female children. Parenthood, for him, may have been viewed as threatening and potentially destructive."

The report also said, "He is subject to being amnesic concerning what he would wish to blot out from his consciousness and very conscience. His credibility leaves much to be desired. In testing, he proved himself to be considerably pathological and impulsive, with feministic characteristics and concealed anger. He has a disdain for others with whom he differs and he is subject to respond with anger when his person is questioned, on whatever basis.

"He handles his conflicts by denying that they even exist. He is not in touch with his feelings and essentially is not comfortable with himself. He has only an authoritarian image of himself as the machismo type of male.

"In terms of mental health and personality functioning, he is either an overt or a repressed sexual invert characterized by expansive egotism and delusions of persecution. He is preoccupied with the irrelevant and is unable to face reality. To suit his whims, he has the faculty to manufacture and convolute circumstances. He seeks attention and approval and is given to denial of truth."

The report continued: "The inanimate movement responses in his Rorschach indicate latent homosexuality approaching homosexual panic; and the depreciated female contents in his projections suggest more than a possibility of homosexuality, latent or otherwise. The animal content in the Rorschach further indicates homocidal tendencies."

In summary, the report stated: "Dr. MacDonald may well be viewed as a psychopath subject to violence under pressure, rather effeminate as an individual and given to overt behavior when faced with emotional stress. There is also, however unclear, a fear in him of what he is subject to do with his hands. . . .

"In essence, Dr. MacDonald is in need of continuous, consistent, psychotherapeutic intervention, coupled with psychiatric attention."

Kernberg has found narcissistic patients to be filled with "intense hatred and fear of the image of a dangerous, aggressive mother," a fear which, he says, "represents a projection of his own aggression, linked to the rage caused by his frustration by mother."

The narcissist's "ideal concept of himself," Kernberg writes, "is a fantasy construction which protects him from such dreaded relationships with all other people . . . and also contains a helpless yearning and love for an ideal mother who would come to his rescue."

Should such a "dreaded relationship" (such as marriage) materialize, the complex defense mechanism which has been constructed within the psyche of the pathological narcissist would come under severe stress, because, as Christopher Lasch notes, such a person perceives the female, "child or woman, wife or mother," as a monster who "cuts men to ribbons or swallows them whole."

Thus, in Lasch's view, "fear of the devouring mother

838

JOE McGINNISS

of the pre-Oedipal fantasy gives rise to a generalized fear of women," and this fear, "closely associated with a fear of the consuming desires within, reveals itself . . . as a boundless rage against the female sex."

On the afternoon of April 6, 1970, Grebner and Ivory and Shaw were questioning MacDonald about a white terry-cloth bathrobe which had been found with blades of grass adhering to the bottom—as if someone had worn it outdoors when the grass was wet and had, perhaps, squatted briefly to place a paring knife and an ice-pick side by side beneath a bush.

"Did you put on that terry-robe at any point in the evening?"

"No."

"Did you ever wear it outside?"

"The robe?"

"Yes."

"Well, maybe to run to get something off the line, you know, or pick up—pick up the paper every morning, but not specifically, no. Now sometimes, you know, maybe the—the kids would dress up in those things and go outdoors and play for a minute, but that was considered good stuff and my mother—my mother, that's a Freudian slip—my wife would have, you know, called them back in and taken it off."

A Freudian slip. Not dissimilar, perhaps, from the other unconscious errors he had made during the April 6 interview, when, three times, he had said "bed" instead of "couch" in describing where his struggle against the intruders had taken place.

On my last day at the condominium, I found more pages of notes in Jeffrey MacDonald's handwriting. The heading said, "Activities—Monday, 16 Feb. 5:30 P.M.—Tues. in Hospital, 17 Feb."

This, too, was part of the detailed account which Mac-Donald had prepared at the request of his military attorney immediately after the April 6 announcement that he was being held as a suspect. The account which, he had told Victor Woerheide at the grand jury, he had put in writing because the events were too painful for him to talk about. This, he had told Woerheide, was the most accurate, most complete, most coherent account of the night of the murders which he had ever compiled. He had not, however, made it available to Woerheide or to the grand jurors. He had not made it available to any investigator. He had given it to his lawyers for their use—not knowing, at the time, what the evidence against him might consist of—and, once it became clear, during the Article 32 hearing, that certain avenues were not to be pursued, this "most accurate" account had lain at the bottom of a cardboard box, covered by dozens of other files.

With the warm Southern California sun of late November shining brightly through the sliding glass doors, I started to read:

> We ate dinner together at 5:45 p.m. (all 4). It is possible I had 1 diet pill at this time. I do not remember, but it is possible. I had been running a weight control program for my unit and I put my name at the top of the program to encourage participation. I had lost 12–15 lbs. in the prior 3–4 weeks, in the process using 3–5 capsules of Eskatrol Spansule (15 mg. Dextroamphetamine) ("Speed") and 7.5 mg. Prochlorperazine (Compazine) to counteract the excitability of the speed. I was also losing weight because I was working out with the boxing team and the coach

told me to lose weight. In any case, the reason I could have taken the pill was two-fold—1) to eat less in the evening when I 'snacked' the most and 2) to try to stay awake after dinner since I was baby-sitting. It didn't work if I did take a pill, because I think I had a ½ hr. nap on the floor from 7:30–8 p.m. after I put Kristy to bed. . . .

The CID knows nothing about the possible diet pill. . . . If I did take the pill, it is conceivable that my urine and blood 11:30 a.m. Tues. would still have some residue. We would have to research the break-down and excretion of what was in the pill. We would also have to find out if the excretion products are definitely different than normal breakdown products of adrenaline from the body, which would be increased in the excitement of the attack, etc. Right now, I don't know if it is definitely possible to identify Dextroamphetamine from pills in the blood and the urine. I think I told the CID the only pills I usually took were aspirin, occas, cold pills, and Tetracycline (anti-biotic). . . . Dr. Henry Ashton, now living in Salt Lake City, Utah, was the group surgeon before I arrived in Sept. 1969. If he remembers, he can testify that the bottle of Eskatrol from my house (with only a few missing) was left in the desk I took over when he left. If necessary, we can then contact the Smith Kline & French representative near here who can testify I never received another large bottle of sample Eskatrol. He did give me some small sample bottles for use in the weight control program. Colette had some diet pills of her own (used before she was pregnant). I think I threw them all out because they made her nervous, but possibly there was an old container left in the medicine cabinet. . . .

Having received a report from the Fort Gordon laboratory that an analysis of Jeffrey MacDonald's blood—
made from a sample taken at 11:40 A.M. on February
17—"did not reveal the presence of any dangerous
drugs or narcotics," Franz Joseph Grebner and all subsequent investigators had simply assumed, with some
justification, that Jeffrey MacDonald's drug consumption had not been a factor in the commission of the
murders.

An examination I made subsequently of the laboratory notes compiled by the Fort Gordon chemist who
had actually performed the tests on MacDonald's blood,
however, revealed that no attempt was ever made to determine from the sample whether Jeffrey MacDonald, in
the hours or days that had immediately preceded the
murders, had been ingesting amphetamines. The chemist had never been instructed to test for the presence of
amphetamines, and, in fact, the equipment available at
the CID laboratory at the time would not have enabled
him to do so. In 1970 these drugs were widely prescribed and were consumed in considerable quantity not
only by individuals attempting to lose weight, but by
students, truck drivers—and physicians—who found it
necessary to remain awake and alert for extended periods
of time. In 1970, amphetamines were not considered a
"dangerous" drug by military authorities attempting to
combat a dramatic upsurge in the use both of hallucino-
gens and of opiates such as heroin and chiefly concerned
with the widespread use of marijuana.

Ten years later, however, the potential hazards associated with Eskatrol consumption had received considerably wider attention. The drug is listed in *Pills That
Don't Work*, the 1981 book by Sidney M. Wolfe, M.D.,
and Christopher M. Coley that is described on its cover

as, "A consumers' and doctors' guide to over 600 prescription drugs that lack evidence of effectiveness."

Wolfe and Coley describe the drug as "not only inef-
fective but also dangerous . . . To use a combination of
an 'upper' and a 'downer' both of which carry significant
risks is asking for trouble." Among the possible side effects listed are: "Insomnia . . . restlessness, nervousness
and dizziness." The authors also state that "psychosis
(insanity) may occur with large doses."

Eskatrol is described in even more detail in the *Physicians' Desk Reference,* a standard medical reference book
published by Medical Economics Company.

"Amphetamines have a significant potential for
abuse," this text states. "In view of their short-term ano-
rectic effect and rapid development of tolerance, they
should be used with extreme caution and only for limited periods of time in weight-reduction programs."

According to his own notes—the notes which Victor
Woerheide had asked him to provide to the grand jury
but which he had declined to do; the notes which had
lain in the bottom of a file drawer since 1970 when
MacDonald had learned that CID testing had failed to
discover the presence of amphetamines in his blood—
MacDonald had lost twelve to fifteen pounds in the
three to four weeks preceding the murders.

That was a lot of weight to lose for an already fit,
twenty-six-year-old Green Beret officer, fresh from paratroop training at Fort Benning. And boxing would not
account for it: his last workout with the boxing team had
come more than three weeks before the killings. Neither
would an odd hour of basketball late on a rainy afternoon produce that sort of weight loss. And there had
been nothing to suggest that MacDonald had embarked
upon a formal diet. (Indeed, he'd been eating cookies

with Ron Harrison on the night of Valentine's Day and drinking a sweet liqueur with his wife two nights later, and—he had said—one of the most appealing features of Hamlet Hospital was that the nurses served him steak for breakfast.)

"Three to five" Eskatrol Spansules over a three-to-four-week period also would not have accounted for the weight loss. Three to five per day, however, could have had a marked effect. That level of consumption could also have had a number of other consequences, such as, according to the *Physicians' Desk Reference*, "marked insomnia, tenseness, and irritability, hyperactivity, confusion, assaultiveness, hallucinations, panic states," and "the most severe . . . psychosis."

"Cardiovascular reactions," the reference book states, "may include chilliness, pallor or . . . headache," all three of which symptoms Jeffrey MacDonald exhibited in the immediate aftermath of the murder of his family.

And it is not only the amphetamine component which can pose hazards. Again, as cited in the *Physicians' Desk Reference,* prochlorperazine—the sedative component of the Spansule—can cause "agitation, restlessness, and reactivation of psychotic processes."

The *Physicians' Desk Reference* also states that the drug was "so prepared that an initial dose is released promptly and the remaining medication is released gradually over a prolonged period." The prescribed dose was one capsule per day, to be taken in the morning.

"If appetite control is desired through evening hours," the *PDR* states, "shift dose to midmorning. Late afternoon or evening medication should be avoided because of the resulting insomnia."

Yet Jeffrey MacDonald—outstanding medical student though he had been—was consuming the drug in a manner contrary to this recommendation. How much he might have been consuming will forever be, to employ a phrase used by Freddy Kassab before the grand jury, "a dark area," but if the "three to five" were a daily dose it would have been enough—taken over a period of three to four weeks—to have caused chronic amphetamine psychosis, many of the symptoms of which MacDonald did, in fact, display. (In the hospital after the murders he also displayed symptoms associated with abrupt cessation of high dosages of the drug, such as [as cited in the *PDR*] "extreme fatigue and mental depression.")

The chapter on amphetamines in *Disposition of Toxic Drugs and Chemicals in Man,* by Randall C. Baselt (Biomedical Publications, 1982) states that "Chronic usage is associated with a high incidence of weight loss, hallucinations, and paranoid psychosis."

An even more detailed analysis of the effects of amphetamines and prochlorperazine is contained in *Goodman and Gilman's Pharmacological Basis of Therapeutics,* a widely used medical text edited by Alfred Goodman Gilman, Louis S. Goodman, and Alfred Gilman and published by Macmillan.

In the chapter titled "Drug Addiction and Drug Abuse," Jerome H. Jaffee, M.D., professor of psychiatry at the University of Connecticut School of Medicine, writes, "the user [of amphetamines] is hyperactive and during a toxic episode may act in response to persecutory delusions. . . . The fully developed toxic syndrome from amphetamine is characterized by vivid visual, auditory, and sometimes tactile hallucinations." (Such as, one cannot help but wonder, a hallucination involving an attack by three armed hippies and a girl with long blond hair holding a candle and chanting "Acid is groovy . . . Kill the pigs"?)

"Tolerance does not develop to certain of the toxic effects of amphetamines on the central nervous system," Dr. Jaffee writes, "and a toxic psychosis may occur after periods of weeks." He also states that "the syndrome may be seen as early as 36 to 48 hours after the ingestion of a single large dose . . . in apparently sensitive individuals, psychosis may be produced by 55 to 75 mg. of dextroamphetamine. With high enough doses, psychosis can probably be induced in anyone."

Other psychopharmacologists have commented that rage reactions are not uncommon in individuals who are abusing amphetamines—particularly when the period of abuse involves sleep deprivation, outside stresses, and, most notably, any predisposition toward psychological instability, such as would be the case with an individual suffering from a narcissistic personality disorder.

"Most observers," Dr. Jaffee writes, "have noted considerable psychopathology in compulsive amphetamine users and their families, which appeared to have antedated the drug use." Whether "considerable psychopathology" existed in the MacDonald family of Patchogue, Long Island, is perhaps another "dark area," but it is fact that the father was given to outbursts of anger and that Jeffrey's only brother was hospitalized after a psychotic episode involving violence.

It is also fact that if Jeffrey MacDonald were taking three to five Eskatrol Spansules daily, he would have been consuming 75 mg. of dextroamphetamine—more than enough to precipitate an amphetamine psychosis.

Chapter 19, "Drug Treatment of Disorders of Mood," of Goodman and Gilman's book discusses side effects of chlorpromazine, the category of drug which includes the prochlorperazine found in Eskatrol Spansules. The author, Ross J. Baldessarini, M.D., professor of psychiatry at the Harvard Medical School, writes that while tolerance to the sedative effects of this drug develops "over a period of days or weeks," it retains a capacity to produce unpleasant side effects, including a syndrome known as akathisia, which is characterized by "the compelling need of the patient to be in constant movement . . . the patient feels that he must get up and walk or continuously move about . . . akathisia can be mistaken for agitation in psychotic patients."

Certainly all reports from Womack Hospital indicate that Jeffrey MacDonald, in the first moments after his arrival—indeed, until Merrill Bronstein began intravenous administration of Vistaril, Nembutal, and Demerol—had felt a powerful urge to get up and walk about and that he appeared to be in a state of high agitation.

Concluding their discussion of Eskatrol Spansules in *Pills That Don't Work,* Wolfe and Coley write that the drug "should have been removed from the market long ago." Late in 1980, as such medications were coming under closer scrutiny from the Food and Drug Administration, its manufacturer, Smith Kline & French, voluntarily ceased the manufacture and distribution of Eskatrol, despite the fact that its estimated retail sales at that time totaled more than $6 million annually.

When Colette MacDonald—pregnant by accident once again—had left for her psychology class that cold and rainy February evening, her husband (whose pallor, fatigue, and changed personality had been noted even by neighbors in the weeks immediately preceding the murders) had been so exhausted, from having worked a twenty-four-hour emergency room shift and then a full day at the office, followed by an hour of basketball and a trip with his daughters to feed the pony, that he had been on the verge of falling asleep without even putting his younger daughter to bed. His condition had been so noteworthy that Colette had commented on it to the friend whom she drove to class.

Yet upon her return he had stayed up with her watching television and sipping Cointreau. And then, even when she had gone to bed, he—having lost sexual interest in her since her pregnancy had begun to manifest itself (impotence and changes of libido are also among the adverse reactions to consumption of dextroamphetamine)—had remained up until 2 A.M. watching the remainder of Johnny Carson and finishing the Mickey Spillane book *Kiss Me Deadly.*

Even then, MacDonald had not been ready for bed. Instead, he said, he had donned a pair of rubber surgical gloves to wash the dishes at 2 o'clock in the morning.

This despite his previous state of exhaustion and notwithstanding the fact that he would have to be up again by 7 A.M. to put in another full day at the office.

And, this also notwithstanding that he had lost fifteen pounds in three weeks, that he was in the midst of devising a plan which would permit him to spend a fair portion of the late winter and early spring in the vicinity of New York City, where his old (or maybe not-so-old) girlfriend, Penny Wells, resided, while pregnant Colette cared for the two daughters and the pony, believing him to be in Russia all the while.

And, all this following an autumn which had brought not only the unexpected pregnancy but the unexpected breakdown of his older brother (following a period of amphetamine abuse) and such other frustrations as the demotion in authority, if not rank, which had ensued upon the departure of his idol, Colonel Kingston, for Vietnam.

He had lost fifteen pounds in three weeks while taking a drug that can cause insanity. He was suffering from short-term physical exhaustion and longer-term emotional stress. His life, in fact, had been one extended period of stress—financial, intellectual, psychological—ever since Colette had become pregnant and he had had to marry her and to leave Princeton early and to get through medical school while being husband to her and father to two daughters, and the glamour and titillation attendant upon his becoming a Green Beret had provided only a temporary escape.

Might it be too much to surmise that since early childhood he had been suffering also from the effects of the strain required to repress the "boundless rage" which psychological maladjustment had caused him to feel toward "child or woman, wife or mother . . . the female sex"?

And that on this night—this raw and somber military-base February Monday night—finally, with the amphetamines swelling the rage to flood tide, and with Colette, pregnant Colette, perhaps seeking to communicate to him some of her new insights into personality structure and behavioral patterns—indeed, possibly even attempting to *explain* him to himself—his defense mechanism, for the first and last time, proved insufficient?

Would it be too much to suggest that in that one instant—whatever its forever unknowable proximate cause might have been—a critical mass had been achieved, a fission had taken place, and that by 3:40 A.M. on February 17, 1970, the ensuing explosion of rage had destroyed not only Jeffrey MacDonald's wife and daughters, but all that he had sought to make of his life?

Perhaps. Yet his bloody footprint had been found on the floor and there were blue threads on the club outside the house and his wife—already dead or so near to it that the difference was of no import whatsoever—had been stabbed in the chest with an icepick twenty-one times after his blue pajama top had been laid across her. And when he had sat down to write the first account of the night's events—knowing that he was now considered the chief suspect—his consumption of a drug which is capable of triggering psychotic rage had been the thing he had felt it necessary to mention first.

3

Though he had denied it under oath during his grand jury testimony, Jeffrey MacDonald had apparently taken a lie detector test during his brief visit to Philadelphia in April of 1970. His own psychiatrist, Dr. Sadoff, had made reference to it during his grand jury testimony, and to the fact that MacDonald "had not come through with flying colors."

Home from California, I put the question to MacDonald in writing. He responded on a tape from Terminal Island.

Ummm . . . I guess it was after my psychological interview. Bernie brought up the fact that he wanted me polygraphed. Actually, I guess it was sort of in the middle of these interviews. I felt uhh . . . you know, sort of *hurt*. I wondered why he wanted 'em . . . and then he explained that perhaps we could use these interviews to head off the Article 32 and the court-martial. That if they came out strong enough, conclusively in my favor, perhaps we could go to the Army *with* them. I said, *fine* . . . if there was a chance for that we would go ahead and do it.

Now, there were two different men. One was John Reid, and the other was Cleve, I think, Backster. They're both well known in polygraph fields. These are not lightweights. These were expensive examinations.

Uuhhh, as I recall it, the first operator was John Reid. He at first seemed very, you know, very professional to me. He explained to me a little bit about the polygraph, what it can do and what it can't do. And then proceeded to hook me up to the machine—told me the area of questioning that we would go into and then he began questioning me.

However, when he began questioning me, it seemed to me that he was basically a prosecutor. He was not satisfied with my results—by that, I don't even really know what the results were, but they were not conclusively proving my innocence . . . and . . . he had a consultation with Bernie, and Bernie uh, sort of abruptly dismissed him. . . . the results were not conclusive of my innocence.

But we moved on, because Bernie really wanted a very positive polygraph test. We went on to the second person, who I believe is Cleve Backster. This is the guy who does the polygraphs and is now famous for polygraphing plants. And he's on Johnny Carson all the time, I believe.

In any case, Bernie now spent a lot of time prepping me for this one—saying that this was much more professional, this guy was bigger in his field than Reid, and that I would find him a lot more congenial, and he would treat me a lot better.

Well, in fact, just the opposite happened. He basically gave me *no* prep, except sort of negative type of prep, in which he said that this machine can detect any sort of lying. . . .

Well, he hooked me up to the machine, and once Bernie was excused from the room, he began going over my sexual history. It was *very* bizarre. He started talking about had I ever had sex with women other than Colette. And I answered that. And then he asked had I ever had sex with men. And then he wanted to know if I . . . if there was a wild orgy the night of the occurrence of the murders.

And I stopped him, and I said uh, I don't understand what we're doing here. I thought this was a polygraph based on my current legal situation—and he says, well, he was just getting me used to the machine and getting a base line ready on truth and falsity.

So I said okay then, let's get back to the point. So then he said okay, and we started going back to some more questions, and he immediately reverted to premarital and extra-marital sexual activities, and unusual sexual activities, and I thought this guy was *crazy*, to tell you the truth. And I said look, I don't think we can continue. And at this point he made some comment about, well, have you considered the insanity defense. And I said, Jesus, that's the most outrageous thing I ever heard. You haven't even completed your polygraph, and now you're telling me that I should be going for an insanity defense. And he said, well, in his judg-

ment, and he said, basically, I've never been wrong
on a major case. Uummm . . . you should start
considering an insanity defense.

When I contacted Cleve Backster to ask for his recollection of the MacDonald polygraph examination, he
said he would not be at liberty to discuss it without written authorization from Jeffrey MacDonald. When I
asked MacDonald to provide such authorization, he refused.

The fact is, on many tapes Jeffrey MacDonald told me
things which, even without the aid of a polygraph, I later
determined to be untrue. He recounted, for example, a
visit he made to the Fort Bragg boxing team "two or
three weeks after I got out of the hospital" in 1970. "I
went over and watched them work out and told them
that I'm sorry, I wouldn't be able to go on this trip to
Russia, and I found the sergeant who was in charge, and
he said he understood completely and I wished him luck,
and, as a matter of fact, he started crying while we were
talking, and then I started crying."

Not only did the boxing coach fail to recall such incident, but the team—as Pruett and Kearns had determined in 1971—was not even planning a trip to Russia.

Once, in discussing Mildred Kassab, MacDonald said
that after the death of her first husband, "She took a boat
from San Francisco to Hawaii and was originally planning on going around the world, but ended up staying in
Hawaii. And she told me many times—many, many
times—both on a couple of occasions when she'd had
too much to drink when Colette was alive and she was
kind of bragging under the influence of wine, but cer-

tainly later on after the tragedy of 1970, when I was at
their house for dinner, she told me in no uncertain terms
that the reason she never went around the world was because she was having so much fun in Hawaii and that she
had balled every houseboy on the boat going from San
Francisco to Hawaii. She then went back to New York,
apparently, and lived in the Plaza Hotel for a period of
weeks or months—got a good room and got an excellent
table and had lunch and dinner there every day, waiting
to meet the right man, and I think that is how she did
meet Freddy Kassab."

MacDonald's mother, of course, had told the grand
jury much the same story, except that in her version Mildred *had* gone around the world for a full year and had
then taken up residence in a high-priced New York hotel
for six additional months, during which time she met
Freddy Kassab, who, as MacDonald's mother recalled,
was from "the South."

The facts are that for four months after her husband's
suicide, Mildred Kassab remained with her children.
Then, leaving them in the care of her sister Helen, she
visited a female friend in California for a week and then
flew to Honolulu, where she remained for three weeks.
She recalls quite specifically arriving home in time to participate, as a class mother, in a group outing which Colette's elementary school class was making to Ebbets
Field, to watch the Brooklyn Dodgers play a baseball
game.

On New Year's Eve of that year, Colette was spending
the night at a friend's house and Mildred—who had at
no time taken up residence at the Plaza—was home
alone with her son, then sixteen. Having earlier declined
an invitation from friends to attend a New Year's Eve
party at a Patchogue restaurant called Felice's, Mildred

changed her mind in midevening, and, shortly before midnight, she and her son did join the group, and she attracted the attention of Freddy Kassab, who was there with friends of his own. Three months later Kassab managed to arrange an introduction.

There was another tape on which MacDonald talked at considerable length and in extraordinary detail about how the night before his wedding he'd had to drive one of the bridesmaids home to New Jersey, but she could not remember where she lived and they had become lost for several hours and as a result he had arrived extremely late for his own bachelor party. I wondered at the time why he had bothered to tell it at all. It was not until months later that I learned where he had really been: back in Patchogue, putting a red-and-black negligee on the front seat of Penny Wells's car.

I finally asked him, once, about the meeting with Penny Wells at the train station in November of 1969. At first he denied—as he had under oath—that any such meeting had occurred. Then he said, "If it did occur, the most that happened is that I ran across Penny. She may have been working in New York at the time, and we ended up getting off the same train or something like that, and I kissed her hello. If I did see her at the train station it was absolutely by chance, and this so-called embrace was simply a kiss hello from an old girlfriend to an old boyfriend."

I did not even bother to ask him about her meeting him at the airport upon the occasion of his June 1971 arrival in California, because by then I had learned, as had Allard Lowenstein ten years before, that, "He'll say anything to anybody."

*   *   *

Thus, there had been no making love on the infield of the Saratoga racetrack during Happy Pappy weekend or a later spring visit to Skidmore. The Saratoga racetrack is open only during the month of August, at a time when Skidmore is not.

And, during the "fifteen days" between the completion of his internship and the date of his reporting to Fort Sam Houston, there had been no vacation to an island he thought might have been Aruba. There had been, in fact, only a single weekend between those two phases of his life—a strained and hectic weekend that had been spent moving Colette and the children from the Bergenfield apartment to Patchogue, where they would be spending the summer.

There had also been no "most memorable" lovemaking session on the couch in the living room of the Kassabs' Washington Square apartment during Thanksgiving vacation of MacDonald's freshman year at Princeton. The Kassabs did not even move to New York City until the summer of the following year. In fact, throughout her freshman year at Skidmore, Colette had not even dated Jeffrey MacDonald: she had continued to see her high school boyfriend, Dean Chamberlain. It was not until her sophomore year that she and MacDonald resumed their relationship.

Thus, the entire, vivid recollection—of his first days at Princeton and the sudden excitement of having become an Ivy Leaguer and the impulsive decision to pursue a career in medicine, all being intertwined with his receipt of that first titillating letter from Colette, and of having rushed, with sweaty palms, up to Skidmore—is false.

A false creation, one might suggest, proceeding from the heat-oppressed brain.

*　　　*　　　*

Of course, I was not the only one to whom he told stories that were not true. Having his nose broken four times in high school, and becoming the first Patchogue High School graduate in more than twenty years to attend an Ivy League college—statements he made to Dr. Sadoff in Philadelphia in April of 1970—these, too, were false.

There was no truth either to the story he told benefactor Bob Stern late one night in August of 1970, toward the end of the Article 32 hearing. This was during the week that the proceedings had been recessed to allow MacDonald to undergo psychiatric interview and testing at Walter Reed Hospital in Washington. In the midst of this trip, he had flown to Philadelphia to visit the Sterns for a weekend.

At that time—three months before he spoke to Freddy Kassab about it on the phone—Jeffrey MacDonald told Bob Stern that he had already tracked down and killed one of the hippies who had attacked him and had murdered his wife and children.

Gradually, I came to learn things about Jeffrey MacDonald from other sources: facts of which not even those who had prosecuted him had been aware.

Such as: he had actually made two trips to California in the summer of 1971. The first, by plane, was when Penny Wells had met him at the airport. But there had been a second trip, after a return to the East, when he had moved out to stay. This second trip was made by automobile and MacDonald had been accompanied by a sixteen-year-old girl—the daughter of family friends from Long Island, whose parents thought she might find it an enriching experience to traverse the United States in the company of the all-American boy they had known so well for so long, and who was struggling so hard now to recover from his recent tragedy.

Throughout the journey—all the way from New York to California—Jeffrey MacDonald had sexual relations with the sixteen-year-old girl.

I learned also that later that summer, not long after Mac-Donald had taken up residence in Huntington Beach, he received a visit from a close friend of his mother's—a woman he had known since childhood. She brought with her her ten-year-old son.

During the course of the visit, which extended over a period of weeks, Jeffrey MacDonald became sexually intimate with his mother's friend. He himself had told me about this during one of my visits to him at Terminal Island. Later, in another part of the country, I located the woman and she confirmed that the story was true, though she was a bit chagrined that he had chosen to make me aware of it.

I asked her what had caused her to terminate the relationship, expecting her to say either that finally the impropriety of the situation had started to bother her, or simply that summer was ending and it was time to go home.

Instead, she said she had left abruptly—before she had planned to—because of two incidents involving her ten-year-old son. The first, she said, occurred when MacDonald—angered by the boy's misbehavior inside his apartment—had carried him outside and dangled him by the feet over the edge of the dock, threatening to drop him head first into the water.

The second incident, the woman said, had occurred later in the summer when she, Jeff, and her son were out for a cruise on his boat. Again, the boy had done something to anger MacDonald. This time, the woman said, MacDonald had grabbed the boy and had told him, in an even more furious and more threatening tone, that upon returning to shore he was going to take the boy's head and hold it over the front of the boat and crush his skull against the dock.

Eventually, I spoke to the boy—now a young adult attending an Ivy League college—about his recollection of these incidents.

"You have to understand," he said, "my parents were divorced and when I was growing up, I hardly ever saw my father. So Jeff was not just like a friend, or even a big brother. Jeff was God to me at that point."

In that context, he said, the first incident had not been unduly alarming. Perhaps just a form of rough-housing that had gone a little too far. But the second episode—the scene on the boat—he said "I remember with real terror to this day." He could not recall what in particular he had done to so anger MacDonald, "but he came at me, yelling, and I remember kind of a fire in his eyes. It *really, really* was scary. I didn't know what he was going to do. In fact, what he did was to throw me in the water—he threw me off the side of the boat while it was moving and I can remember actually feeling relieved that he hadn't done anything more.

"But I will never forget it. I will never forget that look in his eyes. You know, maybe as a kid you perceive things more directly, in a way, than you do as an adult. But ever since that moment on the boat I believed that he must have been guilty. Just from seeing that kind of fire in his eyes. And I did not want to stay around him anymore. I was very frightened and I told my mother I wanted to go home right away. And we did."

4

On November 27, 1979, lawyers for Jeffrey MacDonald filed a brief with the United States Court of Appeals for the Fourth Circuit in which they renewed their argument that MacDonald had been denied his constitutional right to a speedy trial and in which they also cited instances of what they believed to be grievous error on the part of Judge Dupree. Chief among these was Dupree's decision to exclude from trial the testimony of the individuals with whom Helena Stoeckley had discussed her possible involvement in the murders.

Oral argument on these points was heard by a three-judge panel of the appeals court in Richmond, Virginia, in February of 1980. Considerable attention was focused on the speedy trial claim, because it was this which had proved so persuasive in 1976 that a separate panel of the same court had ordered the indictment dismissed.

The question of just what was intended by the framers of the Sixth Amendment when they wrote that every accused was entitled to a "speedy" trial was one which had defied precise judicial analysis for many years.

In 1972, however, the Supreme Court had provided
four specific criteria for use in the evaluation of such
claims. These were: length of delay, reason for delay, the
defendant's assertion of his right, and whether or not
the defendant had been prejudiced by the delay. (*Prejudice* was defined as being any consequence of the delay
which resulted in "oppressive pretrial incarceration,"
which interfered with the accused's right "to minimize
anxiety and concern," in regard to the accusation, or
which created "the possibility that the defense will be
impaired.")

On July 29, 1980, by a 2-to-1 decision, the Fourth Circuit panel found that MacDonald's Sixth Amendment
right to a speedy trial had indeed been infringed upon,
and to such an extent that the jury's verdict should be set
aside, the sentence of three consecutive life terms in
prison should be vacated, and the original indictment
dismissed.

Writing the majority opinion, Justice Francis D. Murnaghan stated that "while we cannot and do not assess
the correctness of the jury's verdict," and while "the required judicial balancing process necessary . . . has been
particularly difficult . . . the vital balancing tips the scales
decisively in favor of finding a violation."

Murnaghan based this finding in part upon his belief
that the two-year delay between the submission of the
final CID report in June of 1972 and the convening of
the grand jury in 1974 had been the result of the Justice
Department's "calloused and lackadaisical attitude."

MacDonald's claim, in Murnaghan's opinion, clearly
met the first three criteria as established by the Supreme
Court. The vital question was the one concerning prejudice, and here the trial testimony of Helena Stoeckley, in

Murnaghan's view, provided the definitive answer. He wrote:

> Had Stoeckley testified as it was reasonable to expect she might have . . . the injury to the government's case would have been incalculably great. The possible reasons why Stoeckley did not so testify are several. But the principal reason she asserted under oath was failure of memory. The government's inexcusable delay of over two years' duration cannot be eliminated as a potential— indeed a probable—cause of that memory lapse.

Though he likened Stoeckley's memory to "a light bulb not screwed tight, blinking on and off," Murnaghan wrote, "Still . . . the unavoidable principle remains that passage of time generally tends to erase memory," and he found that this "substantial proof of prejudice," when combined with "a showing of unreasonable delay," constituted a violation of constitutional rights serious enough to warrant dismissal of the charges.

While the decision, he wrote, was "made more difficult by the terrible crime and by the fact that a jury has found MacDonald guilty after a protracted trial," the court could not condone "a prosecutorial method of obtaining convictions in violation of the fundamental constitutional rights of future generations."

This opinion, in which Justice James M. Sprouse concurred, was dissented from vigorously by Justice Albert V. Bryan, Sr., who wrote:

> [MacDonald's] guilt and sanity were established to the satisfaction of the trial jury beyond a reasonable doubt. Nevertheless, this court absolves him

forever on this hideous offense, shockingly laying his release exclusively on the failure of the government to prosecute within a shorter time than it did.

Conceding that the government's rationale for the two-year delay prior to the convening of the grand jury warranted disapproval, Judge Bryan contended nonetheless that "Nothing in the record warrants the assumption that Stoeckley would have or could have given the testimony the majority would ascribe to her had the government secured its indictment earlier. Stoeckley herself in her trial testimony explains that her inability to recall the pre-dawn events of February 17, 1970 resulted from her consumption, earlier in the evening, of large quantities of drugs; she in no way indicated that *time* had weakened her recollection. . . . Indeed, the record fully upholds the government's contention that any culpable delay on its part had no discernible effect on Stoeckley's testimony."

It was, however, the majority opinion which had the force of law, and so, by midmorning of the day the decision was announced, champagne was flowing freely in the emergency room of St. Mary's.

Also pleased, though not expressing elation, was Jeffrey MacDonald's mother. "All I can say is thank God that in this land we still have some intelligent persons—somebody who can bring justice out of chaos," she said. "It's been ten long years and I'm still angry and frustrated. We've suffered and suffered and suffered, and while I'm joyful, I'm also sorry that there was not a total vindication of his name."

Three thousand miles away, Freddy Kassab termed the decision a "travesty" and said, "I'll still stand by what

I said five years ago. If the courts of this country won't administer justice, I will."

The Justice Department announced its intention to ask for a rehearing before the full Fourth Circuit Court of Appeals, but, on August 22—fifty-one weeks after his conviction—Jeffrey MacDonald was released on bail, pending further legal developments.

He returned to his condominium at 16052 Mariner Drive, where he found his car and boat and Jacuzzi in good working order and Candy Kramer and his mother waiting faithfully.

Even before the brief had been filed with the appeals court, friends of Jeffrey MacDonald had hired a private detective from Los Angeles to conduct an investigation into the case.

The detective's name was Ted Gunderson, he had spent twenty-eight years with the FBI—having retired as head of the agency's Los Angeles division earlier in 1979—and the walls of his Wilshire Boulevard office were crowded with autographed pictures of such people as Gerald Ford, Johnny Carson, J. Edgar Hoover, Ronald Reagan, Jerry Brown, Walter Matthau, Steve Garvey, Roger Staubach, and John Wayne.

Gunderson had begun work immediately, bringing to his task great energy and enthusiasm, and the appeals court decision did not cause the slightest slackening of his pace. As he told the press the day the decision was announced, "We don't want Jeff to be known as a man who was let out on a technicality. We intend to prove his innocence."

Gunderson, in fact, accompanied by a female psychic from the Canadian province of Ontario and working with the cooperation of Prince Edward Beasley, the retired Fayetteville detective, had already made contact with Helena Stoeckley.

On May 1, the trio had located Stoeckley in a J. C. Penney's store in Greenville, South Carolina, where she was trying on nurses' uniforms. The psychic had handed Stoeckley a letter written the night before in which she said, "Five weeks ago, Jeff MacDonald came into my life and my entire world changed. . . . I met a man full of warmth, love, energy and life and I knew that he was innocent and had every right to be cleared."

In the letter, the psychic pledged that MacDonald's friends would support Stoeckley "in every possible way both financially and emotionally" if she would only cooperate with them.

At the time, Stoeckley had said, "I can't now. I wish I could." By October, however, she had expressed a willingness to come to California and discuss matters further with Gunderson. On October 25, after spending five days in a Southern California motel, and having been told by Gunderson that he would help her to resettle in a new location, to find a job, and to start a new life, Stoeckley signed a statement in which she admitted that she and five friends—Bruce Fowler, Greg Mitchell, Don Harris, Dwight Smith, and Allen Mazerolle—all members of a satanic cult (two of whom—Fowler and Mitchell—had been questioned, polygraphed, and dismissed as suspects during the 1971 reinvestigation), had entered 544 Castle Drive during the early morning hours of February 17, 1970, and had murdered Jeffrey MacDonald's wife and children in order to punish MacDonald for his refusal to supply methadone to cult members who were heroin addicts.

On December 18, the Fourth Circuit Court split 5-to-5 on the question of whether to meet in full (*en banc*, as it is known in legal circles) to review the panel's 2-to-1 decision in the MacDonald case. The effect was (as had been the effect of the 3-to-3 split on the same question in 1976) to allow the panel majority's decision to stand.

An exultant Bernie Segal told the press that the vote was "a long-awaited Christmas present for Dr. MacDonald." Ted Gunderson released a copy of Stoeckley's confession to a Fayetteville, North Carolina, newspaper, and told Los Angeles reporters that "She gave names of everybody involved and gave details of the crime. It was a sex-drug-satanic cult and a Manson type murder." Gunderson added that Stoeckley's group had called itself "The Black Cult," and—still active—had committed "at least 13" murders altogether.

On the East Coast, Freddy Kassab repeated, "If the courts won't administer justice, I will, in no uncertain terms. I'll sit just long enough to see what the Supreme Court does. There's no way that I'm going to let him walk around loose."

Shortly before Christmas, MacDonald made a tape and sent it to me.

"I'm sitting out on the dock right now," he said, "having a beer. Trying to tread that fine line between sitting inside a dark room and having some wine and really getting down in the dumps or sitting out in the sun, Southern California–style, and feeling good about life. I don't feel good about life, but I feel a little better than I did a couple of days ago, so I'm sitting in the sun and you're hearing ducks in the background.

"To bring you up to date, Candy and I are doing fine. We've come through, I think, a fairly rough period. I would say basically the problem has been that we're at very different stages. You know, I'm thirty-seven and fighting for a new place in the sun and an income and reacceptance into life or whatever, and Candy at twenty-four bursting forth in the bloom of almost unspoiled youth and beauty.

"We're just at very different points and places, and I'm having a hard time either making her understand it, or whatever. We're just—we're not meshing gears real well, but lately it's starting to come around, I guess because I'm starting to feel a little better.

"She has her own apartment, and that relieved a whole lot of tension and pressure that was unspoken between us, because I have no desire to play the father or the protector right now. I'm just doing too many things and sorting out too many of the past years in my head to totally help her, you know, grow up right now.

"Aaah, let's see. Bringing you up to date on my activities, as incongruous as this sounds, and now seems to me, the Policeman's Benevolent Association of Long Beach has been hounding me to attend all their annual things which occur right around Christmas, so unfortunately—or, fortunately, I guess I should say, as the case may be—over the past four weeks I've been to three functions.

"One was at the bar owned by Dennis Harrah, the lineman for the Rams, which is the big hit in Long Beach now, it's called Legends. And, ah, big Dennis, all six foot six and 260 pounds of him parades around, eyeing the twenty-year-old blondes who sneak in without proof, and the Benevolent Association had a cocktail party there and I went to it. It was extremely uncomfortable, the only thing that really happened of import was that the assistant director for the Long Beach Grand Prix assured me that he wants me back as medical director for next year's race. I've been medical director for the Grand Prix almost since its inception. I think the second year, I took it over, and we've done well by them and they have done well by us with top-flight medical care.

"Then Candy and I went to the Christmas party for the honorary policeman's association and there were five lifetime members, lifetime honorary members, in the history of the association, me being number one for saving a policeman's life who was shot in the stomach and was being mistreated at another hospital. And then Whitey Littlefield who was Frank Sinatra's manager and owner of the beer distributorship for this area, Somerset Distributors, is number two, and there are three other businessmen in town who have become three, four, and five, so there was a big dinner in our honor.

"We had another. Whitey Littlefield, the same guy I just mentioned, has a birthday party each year. His birthday's at Christmas but he holds it early in December, and so we've been to these police parties, so I'm in this kind of strange frame of mind just coming out of Terminal Island and having a very different feeling about police in general, but still being wined and dined by the honorary and Policeman Benevolent Association group of people, and, ah, so I'm sort of masking some feelings as I'm spending some somewhat social evenings doing these things.

"I trust you can hear the Medevac in the background—that's a National Guard helicopter going overhead. Ummm, let's see . . . [he shouts] *Hey, Babe!* [tape recorder clicks off].

". . . Excuse the interruption. I just had a pretty young thing stop by to say hello. God, she looked great, too. She's jogging from Cal State past my house, which is a pretty good jog. She's on about a seven-mile run. . . ."

*   *   *

In March of 1981 the Justice Department filed a petition with the U.S. Supreme Court, asking that the Fourth Circuit speedy trial ruling be reviewed.

Jeffrey MacDonald continued to report to his parole officer once a week. Except for one trip to Las Vegas, where he served as medical director for the Caesar's Palace Grand Prix auto race, he remained confined to the state of California, under the terms of his bail.

He sent me a tape in May:

"A reasonably good friend of mine, Mike Jenkins, was killed recently, and I've been sort of shoring up Pat Kinder, my former head nurse, who was going with him. They were just getting ready to buy a house in Palos Verdes.

"He's this ex–Green Beret, CIA-type, a little paranoid. As a matter of fact, and it's in kind of a strange way, we were getting closer together over a couple of issues. One was helping Ted Gunderson out with, uh, this, um, a rapid deployment force—an antiterrorist force for an Arab government, in which we're providing medical support. And Mike Jenkins was, you know, in on this with me. I finished a report for Ted Gunderson recently, which (a) was fun to do, and (b) it may mean a trip to the Middle East when I'm off bail, and (c) it was interesting kind of work for me—the antiterrorist force based on field medicine.

"So anyway we were working together on that. And also about three weeks before his death I had gotten this call in the middle of the night from Pat Kinder that he had been arrested and [laugh] what should she do about it. And, basically, to make a long story short, he was leaving her house early one morning and there was a police unit nearby and there was—the story diverges here. He says there was a backfire, and the police say they heard a gunshot. So they stopped his van. And of course he always carries a couple of guns, one in the small of his back and one in his sock. He's a little paranoid, like I say. He's an ex-CIA guy for a long time, still identified himself with his code number. Anyway, so they found these guns on him which were not—clearly—not authorized, and so he was arrested. And we had to bail him out of jail in the middle of the night, and Pat Kinder didn't know how to go about doing it. So she called me. And we're old friends anyway and we usually help each other at times of crisis. But [laugh] we eventually got him a lawyer and got the $500, whatever the heck it was, together, and about eight o'clock that morning he was bailed out.

"In any case, he was killed. He was filming a, uh—he's a free-faller, parachuter, and, uh, kind of heavy-duty. He probably has, I don't know, six-seven thousand jumps. And his business is photography. And he's kind of a famous guy for his free-fall photography. He does a lot of advertising for TV and for the media in which, you know, the shots are of, either of other free-fallers or some product or something, but involving parachuting. And so he makes his money as a photographer, basically involving parachute work.

"In any case, he was making a commercial over a lake up near Big Bear. And the production crew wanted him to film it over the land, and he said, no, over the water. So he goes out of the plane and his first chute doesn't open. So he cuts it away, takes his knife out of his, um, his, the calf holster that he always carries a knife in for just that reason. And he cut away the shrouds on his main chute, which were all tangled, and he let it go free. And then he opened his reserve and his reserve didn't fully deploy. And he mildly crashed and burned into the lake. The really strange thing is, and the even more sad part of the story is, is that, he, um, was, apparently okay after he hit the water. The people on the shore had binoculars and they saw him hit the water and they saw him actually stand up, apparently on a sandbar. And they saw him cutting his parachute free. And then they turned their back on him and went to get in a rowboat and row out to him, and when they next turned around he was missing. And they found him out in the lake, drowned. Apparently he stepped off the sandbar trying to walk to shore. And he had two movie cameras on his helmet, and they weighed about forty pounds. And apparently he got underwater and couldn't get above water again once his helmet filled with water, and he drowned.

"The clincher in it, the saddest of all, is that Pat had just taken off to go skiing up in Mammoth. And when she got back there were messages on her answering service to please, not to call anyone, but to call this guy who was her best friend—actually not her best friend but his best friend, who was, a guy who's now a vice-president of a bank out here, and he's kind of a famous guy in the Green Berets. He's called Captain Hook. He's a captain in the Green Berets and in Vietnam got his arm blown off, and he has one of these metal hooks. And he's a free-faller also, and he's a good friend of Jenkins and myself. And he's one of the guys who helped organize this relief mission to Nicaragua and Guatemala that we were doing in the middle seventies. There was a bunch of ex–Green Berets who had gotten together and gotten this relief mission with about 28,000 or 50,000 pounds of medical supplies and dried foods and stuff. And then we were stopped by the CIA because the pilot of our plane was on the outs with the CIA because of some operations in Bangladesh.

"Anyway, it gets very complicated. But the point was, Captain Hook had left a message on Pat's answering service not to call anyone but to call him. And she was replaying the rest of her messages, and among those other messages was a call from Mike, saying don't go skiing, please call me. And of course Pat immediately felt that she was the cause of his death and had she made the call that maybe he wouldn't be dead today, et cetera, et cetera.

"So anyway, I had to sort of support her through this and ended up taking her to the funeral, which was an incredibly moving experience. There was this, um, little chapel on the hillside out, fifteen miles from here inland, and it was filled with all these, oh, I would say it was packed to the brim with, you know, some couples and some young people and some old people and some families. But the majority, like 70 percent of the people there, were these strange assortment of CIA and Green Beret and undercover operatives and a lot of guys who'd been in the service together. And a lot of them kind of strange, and a lot of legends attached to some of these guys. And there wasn't a dry eye in the place. Mike is a fabulous person—*was* a fabulous person—one of these guys who really touched you just by knowing him. He was a high-impact person, without any question, no pun intended."

He then provided an update on his social life, saying he wasn't really seeing Candy anymore but was interested in someone else.

On May 26, 1981, the Supreme Court announced that it would accept the MacDonald case for review, thereby denying him—at least temporarily—total and permanent freedom.

On July 30, Helena Stoeckley wrote Ted Gunderson a letter in which she said:

> It is my opinion that in the preceding months I have been used as a pawn for your convenience and suitability. I also feel that I was coerced into signing a so-called "confession," and that I was exploited by means of false hopes and empty promises. Never have I seen a bigger mockery made of justice or such a shambles made of an investigation. . . .
>
> When I finally agreed to cooperate with you . . . I gave you as conclusive a review of the events of the night in question as I could. You, in turn, misconstrued and distorted all statements I made to you, to be used against me at your convenience.

In November, the *Princeton Alumni Weekly* reported in its notes on the class of '65:

> Sandra O'Connor began her term as a Supreme Court justice with two pending cases of special interest to us. The first is the university's appeal in the U.S. Labor Party case involving Princeton's right to control campus access. The second is the case against *Jeff MacDonald* in which a lower appeals court overturned his 1979 conviction because it said he had been denied the right to a speedy trial. Let's hope for good news on both!

On December 8, the Supreme Court heard oral arguments. Jeffrey MacDonald flew to Washington for the occasion and told reporters, "I've been in this fight since I was twenty-six. The Vietnam war has come and gone and the government is still pursuing me. I've spent all of my emotions and most of my money fighting this. It's been a twelve-year struggle. I have no feelings anymore.

"Brian Murtagh wants to put me in prison, despite the evidence. He is a berserk person being paid with tax money to do this to me. I am the victim of a middle-level bureaucrat run amuck. That gnaws at your innards. I have been told four or five times it was all over. I can't keep bearing this weight."

He then returned to California and purchased a $200,000 condominium at the Mammoth Mountain ski resort, and traded in his Citroën-Maserati for a Jaguar.

He was, by now, dating a twenty-year-old student from Long Beach State University. Her name was Randi Dee Markwith and she was, MacDonald said, "the first person I've felt great with since Colette."

He had met her through her work as a volunteer at St. Mary's Hospital. "It was the day after I'd gone to his lecture on trauma," she told a Long Beach newspaper. "I met him in the hall and said, 'Hi, Dr. MacDonald.' He smiled and said, 'Hi, Randi,' and I couldn't believe it. He knew my name! My heart dropped. My face felt red and hot and I stumbled around for words. I probably said something dumb. . . ."

Despite the difference in age and background, and despite the uncertain future MacDonald faced, romance bloomed quickly. "It was strange," Randi Dee said, "from the very beginning—the sparks we felt. We are both vivacious, energetic people. We both love outdoors and children and music and just being together. We're so in love, so excited and happy with each other."

In March, they decided to get married. "I dragged him into the drugstore and bought some brides' magazines, and he helped me pick out a dress. Then we made out our guest list. I'd call out a name from his address book and he'd say yes or no, whatever.

"We decided on a big wedding in Newport Beach. And we decided on children, two of them. Jeffrey loves children."

On the evening of March 24, 1982, MacDonald invited twenty-four friends to his Huntington Beach condominium. Randi Dee Markwith was already there. Champagne was served in crystal goblets and then four limousines pulled up to the door. Jeff and Randi got into the first limousine—a white one. They pulled out of the Mariner Drive complex and turned left on the Pacific Coast Highway, heading south toward Balboa Island, and their favorite restaurant, where dinner was to be served to the entire group.

It was a perfectly lovely evening in every way. Just before the first course was served, Jeff stood to make a brief speech. He said that despite the fact that there remained "some clouds on the horizon," he and Randi had decided, "to say yes to each other, to say yes to love, to say yes to life." Then he formally announced their engagement.

The food, he reported later, was superb. A choice of entrées: filet mignon, stuffed baby salmon, or veal. The only odd part, he said, was his mother. She would not eat. She did not even sample her main course. Having heard the engagement announcement, she just sat there, throughout the dinner, staring down at her plate, saying nothing.

On March 31, 1982, the U.S. Supreme Court ruled, 6 to 3, that Jeffrey MacDonald's constitutional right to a speedy trial had not been violated.

Writing for the majority, Chief Justice Warren Burger

stated, "The Sixth Amendment right to a speedy trial . . . is designed to minimize the possibility of lengthy incarceration prior to trial, impairment of liberty imposed on an accused while released on bail, and to shorten the disruption of life caused by arrest and the presence of unresolved criminal charges."

In the opinion of the court, the period from 1972 to 1974 could not be counted in any consideration of a speedy trial claim, because throughout that time there were no criminal charges outstanding against MacDonald, the Army having dismissed those which had originally been filed.

"Inevitably," Burger wrote, "there were undesirable consequences flowing from the initial accusation by the Army and the continuing investigation after the Army charges were dismissed. Indeed, even had there been no charges lodged by the Army, the ongoing comprehensive investigation would have subjected MacDonald to stress and other adverse consequences. However, once the charges instituted by the Army were dismissed, MacDonald was legally and constitutionally in the same posture as though no charges had been made. He was free to go about his affairs, to practice his profession, and to continue with his life."

In a footnote, Burger added, "There is nothing to suggest that the Justice Department acted in bad faith in not securing an indictment until January, 1975. . . . Plainly the indictment of an accused—perhaps even more so the indictment of a physician—for the heinous and brutal murder of his pregnant wife and two small children is not a matter to be hastily arrived at either by the prosecutorial authorities or by a grand jury. The devastating consequences to an accused person from the very fact of such an indictment is a matter which responsible prosecutors must weigh carefully. The care obviously given the matter by the Justice Department is certainly not any indication of bad faith or deliberate delay."

In a separate footnote, Burger added: "Our analysis of the speedy trial claim is not . . . influenced by consideration of the evidentiary basis of the jury verdict. The jury that heard all of the witnesses and saw the evidence unanimously decided that respondent murdered his wife and children."

Burger was joined in his opinion by Justices White, Powell, Rehnquist and O'Connor. Justice Stevens filed a separate, concurring opinion, in which he disagreed with Burger's view that MacDonald's speedy trial rights had been in suspension between the Army's dismissal of charges in 1970 and the return of the indictment in 1975. He found, however, that because the murders constituted such a "serious offense" the government was entitled to "proceed cautiously and deliberately before making a final decision to prosecute."

Writing a dissent in which he was joined by Justices Brennan and Blackmun, Thurgood Marshall found that the majority opinion was "not justified by the language of the Speedy Trial Clause or the teachings of our cases, and it is hopelessly at odds with any sensible understanding of speedy trial policies."

Marshall continued: "The majority's analysis is simple: the Speedy Trial Clause offers absolutely no protection of a criminal defendant during the period that a charge is not technically pending. But simplicity has its price. The price, in this case, is disrespect for the language of the clause, important precedents of this court, and Speedy Trial policies. . . .

"Nothing in the language suggests that a defendant must be continually under indictment in order to obtain the benefits of the speedy trial right. Rather, a natural reading of the language (*'In all criminal prosecutions, the accused shall enjoy the right to a speedy and public trial,'*) is that the Speedy Trial Clause continues to protect one who has been accused of a crime until the government has completed its attempts to try him for that crime."

In the MacDonald case, Marshall wrote, he found the question of whether the delay had violated MacDonald's speedy trial right to be "close." Most difficult to evaluate, he said, was the question of prejudice, but he noted that "proof of actual prejudice to the defense at trial is not necessary." The mere potential for prejudice would suffice. In MacDonald's case, Marshall wrote, the record was clear that the delay had caused "substantial" prejudice "including continuing anxiety, intrusive publicity, legal expense, and disruption of a new civilian career," and he added that the proof of actual prejudice at trial "although somewhat speculative" was suggested by the possibility that "Stoeckley's trial testimony would have been less confused and more helpful to MacDonald at an earlier date."

Marshall agreed that "the government's interest in reaching an informed decision whether to prosecute is certainly legitimate," but said, "vague, unexplained references to internal disagreement about prosecution cannot justify more than two years of indecision."

It was, however, once again, the majority opinion which had the force of law and within an hour of its announcement Judge Franklin T. Dupree, Jr., had signed an order revoking MacDonald's bail and federal agents descended upon 16052 Mariner Drive and took him away in handcuffs as a stunned and tearful Randi Dee Markwith stood watching.

He entered the back seat not of a long white limousine as he had just one week earlier, but of a plain gray sedan. And this time, coming out of the Mariner Drive condominium complex, the car turned not left down the Pacific Coast Highway toward Balboa Island, but right, toward the Federal Correctional Institution at Terminal Island from the confines of which Jeffrey MacDonald had enjoyed more than eighteen months of freedom.

During the process of arrest, agents discovered a .44 magnum revolver—the most powerful handgun manufactured in the United States—and a box of ammunition in a nightstand next to his bed. The possession of such a weapon was a violation of the terms of MacDonald's bail, but insofar as he was once again serving three consecutive life sentences for murder, the point was moot. Perhaps, however, Freddy Kassab's repeated threats to "administer justice" personally had not fallen upon entirely deaf ears.

During his first week back in prison, MacDonald wrote me to say that he'd read in the *Los Angeles Times* that Robert Redford was looking for new material and he suggested that Redford be approached about the possibility of playing the role of MacDonald in a movie version of the story.

In June, the Fourth Circuit Court of Appeals heard oral argument on MacDonald's remaining points of appeal.

On July 12 he wrote to say that "despite a chipped toe & sprained ankle (football) I won the July 4th 3-mile run here. Ran a *great* tactical race & dogged this 22 year old Indian for 17 laps (2 steps behind him)—burst past him with 50 yards to go. Won 6 Cokes and a trophy. Time: 19:51."

Four days later he wrote to say that he had just read the transcripts of the oral arguments made in Richmond in June. "No question—we've won. Only question is if there will be a new trial or complete dismissal."

On August 16, however, the same three-judge panel that had ruled in MacDonald's favor on the speedy trial issue found unanimously that the trial had been error-free and that there was "ample warrant" for the verdict.

Even Justice Murnaghan concurred, "albeit not without substantial misgiving," particularly in regard to Judge Dupree's ruling on the Stoeckley witnesses.

"My view," he wrote, "is that the testimony should have been admitted. If such evidence was not persuasive, which is what the government esentially contends in saying that it was untrustworthy, the jury . . . would not have been misled by it."

In the end, however, Murnaghan stated that it would undermine the concept of trial court discretion "were courts of appeal to label as 'abuse of discretion' any action by a district court with which the appellate court disagrees."

Murnaghan concluded his separate but concurring opinion with the statement, "The case provokes a strong uneasiness in me. The crimes were base and horrid and whoever commited them richly deserves severe punishment. The evidence was sufficient to sustain the findings of guilt beyond a reasonable doubt. Still, the way in which a finding of guilt is reached is, in our enduring system of law, at least as important as the finding of guilt itself. I believe MacDonald would have had a fairer trial if the Stoeckley-related testimony had been admitted."

Randi Dee Markwith remained in residence at 16052 Mariner Drive. In the return address on mail she sent out she signed herself as "Mrs. Randi MacDonald." On August 31 she sent me a note which said:

> *I've enclosed some letters that I've written to Jeff & visa [sic] versa. Jeff asked me to send you some, so you could better understand the intense and very beautiful love that Jeff & I share. I've also enclosed a contract which was drawn up by the two of us, and worded by Jeff. It is very meaningful to both of us and it is something that we read often.*

In an eleven-page letter within six days after his appeal for a new trial had been unanimously rejected in Richmond, MacDonald had said to his fiancée:

> *I'm strong and logical and have taken stock in our resources and I feel & believe and know that I (we?) will win. I don't know how soon, how, why, any more, but I will win. I will be free. How "vindicated" I'll be, I don't know, that depends on so many things. It depends on P.R., the new evidence, the strength of my lawyers, investigators, me. It depends on chance (a new witness being found); luck; friends (a pardon?) . . .*
>
> *Vindication can come in many ways—it may be sudden, full, complete. It may be partial in the courts or thru P.R. or thru the book or movie. It may be thru a pardon. I don't know. Can't tell—but I will win, I will be out, I will fight until that is so. . . .*

The "contract" was dated April 12, 1982, which meant that it had been composed less than two weeks after MacDonald's return to prison. In Jeffrey MacDonald's handwriting—the same hand that had written of

Eskatrol twelve years earlier; the same hand which a jury believed had written the word PIG, in Colette's blood, on the headboard of the bed they had shared—the "contract" said:

We, the undersigned, are deeply in love and have agreed to become man and wife forever. We both fully intend for this complete union to occur as soon as it is possible to do so. We both fully intend to have 2 children within our first several years together in order that our children can enjoy our intense love and benefit therefrom as much as possible.

In addition to the above, the undersigned have fully discussed and mutually agree upon another series of binding promises to each other. These promises are part of, but not the total sum of our complete love for each other. These promises were made on or about our fabulous weekend in Palm Springs, during which Jeffrey Robert MacDonald proposed to and was accepted by Randi Dee, the date of which began on Saturday, March 20, in the year of our Lord, 1982. The engagement followed as soon as was humanly possible, namely on March 24, 1982, in a ceremony and gathering of mutual friends, that, by general consensus, was a party of all-time grace, elegance and beauty. The series of binding promises to each other made on that fabulous weekend leading to the engagement party consist of:

(1) Neither party, namely JRM or RDM, will ever go to bed and sleep angry at the partner. Each partner promises to clear the problem prior to

sleep, even to the extent of awakening the other partner and talking thru the night to accomplish the goal of renewing the full feelings of love and respect.

(2) Each partner will always make every effort to be home every night with his/her loved partner/friend/lover/spouse. In the unfortunate event that either partner cannot be home, every effort will be made to call the other partner & say 'I love you.'

(3) Each partner agrees, fully, that if one partner asks a question, a truthful and full answer will be given by the other partner. Each partner agrees that the love shared is so great and so intense that it can overcome any problems that may arise by a full and truthful answer.

(4) Each partner in this lifelong contract of love and fidelity agrees that the single most important thing and person in the world is their respective partner.

(5) Furthermore, each loving partner agrees that our children are part of our love and will share in our love and happiness and growth; and that our loved children are a major part of our universe and will assume a position of importance in our family superseded only by our incredible love for each other, a love so great that it is awesome to both us and observers.

The children, they had decided, were both going to be boys.

Following the decision of the appeals court, Jeffrey Mac-Donald was transferred from Terminal Island to the higher-security federal prison at Lompoc, California. One day, not long afterward, Randi Dee Markwith, having become a stewardess for Pacific Southwest Airlines, paid him a visit to inform him that the engagement was off. She moved out of 16052 Mariner Drive. MacDonald's mother began to clear his personal belongings from the apartment in order that it might be sold. The condominium at Mammoth Mountain was also put up for sale, as were the *Recovery Room* and the Jaguar.

After six weeks at Lompoc, MacDonald was transferred to the Federal Correctional Institution at Bastrop, Texas, to serve the remainder of his term.

Vowing to fight on, he dismissed Bernie Segal as chief counsel and hired a new lawyer from Santa Monica. He also hired a new private investigator from New York City.

Helena Stoeckley, having recanted her recantation, reconfessed in front of television cameras provided by a program called *Jack Anderson Confidential*. From prison, MacDonald urged his new lawyer to explore the possibility of gaining for him a presidential pardon.

"President Reagan," he wrote, "2 pronged attack, orchestrated *carefully*." He suggested that Reagan could be approached either through Jack Anderson, who seemed obviously sympathetic to the cause (if not terribly well informed about the facts) or through the new governor of California, George Deukmejian, who was said to be a friend of Whitey Littlefield's, the beer distributor from Long Beach, and fellow honorary member of the Long Beach Police Officers Association.

From Bastrop, in central Texas, about thirty miles east of Austin, he wrote his new attorney a letter, just as the attorney prepared to visit North Carolina in an attempt to familiarize himself with the case.

. . . Some thoughts on public relations. . . . The Supreme Court should grant a new trial but probably won't, so my only hope is . . . a new trial based on "new" evidence. We'll have to get the evidence, package it, and force a new trial. We'll have to marshall public opinion to do that, I think—and we have to expend good energy that way. . . .

I'm writing this letter to tell you what you already know, and it doesn't require an answer but I wanted to say it. I was innocent in 1970 and I'm innocent now. I spent 7 months in a room in 1970 and a year in prison in 1979–80 and now 7 months more in prison. I'm looking at the rest of my life here, among functional illiterates and vicious people who spend 85% of their time bragging about their crimes. The grotesque monster of the "case" has been on my back for so long I'm not sure what I'd be like without this incredible pressure 24 hours a day. But I would like to find out. The insanity of being here, of being saddled with a "guilty" verdict on these horrendous crimes against my family and myself, of facing the rest of my life behind razor wire, being told to make my bed by thugs with an IQ approaching 60, of watching my Mom aging now incredibly quickly and becoming uncertain in her thought and actions—it is all almost too much to take.

I go over the "ifs" of my case & I can't sleep for 2 nights each time. I can afford no more "if only's"—I need some hope, some new evidence, and a vindication. I have to leave this system, this case, these 12½ years, and return to a real life. I'd like to see my Mom smile again—I'd like to treat patients again—I'd even like a family (that was Randi's gift to me— she got me over that hurdle).

I'm hoping you come back from N.C. with key new evidence. If not, at least a determination, if not a religious fervor, to plunge headlong & 100% into the case, to work day & night, to find the means to overturn this monster I've been saddled with. . . .

The weeks and months keep slipping by—I'm now 39 and have lots of anger to dissipate as I try to resume a life. Remember—this all started when I was 26. I'm sitting here in Texas, in a strange & alien land, in an environment that is 500 fools locked up by 300 borderline retards, on a jr. college campus, but treated like jr. high schoolers, with our campus surrounded by double fences topped with razor wire and barbed wire—all on closed circuit T.V. It is really bizarre.

I need to walk out of here—vindicated, able to hold my head up, able to care for myself & my family. I need that fairly soon.

Lastly, let me say that for 12 years I let the lawyers do it. I paid my way, dearly at times, but I concentrated on my professional career, myself, forgetting Feb. 17, 1970, and tried to live a normal life. That is all gone, and they are saying "forever." My fight now is truly for my life, as it was that night in 1970, only this death will take 30 to 40 years. I don't want, or deserve this. . . . I need to be vindicated—I need to walk out of here, back to life. I would like to smell the flowers again, and I should.

On Monday, January 10, 1983, the Supreme Court, without comment, denied MacDonald's request that it review the Fourth Circuit's rejection of MacDonald's claim that he had not received a fair trial. This brought to an end—after twelve years, ten months, and twenty-four days—the legal phase of the Jeffrey MacDonald case.

Three days later—on the afternoon of Thursday, January 13—the body of Helena Stoeckley was found on a couch in an apartment she had been renting in Seneca, South Carolina. The body, found by a maintenance man who had come to the apartment to install weather stripping, was in a state of decomposition which indicated that she had been dead for several days. Her seven-month-old son—the product of her marriage to Ernie Davis, who was serving a fifteen-year jail sentence for first-degree sexual assault at the time of her death—was found, badly dehydrated but alive, beneath a crib not far from the couch.

From his Bastrop prison cell, MacDonald said he found the death "highly suspicious," but autopsy disclosed that Stoeckley had died of natural causes: pneumonia, brought on by cirrhosis of the liver which, for years, had been diseased with hepatitis.

The manager of the apartment complex in which she had been living said, "She told us a couple of weeks ago that she and the baby had pneumonia." The manager added: "They were going without food. She told me one time she had only peanut butter sandwiches for five days."

From *his* jail cell near Greenville, South Carolina, Ernie Davis charged that his wife's death was the result—at least indirectly—of "harassment" by investigators employed by Jeffrey MacDonald.

"Helena was like a puppet," he said. "These people would pull her strings and make her do whatever they wanted. They'd tell her they talked to people who could place her at the murder and that she'd end up in jail if she didn't confess. Other times, they promised to get her a part in a movie once it was all over. She was just trying to please them. They put things in her head they knew weren't true and had her repeat it in the confessions. She knew it was all lies, but she finally sold out. She said time and time again that if she didn't tell them what they wanted to hear, they'd bother her even more."

Both Ted Gunderson (who was approaching literary agents with the story of how he had "solved" the Mac-Donald murders) and Prince Edward Beasley (who had reached an agreement with a former Fayetteville newspaper reporter that the two of them and Stoeckley would share in the proceeds of a book and possible movie to be based on the proposition that the Stoeckley cult had been responsible for the killings) denied the charges leveled by Ernie Davis.

"Every time Helena gave us statements, it was voluntary," Gunderson said. "The only time she was reluctant was when Ernie was harassing her. And still, she gave us fourteen or fifteen signed statements."

And, ignoring the autopsy findings, syndicated columnist Jack Anderson had written a January 15 column which *The Washington Post* headlined "Evidence Backs the Innocence of MacDonald," in which he said, "My staff has uncovered stacks of evidence that supports the doctor's claim of innocence" (without at any point specifying what the stacks consisted of). Anderson's follow-up piece was headlined, "Death of Trial Witness Looks Suspicious." In this he wrote: "Not long ago, a tragic young woman named Helena Stoeckley stepped out of the shadows to save a man from life in prison. She told my office a story that brought her nothing but grief and threats. Last month she was found dead in her hideout apartment in South Carolina." The column strongly implied that members of Stoeckley's witchcraft cult had been responsible for her death but did not ever suggest how such a cult might use pneumonia and cirrhosis to silence a renegade member.

Encouraged by such evidence of continued support and—as he told a Long Beach newspaper reporter—by "more than 6,500 letters, all but about a dozen of them supportive," Jeffrey MacDonald vowed to fight on.

Dismissing Bernie Segal as "an asshole," he hired a new attorney. And, as ex–FBI agent Gunderson began to give press interviews claiming that the Stoeckley cult was threatening *his* life, MacDonald also employed a new team of private investigators. (Gunderson told a Dallas newspaper that he had received the following deadly message presumed to be from members of the cult: thirteen red roses, thirteen chrysanthemums, and a typed note that read, "Poacher in the grass, Once a cub, the lion sees Shades of death and life," and that as a result he had found it necessary to flee Los Angeles and begin a "life on the run.")

He said that by April 1983 his new attorney would be in court with, "an ironclad case" that would prove his innocence. "We're going to have both barrels loaded," MacDonald said. "We're going to have this thing in a cast-iron mold with perfect evidence." (In the meantime, he said, he was keeping trim in prison by abstaining from dinner. "Too many carbohydrates," he said.)

Not long afterward, however, MacDonald estimated that it would be midsummer at the earliest before his lawyers would be ready to proceed, despite the fact that "We know the people who were in the house that night, and we are on the road to locating them." Later he said no motion would be filed before fall.

The people named by Stoeckley in 1981 were located—not by MacDonald's investigators, however, but by FBI agents and, in February 1983, by a Fayetteville newspaper reporter named Steve Huettel. With the exception of Greg Mitchell, who had died in June of 1982 from liver disease (and who had been investigated and cleared by the CID in 1971 and by the FBI ten years later), all denied any knowledge of the murders.

One called Stoeckley's story "totally insane" and "the craziest thing I've ever heard." Another termed it "the ravings of a madwoman." These two were individuals who, like Mitchell, had been investigated and cleared of involvement, both by the CID in 1971 and by the FBI in 1981 and 1982, following the delivery of Stoeckley's statement to the Justice Department by representatives of Jeffrey MacDonald.

A key figure in the Stoeckley "confession"—one she had not named in prior statements—was Allen Mazerolle, who was traced to a small town in Maine. His denial of involvement was supported by Cumberland County court records, which showed he had been arrested on January 28, 1970, for possession and transportation of LSD and had remained in jail until March 10—thus making his presence in or near 544 Castle Drive during the early morning hours of February 17 a physical impossibility.

"It's ridiculous," Mazerolle said of Stoeckley's allegation. "She was the informer who fingered me to the narcotics agents."

MacDonald, however, still would not admit that it was over. "The Rock won't crumble," he wrote to one admirer, and, after telling me in a collect phone call from Bastrop that he was "80 percent certain" that the Mazerolle court records had been falsified by government agents in an attempt to discredit Stoeckley, he said, "I just believe there will be a major break in the next few months. The things we sensed were there are there. The facts will bear me out. This time, we're going to win."

He also said to a Long Beach newspaper reporter who interviewed him at Bastrop early in 1983: "I have the same nightmares. I still hear Colette's voice, and the sounds in the house . . . I still see the blood. I still wake up in a cold sweat, exhausted."

As long as there is money to pay them, of course, the lawyers and private investigators will be able to keep busy for years. There will always be new "witnesses," new "leads." And, no doubt, there will be money: no small amount of it supplied by that remaining hard core of true believers—those who accept Jeffrey MacDonald at face value; those who did not attend the trial in its entirety (or at all) and who have never taken the time and trouble to read the record; those who are still so mesmerized by the glittery surface of MacDonald's personality (even though he is gaunt now, with graying hair, "a haggard replica of his former self," as one interviewer described him) that their allegiance remains unpolluted by fact.

"He's never going to accept his guilt," Brian Murtagh said not long after the Supreme Court's final decision in the case. "He's never going to just sit in jail. There is a temptation to say, 'The end. This is it. Finished.' But no. Not really. The case is never going to be in a posture where he just quietly sits in jail and lets the years roll by."

5

It is over for me, though. I have reached the end. I have followed the tangled paths as far as possible and they have led me to places where I did not ever want to be.

There was a day, a very hot and humid Saturday in early August, when in the company of two criminologists who were preparing to testify for the defense, I went inside 544 Castle Drive.

I remained for five hours, amid the mustiness, the clutter, and the dust. For the most part it was the little things to which my attention was drawn.

On the dining room floor there was a small wooden figure, about the size of my thumb: a piece of a Fisher-Price toy.

In Kristen's room, under her bed, there was a jumble of Golden Books and dolls and finger paintings which she had made on poster paper, nine and a half years before. There was also a large, rectangular hole in the floorboards where the bloody footprint of her father had been removed.

Across the hall, in Kimberly's room, there was a pair

of white sneakers with holes in the toes. Her bare mattress was still stained by faded blood.

In the master bedroom, at the end of the hall, splinters of wood still lay on the bloodstained shag carpet, and on the windowsill stood a long-dead poinsettia, its pot wrapped in red tinfoil—a remnant of Christmas 1969.

Colette's beige bra, which she had removed as she had changed into her pajamas on the night of Monday, February 16, 1970, still lay on the green chair near the bed. The telephone receiver, smeared with black fingerprint dust, dangled from a dresser alongside.

In the hall bathroom, three toothbrushes hung from a rack and a half-used tube of Crest toothpaste lay curled on the rim of the sink.

There was a calendar in the kitchen with a space next to each date so one could jot reminders of plans.

February 15: "Jeff ER." In Colette's handwriting.

February 16: "Psych."

February 17: "Dinner Ron." Lieutenant Harrison had eaten elsewhere that night.

Next to the kitchen sink was a rack in which, nine and a half years earlier, dishes had been placed to dry: three plates, two cups, and, turned upside down to facilitate the drying process, two liqueur glasses. A bottle of dishwashing liquid—blackened by fingerprint powder, like so many other objects in the house—stood next to the drain.

There was an unopened can of Diet Pepsi on the counter. A pantry contained a large bag of gum drops, a tin of sliced pineapple, and many, many cans of Campbell's soup.

Eventually, I became aware of a noise. A low hum, being emitted by the refrigerator. The CID agent who had opened the apartment that morning told me the refrigerator had never been unplugged. There was a standing order at CID headquarters: every six weeks send an MP to defrost it. For nine and a half years, the Army, as part of its continuing crime scene supervision, had been preserving the food that no one had eaten, that no one would ever eat.

I opened the refrigerator door. There were only two cans inside, both unopened. One contained cranberry sauce, the other ginger ale.

The freezer, however, was crammed with food. A bag of French fries, opened and with half the potatoes gone; a carton of strawberry ice cream, half empty, and next to it a full, unopened carton of chocolate ripple. There were also a box of rainbow trout, two pounds of hamburger meat (at 53 cents a pound), and a package of pork chops, still tightly sealed in supermarket cellophane.

I shut the door. The hum of the refrigerator seemed to grow louder. After a while, I lost all desire to open closet doors or to check under beds, or to make lists of personal effects or household furnishings. I didn't want to find any Christmas tree tinsel on the living room rug, or any threads from a blue pajama top, anywhere.

That night, for the first and only time, I dreamed of Colette. In the dream, she was on the witness stand, testifying, and as she looked across the courtroom at her husband, she cried out: *"Jeff, Jeff, what more do they want from us?! What more do they want us to do?!"*

I told him about the dream the next day, describing in detail its vividness and emotional power. He was sunning himself on the lawn, reading the Sunday papers, which of course were filled with news about the trial.

He looked at me when I had finished as if I had just

told him it was raining in Portland, Maine. Then he mentioned that the Yankees had won the night before.

Then there was the day, months after the trial, that I spent with Paul Stombaugh in his basement office in Greenville, South Carolina—an office filled with notebooks and charts and photographs having to do with the MacDonald case. He showed me a picture I had never seen before. It was a picture taken in the master bedroom of 544 Castle Drive on the morning of February 17. It showed a suitcase on the bedroom floor. The area all around the suitcase was spattered with blood, yet there were not any spatters on the suitcase. To Stombaugh, this suggested that the suitcase had been placed there, near the closet where Jeffrey MacDonald's clothes were kept, after all the blood had been shed. To Stombaugh, it suggested that at least momentarily, before he made the incision in his chest which caused the partial collapse of his lung, Jeffrey MacDonald had been planning to flee.

Many months after the verdict, Stombaugh was still refining his scenario, still working on it as a hobby, like Rubik's Cube. Just one of the many who have grown obsessed.

I have looked at too many pictures that I did not ever want to see.

I have awakened, too many times, between 3 and 4 A.M., thinking about 544 Castle Drive and February 17, 1970, and knowing that my sleep was over for the night.

And, far too often and much too recently, I have maintained contact with people whose pain I did not any longer want to share. I am thinking, in particular, of Jeffrey MacDonald's mother.

Long after I knew the worst about her son—long after I had written it on paper—I called her to ask about the trip he'd taken to Texas during his sophomore year of high school. It was one of the little things that continued to nag at me, because I could just not bring the picture into focus. Like Stombaugh in his basement, I too, I suppose, had grown obsessed.

In any event, she assured me—as I'd known she would—that no family crisis had precipitated his departure. The only problem which arose, she said, was one which developed *because* of it. While she had viewed the episode in an extremely positive light—"an expansion of experience" for her teenaged son—Jeff's father had taken a darker view.

"If the kid wants to go," she recalled him as saying, "that means he doesn't love me. If he likes other people better than the people in his own home, then we've lost him." The longer Jeff had stayed away, the more upset his father had become, growing convinced that "he loves them better than us."

"My husband," said Dorothy MacDonald, "was a very charming man as long as there were people around. He possessed great charisma. He loved to stimulate argument. But after everyone else had gone home, a little of the man who felt rejected by circumstances would start to come out. The rejection he had suffered in his early life would start to get to him, and during the late hours of the evening he would become indignant and morose."

That his younger son had gone to Texas for a two-week visit and had remained for more than four months became a focal point for this anger and self-pity. "But because of his pride, he would never, never, never reveal to Jeff any of that sort of feeling."

We were having this talk during April of 1983: three months after the Supreme Court had rejected Jeffrey MacDonald's final appeal. Yet his mother, like himself, continued to express optimism. Recent developments, she said, had been "very positive." The investigation on the East Coast was "going well." A major letter-writing campaign to members of Congress was under way, and even astrologers had recently begun to inform her that they were picking up "positive vibes."

I really did not want to listen anymore, and there were too many things I could not say: for instance, that I knew her son had killed his wife and children and that Freddy Kassab had told me once that as far back as the Article 32 hearing in 1970, she had said, "Fred, how can you be so *sure* he's innocent?"

So I just took notes while she said, "Right now I feel like a soiled piece of baggage. Life *has* been kind of unusually difficult. I'm not saying that all the things I did as a mother were right. But believe me, *please,* I never intended to cause anybody unhappiness."

I have been, too, to the home of Freddy and Mildred Kassab on Long Island. It is a new house, and much smaller than the one in which they lived in 1970. There is no swimming pool; in the backyard is just a small bed of roses to which Mildred, on nice days, devotes considerable time and energy.

The Quality Egg Company, which employs Freddy Kassab, has moved to Dayton, New Jersey, and Kassab lives alone in a New Jersey apartment during the week. He was sixty-two years old early in 1983, overweight and suffering from emphysema.

They talked to me for hours, and showed me pictures and letters and diaries. At first, I felt—especially when looking at the letters and diaries—the way I could imagine Brian Murtagh feeling as he'd stood at the grave site in September of 1974, waiting for the exhumation to begin: that this was a violation of privacy so gross in dimension that no end, however meritorious, could justify it.

Eventually, however, this squeamishness gave way to an acceptance of the fact that if this was where the path had led me, then, for the moment, this was where I would be. And it was, ultimately, plain and simple sorrow that I felt as I read the words written with such naive excitement so long ago by a girl no older than my own two daughters were now.

From 1957, when Colette was in ninth grade:

Dec. 27—Tonight Judy had a wonderful party. Jeff and I had a "PRAPTIOUS" time, which means, "Wow!" The room was simply loaded with mistletoe, but I didn't let him take advantage very often. When I think of the way he looked at me just before he kissed me, I simply flip.

Later in high school she had written retrospectively of "The times when Jeff and I had serious talks about him loving me. I kept trying to convince him that he doesn't, because I think this is a very temporary thing with him."

And toward the end of that long and painful weekend, the Kassabs showed me the last written message they had ever received from Colette. It was a card, sent from Fort Bragg, just before Christmas of 1969. The printed message said: "May the Good Will and Peace of this Christmas Season be yours Throughout the coming year." She had signed it, "See you soon—Love, Jeff & Colette" and then had written at the bottom: "P.S.

Please get pants for Jeff in 36" instead of 34"—he is gaining weight but doesn't like to feel it!"

That, of course, was before he had started his second moonlighting job and his workouts with the boxing team. And before he had started taking Eskatrol.

On the plane home that night I read a number of the letters Colette had written to her mother from Skidmore. One, in particular, lingers in memory. It was written during the spring of her freshman year, in response to a stern letter from Mildred, warning her to terminate her relationship with her old high school boyfriend, Dean Chamberlain.

While generally considered an affable fellow (except by Jeffrey MacDonald), Dean lacked Jeff's drive, Jeff's flair, Jeff's star quality. He had also lacked acceptance by Princeton and had instead attended, and then withdrawn from, Kutztown State Teachers College in Pennsylvania.

"Look, Colette," Mildred had told her daughter, "don't continue this because you'll end up being big in the local fire department's ladies' auxiliary and pushing a secondhand baby carriage to the village, and I didn't raise you for that." What she had raised Colette for, she continued, was marriage to someone with prospects: someone like Jeffrey MacDonald, who was not only at Princeton but who had already announced his intention to pursue a career in medicine.

In response, Colette had written:

Dear Mom,

> *As mother and daughter we are very alike in some ways and very different in others. It's funny in a way, I guess we are alike physically. For example, we*

both have weak stomachs. We both threw up when reading the other's letter. But what happened to us other than that? Our ideas are so different. I don't mean just in relation to Dean, but in a lot of other things: religion (or lack thereof), prejudices, aim in life, materialism, etc. I'd like to talk to you about all of these things when I come home but I doubt if you will understand.

I'm trying to understand your point of view but it's very hard because what you want you want very, very much and it is the same with me. We both have special interests in mind and I know that you think "it is the best thing" for me. But maybe you don't know all the details or all of the feelings inside me. I'd like to tell you, I'd like you to understand me, but will you?

Next week when I come home it will probably be the last time before summer. I'd like to have everything settled and out in the open. I want to go out and relax. But if you say no even after we talk I won't sneak or defy you. I will, however, know that it is due to a lack of understanding and forgive you. Anything else I have to say had better wait until we talk.

A lot was said, but by the fall Colette had severed her ties to Dean Chamberlain and had resumed her relationship with Jeffrey MacDonald. By the following summer she was pregnant. Within weeks after that she was married to the all-American boy—the man whom her mother had always thought would be the ideal husband for her. Until, "with the last blow he crushed her head like an eggshell."

*   *   *

I saw him once in the fall of 1980. I was in California and he was out of prison on bail. We went to the home of a friend of his for a barbecue supper. Only one thing about the evening stands out: MacDonald, in the kitchen, as the steaks and chops were cooking over charcoal, complaining that the knives were not sharp enough. And then, as I watched, removing them one by one from a drawer and sharpening each blade, precisely and expertly, against a grindstone.

Two weeks later he sent me his children's baby albums. Ever since, I have had them on my desk, within arm's reach: two white, satin-covered volumes, one called "All About Me" and the other titled "Babyhood Years."

They are Kimberly's and Kristen's baby books, filled with Colette's writing about them and also containing locks of their hair. In addition, glued to one page of Kimberly's book is the first of her baby teeth to fall out. The date was November 13, 1969. She was living at 544 Castle Drive.

MacDonald sent me the albums, unrequested, along with hundreds of pieces of fan mail he had accumulated over the years. I'm not sure why. I am also not sure what I should do with them. Maybe I will put them in a safe place for a while.

Under federal law—even having been sentenced to three consecutive life terms in prison—Jeffrey MacDonald could become eligible for parole on April 5, 1991. He will be, then, forty-seven years old. The books are his. I don't imagine he would have much use for them in prison, but should he get out, he might like to have them back, as souvenirs.

The Voice of Jeffrey MacDonald

What's the sense of all this? It's crazy. John Lennon gets shot. It's—it's—I mean there's no sense. I don't pray to "another god." Umm, you know, to a—a god in another world is what I mean.

I—I just believe in life here. Uhh, I—we make our bed and we must lie in it, basically, and um, I think that, you know, man has the ability to create his own environment with, uh—heh!—certain mitigating features, uhh, natural and unnatural disasters.

But there's just gotta be something else. It can't be that life is made up of a series of tragedies and travesties and, and, insanities. Ummm—this country is wacko and it doesn't know it. I—I—I love this country. I *tried* to fight for this country. They wouldn't let me. They kept me at Fort Bragg when I should have been in Vietnam. 'Cause I signed up for the Green Berets. But they weren't sending Green Berets to Vietnam, they were sending tanks to smash villages.

I mean it's—the whole thing is crazy. I mean, good Lord, there has to be more meaning than these, these crazy episodes of life that I apparently have a—an over-abundance of. [Pause.] [Sigh.] Anyway—it's all bullshit.

But I'm gonna just list some of the good things so I don't leave you with that note. The up years were the high school years. Princeton was fabulous: getting back with Colette, and the hitchhiking back and forth to Skidmore, and the lovemaking in the hotel in Saratoga Springs, and being in her arms and getting letters from her and feeling that surge of love, that incredible, indescribable feeling when you're with her and wanting to see her and wanting to come home to see her, and wanting to come home from Columbia Presbyterian, and then fall asleep at the table. And wanting to take her and Kimmy and Kristy down to see the pony. Those are the great things that you remember. That's the greatest of all.

Umm, I suppose I should also just tell you about my disappointments in life. There are three that I can easily remember right now, sitting here. A lot of little disappointments, like everyone, but I think I have three disappointments. One of horrendous magnitude, umm, two of a much lesser magnitude, but the only things that sort of nag at me now.

Umm, number one of course is the inability of me to protect my family on February 17th. Umm, I'm not even going to get into that. I don't like to talk about that. Uhh, that's clearly my Achilles' heel, uh, but it is the major disappointment, uhh, of my life, I think, and, um, what I have to live with, umm, because, like it or not, the fact is had I protected them, then all four of us—all five of us, actually—would be here now, uhh, living some incredible great life, uhh, Colette and I still madly in love and going into New York to see occasional plays from our farm in Connecticut. So that's number one.

The other two disappointments are basically goal-oriented problems, and they're not in the same severity. I don't mean to put them together; it's just that sitting down thinking, there's lots of little things that happened—I wished I'd made a better tackle one time, things like that, I wish I played the instruments still, like clarinet or saxophone—but, um, the only other important, you know, more important thought processes occasionally recur to me: Number one, I wished I had my Princeton degree, and that sounds a little silly and sophomoric, and it may be, but I kind of wish, somehow, that I had my Princeton degree.

Either that I was able to, um, go back somehow and get my degree even now as a physician by doing things or writing papers or examining, or having stayed an extra year then.

Under the exigencies of the situation, uh, we couldn't. It was a financial and partly emotional decision, 'cause we were ready to move on. We were ready not for a senior year that we thought was going to be wasted writing a senior paper and socializing in New York and Philadelphia, but on to medical school and we had an up-and-coming family that we were worried about and wanted to please. But I'd like to have my Princeton degree. I know that sounds materialistic and, and, um, maybe even a little overbearing, but it's true.

And the other thing is, um, in a kind of a strange sense, and um, kind of perverse way, I wished I had the experience of having served in Vietnam. And again, not from the viewpoint of seeing war, and, uh, the mutilation and whatnot, but I think the experience that our generation went through is so traumatic and so important and has shaped the country now for probably the next twenty years, uh, certainly these last ten . . . umm, and I actually grew up thinking that was part of growing up, being in the military, doing your share, carrying your load, umm, so that I wouldn't have minded at all, at all, going to Vietnam. Not in a pro-war fashion, but I would have served proudly and done my best.

I would not have been a warmonger, I don't think, um, but I kind of wish somehow that I had been able to serve my twelve months over there. Um, in a sense a feeling that then I could say to anyone I want, oh, you're an asshole for supporting this next war or you're not an asshole for supporting the war, or vice versa. Any permutation of that.

In other words I think that uh, uh, my perspective is relatively limited on the subject because I didn't go to war. Whereas a lot of people were over there in Vietnam. They did their thing and now they can say whatever they want. They can be for or against the war with a clear mind and a clear conscience.

Of course the corollary of my silly feeling that I should have gone to Vietnam is the fact that a lot of people died in Vietnam and certainly we could have learned that experience without having a lot of able-bodied men and, as a matter of fact, whatever-bodied men, women, and children killed over there.

So I know that's sort of a self-centered and maybe even overly patriotic way of viewing it, but I wish that I had served my country in a combat zone rather than on Fort Bragg.

Of course, the corollary of that also is that maybe then Colette, Kim, and Kris, and uh, our little baby boy, um—Colette was pregnant with a baby boy, as you know—well, maybe you didn't know—um, would be with me today. Maybe I would have served the twelve months in a combat zone and come out a lot better than a half hour or whatever it was in, uh, 544 Castle Drive with at least four intruders.

I still think about that night, you know. I remember Colette was late for class and dashing out the front door and I was already taking care of the kids and putting away the dishes—not putting away the dishes, but getting them into the kitchen and stuff—and she mentioned something about could she stop at the uh, at the uh, the little nearby dairy for milk and I said fine, we needed milk. And, um, it was cold and rainy and Colette ran to the car.

When she got back from classes that night—maybe I've talked myself into it, but it honestly seems like we had a very small-talk type of conversation. It's possible— it *is* possible—that this night Colette said something about, or brought up the bit about Kristy's bed-wetting and asking about it in her child psychology class and I said, "Oh, and what did the professor say?"

I know! I remember the conversation! We *did* have the conversation—I'm just not sure it was that night. But Colette smiled and—and then I added, "I bet he said just what I said he would say." And Colette smiled and said, "You bum, you're always right."

Other than that, there's nothing I can recall about our conversation, uh, except the fact that Colette was tired that night. Umm, she was looking super and, you know, I was in a real—we were in our best time frame ever, and I was in the habit of trying to shore her up about her pregnancy, and I, you know, I was probably even actually saying that, you know, how nice she looked, and she said, "Oh, I just got in and I have rain in my hair and I don't look good at all." She always denigrated herself.

Anyway, she went in and got changed into pj's because she had gotten a little wet in the rain and she sat around on the, uh, um, um, sofa, um, and I was reading for a little while and we talked about essentially nothing things. And we were sitting next to each other, actually touching each other, on the couch.

And that's when she had her liqueur at eleven o'clock or so, and we watched the news and Johnny Carson, and she went to bed as Johnny Carson was coming on, saying she was a little tired.

And the last thing that we ever did together was that I kissed her goodnight and, um, she went padding down the hallway into bed.

She never really looked as pretty in a picture as she was. Colette was not photogenic for some reason, although she had a very fine bone structure and a nice nose. I could never figure out why she wasn't photogenic, because to me she was a brown-eyed beautiful blonde, um, who didn't have the greatest waistline and her legs were a little skinny, but to me she was incredibly beautiful.

Colette wasn't a woman that walked into a room and stopped the room by any means. That was not her at all, or her style even. But she was the kind of woman that the more you looked at her the lovelier she became. Her warmth would come out and her big, brown luminous eyes would take on new meaning, and the little smile that when she was kidding or being cynical or funny, or, you know—her eyes would sparkle and she'd get this little smile, and it was such a beautiful, meaningful face. The only one I could compare her to would be Meryl Streep. She reminds me a great deal of Colette—that sort of quiet beauty about her.

Colette, sort of in a sentence, was to me soft and feminine and beautiful, big brown eyes, very intelligent, quiet sense of humor, not very aggressive, but a magnificent woman. Without any question the neatest woman I ever met. I still see her as the epitome of womanhood.

A fatal vision.

The 1985 Afterword

Let me tell you a story I have not put into this book until now.

Back in the winter of 1980, the first winter after the verdict, when I was still living in a rented house in western New Jersey, obsessed all day every day and all night every night by those haunting, intertwined questions—did he really do it? and, if he did, *how could he have?*—I woke up in the middle of the night with a runny nose.

There wasn't any Kleenex by the bed and I was sleepy and it was cold and I didn't much feel like getting up in the dark and walking down the hall to the bathroom, so I tried just wiping my nose with the back of my hand. But it kept running, so I finally gave in, got up, shuffled down to the bathroom, felt around on top of the toilet, found some Kleenex, wiped my nose, and stepped to the sink to rinse off my hands.

As I switched on the bathroom light and looked in the mirror, I saw that it had not been a runny nose but a bloody nose, and that I was now standing at the sink of my hall bathroom with my hands covered in blood. And then it came to me what day it was, and I ran back to the bedroom to check the time; it was 3:30 A.M. on the morning of February 17, 1980—ten years to the minute from the time that Jeffrey MacDonald had stood at *his* hall bathroom sink at Fort Bragg with the blood of his wife and children on his hands.

I did not get back to sleep that night, and when the chill dawn finally crept into the February sky, three hours and four cups of coffee later, I considered again—this time more seriously—abandoning the entire project that eventually became *Fatal Vision*.

I tell this story now so that you may have some sense of just how deep my involvement in this business really was, and that you may understand that it was more wishful thinking than statement of fact when, three years ago, I wrote, at the start of the last chapter of the book: "It is over for me now, though. I have reached the end."

I wanted very much for it to be over. I still do. But by now I have come to accept that it is not over for me— nor for anyone whose life has been touched by the tragedy of the MacDonald murders or by the seductive and destructive personality of Jeffrey MacDonald over the fifteen years during which he has fought to avoid punishment for his crimes.

Even today, as I write this, lawyers for MacDonald are appearing in the Fourth Circuit Court of Appeals in Richmond, Virginia, arguing that Judge Franklin T. Dupree, Jr. was in error last March when he denied Mac-Donald's motion for a new trial, a motion based on the alleged discovery of "new evidence."

Pending a future ruling by the appeals court, which is already on record as having praised Judge Dupree's conduct of the trial and as having found there to be ample evidence to support the jury's verdict of guilt—factors which make it most unlikely that a new trial would ever be awarded—it is Judge Dupree's 110-page opinion, published in March of 1985, which stands as the last word, legally, on the case.

After subjecting each of MacDonald's claims to exhaustive scrutiny, Judge Dupree wrote in his conclusion:

> Almost nine years passed between the . . . murders and the time the case came on for trial. . . . The parties on both sides . . . fully availed themselves of the opportunity before trial to investigate the crime scene and to develop the evidence which was introduced at a trial lasting almost seven full weeks. . . .
>
> Over five years have now passed since the trial, more investigation has been undertaken and more evidence introduced into the record, but the result is still the same. The court has been unable to . . . conclude that the government suppressed any evidence favorable to MacDonald, either before, during or after trial.
>
> The case has attracted an astonishing amount of publicity. Helena Stoeckley [and others] were drawn to the case and have contributed to a factual charade which has allowed it to continue for more than a decade and a half. Their "confessions" have been shown to be unbelievable, and . . . even if the government were again called upon to present its evidence at a new trial and MacDonald was able to put all . . . of his new evidence before a second jury, the jury would again reach the almost inescapable conclusion that he was responsible for these horrible crimes.

And so it seems all but certain that finally, after more than fifteen years, the criminal case against Jeffrey Mac-Donald is over. But that does not mean the story has ended. I think back again to what Brian Murtagh said early in 1983: "He's never going to accept his guilt. . . . The case is never going to be in a posture where he just quietly sits in jail and lets the years roll by."

Indeed, in the years since the publication of *Fatal Vision*, MacDonald has been anything but quiet: he has given interviews, filed lawsuits, published a monthly "newsletter," and sought donations to his "Defense Fund"; he has often seemed as obsessed with public reaction to the book and the subsequent NBC mini-series as he has been with attempting to overturn his convictions. It is almost as if the appearance of the book and the mini-series looms as large in his mind as the murders and the jury's verdict of guilty. Indeed, the lead paragraph of one recent newspaper interview actually said: "During the last fifteen years, Jeffrey MacDonald has lived through three events he describes as devastating." The first was the murders, the second his conviction, and the third the publication of this book. That he could equate three such events in terms of their impact upon him might strike one as odd until one again considers the nature of the man.

The philosopher David Kelley, writing in the August 1985 issue of *Harper's* magazine ("Stalking The Criminal Mind"), refers to recent work by Samuel Yochelson and Stanton Samenow, who conducted a fifteen-year study of criminals at a federal psychiatric hospital in Washington, D.C., in an attempt to explore the link between crime and psychopathy. Much of what Yochelson and Samenow discovered has a certain resonance when compared with earlier speculation on the degree to which MacDonald may have harbored repressed rage associated with the disorder known as pathological narcissism, a form of psychopathic illness.

The greatest fear of the psychopathic patients interviewed by Yochelson and Samenow was of what they termed "the zero state." As Kelley writes: "This sense of complete and profound worthlessness was something all of their patients had experienced and went to great lengths to repress. They protected themselves against it by a kind of grandiosity, a conception of themselves as supermen, as effortless heroes able to achieve great ends by unconventional means. Their chief method of sustaining this self-image was to exert control over others. By forcing others to bend to his will—intimidating them, manipulating them through lies and cons—the psychopath makes society affirm a view of his potency that he cannot affirm by looking within."

The attempt to manipulate "through lies and cons" was—it seems clear to me now in retrospect—something Jeffrey MacDonald engaged in with me. Appearance of this book was forceful proof that he had not succeeded. That this would provoke a response more intense than the normal disappointment or irritation of a subject when he finds the portrayal of him in print not all he had allowed himself to hope for seems to me a function of—and a graphic illustration of—MacDonald's condition of mind.

Indeed, as David Kelley writes: "Anything that suggests a lack of control over the world threatens to bring on the zero state. According to Samenow, 'The threat of being less than top dog, the possibility that he won't achieve unusual distinction, the chance that things will not go as he wants constitute a major threat to the criminal, almost as though his life were at stake. From his standpoint it is, because *the puncturing of his inflated self-concept is psychological homicide'* [emphasis added]."

Kelley goes on to say: "Anyone trying to understand the case of Jeffrey MacDonald should find that a chilling observation."

His reference, I am sure, is to Colette's growing insight into MacDonald's personality and to the probability that her new awareness led her to confront him in a way that made him feel his "inflated self-concept" was at risk. Thus, feeling in that particular—but very real—psychological sense *that his own life was at stake,* he killed her. And as has been amply and painfully demonstrated, in the same explosion of rage and its aftermath, he killed his daughters as well.

But I would suggest that Kelley's observation also goes a long way toward explaining the depth of MacDonald's rage against this book and against me, the author. For what, really, has *Fatal Vision* done? Demonstrated that MacDonald murdered his family? It was the prosecutors who did that at trial. It was the jury's verdict, not the publication of this book, that convicted him of murder. And it is not simply that I have come to agree with the verdict that so angers MacDonald today. It is rather his perception, expressed in the same newspaper interview mentioned earlier, that I portrayed him as a "creep," with "latent homosexual tendencies, a subhuman type of person . . ."

Actually, judging from so many of the thousands of letters I have received since this book's publication, I don't think I portrayed him that way at all. The question of his sexuality seems of concern only to him, not to readers of the book and certainly not to me; and the emotions most often expressed by those who write to me are sadness, confusion, dismay. In their grief for the tragic fates of Colette and Kimberly and Kristen they also feel something approaching compassion for MacDonald himself: a man who could have had so much, who could have given so much, who could have done so much, had he not suffered from this mysterious and indefinable flaw.

To view him as such is a long way from calling him simply a "creep" or "a subhuman type of person." It is not most readers of *Fatal Vision* nor I, but he who introduces that sort of characterization and then uses it to fuel his anger. I think the observations of people like Kelley and Samenow and Yochelson offer valid insights into why this might be so: namely, that I have punctured his inflated self-concept; revealed him to be less than a superman and not very heroic; and committed, through publication of *Fatal Vision,* an act of psychological homicide.

Yet of course Jeffrey MacDonald is not dead, neither psychologically nor physically. Thus it is not he but his wife and daughters who are, in this case, the victims of homicide. MacDonald lives on—to argue, to fume, to fret, to accuse, to rant and rage against what he perceives as the monumental unfairness of a system (of which I now seem to have become a part) that has denied his superhuman qualities and punished him, like any ordinary mortal, for having committed such grievous crimes.

He lives on in the Bastrop Federal Correctional Institution, not far from Austin, Texas. I am told by people who have visited him that conditions are rather more comfortable there than in many of the prisons to which a man might be consigned for having murdered a pregnant woman and two little girls. I am told there is a softball field that he tends from time to time as part of his prison work. I am told he has his own room with ther-mostatically controlled air conditioning to protect him against the draining Texas heat.

In a recent edition of his "newsletter" he is pictured on the front page—in fact, in all copies of the newsletter I've seen, MacDonald has been pictured on the front page—in neatly pressed prison khakis, smiling winsomely as he poses underneath what appears to be a shade tree in a courtyard. Victory, he continues to insist—and, I'm sure, will always insist—is just around the corner. Just one more "witness," one more "new discovery," one more piece of "evidence," and suddenly all the facts painstakingly compiled over fifteen years will be washed away and he will emerge from his confinement, clean and pure, restored and radiant, vindicated at last.

That won't happen, of course. Truth is truth, and when it cuts this deep it can't be overcome by hype. And guilt is guilt, and it doesn't go away either—no matter how often or how strenuously it is denied. Which is not to say that the denial will not continue. As long as there is anyone left to listen, Jeffrey MacDonald will deny. And as long as he wants to keep me involved—through litiga-tion, accusation, distortion of fact—I will remain so.

Of all the work I've ever done, this book, *Fatal Vi-sion,* is that of which I am most proud. I am grateful that I was able to learn the truth and ultimately to accept it—no matter how painful it was—and be as content as a writer can ever be with the form in which I was able to put it. I am grateful, too, for the friendships I have made during my years of immersion in this project—years that did not end with the initial publication of the book.

I am grateful most of all to Freddy and Mildred Kassab, who today live in New Jersey, where Freddy still works for the Quality Egg Company, and who continue their fight to be sure that Jeffrey MacDonald will not be paroled when he first becomes eligible—only five years from now. And to Brian Murtagh, who has left the Justice Department and now works as an assistant United States Attorney in Washington, D.C., but who continues to fight every legal skirmish that arises in the MacDonald case with the same degree of passion and commitment that has infused his career for the past fifteen years. And to Jim Blackburn, now in private practice in Raleigh, and a man frequently mentioned as a possible candidate for major political office. The somber eloquence of his 1979 summation to the jury lingers clearly in memory.

With them, and with the dozens of others who also have been affected by this tragedy, I share the awareness that it will never be over for any of us as long as our own lives continue.

—Joe McGinniss

The 1989 Epilogue

"Yet why not tell it like it happened?"
—Robert Lowell

This book so angered Jeffrey MacDonald that he sued me in August, 1984. The suit, which originally received little attention, considering the constitutional questions it raised, proceeded to trial in July, 1987. A mistrial was declared when the jury found itself unable to reach a verdict, and the case was later settled out of court.

In its issues of March 13 and March 20, 1989, *The New Yorker* magazine printed a two-part article entitled "The Journalist and the Murderer" by a staff writer named Janet Malcolm. The first part opened with the declaration: "Every journalist . . . knows that what he does is morally indefensible. He is a kind of confidence man, preying on people's vanity, ignorance, or loneliness, gaining their trust and betraying them without remorse."

Malcolm's focus was my journalistic relationship with Jeffrey MacDonald over the four years before *Fatal Vision* was published. Charging that I had "deceived," "betrayed," and "devastated" this convicted murderer and that my letters to him during the process of research constituted a "written record of . . . bad faith," she attempted to employ this most atypical relationship between an author and his principal subject as a paradigm for the standard journalistic encounter—one which, somewhat idiosyncratically, she seems to view as the equivalent of "a love affair," doomed to end badly.

Other publications, such as *The Village Voice,* have already commented upon Malcolm's "asperity" and "quaint devotion to Freudian dogma," both of which qualities are much in evidence in her commentary. And she is, of course, entitled to her opinions—such as that she "cannot learn anything about MacDonald's guilt or innocence" from the physical evidence that led to his conviction or that "we have all dreamed about the violent deaths of our families"—however whimsical they may be.

But so numerous and egregious are her omissions, distortions and outright misstatements of fact, that I feel compelled to set the record straight. And in this matter, largely (and ironically) as the result of MacDonald's lawsuit, there is a public record, vast portions of which Malcolm chose to ignore.

I first met MacDonald because I wanted to write a newspaper column about him. I'd arrived in Los Angeles in June, 1979, to spend several weeks as "writer in residence" at the *Herald-Examiner* and had read that the Long Beach Police Officers Association was planning a dinner-dance to raise funds for his defense.

The item triggered an old, vague memory: this was the Green Beret doctor from Fort Bragg whose wife and two young daughters had been slaughtered in their home back in 1970. I recalled something about him saying that hippies had done it; then that he'd been charged;

then that the charges had been dropped. But now, nine and a half years later, he was to return to North Carolina to stand trial for the murders—a circumstance sufficiently unique to warrant an eight-hundred-word column, assuming he would be willing to talk.

He was, and I drove down to meet him. Toward the end of our conversation, he broached the idea that I might write not merely a newspaper column but a whole book about him. As he later testified at deposition, "I believe that I was the one who initiated the discussion. I believe that I said, 'Would you be interested in the possibility of writing a book on this case?'"

What he didn't tell me, but later admitted under oath, was that he'd already scheduled a meeting with Joseph Wambaugh for later that day to discuss the same proposition. Wambaugh, immersed in other projects, turned him down.

At deposition, MacDonald also recalled telling me, "You're the kind of guy I've been looking for for nine years." When asked what he meant, he testified: "[McGinniss] appeared to be comfortable for me to be around. He appeared very bright; cynical. . . funny, easy to work with; had prior successful books; had proper contacts in publishing circles; had expressed enthusiasm to me and appeared to be very receptive to a fair reading of the facts."

Now—noting that from the start he sensed I was "cynical," but somehow interpreted that as advantageous rather than inimical to his interests—one might think that were I interested in "seducing" this man (in Malcolm's use of the term as it applies to journalistic conduct), I would have made certain that the one thing I *did* write about him—my *Herald-Examiner* column—

would be sufficiently flattering as to lull him into a false sense of security.

One would think that, as Malcolm's exemplar of "the journalist—who [seems] so friendly and sympathetic, so keen to understand [the subject] fully, so remarkably attuned to his vision of things," I would have taken pains not to blow my cover, as it were, for the sake of a newspaper column.

Such was not the case. As MacDonald later told a *Washington Post* reporter, "I read the column and it's about [my] boat, it's about my blond stewardess girlfriend and it's about [my] condominium . . . I call him and I say, 'Joe, this is a piece of crap' . . . I said, 'Joe, I'm really disappointed. I thought we had a whole different kind of relationship . . .'"

No such conversation, in fact, ever took place, but when he testified at the trial of his civil suit against me, MacDonald admitted my column had provoked "feelings of annoyance . . . I was annoyed that the exact three things that I had hoped would not be mentioned in the column were mentioned in the first paragraph."

This point seems not only to set the agenda for so much that followed between MacDonald and me but also to undermine Malcolm's basic premise—namely, that the journalist invariably practices "deception" upon his or her subjects, "preying" on their "vanity, ignorance, or loneliness." Vain he may have been, but in June, 1979, when I first wrote about him to his displeasure, Jeffrey MacDonald was neither lonely nor ignorant.

He was, however, hungry for money, as was his lawyer, which led to the arrangement between us that—all by itself—should have (but didn't) rendered this relationship unsuitable for what Malcolm termed her "re-

flections." It was not, as she wrote, a "grotesquely magnified version of the normal journalistic encounter," but
something quite exceptional. I don't think she could
have chosen a worse example if she'd tried—which she
didn't.

Later that June, I met with MacDonald's lawyer, Bernard Segal. We agreed that MacDonald would receive a
minority share of the proceeds of any book I might write
about him in return for granting me complete and exclusive access to him and his legal staff throughout the trial
and, upon the trial's conclusion, access to all documents
related to the case, as well as his assurance of continuing
cooperation.

There was no commitment, indication, or even hint
that my book would portray MacDonald as innocent. Indeed, having no idea what the story would turn out to
be—was he a murderer or not?—I could hardly have offered such assurances.

MacDonald himself, testifying at both deposition and
the trial of our civil suit, conceded that from the start he
recognized he would have no control over what I would
write.

"Do you recall in your discussion with Mr. McGinniss," my lawyer asked at deposition, "[his] telling you
that he would only write the book on the condition that
he had total control over what he published and could
publish the truth as he saw it?"

"Not in those words," MacDonald replied.

"Do you recall any similar sentiment or words to that
effect?"

"Yes," MacDonald conceded.

At our civil trial, my lawyer, Daniel Kornstein, asked
MacDonald, "You did expect Mr. McGinniss to hear

other sides, other versions adverse to yours about the story?"

"Yes, that's true," he said.

"And . . . you never, during these preliminary conversations, told Mr. McGinniss that you wanted him to write a book portraying you as innocent, did you?"

"No, I did not," MacDonald said.

"And you understood that it was possible that Mr. McGinniss might come to a contrary conclusion?"

"Yes."

"Did you ever consider what might happen if Mr. McGinniss concluded that you were guilty instead of innocent? Did that thought ever cross your mind?"

"I'm sure that crossed my mind. I can't recall it specifically happening, but it must have occurred at some time."

"And when the thought crossed your mind, did you also think whether or not Mr. McGinniss would have the right to conclude that you were guilty?"

"Mr. McGinniss could conclude what he wanted, if it was fair and honest and accurate and nonfiction."

"And he could write about it that way in the book, couldn't he?"

"That was my understanding."

How much clearer can it be that from the start—long before any "friendship" entered into the equation—MacDonald was aware he was taking a risk? But—as is the case with many psychopaths—he was so convinced of his own ability to manipulate, to persuade, to seduce, that he did not see it as such.

What we are talking about here is not only pathological narcissism but what I would term "pathological optimism."

*   *   *

With the understanding that further details would soon be arranged, I arrived in Raleigh, North Carolina, where MacDonald was about to stand trial, and found him and his aides residing in a fraternity house on the campus of North Carolina State University. A room was made available to me and I began my reportorial work as negotiations between Segal and my literary agent at the time, Sterling Lord, proceeded.

When asked at deposition to describe his recollection of my relationship with him during his murder trial, MacDonald testified, "We had meals together. He was living in the same fraternity house that we were living in, so I saw him on a daily basis. And I remember that he was—I would characterize it as sort of hanging around. He was always in the background with a—with a pad and a pencil."

"And was this consistent with your expectations of what you wanted the person writing the book to do?" my lawyer asked.

"Yes," MacDonald replied.

This is consistent also with effective reporting technique as described by its practitioners for generations. Gay Talese wrote in the preface to his collection of profiles, *Fame and Obscurity,* in 1970: "I try to follow my subjects unobtrusively while observing them in revealing situations." And in Tom Wolfe's 1973 introduction to *The New Journalism* he writes: "Most good journalists who hope to get inside someone else's world and stay there awhile come on very softly and do not bombard their subjects with questions . . . Your main problem as a reporter is, simply, managing to stay with whomever you are writing about long enough for the scenes to take place before your own eyes. There are no rules or craft secrets . . . that will help a man pull this off; it is completely a test of his personality."

To me, the problem of the reporter and the subject seems analogous to that posed by Heisenberg in his formulation of the "uncertainty principle," which states that any attempt to measure precisely the velocity of a subatomic particle will knock it about in an unpredictable way, thereby altering the very force that the experimenter had sought to quantify. The reporter, by his very presence, causes a change in the behavior of the person about whom he eventually hopes to write. His goal should be to minimize this alteration.

I might add that the presence of machinery, be it full-sized television camera or pocket-sized tape recorder, invariably aggravates this problem, making the reporter's presence more intrusive and rendering less authentic the eventual portrait. That's an opinion shared by *The New Yorker*'s Lillian Ross, who has written: "Does a tape recorder used in reporting help reveal any truth? I don't believe so. In fact, I believe that a tape recorder gets in the way of your response to a person, and it is this response that gives an interview its authenticity. Tape recorders almost always take the life out of your response to a person, and the response of the person to the tape recorder may deaden things further . . . Furthermore, the practice of depending on a tape recording makes for a lifelessness in the way you report. It makes *you* lazy and inert."

On July 16, 1979, about a week after the murder trial had begun, Segal and my agent, Lord, representing MacDonald and me, signed an agreement which specified that in return for granting me "exclusive story rights" to his life, MacDonald would receive twenty percent of the first $150,000 paid to me by any publisher for a book about him and thirty-three percent of any proceeds beyond that. In addition, the agreement stated that MacDonald would receive forty percent of any motion picture or television proceeds.

By the end of the month, Lord had reached agreement with the Dell Publishing Company for publication of both hardcover and paperback editions of the book. There was, however, a significant caveat: MacDonald would have to sign a release prepared by Dell's lawyers in which he promised not to sue. He did sign on August 3, 1979, with Segal signing as witness. At no time did I sign any agreement with MacDonald in regard to what the book's contents would be, nor did I ever, orally or in writing, grant him any rights of approval or review. Indeed, the whole purpose of the release was to assure just the opposite: that I would be free to write whatever I came to believe to be true.

The release said:

Dear Joe:

I understand you are writing a book about my life centering on my current trial for murder. . . .

Accordingly, I hereby grant to you the exclusive right to use my name, portrait and picture in and in connection with the publication of an untitled work about my life and the trial in which I am a defendant for murder . . . You may include in the book any incidents, characters, dialogues, actions, scenes and situations that you desire.

In the next paragraph, Segal inserted the phrase in brackets.

I realize, of course, that you do not propose to libel me. Nevertheless, in order that you may feel free to write the book in the manner that you may deem best, I agree that I will not make or assert against you, the publisher or its licensees or anyone else involved in the production or distribution of the book any claim or demand whatsoever based on the ground that anything contained in the book defames me [provided that the essential integrity of my life story is maintained].

The next and last relevant paragraph said:

I hereby release, discharge and acquit you from any and all claims, demands or causes of action that I may hereafter have against you—whether for libel, invasion of right of privacy, or anything else—by reason of anything contained in the book or in the publicity or advertising pertaining thereto.

As August passed, my jounalistic relationship with MacDonald (which in all other ways was so unusual) took on the inevitable personal aspect. As Tom Wolfe has written: "If a reporter stays with a person or group long enough, they—reporter and subject—will develop a personal relationship of some sort, even if it is hostility. More often it will be friendship . . ."

This has happened to me with almost everyone upon whom I have reported in depth. As journalist Marshall Frady has said of his own subjects (who have included Billy Graham, George Wallace, and Wilbur Mills among others), "I like 'em all when I'm with 'em. It's only when I sit down at the typewriter that I realize what sons of bitches they really are."

Not all, of course, are sons of bitches. Some of the best friends I have are people about whom I've written, but there was never any ambiguity about the nature of the relationship when it began: I was journalist and he or she was subject and we were entering into a relationship from which each hoped to gain. (Only MacDonald, however, has ever benefited financially.)

By the time of his conviction, I had come to like Jeffrey MacDonald enormously. I had spent vast amounts of time observing him in court and listening to him testify and also much time with him under less stressful circumstances. I'd laughed, jogged, eaten, drunk, browsed through bookstores and talked sports with him. I had come also to know and to like his mother, his friends from high school, college, the Army, the hospital in California where he had worked—all of them people who professed belief in his innocence.

Can it be surprising that I found myself wanting to believe the same? Day after hot, humid day I would sit in court looking at crime-scene photographs that depicted the carnage inflicted upon MacDonald's wife and daughters. Then, within the hour, he'd be chatting affably with me. Each time, my reaction was the same: *this* man could not have done *that* to those people.

Yet every day the evidence mounted. Concrete physical evidence; unambiguous, clear. It could not be, yet it was. He could not have, yet he did. The evidence demonstrated that Jeffrey MacDonald, this gracious, charming, affable man, had fractured the skull of his pregnant wife with a club; had broken both of her arms with a club; had stabbed her sixteen times in the neck and chest with a knife; had shattered the skull of his five-year-old daughter with a club; had stabbed her in the throat eight to ten times with a knife; had hit her again so hard with the club that he'd shattered an entire side of her face, leaving a piece of cheekbone protruding through the skin; and then, with full awareness of what he was doing, had walked into the bedroom of his two-year-old daughter and, laying her across his lap, had stabbed her twelve times in the back with a knife and four times in the chest and once in the neck and then, again, fifteen times in the chest with an icepick.

I can tell you one thing: there was no "seduction" going on. At least not on my part. There was only my struggle to hold myself together in the face of this mounting horror.

To say there was ambivalence, to say there was conflict between what my head told me must be true and what my "heart," for lack of a better word, told me could not be, would be to make the greatest understatement of my life.

Yes, I'd been persuaded he must have done it. But yes, I cried, as did some of the jurors themselves, when their foreman pronounced their guilty verdict.

Let me now discuss the letters I wrote MacDonald in the months that followed, letters from which Janet Malcolm has quoted copiously. These were compassionate, anguished, and utterly genuine—and, I should say (since Malcolm pointedly does not) always written in response to equally anguished, tormented letters from him.

For six months following his conviction, maybe seven or eight, finding myself confronted by the most awful set of circumstances I'd ever known as a writer, and all the while being beseeched by this charming and persuasive man to believe in him, I wrestled with not only the question of his guilt but with another that was in some ways more disturbing: *if he could have done this, how could I have liked him?*

The "Afterword" to this edition, with its tale of my February 17, 1980, bloody nose, may have given some sense of how totally consumed I was by what I'd gotten into. For three years, almost every night, I would awaken within minutes of three A.M. and lie in bed imagining, thinking, wondering—trying to come to terms with what had gone on inside that apartment at that hour on that night. Seldom would I get back to sleep before the sky lightened. These were not things about which I could speak to anyone but my wife, and even to her only on rare occasions.

This was not a question of saying, "Oh, well, I guess he's guilty, so probably I ought to stop being friendly and let him know what I think." We are talking here of psychological crisis of major proportions. Sweats, chest pains, the insomnia, fits of depression.

And this wasn't just some private nightmare I was locked into: there was this *book* I had to write.

Recall here the words of Cleckley which I encountered for the first time in the fall of 1980: "Only very slowly and by a complex estimation or judgment based on multitudinous small impressions does the conviction come upon us [in regard to the psychopath] that, despite these intact rational processes, these normal emotional affirmations and their consistent application in all directions, we are dealing . . . not with a complete man at all but with something that suggests a subtly constructed reflex machine which can mimic the human personality perfectly."

It took me a long time to accept that MacDonald could be the charming and apparently caring man I'd come to know (or thought I did) during the summer of

1979, and, at the same time, be what the psychiatrist Otto Kernberg has described as "an enraged empty self—the hungry wolf out to kill, eat and survive . . ."

My learning process, in that regard, did not even begin until the end of the trial. It intensified once I won cooperation both from the federal prosecutors and from MacDonald's in-laws, Alfred and Mildred Kassab (none of whom, incidentally, feel in the slightest betrayed), and continued until I had finished work on the book in spring of 1983.

During this period of turmoil, I was not about to sit down and kick things around with him conversationally.

In her *New Yorker* articles, Janet Malcolm writes that my letters, "assuring MacDonald of . . . friendship" continued until "close to the publication" of this book, by which time, she says, I apparently felt I "could afford to be a bit cold and careless."

That statement is false. By spring of 1980, as I found myself moving beyond the magnetic field of MacDonald's personality and as my research turned up new information—none of it favorable to him—the tone of my letters shifted markedly. He still was my subject, about whom I would have to learn more if I was ever to reconcile the apparently irreconcilable. (As Barbara Grizzuti Harrison has written: "To try, in print, to reconcile irreconcilable differences is noble work, it is . . . labor to be proud of.") It was necessary to keep lines of communication open, but because I no longer felt it I could no longer express much personal warmth or sympathy for his predicament.

In July of 1980 MacDonald's conviction was overturned by an appellate court—not because he was innocent but on grounds that the government had taken too long to bring charges against him. He was released from prison. Malcolm might think my continuing "seduction" or "conning" of him would have had me on the first flight west, eager to greet him as he walked out through the prison gates.

But no such thing happened. To fly to California and feign happiness at his release in order to assure his continuing cooperation seemed repugnant, given my feelings at the time. I am perfectly capable of suspending judgment while gathering information, or even of suppressing troublesome feelings in order to more fully report—as I think any good journalist has to be—but I cannot fake what I do not feel.

I liked MacDonald when I was with him during his murder trial. I felt sorry for him for months afterward and wrote him letters genuinely expressing that sorrow, even after I'd formed my opinion as to his guilt. Those letters—far from being my attempt to con him—represent the degree to which he'd succeeded in conning me.

It was not until October of 1980, when a publicity tour for *Going to Extremes*, my just-published book about Alaska, required it, that I next went to California. On October 1, I met Bernie Segal and an assistant of his named Sara Simmons for a drink at the Top of the Mark hotel in San Francisco. That night, in my notebook, I wrote: "They sense I feel he's guilty." Not an impression, I suggest, that a con artist would be seeking to create. (That notebook entry, as well as the excerpts from testimony that follow, were all in the public record and available to Janet Malcolm, but in her articles she omitted any reference to them.)

My recollection of the conversation, given under oath, is that Simmons, apparently troubled by something in my manner, asked, "You don't think there is any chance that Jeff is guilty?" I replied, "I don't know what I think." She then said, "But don't you think you have a moral obligation to Jeff?" I responded, "I think I have a moral obligation to the truth."

Bernie Segal, MacDonald's lawyer, remembered it slightly differently. At the 1987 civil trial, he testified, "My recollection is that Sara asked more directly, 'Joe, is your book going to be [sic] that Jeff is guilty?'" He then said, "Joe was evasive—that is, 'Well, you know, I can't say everything now, and you'll have to wait.'"

Whatever the actual words, alarm bells began ringing so loudly that Segal immediately called MacDonald, who just as quickly, Segal testified, "expressed his dismay. He was upset to learn that I believed that Joe McGinniss was actually writing . . . a negative book."

On the same trip—it was, I believe, the next day—I gave an interview to the San Francisco *Chronicle*. When the reporter asked if I thought MacDonald was guilty, I said, "I can't talk about what I think. At the end of the book, the reader can draw a reasonable conclusion. I spent a great deal of time with both sides and got full cooperation."

These are not the words of a perfidious journalist seeking to lull a naive subject into continuing cooperation. Indeed, the combination of Segal's call and the newspaper story, which was published on October 12, so worried MacDonald that only two days later he wrote me a letter expressing concern.

"I had just finished a strange conversation with Bernie," he wrote, "in which he was telling me how he sort of confronted you with some sort of request as to how you view my guilt or innocence. I pooh-poohed him, thinking he was exaggerating his statements and your lack of response. Reading your quotes [in the October 12 article] gave his version of your meeting a new weight and sobered me significantly . . . I hadn't expected comments like that from you and don't really know what to make of them."

That letter, which was sent to me *almost three years* before the publication of *Fatal Vision*, was, like so much else in the public record, ignored by Malcolm.

Despite the warning flags I had held up, MacDonald—more than a full year later—signed a second release, this one requested by a producer in connection with the *Fatal Vision* mini-series but clearly covering the book as well.

With no additions or deletions, MacDonald granted me the "unlimited right" to "describe, impersonate, simulate, depict and portray" him, and to "make use of any episodes in [his] life" as I, in my "sole discretion deem proper." The release also stated that I "may exercise all or any of the rights herein granted . . . without claims, demands or causes of action, whether for libel, defamation, violation of right of privacy or infringement of any literary or other property right or otherwise" insofar as MacDonald was concerned.

And there is more. In addition to the releases, MacDonald sent me many letters in which he reiterated his awareness that he had no control over the content of my book. Examples from the public record, available to but ignored by Malcolm, include:

—April 14, 1982: "I haven't ever asked you for any favors re: the book and I don't normally think it's my place to do so." MacDonald then acknowledged his recognition that he did not have "any right to review material or anything else," and added, "I never ask you what you are writing or how you feel about anything, i.e., me, Bernie, evidence, et cetera, et cetera. . . ."

—April 27, 1982 (following a meeting with an associate of F. Lee Bailey's in which MacDonald tried unsuccessfully to persuade Bailey to take his case): "Bailey's associate was totally aghast that I had no artistic control over the book . . ."

—August 22, 1982: "I had made myself a promise not to question you on the book. I've told you, and I mean it, that I have decided to go with you . . . without any controls to protect me, as I could have gotten with a lesser writer . . ."

The August 22 letter came after a phone call in which, for the first time, MacDonald *had* asked me how the book would portray him. I had declined to answer. In his letter, apropos of the phone conversation, he wrote that "Randi [his fiancée at the time] was stunned by your refusal to be committal," but added that he'd overcome his original uneasiness about the conversation, saying, "Now I'm better. I think I've sorted things through."

That comment seems to me further evidence of the "pathological optimism" alluded to by the Army psychiatrist who testified at the grand jury that MacDonald, "if presented with twenty pieces of data . . . is capable of seeing only three or four and drawing his conclusions from those." This seems particularly apparent given that his call came only nine days after he'd received a clearly ominous letter from Segal.

In response to MacDonald's increasing pressure to learn how the book would portray him, I had sent him a couple of deliberately unilluminating paragraphs. This was a quite conscious effort on my part to keep him from interfering with my completion of the work. He had for-

warded the brief excerpt to Segal and the lawyer had
written: "I read the extract from Joe's draft. It's unre-
vealing about what he really thinks about the principal
subject of the book, you, and about the tone (really innocent; probably innocent; suspiciously guilty; outrageously guilty, but clever and should get away with it)
that the book will finally take. Truthfully, I don't know
of any valid journalistic reason for Joe to be so guarded
on the tone of the book, except one. That one reason is
he is (and has been) vacillating on where he personally
comes out on you and your case . . ."

At the 1987 trial of MacDonald's lawsuit, Daniel Kornstein questioned Segal about this letter.

"Did you believe that [Joe] was vacillating over what
he was going to write?"

"Yes," Segal replied. "Some days he believed one way,
it seemed to me, and other days he moved away from it.
*He never indicated, however, at any time from the October,
1980 meeting on that he was still the so-called staunch believer in Jeffrey MacDonald's innocence . . .*"

This testimony by MacDonald's own lawyer is perhaps the clearest evidence of all that Janet Malcolm's
statement that MacDonald "was led to believe by Mc-
Ginniss that the book would support his claim [of inno-
cence]" is false.

And there were still more revealing letters from him
to me, unreported by *The New Yorker*.

In December, 1982, I informed MacDonald that I
had completed my manuscript. He wrote back that the
news left him with feelings of ". . . anxiety about how
and what you've said. I don't really even know the
style, much less the content." That does not strike me
as the reply of a man who for three and a half years had

been misled into thinking he would be favorably portrayed.

On February 9, 1983, he wrote, while asking if he could see an advance copy of the manuscript: "It was one thing not to have control over the book/contents/you. I granted you that and I have lived with it . . ."

And on February 17, in the same context, he conceded: "It is *not* my right, as per our agreement, to tell you what to write, or have veto power, etc. etc."

At the very least, this record provides valid basis for adopting a view of my relationship with MacDonald quite different from the extremely myopic one proffered by Malcolm.

As I see it, what really happened was that from the moment he first laid eyes upon me, MacDonald tried to con *me,* and through me—as, later, through Janet Malcolm—the public.

With her, he may have succeeded to a degree, in that she has written, after confessing her inability to confront the physical evidence, "MacDonald may be a murderer or he may be an unjustly convicted man." But that may be just another version of the old story of the lady and the convict. There are women who develop a fascination with men convicted of violent crimes—especially violent crimes against women.

Certainly, Malcolm's portrayal of MacDonald—"handsome, tall, blond, athletic," and of his "poise" (not to mention his "preternatural equipoise"), his "intelligence," the "intensity of his listening," the way he "bristled with tense aliveness," his "physical grace," the way he handled a *doughnut,* for heaven's sake, "breaking off pieces and unaccountably keeping the powdered sugar under control—with the delicate dexterity of a veterinarian fixing a broken wing" (this from a woman herself so delicate that she could not bring herself to look at some of the other things MacDonald had broken, like the arms and skull of his wife and the skull and face of his five-year-old daughter)—suggests a certain degree of emotional involvement.

Indeed, she refers to her correspondence with MacDonald, like all correspondence, as "a kind of love affair . . . tinged by a subtle but palpable eroticism." But that, as they say, is another story.

MacDonald sued me in 1984 on grounds of fraud, breach of contract, breach of the covenant of good faith and fair dealing, and intentional infliction of emotional distress. He claimed that I had "intentionally and cynically" led him to believe that I was "convinced" of his innocence and that I was "writing the planned book from that point of view." He also claimed that the book contained "numerous false statements of fact and false implications" and that because it had failed to "set forth his innocence," I had not "maintained the essential integrity of his life story." He further claimed that I'd caused him to suffer "mental anguish . . . nausea, weight loss . . . nightmares . . . shame, embarrassment and humiliation . . . loss of support by friends and associates . . . anxiety caused by hate-mail . . . difficulties in relating to and dealing with prison personnel and fear and anxiety regarding physical well-being due to adverse inmate reaction to falsehoods published in *Fatal Vision*."

Leaving aside the irony that my "cynicism" was one of the qualities that supposedly had first made me seem an attractive journalistic prospect, and the further irony that a man convicted of murder could argue that in order to maintain the "essential integrity" of his life story a book about him would have to proclaim his innocence, I felt that the whole thing was simply a libel suit in disguise. But given that he'd signed two releases that precluded him from suing on *any* grounds, it didn't seem to matter what he called it.

I quickly learned differently when my publisher's insurance company said that because it was not labeled as a suit for either libel or invasion of privacy the company did not have to provide the coverage guaranteed me under my publishing contract. (G.P. Putnam's had replaced Dell as hardcover publisher.)

I had to sue the insurance company in Federal District Court in New York City. In November, 1986, Judge Robert Sweet ruled in my favor, saying, "the court must look past the labels . . . to the facts . ." Making it clear he was expressing no opinion on the merits of MacDonald's claims but only their nature, Judge Sweet added: "The essence of these allegations . . . is that MacDonald did not receive a book which portrayed the 'full and true' story, equating truth with innocence. Since McGinniss wrote a book which did not fully support MacDonald's version of the story, McGinniss allegedly lied when he represented that he was writing the 'true' story. The focus in these pleadings is MacDonald's and McGinniss' contrary views of the truth of the book . . . The pleadings . . . focus almost exclusively on the falsity of the book . . . The facts are based upon, and at times indistinguishable from, an allegation of libel."

Eight months earlier, in Los Angeles, Federal Magistrate James McMahon, presiding over a pretrial hearing in the civil suit, also found it to be "a hidden libel case." Using even stronger language, Magistrate McMahon said what MacDonald had apparently wanted was a "kept journalist," and, later, "what he wasn't interested in was a journalist. It was rather a publicist was what he wanted—a PR man."

The magistrate asked rhetorically, "So [McGinniss's] obligation in entering into this contract in a hotly contested murder trial where everybody recognized there was a significant chance of conviction as well as a significant chance of acquittal was to be totally up front with MacDonald at all times, and at the point where some evidence seemed to him to be convincing he was supposed to say, 'Jeff, I now think you're guilty so I have to walk out of here'?"

He added that the complaint made it "sound like MacDonald's a spurned lover and he wants to blacken McGinniss's reputation . . . This whole lawsuit smells like a grudge suit."

None of these proceedings is even alluded to by Janet Malcolm. Yet she writes in copious—and often erroneous—detail about the eventual trial, which she did not attend. (I might add that neither I nor anyone else about whom Malcolm wrote and to whom I've subsequently spoken was ever contacted by a *New Yorker* fact checker.)

That the case even got to trial was the result of another judge's befuddled misreading of the first release MacDonald signed. William Rea, a man only recently appointed to the federal bench by Ronald Reagan, apparently interpreted Segal's handwritten addition to the single paragraph of the 1979 release as somehow obligating me to tell the story the way MacDonald wanted it told, in order to maintain the "essential integrity" of his life.

Judge Rea failed to grasp the most obvious fact: that a release can only enlarge, not diminish, a writer's freedom. A modification of it may limit the degree to which that freedom is increased, but cannot leave the writer with less than if there had not been one. He also disregarded not only the unmodified paragraphs of the original release, but the entire 1981 release. Ruling that there were "genuine factual issues to be resolved," he denied my motion for summary judgment. He also ruled that there were no First Amendment issues involved in the dispute. And, finally, that MacDonald—though serving three consecutive life sentences for murder—should be let out of prison each morning in order to attend the trial.

The trial lasted six weeks, starting in July, 1987. From the first, it was an exercise in total confusion. *The American Lawyer,* the only periodical to cover the trial in any depth, termed it "amorphous and unwieldy" due to "the judge's failure to define the case." The suit, according to the magazine, "[sounded] like a libel action, but the similarity eluded . . . William Rea . . . When Judge Rea chose to ignore the constitutional issues . . . he left the author shorn of his First Amendment protections."

What the judge did permit, despite the fact that MacDonald's convictions had by then been upheld even by the United States Supreme Court, was for him to assert his innocence. On the other hand, I was not allowed to introduce evidence that demonstrated his guilt.

Also, despite his ruling that this was not a libel suit and that no First Amendment defenses would be allowed, Judge Rea permitted extensive inquiry into the alleged "false statements and implications" in the book. None was found. The book's "essential integrity" was maintained.

Malcolm (who, having not attended the trial, apparently relied heavily on MacDonald's lawyer as a source for her impressions) reported that on cross-examination by this "pitiless" man, I was "mauled . . . until there was little left of [me] . . ." that I had my "liver ravaged" by his "relentless and pitiless interrogation" and that on at least one occasion he found himself "going straight for [my] exposed throat."

Her graphic descriptions are in sharp contrast to those of the *American Lawyer* reporter, who was there, and who wrote simply that I answered questions in a "soft, almost academic manner."

The cross-examination that did impress *The American Lawyer* was that of MacDonald, conducted by my extremely accomplished lawyer, Kornstein. This, the reporter found "incisive and at times devastating." Of it, Malcolm printed not a word. What she did write about Kornstein was that "he frequently humiliated a young associate; in one instance, the associate made what Kornstein perceived as a mistake while examining a witness, and Kornstein peremptorily ordered him to sit down."

Well, I was there—all day, every day—and I can tell you this never happened. Mark Platt, the associate in question, who continues to work for the firm of Kornstein, Veisz and Wexler in New York, can tell you the same. This is, quite simply, not true. I can only surmise that Malcolm published the statement to try to harm Kornstein's reputation, perhaps out of pique she felt after he declined to be interviewed by her.

(Clearly, she feels that such a refusal offers her the journalistic equivalent of a license to kill. After I'd broken off contact with her following a single extremely peculiar interview, she wrote: ". . . as McGinniss had come to see MacDonald with the eyes of the government prosecutors, so I, as I proceeded with my researches, had come to regard McGinniss with the eyes of [MacDonald's lawyer] and his staff. I was more fortunate than McGinniss precisely because of his refusal to speak with me: by banishing me, he had freed me from the guilt I would otherwise have felt.")

Not being there, of course, can put any reporter at a distinct disadvantage, which Malcolm's account of the trial amply demonstrates. Nowhere is this clearer than in her sketchy and misleading account of the testimony of Joseph Wambaugh which, she writes (offering no documentation whatsoever), "everyone later agreed was the pivotal moment of the trial."

Bypassing the question of how a trial that ends in a hung jury can have a "pivotal" moment, let us look at some of what Wambaugh said that Malcolm chose not to report. He offered his opinion that:

"It's necessary to form a personal relationship with the subject you're interviewing.

"The author has total discretion to write his book as he sees fit, whether or not he's a friend of the subject.

"One should never disclose one's views because it may shut off further communication."

He later added—speaking in particular of one's dealings with a psychopath, which he considered MacDonald to be—"I would always allow a subject to think that he is manipulating me even when I had all sorts of evidence to cast doubt on what he's telling me. I would continue to pretend to believe it and encourage him to talk."

When asked whether "an author should disclose everything that he is thinking to his subject," Wambaugh replied, "An author would be a fool to do that."

Wambaugh also offered impressions of MacDonald based on his meeting, which had taken place the afternoon of the day I'd first met MacDonald. "I found him to be extremely glib . . . I had never met anyone quite as glib I don't think, and I was astonished by the manner in which [his] story was delivered. He was describing events of consummate horror, but he could discuss the murders in quite graphic detail . . . in a very detached and glib and easy manner . . . I have interviewed dozens and dozens of people who were survivors of horrible crimes, some immediately after the event and some many years after, including the parents of murdered children, and I have never in all of my experience encountered someone who could describe an event like that in the almost cavalier manner that Dr. MacDonald described it."

Asked if MacDonald had expressed any reaction at the close of the meeting, Wambaugh said, "He said he thought that I'd be the man to do the job and that we could work together."

This happened to be precisely the same sentiment MacDonald had expressed to me only hours before. So once again the question arises of who, from day one, was seducing whom?

Other witnesses whose testimony Malcolm did not report included a medical doctor and professor of pharmacology who testified that the amount of amphetamine MacDonald's own notes indicated he might have taken over the weeks that led up to the murders would have been more than enough to precipitate a rage reaction, or "amphetamine psychosis."

There was also Joseph Barbato, the Army chemist who actually had performed the drug tests on MacDonald's blood. Barbato unequivocally laid to rest any suggestion that the Army's testing, given the equipment used and tests performed, could have detected the presence of amphetamines. MacDonald, according to Barbato, would have had to have taken a "lethal dose—he'd have to have the vial of pills still in his mouth" for the tests to show any evidence of amphetamine consumption.

Thus, the theory offered toward the end of *Fatal Vision* that amphetamine use might have played a role in MacDonald's commission of the murders was not only vindicated but strengthened.

It was, however, Cleve Backster, the polygraph expert who'd administered a private examination in Bernard Segal's Philadelphia office in April of 1970—and to whom MacDonald had consistently denied me access by refusing to sign a release allowing Backster to talk to me—who provided perhaps the most damning testimony.

After Kornstein located Backster in San Diego and served him with a subpoena, the polygraph expert—sworn to silence for seventeen years—testified at trial: "The results [of MacDonald's examination] were very unambiguous. They were not borderline at all. In my opinion he was being deceptive . . . concerning the questions relating to the crime [and so] I told him I could not be of help to him in his defense because he had failed the polygraph test . . ."

None of this was reported by Janet Malcolm. All of it further confirmed MacDonald's guilt. That guilt, for some reason, is something Malcolm remains unwilling to accept. Despite dozens of volumes of court documents that contradict her, she's even gone so far as to write: "investigators spent years working over the MacDonald murders and end[ed] up with no certain answer to the question of what 'really' happened." And that to try to "learn anything about MacDonald's guilt" from the evidence "is like looking for proof or disproof of the existence of God in a flower."

But perhaps the most remarkable of Malcolm's omissions and misinterpretations concerned the trial's outcome. She wrote that "five of the six jurors were persuaded that a man who was serving three consecutive life sentences for the murder of his wife and two small children was deserving of more sympathy than the writer who had deceived him," and that MacDonald's lawyer "succeeded in causing five (out of the six) jurors . . . to accept his version of the MacDonald-McGinniss encounter."

Again, however, her version is contradicted by fact. At trial's end, Judge Rea gave the jurors sixty-nine pages of instructions and a "Special Verdict Form" that contained thirty-seven questions, telling them to answer each one in order and not to proceed to a new one until unanimous agreement on the prior question had been reached. Then, as the jury began its deliberations, William Rea boarded a plane for Hawaii, telling all concerned that they could try to reach him by phone if any problems arose.

The first question on the form concerned not me but MacDonald, asking whether he had "performed all of the obligations and conditions imposed on him under the contract."

One of the jurors answered "no" to this question. She contended that MacDonald had violated the exclusivity provision by cooperating with other authors (copies of a book proclaiming his innocence were actually on sale throughout Los Angeles during our trial); that he'd violated his agreement to cooperate fully by not permitting me access to Backster; and that—most flagrantly—he'd breached the contract by lying about the murders.

Others were unsure how to answer. The forewoman,

Elizabeth Lane, whom Malcolm quotes extensively (but not on this point), wrote in a letter to the Los Angeles *Times*, "I myself changed my mind twice on this very crucial issue."

According to *The American Lawyer*, Lane said "she was puzzled about whether the jury should consider the releases and competing book in answering this question," but because Judge Rea had not instructed them to do so, "we did not consider them."

Having thus disregarded the releases—due to absence of instruction from the judge—five jurors eventually agreed to answer "yes" to Question One in order to get on with their deliberations. But the sixth, Lucille Dillon, refused to change her opinion, saying, "An author must have total freedom to write the truth," and "I don't see how McGinniss did wrong."

And so on that question and on that question alone—one which did not even relate to my conduct or to the content of my book but to *MacDonald's* conduct—the vote was 5–1. Out of that has arisen a widespread misconception—fostered by Malcolm—that "the jury voted five to one for MacDonald."

"There was an enormous assumption that we were in sympathy with MacDonald and we were going to give him the earth," the forewoman told *The American Lawyer*. "It wasn't true." She said the jury had found Judge Rea's instructions and the verdict questions "extremely confusing" and added, "I would like to have [said] at the outset that MacDonald got what he asked for and McGinniss did what he said he'd do, but we were asked to go through all the legal points. Maybe we got caught up in a thicket of legalities."

Whatever she later told Malcolm, the forewoman wrote in her letter to the editor on August 26, 1987, that Lucille Dillon "was not . . . the only juror 'sympathetic' to . . . McGinniss, and we other five jurors were not all in favor of Jeffrey MacDonald."

Needless to say, in *The New Yorker* articles written by Malcolm, edited by her husband, and published by her extremely close friend Robert Gottlieb, those sentiments were not reported.

The fact is, the jurors never got beyond their disagreement over that first of the thirty-seven questions, and Judge Rea had to be summoned from Hawaii to declare a mistrial. That outcome left alive an extremely troubling constitutional issue. As Kornstein put it in a letter sent to a number of journalists at the close of trial:

> *For the first time a disgruntled subject has been permitted to sue a writer on grounds that render irrelevant the truth or falsity of what was published . . . Now, for the first time a journalist's demeanor and point of view have become an issue to be resolved by jury trial . . . The MacDonald claim suggests that newspaper reporters, as well as authors, can and will be sued for writing truthful but unflattering articles should they ever have acted in a fashion that indicated a sympathetic attitude toward their subject.*

It seemed apparent that Judge Rea had learned nothing during the six weeks of testimony and that any retrial in front of him would be just as much a mishmash as had been the first. Indeed, there was the prospect of an endless series of mistrials, stretching toward infinity, due to endless confusion over just what the relevant issues were. There was also the sobering possibility that a jury instructed by such a judge—who would permit no First Amendment defenses in a trial about the content of a book—might return a finding for MacDonald, thereby setting the very precedent about which Kornstein had expressed concern.

From the day he'd filed his suit, I had instructed that no further payments be made to MacDonald, on grounds that by suing he had breached his agreement not to sue. By trial's end, approximately $100,000 that otherwise would have been paid to him by my agent had accumulated in an escrow account.

In November, faced with the prospect of a retrial that again would take me three thousand miles from wife and family and again would disrupt work on the book that became *Blind Faith,* I agreed to release the money in escrow, drop my counterclaims against MacDonald, and permit my publisher's insurance company to pay an additional $225,000 in order to dispose of the case.

I doubt that anyone would feel good about seeing $325,000 given to a murderer, and I did not. On the other hand, I wanted to rid myself of him—not to mention Judge Rea and his obtuseness. MacDonald was in prison for life. Having the ability to reach out from behind bars and so disrupt my own life was something that gave him great pleasure. I wanted all that to stop.

And so, in November of 1987, the lawsuit was disposed of through a settlement in which MacDonald dropped all claims. That matters could have progressed to the point where any payment seemed necessary was horribly distasteful to me, but subsequent developments left me feeling not quite so chagrined.

MacDonald's lawyer—apparently looking for income tax advantages—insisted that the money not be paid until January, 1988. In the interim, MacDonald's father-in-law, Fred Kassab, filed suit against him, claiming that—as in the Son of Sam law—no murderer should profit from his crime. In the final disposition of that case, a California judge reapportioned the payment so that MacDonald only received $50,000, not $325,000, and awarded almost $85,000 to the Kassabs. (MacDonald's lawyer collected most of the rest as his fee.)

So the net result was that—not even taking into account additional legal expenses—MacDonald wound up with less than half the money he would have received if he'd never sued me in the first place. Indeed, with less money than the Kassabs. And no new and dangerously restrictive precedents governing the conduct of reporters were set.

As I try to put these past ten years in perspective, I think sometimes of what Milton wrote in *Areopagitica,* his "Speech for the Liberty of Unlicensed Printing to the Parliament of England," in 1644:

> For books are not absolutely dead things, but do contain a potency of life in them to be as active as that soul was whose progeny they are; nay, they do preserve as in a vial the purest efficacy and extraction of that living intellect that bred them . . . unless wariness be used, as good almost kill a man as kill a good book. Who kills a man kills a recognizable creature, God's image; but he who destroys a good book, kills reason itself, kills the image of God, as it were, in the eye . . .
>
> We should be wary therefore what persecutions we raise against the living labors of public men, how we spill that seasoned life of man, preserved

and stored up in books; since we see a kind of homicide may be thus committed."

I also think back to a letter I received in January, 1986, from a former criminal investigator named Richard Caniell, a resident of British Columbia.

Mr. Caniell, with whom I was not and am not acquainted, wrote in part:

> I think it is fairly axiomatic that society has an enormous need, as well as interest, in all the truth it can gain about such crimes [as MacDonald's] and particularly their motives . . . Yet how can we gain the needed insights if the criminals, or those who defend them, subvert, hide or destroy relevant evidence so that we never come to understand how such horrible crimes could be done by a person such as Doctor MacDonald . . .
>
> In a very real sense, whether one is appointed by government, law enforcement bureaus or Life, itself, certain persons are called forward as undercover agents to investigate crucially important crimes. They are required to enter a variety of alien or enemy territories for the purpose of gaining vital information as to the ways and means used by adverse, hostile or criminal forces for injurious or illegal purposes. A disguise, in such matters, of one sort or another, becomes mandatory. In every case such undercover work is literally impossible without inducing trust in those to be investigated; a trust which, by its very nature, must be abused or betrayed in service to a larger purpose of reporting the truth . . .
>
> It seems to me at the point you were forced to

conclude that MacDonald was guilty you were required, by service to the truth you had agreed to
serve in your writing, to do everything possible to
reach through the remaining mystery. MacDonald
claims it is against his personal interest that you
acted, yet it is in the public interest that you did
precisely what you did . . .

Isn't his complaint fundamentally based on the
continuance of his intent to make the story you
wrote part of his cover-up? Having induced your
trust, he meant to cooperate only insofar as it
served his interests . . . In the end [he] seems to be
saying you tricked him, took advantage of him, in
order to learn the truth and reveal it. If this is pun-
ishable, then we need new laws. Have you, have
we, an action against him for inducing our trust?
May we sue him for lying to us, for misleading us,
for hiding evidence, for endeavoring to drive society out of its mind? . . .

The answer is no, we may not. But at least, despite his
own litigiousness and the acquiescence of some courts
and the fawning of the occasional magazine writer, we
may continue to see him for what he is. Not that it's a
pretty sight. And not that the work I had to do in order
to view it was ever joyous.

With some stories, that's just the way it is. If you are
going to be a non-fiction writer you must be willing to
go where the story leads you, even if it isn't where you
want to be. And, as the occasion demands, you must be
willing to publish unpleasant truths—rather than pleasant untruths—about your subject.

At the very least, I hope that anyone who has read
Fatal Vision can recognize that—contrary to Janet Mal-

colm's assertion—I did not suffer from an "incapacity" for "looking at this horror squarely."

That much, for ten years, I know I've done.

> —Joe McGinniss
> Williamstown, Mass.
> April, 1989

SELECTED REFERENCES

Baselt, Randall C. *Disposition of Toxic Drugs and Chemicals in Man*. Davis, Calif: Biomedical Publications, 1982.

Cleckley, Hervey, M.D. *The Mask of Sanity*. St. Louis: C.V. Mosby Company, 1976.

Gilman, Alfred Goodman, Louis S. Goodman, and Alfred Goodman. *Goodman and Gilman's Pharmacological Basis of Therapeutics*. New York: Macmillan, 1980.

Kernberg, Otto, M.D. *Borderline Conditions and Pathological Narcissism*. New York: Jason Aronson, Inc., 1975.

Lasch, Christopher. *The Culture of Narcissism*. New York: W.W. Norton & Company, Inc., 1978.

Physicians' Desk Reference. Oradell, N.J.: Medical Economics Company, 1977.

Wolfe, Sidney M., M.D., Christopher M. Coley, and the Health Research Group founded by Ralph Nader. *Pills That Don't Work*. New York: Farrar, Straus & Giroux, Inc., 1981.

Available for the first time as an e-book
from *New York Times* bestselling author

Joe McGinniss

CRUEL DOUBT

One hot summer night in 1988, Bonnie Von
Stein's second husband was murdered in their bed,
Bonnie herself stabbed, beaten, and left for dead
beside him. It looked like a brutal but tragically
ordinary case: Von Stein was newly wealthy, and
his estranged stepson Chris was a drop-out drug
user with a need for money and a tenuous grasp
on reality. But then mystifying new leads
suggested the crime could be a real-life enactment
of a bizarre Dungeons and Dragons fantasy
adventure, implicating the game's Dungeon
Master and perhaps Bonnie's teenage daughter...

**"McGinniss is the Alfred Hitchcock
of the true-crime genre,
a genre he often transcends."
—*Boston Globe***

Available wherever e-books are sold or at
penguin.com